RAND McNALLY
PHOTOGRAPHIC WORLD ATLAS

A Traveler's Portrait of the World

RAND McNALLY
PHOTOGRAPHIC
WORLD ATLAS

Rand McNally & Company
Chicago • New York • San Francisco

Rand McNally
Photographic World Atlas

General manager: Russell L. Voisin
Managing editor: Jon M. Leverenz
Editor, writer: Elizabeth G. Fagan
Cartographic editor: V. Patrick Healy
Art directors: Gordon Hartshorne, Bill Pieper
Designer: Linda Kolarich
Production editor: Laura C. Schmidt
Production manager: John R. Potratz

Photograph Credits

Christopher Arnesen/Aperture PhotoBank: 24 bottom, 50, 51, 53 bottom right, 74, 79 bottom, 91. David Barnes/Aperture PhotoBank: 39 bottom right, 152 top right. Nathan Benn/Aperture PhotoBank: 35 bottom right, 104 left, 146 top. Campbell & Boulander/Aperture PhotoBank: 105 bottom, 157 middle left. Byron Crader/Ric Ergenbright Photography: 47 bottom, 89, 160 bottom left. Chad Ehlers/Aperture PhotoBank: 135 top right. Ross Ehlert/Viesti Associates: 125 bottom. Ric Ergenbright/Ric Ergenbright Photography: cover (Le Mont-Saint-Michel, France), 10, 11, 14 bottom, 15 top, 28 bottom, 29 top left, 32 right, 33 bottom, 35 top, 39 top, 60, 63, 72, 73, 75 bottom, 103, 110, 114 right, 125 top, 126 top, 127. Tim Fitzharris/Aperture PhotoBank: 128 bottom. Ken Graham/Aperture PhotoBank: 94 bottom. Robert Ivey/Ric Ergenbright Photography: 88, 90 bottom, 112 top. Wolfgang Kaehler/Aperture PhotoBank: 95. Stephen J. Krasemann/Aperture PhotoBank: 81. Greg Lawler/Aperture PhotoBank: 58. Will McIntyre/Aperture PhotoBank: 28 top left. David Muench/Aperture PhotoBank: 122. Floyd Norgaard/Ric Ergenbright Photography: 77. Ken Ross/Viesti Associates: 59, 124, 134 bottom, 156 top. James Randklev/Aperture PhotoBank: 140 top right. Ron Sanford/Aperture PhotoBank: 25 top right. Kevin Schaper/Aperture PhotoBank: 101. George Schwartz/Ric Ergenbright Photography: 153 bottom left. Monserrate J. Schwartz/Ric Ergenbright Photography: 141 bottom left. Masa Uemura/Aperture PhotoBank: 140 bottom. Joe Viesti/Viesti Associates: 13, 18, 19, 34 bottom, 38 top, 42 bottom, 43 top, 46 right, 61, 100, 102 bottom left, 107, 113, 123, 129. Art Wolfe/Aperture PhotoBank: 134 top. Reprinted from **World Atlas of Nations**, copyright © 1988 by Rand McNally & Company, used with permission: 12 bottom, 62. Reprinted from **This Great Land**, copyright © 1983 by Rand McNally & Company, used with permission: 147 bottom left, 156 bottom, 157 top. All other photographs reproduced from **Rand McNally Pictorial World Atlas**, copyright © 1980 by Rand McNally & Company, used with permission. Portions of text revised from previously published text and used with permission from Intercontinental Book Productions Limited.

Rand McNally Photographic World Atlas
copyright © 1989 by Rand McNally & Company.

Maps from **The New International Atlas**, copyright © 1989 by Rand McNally and Company.

Library of Congress Catalog Card Number: 89-42683
ISBN: 0-528-83363-4

Contents

In this Atlas

Do you know where the nation of Burkina Faso is? How about Vanuatu? And what about Belize?

What does Malta look like? How flat is the altiplano of Peru and Bolivia? And how bright are the lights of Chicago at night?

If you were traveling to Nepal, what kinds of people would you expect to find there? And what if you were going to Melanesia – what would the residents be like?

At any given moment, the minds of most people are concerned primarily with their immediate world: professionals with their budgets, deadlines, and demanding bosses; farmers with their animals, crops, and the weather; and students with their exams, grades, and social lives.

Think, though, of yourself in relation to the earth, with its circumference of 24,902 miles (40,075 kilometers) and diameter of 7,926 miles (12,756 kilometers). That measurement represents a surface area of nearly 200 million square miles (about 500 million square kilometers).

Now think again. Think of the vast expanses of the Pacific Ocean, which, in places, is deeper than Mount Everest is high and covers one-third of our planet. Think of the ancient pyramids of Egypt and the sophisticated culture they represent – a culture that existed thousands of years before humanity harnessed the electric power that could have helped construct those same pyramids. Think of the peoples

in the isolated corners of the world who continue to live as they did in the Stone Age and who worship the airplanes they occasionally see and hear flying overhead. In other words, think of the enormous size, long history, and endless variety of the planet earth.

There's a whole world out there – and it's all here in your *Rand McNally Photographic World Atlas*.

The atlas is divided into sections that cover each major region of the world. In most cases, the regions coincide with the continental divisions of the earth. Thus, you will see sections on Europe, Asia, Africa, South America, and North America.

You will also find, however, sections covering the Soviet Union, Oceania, Middle America, and the Polar Regions. These regional divisions do not fit in with the traditional continental scheme of the earth – a scheme that may no longer be ideal for most purposes.

The Soviet Union, for example, straddles two continents and is of such stature physically and politically that it merits its own section.

Australia alone is a continent, but no atlas would be complete without New Zealand and the widely scattered islands of the Pacific Ocean. This section therefore encompasses all of Oceania.

The two Americas are increasingly divided into three: the largely English-speaking North, the Spanish- and Portuguese-influenced South, and the patchwork of predominantly Latin

mainland states together with the Caribbean and other islands that make up Middle America. Within this atlas, these divisions allow more expansive treatment of each region.

Finally, the most complete of atlases include not only Antarctica but also the vast, frozen expanses of the North Pole.

Following is an overview of what you can expect to find in your *Rand McNally Photographic World Atlas*.

Photographs

This atlas brings you a visual presentation of the world with nearly 175 full-color photographs. As a whole, they work to illuminate the wide variety that is the planet earth.

Captions

An extended caption accompanies each photograph. These captions inform you not only of the location and description of each photograph but also provide some insight into the meaning of each. Browsing the photographs and reading the captions of your *Rand McNally Photographic World Atlas* will educate as well as entertain you.

Maps

The regional sections conclude with full-color maps. These maps represent some of the highest cartographic standards available in print. Mainly on two scales, the smaller (1:12,000,000) presenting the continents as a whole on one or more maps; the larger (1:3,000,000)

showing countries or areas in greater detail. The maps emphasize political features and show the main physical characteristics.

Profiles

The profiles begin each regional section by acquainting you with the location and size; landscape; climate; and history, politics, and economy of the area. They give you the "big picture" of the region.

Countries

Following each profile is an alphabetic list of the countries in the region – except, of course, in the Soviet Union and Polar Regions sections. Here you can find a brief overview of every independent nation and of some major foreign-ruled territories.

Portfolios

Your *Rand McNally Photographic World Atlas* presents expanded sections on Europe and the United States – two regions that appeal especially to many travelers. In the portfolios, you will find these two places subdivided into regions, each with a wide variety of photographs to give you a closer look.

Index

Found at the end of the book, the index is an alphabetic list of the names appearing on the maps that gives a page reference, coordinates, and, where applicable, a symbol indicating the nature of the feature.

World Index Map

A-519500-964

Legend to Maps

Inhabited Localities

The symbol represents the number of inhabitants within the locality

1:3,000,000	•	0—10,000	1:12,000,000	·	0—50,000
1:6,000,000	○	10,000—25,000		⊛	50,000—100,000
	⊛	25,000—100,000		⊡	100,000—250,000
	⊡	100,000—250,000		⊡	250,000—1,000,000
	▣	250,000—1,000,000		■	>1,000,000
	■	>1,000,000			

⬚ Urban Area (area of continuous industrial, commercial, and residential development)

The size of type indicates the relative economic and political importance of the locality

Écommoy	Lisieux	**Rouen**
Trouville	**Orléans**	**PARIS**

Hollywood □   Section of a City, Neighborhood
Westminster

Bîr Safâjah °   Inhabited Oasis

Capitals of Political Units

<u>**BUDAPEST**</u>	Independent Nation
<u>Cayenne</u>	Dependency (Colony, protectorate, etc.)
GALAPAGOS (Ecuador)	Administering Country
<u>Villarica</u>	State, Province, etc.
<u>White Plains</u>	County, Oblast, etc.

Alternate Names

Basel	**MOSKVA**	English or second official language names are shown
Bâle	**MOSCOW**	in reduced size lettering
Ventura	Volgograd	Historical or other alternates in the local language
(San Buenaventura)	(Stalingrad)	are shown in parentheses

Transportation

1:12,000,000	1:3,000,000 1:6,000,000	
———————	——————	Primary Road
	——————	Secondary Road
- - - - - - -	- - - - - - -	Minor Road, Trail
+++++++++	+++++++	Primary Railway
	✈	Airport

MACKINAC BRIDGE	Bridge	- - - - -	Shipping Channel
GREAT ST. BERNARD TUNNEL	Tunnel	*Canal du Midi*	Navigable Canal
TO CALAIS	Ferry		Intracoastal Waterway

Metric-English Equivalents

Areas represented by one square centimeter at various map scales

1:3,000,000
900 km²
348 square miles

1:6,000,000
3,600 km²
1,390 square miles

1:12,000,000
14,400 km²
5,558 square miles

Meter=3.28 feet   Meter² (m²)=10.76 square feet
Kilometer=0.62 mile   Kilometer² (km²)=0.39 square mile

Political Boundaries

International (First-order political unit)

1:3,000,000
1:6,000,000
1:12,000,000

———·——·——   Demarcated, Undemarcated, and Administrative

— · · — · · —   Disputed de jure

— — — —   Indefinite or Undefined

——————   Demarcation Line

Internal

——————— Guaira   State, Province, etc. (Second-order political unit)

WESTCHESTER   County, Oblast, etc. (Third-order political unit)

ANDALUCIA   Historical Region (No boundaries indicated)

Miscellaneous Cultural Features

PARQUE NACIONAL CANAIMA ▲	National or State Park or Monument	⊥ STEINHAUSEN	Church, Monastery
FORT CLATSOP NAT. MEM. ▲	National or State Historic(al) Site, Memorial	∴ UXMAL	Ruins
BLACKFOOT IND. RES.	Indian Reservation	⊻ WINDSOR CASTLE	Castle
FORT DIX	Military Installation	∕ AMISTAD DAM	Dam
▲ TANGLEWOOD	Point of Interest (Battlefield, cave, historical site, etc.)		

Hydrographic Features

	Shoreline	*The Everglades*	Swamp
	Undefined or Fluctuating Shoreline	SEWARD GLACIER	Glacier
Amur	River, Stream	*L. Victoria*	Lake, Reservoir
	Intermittent Stream	*Tuz Golu*	Salt Lake
<<< L	Rapids, Falls		Intermittent Lake, Reservoir
	Irrigation or Drainage Canal		Dry Lake Bed
	Reef	(395)	Lake Surface Elevation
764 ▽	Depth of Water		

Topographic Features

			Lava
Mt. Kenya △ 5199	Elevation Above Sea Level		Sand Area
76 ▽	Elevation Below Sea Level		Salt Flat
Mount Cook ▲ 3764	Highest Elevation in Country	**A N D E S** KUNLUNSHANMAI	Mountain Range, Plateau, Valley, etc.
Khyber Pass ⊐⊏ 1067	Mountain Pass		
133 ▼	Lowest Elevation in Country	BAFFIN ISLAND NUNIVAK ISLAND	Island

Elevations and depths are given in meters
Highest Elevation and Lowest Elevation of a continent are underlined

POLUOSTROV KAMČATKA
CABO DE HORNOS   Peninsula, Cape, Point, etc.

ARCTIC   OCEAN

Beaufort   Sea

GREENLAND
(Den.)

Thule

VICTORIA
ISLAND

Baffin
Bay

BAFFIN ISLAND

Godhavn

Davis Strait

Angmagssalik

Norwe

UNITED STATES
Arctic   Circle

Inuvik

Mackenzie

Godthåb

Reykjavik

ICELAND

FAEROE
ISLANDS
(Den.)

Sea

U.S.S.R.

Bering Strait

Nome

Yukon

Fairbanks

Yellowknife

Glasgow

UNIT

Anchorage

Mount
McKinley
6194

Juneau

Churchill

Hudson
Bay

Goose Bay

Dublin

KING

IRELAND

LO

Bering Sea

Gulf of
Alaska

C A N A D A

Edmonton

NEWFOUNDLAND

St. John's

ALEUTIAN   ISLANDS

Vancouver

Calgary

Winnipeg

Lake
Superior

Québec

Halifax

ROCKY MOUNTAINS

Seattle

Lake
Huron

St.
Lawrence

Montréal

ATLANTIC   OCEAN

Portland

Minneapolis

Ottawa

Toronto

L. Ontario

Boston

Porto

NORTH AMERICA

CHICAGO

DETROIT

L. Erie

Lake
Michigan

NEW YORK

PORTUGAL

M

San Francisco

Salt
Lake City

Denver

St.
Louis

APPALACHIAN MOUNTAINS

PHILADELPHIA

Washington

Lisboa

SPA

AÇORES AZORES
(Port.)

GIBRALTAR
(U.K.)

Wes

PACIFIC

UNITED STATES

Rabat

LOS ANGELES

Phoenix

Dallas

Atlanta

BERMUDA
(U.K.)

ARQUIPÉLAGO
DA MADEIRA
(Port.)

Casablanca

MOROCCO

San Diego

El Paso

Rio Grande

Houston

New
Orleans

OCEAN

MIDWAY ISLANDS
(U.S.)

Mississippi

ISLAS CANARIAS
CANARY ISLANDS
(Sp.)

Monterrey

Gulf of Mexico

Miami

BAHAMAS

Tropic of Cancer

CABO SAN LUCAS

MEXICO

La Habana

WESTERN
SAHARA

HAWAIIAN

Honolulu

CIUDAD
DE MÉXICO
MEXICO CITY

CUBA

DOMINICAN
REPUBLIC

S

MAURI-
TANIA

JOHNSTON ATOLL
(U.S.)

ISLANDS

Guadalajara

HAITI

PUERTO RICO (U.S.)

Nouakchott

GUATEMALA

BELIZE

Port-au-Prince

JAMAICA

Santo
Domingo

San Juan

Tombouctou

P

Guatemala

San Salvador

HONDURAS
Tegucigalpa

GUADELOUPE (Fr.)

SENEGAL

Dakar

15°

ÎLE CLIPPERTON
(Fr.)

EL SALVADOR

Managua

NICARAGUA

Caribbean
Sea

MARTINIQUE (Fr.)

BARBADOS

GAMBIA
Banjul

Bamako

GUINEA-BISSAU

M

O

TRINIDAD AND
TOBAGO

GUINEA

Conakry

L

San José

COSTA
RICA

Panama

Port of Spain

SIERRA
LEONE

Freetown

IVORY
COAST

Ouaga

Y

PANAMA

VENEZUELA

Caracas

GUYANA
Georgetown

Monrovia

Yamoussouk

Abidjan

N

LINE ISLANDS

Medellín

Bogotá

Paramaribo

SURI-
NAME

FRENCH
GUIANA

LIBERIA

PHOENIX
ISLANDS

Cali

COLOMBIA

E

Quito

Equator

ECUADOR

Amazon

Belém

Equator

S

Guayaquil

Iquitos

Manaus

Fortaleza

I

ARCHIPIÉLAGO DE COLÓN
GALAPAGOS ISLANDS
(Ec.)

Trujillo

ANDES

Madeira

CABO DE SÃO ROQUE

Natal

A

PERU

B R A Z I L

Recife

TOKELAU
(N.Z.)

ÎLES MARQUISES

Lima

SOUTH AMERICA

Salvador

ATLANTIC   OCEAN

15°

WALLIS
AND
FUTUNA
(Fr.)

W.
SAMOA

AM.
SAMOA

ÎLES

Arequipa

La Paz

Goiânia

Brasília

FIJI

Apia

TUAMOTU

BOLIVIA

Belo Horizonte

NIUE
(N.Z.)

ÎLES DE LA SOCIÉTÉ
SOCIETY ISLANDS

Sucre

COOK
ISLANDS
(N.Z.)

FRENCH
POLYNESIA

PARAGUAY

SÃO PAULO

RIO DE JANEIRO

TONGA

Tropic of Capricorn

Asunción

Santos

Curitiba

PITCAIRN
(U.K.)

Antofagasta

ISLA
SAN AMBROSIO
(Chile)

Porto Alegre

ISLA DE PASCUA
EASTER ISLAND
(Chile)

CHILE

Paraná

International Date Line

Co. Aconcagua
6959

Córdoba

URUGUAY

ARCHIPIÉLAGO
JUAN FERNÁNDEZ
(Chile)

Valparaíso

Santiago

Rosario

BUENOS AIRES

Montevideo

ARGENTINA

Mar del Plata

PACIFIC

Concepción

Bahía Blanca

CHATHAM ISLANDS
(N.Z.)

OCEAN

FALKLAND ISLANDS
ISLAS MALVINAS
(U.K.)

Punta Arenas

SOUTH GEORGIA
(U.K.)

CABO DE HORNOS
CAPE HORN

Drake   Passage

SOUTH ORKNEY
ISLANDS
(B.A.T.)

Antarctic Circle

ANTARCTIC
PENINSULA

Bellingshausen Sea

Weddell   Sea

Ross Sea

Vinson Massif
4897

MARIE BYRD LAND

A   N   T   A   R

ROSS ICE SHELF

One centimeter represents 750 kilometers.
One inch represents approximately 1200 miles.
Robinson Projection
Scale 1:75,000,000

Europe
Profile

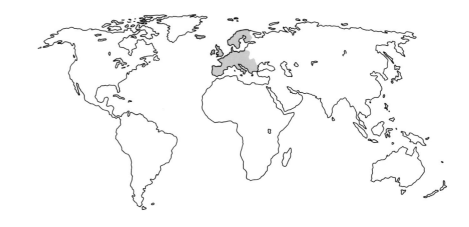

Location and Size

Europe is situated in the Northern Hemisphere. From its northern tip at North Cape, Norway, to its southern point at the island of Crete in the Mediterranean Sea, Europe extends some 2,500 miles (4,000 kilometers). From the west to east borders, Europe extends from the western Portuguese coast to the boundaries of the Black Sea in Romania, approximately 2,100 miles (3,400 kilometers) across. Beyond the mainland, Iceland, the Azores, and parts of Ireland lie even farther west. With over 30,000 miles (48,000 kilometers) of coastline, Europe is an intricate continent with large areas of ocean and sea reaching in everywhere.

Landscape

The three main physical regions of Europe are two areas dominated by uplands – one in the northwest and one in the south – and one lowland area in the east and west. Rarely are found open expanses of monotonous landscape such as are found in some other continents. Not even the lowlands surrounding the Baltic Sea are as expansive as the interior lowlands of North America, the Great Siberian Plain, or Amazonia.

The uplands of the north and west are the remains of a chain of mountains formed in the Caledonian Age about 350 million years ago. Today these mountains reach heights of more than eight thousand feet (two thousand meters) in Norway and more than four thousand feet (one thousand meters) in Scotland.

But not all of this part of the European continent is mountainous. Parts of Sweden and all of Finland, for example, have been reduced over the ages by erosion to their present flat terrain.

The mountains of Iceland were mainly produced by more recent volcanic activity. Iceland is one of the few places in Europe that is still volcanically active.

The largest area of the three major regions is the lowlands that lie east and west across Europe. Geographically they are younger than the northern uplands but older than much of the area to the south. The landscape often has a gently rolling appearance, being a succession of low hills or *scarps* with valleys or *vales* between them. Such landscapes are found in Britain and northern France, generally reaching less than 500 feet (150 meters) above sea level.

The mountains of the south are among the youngest regions of the continent, created less than 100 million years ago. They are a part of a great expanse of mountains that runs west to east from northern Spain, across Italy, Switzerland, Austria and the Balkan countries, and then on into the Soviet Union and Asia. These are the highest mountains in Europe, rising to more than fifteen thousand feet (four thousand meters) at Mont Blanc.

Other older upland areas are also found in southern Europe. The south-central parts of France and parts of central and southern Germany and western Czechoslovakia are eroded mountain systems that were formed about 200 million years ago. In the Massif Central of France, these rise to more than six thousand feet (almost two thousand meters).

In very recent geological times, northern Europe and the higher parts of the southern mountain areas have been covered with ice. Much smaller areas of northern and mountain Europe are glaciated today. At its maximum advance, the ice covered most of the northern continent. It eroded the landscape in many places, and today such features as the Norwegian fjords and the Scottish lochs are evidence of this glaciation. In other places, the ice carried and then deposited much fertile soil that is today the basis of some of the rich farmlands of the central lowlands.

Europe is a continent of comparatively short rivers, and no location in the whole continent is more than about 400 miles (650 kilometers) from the sea. The most important rivers in the western portions begin in the Alps or other central mountains. The largest of these rivers is the Danube, rising in southern Germany and flowing eastward to the Black Sea. Others include the Rhine, Rhône, Saône, Po, Elbe, and Vistula. The major rivers of Eastern Europe flow mostly to the south.

Left: A familiar sight to residents and visitors alike, the many castles of Europe once housed the lords of the land. This small castle is on Loch Linnhe, in Scotland's western coastal region.

Right: One of the Alps' many branches, the Bernese Alps run through south-central Switzerland. Shown here is a peak known as the Eiger.

Europe

Climate

Europe lies on the west side of the world's largest land mass, Eurasia, almost entirely north of 40° – that is, north of southern Italy – and south of the Arctic Circle. Since no mountains run parallel to the Atlantic coast except in Norway, maritime air masses pass well into the central parts of the continent. Thus, most of Europe experiences very temperate climates.

The average temperature in western Europe seldom falls below 32°F (0°C). Rainfall is spread fairly evenly throughout the year with no marked wet and dry seasons. Rainfall totals are almost all above 22 inches (550 millimeters) per year and much higher in upland areas of the west coast.

Southern France also experiences average monthly temperatures always above 32°F (0°C). In some places, particularly in the eastern Mediterranean area, the average monthly temperature in the summer can easily reach as high as 80°F (27°C).

In Eastern Europe and much of Scandinavia, winters are colder, with average monthly temperatures falling below 32°F (0°C) in midwinter. In the north of this region, average monthly summer temperatures may only rise to 62°F (17°C). In Romania and Bulgaria, they may rise to above 75°F (24°C), giving these regions the highest temperature range in Europe – a result of their position farther away from the moderating effects of the ocean.

In the extreme north of Scandinavia and Iceland, polar climates exist where no month has average temperatures higher than 50°F (10°C).

History, Politics, and Economy

Europe has been the birthplace of many major developments in Western civilization from the beginning of recorded history. From the democratic principle originating in Greece to other great concepts such as parliamentary government in the United Kingdom, Europe has contributed many fundamentals that have been adopted by countries throughout the world. The growth of the industrial, and hence, the technological age started in Europe, and it can be argued that Europe's influence in the world has been collectively greater than any other continental area.

Within twenty-five years, Europe was torn apart by two different wars that

Above left: Greek windmills such as this one on Crete pump water to irrigate olive, grape, and grain crops.

Above: Venice, a seaport in northeast Italy, is one of the world's treasure houses of art and architecture.

Left: The changing of the guard at Buckingham Palace, London, is popular with tourists.

Opposite, bottom: Often called the "Land of Fire and Ice," Iceland is an island of contrasting features, as exemplified by the geysers shown here against a backdrop of snow- and glacier-covered mountains. Volcanoes, lakes, a mountainous lava desert, sulfur springs, canyons, waterfalls, and fast-flowing rivers are also found throughout the island, and areas such as these make up almost 80 percent of Iceland's total area. Population is concentrated on the 7 percent of the island that borders the sea.

Left: Historic Aragon, in northeastern Spain, is arid and sparsely populated. The only city of any size in the region is Zaragoza. These women are traditionally dressed for the Fiesta del Pilar, held annually in Zaragoza to honor the Virgin Mary.

Europe

Profile continued

embroiled much of the rest of the world. In the aftermath of the two wars, Communist governments were established in much of Europe, and the continent was divided into Communist and non-Communist nations, or Eastern and Western Europe as we know them today. In 1949, ten Western European nations joined the United States and Canada to form the North Atlantic Treaty Organization (NATO), designed to unify Western countries in defense. Similarly, in 1955, the Soviet Union and most of the other Eastern European countries formed what was called the Warsaw Pact for the same purposes.

In 1958, the European Economic Community (EEC), or Common Market, was established to help integrate the economies of Western Europe by forming common price levels. Although it has not solved all the economic concerns facing its member countries, the Common Market is considered to be a

success because much of the economic growth of Western Europe in the decades since its inception can be attributed to the union. In the late 1980s, the Common Market expanded, with Spain and Portugal becoming its newest members.

Although, from the late 1940s through the early 1960s, Europe was engulfed in Cold War tension between the East and West, since then its statesmen have struggled to forge a lasting peace through various trading links and economic agreements. One such agreement involved all of Europe and the United States. Named the Helsinki Agreement, it was signed in 1975. In it, almost every European nation, the United States, Canada, and Cyprus pledged to cooperate on matters of economics, peacekeeping, and human rights.

Since the late 1970s, many European nations have suffered from recession, inflation, and high unemployment.

Opposite, top: Hammerfest, Norway, is sometimes called the world's northernmost town. Here the sun never sets from May to August and never rises from November to February.

Opposite, center: Since the 1600s, northern Bohemia, Czechoslovakia, has been a leader in the craft of glassmaking. Shown here is the Světlá glassworks.

Opposite, bottom: Built in the latter part of the nineteenth century, scenic Kylemore Abbey is in County Galway, Ireland, near the town of Letterfrack.

Above: The Lot River valley in southwestern France is a fertile region dotted with vineyards and small towns.

Right: The glittering nightlife of Monte Carlo draws thousands of tourists to Monaco each year, making this Riviera resort a major contributor to the principality's tourism-based economy.

15

Kilometers ⊢──────────────────┤ Km.
              0   200   400   600

Statute Miles ⊢──────────────┤ Mi.
              0   200   400   600

Scale 1:12,000,000

One centimeter represents 120 kilometers.
One inch represents approximately 190 miles.
Miller Oblated Stereographic Projection

Europe
Countries

Albania

The People's Socialist Republic of Albania established a Communist government in 1944, and since then it has severed ties with one-time allies – Yugoslavia, the Soviet Union, and most recently China. In 1967 religious institutions were banned, and Albania claims to be the first atheist state.

Andorra

Andorra, a duty-free shopping mecca, lies between France and Spain, with Spanish the predominant language. A mild climate complements the mountainous terrain of this attractive and antiquated country. Andorrans have a high literacy rate but no formal constitution, no armed forces, and no political parties.

Austria

Known for its beautiful ski resorts and clean cities, Austria is an attraction for tourists from around the world. With low unemployment, this country has a strong economy. After World War II, the government nationalized some industries; today the economy is a blend of state and privately owned industry. Vienna (Wien), its capital city, is one of the great cultural centers of Europe.

Belgium

A founding member of the EEC, Belgium now plays host to the organization in its capital, Brussels (Bruxelles). Positioned between France and the Netherlands, Belgium borders on the North Sea. The economy and population have been affected by Belgium's central location. Industry was early established as the economic base.

Bulgaria

The mainly mountainous People's Republic of Bulgaria is just south of Romania, bordering on the Black Sea. The climate is similar to that of the American Midwest. A Communist government has been in power since the 1940s.

Channel Islands

Set in the Atlantic Ocean, some 90 miles (140 kilometers) south of the British mainland, the Channel Islands are part of the United Kingdom. English is the predominant language, though a form of Norman-French is also spoken.

Czechoslovakia

An industrialized nation, Czechoslovakia has a centralized economy and one of the highest standards of living of the Eastern-bloc countries. Most people are Roman Catholic, and the government licenses and pays the clergy.

Denmark

Denmark is made up of the Jutland Peninsula and more than four hundred islands, about one hundred of which are inhabited. In addition to these islands, Greenland and the Faeroe Islands are also part of Denmark. Despite limited natural resources, Denmark has a diversified economy.

Faeroe Islands

This group of more than twenty islands belongs to Denmark and is situated 310 miles (500 kilometers) southeast of Iceland in the northern Atlantic Ocean. The name Faeroes is taken from the Danish for "sheep islands," and sheep farming has been a major occupation.

Finland

The most northerly country of mainland Europe, Finland has a low-lying, forested, and lake-filled landscape. The winters are so long and severe that even the capital, Helsinki, in the south of the country, is icebound. Northern Finland has periods of continuous daylight in summer and darkness in winter. Much of Finland's economy is supported by its rich forests.

France

The largest country in Western Europe, France is a major tourist country, famed for its capital, Paris. France has long contributed to learning and the arts. In 1981 France elected a Socialist president. The country is highly developed, and it remains one of the leading powers of Europe.

Germany, East

Also known as the German Democratic Republic, East Germany has a high standard of living, and citizens benefit from extensive educational and social-insurance programs. Postwar economic expansion emphasized industry, and today the country is one of the world's largest industrial producers.

Germany, West

Also known as the Federal Republic of Germany, West Germany has about four times the population of East Germany. Despite the destruction of World War II, and Germany's division into two countries, West Germany has one of the world's strongest economies.

Gibraltar

Occupying a narrow peninsula on Spain's southern coast, the British colony of Gibraltar has a mixed population of Italian, English, Maltese, Portuguese, and Spanish. A number of British military personnel are also present.

Greece

This mountainous country at the extreme southeast of Europe relies heavily on maritime trading and tourism. Greece has one of the largest merchant fleets in the world. Greeks are united by a language that dates back three thousand years.

Hungary

This landlocked, Eastern-bloc nation is a socialist republic composed of Magyar tribe descendants. Gypsies and Germans also compose a minority in a country where flat plains dominate and varied terrain is seldom seen. Agriculture is almost completely socialized.

Iceland

Just south of the Arctic Circle, this volcanic island in the North Atlantic was formerly part of the Danish realm. Fish, found in the island's rich coastal waters, is the main natural resource and export. Located in the Land of the Midnight Sun, Iceland has periods of twenty-four-hour daylight in June.

Ireland

The country of Ireland occupies most of an island in the Atlantic Ocean that sits next to the United Kingdom. The north of this island is part of the United Kingdom, and there has been much conflict over its control. Ireland has a long literary tradition and has contributed greatly to world literature. The economy

Right: Tourism has become important to the Mediterranean island nation of Malta. Popular among visitors is the Blue Grotto, situated on the main island, southwest of the town of Zurrieq.

is diversified, but agriculture – aided by fertile, rolling land suitable for farming – continues to play an important role.

Isle of Man

Set in the middle of the Irish Sea, this attractive island relies heavily on tourism as its economic base. The residents raise only a minimum of crops as well as some sheep and cattle.

Italy

The birthplace of the Renaissance, Italy has made substantial contributions to world culture and art. Italy is a long, boot-shaped peninsula that stands in the Mediterranean Sea at the southern tip of central Europe. The islands of Sicily and Sardinia are also part of Italy, and Rome is the capital city. The Italian economy is based on private enterprise, although the government is involved in some industrial and commercial activities.

Liechtenstein

Most of Liechtenstein, one of the world's smallest nations, is covered by Alps, but it features a mild climate. The last few decades have seen the economy shift from agricultural to highly industrialized. Women did not gain the right to vote in this nation until the 1980s.

Luxembourg

The Grand Duchy of Luxembourg is a central European nation governed by a constitutional monarchy. Most Luxembourgers are a blend of Celtic, French, and German stock. German and French are the official languages, as is Luxembourgish, an indigenous German dialect.

Malta

Situated between Europe and Africa, this Mediterranean island is a hilly country. One of the most densely populated places in the world, Malta is home to a diverse group of Arabs, Normans, Sicilians, and English.

Monaco

The Principality of Monaco is found at the southern tip of France, bordering on the Mediterranean Sea. A popular tourist haven, Monaco is famous for it gambling casinos in Monte Carlo.

Netherlands

Often referred to as Holland, the Netherlands is a low-lying kingdom bordering the North Sea. It has one of the highest population densities in Europe. Much of the Netherlands lies below sea level – behind protecting dikes and sea walls – and some of its richest farmlands have

been reclaimed from the sea through artificial drainage. A variety of manufacturing strengths – notably the metal, chemical, and food-processing industries – fuel the prosperous economy.

Norway

An independent kingdom since 1905, Norway has been closely linked with neighbors Sweden and Denmark throughout its history. Famed for its mountains and fjords, most Norwegian land is unproductive. In 1967, the government initiated a wide-ranging social-welfare system.

Poland

The Polish People's Republic borders on the Baltic Sea and is surrounded by the Soviet Union, Czechoslovakia, and East Germany. Government policies since the war have transformed Poland from an agricultural nation into an industrial producer. Shortages in consumer goods have been chronic since the 1970s, when debts to the West were compounded by the failure of Polish goods in the market. Poland has a mostly flat terrain, except for mountains in the south.

Portugal

Together with Spain and Gibraltar, Portugal is situated on the Iberian Peninsula. The Atlantic islands of Madeira and Azores are also part of Portugal. A variety of social and political ills have contributed to Portugal's status as one of the poorest nations in Europe.

Romania

When Romania became a Communist country in the 1940s, the government began to turn the country from agriculture to industry. Although Romania remains less developed than many other European countries, it has experienced some post-war growth.

San Marino

Founded in the fourth century, San Marino claims to be the world's oldest republic. Surrounded completely by Italy, it has strong ties to the Italians and combines Latin, Adriatic, and Teutonic roots.

Spain

One of the largest yet least developed countries of Western Europe, Spain, together with Portugal and Gibraltar, occupies the Iberian Peninsula. Despite the effects of recent worldwide recessions, Spain has benefited greatly from an economic-restructuring program that

began in the late 1950s. Spain's terrain is mainly composed of a dry plateau area; mountains cover the northern section, and plains extend down the country's eastern coast.

Sweden

The Scandinavian kingdom of Sweden is one of the most prosperous countries in Western Europe. With one of the highest standards of living in the world, Swedish government provides exceptional benefits for most citizens, including free education and medical care, pension payments, four-week vacations, and payments for child care. The nation is industrial and bases its economy on its three most important resources: timber, iron ore, and water power. Most farms are part of Sweden's agricultural-cooperative movement.

Switzerland

This landlocked, central European country is known for the Alps and other mountains that cover nearly 70 percent of the terrain. Most of Switzerland is unsuitable for agriculture, but tourism thrives here. Switzerland is also an international banking and finance center.

United Kingdom

England, Scotland, Wales, and Northern Ireland compose the United Kingdom, which occupies most of the British Isles. The Industrial Revolution developed

quickly in Great Britain, and the country continues to be a leading world producer. London is well known as an international financial center. The varied terrain is marked by several mountain ranges, moors, rolling hills, and plains. The climate is tempered by the sea and is subject to frequent changes. The United Kingdom administers many overseas possessions, remnants of its powerful empire.

Vatican City

A tiny sovereign state within the city of Rome, the Vatican provides an independent base for the headquarters of the Roman Catholic church. Governed by the Pope, it has its own coins and stamps, and a radio station that broadcasts in thirty-one different languages. The Vatican City is the smallest independent state in the world.

Yugoslavia

The population in Yugoslavia is one of the most diverse in Eastern Europe. Although Yugoslavia became a Communist republic in 1945, there has been a shift to encourage Western trade and broaden political and cultural exchanges, a result of United States aid from the 1940s to the 1960s. Since 1945, the economy has made a successful transition from agriculture to industry, although agriculture – aided by the moderate climate along the Adriatic – continues to play an important role.

One centimeter represents 60 kilometers.

One inch represents approximately 95 miles.

Scale 1:6,000,000

Lambert Conformal Conic Projection

Kilometers

Statute Miles

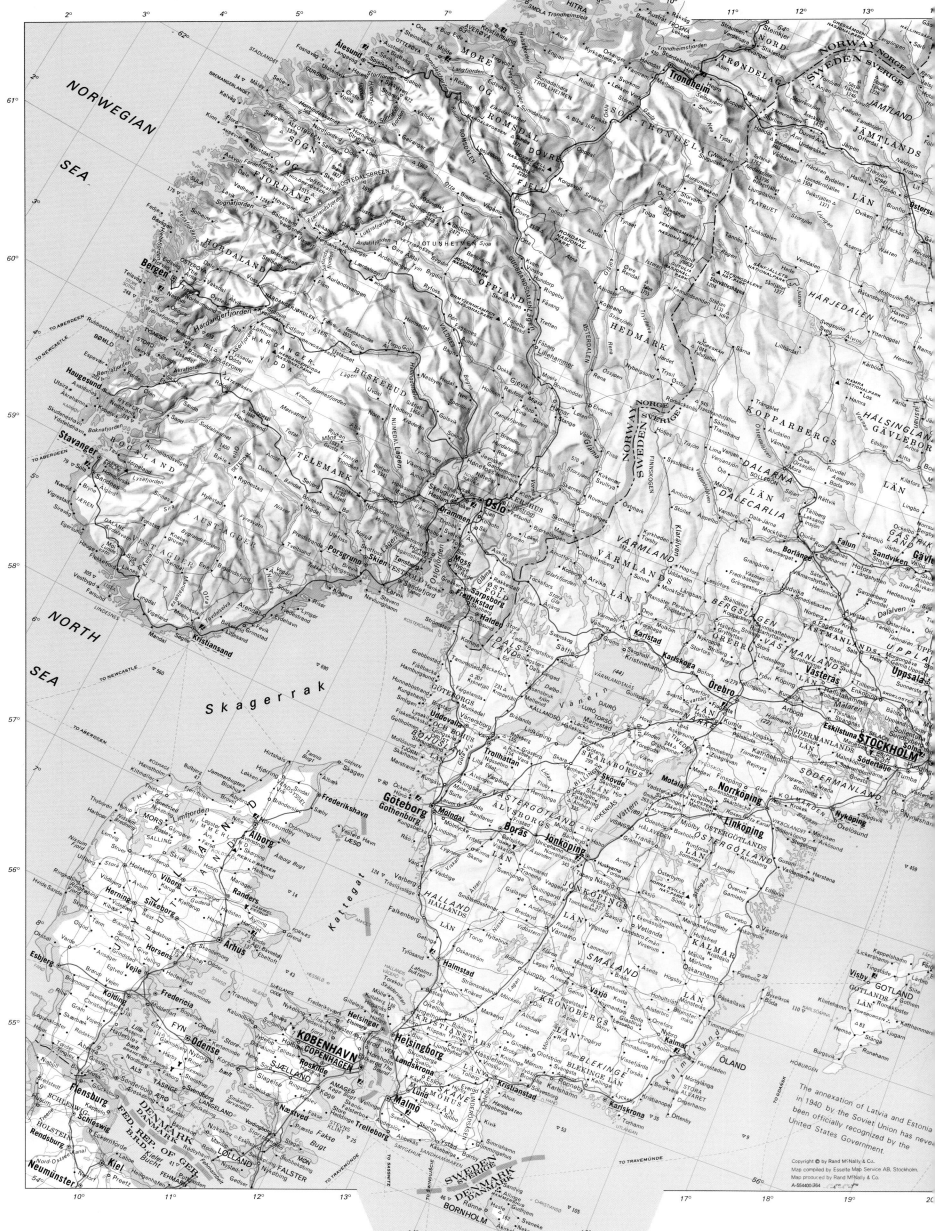

The annexation of Latvia and Estonia in 1940 by the Soviet Union has never been officially recognized by the United States Government.

Copyright © by Rand McNally & Co.
Map compiled by Esselte Map Service AB, Stockholm.
Map produced by Rand McNally & Co.
A-554400-364

Europe
Scandinavia

The term Scandinavia has been used for centuries to refer to the northernmost countries of Europe. In the 1980s, Scandinavia has continued to live up to its reputation as a prosperous and innovative corner of the world. Its nations remain world leaders in the search for solutions to such problems as health care, environmental planning, industrial democracy, and the redefinition of age and sex roles.

Visitors might find some contradictions in the nations of Scandinavia. They are alike yet different, sophisticated but simple. Scandinavia boasts vast open spaces and intimate cities; an advanced economic society, yet one that includes a race of nomadic herdsmen.

Think of Scandinavia and you think of the great outdoors, where mountains, lakes and forests combine in one marvelous year-round winter sports center. Water is ever-present, from Sweden's thousands of lakes, to Norway's spectacular fjords and glaciers, from Finland's sailing waters to the sea around Denmark. Trees too stretch away

as far as the eye can see, especially in Sweden, the largest country.

In northern Scandinavia, there are prolonged hours of summer daylight and long winter nights. Here the reindeer-herding Lapps cope with the extremes of almost continual summer light and winter darkness. For the most part, however, the populations of Norway, Finland, and Sweden are concentrated in the south.

The Scandinavian capitals are places of warmth and sophistication. Few can resist the charm of Denmark's Copenhagen, a cosmopolitan city with much to offer. Stockholm epitomizes Swedish style and cleanliness, the old town with its narrow streets and cluttered shops contrasting with the modern business center and spacious lakeside suburbs. Oslo, the Norwegian capital, is a major port and the cultural heart of Norway. It is a well-planned metropolis, with wide, straight streets. Helsinki, in Scandinavia's most unspoiled country, Finland, mixes modern amenities with a picturesque setting.

Far left, top: Olavinlinna, in Savonlinna, Finland, is one of the largest castles in northern Europe. Savonlinna is on an island in the Lake Saimaa region of southeast Finland.

Far left, bottom: The area surrounding Sergels Torg in Stockholm, Sweden, is a showplace of contemporary Swedish architecture.

Left: This youthful resident of Turku, Finland, displays the fair skin, blue or gray eyes, and blond or light brown hair of many Scandinavians.

Below: The Romsdal of Norway is characterized by steep, jagged peaks. A beautiful area, it lies on the western coast, south of Trondheim.

Opposite, top: The fjords of Norway are the legacy of the glaciers that once covered the region. After the glaciers melted, their eroded valleys flooded with seawater.

Opposite, bottom: The Tivoli gardens are an entertainment center in Copenhagen, Denmark. Opened in 1843, they feature restaurants, walkways, a concert hall, and a bandstand.

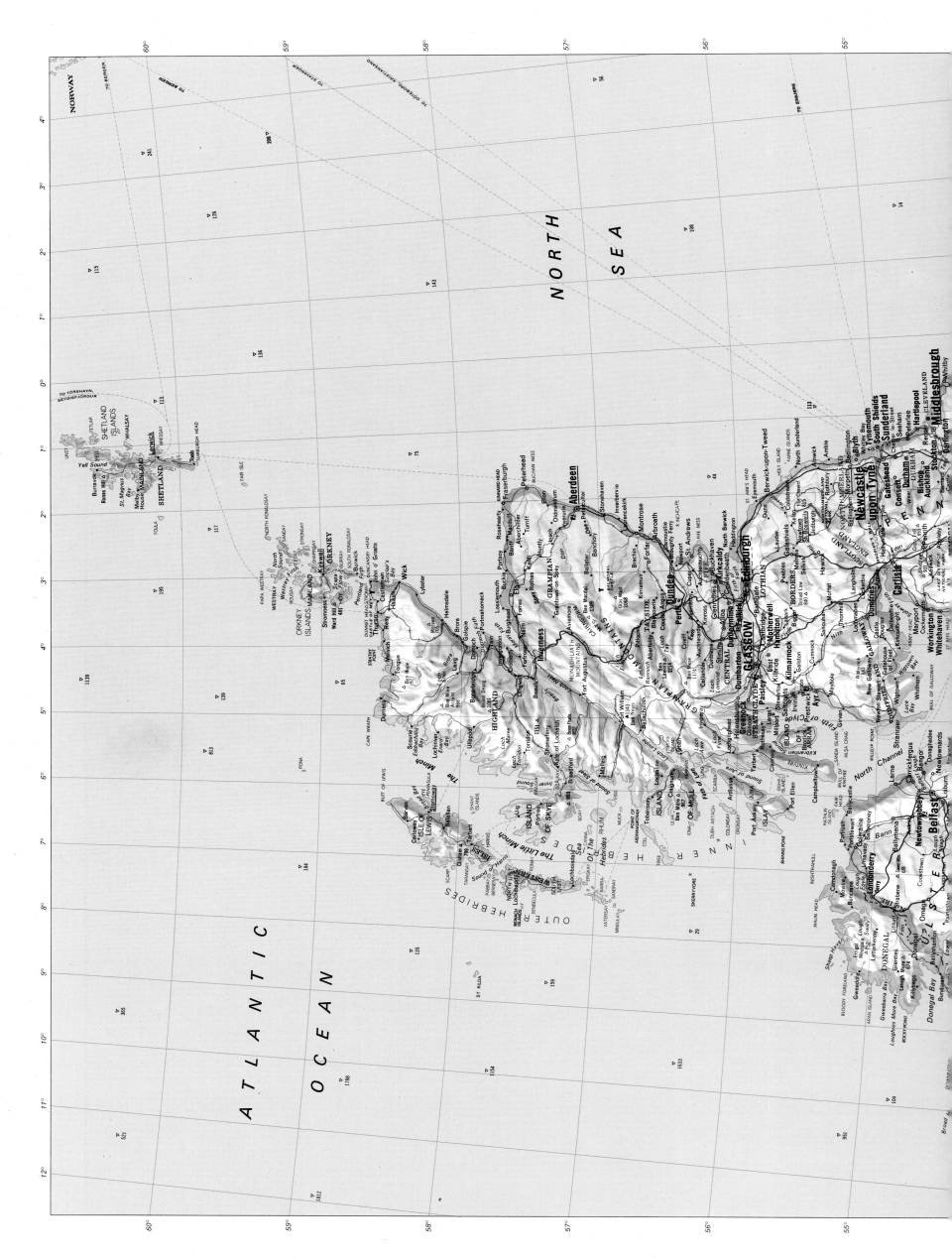

NORWAY

TO BERGEN

TO STAVANGER

NORTH SEA

ATLANTIC OCEAN

SHETLAND ISLANDS

ORKNEY ISLANDS

OUTER HEBRIDES

ISLE OF SKYE

ISLE OF LEWIS

HIGHLAND

GRAMPIAN

GRAMPIAN MOUNTAINS

Aberdeen
Peterhead
Fraserburgh

Inverness

Wick

Dundee
Perth

GLASGOW
Edinburgh
Paisley
Motherwell
Hamilton
Kilmarnock

STRATHCLYDE
CENTRAL
LOTHIAN
BORDERS
DUMFRIES AND GALLOWAY

Carlisle
Dumfries

Newcastle upon Tyne
Sunderland
Gateshead
South Shields
Hartlepool
Middlesbrough
Stockton
Darlington
Durham
Consett

Belfast
Londonderry
DONEGAL
ULSTER

26

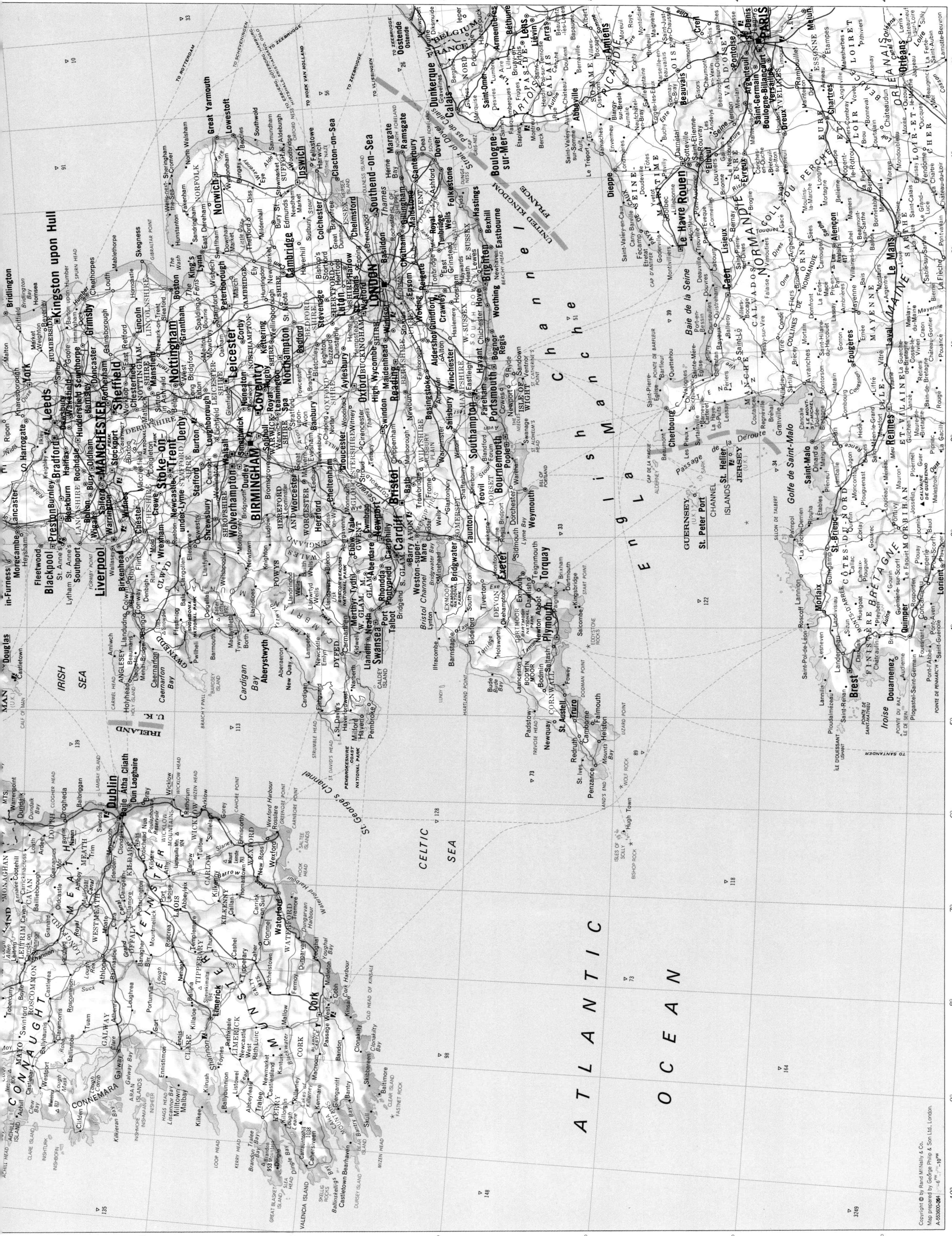

British Isles

ATLANTIC OCEAN

CELTIC SEA

IRISH SEA

English Channel

La Manche

St. George's Channel

UNITED KINGDOM

IRELAND

U.K.

FRANCE

BELGIUM

NORMANDIE

BRETAGNE

LONDON

Paris

Dublin

Baile Átha Cliath

Dún Laoghaire

Kingston upon Hull

Manchester

Liverpool

Birmingham

Leeds

Sheffield

Nottingham

Leicester

Coventry

Stoke-on-Trent

Bristol

Cardiff

Swansea

Newport

Plymouth

Exeter

Southampton

Portsmouth

Bournemouth

Brighton

Southend-on-Sea

Ipswich

Norwich

Cambridge

Peterborough

Northampton

Oxford

Reading

Luton

Colchester

York

Bradford

Preston

Blackpool

Lancaster

Chester

Wolverhampton

Worcester

Gloucester

Bath

Weston-super-Mare

Torquay

Great Yarmouth

Grimsby

Lincoln

Doncaster

Derby

Shrewsbury

Hereford

Aberystwyth

Caernarfon

Douglas

MAN

Cork

Limerick

Galway

Waterford

Wexford

Rosslare

CONNAUGHT

LEINSTER

MUNSTER

MEATH

Cherbourg

Le Havre

Rouen

Caen

Rennes

St-Malo

St. Helier

St. Peter Port

GUERNSEY

JERSEY

CHANNEL ISLANDS

Calais

Dunkerque

Boulogne-sur-Mer

Dieppe

Amiens

Arras

Lens

Béthune

Versailles

Chartres

Le Mans

Orléans

Brest

Quimper

Lorient

Morlaix

ISLE OF WIGHT

ANGLESEY

Kilometers
0 50 100 150 Km.

Statute Miles
0 50 100 150 Mi.

Scale 1:3,000,000

One centimeter represents 30 kilometers.
One inch represents approximately 47 miles.
Conic Projection, Two Standard Parallels

Copyright © by Rand McNally & Co.
Map prepared by George Philip & Son Ltd., London

27

British Isles

Many Western nations have experienced sluggish economies in the 1980s, and those of the British Isles are no exception. Visitors still flock to these countries, however, to be charmed by their long histories and rich cultures.

London still represents England to those who have ventured no farther than Piccadilly Circus and the Tower, Buckingham Palace and Westminster Abbey. But England stretches from the glorious West Country coast through soft Cotswold villages and the sweeping landscapes of the Northumberland moors.

In the north, Scotland combines a fierce love of tradition with the modern pace of industrial life. This land of lochs and mountains offers the cosmopolitan delights of the capital, Edinburgh, and the wild beauty of the highlands and islands as typified by remote crofts and grey fishing villages.

Ireland, too, is a place of beauty and contrasts, made all the more apparent and heartbreaking by internal conflict. But everywhere, from the northern loughs to the southern mountains, from urbane Dublin to the comparative poverty of the west, this land of Yeats and Shaw exudes a sense of hospitality and pride.

And in Wales, that same warmth is extended in the Celtic tongue, through Cardiff – the capital and largest city – and the industrial valleys of the south to Snowdonia.

Above, left: An international center for commerce as well as for culture, London is the most populous city in Europe. Two types of public transportation help keep the city bustling: the double-decker bus and the underground train system known as the tube.

Above: Shown here is Melrose Abbey in Roxburghshire, Scotland. Although largely ruined, Melrose is said to be the most picturesque of the Scottish abbeys.

Left: The Houses of Parliament and Big Ben are well-known London landmarks. Situated on the banks of the Thames, this government complex was constructed in the mid 1800s.

Left: County Kerry, in the extreme southwest of Ireland, is a land that features, among other sights, green pastures and rugged coastlines. Shown here is the Ring of Kerry road, which affords the traveler many miles of scenic landscape.

Below: Caerphilly Castle, in Glamorgan, Wales, was constructed in the thirteenth century. It is situated in the town of the same name, just north of Cardiff.

Bottom: Typical of the small towns of the English countryside is Shaftesbury, west of Salisbury, in the southern county of Dorset. Shaftesbury has a long history, and there are a number of sights in the surrounding region.

29

Kilometers

Statute Miles

| 0 | 50 | 100 | 150 |

Km.

| 0 | 50 | 100 | 150 |

Mi.

Scale 1:3,000,000

One centimeter represents 30 kilometers.
One inch represents approximately 47 miles.
Copyright © by Rand McNally & Co.
Made in U.S.A.
Conic Projection, Two Standard Parallels.

West Germany, Austria & Switzerland

West Germany's strong economy has persisted, largely because of the nation's cooperation with the EEC. Its recovery after two devastating wars has been remarkable, and today, West Germany not only dominates this part of the map, but it also remains a leader in the world economy.

Yet the industrial landscapes of the Ruhr and Saarland are only as representative of this multifaceted country as the vine-clad slopes of the Rhine and Mosel rivers, the nightlife of Hamburg's famous Reeperbahn, the romance of Heidelberg, and the fairy-tale scenic splendors of Bavaria.

A cultural giant, this country can claim to have produced such writers as Goethe and Schiller and to have an especially powerful musical inheritance in the works of Beethoven and Brahms.

Germany's former traditional capital, Berlin, since 1961 divided by the concrete wall built by the East, retains a particular significance for West Germany and East Germany alike.

Although it is officially neutral, Austria in the late 1980s maintains its position as a prosperous link between Eastern and Western Europe. Also unaligned, Switzerland continues to be one of the most economically and politically stable countries in the world. Its mountainous terrain has caused it to rely on economic contributors other than agriculture, tourism primary among them. Though they may lack size and power in the world economy, West Germany's neighbors offer outstanding scenery, long cultural traditions, and solid worth for vacationers.

Austria's renowned cultural centers of Vienna (Wien), Innsbruck, and Salzburg are equalled in appeal by the mountainous Tirol region, winter sports centers, and health spas. Music lovers are drawn to seasonal festivals held in Austria. Shoppers will appreciate fine Austrian craftsmanship. Porcelain, leather goods, and clothing are fine examples and popular purchases.

In Switzerland – home of financial wizards, precision watch making, and dairying – the scenery is no less spectacular. Beautiful Lake Geneva consistently draws tourists. There are beautiful lakes, lined with palm trees, in the south. Splendid peaks such as the Matterhorn are perhaps more expected sights to visitors. And the ski resorts of St. Moritz and Davos are world famous. Because Switzerland is so compact, a traveler can see many of its different facets in a short time.

Left: Salzburg, Austria, draws tourists interested in the surrounding scenery and the city's rich architectural and cultural histories. Situated in north-central Austria, near the West German border, Salzburg dates from Roman times. This castle, which once afforded a panoramic view to its lords, now attracts friendly visitors rather than invaders.

Above: Much of West Germany, Austria, and Switzerland is mountainous, but between the peaks of central Europe lie many fertile valleys that are suitable for farming. These countries produce wine, fruits, vegetables, and other crops. Additionally, the raising of livestock and fodder is important. Here, hay is harvested in the region of western Austria called Tirol.

Far left: The Alps of Switzerland have prevented some types of economic development in the small country but have also contributed to the nation's growth: tourism, including outdoor recreation, is second only to manufacturing in importance.

Left: Heidelberg, on the Neckar River in southwestern West Germany, attracts both tourists and students to its historic sites and fine university.

Below: Dominating the landscape of central Europe, the Alps form the youngest and most extensive mountain system on the continent. The range's many arms reach into France, Italy, Switzerland, Germany, Austria, Yugoslavia, and Liechtenstein. Shown here are central Austria's Dachsteins.

The Netherlands, Luxembourg & Belgium

No longer banded together as an economic threesome, the Benelux countries of Belgium, Luxembourg, and the Netherlands remain a delightful entity while retaining their individual charm. Founding members of the EEC, these countries have profited from the coalition, and in recent years, the Netherlands, Luxembourg, and Belgium have enjoyed relative economic stability.

Situated at the mouth of the Rhine, the Netherlands is rightly called "the gateway to Europe." Known the world over as a land of cheese, canals, and bulbs, more importantly it boasts busy seaports, and Amsterdam, the friendly capital, is a world center for diamond cutting.

Among the sights to see in the Netherlands are treasured remnants of the past. Most old city centers are protected from redevelopment, and everywhere there are museums and collections. The Netherlands is a land taken back from the sea, and it is not surprising that marine sports are popular pastimes. The sand beaches and dunes that run nearly the whole length of the coast are well suited for such activities. Shoppers may be interested in the diamonds that are a

relative bargain here; or, for those with less in their budget, Delft china, bearing the official imprint, is also found.

Belgium, now destined to be home to EEC bureaucrats, is notable for its capital, Brussels (Bruxelles), with its magnificent market place, and for the medieval pearl of Bruges (Brugge). The wooded heights of the Ardennes region are a hiker's and a gastronome's delight. Belgium boasts a short, sandy coastline of wide beaches and sand dunes, lined with a long succession of resorts. Traditional festivals are popular and keenly supported in Belgium. Belgian handmade lace, embroidery, and glassware can be found in shops throughout the country, but smart buyers avoid souvenir shops.

Rolling on into Luxembourg, the traveler finds a land of magic castles, rivers, forests, and enchanting towns. This is one of the smallest nations in Europe, but it has one of the highest standards of living on the continent, and it holds its own for the tourist. Popular sights are the ruined fortresses that are scattered throughout the countryside and the narrow cobbled streets and medieval houses of Luxembourg's cities.

Above: Although the Netherlands' use of windmills for power is now minimal, they remain a common sight.

Right: Unlike many other European cities, Bruges (Brugge), Belgium, has remained largely unchanged since medieval times.

Below: Wiltz, Luxembourg, in the north-central region of the country, boasts a twelfth-century castle.

Europe
Eastern Europe

Traveling in Eastern Europe may intimidate some people, but for those who do include Poland, Czechoslovakia, Hungary, and nearby countries on their itineraries, the adventure can be well worth the effort. Rich in history and culture, the nations of Eastern Europe provide a view of the Continent that is slightly different from that offered by Western Europe.

Since the late 1940s, many of the nations of Eastern Europe have been under Soviet influence. Though they lag behind Western European countries, they are developed, industrial nations. In these Soviet satellite countries, the vast rolling estates and artistic splendors that characterized Central Europe before World War I have disappeared.

The Hungarian Magyars, once part of two great empires, still mainly work the land, however, retaining their old traditions and culture. Budapest, Hungary's capital, has been called the most romantic city in Europe.

A land of great scenic attractions, with its extensive Bohemian forests and magnificent Carpathians, Czechoslovakia too is in many ways outwardly unchanged. Many beautiful buildings are now being restored in the capital, Prague (Praha), one of Europe's most charming, relatively undiscovered cities.

Poland, a once mighty nation that was partitioned in the eighteenth century, regained its sovereignty only to lose it to Nazi Germany during the opening weeks of World War II. Warsaw (Warszawa), though devastated in the war, is today a modern, thriving metropolis and Poland's largest city. Cracow (Kraków), on the other hand, suffered little damage during the war and retains many of its fine old structures.

Top right: The old section of Warsaw (Warszawa) was enclosed in walls built in 1380. The city was destroyed in World War II, but much of this section has been restored in its original style. Situated on the Vistula (Wisła) River, Warsaw is Poland's political, financial, and cultural center.

Above: Hungary has had more success with its collective and state farms than have other Eastern European countries.

Right: St. James (Jakuba) church is one of the historic sites in Prague (Praha), Czechoslovakia, to remain intact despite Europe's many wars.

Kilometers | 0   50   100   150 Km.

Statute Miles | 0   50   100   150 Mi.

Scale 1:3,000,000

One centimeter represents 30 kilometers.
One inch represents approximately 47 miles.

Lambert Conformal Conic Projection

France

The largest country in Europe, France is also an industrial and agricultural leader. As is the case with many of its neighbors, France's participation in the EEC has contributed much to its success in recent decades. It is not without its share of problems, however, as the inflation and unemployment that trouble other Western European nations persist in France as well.

Yet, France has so much in its favor for tourism that less well-endowed countries might be forgiven a passing resentment at such good fortune. Rich in history and culture, with a pleasing position and climate, it is no wonder that travelers continue to place France high on their lists of places to visit.

Despite its size and wealth, France is predominantly a nation of small towns and villages where home and family, the church, and trade rule supreme.

Is it not strange then, that a land so indisputably rural, with a still large and vociferous peasantry, should be renowned the world over for its enviable chic and its undoubted sophistication? Thus the influence of the capital, Paris, is asserted far beyond its own region. Indeed, its dictates in the world of fashion and the arts are followed more slavishly in London and New York than in its own country.

France has been in the forefront of true Western culture for centuries, and Paris itself has been the cradle of writers and artists too numerous to mention. Look around at the museums, galleries, artistic treasures and monuments, and you can see the past glory of the mighty French Empire, the golden Bourbons and the military might of Napoleon, all part of an historic heritage that continues unbroken to the present day, despite the major upheaval of the Revolution in 1789.

France in the 1980s is strongly placed on the economic front with its major manufacturing centers at Lille, Lyons, and Paris and the port of Marseille in the south. But it is for its splendid beaches that the Riviera coast is best known; the elegant resorts of Nice and Cannes vying with St. Tropez and its starlet strip. Farther west the wild, swampy Camargue region with its roaming horses and wealth of wildlife is a great attraction for naturalists. Inland, the ancient towns of Arles, Avignon, and Nîmes are much visited.

The southwest also has fine beaches, the forests of the Landes area and, above all, Bordeaux, the greatest wine area in the world. Others may prefer the wilder Brittany coastline, the quiet charm of the Loire region with its magnificent châteaux or the gently pastoral area of the Dordogne.

Above: Paris and its environs constitute the second largest metropolitan area in Europe. The city on the Seine has long been a world center for business, art, religion, education, and tourism. Shown here is the Eiffel Tower, a symbol of French achievement.

Below: The valley of the Loire River, the longest river in France, is famous for vineyards and for the châteaux built during the fifteenth and sixteenth centuries. The Château de Chenonceaux, shown here, is considered by many to be the Loire's prettiest château.

Top: The fields in the foothills of the Pyrenees contribute to France's stature as the leading agricultural nation of Europe.

Above: The Bordeaux area in the southwest is well known for wines. Here grapes are harvested at one of the region's vineyards.

Right: A popular resort area, the subtropical Côte d'Azur runs along the Mediterranean from Cannes to Italy.

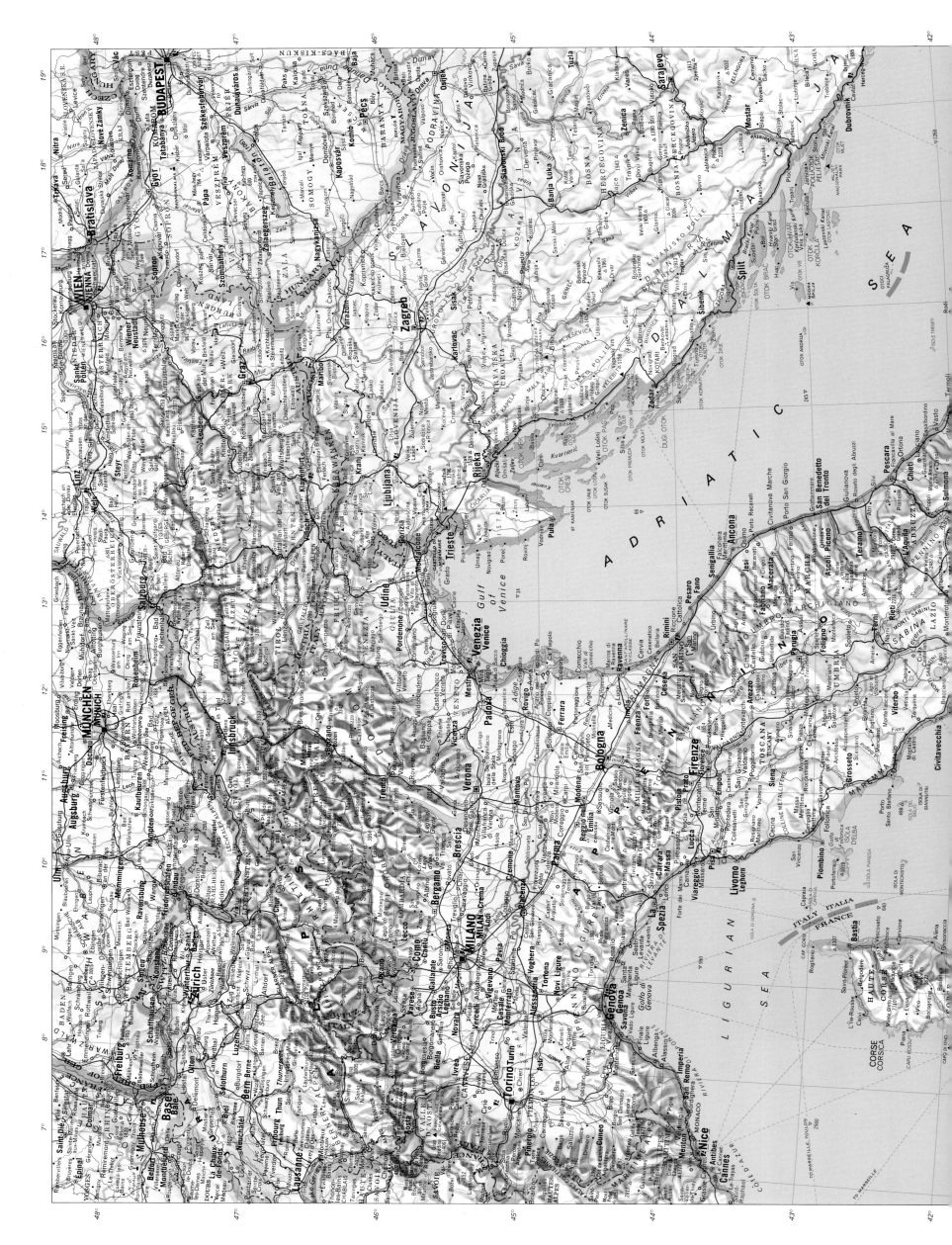

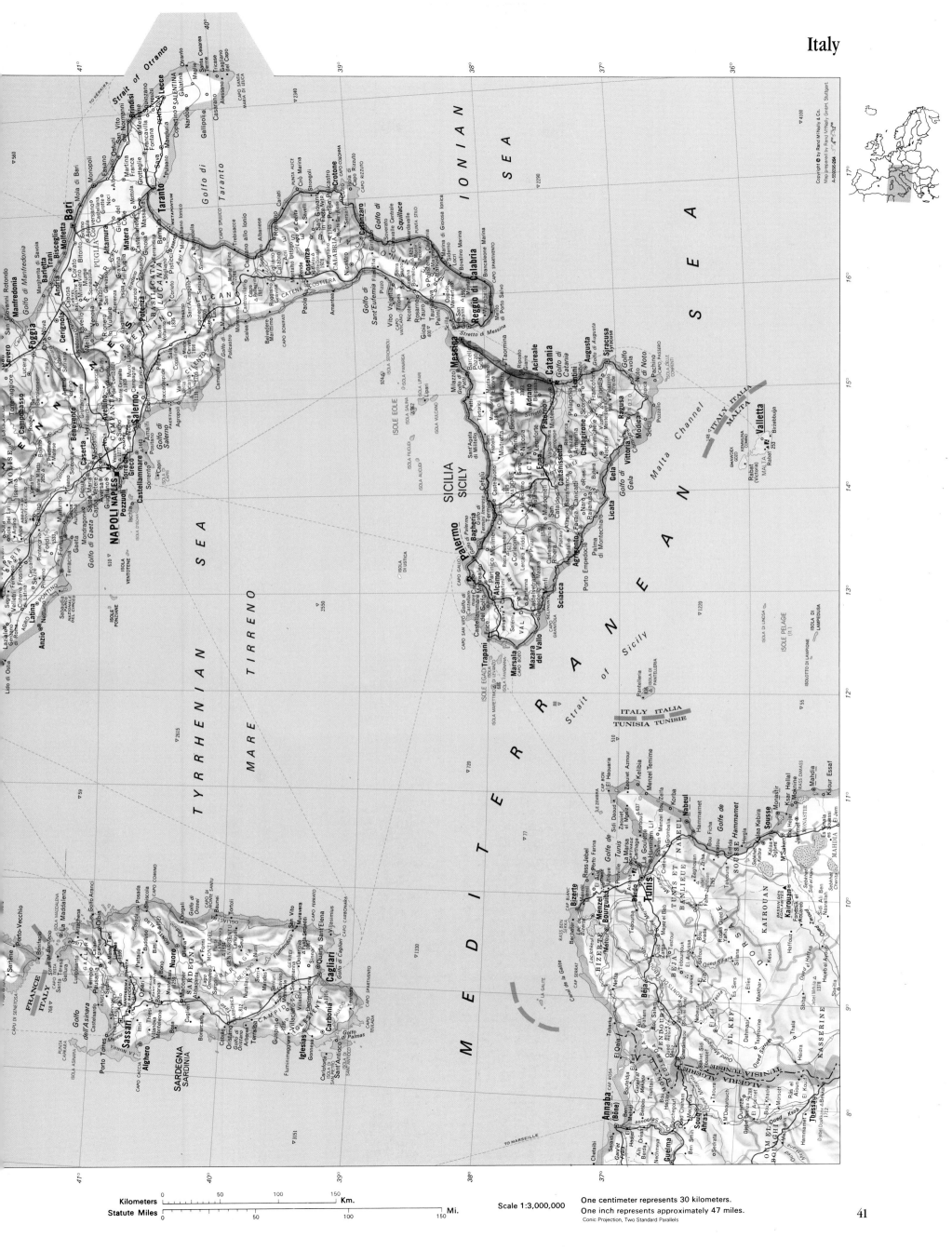

Italy

Italy's skilled and abundant work force has proved to be one of the country's greatest assets. The nation has accomplished something of an economic miracle since 1950, and in the late 1980s, it remains prosperous. Like its people, Italy can be by turns volatile and subdued, extremely wealthy or disturbingly poor, spontaneous and welcoming or difficult to know. It is, above all, a cultural colossus where the influence of the Roman Catholic church is all-pervasive.

At its peak during the Roman Empire, which spread its influence throughout the world, Rome (Roma) itself – the Eternal City – contains more architectural and artistic masterpieces than any other place in the world. At Rome's heart is the Basilica of St. Peter and the Vatican, home of the Roman Catholic church. Rome also has such favorite haunts as the Trevi Fountain and the Spanish Steps.

Golden Florence (Firenze), in Tuscany, birthplace of the Renaissance, combines a wealth of priceless treasures in its buildings and museums with the prosperity of a modern city. Among the sights are classic monuments, like Michelangelo's David, and historic architecture, such as the sixteenth-century Ponte Vecchio.

Venice (Venezia) remains a popular attraction despite its environmental problems. The Grand Canal cuts a backwards S-curve through the city, and modes of travel are limited to motorboats, waterbuses, and the famous gondolas. Tourists can also venture on foot, using the more than four hundred foot bridges that cross the smaller canals. On the many islands that make up the city are found historic squares, the most famous of which might be the Piazza San Marco.

Then there is Milan (Milano), Italy's economic pulse, with much of the new industrial development centered north of the old city. The metropolitan area of Milan is Italy's most populous. The Milan Cathedral is truly awe inspiring, and other attractions include da Vinci's *The Last Supper.* Milan is home to La Scala, one of the world's most renowned opera companies.

And there is more to this country of hot summers and superb scenery. Positano on the fashionable Costa Amalfitina, the artistic haven of Portofino and the Italian coast resorts all have much to offer. Inland, the Italian Lakes lie serenely at the foot of the Alps, while to the northeast are the dramatic Dolomites (Dolomiti) with their famous skiing resorts. To the south is historic Palermo, on Sicily.

Above: Portofino is chief among the resort and fishing towns that line the northwest coastal region known as the Italian Riviera. The beauty and climate of the region draw many visitors.

Left: Umbria – a region in the Apennines – is a land of scenic vistas and medieval cities. Considerable agricultural activity produces grapes, sugar beets, olives, and livestock.

Above: The many eras of Rome's long history are reflected in the buildings, squares, and streets of the city. The Piazza Navona was built in the sixteenth and seventeenth centuries.

Far left: The Dolomites' limestone peaks rise above Cortina d'Ampezzo in northeast Italy. This eastern branch of the Alps is popular with tourists, especially those interested in mountaineering.

Left: Venice (Venezia) consists of more than 118 islands in a large lagoon. The main water thoroughfare is the Grand Canal, but narrow canals separate most of the islands.

ATLANTIC

OCEAN

Bay of Biscay

10° 9° 8° 7° 6° 5° 4° 3° 2°

43°

42°

41°

40°

39°

38°

37°

36°

35°

CABO ORTEGAL
Ria de Ortigueira
PUNTA DE LA ESTACA DE BARES
CABO PRIOR 160 El Ferrol
Ria de Betanzos del Caudillo
La Coruña
CABO TOURIÑAN 2798
CABO DE FINISTERRE

Vivero Ribadeo
PEÑAS
Avilés Gijón
Oviedo
Santander
CABO DE AJO
CABO MACHICHACO
Donostia
San Sebastián
Bilbao
Baracaldo
EUSKAL
HERRIKO
Vitoria Gasteiz

GALICIA
Santiago de
Compostela
Pontevedra
Vigo

Lugo

ASTURIAS
CANTABRICA
CORDILLERA
CANTABRIA

Miranda
de Ebro
LA RIOJA
Logroño

León
Ponferrada

SPAIN
ESPAÑA
PORTUGAL
MINHO
Braga
Guimarães

Zamora
Valladolid
CASTILLA
LEÓN
Palencia
Burgos

Soria

Porto
Vila Nova de Gaia

TRÁS-OS-MONTES
Bragança

DOURO
Douro

Salamanca
Segovia
MADRID
Guadalajara

Coimbra
BEIRA

Guarda
ESTRELA
SIERRA DE GATA

Ávila

MADRID
Alcalá de Henares
Leganés
Parla Getafe
Aranjuez
Cuenca

LITORAL
CABO MONDEGO
Figueira da Foz

BEIRA
BAIXA

Plasencia
Talavera
de la Reina
Toledo

CASTILLA-LA MANCHA

Leiria
Fátima

Tagus Tejo
Castelo Branco

Cáceres
Tagus Tejo

ESTREMADURA
Tagus Tejo
LISBOA LISBON
Setúbal
Barreiro

Santarém

EXTREMADURA
Mérida
Badajoz

Don
Benito
Guadiana
LA SERENA

Ciudad Real
Puertollano
Valdepeñas
Albacete
LA MANCHA

CABO DA ROCA
CABO ESPICHEL

Évora

ALENTEJO
PORTUGAL

SIERRA
MORENA

CABO DE SINES
Santiago do Cacém

Beja

SIERRA
Guadalquivir
Córdoba

Jaén
Úbeda
Linares

BÉTICOS

ALGARVE
Lagos Faro
CABO DE SÃO VICENTE
CAPE ST. VINCENT

Huelva
Sevilla
Seville

Morón de
la Frontera
Antequera

Granada
SIERRA NEVADA
Almería
CABO DE GATA

Sanlúcar de
Barrameda
Jerez de la Frontera
El Puerto de Santa María
Cádiz
San Fernando

Utrera

Málaga
COSTA DEL SOL

ALBORÁN SEA

ATLANTIC

Algeciras
La Línea
Gibraltar (U.K.)
EUROPA POINT
PUNTA DE TARIFA Tarifa
Strait of Gibraltar
Estrecho de Gibraltar

OCEAN

Tánger
Tangier
CAP SPARTEL
Ceuta (Sp.)

Tétouan

Larache

Melilla (Sp.)
Nador

MOROCCO
AL-MAGREB
RIF

Copyright © by Rand McNally & Co.
Map prepared by Rand McNally GmbH, Stuttgart.
A-559900-264 −18 −12

MEDITERRANEAN SEA

Golfe du Lion

ILLES BALEARS
BALEARIC ISLANDS

MALLORCA
MAJORCA

MENORCA
MINORCA

ALGERIA
ALGÉRIE

ATLAS MOUNTAINS TELLIEN

ATLAS TELLIEN

PLAINE DU HODNA

Kilometers 0 50 100 150 Km.

Statute Miles 0 50 100 150 Mi.

Scale 1:3,000,000

One centimeter represents 30 kilometers.
One inch represents approximately 47 miles.

Conic Projection, Two Standard Parallels

45

Spain & Portugal

Despite their physical togetherness and intermingled histories, Spain and Portugal are two very different countries. Recently, Spain – the larger and more prosperous of the two – and Portugal have become members of the EEC and should benefit economically as a result.

At its heart, Spain remains the land of Hemingway, where bulls still run in the streets of Pamplona – and the land of El Greco, whose magnificent paintings in Toledo are matched by the town's spectacular location. Home to the plundering conquistadors, the civilizing Moors, and the feared Spanish Inquisition, Spain continues to be, above all, a land where holy processions and modern celebrations combine in annual outbursts of gaiety and reverence throughout the country.

The vast hotel blocks on the highly commercialized Costas Brava and del Sol contrast starkly with the unchanged life-style of the interior where hilltop villages and vast plains give way to thriving, historic cities.

But Portugal, with its softer landscape, gentle people, white-walled villages and haunting fado music, has a special appeal. Undisturbed by the last two great wars, Lisbon (Lisboa), the capital, retains much of its past glory, the elegant nineteenth-century buildings and boulevards contrasting sharply with the winding alleys of the old Arab quarter, the Alfama. The city has been the Portuguese capital since 1256.

Close by, the dignified resorts of Estoril and Cascais provided a pleasant exile for many of Europe's deposed ruling families, suitably near to the old royal palaces at Byron's beloved Sintra, and Quelez. Along the coasts, brightly painted small boats, often crewed by men in traditional garments, still go out to fish in the time-honored way.

Above: Fishing has long been one of Portugal's most important industries, and fishing towns such as Sezimbra, shown here, line the extensive Atlantic coast. Sardines, cod, and shellfish are most important.

Left: Barcelona, the second largest city in Spain, lies in Cataluña, on the northeastern Mediterranean coast. The city dates from Carthaginian times and contains many historic sites, including the Barcelona Cathedral, shown here.

Right: Shown here are almond trees in Alicante province, in southeastern Valencia. This part of Spain is a fertile Mediterranean region that produces a variety of crops.

Greece & Yugoslavia

In many ways remarkably different – historically, politically, and ethnically – Greece and Yugoslavia jointly represent southeastern Europe. Economically stagnant for many years, Greece has benefited in recent years from its membership in the EEC. Yugoslavia, a Soviet satellite nation, has a developed economy.

Greece, home of some of Europe's earliest civilizations, relies heavily on tourism. Today, the glory that was Greece is still seen in breathtaking ancient ruins. Placed atop the rock of the Acropolis, the classical architectural simplicity of the Parthenon represents the high point of the great age of Athens (Athínai), the modern capital.

The islands of Greece, with their sunny beaches and blue waters, continue to be popular tourist destinations. Crete (Kríti), the largest of the islands, was home to the Minoans, who represented one of Europe's earliest civilizations. Many ancient ruins still exist.

Tourism is increasing in the less commercially developed yet spiritually resilient Yugoslavia. The largest of the Balkan countries, Yugoslavia has made a successful transition from agriculture to industry. Belgrade (Beograd), its capital, and Zagreb are growing industrial centers.

To the tourist, the country is perhaps best known for its beautiful Adriatic coastline, although Yugoslavia offers much more in a complex medley of peoples, religions, and traditions. Serbs, Croats, Slovenians, Macedonians, Montenegrans – not to mention groups of Albanians, Hungarians, and Gypsies – have maintained their own cultures, providing visitors with fascinating discoveries and endless variety.

Above: The Erechtheion, on the Acropolis in Athens (Athínai), is a symbol of the mastery of Greek architecture. Construction on this temple was completed around 410 B.C.

Top right: In the Julian Alps, near the Austrian border, lies scenic Lake Bled, Yugoslavia. This corner of Slovenija is a popular resort region.

Middle right: The narrow Corinth Canal connects the Gulf of Corinth with Saronikós Bay, thereby eliminating journeys by water around the Peloponnese peninsula of Greece. Freight trains such as this are a regular sight on the canal's bridge.

Right: The Bay of Kotor and the town of the same name are found in Montenegro, Yugoslavia. This inlet on the Adriatic is a prime port and tourist destination.

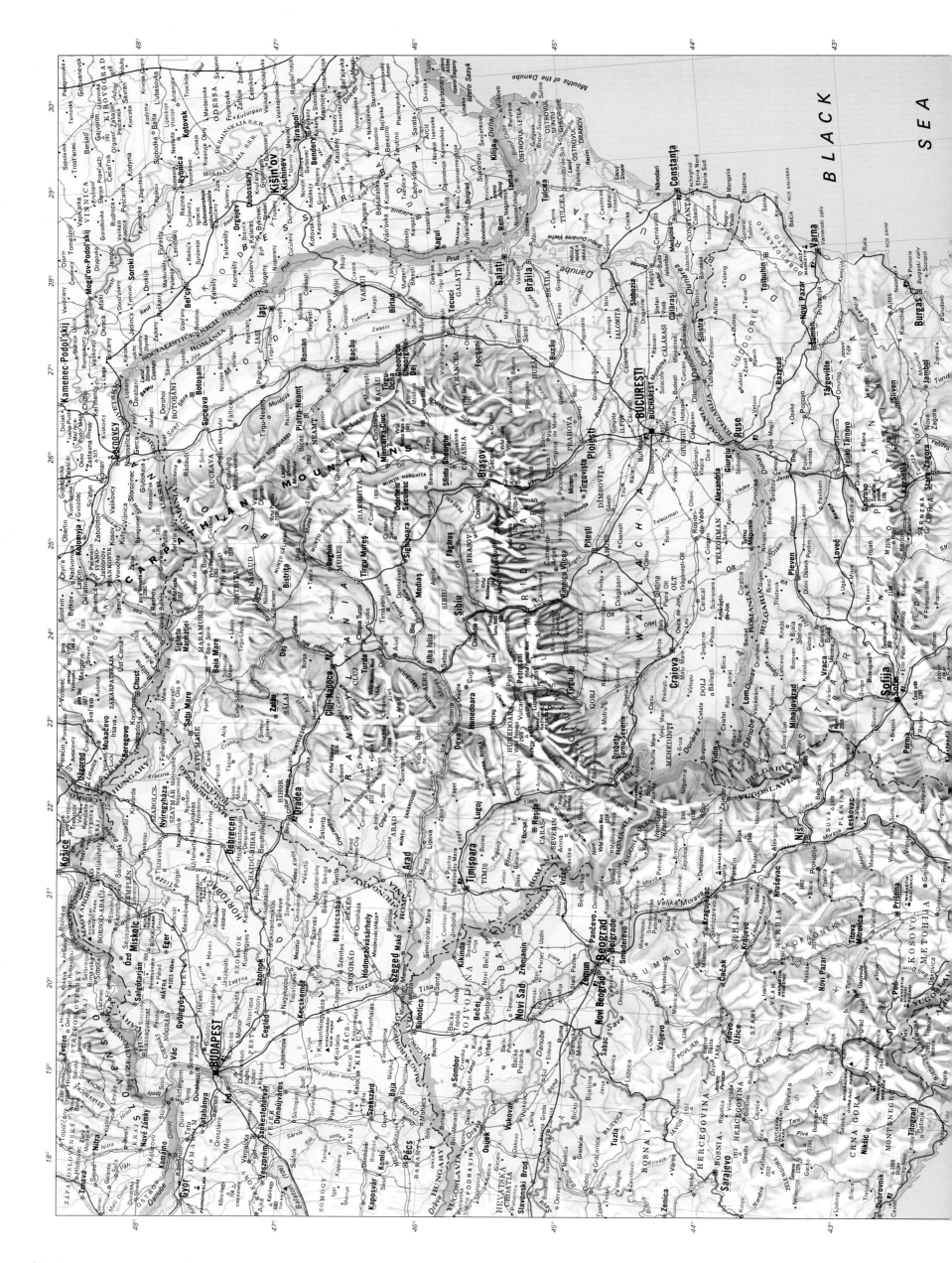

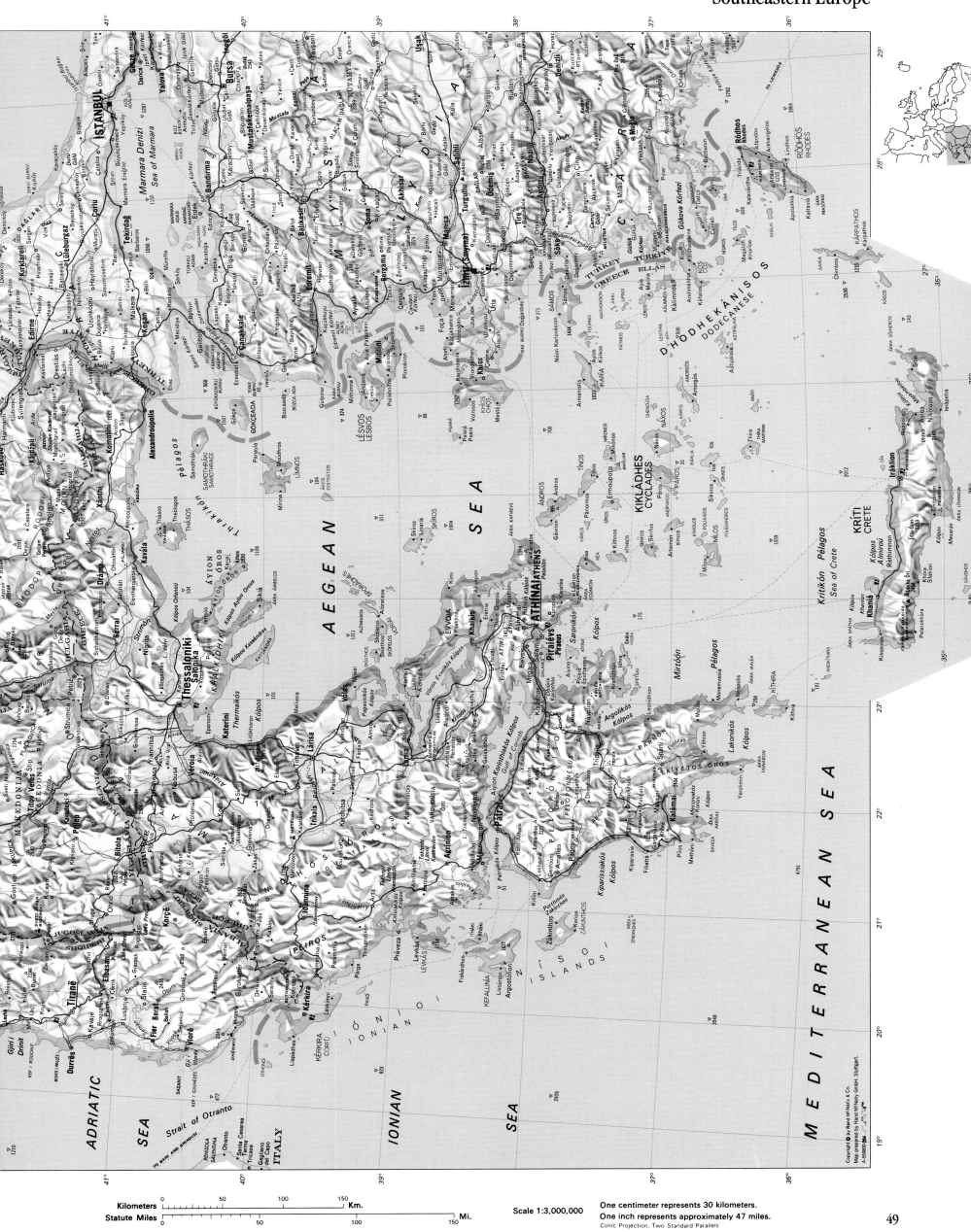

ADRIATIC SEA

IONIAN SEA

AEGEAN SEA

MEDITERRANEAN SEA

Sea of Marmara

Marmara Denizi

Strait of Otranto

ITALY

TO BARI AND BRINDISI

ISTANBUL

Bursa

Edirne

Thessaloniki
Salonika

ATHÍNAI ATHENS
Piraiévs
Piraeus

Pátra

İzmir (Smyrna)

RÓDHOS
RHODES

KRÍTI
CRETE
Iráklion

KIKLÁDHES
CYCLADES

DHODHEKÁNISOS
DODECANESE

GREECE
ELLÁS

TURKEY
TÜRKIYE

KÉRKIRA
CORFÚ

NÍSOI IÓNIOI
IONIAN ISLANDS

Kikion Pélagos
Sea of Crete

Kritikón Pélagos

Gulf of Corinth
Aíyion Korinthiakós Kólpos

PELOPÓNNISOS

TíRANÉ

JUGOSLAVIJA

MAKEDONIJA

BULGARIA

ALBANIA
SHQIPËRIA

Tiranë

Kilometers   0   50   100   150   Km.
Statute Miles   0   50   100   150   Mi.

Scale 1:3,000,000

One centimeter represents 30 kilometers.
One inch represents approximately 47 miles.
Conic Projection, Two Standard Parallels

Soviet Union
Profile

Location and Size

The Soviet Union sits between Europe and Asia and is the largest country in the world – more than twice the size of any other nation. Extending from the Taymyr (Tajmyr) Peninsula in the north to Taškent, next to the Afghan border in the south, the central Soviet Union extends some 3,000 miles (4,800 kilometers). From the west to the east, the Soviet Union stretches from the Czechoslovak border to the Bering Strait, thus wrapping nearly halfway around the globe in the Northern Hemisphere. Beyond the mainland, there are many islands in the Arctic Ocean that belong to the Soviet Union.

The huge distances of the Soviet Union can be envisioned in terms of time. When it is eight o'clock in the morning in Moscow (Moskva), it is six o'clock in the evening in the eastern Cukotskij Peninsula. With a total area of nearly nine million square miles (more than twenty-two million square kilometers), 25 percent of the country is in Europe, 75 percent in Asia. For such a land mass, the Soviet Union has only

limited stretches of coastline that are ice free throughout the year. In the northwest, only a small part of the Arctic coast is free of ice all year. In the west, parts of the Baltic freeze in the winter, but most of the Black Sea coast and its ports remain open all the time. The north-flowing rivers are frozen for up to seven months each year.

Landscape

Most Soviet land borders are in mountainous parts of the country. The south and east are the highest areas, while the northern, central, and western parts are dominated by plains.

European Soviet Union consists in the east of the Great European Plain. Only the Central Russian Uplands, the Valdai (Valdajskaja) Hills – rising to 1,125 feet (346 meters) northwest of Moscow – and the uplands of the Kola (Kol'skij) Peninsula – rising to 3,907 feet (1,191 meters) – stand above this. The lower plains continue eastward through the basins of the rivers Don, Volga, and North Dvina to the Ural (Ural'skije) Mountains, which form the only major

north-south divide in the western Soviet Union.

To the south of this lowland region lies the Black Sea, with its outlet to the Mediterranean, and the Caspian Sea, which is a focus of inland drainage. The Carpathian Mountains on the Romanian border rise to 6,762 feet (2,061 meters), and the Caucasus Mountains (Bol'Soj Kavkaz) between the Black and Caspian seas rise to 18,481 feet (5,633 meters).

East of the Caspian Sea lies the Turanian (Turanskaja) Plain and an area of inland drainage focusing on the Aral (Aral'skoje) Sea. Uplands surround this whole region, particularly to the south and east, where the boundaries with Afghanistan and China lie within the Pamir and the Tien Shan ranges. Here the highest point in the Soviet Union, Communism (Kommunizma) Peak, rises to more than 24,500 feet (almost 7,500 meters). East and northeast of the Turanian Plain are the Lake Balkhash (Balchaš) basin and the Kazakh (Kazachskaja) uplands.

West of the Yenisey (Jenisej) River and east of the Urals is an extensive plain known as the Western Siberian

Lowlands. This has a total area of over one million square miles (2.5 million square kilometers) and constitutes the largest single area of plain land in the world.

The landscape east of the Yenisey is more varied and elevated. The central Siberian Uplands between the Yenisey and Lena rivers is generally above 1,000 feet (300 meters) and in the south reaches to above 10,000 feet (3,000 meters) in the Sayan (Sajany) and Yablonovy (Jablonovyj) mountains. The Putoran (Putorana) Mountains in the north rise to a maximum height of 5,581 feet (1,701 meters). The remote region east of the Lena River is dominated by a series of mountain ranges that reach a maximum of 15,584 feet (4,750 meters) in the Kamchatka (Kamčatka) Peninsula.

The Soviet Union is a land of great rivers draining in four directions. In the west are comparatively short rivers – such as the Don, the Dnepr, and the Dvina – flowing to the Black or Baltic seas. In the east, the Amur and many smaller rivers flow eastward to the Pacific. About half the country is drained northward by the Ob', Yenisey, and Lena

Left: Suzdal', north of Vladimir, was founded in 1028 and is the site of many historic buildings. These women are dressed in the traditional clothing of this region in the east-central Soviet Union.

Right: St. Basil's Cathedral, Moscow, was commissioned by Ivan the Terrible and erected in the mid sixteenth century. This church just south of Red Square epitomizes historic Russia.

river systems. The Volga and Ural flow to the Caspian Sea, and the Amu Darya (Amudarja) and Syr-Darya to the Aral Sea, forming the largest inland drainage basin of the world.

Climate

The Soviet Union is the most extensive west-east land mass in the world. It is a continent surrounded by both land and seas, encompassing huge mountain ranges and massive plains. Overall, the country's climates are characterized by large temperature fluctuations and low precipitation.

The southern parts of Soviet Central Asia experience a midlatitude desert climate. Over a large area, the average monthly temperature in January falls to 14°F (-10°C) but in July rises to 86°F (30°C). Nowhere does annual precipitation rise above eight inches (two hundred millimeters), and it is often far less.

In a broad belt from the southern Ukraine (Ukrainskaja) to the Mongolian and Chinese borders lies an area of dry midlatitude steppe climate. The temperature range here is higher in the east than in the west. Low annual rainfall, less than sixteen inches (four hundred millimeters), comes mainly in the summer.

In the extreme north of the country, polar climates extend from west to east. Most places in this area have at least one month when the average temperature is above freezing, but no month's average rises above 50°F (10°C).

Between these southern desert-steppe and the northern polar climates, most of the Soviet Union has a more humid climate with a wide annual temperature range. In the west, the July average temperature may approach 72°F (22°C) with the winter average going as low as 14°F (-10°C). Precipitation, with a summer maximum, comes throughout the year and may total twenty-eight inches (seven hundred millimeters). This decreases farther east and the temperature range increases.

History, Politics, and Economy

The region that is now the Soviet Union was inhabited as early as the Stone Age. The area has been a changing land that has undergone successive invasions by the Scythians, Sarmatians, Goths, Huns, Bulgars, Slavs, and others.

By A.D. 989, Byzantine cultural influence had become predominant. Various groups and regions were slowly incorporated into a single state. In 1547, Ivan IV was crowned czar of all Russia, beginning a tradition of czarist rule. This tradition lasted until the Russian Revolution in 1917, when the Bolsheviks came to power and named Vladimir Ilyich Lenin as head of the first Soviet government. After the Revolution, the Bolsheviks established a Communist state and weathered a bitter civil war, consolidating their power in 1920. On December 30, 1922, the Union of Soviet Socialist Republics was born. The word *soviet* means *council* in Russian, and it was used because government councils make up the system of government. The word *socialist* was used instead of *communist* because the Russians believed that communism was an ideal political and economic state not yet achieved.

Joseph Stalin succeeded Lenin as head of state in 1924 and initiated a series of political purges that lasted through the 1930s. The Soviet Union later became embroiled in World War II and lost over twenty million people. Suffering widespread destruction of both city and countryside, the Soviets emerged from the war with extended influence, however, having annexed part of Finland and many Eastern European nations. In the late 1940s and 1950s, a period of lasting international tension and mistrust erupted between the Soviet Union and the West. This period is known as the Cold War.

Following Stalin's death in 1953, the Soviet Union experienced a liberalization of policies under Nikita Krushchev. In 1964, Krushchev was ousted from power and Leonid Brezhnev took control. Throughout his reign, Brezhnev worked to consolidate and strengthen the power of the Secretariat and Politburo of the Communist party. He also pursued a policy of détente with the West. In 1982 Brezhnev died, and Soviet leadership was passed on to Yuri Andropov, who died in 1984. Leadership then went to Konstantin Chernenko, who died in 1985. Mikhail Gorbachev, the youngest Soviet leader in decades, took office in 1985 and has initiated many reforms in human-rights policies as well as international diplomacy with the West. In the late 1980s, a period of openness, or *glasnost*, has characterized Soviet society.

As an industrial power, the Soviet Union ranks second only to the United States. Mining, steel production, and other heavy industries predominate. The Soviet Union is self-sufficient in coal, petroleum, natural gas, and iron ore; it is also a world leader in timber production. Although this huge nation is so richly endowed with minerals and other natural resources, the Soviets lag in the development of advanced technology, particularly in availability of consumer goods.

The Soviet economy is controlled by the state, and economic policies are administered through a series of five-year plans, which emphasize industrial and technological growth. The Soviets suffer from low productivity, energy shortages, and a lack of skilled labor, however, and these are problems the government hopes can be eased by greater use of technology and science.

In agriculture, the Soviets produce more wheat, cotton, potatoes, and sugar than any other nation in the world. There are three types of Soviet farms: collective farms, state farms, and private garden plots. Garden plots produce as much as 60 percent of the nation's potato supply. Most bigger field crops are grown on collective and state farms. Though the country contains some of the world's most fertile land, long winters and hot, dry summers keep many crop yields low. This has forced the Soviets to import some farm products from the West, especially feed grains. In 1980 and 1981, the United States refused to sell grain to the Soviets in protest of its invasion of Afghanistan. The Soviet Union is also a leading nation in the fishing industry and the exportation of caviar.

Right: Leningrad, on the Gulf of Finland in the northeast Soviet Union, is the nation's second largest city. Originally named St. Petersburg, the port city was built in 1703 by Peter the Great and served as the Russian capital until 1918. Shown here is Peterhof, formerly the czar's summer residence and now a museum, situated just outside modern Leningrad.

Top left: A basket of caviar is carried for weighing in Ust'-Kamčatsk. The livelihood of many residents of this peninsula on the Bering Sea depends upon world demand for this delicacy.

Top right: State farms are owned by the Soviet government and employ salaried workers. Collective farms are run by their members. These two types of farms account for most of the major crops grown in the Soviet Union. Here, wheat is harvested on a state farm.

Above: Situated in the northwest, southeast of Leningrad, Novgorod is first mentioned in documents dating from the 800s. One of the oldest cities in the Soviet Union, Novgorod has preserved some of its historic sites, including this eleventh-century church.

Right: Jalta, a Ukrainian city on the Black Sea, is a leading Soviet resort. It is situated on a peninsula known as the Crimea — a subtropical region that was first settled by ancient Greeks.

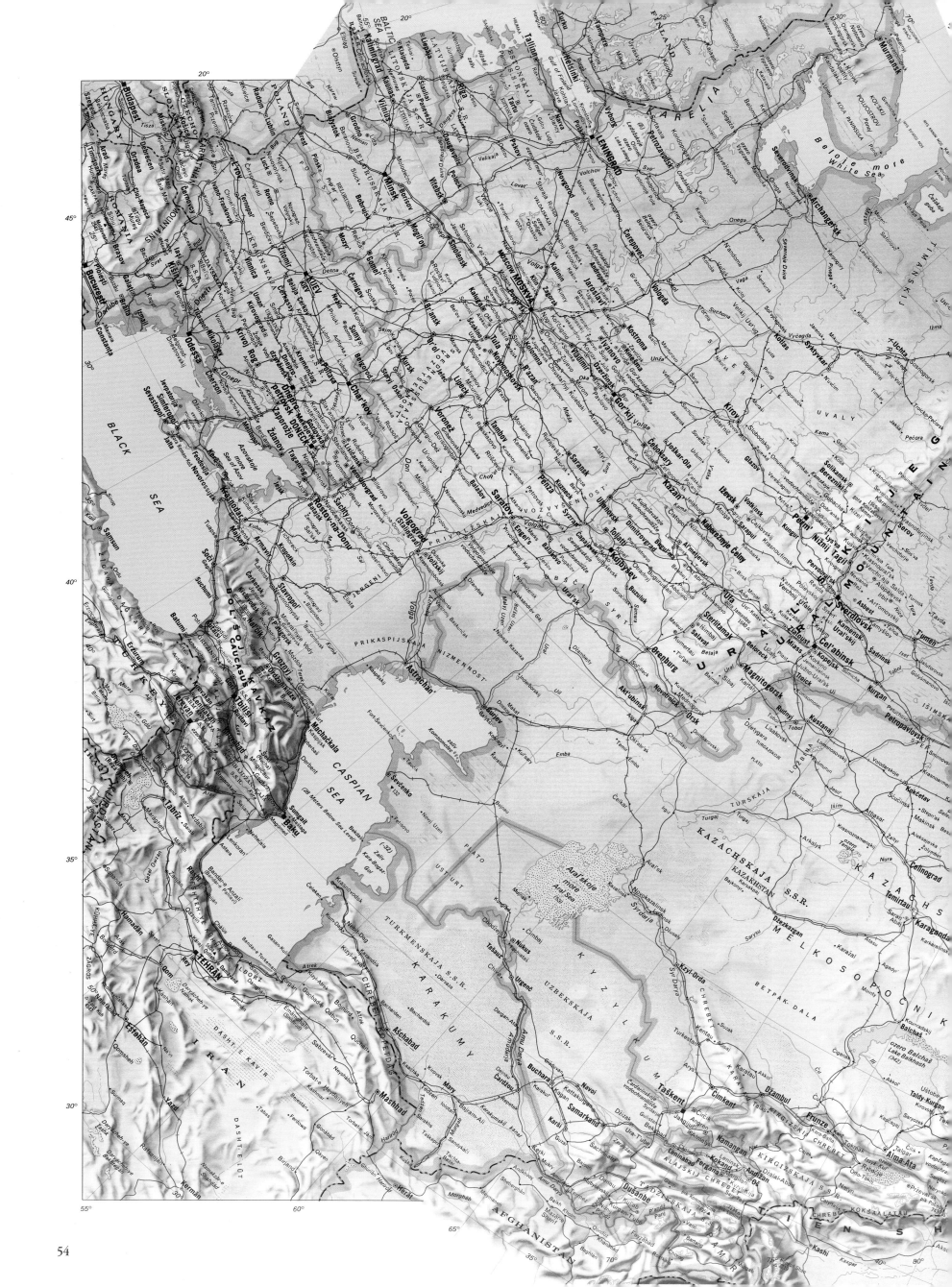

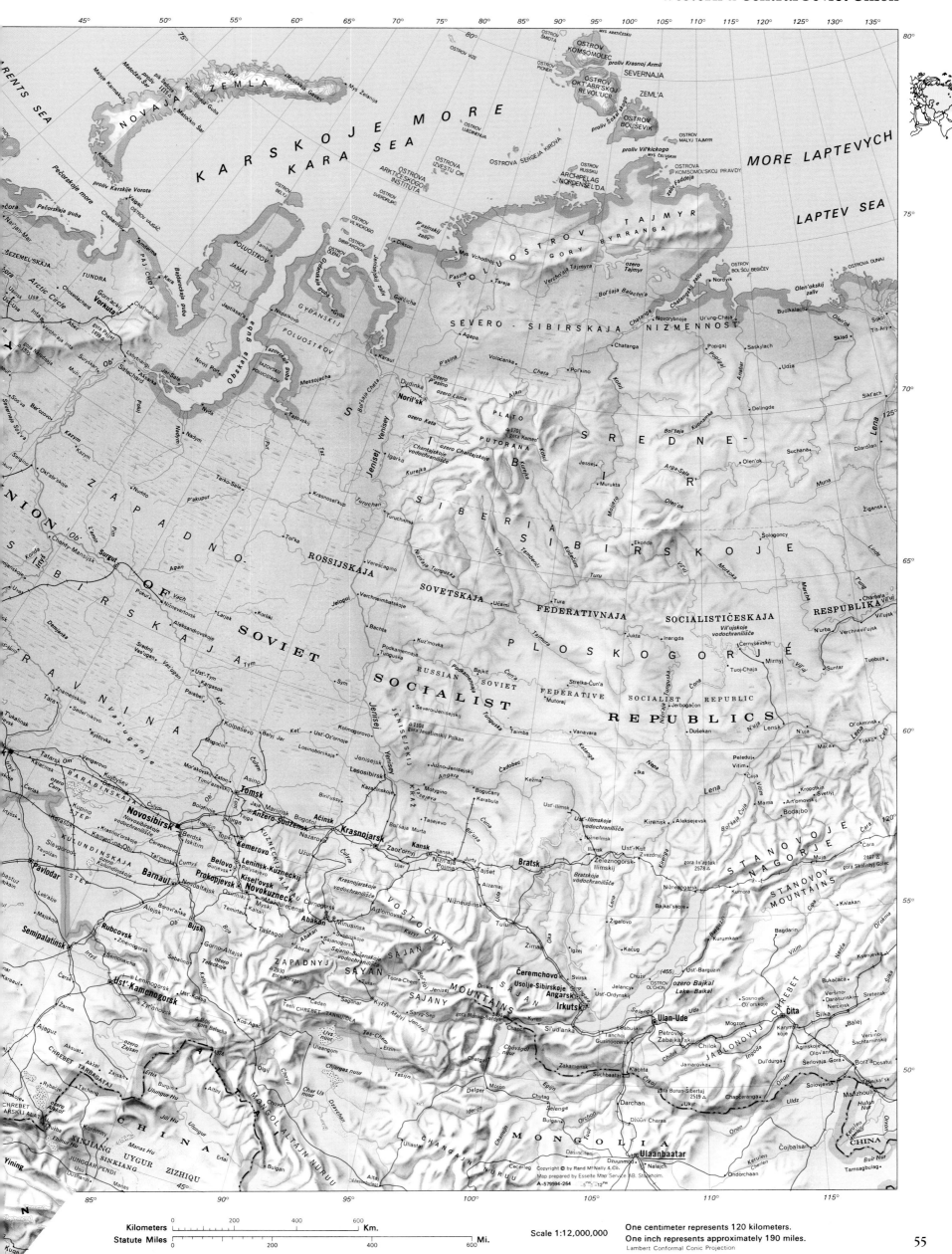

Kilometers
Statute Miles

0   200   400   600   Km.
0   200   400   600   Mi.

Scale 1:12,000,000

One centimeter represents 120 kilometers.
One inch represents approximately 190 miles.

Copyright © by Rand McNally & Co.
Map prepared by Esselte Map Service AB, Stockholm.
A-579594-264

Lambert Conformal Conic Projection

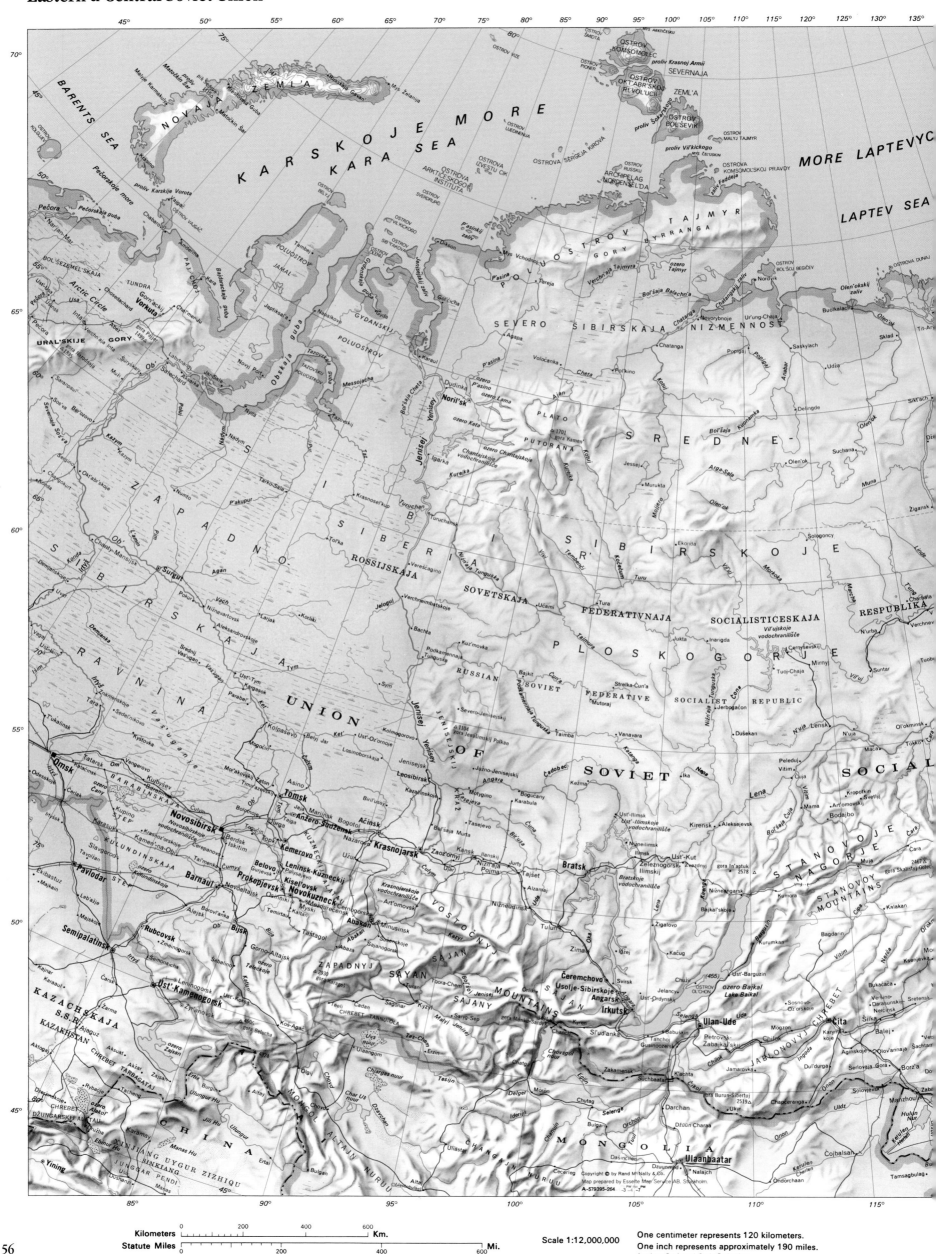

Kilometers
Statute Miles

0   200   400   600   Km.

0   200   400   600   Mi.

Scale 1:12,000,000

One centimeter represents 120 kilometers.
One inch represents approximately 190 miles.

Lambert Conformal Conic Projection

VOSTOCNO-SIBIRSKOJE MORE

EAST SIBERIAN SEA

Chukchi Sea

Bering Sea

OSTROVA

OSTROVA DE-LONGA

OSTROV KOTELNYJ

OSTROV NOVAJA SIBIR

proliv Longa

OSTROV VRANGELA

Arctic Circle

SIBIRSKIJE OSTROVA

L'ACHOVSKIJE OSTROVA

proliv Dmitrija Lapteva

Janskij zaliv

SANT LAWRENCE ISLAND

SAINT MATTHEW ISLAND

NUNIVAK ISLAND

MYS SVJATOJ

Bol'soj Anjuj

Malyj Anjuj

AN'UJSKIJ CHREBET

ANADYRSKOJE PLOSKOGORJE

zaliv Kresta

Anadyrskij zaliv

MOMSKIJ CHREBET

CHREBET ČERSKOGO

KOLYMSKAJA NIZMENNOST

JUKAGIRSKOJE PLOSKOGORJE

KORJAKSKOJE NAGORJE

CHREBET

SIBERIA

CHREBET SUNTAR-CHAJATA

CHREBET SETTE-DABAN

Magadan

Taujskaja guba

Šelichova zaliv

SREDINNYJ CHREBET

STANOVOJ CHREBET

Lena

Jakutsk

Pokrovsk

ALDANSKOJE NAGORJE

CHREBET DŽUGDŽUR

Ochotsk

POLUOSTROV KAMČATKA

KAMCHATKA

Petropavlovsk-Kamčaskij

KOMANDORSKIJE OSTROVA

SEA OF OKHOTSK

OCHOTSKOJE MORE

OSTROV ION

Pervyj Kuril'skij proliv

Severo-Kuril'sk

REPUBLICS

BURINSKIJ CHREBET

Komsomol'sk-na-Amure

Svobodnyj

Belogorsk

Blagoveščensk

Chabarovsk

SANTARSKIJE OSTROVA

Sachalinskij zaliv

OSTROV SACHALIN

SAKHALIN

KURIL'SKIJE OSTROVA

KURIL ISLANDS

proliv Kruzenšterna

proliv Friza

Uglegorsk

Sovetskaja Gavan

Južno-Sachalinsk

zaliv Terpenija

MYS TERPENIJA

Tatarskij proliv

Habomai, Shikotan Kunashiri, and
Etorofu, occupied by the U.S.S.R.
since 1945, are claimed by Japan
pending a final peace treaty.

SICHOTE-ALIN

DA HINGGAN LING

NEI MONGGOL ZIZHIQU

MONGOLIA

CHINA

MANCHURIA

HEILONGJIANG

Bei'an

Yichun

Hegang

Jiamusi

Shuangyashan

Qiqihar Tsitsihar

Harbin

Mudanjiang

Suifenhe

Art'om

Vladivostok

Nachodka

La Perouse Strait

Wakkanai

REBUN-TO

RISIRI-TO

HOKKAIDO

Asahikawa

Kushiro

Otaru

Sapporo

Tomakomai

Muroran

Hakodate

SEA OF JAPAN

Aomori

Hirosaki

Akita

Morioka

Hachinohe

JAPAN

HONSHU

PACIFIC OCEAN

57

Asia
Profile

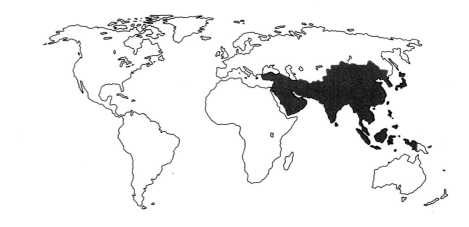

Location and Size

Asia is the largest continent in the world, covering an area of 17,159,995 square miles (44,444,100 square kilometers). It spreads over 33 percent of the world's total land surface and is connected to both Europe and Africa. With the highest population in the world – nearly three billion people – Asia holds about 59 percent of the world's total population.

This vast continent can be divided into six main regions: western Asia, which encompasses Iran, Afghanistan, Cyprus, Iraq, Israel, United Arab Emirates, Yemen, Turkey, Jordan, Kuwait, Lebanon, Oman, Saudi Arabia, and other middle eastern countries east of the Suez Canal; eastern Asia, which includes Japan, North and South Korea, and most of China; southern Asia, including India, Pakistan, Nepal, Bangladesh, Bhutan, Sri Lanka, and Maldives; southeastern Asia, which groups Indonesia, Malaysia, New Guinea, the Philippines, Singapore, Vietnam, Laos, Thailand, Kampuchea, Burma, and Brunei; central Asia, encompassing Mongolia and the autonomous Chinese regions of Tibet and Sinkiang (Xinjiang); and finally, Soviet Asia, clustering Siberia and all the Asian republics of the Soviet Union. Asia is a diverse continent filled with many races, religions, languages, political systems, and cultures.

Landscape

Asian landscape comprises many high mountain ranges, plateaus, basins, island clusters, and lowlands. Mountains predominate, and Asia's tallest peaks are in the Himalayas – the highest of which soar to more than twenty-nine thousand feet (almost nine thousand meters). The lowest point in Asia is 1,296 feet (395 meters) below sea level, at the Dead Sea in Israel.

Southwest Asia tends to be rugged and mountainous, reaching 18,387 feet (5,604 meters) in the Elburz (Alborz) Mountains of northern Iran. Also within this region lie some extensive plateaus, such as the Plateau of Iran. Parts of this region are prone to earthquakes; in 1988, the Soviet republic of Armenia (Arm'anskaja) suffered a devastating earthquake in which more than fifty

thousand people lost their lives.

South of this area is geographically more complex. Its western region is part of the great Rift Valley, which extends from East Africa to Syria. The mountains of the Arabian Peninsula rise to 12,336 feet (3,760 meters). East of these mountains, the landscape falls across the great desert expanse of the Arabian Peninsula to the lowland belt occupied by the Persian Gulf and the southeast-flowing Tigris and Euphrates rivers.

Central Asia is perhaps the most remote and physically brutal area in the world. Bounded in the north by the Tien Shan and the Sayan (Sayany) Mountains, it extends southward across western China, Mongolia, and Tibet to the Himalayas. Within Sinkiang Province, China, the Turfan (Turpan) Depression descends to a level of 505 feet (154 meters) below sea level. In contrast, the highest peaks of the Himalayas are also found here. Encircled by mountains, the area's heartland is a series of plains, predominantly uninviting dry lands including the Takla Makan (Taklimakan) and Gobi deserts, and the Plateau of Tibet.

Farther east lie the large river valleys

of eastern Asia, flanked by the hills and low tablelands of eastern China. The surrounding islands – including Japan and Taiwan – are essentially the tops of a great mountain ridge rising steeply from the floor of the Pacific Ocean. These islands, among others, are in a region known as the Ring of Fire, a zone of active volcanoes and frequent earthquake activity.

South of the mountains of central Asia lies the Indian subcontinent, which is composed of two distinctly different areas. Much of the Deccan Plateau – a triangular-shaped tabletop that occupies

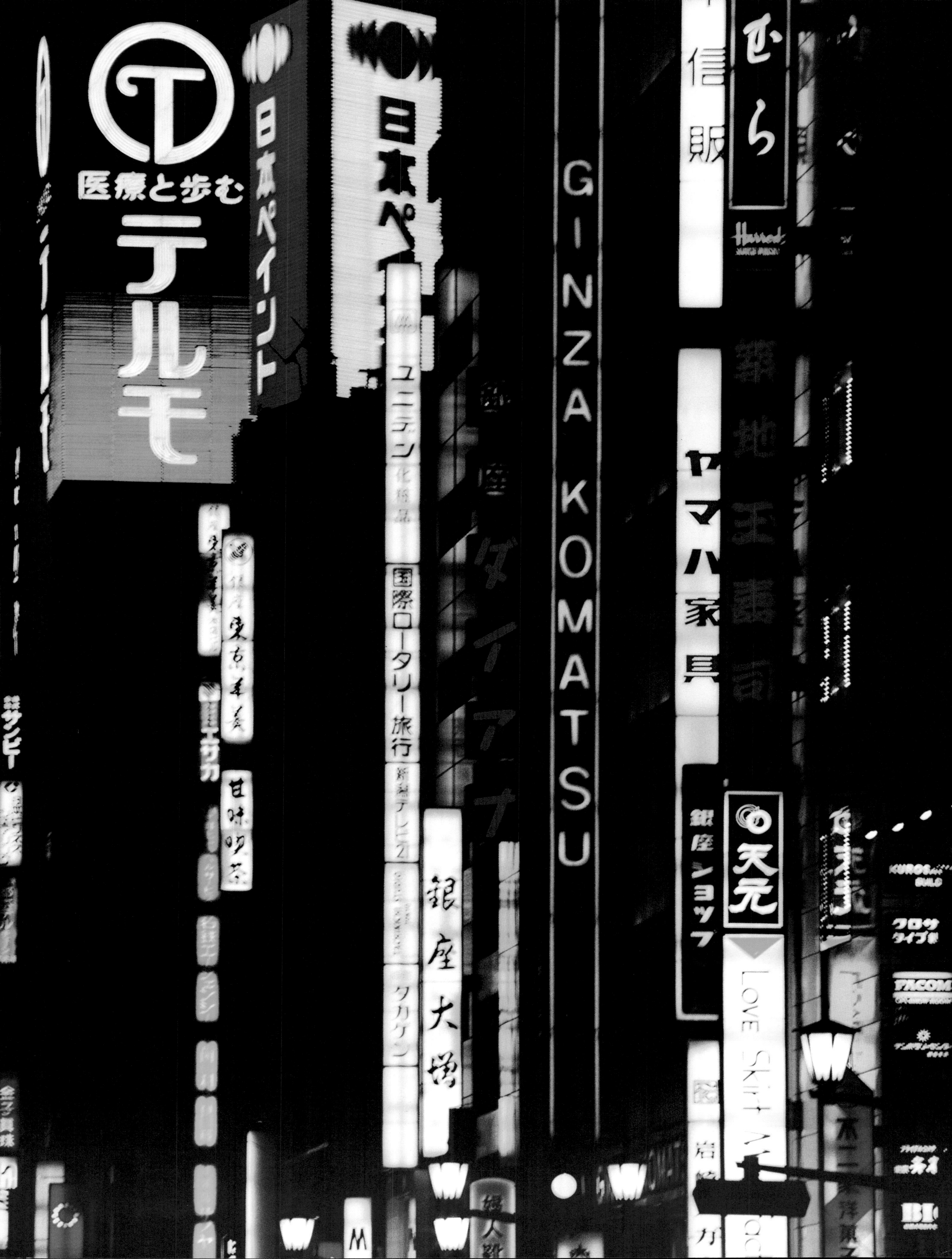

テルモ
医療と歩む
日本ペイント
GINZA KOMATSU
信販
GINZA
ユニデン化粧品
国際ロータリー旅行
銀座大學
ヤマハ家具
銀座ショップ
天元
Love Skirt
Harrod

the southern parts of the peninsula – lies at 1,650 feet (500 meters) to 2,300 feet (700 meters). Its margins rise in the Western and Eastern Ghāts to greater heights – 8,842 feet (2,695 meters) and 5,512 feet (1,680 meters) respectively. Between the Deccan and the Himalayas are the great valleys of the Indus, Ganges (Ganga), and Brahmaputra (Yaluzangbujiang) rivers.

South of China and east of India lies the intricately shaped peninsula of Southeast Asia and the islands beyond. The northern flanks are mountainous. A large number of rivers flow southward across broad plains in Burma, Thailand, and Kampuchea.

Climate

Asia can be divided into three different climate types: monsoon, dry, and cold. The first climate type, monsoon, is predominant in southern, southeastern, and eastern Asia. In the summer, mainland Asia heats up rapidly. As heat builds up, warm air rises and creates low-pressure centers. High-pressure centers above the Pacific and Indian oceans force humid air inland, bringing heavy rains. This occurs mostly during the summer months. During the season of winter monsoons, the opposite occurs. Because the land cools off much more quickly than the surrounding waters, a high-pressure zone develops, forcing continental winds to blow offshore from inland Asia. Monsoon areas are generally warmer in summer and colder in winter than other areas of similar latitude and geographic type.

Temperatures range considerably within monsoon regions. To the north of the equator, summers tend to be hot and humid, with average temperatures reaching 80°F (27°C), while winters are cool and dry (50°F/10°C). The rest of Asia tends to be fairly temperate with the north being generally cooler than the south.

The second climate type, dry, is found in parts of southeast and central Asia. Here, rainfall varies from less than one inch (twenty-five millimeters) annually in some Soviet Asia desert regions to up to twenty inches (five hundred millimeters) annually in the western regions near the Mediterranean Sea.

The third climate type, cold, is found in most of Soviet Asia, to the north. Here, summers tend to be shorter and rainfall less. In the far northern region of Asia, polar climates exist where the subsoil is permanently frozen year-round.

History, Politics, and Economy

Asia has been the home of many great civilizations: the Sumerians, who thrived in Mesopotamia over five thousand years ago; the great Indus Valley culture, which existed over four thousand years ago; the Chinese dynasties, which culminated in the Chou some two thousand years ago; and the empire of Alexander the Great, at its peak seven hundred years later.

Asia has also been the birthplace of many great religions in the world: Buddhism was founded in India and Confucianism in China in the sixth century B.C.; Christianity began in Palestine and Islam in Arabia in the sixth century A.D.

Great empires have come and gone and centuries of wars have swept the area. The Byzantine Empire flourished in the fourth century. The Mongols, led by Genghis and Kubla Khan, dominated vast regions in the thirteenth century. In the sixteenth century, Ottomans ruled parts of eastern Asia. These empires were followed by those of the British, French, and Dutch, and other invaders, who moved in to establish outposts. Today, the remnants of foreign domain have crumbled, and the continent is made up of independent countries.

The people of Asia differ greatly in their life-styles, languages, religions, and politics – more so than in any other single continent. As evidenced by the Tibetans who never leave their mountain aeries and the Arab teenagers who commute by jet to shop in Europe's capital cities, Asians experience very different existences.

Asia's politics are equally diverse. In India, the great leader Mahatma Gandhi preached a doctrine of religious tolerance and civil disobedience that changed his nation forever. Gandhi is regarded as the founder of India's independence movement, and in 1947 he prevailed upon Great Britain to grant India its autonomy. This event changed the course of history for India.

The Chinese Revolution in 1911 brought the downfall of the Manchu dynasty and set about a Nationalist government. This revolutionary force, also called Kuomintang, was aligned with the Chinese Communist party and led by Sun Yat-sen and later by Chiang Kaishek. Tension grew between the Communists and Nationalists until fighting broke out and many Communists were executed. Remaining Communists reorganized under Mao Zedong, and the Communist-Nationalist conflict continued, along with Japanese invasion and occupation. By 1949, Communists controlled most of the country, and the People's Republic of China was proclaimed. Mao died in 1976, but his legacy lives on.

After over two centuries of isolation from the West, Japan began to adopt Western technologies and legal systems, stressing industrialization and education in 1853. After a military expansion that included the annexing of Korea in 1910, Japan became a British ally in World War I. Japan invaded China in 1937, then attacked United States military bases in Pearl Harbor, Hawaii, in 1941. After the United States dropped atomic bombs on Hiroshima and Nagasaki in 1945, Japan surrendered. Since the war, however, Japan has flourished economically and has become a model of the West.

Because the nations of the region are so diverse, the economic outlook for Asia in the late twentieth century is a varied one. Asia now includes a new, rising economic generation in the Middle East and in Japan, South Korea, Taiwan, Singapore, and Hong Kong. China and India embrace rich histories yet have unrealized economic potential in the modern world. Many Asian countries are still Third World nations, clinging to a minimal existence.

Asia
Countries

Afghanistan

Formerly a kingdom, Afghanistan has been a republic since 1973. A terrain of mountains and valleys separates the desert region of the southwest from the more fertile north. Increased development has made natural gas an important export. Since the Soviet invasion in 1979, continued conflict and guerrilla fighting has plagued the nation, and in 1988 the Soviets agreed to remove military forces. Political factions make it unlikely that social and economic conditions will improve quickly.

Bahrain

Composed of thirty-three small islands in the Persian Gulf, this Middle Eastern country has a fierce desert climate. Many of the country's islands are barren and the population is concentrated in the capital city. The oil economy has resulted in an influx of foreign workers and considerable westernization. Friendly international relations and political allegiance to the Arab League characterize the current government.

Bangladesh

The people, mostly peasant farmers, are among Asia's poorest and most rural. With a relatively small area and a high birthrate, the country is also one of the world's most densely populated. The country has yet to recover from damage sustained in a 1971 civil war and a 1985 tidal wave. Farm output fluctuates greatly, subject to frequent monsoons, floods, and droughts. Partially a result of this, the nation's food shortages have not been assuaged.

Bhutan

This small landlocked Himalayan state is independent, but neighboring India officially guides its foreign affairs. The mountainous terrain of Bhutan has long isolated the nation from the outside world. The population is largely rural, with small villages that have grown up around monastery fortresses. Partially due to its physical isolation, Bhutan has one of the world's least developed economies and is dependent on foreign aid. Mining and tourism are developing.

British Indian Ocean Territory

Formed in 1965 from a number of scattered islands in the western Indian Ocean, this British colony today comprises the Chagos Archipelago, some 1,000 miles (1,700 kilometers) southwest of Sri Lanka. The small population mainly fishes and grows food crops.

Brunei

Independence was gained from Britain in 1984. Today the nation is ruled by a sultan, who, as a result of significant oil and natural gas income, is generally regarded as the wealthiest person in the world. Situated on northeastern Borneo, Brunei is generally flat and covered with dense rain forests.

Burma

A Socialist republic since 1974, Burma left the then British Commonwealth in 1948 to become an independent federal country. The terrain is marked by mountains, rivers, and forests; the climate is tropical. Sporadic uprisings continue, often carried out by ethnic minorities.

Burma has been beset with economic problems, caused mainly by the significant destruction it suffered during World War II and by postindependence instability. Agriculture continues as the economic mainstay.

China

One of the oldest civilizations on earth, China has a very long history and has contributed much to world culture. The People's Republic of China has been a Communist state since 1949. China's terrain is varied: two-thirds consists of mountainous or semiarid land, with

Below: **The desert and semiarid regions of northwestern India contrast with the rest of the mostly tropical country. Here, near Pushkar, Rājasthān, camels and other animals are traded during a religious festival held since the fourth century.**

fertile plains and deltas in the east. China has the largest population of any country in the world. Since Communist leader Mao Zedong's death in 1976, foreign trade and contact have expanded. A current economic plan focuses on growth in agriculture, industry, science and technology, and national defense. In 1979, the United States recognized Beijing – rather than T'aipei on Taiwan – as China's capital.

Christmas Island
Lying 210 miles (350 kilometers) south of Java in the eastern Indian Ocean, Christmas Island is now under Australian sovereignty. The extraction of phosphates is the island's major industry.

Cocos Islands
These islands lie six hundred miles (one thousand kilometers) west of Christmas Island. Their control was passed from Singapore to Australia by the British government in 1955.

Cyprus
This eastern Mediterranean island became independent from Britain in 1960. Since then, its history has been marked by Greek-Turkish conflict. Cyprus is marked by a fertile central plain bordered by mountains in the southwest and north. Relocation of Greek Cypriots in the south and Turkish Cypriots in the north has severely disrupted the economy. Greek Cypriots have made progress, expanding agriculture to manufacturing and tourism. Turkish Cypriots remain agriculturally based and dependent on Turkey.

Hong Kong
One of the world's most densely populated areas, Hong Kong is a British colony that was leased from the Chinese in 1898 for a period of ninety-nine years. Low taxes, duty-free status, an accessible location, and an excellent natural harbor have helped make Hong Kong an Asian center of trade. The islands are hilly and tropical.

India
India has a history of civilization that dates back to about 2,500 B.C. The population is composed of two main ethnic groups: the Indo-Aryan and the Dravidian. Hindus are the religious majority, but the country has one of the world's largest Muslim populations. Hindi is the official language. Although economic conditions have improved since India became independent in 1947, poverty, unemployment, underemployment, and civil strife continue to plague the nation. In 1984, Prime Minister Indira Gandhi was assassinated, and conflicts continue.

Indonesia
Java (Jawa), Sumatra (Sumatera), Sulawesi (Celebes), and most of Borneo (Kalimanatan) are the largest islands in this independent republic, which is the fifth most populous nation in the world. Overpopulation threatens the economy and food supply. Economic and political instability led to an attempted Communist coup in 1965, and the government has since outlawed the Communist party, cut its ties with China, and strengthened relations with Western powers.

Iran
Set between the Persian Gulf and the Caspian Sea, Iran (formerly Persia) has a history dating back several thousand years. Nearly all Iranians are Aryan and Muslim, mainly of the Shiite sect. The country is an Islamic republic, with law based on Islamic teachings. Aridity and a harsh mountain-and-desert terrain result in population concentrated in the west and north. Iran's previously rapid economic development has slowed as a result of a 1979 revolution and ongoing war with Iraq. Small-scale farming, manufacturing, and trading appear to be current economic trends. Oil remains the most important export, and trade of Persian carpets continues.

Iraq
This former kingdom became a republic in 1958. It is centered on the fertile basin of the Tigris and Euphrates rivers, where civilizations such as the Sumerian, Babylonian, and Parthian once existed. Oil is the mainstay of Iraq's economy. Despite its wealth, the Iraqi economy, like the Iranian, has been drained by the continuing Iran-Iraq war.

Israel
Israel comprises much of the region of Palestine, the site of most biblical history. Most Israelis are Jewish, and the non-Jewish population is predominantly Arab and Muslim. Hebrew and Arabic are the official languages, and both are used on documents and currency. Despite drastic levels of inflation and a constant trade deficit, Israel has experienced economic growth. Taxes are a major source of revenue, as are grants and loans from other countries and

Right: The Bhote, an ethnic group related to Tibetans, comprise many different populations whose cultures have developed in isolation from one another. These Bhote come from Yakba, a village in western Nepal.

income from tourism. The nation of Israel was established in 1948. Torn by war since then, Israel remains steeped in conflict with many of its neighbors over territorial rights.

Japan

One of the world's leading industrial powers, Japan is remarkable for its economic growth rate since World War II, especially considering its lack of natural resources. After Japan surrendered to the United States at the end of World War II, industry became the country's chief occupation. It has since become famous for its innovative technology. Japan's mountainous terrain includes both active and dormant volcanoes, and earthquakes sometimes occur. Japan's culture blends East and West, with karate, tea ceremonies, and kimonos balanced by baseball, fast food, and business suits. Japan has gained much attention as an economic power, but lack of military might could stifle its authority in the world marketplace.

Jordan

The modern Arab kingdom of Jordan was established in 1949. A nation of few natural resources, Jordan has suffered further economic damage from an influx of refugees and the chronic political instability of the Middle East. In a 1967 war with Israel, Jordan lost the economically active West Bank, which made up about half the country's farmland. Agri-

culture remains the most important activity, however, and tourism has helped the weak, foreign-aid-dependent economy.

Kampuchea

The Khmer, one of the oldest peoples in Southeast Asia, constitute the major ethnic group in Kampuchea, formerly known as Cambodia. The population has declined significantly since the mid-1970s as a result of war, famine, human-rights abuses, and emigration; the nation has suffered economically for the same reasons. Several insurgent groups, including the Khmer Rouge, have continued guerilla warfare against the Vietnamese-installed government.

Korea, North

The northern part of the Korean peninsula is a Socialist republic and maintains one of the world's largest armies. Despite its ties to the Soviet Union and China, North Korea strives for an independent foreign policy based on self-reliance. The government discourages religious activity. The division of the Korean peninsula after World War II left North Korea with most of the industry and natural resources but little agricultural land and few skilled workers. The country has succeeded in becoming one of the most industrialized nations in Asia and is overcoming its agricultural problems. The Soviet Union and China have contributed aid.

Korea, South

The southern part of the Korean peninsula is officially known as the Republic of Korea. Its economy is more evenly based than that of the north, and most trade is with Japan and the United States. Population is much more dense in the south than it is in the north, as a result of massive migration to the south after World War II. Internal unrest has led to demands for wider democracy and reunification of Korea. South Korea has recently gained attention as a growing economic force.

Kuwait

Kuwait is one of the world's largest oil producers, a fact that has transformed it from a poor nation into an affluent one. Poised at the tip of the Persian Gulf, Kuwait must always be sensitive to the interests of its many neighbors. Though it strives to remain politically neutral, the ongoing Iran-Iraq war has created problems for Kuwait. The nation's prosperity has drawn emigrants from the Persian Gulf and beyond, giving it a diverse population.

Laos

Formerly part of French Indochina, this landlocked country is now an independent Socialist republic. It is one of the least developed countries of Southeast Asia, and agriculture remains the mainstay of the economy. Many Lao, opposed to the Communist rule, have fled the

Above: The highest mountains in the world, the Himalayas dominate central Asia. Extending roughly 1,550 miles (2,500 kilometers), they cut through Pakistan, India, China, Nepal, and Bhutan. Their formidable terrain and climate limit settlement, but in some places, humans manage to grow crops such as these apricots, laid in the sun to dry in northern Pakistan.

country for refuge in Thailand and the United States.

Lebanon

This small republic borders the Mediterranean Sea and has long been a center of commerce; however, prolonged fighting, beginning with the 1975 civil war, has greatly damaged all economic activity. Islam is the majority religion, although Christianity continues to be a strong presence. Palestinian refugees have settled in Lebanon since the creation of Israel in 1948, many of them living in refugee camps. International attempts to reconcile warring factions, including a peace agreement signed by faction leaders in 1986, have been unsuccessful.

Macao

Two islands and a part of a peninsula form this Portuguese territory on China's coast. Tourism, gambling, and light

Right: Shown here is the Marble Temple (Wat Benchamabophit), a Buddhist temple in Bangkok (Krung Thep), Thailand. Buddhism, Hinduism, and Islam are the principal religions of Asia.

industry help make up Macao's economy. Although the government is nominally directed by Portugal, any policies relating to Macao are subject to China's approval. Macao is the oldest European settlement in the Far East.

Malaysia
Malaysia's location at one of Southeast Asia's maritime crossroads has left it with a diverse population, including Malays, Chinese, Indians, and native non-Malay groups. Composed of the Malay Peninsula and parts of northern Borneo in the South China Sea, Malaysia has one of the healthiest economies in the region, supported by multiple strengths in agriculture, mining, forestry, and fishing. The nation is one of the world's leading producers of rubber, palm oil, and tin, and one of the Far East's largest petroleum exporters.

Maldives
Now an independent republic, this collection of 1,200 coral atolls lying southwest of Sri Lanka was a British protectorate until 1965. Tourism and fishing are the main activities. Nearly all residents are Sunni Muslims.

Mongolia
This Socialist republic is a sparsely populated, landlocked country lying between the Soviet Union and China. Situated in the heart of Asia, Mongolia supports the Soviet Union, and Soviet troops are stationed throughout the land. The traditional nomadic way of life of many Mongols is becoming less common as recent government policies have led to urbanization and settled agriculture. Mongolia's economy, long based on the raising of livestock, has been shaped by the ideal grazing land found in most of the country.

Nepal
Landlocked between Tibet and India, Nepal is a Himalayan kingdom. This nation has one of the least developed economies in the world, with agriculture the most important activity. Most of Nepal is covered by the Himalayas, the tallest mountains in the world – a fact that hinders it economically by curbing agriculture and that helps it by encouraging tourism. There are no political parties in Nepal.

Oman
Situated on the Persian Gulf, Oman's land borders are undefined and in dispute. Oil production is the economic mainstay, but oil supplies in Oman are not as vast as those in other Arab states, and the government is seeking to diversify. Oman is a moderate, pro-Western Arab state, and a desert climate prevails over most areas.

Pakistan
The Islamic Republic of Pakistan remains an agricultural economy. Spurred by poor living conditions and a lack of jobs, many Pakistanis work abroad. Pakistan remains troubled by population growth, unskilled labor, a trade deficit, and an influx of refugees fleeing the war in Afghanistan. Subsequent political activity in Pakistan has included martial law and accusations of government corruption.

Philippines
Only one-tenth of the seven thousand islands in the Republic of the Philippines are inhabited. The Philippines is primarily an agricultural nation, relying on rice, sugar, coconuts, and wood. Manufacturing is developing through government incentives. A dependence on imported goods, along with inadequate but growing power and transport systems, has hampered growth. Since the election of Corazon Aquino, the country has been plagued by coup attempts, leftist insurgency groups, and unresolved social and economic problems.

Qatar
The State of Qatar relies on oil to fuel its economy, and extensive reserves of natural gas await exploitation. Qatar became independent in 1971 after failing to agree on the terms of a union with eight Persian Gulf sheikdoms. Despite a political trend toward a modern welfare state, Qatar retains many elements of a traditional Islamic society.

Saudi Arabia
Saudi Arabia is inhabited primarily by Arab Muslims, but some Bedouin tribes roam this hot, arid region. Agriculture is severely limited, and the country must import nearly all its food. A dominant member of the Organization of Petroleum Exporting Countries (OPEC), Saudi Arabia is the world's leading exporter of petroleum. It possesses the largest concentration of known oil reserves in the world. The country maintains strong diplomatic and economic ties with Western nations.

Singapore
Singapore is one of the most densely populated nations in the world, with most of the population living in the city of Singapore on Singapore Island. The island nation at the tip of the Malay Peninsula is a leading Asian economic power and a world leader in petroleum refining. Cool breezes and a tropical climate make Singapore an attractive spot for tourists. Singapore's society is characterized by a mixture of Western and traditional customs and dress.

Sri Lanka
Formerly known as Ceylon, the Democratic Socialist Republic of Sri Lanka is an island off India. The economy is based on agriculture, which employs nearly half the people. Sri Lanka is sponsoring several internal-development programs; however, continuing high

government subsidy and welfare policies threaten economic growth. Tensions between ethnic groups have often erupted in violence.

Syria

Syria is a developing country with great potential for economic growth. Oil is the major natural resource. The majority is Sunni Muslim, and Islam is a powerful cultural force. Tensions over land disputes between Syria and Israel erupted in war in 1967 and 1973 and remain unresolved.

Taiwan

Taiwan – or the Republic of China – is an eastern Asian island off the coast of mainland China in the South China Sea. Since World War II, Taiwan's economy has changed from agriculture to industry, and today technology and heavy industry are emphasized. T'aipei, Taiwan, has been proclaimed the capital of Nationalist China, a separate nation from mainland China, but nearly all nations view Taiwan as part of the People's Republic of China.

Thailand

Formerly called Siam, Thailand is a southeastern Asian kingdom with a tropical climate. It has been under military rule since 1976. With an economy based on agriculture, Thailand exports large quantities of rice each year. The cost of caring for thousands of refugees from the Vietnam war has been a major drain on the economy. Thai society is rural, with most people living in the rice-growing regions. The government has sponsored a successful family-planning program, which has greatly reduced the annual birthrate.

Turkey

The Republic of Turkey was restored to civilian rule in 1983 after control by Turkish generals. Military rule came about as a result of a fledgling government and years of terrorism, flared by disputes with Greece over Cyprus. The government owns and controls many important industries, transportation services, and utilities. Most people are farmers and the population is mainly Sunni Muslim.

United Arab Emirates

Most residents are not U.A.E. citizens, but Westerners and Asians attracted by jobs in the oil industry. With one of the highest per capita incomes in the world, this small urban federation situated on the Persian Gulf provides free medical and educational facilities. The nation is divided into seven independent states. Because each emirate has a great deal of control over its internal affairs and economic development, the growth of federal powers has been slow.

Vietnam

Vietnam is a war-torn nation composed mostly of ethnic Vietnamese. The official language is Vietnamese, but a history of foreign intervention is reflected in wide use of French, English, Chinese, and Russian. Communist Vietnamese gained control over North Vietnam in 1954, and in 1975, they were victorious in unifying the north and south into a Socialist republic. Economic problems have increased since the Vietnam War, and the country remains dependent on Soviet and Eastern-bloc aid.

Yemen

At the southwest tip of Arabia, the Yemen Arab Republic – or North Yemen – has a terrain suited for agriculture, the backbone of the nation's economy. Border clashes have erupted with South Yemen, but the governments of both North and South Yemen want to unify Yemen.

Yemen, People's Democratic Republic of

Formerly controlled by Britain, the People's Democratic Republic of Yemen – also referred to as South Yemen – was established in 1970 after a Marxist takeover. Petroleum products are South Yemen's major industrial export. Military leaders assumed control of the country in 1974.

Below: The Troglodyte dwellings shown here are found in Turkey's Cappadocia region. The Troglodytes were a primitive people who inhabited the caves and tunnels of rocky hillsides. They were given their name by the ancient Greeks.

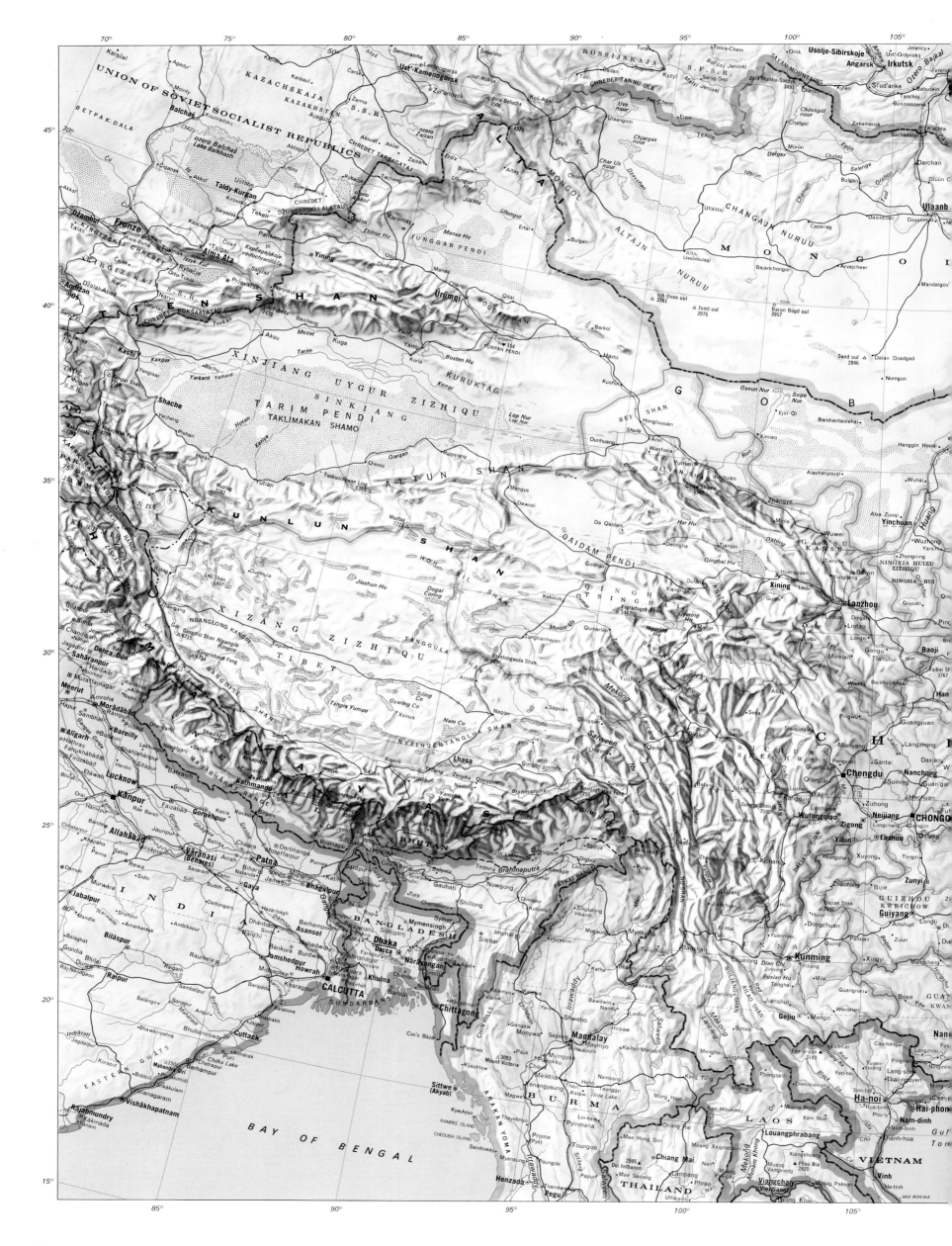

SEA OF OKHOTSK

U.S.S.R.

S.F.S.R.

OSTROV SACHALIN
SACHALIN
SAKHALIN

La Perouse Strait

HOKKAIDO

Sapporo

Asahikawa

Kushiro

Obihiro

Hakodate

Chabarovsk

Vladivostok

Ussurisk

Art'om

Nachodka

MANCHURIA

HEILONGJIANG
HEILUNGKIANG

Harbin

Qiqihar
Tsitsihar

Jiamusi

Shuangyashan

Yichun

Hegang

DA HINGGAN LING

XIAO HINGGAN LING

SICHOTE ALIN

Aomori

Hirosaki

Akita

Morioka

Hachinohe

SEA OF JAPAN

JAPAN

Sendai

Niigata

Changchun

Jilin
KIRIN

NORTH KOREA

P'yŏngyang

Ch'ŏngjin

Kimch'aek

Hamhŭng

Hŭngnam

Wŏnsan

CHANGBAI SHAN

Paektu-san 2744

Kanazawa

Nagano

Utsunomiya

Mito

TOKYO

Kawasaki

Yokohama

Yokosuka

NEI MONGGOL ZIZHIQU
INNER MONGOLIA

Baotou

Hohhot

Zhangjiakou
Kalgan

BEIJING
PEKING

TIANJIN
TIENTSIN

SHENYANG
MUKDEN

Fushun

Anshan

Dandong

Sinŭiju

LIAONING

SOUTH KOREA

SOUL
SEOUL

Inch'ŏn

Taejŏn

Taegu

Pusan

HONSHU

Nagoya

Kyoto

Kobe

OSAKA

Nara

Wakayama

Hamamatsu

Shizuoka

Taiyuan

SHANXI
SHANSI

Shijiazhuang

Baoding

HEBEI
HOPEH

Tangshan

Dalian

Lüshun
(Port Arthur)

Korea Bay

Bo Hai

Yellow Sea

Mokp'o

Kwangju

Yŏsu

Hiroshima

Kitakyūshū

Fukuoka

Matsuyama

Kōchi

SHIKOKU

KYŪSHŪ

Nagasaki

Kumamoto

Miyazaki

Kagoshima

Jinan
Tsinan

SHANDONG
SHANTUNG

Qingdao
Tsingtao

Weifang

Zhengzhou

HENAN
HONAN

Xuzhou

JIANGSU
KIANGSU

Lianyungang

EAST CHINA SEA

RYUKYU ISLANDS
NANSEI SHOTŌ

SATSUNAN SHOTŌ

Naha

OKINAWA-JIMA

Luoyang

Nanyang

Hefei

ANHUI
ANHWEI

Nanjing

Wuxi

Suzhou

SHANGHAI

HUBEI
HUPEH

WUHAN

Huangshi

Hangzhou

Ningbo

ZHEJIANG
CHEKIANG

Shaoxing

PACIFIC OCEAN

Changsha

HUNAN

Nanchang

JIANGXI
KIANGSI

Jingdezhen

Wenzhou

Tropic of Cancer

Guilin

Hengyang

Ganzhou

FUJIAN
FUKIEN

Fuzhou

Chilung

T'aipei

Hsinchu

T'aichung

TAIWAN

GUANGDONG
KWANGTUNG

Guangzhou
CANTON

Zhangzhou

Xiamen
Amoy

Shantou
Swatow

Quanzhou

T'ainan

Kaohsiung

Kowloon Jiulong

Victoria Xianggang

Macau
Aomen

HONG KONG
(U.K.)

Maoming

Zhanjiang

Haikou

HAINAN

PHILIPPINES

LUZON

Bashi Channel

BATAN ISLANDS

Luzon Strait

Balintang Channel

BABUYAN ISLANDS

PHILIPPINE SEA

SOUTH CHINA SEA

Kilometers
0   200   400   600   Km.

Statute Miles
0   200   400   600   Mi.

Scale 1:12,000,000

One centimeter represents 120 kilometers.
One inch represents approximately 190 miles.
Lambert Conformal Conic Projection

INDIA
Kalemyo
Falam
Pawdwin
Shanshui
Yuanjiang
CHINA
Gejiu
Mengzi
Wenshan
Qilin
GUANGDONG
Chao'an
Chao'an
Juidong
Wuzhou
GUANGZHOU
CANTON
Jieyang
Zhao'an
Shantou
Swatow
CHITTAGONG
BANGLADESH
Cox's Bazar
Paletwa
Mount Victoria
3053
Pauk
Minbu
Kyaukpyu
RAMREE ISLAND
CHEDUBA ISLAND
Sandoway
Sittwe
(Akyab)
ARAKAN YOMA
BURMA
Gangaw
Monywa
Shwebo
Ye-u
Myingyan
Kyaukse
Meiktila
Thazi
Pyinmana
Toungoo
Prome
Henzada
Myaungmya
Bassein
Ma-ubin
RANGOON
Syriam
Pegu
Moulmein
Gulf of Martaban
Mandalay
Maymyo
Lashio
Hsipaw
Ke-tu-mang
Mong Hsat
Chiang Rai
Doi Inthanon 2595
Chiang Mai
Lampang
Phrae
Nan
YUNNAN
Simao
Meng-la
Muang Sing
Muang Ngoy
Phongsali
Dien-bien-phu
Black Da
Son-la
Lang-son
Cao-bang
Tuyen-quang
Nam-quan
Mong-cai
HA-NOI
Hoa-binh
Phu-ly
Nam-dinh
Thanh-hoa
Hai-phong
Cam-pha
Hon-gai
Hon-me
Haikou
HAINAN
Dongfang
Wuzhi Shan 1867
HAINAN DAO
Baoting
Yaxian
Beihai
Zhanjiang
DONGHAI DAO
LEIZHOU BANDAO
Xuwen
Qiongzhoukaixia
Nanning
ZHUANGZU
Chongzuo
Yulin
GUANGXI
Guixian
Liuzhou
Guiping
Xijiang
Foshan
Aomen Macau
VICTORIA XIANGGANG
HONG KONG (U.K.)
New Kowloon Xinjiulong
Zhaoqing
Hepu
TUNGSHA TAO
PRATAS ISLAND
(Tai)

LAOS
Xam Nua
Louangphrabang
Muang Xaignabouri
Muang Xiangkhoang
Phou Bia 2820
Vangviang
VIANGCHAN (Vientiane)
Nong Khai
Udon Thani
Nakhon Phanom
Savannakhét
Sakon
Vinh
Ha-tinh
Dong-hoi
MUI RON-MA
VIETNAM
CHAÎNE ANNAMITIQUE

BAY OF BENGAL

Preparis North Channel
PREPARIS ISLAND
Preparis South Channel
COCO CHANNEL
COCO ISLANDS

THAILAND
Tak
Sukhothai
Phitsanulok
Uttaradit
Loei
Khon Kaen
Kalasin
Roi Et
Nakhon Sawan
Uthai Thani
Chaiyaphum
Nakhon Ratchasima
Muang Nam Khong
Ubon Ratchathani
Sisaket
Saravan
Attapu
Kontum
Pleiku
Muang Không
Hue
Da-nang
Quang-tri
Tam-ky
Quang-ngai
Ngoc Linh 2598
An-nhon
Qui-nhon
XISHA QUNDAO
PARACEL ISLANDS (China)

ANDAMAN ISLANDS (India)
NORTH ANDAMAN
MIDDLE ANDAMAN
BARATANG ISLAND
SOUTH ANDAMAN
Port Blair
LITTLE ANDAMAN

ANDAMAN SEA

MALI KYUN
KADAN KYUN
Mergui
MERGUI
LETSÔK-AW KYUN
ARCHIPELAGO
LANBI KYUN
KANMAW KYUN
SAGANTHIT KYUN
Tavoy
Tenasserim
Prachuap Khiri Khan
Chon Buri
Rayong
Chanthaburi
Sattahip
KO CHANG
Hua Hin
Phetchaburi
Ratchaburi
Suphan Buri
Kanchanaburi
Nakhon Pathom
KRUNG THEP
BANGKOK
Lop Buri
Ayutthaya
Saraburi
Prachin Buri
Aranyaprathet
Battambang
Poipet
THIU KHAO PHETCHABUN
THIU KHAO DONGRAK
PHANOM DONG RAK
Mun
Nam
Choam Khsant
Chaiyaphum
Muang Pakxé
Stœng Trêng
Lac-giao
Da-lat
Nha-trang
Phan-rang
Phan-thiet
Ban Me Thuot
Loc-ninh

BILAUKTAUNG RANGE
DAWNA RANGE

Chumphon
Ranong
ISTHMUS OF KRA
Surat Thani
KO PHANGAN
KO SAMUI
Nakhon Si Thammarat
Phuket
Phangnga
KO PHUKET
Trang
Kantang

KAMPUCHEA
(CAMBODIA)
Pouthisat
Kampong Chhnang
Tônlé Sab
Siěmréab
Kampong Thum
Krâchéh
Phnum Aôral 1771
PHNUM PÉNH
Kampong Cham
Svay Riěng
Krŏng Kaôh Kŏng
Kâmpôt
Chhâk Kâmpóng Saôm
Kâmpóng Saôm
DAO PHU-QUOC
Ha-tien
Ha Tien
Long-xuyen
My-tho
Rach-gia
Cân-tho
Bac-lieu (Vinh-loi)
Vinh-long
Khanh-hung
Quan-long
MUI CA-MAU
CON SON
THANH-PHO HO CHI MINH (SAI-GON)
Bien-hoa
Gia-dinh
Vung-tau
Phuoc-le
Tây-ninh

Gulf of Thailand

SOUTH CHINA
SEA
NANSHAN ISLAND
SPRATLY ISLAND
BARQUE CANADA REEF
INVESTIGATOR SHOAL
PALAWAN
Puerto Pri...

NICOBAR ISLANDS (India)
TARĀSA DWIP
TILLANCHĀNG DWIP
KATCHALL ISLAND
CAMORTA ISLAND
LITTLE NICOBAR
GREAT NICOBAR
Ten Degree Channel
CAR NICOBAR ISLAND
NANCOWRY ISLAND
Great Channel

NORTH LUCONIA SHOALS
BALABAC STRAIT
BALABAC ISLAND
PULAU BANGGI SULU
PULAU JAMBONGAN
Kota Belud
Kota Kinabalu (Jesselton)
Gunung Kinabalu 4094
Ranau
Beaufort
Tenom
Labu
Lahad Datu

PULAU BREUEH
Sabang
PULAU WE
Banda Aceh
Sigli
Bireuen
Lhokseumawe
Idi
PULAU SIMEULUE
Meulaboh
Takengeun
Tangsa
Gunung Abongabong 2985
Belawan
Tebingtinggi
Medan
Binjai
Pematangsiantar
Danau Toba
Tarutung
Sibolga
KEPULAUAN BANYAK
PULAU NIAS
Gunungsitoli
Padangsidempuan
Rantauprapat
PULAU BATU
TANAHMASA
TANAHBALA
Natal
KEPULAUAN MENTAWAI
PULAU SIBERUT
Muarasiberut
Pariaman
Padang
PULAU PAGAI UTARA
PULAU PAGAI SELATAN
Sungaipenuh
Gunung Kerinci 3800
Lubuklinggau
Perabumulih
Lahat
PULAU ENGGANO
Bengkulu
Gunung Dempo 3159
Curup
Baturaja
Kotabumi
Menggala
TANJUNG CINA
Kotaagung
Tanjungkarang
Telukbetung
SELAT SUNDA
PULAU MEGA

Banda Aceh

George Town (Pinang)
PULAU PINANG
Butterworth
Taiping
Ipoh
Gunung Tahan 2187
Alor Setar
Kota Baharu
PULAU REDANG
Kuala Terengganu
Kelang
Kuala Lumpur
Seremban
Melaka (Malacca)
Muar
Batu Pahat
Kluang
Keluang
Johor Baharu
SINGAPORE
PULAU BINTAN
Tanjungpinang
KEPULAUAN RIAU
PULAU BATAM
Kuantan
Segamat
Port Dickson
Pelabuhan Kelang
PULAU LANGKAWI
Sungai Petani
Kangar
Pattani
Sai Buri
Songkhla
Hat Yai
Yala
Sabang

Strait of Malacca
Selat Malaka
MALAYSIA
MALAYA

INDONESIA

Pakanbaru
Rengat
PULAU SINGKEP
KEPULAUAN LINGGA
PULAU LINGGA
Mempawah
Singkawang
Sambas
Kuching
SARAWAK
Sibu
Rajang
Kapit
Belaga
Gunung Murud 2423
PEGUNUNGAN IRAN
Tanjungredep
Gunung Niut 1701
Sintang
Semitau
PULAU KARIMATA
KEPULAUAN TAMBELAN
KEPULAUAN ANAMBAS
PULAU TIOMAN
KEPULAUAN BUNGURAN SELATAN
KEPULAUAN NATUNA BESAR
Ranai
KEPULAUAN BUNGURAN UTARA
PULAU LAUT

SUMATERA
SUMATRA
Jambi
Batanghari
Sawahlunto
Payakumbuh
Bukittinggi
Pekanbaru
Muarabungo
Muaratebo
Bangko
Sarolangun
Palembang
Pangkalpinang
BANGKA
PULAU BANGKA
Selat Bangka
PULAU BELITUNG
BELITUNG
Tanjungpandan
Muntok
Selat Karimata
Karimata Strait
TANJUNG SELAKAU
Ketapang
Pontianak
KALIMANTAN
BORNEO
PEGUNUNGAN SCHWANER
Bukit Raya 2278
Sampit
Pangkalanbun
Kualakapuas
Muaratewe
Kahayan
Barito
Palangkaraya
Amuntai
Banjarmasin
Martapura
Kandangan
Sampit
TANJUNG PUTING
PULAU LAUT
Samarinda
Balikpapan
Mahakam
Longiram
Kelai
Kelabit 2053
Kong Kemul
Muaratewe
Kelolokan
TANJUNG DATU
Longbawan

GREATER SUNDA ISLANDS

BRUNEI
Bandar Seri Begawan
Miri
Seria
Lutong
Bukit Pagon 1850
Lawas
Niah
Marudi
MALAYSIA
Mukah
Belaga

LAUT JAWA
JAVA SEA
KEPULAUAN KARIMUNJAWA
PULAU BAWEAN
MADURA
Bangkalan
Sumenep
Pamekasan
Kangean
KEPULAUAN KANGEAN
MASALEMBO-BESAR
Laut Bali
Bali Sea

Equator

INDIAN OCEAN

JAKARTA
Bogor
Cianjur
BANDUNG
Sukabumi
Garut
Tasikmalaya
Purwakarta
Cirebon
Tegal
Pekalongan
Cilacap
Purwokerto
Kebumen
Magelang
Gunung Slamet 3428
Yogyakarta
Surakarta
SEMARANG
Salatiga
Madiun
Kediri
Kudus
Rembang
SURABAYA
Pasuruan
Malang
Probolinggo
Situbondo
Banyuwangi
Jember
Singaraja
Denpasar
LOMBOK
Mataram
SUMBAWA
Sumbawa Besar
Praya
Gunung Rinjani 3726
BALI
JAWA
JAVA
Purwakarta
TANJUNG CANGKUANG
SELAT BALI
LES...

CHRISTMAS ISLAND (Austl.)

Kilometers
0   200   400   600   Km.

Statute Miles
0   200   400   600   Mi.

Scale 1:12,000,000

One centimeter represents 120 kilometers.
One inch represents approximately 190 miles.
Lambert Conformal Conic Projection

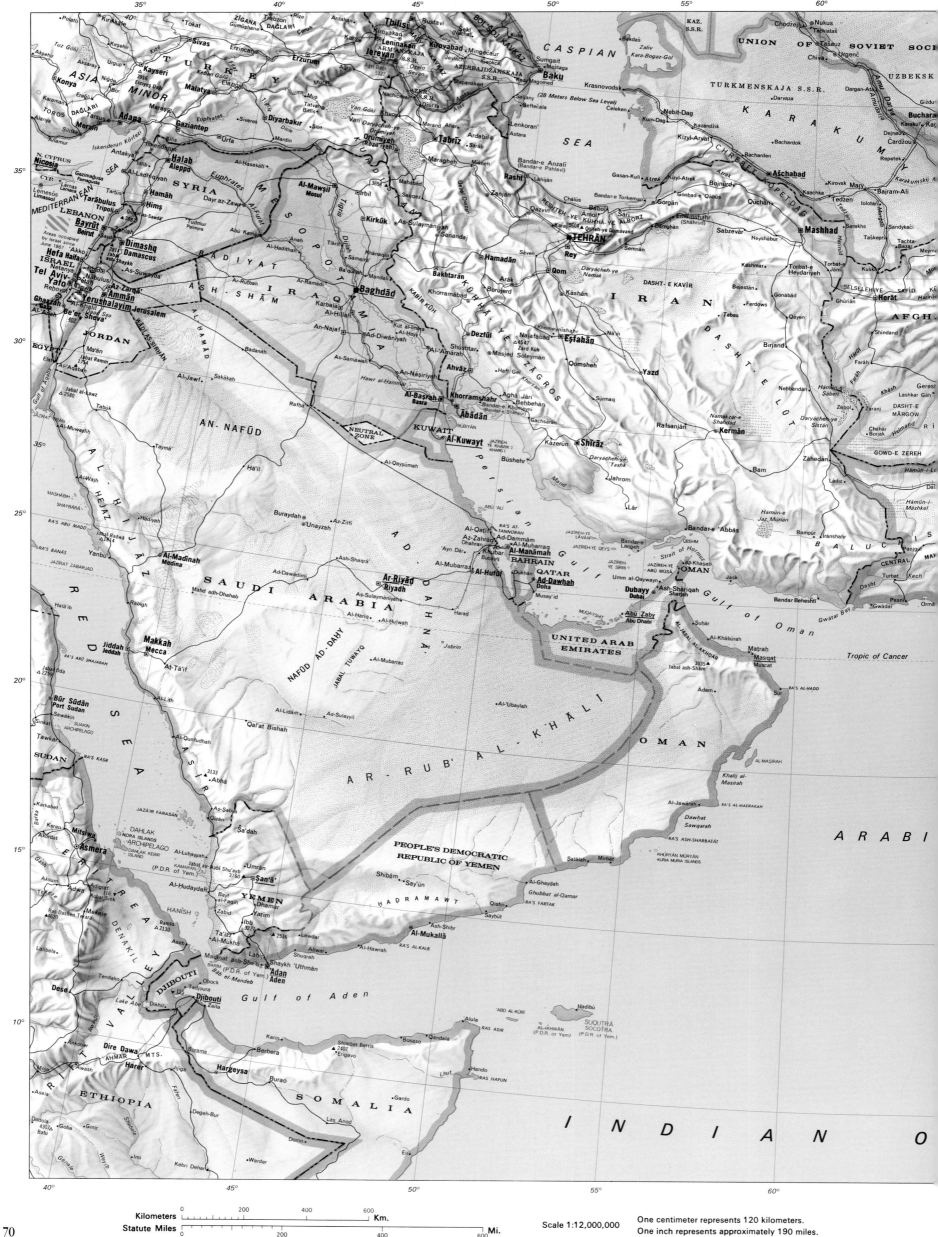

35°   40°   45°   50°   55°   60°

Polatlı Kırıkkale 40° Tokat ZIGANA Trabzon Rize Ardahan BOL. SOL. KAVKAZ CASPIAN Zaliv Chodžejli Nukus Tachiataš
Kırşehir Sivas DAĞLARI Gümüşhane Ardahan Rustavi Tbilisi Sumqait Kara-Bogaz-Gol UNION OF TAŞ SOVIET SOCI
Aksaray Ürgüp TURKEY Erzincan Erzurum Muş LENINAKAN ARM. S.S.R. Kirovakan Kirovabad Mingečaur SEA Chiva Urgenč
Konya Kayseri 3916 Keban Gölü Ağrı Dağı Jerevan Stepanakert Baku Krasnovodsk TURKMENSKAJA S.S.R. Darvaza UZBEKS
ASIA Karaman Niğde Elazığ 5122 AZERBAJDŽANSKAJA Kum-Dag Kizyl-Arvat Kazandžik Mary Bucharo
MINOR TOROS DAĞLARI Malatya Diyarbakır Mardin Siirt Van Gölü Orūmiyeh Tabrīz Ardabīl S.S.R. Gasan-Kuli Atrek Kizyl-Atrek Nebit-Dag K A R A K U M Čardžou
Adana Tarsus Gaziantep Urfa Euphrates Al-Hasakah Maragheh Zanjan Rasht Lenkoran' Astara Bojnūrd CHREBET KOPETDAG Bachardok Tedžen Iolotan
Mersin İskenderun Körfezi Antakya Kilis Aleppo Al-Mawsil Irbil As-Sulaymānīyah KŪHHĀ-YE ALBORZ Āmol Sārī Gorgān AŠCHABAD Kaachka Sarakhs Tachta-Bazar
N. CYPRUS Nicosia Lārnax Famagusta SEA Al-Lādhiqīyah Hamāh Dayr az-Zawr Al-Hadīthah Kirkūk Sanandaj Qazvīn Chālūs Bābol Damghān Shāhrūd Neyshābūr Mashhad Torbat-e Jām
CYP. Lemesós Ţarţūs Aleppo Ḥimş Palmyra Tikrīt Dijlah Sāmarrā' Khānaqīn Hamadān Sāveh TEHRĀN Semnān Sabzevār Kashmar Torbat-e Heydarīyeh
Ţarābulus LEBANON Bayrūt Beirut Dimashq Damascus BADIYAT Ar-Ramādī Ba'qūbah Bakhtarān Arāk Qom Rey Daryācheh-ye Namak Gonābād Ghūrīan HERĀT AFGH
Tripoli Hefa Haifa ISRAEL Tel Aviv Yafo Az-Zarqā' ASH-SHĀM Al-Hadīthah Baghdad Karbalā' An-Najaf Khorramābād Borūjerd Eşfahān DASHT-E KAVĪR Ferdows Bejestān Qāyen
Yerushalayim Jerusalem Al-Khalīl AMMĀN JORDAN Ar-Rutbah Al-Hillah Kūt al-Imāra Ad-Dīwānīyah Dezfūl Najafābād Khomeynīshahr 4547 Masjed Soleymān Shūshtar Yazd Tabas Birjand Khāsh
Be'er Sheva' 502 EGYPT Ma'ān An-Nāsirīyah As-Samāwah Al-Amārah Ahvāz Haft Gel Khorram Zard Kūh Qomsheh Nā'īn Nehbandān Hāmūn-i DASHT-E Zābol Zaranj
30° 'Aqaba Jabal Ramm An-Najaf Badanah Hawr al-Hammār Al-Başrah Basra Aghā Jārī Behbehān Gachsārān Rafsanjān Kermān MĀRGOW Chāh Hāmūn-e Sāberī 30°
Al-'Aqabah Tabūk Jabal al-Lawz Sakākah Rafha Khorramshahr Ābādān Bandar-e Māhshahr Sīrjān Bam Lādiz GOWD-E ZEREH Hāmūn-i Māshkel Mīrjāveh
An-Nāfūd Al-Jawf KUWAIT Būshehr Daryācheh-ye Tashk Zāhedān BALUCHIS
MASHĀBĪH SHAYBĀRĀ NEUTRAL ZONE Al-Kuwayt Kāzerūn Shīrāz Jahrom Lār Bandar-e 'Abbās Īrānshahr Khāsh CENTRAL
RA'S ABŪ MADD Taymā' Ḥā'il Az-Zilfī ABŪ 'ALĪ Bandar-e Lengeh Bampūr Turbat Kech
25° Al-Wajh HEJAZ Buraydah 'Unayzah JAZĪREH-YE KHĀRK RA'S AT-TANNŪRAH Al-Qatīf Az-Zahrān Ad-Dammām JAZĪREH-YE LĀVĀN JAZĪREH-YE QEYS Strait of Hormuz AL-KHASAB Mināb Jāsk Bandar Beheshti Gwātar Bay Gwādar Ormā 25°
JAZĪRAT ZABARJAD Yanbu' Al-Madīnah Medina Ash-Shaqrā' Dhahran Al-Mubarraz BAHRAIN Al-Manāmah Al-Muharraq JAZĪREH-YE SIRRĪ Dubayy Dubai OMAN RA'S AL-HADD
AL-HIJĀZ Rābigh Al-Hariq Mahd adh-Dhahab Ad-Dawhah Doha QATAR Umm al-Qaywayn Ash-Shāriqah Sharjah Sur JABAL ASH-SHĀM 3035
Jiddah Jeddah Makkah Mecca SAUDI ARABIA Ar-Riyāḍ Riyadh Al-Hufūf Dukhān Abū Zaby Abu Dhabi Şuḥār Al-Khābūrah Matraḥ Muscat Tropic of Cancer
20° Al-Tā'if AD-DAHNĀ' Harad Jabrin Musay'id UNITED ARAB EMIRATES Adam Masqat Muscat 20°
Al-Lith NAFŪD AD-DAHY JABAL TUWAYQ Al-Mubarraz RA'S AL-HADD
Būr Sūdān Port Sudan Al-Qunfudhah As-Sulayyil RA'S AL-MADRAKAH
SUDAN RA'S ABŪ SHAJARAH Qal'at Bishah Al-'Ubaylah Al-Jawārah Dawhat Sawqarah
RA'S KASR ASĪR 3133 Abha Al-'Ubaylah AR - RUB' AL - KHĀLĪ OMAN Al-Khalīj al-Maşīrah
15° Mitsiwa JAZĀ'IR FARASAN DAHLAK As-Sarw Qizān Al-Ghaydah KHŪRYĀN MŪRYĀN Al-Maşīrah 15°
Asmera DAHLAK KEBIR ISLAND (P.D.R. of Yem.) Jabal al-Nabi Shu'ayb 3760 Umrān San'ā' PEOPLE'S DEMOCRATIC REPUBLIC OF YEMEN Shibām Say'ūn Salālah Mirbāt KURIA MURIA ISLANDS RA'S ASH-SHARBATĀT
ERITREA HANISH YEMEN Dhamār HADRAMAWT Qishn RA'S FARTAK
Mekele Ramlo 2516 Al-Hudaydah Bayt al-Faqīh Yarīm Ibb 3323 Lawdar Ghubbat al-Qamar
DENAKIL Ta'izz Zabid Al-Mukhā Ahwar Shuqrah Sayhūt Ash-Shihr Al-Mukallā RA'S AL-KALB
10° Lalibela Shaykh 'Uthmān Al-Hawrah ABD AL-KŪRI Hadibū SUQUTRA SOCOTRA (P.D.R. of Yem.) 10°
Dese Maqarin ash-Sha'b (P.D.R. of Yem.) Adan Aden AL-IKHWĀN (P.D.R. of Yem.)
Tendaho DJIBOUTI Djibouti Zeila Gulf of Aden 'Alula RA'S ASIR ALI-IKHWĀN (P.D.R. of Yem.)
Lake Abe Dikhil Obock Tadjoura Karin Bosaso Qandala
Dire Dawa Borama Berbera Shimber Berris 2407 Erigavo Hando RA'S HAFUN
AHMAR MTS. Harer Jijiga Hargeysa Burao Gardo Las Anod
ETHIOPIA SOMALIA INDIAN O
Goba Ginir Domo Degeh-Bur Warder

40°   45°   50°   55°   60°

70

Kilometers 0   200   400   600 Km.
Statute Miles 0   200   400   600 Mi.

Scale 1:12,000,000

One centimeter represents 120 kilometers.
One inch represents approximately 190 miles.
Lambert Conformal Conic Projection

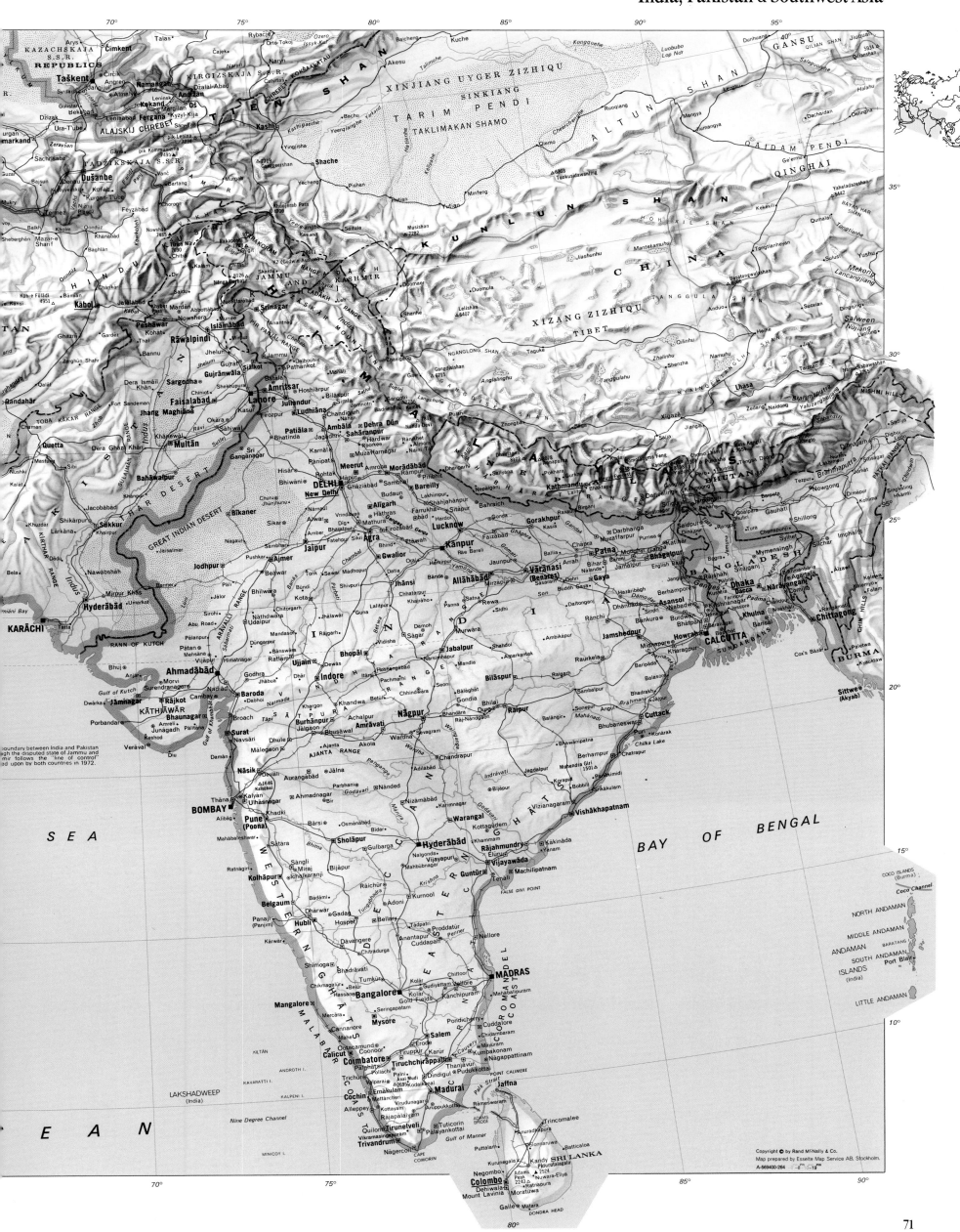

Africa
Profile

Location and Size

Africa is the second largest continent – after Asia – and constitutes 22 percent of the earth's land area. Yet it seems that few people realize just how huge Africa is. The entire United States could be placed in just the Sahara Desert, which extends 3,200 miles (5,150 kilometers) across northern Africa. The continent sits astride the equator and reaches north-to-south distances of some 4,900 miles (7,900 kilometers) and, at its widest, east-to-west expanses of about 4,450 miles (7,100) kilometers.

Africa is geographically connected to Asia by the Suez (Suways) Canal and to Europe by the Strait of Gibraltar. The waters surrounding Africa include the Atlantic Ocean to the west, the Indian Ocean to the east and south, and the Mediterranean Sea to the north. Africa includes not only the mainland area, but it also comprises a number of large and small islands in these surrounding waters. Madagascar is the most significant of these.

At the northernmost point of mainland Africa is Cape Ben Sekka, Tunisia, while at the southernmost point is Cape Agulhas, South Africa. At its farthest eastern border is found Cape Hafun, Somalia, and to the west is Cape Vert, Senegal.

Landscape

Africa is an ancient, mammoth plateau of crystalline minerals dating back over 3.2 billion years. On top of this platform sits a vast area of mountains, deserts, rain forests, and plains that is mostly lower in the north and west and higher in the east and south.

It is easy to see how some of Africa's outstanding landscape features have influenced its history and development by preventing human migration and exploration. For example, Africa has remarkably straight coastlines with very few harbors, inlets, or bays – a fact that hindered seafaring explorers. The world's largest desert, the Sahara, dominates the landscape in northern Africa, preventing penetration from that direction. The majority of African rivers are largely unnavigable, and coastal swamps, mountain ranges, and forests have further discouraged foreign conquerors.

Africa lacks the huge mountain ranges of most other continents; the spectacular Rift Valley in the eastern third of Africa provides the greatest land relief. This majestic trough cuts into the earth from the Dead Sea in the Middle East southward to Mozambique and Swaziland, extending approximately 4,300 miles (6,900 kilometers). In the deepest spot of the Rift Valley, the walls rise up more

Left: The nomadic, cattle-herding Masai people of East Africa forage over the lands of southern Kenya and Tanzania, paying little attention to national boundaries and resisting permanent settlement and integration into the economy. Trade among the Masai is based on cattle, which provides food and leverage for other types of exchanges. These young Masai women are dressed in typical garb.

Right: Contrary to popular belief, Africa is more a land of plains and deserts than it is of jungles. Grassland containing scattered trees and other hardy plants, or savanna, covers much of eastern, central, and southern Africa. Here the sun sets behind an acacia tree on the East Africa savanna.

than 10,500 feet (3,200 meters).

Most of the continent's great natural lakes are found in or around the Rift Valley. Lake Victoria, lying between the two main valleys, has a surface area of nearly 26,830 square miles (69,500 square kilometers) and is second only to Lake Superior as the world's largest freshwater lake.

Close to the Rift Valley are a number of mountainous areas, some of which contain active volcanoes. Here is found Africa's highest point: Mount Kilimanjaro, at 19,340 feet (5,895 meters). The mountainous Ethiopian Plateau contains some of the highest elevations in Africa.

The north is marked by semiarid, mountainous regions. In the northwest, the barrier of the Atlas Mountains of Tunisia, Morocco, and Algeria, rising to 13,665 feet (4,167 meters), effectively divides the coastal strip from the Sahara.

Finally, at the bottom of the continent, the Drakensberg Mountains of Lesotho and South Africa reach heights of more than ten thousand feet (three thousand meters). This range is part of the escarpment that forms the southern edge of the continental plateau.

In many parts of Africa, comparatively short rivers flow to the Atlantic and Indian oceans. The major exception in both size and destination is the Nile, the world's longest river, which flows northward for 4,160 miles (6,700 kilometers) from the East African lakes to the Mediterranean Sea.

In West Africa, the Niger follows a circuitous course for 2,595 miles (4,190 kilometers) between the highlands of Sierra Leone and its delta in Nigeria. The Congo (Zaire) is the main channel of equatorial Africa. In the southeast, the Zambezi (Zambeze) flows for 1,615 miles (2,600 kilometers) from Angola eastward to the Indian Ocean, cascading over the Victoria Falls en route. All African rivers contain similar waterfalls and cataracts, where they drop from one plateau to another.

Climate

Since Africa sits on the equator, climatic conditions are mirrored on the opposite sides of 0° latitude. In the extreme north of Morocco, Algeria, and Libya, as well as the southern tip of South Africa, the climate is subtropical. Summers here are dry, with the highest monthly average temperature above 72°F (22°C) and no winter average monthly temperature below 50°F (10°C). The South African plateau has a cooler subtropical climate with no dry season and most of its rainfall in summer.

In a belt of central and western Africa close to the equator, and on the east coast of Madagascar, rain falls throughout the year with total accumulation in excess of 60 inches (1,500 millimeters) and often more than 100 inches (2,500 millimeters). Monthly average temperatures never fall below 64°F (18°C) and reach just above 80°F (27°C) at their maximum.

Tropical savanna lands are found in much of eastern and south-central Africa. Here, precipitation is less and, although temperatures never fall below 64°F (18°C) in any month, they show a greater seasonal range than in other parts of Africa.

North and south of the savanna lands lie semiarid and true desert climates such as that of the Sahara Desert. Average monthly summer temperatures in the arid regions may reach 98°F (37°C), while winter temperatures average 59°F (15°C). Precipitation, often negligible, rarely exceeds an average of five inches (125 millimeters). When rain does fall, it is brief but torrential.

Overall, two factors influence African climates. First, 75 percent of the continent has a water supply problem. Average rainfall amounts throughout the continent seem sufficient but, except in equatorial areas, rainfall varies from year to year and creates great difficulties. Second, because so much of Africa – outside of the deserts – is of mid- to high-level elevation, consistent high temperatures are more the exception than the rule. Thus, while the temperature on the Kenyan coast may be unpleasantly high, regions that are farther west – still on the equator but 5,000 feet (1,500 meters) above sea level – the temperature is lower.

History, Politics, and Economy

Modern humankind's research has uncovered evidence suggesting that Africa may well have been the birthplace of the first humans. Sites in East Africa, especially in Tanzania and Kenya, have produced the oldest human remains, some of them thought to be more than two million years old. Many civilizations and empires have flourished and disintegrated during the long course of Africa's history.

The Stone Age probably began in Africa. Many Stone Age peoples were hunter-gatherers; that is, they foraged the land, without engaging in organized agriculture. Some hunter-gatherer societies still exist in remote regions of Africa, the most well-known of which might be the San of the Kalahari Desert.

The culture of ancient Egypt was one of the world's first great civilizations. Although the valley of the Nile has been inhabited for more than twenty thousand years, the classic period of the ancient civilization began about 3100 B.C. and reached its peak about 1400 B.C. The rise of Rome eventually ushered in the demise of ancient Egyptian power.

Elsewhere in Africa, other agricultural civilizations sprang up. About the time of Christ, a huge north-to-south migra-

Right: Africa is the least urbanized continent, and in many nations, the capital city is the only sizable urban center. Harare, shown here, is the capital and largest city of Zimbabwe, a subtropical republic in southern Africa.

Above: The native section of North African cities is sometimes referred to as the Casbah. These women in the Casbah of Tétouan, Morocco, are veiled in accordance with the ancient Islamic custom of purdah, which assures the seclusion of women from public observation. Some North African Muslims have abandoned purdah.

Top, right: Mount Kilimanjaro, in Tanzania, soars above these giraffes in nearby Amboseli National Park, Kenya. Africa's highest peak, Kilimanjaro is always covered with snow.

Right: Ngorongoro Crater lies in the volcanic region of northeastern Tanzania. In the crater is found one of the heaviest concentrations of wildlife in Africa, including these zebras.

Africa

Profile continued

Below: Table Mountain, shown here, rises behind Cape Town, South Africa. The mountain is sometimes covered by a gray-white cloud, referred to locally as "the tablecloth."

Below: Table Mountain, shown here, rises behind Cape Town, South Africa. The mountain is sometimes covered by a gray-white cloud, referred to locally as "the tablecloth."

tion of black Africans began, bringing agriculture to central Africa.

In the seventh century, Islam began to spread from the Middle East across northern Africa and down into East Africa. Later on, after about 1100, Arab traders began to settle along the eastern African coast, in what is now Kenya, Mozambique, Somalia, and Tanzania. They thrived on trade with China, India, and Indonesia.

By about 1000, West African society had emerged. Early West Africans were generally governed by single chiefs, often men who were thought to hold divine rights or special powers. They lived in autonomous, tightly knit groups that were close to each other and fought often. The kingdom of Ghana dominated West Africa by 1000; it was succeeded by the Mali Empire in the 1200s and the Songhai Empire by 1500.

Portuguese exploration of the western African coast began in the 1400s. Soon, trade was established with Africans, with several commodities exchanged, among them European guns and African slaves. After the New World was discovered and then colonized, the demand for slaves accelerated.

By the nineteenth century, about ten million Africans had been forced from their homeland and placed into slavery in the New World. Many died on the long and crammed voyages to America; others resisted and were killed. Areas known for slave trade – such as Ghana with its powerful Ashanti kingdom – flourished

economically, and the slave trade was dependent upon the toleration and cooperation of these African entrepreneurs. For those who remained in Africa, the slave trade brought new sources of revenue and technology from the West. Britain abolished slavery in 1807, and other countries followed suit soon thereafter.

There were other groups, however, that refused to tolerate slavery. Additionally, large regions of Africa experienced little or no European influence until after 1800.

During the nineteenth century, exploration of the African interior increased, as did European involvement in African economic affairs. A great rivalry began among the European nations in the opening up of the Dark Continent. By 1900, Britain, France, Portugal, Spain, Germany, and Italy laid claim to most of the land.

African nationalism rose greatly after World War II. In 1951, only three African countries were independent. From 1956 to 1968, thirty-eight independent countries emerged, many changing their colonial names to African names. Most African nations won their independence peacefully, unlike many nations in other parts of the world.

Today, most African governments are marked by the problems that face many developing nations: poverty, illiteracy, disease, and food shortages. Additionally, unstable governments and ethnic tensions have led to dictatorships, military

takeovers, and civil unrest. Most African nations remain agricultural, Third World countries, with South Africa having the only developed, industrial economy on the continent.

South of the Sahara, widespread famine is a most serious issue, and it is accompanied by the related problem of overpopulation. In the early 1980s, a widespread and long-lasting drought struck the middle of Africa. Its effects were felt most by the already poverty-stricken nomadic and seminomadic peoples of the area. Accustomed to living just above the starvation level even in the best years, these people died by the hundreds of thousands. Worldwide efforts to rush relief to the famine victims resulted in vast amounts of food finding its way to mid-Africa, but it is believed that inefficient government agencies slowed food distribution.

In southern Africa, racial tensions continue, especially in South Africa. Despite efforts of the government to set up black "homelands," and constitutional reforms that allow a minimum political role for nonblack minorities, the large black majority has become increasingly restive. Strikes, job actions, demonstrations, and other forms of civil disobedience are widespread, and the death toll of blacks is growing amid increasing international scrutiny.

Namibia and Angola continue to suffer from problems left over from colonial days. Angola, long a Portuguese colony, is finding it difficult to achieve

and maintain its status as an independent republic, while Namibia has been trying to free itself from imperialism since World War I.

To the north, Nigeria – with its enormous oil deposits – made what appeared to be great economic strides in the 1970s. But the collapse of the world market for oil in the 1980s made it especially vulnerable; it suffered from the same kinds of problems faced by industrial nations in economic recession while trying to cope with the strains present in a developing nation.

Despite North Africa's cultural link with the Middle East, its colonial past ties it to the rest of the African continent. As in other parts of Africa, colonies were demarcated by artificial borders that had more to do with foreign treaties and agreements than with indigenous ethnicity or tribal allegiance. The land of the region has fostered a nomadic life-style, and the foreign-imposed boundaries prevented people from following their traditional way of life. When independence was finally achieved, the artificial boundaries remained, sometimes uniting diverse peoples into a single nation, and sometimes separating a single people by an international border. Dissension was often the result; many borders were finalized only recently, and many remain in dispute. Libya's Bedouin tribes, for example, long presented a unified resistance to the imposition of what they viewed as artificial borders.

Algeria

Algeria is the second largest country in Africa, but 90 percent of it lies in the Sahara Desert. A French possession until 1962, Algeria's oil and natural gas provide most of its revenue. The nation enjoys political stability, free medical care, and a greatly improved educational system.

Angola

Situated on the southwest coastline of Africa, Angola was a Portuguese territory until 1975. It is now a Socialist republic. A civil war, the resultant departure of skilled European labor, and continuing guerilla activity have taken their toll on Angola's economy. Most people are subsistence farmers, although Angola is also a large oil producer.

Benin

Lying on the Gulf of Guinea, Benin was formerly called Dahomey. It is now a Socialist republic, having gained independence in 1960. Political instability has been both the cause and effect of Benin's economic problems. The agricultural economy remains largely undeveloped.

Botswana

Botswana is a landlocked republic in southern Africa that gained independence from Britain in 1966. Though limited by the Kalahari, agriculture and the raising of livestock are the primary activities. Since the early seventies, the economy has grown rapidly, with diamond mining the focus.

Burkina Faso

Landlocked Burkina Faso – formerly Upper Volta – is under military rule. The West African nation became independent from France in 1960. The agricultural economy suffers from frequent droughts and an underdeveloped transportation system. Most people are subsistence farmers.

Burundi

Set in the highlands of East Africa, Burundi is a small, densely populated land where subsistence farming is most important. The nation became an independent monarchy in 1962 but is now a republic. Tourists are drawn to Burundi's pleasant climate and hilly terrain.

Cameroon

Cameroon, once controlled by France and the United Kingdom, claimed its independence in the early 1960s. Most of the people in the central African republic live by subsistence farming. Recent economic plans have focused on agriculture, industry, and the development of oil deposits.

Cape Verde

These islands off the west coast of Africa have been independent from Portugal since 1975. The volcanic, mountainous terrain features few resources and low rainfall; thus the economy remains underdeveloped. The tropical climate, however, has helped tourism.

Central African Republic

This republic was once called French Equatorial Africa and remained under French rule until 1960. Fertile land, extensive forests, and mineral deposits provide adequate bases for agriculture, forestry, and mining. Economic development remains minimal, however, impeded by poor transportation routes, a landlocked location, lack of skilled labor, and political instability.

Chad

The Republic of Chad has one of the lowest population densities in Africa. Nomadic Arab herdsmen roam the dry lands with their animals in the north. In the south, black Africans grow some commercial crops. Independence from France was gained in 1960; conflicts between the north and south have marked Chad's politics since then.

Comoros

An Islamic republic, Comoros is an island nation situated between Madagascar and southwestern Africa. The nation was formerly ruled by France and gained independence in 1975. The economic mainstay is agriculture, and most Comorans practice subsistence farming and fishing.

Congo

The Congo is a Socialist republic that sits on the equator and is largely clothed in equatorial rain forest. Brazzaville was the commercial center of the former colony of French Equatorial Africa; the Congo became independent in 1960. It now benefits economically from the early groundwork laid for service and transport industries.

Djibouti

Set on the Gulf of Aden in East Africa, the Republic of Djibouti is mainly a stony desert. Traditional nomadic herding continues as a way of life for many Djiboutians. Formerly under French control, the nation became independent in 1977.

Egypt

Occupying the extreme northeast corner of Africa, Egypt is a Socialist republic that is mostly desert. The nation has a very long and rich history but today suffers from wars, shifting alliances, and limited natural resources. Agriculture, centered in the Nile Valley, remains an

Right: Most Ethiopians are subsistence farmers who live in small villages such as this one. These villages range in size from a few people to several hundred and feature small stone houses or mud huts with thatched roofs.

Africa

Countries continued

economic mainstay. Offshore petroleum will most likely continue its economic role, and tourism is a contributor as well.

Equatorial Guinea

On Africa's west coast near the equator sits Equatorial Guinea. Previously a Spanish colony, the republic gained independence in 1968. The economy is based on agriculture and forestry.

Ethiopia

Formerly known as Abyssinia, Ethiopia has a very long history. Until 1975, it was a kingdom ruled by a house said to be descended from King Solomon and the Queen of Sheba. Today, Ethiopia is a Socialist republic. Political instability and drought have taken their toll on Ethiopia's agricultural economy. Subsistence farming remains a major activity, though much arable land is uncultivated.

Gabon

Covered with dense rain forests, Gabon is a republic that sits on the equator in West Africa. Formerly controlled by several European nations, Gabon gained independence from France in 1960. The most important activities are oil production, forestry, and mining, although many people continue subsistence farming. The economy depends on foreign investment and imported labor.

Gambia

This narrow strip of land stretches along either bank of the Gambia (Gambie) River in West Africa. Formerly under British rule, the nation achieved independence in 1965 and became a republic in 1970. Gambia's economy relies on peanut production, but fishing and tourism have expanded in recent years.

Ghana

Formerly known as the Gold Coast, Ghana was one of the first countries to achieve independence from Britain in 1957. This West African country is predominantly agricultural, but its natural resources are diverse. Periods have unrest have resulted in the present military government.

Guinea

Ruled by France until 1958, Guinea is West Africa's most mountainous country. Agriculture is important, along with mining. In recent years, the military set up a provisional government and banned political parties.

Guinea-Bissau

Formerly a Portuguese province, this Atlantic coast republic has been independent since 1974. The economy is underdeveloped and dependent upon agriculture.

Ivory Coast

Until 1960, Ivory Coast was under French rule, but it is now an independent republic. It is potentially one of the richest countries of West Africa. Once solely dependent on the export of coffee and cocoa, Ivory Coast now produces and exports a variety of agricultural goods. Petroleum, textile, and apparel industries contribute to the strong economy.

Kenya

Straddling the equator in East Africa, Kenya became independent from Britain in 1963. Scenic terrain, tropical beaches, and abundant wildlife have given this republic a thriving tourist industry, and land has been set aside for national parks and game preserves. Agriculture, including the raising of livestock, is the leading economic contributor. Recent administrations have pursued a policy of Africanization, under which land and other holdings have been transferred from European to African hands.

Lesotho

Lesotho is a small, landlocked constitutional monarchy that is dependent economically upon South Africa, which surrounds it. Agriculture remains at the subsistence level, and livestock raising is important.

Liberia

This is the oldest independent country in West Africa, having been established in 1822 as an American settlement for freed slaves and granted independence twenty-five years later. The nation is a republic but is currently under martial rule. Liberia owes its healthy economy largely to an open-door policy, which has made its extensive resources attractive to foreign nations.

Libya

This North African nation is a Socialist republic that is under the leadership of Colonel Mu'ammar al-Qadhafi. The discovery of oil in 1959 propelled Libya from the ranks of the world's poorest nations to one of its leading oil producers. Most of Libya is covered by the Sahara Desert, and the limited agriculture has been further hurt by Libyan farmers migrating to the cities. Libya's support of terrorist activities led to a controversial United States air strike against the country in 1986, and several nations have instituted economic sanctions against the nation.

Madagascar

Lying some 240 miles (400 kilometers) off the southeastern African coast, Madagascar is an island in the Indian Ocean. It gained independence from France in 1960 and is now a republic.

Above: Ghana was one of the first African countries to become independent from European rule. A variety of crops are grown and traded here, as this street market shows, but cocoa is the most important export.

Right: The oasis town of Béchar, Algeria, is situated in the foothills of the Atlas Mountains. These coastal mountains prevent moisture from reaching inland and thereby contribute to the arid conditions of the huge Sahara Desert.

Below: The city of Aswān marked ancient Egypt's southern frontier. Now known for the nearby Aswān High Dam (As-Sadd al-'Alī), this city on the Nile River has a hot, dry climate and is a popular winter resort.

Right: These Nigerians are fishing in the Niger River, an important activity in this region. Though relatively small in area, Nigeria is the most populous African nation.

Madagascar is chiefly an agricultural nation, with the majority of the work force engaged in farming or herding.

Malawi

This landlocked republic in East Africa became independent from Britain in 1964. Malawi relies almost entirely on agriculture, though production is limited.

Mali

Formerly under French control, the Republic of Mali gained independence in 1960. One of the world's poorest nations, Mali depends primarily on agriculture but is limited by a poor climate and a desert terrain. Mali is a landlocked nation in West Africa.

Mauritania

This largely dry desert faces the Atlantic Ocean in West Africa. Mauritania was ruled by France until 1960; it is now under provisional military rule. The economy is based on agriculture, with many farmers producing only subsistence-level output.

Mauritius

This group of islands in the Indian Ocean five hundred miles (eight hundred kilometers) east of Madagascar is a parliamentary state, having gained independence from France in 1968. Sugar remains fundamental to the economy.

Mayotte

One of the Comoros Islands situated in the Mozambique Channel, Mayotte is a territorial collectivity of France. Unlike the mostly Muslim population of the other islands, most residents of Mayotte are Roman Catholic descendants of Malagasy immigrants.

Morocco

The Kingdom of Morocco has been independent from France since 1956. The nation is situated at the extreme northwest of the continent, on the Atlantic Ocean and Mediterranean Sea. Although agriculture employs much of the work force and is an important activity, the nation depends on mining for most of its income. Severe drought, rising dependency on imported oil, and a costly war in Western Sahara have slowed productivity, while investment by Arab countries has bolstered the economy.

Mozambique

This former Portuguese territory is now a Socialist republic that has been independent since 1975. Stretching along the southeast coast of Africa, Mozambique has an underdeveloped economy that is centered around agriculture and transport services. Continued guerrilla fighting, severe drought, and subsequent food shortages have created a crisis situation in Mozambique.

Namibia

Situated on the southwest tip of Africa, Namibia is governed by South Africa. The economy rests on the mining of diamonds, copper, lead, and other minerals. Agriculture makes a marginal contribution. South Africa has refused international orders to withdraw from the nation; negotiations for independence continue.

Niger

This landlocked nation in West Africa is now under a provisional military government, but it became independent from France in 1960. Niger's economy is agricultural, although arable land is scarce and drought common. Civilians now take part in the political system.

Nigeria

Africa's most populous nation, Nigeria was under British rule until 1960. The West African nation has suffered from civil war and political instability since independence and is now under a provisional military government. Nigeria's economy is based on mining and agriculture; petroleum is very important, but oil revenues have been declining.

Réunion

Réunion – an island in the Indian Ocean some 560 miles (900 kilometers) east of Madagascar – is an overseas department of France. Réunion's traditional sugar crop continues as its economic mainstay, although commercial fishing and shellfish are also important.

Left: **The pyramids at Giza (Al-Jīzah), Egypt, were constructed between 2650 and 2550 B.C. and remain one of the wonders of the ancient world. The pharaohs for whom they were erected employed vast numbers of people and primitive tools to create these architectural wonders and such others as the tomb of Tutankhamen and the huge temples at Luxor (Al-Uqṣur) and Karnak (Al-Karnak).**

Left: Olduvai Gorge, Tanzania, has been the site of numerous archaeological digs. After World War I, animal fossils were discovered here, but it was not until the Leakeys found evidence of human remains that investigation of the gorge began in earnest. Since then, Olduvai Gorge has yielded many fossils and artifacts that evidence thousands of years of prehistoric habitation. The earliest remains at Olduvai are estimated to be about two million years old.

Rwanda

This landlocked East African republic was under Belgian rule and became independent in 1962. Agriculture is the major activity, although plagued by the erosion and overpopulation of arable land. Tourism is small but growing.

St. Helena

This small volcanic island 1,200 miles (1,900 kilometers) west of the African mainland is a British colony. A number of other islands are associated with it, particularly Ascension Island, 700 miles (1,100 kilometers) to the northwest.

São Tomé and Príncipe

These islands off western Africa were formerly under Portuguese administration, having gained independence in 1975. Cocoa dominates São Tomé and Príncipe's economy.

Senegal

Senegal, situated on the western coast of Africa, was under French rule. It became an independent republic in 1960. The mainstays of the economy are petroleum, agriculture, fishing, and mining. Tourism is a rapidly growing new industry.

Seychelles

This group of more than one hundred islands in the Indian Ocean, some 1,000 (1,600 kilometers) east of the Kenyan coast, was formerly a British colony. Seychelles achieved independence in 1976. The basis of the economy is tourism, with foreign visitors attracted by the tropical climate, white-sand beaches, and exotic flora and fauna found on the islands.

Sierra Leone

Sierra Leone is a West African republic that was under British domination until 1961. The nation is one of the world's largest producers of industrial and commercial diamonds. Poor soil, a fluctuating tropical climate, and traditional farming methods keep crop yields low.

Somalia

Jutting along the northeast corner of Africa, Somalia is a Socialist republic. The economy is based in agriculture, though activity is restricted to the vicinity of the rivers and certain coastal districts. The region was once under British and Italian domination, and it became independent in 1960.

South Africa

The discovery of gold and diamonds in South Africa in the late 1800s shaped this republic's prosperous economy. Mining remains a mainstay, as does agriculture; the nation is almost self-sufficient in food production. Today, South Africa is one of the richest and most developed nations in Africa, yet, in spite of increased racial tension and violent conflicts, the white-run, Afrikaner government continues to suppress the black majority population with its apartheid system.

Sudan

A republic in northeastern Africa, Sudan overcame British administration in 1956. A series of military coups since that time has burdened the country with economic and political instability. The economy is based on agriculture. Irrigation has made arid Sudan a leading producer of cotton, although the land is vulnerable to drought.

Swaziland

The Kingdom of Swaziland is a small, landlocked country in southern Africa, which became independent from British rule in 1968. Most Swazi are subsistence farmers. Europeans own nearly half the land and raise most of the cash crops.

Tanzania

Independent since 1961, Tanzania is an East African republic. Agriculture accounts for most export earnings and employs 80 percent of the work force. Yet two-thirds of the land cannot be cultivated because of lack of water and tsetse-fly infestation.

Togo

This West African republic has suffered internal strife and a military dominance since separating with France in 1960. Togo has one of the world's largest phosphate reserves. Although Togo is an agricultural nation, farmland is scarce.

Tunisia

The Republic of Tunisia sits at the tip of northern Africa. It became independent from France in 1956. The economy is based in agriculture and oil. Tourism is growing despite an unemployment problem.

Uganda

This East African republic sits on the equator. Political instability has marked the government since independence from Britain came in 1962. Despite attempts to diversify the economy, the country remains largely agricultural.

Western Sahara

Occupied by Morocco, Western Sahara sits on the northwest corner of Africa, facing the Atlantic Ocean. Most of the nation is desert, with a rocky barren soil that severely limits agriculture. In Western Sahara are found valuable phosphate deposits – the source of most export income.

Zaire

This central African republic was under Belgian domination until 1960. Mining has supplanted agriculture in economic importance and now dominates the economy. Agriculture continues to employ most Zairians, however, and subsistence farming is practiced in nearly every region. The government has stabilized under the present administration.

Zambia

Landlocked in southern Africa, Zambia became an independent republic in 1964. The economy is based in copper, which is the major export. Declining copper prices and a severe drought are problematic.

Zimbabwe

Zimbabwe is a landlocked republic in southern Africa that became free of British rule in 1980. Despite Zimbabwe's move toward stability since independence, some internal unrest continues. The nation's natural resources have played a key role in its sustained economic growth. The subtropical climate supports the exportation of many agricultural products and makes large-scale cattle ranching feasible.

ARQUIPÉLAGO DA MADEIRA
MADEIRA ISLANDS
(Portugal)

PORTO SANTO

Funchal MADEIRA

30°

SPAIN **Málaga**
Algeciras Gibraltar
Strait of Gibraltar (U.K.)
Tanger (Sp.) ISLA DE
Tanger ALBORÁN
(Sp.)
Larache
Ksar-el-Kebir Al-Hoceima **Melilla**

Kenitra Ouezzane **Melilla**
Mohammedia Taza
Rabat Salé Ouida
Casablanca Meknès **Fès**
Dar-el-Beïda El-Jadida
Safi Khouribga M O R O C C O

ÍLHAS SELVAGENS
(Mad. Is.)

Essaouira Youssoufia Beni-Mellal
Oued Oum er CAP RHIR

ISLAS CANARIAS
CANARY ISLANDS
(Spain)

Agadir ANTI-ATLAS Ouarzazate Erfoud **Béchar**

LA PALMA Santa Cruz
de la Palma LANZAROTE
Pico de Teide
GOMERA 3718 TENERIFE **Santa Cruz de Tenerife** Arrecife
HERRO **Las Palmas de Gran Canaria**
GRAN CANARIA FUERTEVENTURA Sidi Ifni HAMADA DU DRA'A

CAP JUBY **Tarfaya**

25°

El Aaiún As Saquia al Hamra
Laayoune Smara Tindouf

CAP BOJADOR

Tropic of Cancer

W E S T E R N
S A H A R A

Western Sahara has been occupied
by Morocco

Bir Mogreïn

CAP BARBAS

Kediet ej Jill
Fdérik ▲ 915

20°

La Goueïra Nouâdhibou
RÁS NOUÂDHIBOU

Taoudenni

A T L A N T I C

Atâr Chinguetti
ET TÎDRA O U A R Â N E
RÁS TIMIRIST Nouâmghâr ADRAR M A U R I T A N I A
Akjoujt I J Â F E N E

Nouakchott

Boutilimit

Tidjikja
SÃO ANTÃO Moudjéria Tichît
SÃO VICENTE **Mindelo**
SANTA LUZIA A O U K Â R
SÃO NICOLAU SAL Araouane
CAPE VERDE BOA VISTA

Saint-Louis Rosso Aleg Kiffa Tamchaket Oualáta M A L I
15° Dagana Podor Bogué 'Ayoûn el 'Atroûs Oualáta
BRAVA SANTIAGO MAIO Louga Kaédi Tombouctou Bamba
FOGO **Praia** Linguère Matam Mbout Timbuktu
CAP VERT Vallée du Ferlo Sélibaby Néma Lac Faguibine
Dakar **Thiès** Sine Diourbel S E N E G A L Bakel Kayes Yélimané Nioro du Sahel Goundam Niger Gao
Rufisque Saloum Kidira Niafounké
Kaolack Bafoulabé S S U D A
Georgetown Tambacounda Kita Koulikoro Niono Djenné U Douentza Hombori Tondo
Banjul Gambia Kéniéba Kayes Ségou Bani San H Mopti ▲ 1155
GAMBIA Vélingara Kédougou Bafing Sikasso MASSINA E
Ziguinchor Kolda **Bamako** Koutiala A
Gambie Bafatá Kta Bougouni **BURKINA FASO**
10° **GUINEA-** **Bissau** Corubal Labé Siguiri Dédougou **Ouagadougou**
BISSAU Bolama Tinkisso Kouroussa Sikasso Bobo Leo Fada
ARQUIPÉLAGO Bubaque F O U T A G U I N E A Koudougou Tenkodogo
DOS BIJAGÓS Boké D J A L O N Dabola Niger Bougouni Bolgatanga Dapango
Kindia Mamou **Kankan** Bouna Wa
Dubréka Faranah Odienné Korhogo GHANA Tamale
Conakry Port Loko SIERRA Kissidougou Yendéré **Bobo Dioulasso** Yendi
Maken Bolgatanga Bassari
Freetown Lungi LEONE 1945 Macenta Touba **IVORY COAST**
Móyemba Pendembu Nzérékoré Bondoukou
Bo Volinjama Man **Bouaké** Suryani
SHERBRO ISLAND Bonthe Kenema Mont Nimba Katiola Kumasi
Lofa 1752 Daloa Bouaflé Abengourou
Robertsport Saint Paul Ghanga Yamoussoukro Obuasi Kade Koforidua
Monrovia L I B E R I A Cavally Dalca Gagnoa Oda Keta
Marshall Buchanan Dunkwa **Accra**
Cestos Tchien **Abidjan** Asamankese
River Cess San-Pédro Grand-Bassam Winneba
Greenville Grand **Cape Coast**
Sastown Cess Port-Bouët **Sekondi-Takoradi**
Harper Tabou GROWA POINT CAPE THREE POINTS

O C E A N

5°

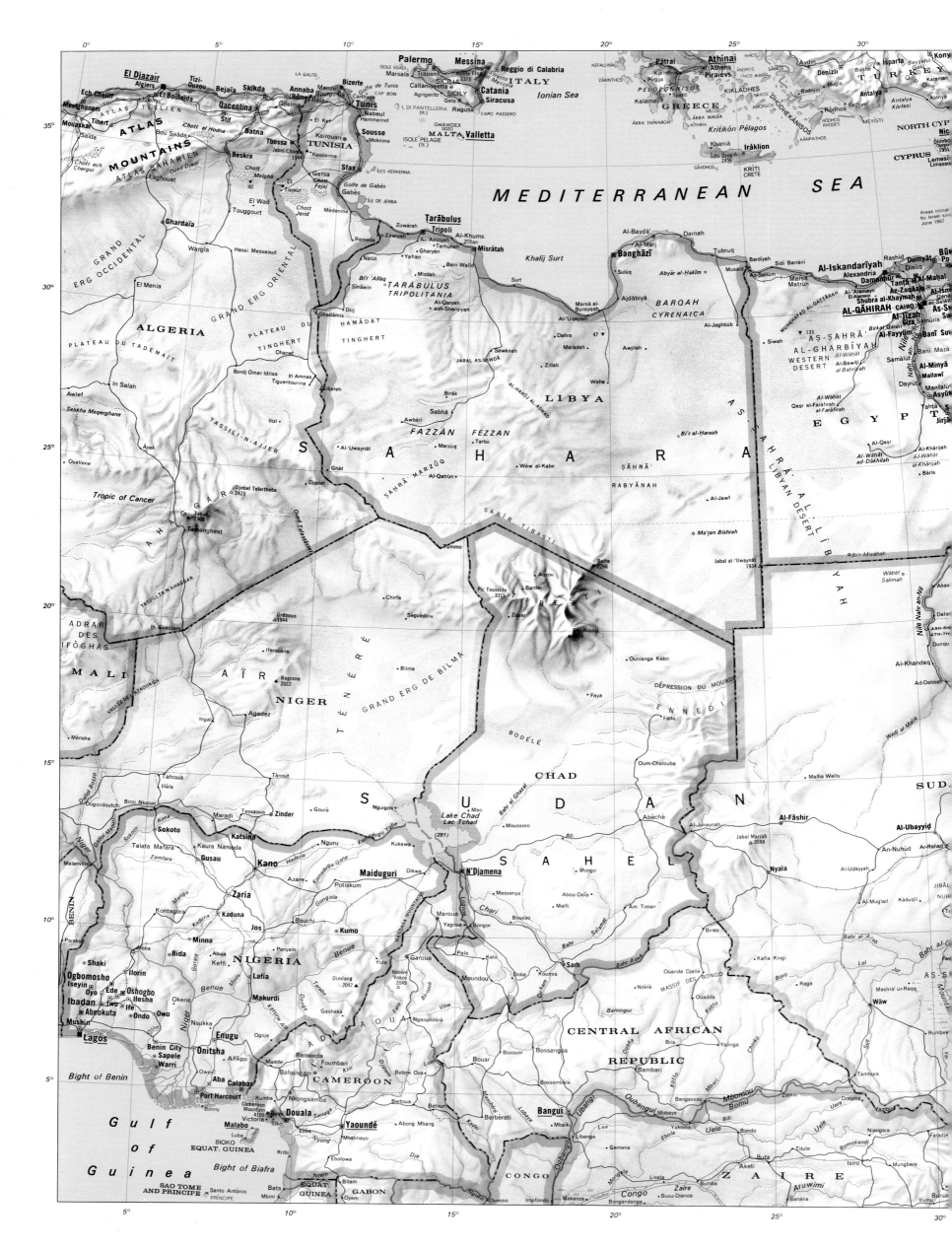

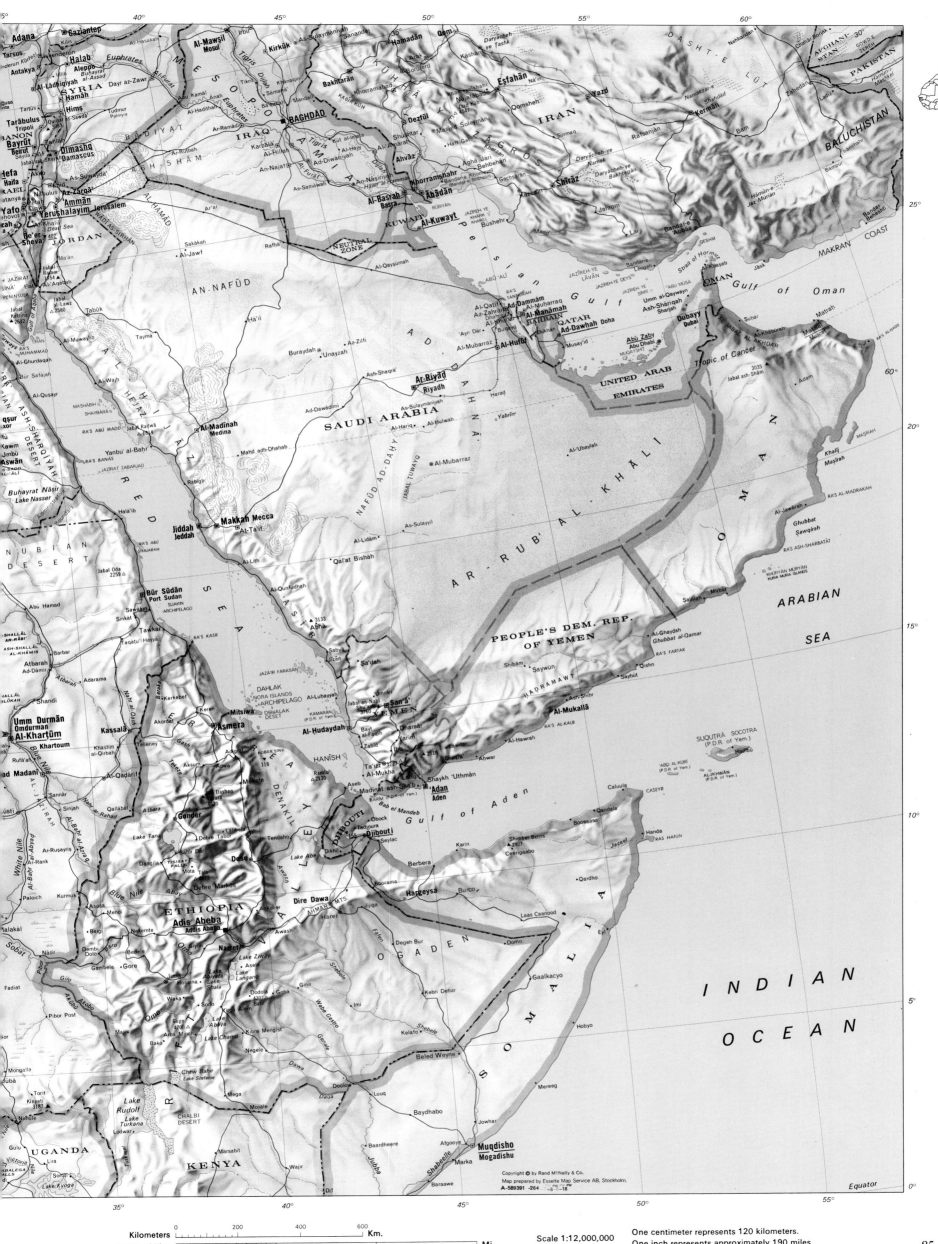

Kilometers
Statute Miles

Scale 1:12,000,000

One centimeter represents 120 kilometers.
One inch represents approximately 190 miles.
Miller Oblated Stereographic Projection

5°
10°
15°
20°
25°
30°
0°
5°
10°
15°
20°
25°
30°
SAO TOME AND PRINCIPE
PRINCIPE
Santo Antônio
SÃO TOMÉ
São Tomé
ANNOBÓN (Equat. Gui.)
EQUATORIAL GUINEA
Bata
Mbini
Libreville
GABON
CAP LOPEZ
Port Gentil
Lambaréné
Ogooué
CAMEROON
CONGO
Brazzaville
Pointe-Noire
CABINDA (Angola)
Cabinda
KINSHASA (LÉOPOLDVILLE)
Matadi
Boma
Congo
Zaire
ZAIRE
Mbandaka (Coquilhatville)
Kisangani (Stanleyville)
STANLEY FALLS
Bandundu
Kikwit
Kananga (Luluabourg)
Mbuji-Mayi (Bakwanga)
Kasai
Lac Mai-Ndombe
Lake Albert
Lake Edward
Lake George
Lake Kivu
RWANDA
Kigali
BURUNDI
Bujumbura
Bukavu
Kalemie (Albertville)
Lake Tanganyika
MONTS MITUMBA
KATANGA
Kolwezi
Likasi (Jadotville)
Lubumbashi (Elisabethville)
Lake Mweru
Lake Bangweulu
ZAMBIA
Kitwe
Ndola
Chingola
Luanshya
Kabwe (Broken Hill)
Lusaka
Zambezi
Livingstone
VICTORIA FALLS
Lake Kariba
ZIMBABWE
Harare (Salisbury)
Bulawayo
Gweru
Masvingo
ANGOLA
Luanda
PONTA DAS PALMEIRINHAS
Malanje
Lobito
Benguela
Huambo (Nova Lisboa)
Serra Môco 2620
CABO DE SANTA MARIA
Lubango
Namibe
Tombua
PONTA DA MARCA
Foz do Cunene
Cunene
Cuando
Cubango
Okavango
CAPRIVI ZIPFEL
ATLANTIC
OCEAN
OVAMBOLAND
Etosha Pan
Tsumeb
KAOKO VELD
CAPE FRIA
NAMIBIA
NAMIB DESERT
Otjiwarongo
Ugab
2574 Brandberg
DAMARALAND
Windhoek
Swakopmund
Walvisbaai
Walvis Bay (S. Afr.)
Tropic of Capricorn
(S. Afr. Admin.)
HOLLANDSBIRD ISLAND (S. Afr.)
GREAT NAMAQUALAND
Keetmanshoop
Lüderitz
Orange
Oranjemund
Alexander Bay
Port Nolloth
BUSHMAN LAND
KAUKAU VELD
OKAVANGO DELTA
Maun
Lake Ngami
Makgadikgadi
BOTSWANA
KALAHARI DESERT
Serowe
Gaborone
Molepolole
Francistown
BOPHUTHATSWANA
Pretoria
JOHANNESBURG
Vereeniging
Kimberley
Bloemfontein
LESOTHO
SWAZILAND
Pietermaritzburg
Durban
TRANSKEI
East London
Oos-Londen
Port Elizabeth
SOUTH AFRICA
GREAT KAROO
Cape Town
Kaapstad
Stellenbosch
Paarl
CAPE OF GOOD HOPE
CAPE AGULHAS
CAPE SAINT FRANCIS
Uitenhage
Mosselbaai
Oudtshoorn
LITTLE KARROO
Springbok
Upington
The United Nations declared an end to the mandate of South Africa over Namibia in October, 1966. Administration of the territory by South Africa is not recognized by the United Nations.

INDIAN OCEAN

Equator 0°

SEYCHELLES

PRASLIN ISLAND
LA DIGUE
SILHOUETTE
Victoria
MAHÉ ISLAND
5°

AMIRANTE ISLANDS (Sey.)
ÎLE DESROCHES (Sey.)
PLATTE ISLAND (Sey.)

ALPHONSE ISLAND (Sey.)
COETIVY ISLAND (Sey.)

PROVIDENCE ISLAND (Sey.)
ALDABRA ISLAND (Sey.)
COSMOLEDO I. (Sey.)
SAINT PIERRE ISLAND (Sey.)
CERF ISLAND (Sey.)
10°
ASSUMPTION ISLAND (Sey.)
ASTOVE ISLAND (Sey.)
FARQUHAR GROUP (Sey.)
AGALEGA ISLANDS (Mauritius)

SOMALIA
Shabeelle
Baraawe

Mado Gashi
Ulib
Jamaame
Garissa
Kismaayo Jumboo
Buur Gaabo
PATE ISLAND
Lamu
Kipini
Malindi

Mount Elgon
Kitale
Eldoret
Marsabit
Meru
Kitui
NAIROBI
Machakos
Konza
KENYA
Mombasa

SERENGETI PLAIN
Arusha
Mount Kilimanjaro

MASAI STEPPE
Tanga
Zanzibar
ZANZIBAR
Dar es Salaam

TANZANIA
Dodoma
Morogoro

MAFIA ISLAND
Kilindoni

KIPENGERE RA.
Njombe
Songea
Tunduru

Lake Nyasa
Lake Malawi

ÎLES GLORIEUSES (Reunion)

CAP D'AMBRE
SAINT-SÉBASTIEN
CAP
Antsiranana

Mikindani
Mwara
Masasi
Ruvuma
CABO DELGADO
Palma
Mocimboa da Praia

COMOROS
Moroni
Fomboni
Mutsamudu
MWALI
NZWANI
Dzaoudzi
MAYOTTE (Fr.)

NOSY MITSIO

NOSY BE
Hell-Ville
Ambilobe
Vohimarina

MALAWI
Lilongwe
Lake Chilwa
Zomba
Blantyre

Ibo
Quissanga
Pemba

Montepuez
Nampula

MASSIF DU
TSARATANANA
Sambava
Antalaha

ARCHIPEL DES COMOROS

NOSY LAVA
Analalava
Baalanana
Andapa

Baie de Narinda
Antsohihy

Nacala
Moçambique

Mozambique

MOZAMBIQUE
Zambeze
Quelimane

Angoche
ILHA ANGOCHE
Moma
Pebane

Helodranon' i Mahajamba
Mahajanga
Lac Kinkony
Soalala
Marovoay
Mampikony

PRESQU'ÎLE DE MASOALA
CAP EST

ÎLE CHESTERFIELD (Reunion)
Besalampy

ÎLE JUAN DE NOVA (Reunion)

Tsaratanana
NOSY BORAHA
Ambodifototra

Beira
Dondo
Nova Sofala

NOSY BARREN
Tambohorano
Maintirano

Morafenobe
Maevatanana
Andriamena
Fenoarivo Atsinanana

Ambatondrazaka
Toamasina

Bartolomeu Dias
Nova Mambone

MADAGASCAR
Belo
Tsiribihina
Miandrivazo
Ankavandra

Tsiroanomandidy
Ankazobe
Antananarivo
Vohibinany

Vilanculos
ILHA DO BAZARUTO
PONTA SÃO SEBASTIÃO

BASSAS DA INDIA (Reunion)

Morondava
Mahabo
Malaimbandy
Ambatolampy
Vatomandry

Antsirabe
Mahanoro

Massinga
Morrumbene
PONTA DA BARRA
Inhambane

Mandabe
Manja
Ambositra
Nosy Varika
Mananjary

ÎLE EUROPA (Reunion)
CAP SAINT-VINCENT
Morombe
Mangoky
Beroroha
Pic Boby 2654
Fianarantsoa
Ampalaza
Manakara

Port Louis
Curepipe
Mahébourg
MAURITIUS
20°

Le Port
Saint-Denis
Saint-Paul
Saint-Pierre
RÉUNION (Fr.)

MASCARENE ISLANDS

Andranovory
Ankazoabo
Betioky
Toliara
Manja

Betroka
Vangaindrano
Farafangana

Tropic of Capricorn

Ampanihy
Bekily
Midongy Sud

Mozambique Channel

Androka
Tsihombe
Ambovombe
Faradofay

CAP SAINTE-MARIE

Xai-Xai

INDIAN OCEAN

Kilometers
0   200   400   600   Km.
Statute Miles
0   200   400   600   Mi.

Scale 1:12,000,000

One centimeter represents 120 kilometers.
One inch represents approximately 190 miles.

Miller Oblated Stereographic Projection

Oceania
Profile

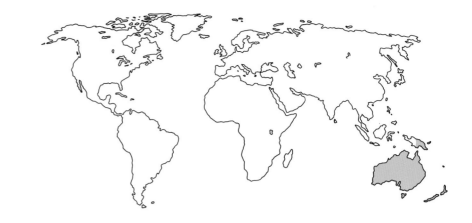

Location and Size

Oceania comprises Australia, New Zealand, Papua New Guinea, and a number of island countries scattered over the southern and central Pacific Ocean. Together, the three countries mentioned above make up nearly 99 percent of the total land area and contain nearly 92 percent of the total population of all Oceania. The continent of Australia alone contains over 90 percent of the total land area and nearly two-thirds of the total population.

The principal Pacific islands and island groups within Oceania may be grouped into three areas: Melanesia, Micronesia, and Polynesia. Occupying the smallest area, Melanesia lies closest to Australia. It extends northwest to southeast, from Papua New Guinea to the Solomon Islands, New Caledonia, Vanuatu, and Fiji. Melanesia means the "black islands."

Micronesia, meaning the "little islands," contains no islands as large as the main ones of Melanesia but is composed of tiny atolls. Polynesia – meaning "many islands" – covers the largest area of the three. Some of these islands are associated politically with the United States, France, or Chile.

Australia extends nearly 2,300 miles (3,700 kilometers) north to south, from Cape York Peninsula in Queensland to South East Cape in Tasmania. Its west-east expanse is similar, stretching from the Western Australia coast near Carnarvon to the Pacific margins of Queensland and New South Wales. Australia is the only continent in the world that is also a country; though it is the world's smallest continent, it is one of its biggest countries. Situated entirely in the Southern Hemisphere, Australia straddles the Tropic of Capricorn.

Landscape

For the most part, Australia is a vast, undulating desert plateau. The great exceptions are: the eastern mountains, or the Great Dividing Range, extending from Cape York Peninsula in the north to Victoria in the south; the lowland area of the central basin, extending from eastern South Australia to the Gulf of Carpentaria; and the plains that are found around most of the coast. Australia has proportionally more desert area than any other continent, and water sources are a great problem in much of the nation.

Australia's rivers fall into two main types. Many comparatively short rivers flow toward the east coast from the divide of the eastern highlands. More major river systems cross parts of the interior, with the Murray and its tributaries the largest. These rivers have a large discharge in their headwaters but lose much as they flow westward across the drier interior lands of the central basin. Parts of this area are drained by rivers that dry up in the hot season or reach lakes whose surface areas vary greatly throughout the year.

A distinctive water feature of Australia is its series of artesian basins. The Great Artesian Basin underlies much of western Queensland, northeastern South Australia, and northwestern New South Wales, extending for 600,000 square miles (1,554,000 square kilometers). In these basins, rainfall in the surrounding areas percolates underground and is stored under such great pressure that it gushes to the land surface through any opening. One needs only dig a hole in the ground to bring the water back to the surface. Artesian water does not, therefore, need to be pumped.

Farther south, the artesian Murray River basin occupies a smaller area. Western Australia has four smaller basins around its coastal margins. In general, the water in these basins is too salty for humans to drink.

The Great Barrier Reef, the world's largest coral reef, extends some 1,200 miles (1,930 kilometers) along Australia's northeastern coast. Although its name implies that it is one giant reef, the Great Barrier Reef is actually a series of more than 2,500 reefs. It is composed of more than three hundred species of corals in a dazzling array of colors and shapes. Its unique beauty and year-round warm waters attract many tourists, snorkelers, and skin divers from around the world.

New Zealand is a long narrow strip of land, divided into two islands by Cook Strait. The land is mostly mountainous and no location is more than 80 miles (130 kilometers) from the sea. The most rugged regions are found in the Southern Alps of South Island; North Island is slightly less mountainous but contains volcanic regions. Fertile, narrow plains

Left: The photogenic skyline of Sydney, Australia, features the Sydney Opera House and the Sydney Harbor Bridge. This metropolis on the southwestern coast is Australia's oldest and most populous.

Right: French Polynesia's reputation as a tropical paradise is well founded and over the years has attracted, among others, the mutinous crew of the *Bounty* and French painter Paul Gauguin. Here, the island of Bora-Bora rises in the distance.

lie along some coastal areas.

Most other areas in Oceania are tropical, volcanic islands, filled with a variety of vegetation and animal life. Other islands are simply a series of coral atolls, such as the Gilbert Islands.

Climate

There are three main climates in Australia. Only the temperate humid climate is at all attractive to white settlers who are found only in limited parts of the country. Nowhere in the temperate areas does the average temperature of the coldest winter month, July, fall below freezing, and in summer the averages rise above 64°F (18°C), reaching above 72°F (22°C) in places. The extreme southwest of Western Australia has a Mediterranean type of climate, with summer temperatures reaching the

higher levels and a marked lack of summer rain.

Farther east, in southern South Australia and parts of western Victoria, similar summer temperatures prevail and the rainfall – mainly in the winter – is greater. Still in the temperate group, the east coast climate – from Tasmania to the central Queensland area – shows more even distribution of rainfall in the south. In the south, the highest monthly average temperatures are below 68°F (20°C), but in the north they are well above 72°F (22°C).

The northern coastal areas of the country experience tropical climates, in which even the coolest month has an average temperature 64°F (18°C). Here there is a marked summer maximum in the rainfall, with totals exceeding eighty inches (two thousand millimeters) in places.

The great heartland of Australia – from the Indian Ocean in the west, eastward to the interior slopes of the highlands of the Pacific-bordering states – is an area of marked rainfall deficiency with higher average temperatures than elsewhere in the continent. In the most arid central parts, precipitation rarely exceeds ten inches (250 millimeters). Here, the summer temperature may reach 80°F (27°C) and in the winter drops only to 54°F (12°C). Bordering this region, less extreme climates may be found.

Because Australia is south of the equator, its warmest months are December through March and its coldest are June through September. In other words, the seasons are the reverse of those in the Northern Hemisphere.

As a result of the moderating effects of the ocean, New Zealand experiences

a mild climate with slight seasonal variations. It is subtropical in the north and temperate farther south. The islands of Oceania lie within the tropics, so they experience warm climates.

History, Politics, and Economy

The first humans who lived in the western Pacific around thirty thousand years ago were Aboriginals who established a hunter-gatherer society. Migration from Malaya-Indonesia was helped by the natural land bridges that formed with the shallow sea level of the ice ages. Further migration occurred from Micronesia and Melanesia to Polynesia around 1,000 B.C.

Situated on the opposite side of the globe from Europe, this part of the world was among the last places to be visited by the European explorers. Ferdi-

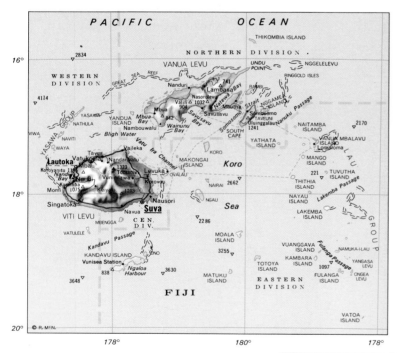

Above, right: These residents of Malakula, Vanuatu (New Hebrides), experience a tropical rain-forest climate year-round.

Right: West of Ayers Rock in the Australian Outback is a group of rocks known as the Olgas. They differ from the Rock in appearance and texture, yet they too display the types of ancient Aboriginal paintings for which the Rock is known.

Opposite: The Isle of Pines, shown here, is one of the several islands that make up New Caledonia. The climate and culture of this French territory attract tourists.

nand Magellan was one of the first to arrive in Oceania when he discovered Guam in 1521.

In 1606, Dutch navigators landed on the northern Australian coast and the Cape York Peninsula. Little impressed by the hot lands, the Dutch took no further interest in this area, which they called New Holland. Some eighty-two years later, the English explorer William Dampier reached the barren wastes of the northwestern coast, and reported unenthusiastically of his finds on his return home. Captain James Cook sailed to Oceania on three voyages – from 1769 to 1779 – and explored Tahiti and New Zealand before reaching Australia. He subsequently laid formal claim to Australia for Great Britain.

Interest in this distant land did not grow, however, until after Great Britain had lost its American penal colonies a few years later. The earliest colony, Port Jackson (now Sydney), in New South Wales, was founded in 1788, and many of the early white residents were British convicts.

For the next thirty years or so, the Blue Mountains presented an impenetrable barrier to westward expansion. Then, beginning in the early 1800s, a squatter movement spread the population to other parts of the island. During subsequent years, many new settlements were established: Tasmania in 1803, Brisbane in 1824, the Swan River colony in the distant southwest in 1829, Melbourne in 1835, and Adelaide in 1836. In turn, settlements became provinces

or colonies: Tasmania (1825), Western Australia (1831), South Australia (1834), Victoria (1851), and Queensland (1859). By 1850 the population had risen to just over 400,000. But it was not until the early 1860s, when the population had risen to over one million, that the first south-north crossing of the country was made.

The first attraction of the new lands was for farming. Merino sheep from Spain soon flourished here and produced the world's finest wool. But with the discovery of gold in 1850, mineral prospecting received a great lift, and many new mining settlements were established.

In 1901, the Commonwealth of Australia claimed independence from the British crown. The nation fought on the side of the British during both world wars.

Today, more attention is being paid to the rights of the indigenous Australian Aboriginals, who number about 160,000. Most are of mixed descent – part Aboriginal, part Anglo – and live on special reserves or on the fringe of white society. To some extent, they maintain their traditional life-style, particularly in art and religion.

The Commonwealth of Australia is a parliamentary state, with a constitution similar to that of the United States. The nation is divided into six states and presides over two territories.

Australia's economy is similar to economies in other developed nations, characterized by a postwar shift from

agriculture to industry and services, and problems of inflation and unemployment. Wool is a major export, and livestock raising takes place on relatively flat, wide grazing lands surrounding an arid central region. Commercial crop raising is concentrated on a fertile southeastern plain. Plentiful mineral resources such as gold, cobalt, copper, manganese, silver, tin, and tungsten provide for a strong mining industry.

New Zealand has a history similar to that of Australia. Captain James Cook first charted the islands in the late 1700s. European settlement was hindered by the fierce Maori, the original settlers, thought to have migrated from Polynesia around A.D. 1000. Nonetheless, European traders and hunters began to arrive, and after an 1840 treaty with the Maori, British rule was established and more settlers were drawn to the islands. Independence came in the 1940s. Today, the population is mainly white, but the number of Maoris, unlike the Aboriginals of Australia, is growing.

Like Australia, New Zealand is a parliamentary state, but it has no written constitution. The nation recognizes Britain's Elizabeth II as queen of New Zealand.

Farming and farm-related industries dominate New Zealand's developed economy. The raising of livestock, particularly sheep, is especially important. The number of livestock on the islands is far larger than the number of people.

After Captain James Cook's exploratory voyages in the late 1700s, the British

and French began to settle on some of the islands of Oceania. Many of the indigenous cultures were altered by European missionaries who came to the region in the nineteenth century. By 1900, the region had mostly come under European dominion.

Japan occupied much of Oceania during World War II, and the South Pacific became a hot battlefield, particularly around New Guinea and the Solomon Islands. After the war, some of the islands were placed under the United Nations trusts until they could achieve self-government. The first nation to realize independence was Western Samoa in 1962; it is now a constitutional monarchy. In 1970, Fiji and Tonga also became independent. Independence soon followed for Papua New Guinea (1975), the Solomon Islands and Tuvalu (1978), Kiribati (1979), and Vanuatu (1980).

For the most part, independence for the island nations of Oceania came peacefully. Recently, however, violence has erupted in New Caledonia's struggle for independence. A group of indigenous Kanaks refuses to discuss limited autonomy with France and will not accept anything less than full independence for New Caledonia.

Today, some of the island nations – such as Fiji, Kiribati, and Nauru – are republics. Some – such as New Caledonia, French Polynesia, and Guam – are administered by Western nations. The islands struggle to make their way in the world economy, and increased tourism in Oceania has helped.

Oceania
Countries

American Samoa

The Samoan Islands are a Polynesian group approximately midway between Australia and Hawaii. The eastern islands have been an unincorporated territory of the United States since 1900. Fishing, especially for tuna, is important, providing the major export item. Other exports include pet foods and native crafts.

Australia

The Land Down Under is the smallest of continents and one of the world's largest countries. Relatively dry (one-third of the land is desert) and thinly populated, this island was originally settled by British convicts, though native Aboriginals have existed on the land for over thirty thousand years. Sheep raising is an important activity, and wool is a major export. Australia fought on the side of the British in both world wars, and postwar years have seen increased attention paid to the rights of the dwindling Aboriginal population.

Cook Islands

Widely scattered throughout the southwest Pacific, these Polynesian islands are mostly of volcanic origin. First discovered in 1773 by Captain James Cook, they were a British protectorate, then a New Zealand territory. Since 1965, however, the Cook Islands have been self-governed.

Fiji

Fiji is a group of nearly 850 islands in the South Pacific. Little is known about Fiji before the arrival of Europeans, though early Melanesians probably migrated there from Indonesia, followed by Polynesian settlers in the second century. Only about one hundred of the islands are inhabited, and traditional sugar cane growing is a principal economic activity. Tourism is growing, and expansion of forestry is planned. The land is characterized by mountains, valleys, and rain forests.

French Polynesia

These South Pacific islands are an overseas French territory and are spread over roughly 1.5 million square miles (3.9 million square kilometers). The territory includes the Marquesas (Marquises) Islands, the Society (Société) Islands, the Tuamotu Archipelago, the Gambier Islands, and the Austral (Australes) Islands. The Marquesas, known for their beauty, form the northernmost group. The Society Islands include Tahiti and Bora-Bora, both popular tourist spots. Pearls, copra, and precision instruments are exported, while coconut, mother-of-pearl, and tourism are also economic contributors. Most inhabitants are Polynesian, with minorities including Chinese and French. The climate is tropical. The French use several of the islands for nuclear testing.

Guam

This largest and most southerly island in the Marianas Archipelago of Micronesia is an unincorporated territory of the United States, ceded from Spain in 1898. It is the United States' most westerly Pacific outpost and is of major strategic importance both as a naval and air base. About a quarter of the present population is United States service personnel and their families. The native population is mainly of Malay origin. Agriculture is a primary activity.

Kiribati

The people of Kiribati, a nation of thirty-three islands in the central Pacific, are mostly Micronesian. Almost all the population lives on the Gilbert Islands in small villages. The official language is English, but Gilbertese is also spoken. With a relatively small land area and few natural resources, Kiribati natives live a subsistence existence. The islands are mostly coral reefs, and the climate is tropical. Kiribati was formerly part of the Gilbert and Ellice Islands; it became independent in 1979. The nation is dependent on economic aid from Australia, New Zealand, and Great Britain.

Nauru

A tiny Micronesian coral island approximately 8.1 square miles (21 square kilometers) in area, Nauru's core contains extensive deposits of high grade phosphates, its sole export. With limited agriculture, nearly all food must be imported. Once governed by Australia, Nauru gained independence in 1968, then gained control of European interests in the phosphate industry in 1970. Most inhabitants are of mixed Polynesian, Melanesian, and Micronesian stock, and the climate is tropical. The government is establishing trust funds to support islanders when the phosphate resources are depleted.

New Caledonia

New Caledonia is a French overseas territory and includes the Isle of Pines and the Loyalty (Loyauté) and Bélep islands. The principal economic activity, the mining and smelting of nickel, has decreased over the years. Copra and coffee are exported, and tourism is important. New Caledonia, the main island, is mountainous, and all the islands are tropical in climate. Most inhabitants are Melanesians, or Kanaks, but there are some French, Asian, and Polynesian inhabitants. Violence erupted in the 1980s, stemming from the desire of the Kanaks for independence.

New Zealand

New Zealand consists of two large islands – North Island and South Island – and many smaller islands scattered throughout the South Pacific. The scenic terrain is greatly varied, ranging from fjords and mountains to a volcanic plateau. Manufacturing, including food-processing and paper industries, is an expanding economic sector, as is tourism. New Zealand supported Britain in both world wars; advancing the rights of the Maori population has become a priority.

Niue

Geographically within the Cook Islands, Niue's area is more than that of all the other islands in that group together, but its population is much smaller. It achieved self-government in 1974 but is economically dependent upon its mother country, New Zealand. Copra, sweet potatoes, and bananas are the main crops.

Norfolk Island

An Australian territory 900 miles (1,400 kilometers) east of the New South Wales coast, this island was originally used as a penal settlement. In 1856, 194 *Bounty* descendants moved from Pitcairn to Norfolk Island. Today, Norfolk's attractive scenery, beaches, and climate have encouraged tourism.

Pacific Islands,
Trust Territory of the

Following World War II, the United States was appointed by the United Nations to act as trustee of all formerly Japanese-mandated islands in the Pacific

Right: South Island is the larger, more mountainous, and less populated of the two major islands that make up New Zealand. Shown here is Queenstown, on Lake Wakatipu.

Below: This Aboriginal man is drawing on the Wessel Islands in a manner largely unmodified since the Stone Age.

92

Below: Some of the geysers and hot springs of New Zealand's North Island have been harnessed to produce electricity. Shown here is Pokutu Geyser.

Bottom: Sheep and cattle farming are all-important to New Zealand. Here cattle graze near Mount Egmont (Taranaki) on North Island.

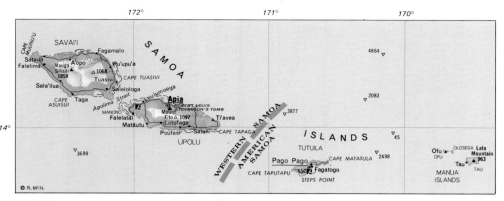

between 1° and 22° north, and 130° and 172° east. These Micronesian islands – over 2,100 atolls and smaller islands – are mainly in the Caroline, Marshall, and Marianas groups and are scattered over three million square miles (eight million square kilometers) of ocean. Each district has its own elected local government.

Papua New Guinea

This nation consists of the eastern half of New Guinea Island, plus New Britain, New Ireland, Bougainville, and six hundred smaller islands. Terrain includes swamps, mountains, broad valleys, volcanoes, and rain forests. It is thought that New Guinea has been inhabited for thousands of years. Almost all inhabitants are Melanesians. More than seven hundred languages are spoken, but most people also speak Motu or a dialect of English. After being occupied by the Japanese in World War II, Papua and New Guinea were united as an Australian territory. The nation became independent in 1975; it has close ties with Australia.

Pitcairn

Lying approximately midway between New Zealand and Panama, Pitcairn is a Polynesian island whose population is declining. Its original inhabitants, who arrived in 1767, were nine mutineers from the *Bounty*, who brought with them eighteen Tahitians. In 1856, the entire population of 194 moved to Norfolk Island, but some returned soon afterward. Pitcairn is a British dependency.

Solomon Islands

Comprising one of the largest island groups in Melanesia in the southwest Pacific, the Solomons are mountainous, forested, and contain low-lying coral atolls. The climate is warm and damp, with heavy annual rainfall. The population is primarily rural, and much of its social structure is patterned on traditional village life. The economy is based on subsistence farming. The area was the site of fierce battles between the Japanese and Allied forces during World War II. In 1978, the islands became a sovereign nation.

Tokelau

Made up of three Polynesian atolls three hundred miles (480 kilometers) north of Western Samoa, Tokelau totals only four square miles (ten square kilometers) in area. An island territory of New Zealand, the country relies heavily on its mother country for economic aid.

Tonga

Due east of Fiji, Tonga consists of about 150 coral and volcanic islands. Most of the islands are coral reefs, but many have fertile soil. Almost all Tongans are Polynesian, and about two-thirds of them live on the main island of Tonga-tapu. The climate is subtropical. Tonga's economy is dominated by both subsistence and plantation agriculture. This Polynesian nation was a British protectorate until it became independent in 1970.

Tuvalu

Tuvalu consists of nine islands, most of them atolls surrounding lagoons. There is little cultivable soil, and fishing is a major activity. Tuvalu has minimal manufacturing and no mining. The climate is tropical, and most people are Polynesian. Tuvaluans weave mats and baskets for export, and they speak Tuvaluan, derived from Polynesian. The island group became independent from Great Britain in 1978.

Vanuatu

Formerly a joint territory of Britain and France known as the New Hebrides, Vanuatu became independent in 1980. The economy is based on agriculture, and copra is the primary export crop. Fishing is also important, as is the growing tourist industry. Most residents are of Melanesian descent, but there are minorities of Asians, Europeans, and Polynesians. Languages include English and French, the languages of former rulers; and Bislama, a mixture of English and Melanesian.

Wallis and Futuna

The Wallis Islands, Futuna, and Alofi are grouped 380 miles (600 kilometers) northwest of Fiji within Polynesia. Formerly a French protectorate, they are now an overseas territory of France and are mandated by their own internal government. Farming is important, as is fishing.

Western Samoa

Four inhabited Polynesian islands and a number of smaller ones northeast of Fiji and west of American Samoa make up Western Samoa. Bananas, coconuts, and tropical fruits are the most important crops grown and exported. Formerly administered by New Zealand, Western Samoa gained independence and self-government in 1962. Most Western Samoans are of Polynesian descent, and a significant minority is of mixed Samoan and European heritage.

Above: The scattered islands of Oceania contain several distinct indigenous groups. Micronesians generally have dark brown skin and straight black hair. Polynesians are tall, with light brown skin and black hair. Melanesians have dark brown skin and very curly hair, evidenced by these natives of Fiji.

Right: Most New Zealanders are native-born descendants of British immigrants, like this schoolboy. Maoris, of Polynesian descent, were the original settlers, but today they make up less than ten percent of the population.

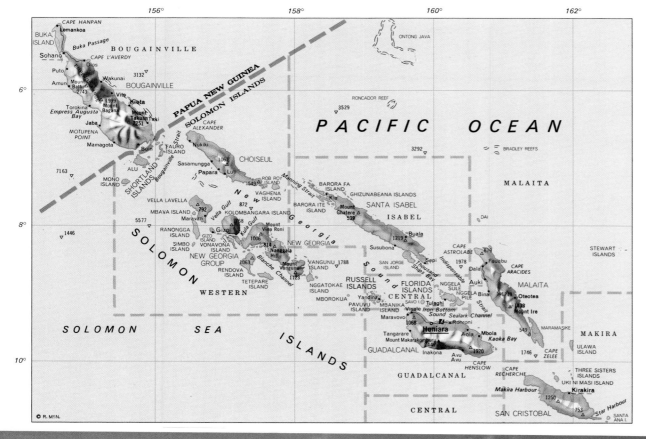

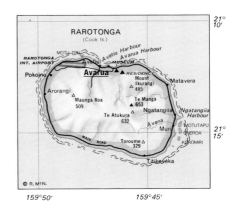

Below: Some of the islands of Oceania are coral atolls built on volcanic bases, and some are formed from the tips of volcanoes on the ocean floor. The volcanic Austral Seamounts are part of French Polynesia. Shown here is the opening from a collapsed volcano, or a caldera, on Rapa.

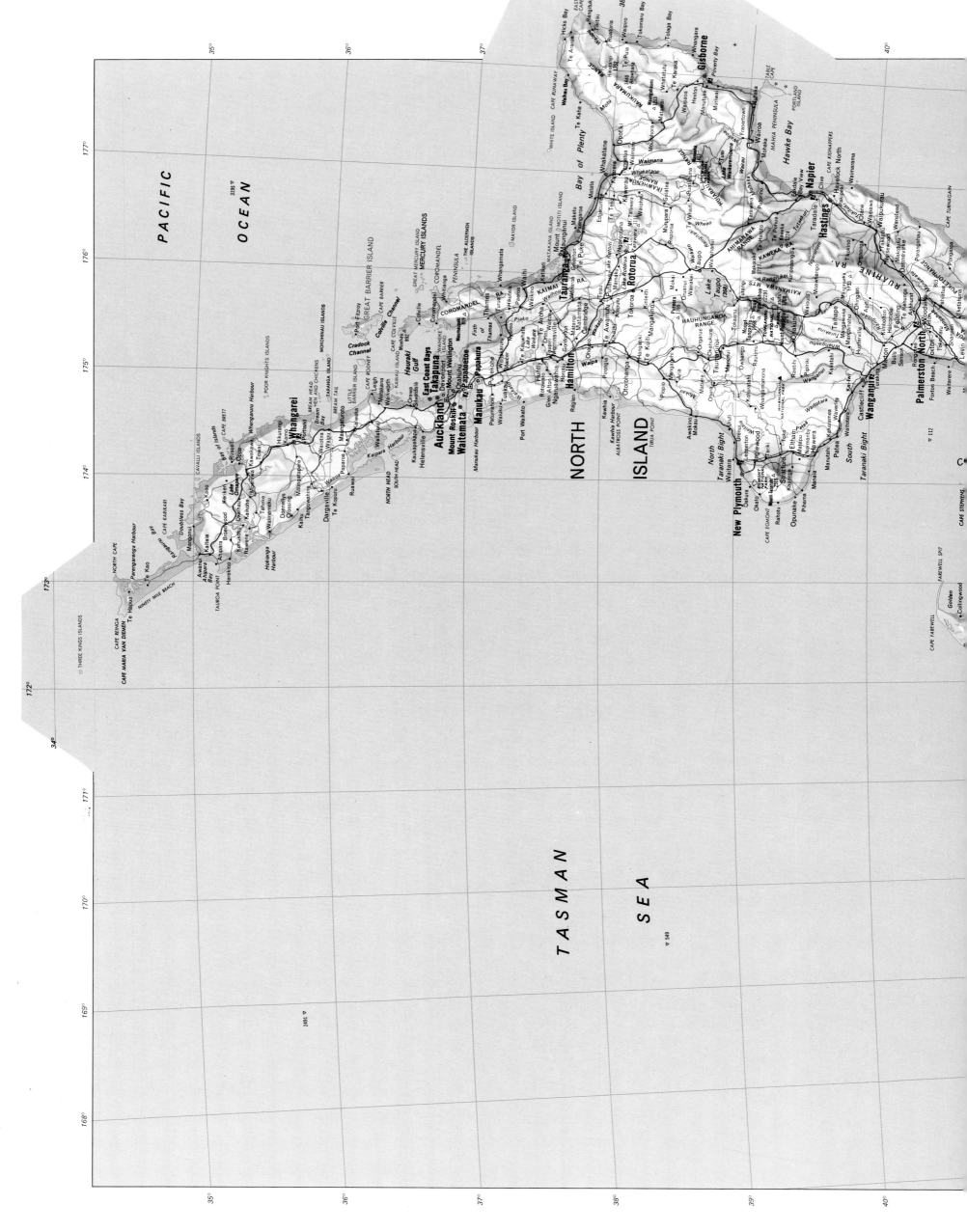

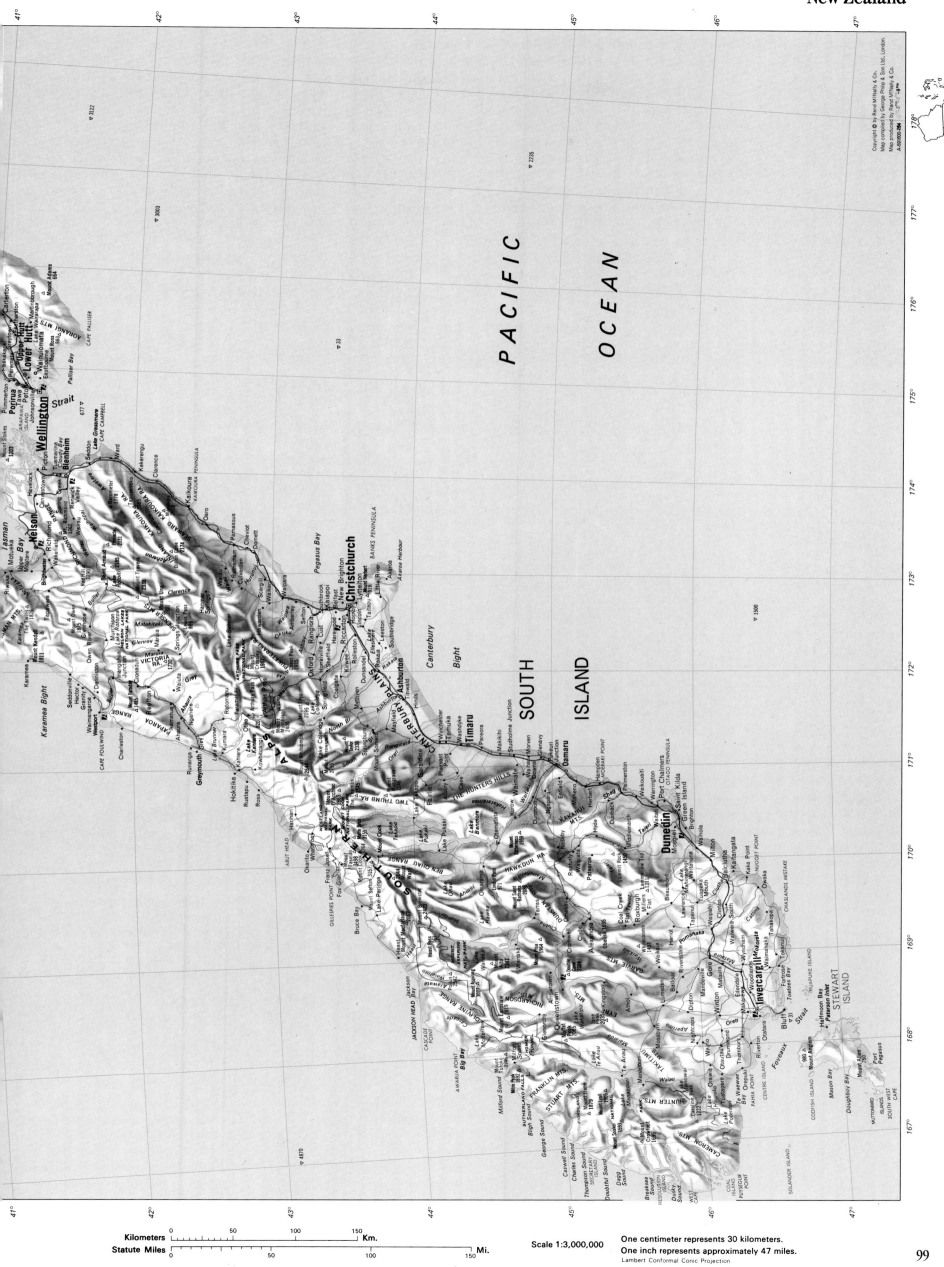

New Zealand

PACIFIC

OCEAN

SOUTH

ISLAND

Wellington
Nelson
Blenheim
Christchurch
Timaru
Oamaru
Dunedin
Invercargill

STEWART
ISLAND

Kilometers |0   50   100   150| Km.

Statute Miles |0   50   100   150| Mi.

Scale 1:3,000,000

One centimeter represents 30 kilometers.
One inch represents approximately 47 miles.

Lambert Conformal Conic Projection

99

Middle America
Profile

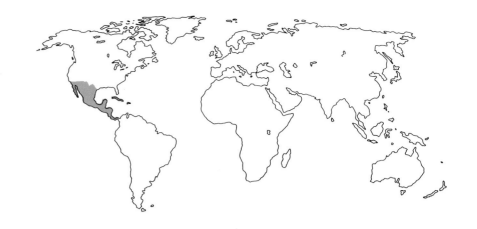

Location and Size

The term *Middle America* refers to Mexico, Central America, and the Caribbean and Atlantic island countries south of the continental United States. *Middle America* therefore includes much more territory than *Central America*. The northwest-to-southeast extent of the mainland is some 3,000 miles (4,800 kilometers). Yet this region is never more than 750 miles (1,200 kilometers) in west-east extent in Mexico and is often far narrower.

Middle America includes the islands of the Bahamas, the Greater and Lesser Antilles, and others lying in the seas between the mainland of the two Americas. These islands, which number about one thousand, are sometimes collectively called the West Indies, and they range in size from Cuba – at more than forty-two thousand square miles (more than 110 thousand square kilometers) – to Saba – at five square miles (thirteen square kilometers).

Landscape

Middle America may be divided into three main physical areas. In the north – in much of Mexico as far south as the Isthmus of Tehuantepec – the great mountain system of western North America continues. The Sierra Madre Occidental runs parallel to the Pacific coast and rises to a maximum of 13,994 feet (4,265 meters). The Sierra Madre Oriental runs parallel to the Gulf of Mexico and rises to greater heights in some of the volcanic peaks, such as Popocatépetl at 17,887 feet (5,452 meters). Between these two ranges, a complex plateau lies at heights of between four thousand feet (1,200 meters) and eight thousand feet (2,400 meters).

To the west of these lies the great depression occupied by the Gulf of California and the elongated Baja California peninsula, an extension of the coastal ranges of the United States.

The southern mainland section of Middle America is physically far more complex. In its northern province, between Tehuantepec and Nicaragua, a series of mainly west-to-east mountain ridges lies across the isthmus from a high volcanic plateau on the Pacific fringe. Each line of mountains is highest in the west. There are limited coastal lowlands in this area, except in the great Yucatan Peninsula, which is an extensive low limestone plain. The mountains of southern Nicaragua, Costa Rica, and Panama are separated from the others by the depression containing Lakes Nicaragua and Managua. These mountains present a formidable barrier to movement across the isthmus, running northwest to southeast, then west to east.

The third physical province is that of the islands, which can be subdivided. To the north lies the line of coral reefs that make up the Bahamas. Then the often-large islands of the Greater Antilles are an eastern continuation of the mountains of southern Mexico, Guatemala, and Honduras. Finally, the Lesser Antilles are mainly a volcanic arc. They are a northeastern extension of the South American Andes. There are also a number of coral islands in this vast area. Thus, the West Indian islands show a great variety of physical features: active volcanoes, extinct volcanoes, coral islands, and mountainous islands.

Climate

Virtually all of Middle America lies within the tropics. The close proximity to the seas and the range of altitudes account for the variety of climates.

Mexico, north of the Tropic of Cancer, experiences dry climates. In the northwest and north-central parts lies a subtropical desert area where the monthly average temperature never drops below 32°F (0°C), but where rainfall is below ten inches (250 millimeters). Central and northeastern Mexico has a subtropical steppe climate in which similar temperatures are accompanied by higher rainfalls, up to twenty-four inches (six

Left: Leaping from heights of 140 feet (40 meters), the cliff divers of Acapulco, Mexico, are but one of the attractions of this seaport on the Pacific Ocean. Acapulco's climate, atmosphere, deep-sea fishing, and beautiful beaches also contribute to its stature as a leading vacation destination.

Right: Belize, the most sparsely populated nation of Central America, lies on the Caribbean Sea next to Mexico and Guatemala. Its mostly low-lying terrain was once heavily forested; timber production, however, has depleted this resource. Here, a remaining wooded area lies below a conical karst hill, formed by erosion of water-soluble rock.

hundred millimeters).

Except in the high mountain areas, the remainder of the mainland experiences tropical rainy climates and is wetter on the east coast – except in the Yucatan Peninsula – than on the west. Here is the rain forest area where average monthly temperatures may be around 77°F (25°C) for much of the year, and rainfall exceeds 100 inches (2,500 millimeters). In the drier savanna areas of the west, rainfall is only around one-third of this amount.

Many of the islands experience a similar tropical savanna type of climate, though parts, such as the northern coastal strip of Hispaniola and Puerto Rico, have far higher rainfalls. Hurricanes are an occasional menace.

History, Politics, and Economy

The history of Middle America dates back to the early settlements of Indians who migrated from north to south through the Americas about 10,000 B.C. Developing rich civilizations, their descendants included the Maya of Central America and Mexico; the Aztecs and Toltecs of Mexico; and the Arawak, Lucayo, and Carib peoples of the Caribbean.

In 1492, Christopher Columbus discovered Middle America when he landed on a small island in the Caribbean Sea. Spanish settlement of the New World began in the Caribbean in the same year, when one of Columbus's ships was wrecked and several men were left on

Haiti. Like many early settlements, this one ended unsuccessfully for Europeans when all of the men perished.

In 1513, Vasco de Balboa crossed the Isthmus of Panama and discovered the Pacific Ocean. Soon after, Hernán Cortés launched an expedition to conquer the Aztec Empire, and he succeeded in the early 1520s. Mexico and much of Central America soon became a viceroyalty of Spain. In 1525, Spanish conquistadors established the city of San Salvador in El Salvador. But wars, enslavement, and disease were all factors that thinned the Indian population, and Central America became a relatively impoverished place.

European influence in Middle America from 1500 onward was essentially by two groups. The mainland was part of

an area allocated to Spain under the 1493 agreements between Spain, Portugal, and the Pope; the Caribbean islands were part of the area largely left to the Dutch, French, and British.

Independence movements developed early in the nineteenth century. Mexico was the first mainland country to experience revolution, gaining independence from Spain in 1821. In that same year, five Central American nations gained independence from Spain and later became part of the Federation of Central American States, which lasted for only fourteen years. In 1838, Nicaragua, El Salvador, Honduras, Costa Rica, and Guatemala became autonomous nations. Panama remained part of Colombia until 1903, and in 1981, Belize finally achieved

Opposite, top left: Carnival is a pre-Lenten celebration that includes parades and feasting, held in many Catholic countries. Its festivities appeal to both tourists and residents, as these revelers on St. Vincent demonstrate.

Opposite, top right: Mexico City (Ciudad de México) is the capital and fastest-growing city of the nation. It is among the top five most populous cities in the world. In 1985, the city suffered a major earthquake, which caused much damage and killed thousands.

Opposite, bottom left: The destruction of a 1976 earthquake is still evident in Antigua, Guatemala — a city situated in a valley surrounded by several volcanoes.

Opposite, bottom right: The sugar industry is the heart of the Cuban economy. It employs nearly 500 thousand workers, including these men, and sugar accounts for almost 90 percent of all export income. The industry has been nationalized since 1959.

Left: On the San Blas Islands off the northeastern coast of Panama live the Cuna, an Indian people. They moved to the islands from the mainland in the nineteenth century. Until the 1960s, they prohibited strangers from spending the night on their land.

103

independence from Great Britain.

Since independence, Mexico has experienced periods of difficulty. It lost considerable territory, including Texas, to the United States during the Mexican War. Subsequent years saw power change hands frequently as liberals demanding social and economic reforms battled conservatives. A brief span of French rule in the mid 1860s interrupted the struggle. Following a revolution that started in 1910, a new constitution was adopted in 1917, and progress toward reform began, culminating in the separation of church and state and the redistribution of land.

The road to prosperity and stability has been rocky for many Central American nations. Resentment about the growing United States influence and control in Central America started to rise in the early nineteenth century. It was fueled by the construction of the Panama Canal in 1914 and the growth of the United States-controlled banana industry.

Military dictators ruled the Central American region until the mid 1940s, when a revolution in Guatemala temporarily halted this trend. The rest of the region made steps toward democracy throughout the 1950s but returned toward a trend of military rule in the 1960s.

For many years, large landowners and political leaders monopolized the valuable land that produced the thriving export crops of Central America. As the economy grew, pressures mounted for democratic reform and economic equality. Tensions between government and its citizens increased and were exacerbated by numerous controlled elections. Many began to support radical, left-wing groups that championed violence as a means to social and political change. In 1979, the Sandinista guerrillas overthrew the Samoza dictatorship in Nicaragua. Then, violence in El Salvador and Guatemala broke out virtually ending tourism and foreign investments.

In 1983, Manual Antonio Noriega became head of the National Guard in Panama, overthrew the government, and installed a figurehead as president. In the meantime, the Panamanian people suffer from the effects of a depressed economy and the loss of democratic rule to a military junta. Corruption in government and a growing drug trade are threatening Panama's current steps toward prosperity and democracy. In Nicaragua, international efforts to end the Sandinista-contra war have been fruitless.

Most Caribbean nations remained under foreign rule until after World War II, and some of them are still administered by other countries. Major exceptions include Cuba, Haiti, and the Dominican Republic.

Cuba became independent from Spain in 1902. In 1952, Sergeant Fulgencio Batista seized power in a coup that established an unpopular and oppressive regime. A group opposed to Batista gained support, and in 1959, he fled the country, leaving its leadership to Fidel Castro and the Communist party.

By 1804, Haiti had achieved independence from France. In 1957, François Duvalier came to power and later declared himself president-for-life. His rule was marked by repression, corruption, and human-rights abuses. His son succeeded him but fled the country in 1986. A new constitution was approved in 1987, but instability continues.

In 1844, the Dominican Republic broke away from Haiti and became independent. The nation has experienced periods of instability and United States intervention, and various presidents have been installed.

Jamaica, at one time the most important sugar and slave center in the New World, became independent from the United Kingdom in 1962. Since then, the nation has faced problems of unemployment, inflation, poverty, and periodic social unrest.

Puerto Rico is affiliated with the United States as a commonwealth. For many years, the island has been allowed to determine its own status. In referenda and public opinion polls, residents have voted to maintain the status quo. There are, however, strong political movements for both statehood and independence.

As politics have changed, so have the economies of Middle America. Mining and subsistence farming have been the traditional activities of most Mexicans. The extraction of petroleum, natural gas, and other minerals has to a large extent replaced silver as a leading mining endeavor. World recessions and fluctuating oil prices have taken their toll on Mexico, and in the early 1980s, the nation was close to bankruptcy. Austerity plans and foreign aid are expected to revitalize the economy.

Cotton, sugar, meat, coffee, and bananas have been major exports in the agricultural economies of Central America. In Nicaragua, years of political instability, a large foreign debt, and a civil war have hindered prosperity. Honduras, Guatemala, and Belize remain underdeveloped. Political instability, a low literacy rate, high population density, and high unemployment have hindered El Salvador. Panama has benefited economically from the strategic Panama Canal, but the nation remains troubled.

Many West Indian economies are also steeped in agriculture, with tropical fruits, spices, sugar, coffee, and cacao major crops. There is considerable mining activity on some islands, and some industry as well. Income stemming from tourism is crucial to many Caribbean economies.

Below: The Bahamas are coral islands, and their thin soils are not well suited for agriculture. A few crops are grown, however, including the bananas being harvested here. Climate is the islands' most important resource, and tourism is the economic mainstay.

Above: Coral reefs and submarine volcanoes have formed the islands of the Caribbean. Many of the coral islands tend to be flat and low-lying; those of primarily volcanic origin tend to be rugged. Shown here is volcanic Saba, in the Leeward Islands.

Anguilla

Anguilla was associated with St. Christopher and Nevis until 1976. The smallest of the Leeward Islands – thirty-five square miles (ninety-one square kilometers) – it is a dependent territory of the United Kingdom. While it enjoys internal self-government, the United Kingdom is responsible for defense and foreign affairs. It is a low coral island with poor soils. Sea salt and fruits are the main products.

Antigua and Barbuda

Tourism is the principal economic contributor of this Caribbean nation composed of the islands of Antigua, Barbuda, and uninhabited Redondo. It gained independence from the United Kingdom in 1981. The climate is tropical. Most Antiguans are descendants of black African slaves brought by the British to work sugar-cane plantations. Formed by volcanoes, the low-lying islands are flat and ringed with white-sand beaches.

Aruba

This self-governing possession of the Netherlands is a beautiful Caribbean island that is home to white sands and a booming tourist industry.

Bahamas

The Bahamas comprise some seven hundred coral islands and cays north of Cuba and east of Florida. Only about twenty-nine of the islands are inhabited, and most of the people live on Grand Bahama and New Providence. Blacks are the majority, mainly descendants of

slaves routed through the area or brought by British Loyalists fleeing the American colonies during the revolutionary war. With its semitropical climate, tourism is predominant in the Bahamas. Because it is a tax haven, the country is also an international finance center. The Bahamas achieved independence from Great Britain in 1973.

Barbados

The Caribbean island of Barbados became independent from the British in 1966. Barbados's pleasant tropical climate and its land have determined its economic mainstays: tourism and sugar. Sunshine and year-round warmth attract thousands of visitors and provide an excellent environment for sugar cane cultivation. The coral island's terrain is mostly flat. It is one of the world's most densely populated countries, and most citizens are black descendants of African slaves.

Belize

Central American Belize has a mixed populace, including descendants of black Africans, Spanish-Indians, and Indians. Population is centered in six urban areas along the coast. Sugar is the major crop and export. Formerly known as British Honduras, its name changed to Belize in 1973. In 1981, it gained independence from Great Britain. The hot, humid climate is offset by sea breezes.

Bermuda

Bermuda is made up of North Atlantic islands, 650 miles (1,046 kilometers)

Below and bottom: To many, the Caribbean means sandy beaches, such as this one on St. Thomas. Snorkeling and windsurfing are popular. Cruises have gained momentum as a way to enjoy leisure travel.

Middle America

Countries continued

east of North Carolina. This dependent territory of the United Kingdom features beautiful beaches and scenic, hilly countryside, which invite a thriving tourist industry. The population is mainly black descendants of African slaves but also includes Portuguese, British, Canadian, Caribbean peoples, and some United States military staff. The archipelago consists of many small islands and islets. About twenty are inhabited, several of which are connected by bridges and collectively known as the island of Bermuda.

Cayman Islands
Grand Cayman is the most important of the three coral islands that compose this British dependency some 200 miles (320 kilometers) northwest of Jamaica. Tourism is important to the islands, as is international banking.

Costa Rica
Costa Rica has one of the most prosperous economies of all Central American countries. Agriculture remains important, producing coffee and bananas. Much of the area is forested, and the mountainous central region is bordered by coastal plains on the east and west. The climate is semitropical to tropical. In the 1980s the country has worked to promote peaceful solutions to armed conflicts in the region.

Cuba
The Republic of Cuba is ruled by its Communist party. It is economically

dependent on sugar, but the island also possesses mineral deposits, including oil and nickel. Mountains, plains, and scenic coastlines make Cuba one of the most beautiful islands in the West Indies; it is also the largest island in the Caribbean. The climate is tropical. Most Cubans are descendants of Spanish colonists, African slaves, or a blend of the two.

Dominica
This Caribbean island is volcanic in origin, though the soil is suitable for farming. Mountains and dense forests, however, limit cultivatable land. Hurricanes also hinder production. Its tropical climate and scenic landscape create a basis for tourism. Dominica gained independence from Great Britain in 1978. A small indigenous Carib Indian population is concentrated in the northeastern part of the island and maintains its own customs and life-style.

Dominican Republic
The Dominican Republic forms the eastern two-thirds of the Caribbean island of Hispaniola. The mixed population includes minorities of Haitians, other blacks, Spaniards, and European Jews. Agriculture remains important, with sugar the main crop. The mountainous terrain, however, limits arable area. Aided by a warm, tropical climate, tourism is growing.

El Salvador
Right-wing death squads, poverty, political unrest, and human-rights abuses

plague this war-torn country in Central America. With high population density and high unemployment, economic conditions remain very bad in El Salvador. The United States has played a major role in furnishing military and economic aid to the government. The climate is tropical.

Grenada
Rich volcanic soils and heavy rainfall have made agriculture the chief economic activity. Also known as the Isle of Spice, Grenada is one of the world's leading producers of nutmeg and mace. Many tropical fruits are also raised, and the small plots of peasant farmers dot the hilly terrain. Tourism is another economic contributor, with visitors who are drawn by the beaches and tropical climate of this Caribbean island. After the United States led an invasion that deposed a Marxist regime, a new government was installed in 1984.

Guadeloupe
One of the four overseas departments of France, Guadeloupe is a group of two main and five smaller islands. The main western island is dominated by an active volcano; the eastern island is much flatter. They are all situated between the British Leeward Islands and Dominica in the Caribbean. Bananas, sugar, rum, and pineapples are the principal products and export items.

Guatemala
This mountainous Central American

country sits below Mexico between the Pacific Ocean and the Caribbean Sea. Largely undeveloped, Guatemala consists of northern rain forests and grasslands. A 1976 earthquake resulted in heavy loss of life and property. Since a 1983 coup, military rule has been established, although some reforms are being made.

Haiti
Occupying the western third of Hispaniola in the central Caribbean, Haiti has an overall mountainous terrain and a tropical climate. Haiti's economy remains underdeveloped and its politics unstable. Most people are poor and rely on subsistence farming, though productivity is hampered by high population density in productive regions. Coffee is a main commercial crop and export. Voodooism, which blends Christian and African beliefs, is still practiced.

Honduras
Central American Honduras has an underdeveloped economy based on banana cultivation. Mostly mountainous with lowlands along some coastal regions, Honduras has a temperate to tropical climate. Since the 1950s, civilian

Below: As is the case with many other Caribbean islands, most of the residents of Antigua are the descendants of black African slaves brought here by Europeans to work sugarcane plantations. Today, the island depends upon tourism.

governments have alternated with military coups and rule. Controversies focus on issues of poverty, land distribution, and a border dispute with El Salvador. The country has been an important base for United States activities in Central America, evidenced by ongoing United States military maneuvers in the area.

Jamaica

Despite periodic unrest, this Caribbean island is a popular tourist spot. Its mountainous inland region is surrounded by coastal plains and beaches, and its tropical climate is tempered by ocean breezes. Most Jamaicans are of African or Afro-European descent. Sugar cane and bananas are principal crops, and more than a third of the population is engaged in farming. A 1988 hurricane damaged much of the island.

Martinique

Situated near Dominica, the Caribbean island of Martinique is an overseas territory of France. The north is dominated by a volcano that is responsible for one of the worst natural disasters of modern times; on May 8, 1902, its eruption killed forty thousand people. Bananas, sugar, and rum are its main exports.

Mexico

By far the largest Middle American country, Mexico is also among the most northerly. Mexico's terrain and climate are greatly varied, ranging from tropical jungles along the coast to desert plains in the north. Most Mexicans are mestizos, descended from Indians and the Spaniards who conquered Mexico. The nation is a leading producer of petroleum and silver; a growing manufacturer of iron, steel, and chemicals; and an exporter of coffee and cotton. Drawn by archaeological sites and warm, sunny weather, foreign visitors often tour Mexico. Mexico has been troubled by inflation, declining oil prices, and rising unemployment.

Montserrat

This scenically attractive island is a British colony situated southwest of Antigua and northwest of Guadeloupe. The economy is heavily dependent on British aid.

Netherlands Antilles

The Netherlands Antilles are composed of two groups: the three islands of Aruba, Curaçao, and Bonaire; and St. Martin, St. Eustatius, and Saba. The islands are self-governing territories of the Netherlands, and the two groups are separated by many miles of sea. Over 92 percent of the population lives on Aruba and Curaçao. Tourism is important.

Nicaragua

Nicaragua is Middle America's second largest country and is situated between Honduras and Costa Rica. The terrain includes a low-lying Pacific region, central highlands, and a flat Caribbean area. The climate is tropical. Nicaragua is chiefly an agricultural nation, and it relies on the production of textiles, coffee, and sugar. Political unrest and poverty plague the country.

Panama

Linking North America and South America, Panama has been a strategic center for trade and transportation. The 1914 opening of the Panama Canal, connecting the Atlantic and Pacific oceans, has provided additional revenue and jobs; the canal area is now Panama's most economically developed region. Panama has a mountainous interior and a tropical climate. A military government rules in Panama. In 1988, civilian-military clashes arose.

Puerto Rico

This Caribbean island is marked by mountains, lowlands, and valleys. A rising population has caused poverty, housing shortages, and unemployment. Puerto Rico is a commonwealth of the United States, and many Puerto Ricans live in the United States, mostly in New York and other large cities. Most of the population is descended from Spaniards and black African slaves. Once dependent on such plantation crops as sugar and coffee, Puerto Rico is now reliant upon manufacturing.

St. Christopher and Nevis

The Caribbean islands of St. Christopher, often called St. Kitts, and Nevis became independent from British control in 1983. The rural, black population is concentrated along the coasts. Agriculture is a mainstay, with sugar cane the main crop, and tourism is enhanced by the tropical climate, beaches, and scenic mountainous terrain.

St. Lucia

This Caribbean island gained independence from Great Britain in 1979 and has remained politically stable since. Banana and cocoa growing are important activities. Tourism is becoming increasingly important, with visitors drawn by the tropical climate, scenic mountainous

terrain, and beaches. During the colonial period, the island frequently shifted from British to French control, and its culture reflects both British and French elements.

St. Vincent and the Grenadines

These Caribbean islands were once possessions of Great Britain but have been independent since 1979. St. Vincent is the largest island, and about one hundred smaller islands make up the Grenadines. The population is mainly descended from black African slaves. The terrain is mountainous, with coastlines marked by sandy beaches. The climate is tropical.

Trinidad and Tobago

Situated very near the coast of Venezuela, the two Caribbean islands of Trinidad and Tobago form a single nation. Trinidad has nearly all the land mass and population. About 80 percent of all Trinidadians are either black African or East Indian, and about 20 percent are European, Chinese, and of mixed descent. Although tourism and agriculture are important, the economy is based on oil. The nation became independent from British control in 1962.

Turks and Caicos Islands

These two groups of islands are a British dependent territory lying southeast of the Bahamas. Only six are inhabited. Until 1976, they were associated with

Above: The remains of Spanish colonists' fortifications against English, French, and Dutch attack can still be seen on Puerto Rico. Shown here is El Morro in San Juan.

the Cayman Islands. Fishing is the most important activity, but tourism has been increasing.

Virgin Islands, British

This dependent territory of Great Britain lies in the Caribbean Sea and is made up of many islands, islets, rocks, and cays. Most are of volcanic origin. The two major islands, Tortola and Virgin Gorda, along with Anegada and Jost Van Dyke, contain most of the population. Standards for education and health are among the highest in the Caribbean. Tourism is the economic mainstay, but a variety of tropical crops are grown.

Virgin Islands, United States

Constitutionally an unincorporated territory of the United States, this group of Caribbean islands is made up of St. Thomas, St. Croix, St. John, and about fifty other smaller islands. Tourism is now the base of the economy, although agriculture is also important. Additionally, St. Croix has mineral-processing plants, and St. Thomas is an important commercial center. Standards for health and education are quite high, and the climate is very pleasant.

ATLANTIC OCEAN

WEST INDIES

GREATER ANTILLES

CARIBBEAN SEA

LESSER ANTILLES

VENEZUELA

COLOMBIA

BRAZIL

Kilometers | 0 200 400 600 Km.

Statute Miles | 0 200 400 600 Mi.

Scale 1:12,000,000

One centimeter represents 120 kilometers.

One inch represents approximately 190 miles.

Oblique Conic Conformal Projection

109

South America
Profile

Location and Size

The dividing line between Middle and South America lies at the Colombian-Panamanian border, the narrowest land bridge dividing the Pacific Ocean from the Caribbean Sea. The north-south extent of the continent is 4,600 miles (7,450 kilometers). The west-to-east extent varies greatly, but in the central equatorial regions – from northern Peru to eastern Brazil – it extends some 3,200 miles (5,150 kilometers).

South America is essentially triangular in shape. The north and east coasts are comparatively straight, but the west coast has a straight southern part and then a convex northern part.

Although the coastline of South America is largely uncomplicated, the continent includes a number of offshore islands. The Falkland (Malvinas) Islands are to the southeast, off the shore of southern Argentina. The Galapagos Islands (Archipiélago de Colón) – home of a variety of unusual wildlife – are to the west, off Ecuador. The Chonos Archipelago is to the southwest, off the rugged coast of Chile. And finally, the remote Tierra del Fuego lies at the southernmost tip of Argentina.

Landscape

South America can be divided into eight distinct physical regions, four of which are essentially lowlands and the rest uplands. Within each of these two groups is a dominant member: the Amazon (Amazonas) Basin is by far the most extensive lowland area and the Andes Mountains the most extensive upland area. Three of the lowland regions are river basins, and one is coastal plain. The upland areas are, for the most part, rugged and mountainous.

The Amazon Basin is an extremely low-lying area dominated by dense tropical rain forest. It covers a part of central and eastern South America that is almost as big as the entire United States. The main rivers discharge more water than any other single system in the world. The Amazon itself is some 3,900 miles (6,275 kilometers) long.

The continent's second largest river system is dominated by the Paraná, Paraguay (Paraguai), and Uruguay (Uruguai) rivers. These reach the sea via the Río de la Plata, which is really an inlet of the Atlantic Ocean that extends some 205 miles (330 kilometers) inland at the border of Uruguay and Argentina.

The third, but far smaller, river basin is that of the Orinoco in the north. This river drains a smaller area than the Amazon, from which it is divided by an extremely low watershed. The rivers in this region drain the eastern and northern flanks of the Andes as well as the Guiana Highlands. Most of this region is known as the llanos and is dominated by vast swamplands.

The last area of lowland, along the Pacific coastal fringes, is the most fragmented. The coastal plains are widest in the extreme north and parts of Chile, where they may reach fifty miles (eighty kilometers) at their maximum. The humid regions of these lowlands are crossed by a number of short rivers that plunge steeply westward from the Andes.

The magnificent Andes run parallel to the Pacific coast. They are second only to the Himalayas in their towering heights, and they form the longest chain of peaks in the world. In the south, there is one main ridge; in the north, however, there are several ridges, with large valleys and the flat altiplano of Bolivia and Peru between them. At its widest, the whole range stretches for about 310 miles (500 kilometers) from west to east. The Andes chain contains a number of active and extinct volcanoes and is still an active region of earthquakes – it is part of the Ring of Fire, a narrow zone of frequent geologic activity that encircles the Pacific Ocean. Mount Aconcagua in Argentina rises to 22,831 feet (6,959 meters), the highest point in the Western Hemisphere.

South and east of the Amazon lies the second largest upland area, the triangularly shaped Brazilian Highlands. These rise quite steeply from the Atlantic coast and then slope gently into the interior. These highlands are far older than the Andes; thus they are lower.

The smaller Guiana Highlands to the north, between the Orinoco and Amazon basins, rise steeply from the former and then slope gently toward the north.

The plateau that is Patagonia lies in southern Argentina. It is a lower, irregular, windswept tableland that rises to a variety of heights.

Climate

Extending from the world's largest equatorial basin to the most southerly point in the Southern Hemisphere outside Antarctica, South America exhibits a wide range of climates. East of the Andes

Right: The Sierra of Peru is a high-altitude region of gentle slopes surrounded by the towering peaks of the Andes. Land suitable for farming is found between the mountains, and this is where about half of the population lives. Shown here is a farming community near the Urubamba, a river that is used extensively for irrigation.

Opposite: Brazil's natural resources make it a leading producer of hydroelectric power, with potential for further development. Forming part of the border between Brazil and Argentina, the spectacular Iguassu (Iguaçu) Falls would provide great power if harnessed.

and north of 20°S is a large area that experiences equatorial and tropical climates. These make for dense rain forests near the equator and the savanna of Venezuela, Guyana, Suriname, French Guiana, and the Brazilian interior. This region of rain forest is the largest in the world, but it is threatened by encroaching civilization, especially in Brazil. Average monthly temperatures never fall below 64°F (18°C). Rainfall at its maximum exceeds 100 inches (2,500 millimeters). Similar humid tropical climates are also found on some of the Brazilian coastal fringes and some of the Colombian coast.

Hot or warm climates are found along some of the Pacific coastal lowlands south of the equator and in a small area of about the same latitude on the other side of the Andes. Here, rainfall is mainly below five inches (125 millimeters) per year, and average monthly temperatures reach the low 80°sF (high 20°sC) in the north and the mid 70°sF (mid 20°sC) in the south. Patagonia is an area of midlatitude desert, where rainfall rarely reaches ten inches (250 millimeters) and average temperatures range between 66°F (19°C) and 32°F (0°C). Steppe climates are found in a north-south belt east of the Andes near the Tropic of Capricorn, in northeastern Brazil, and in a small coastal area of Venezuela.

Warm and cool temperature climates dominate the Pacific coastlines south of the Tropic of Capricorn and the southern parts of Brazil and Uruguay. Along the Pacific, the north of this region experiences a Mediterranean climate while farther south it becomes cooler and much wetter. The climate in the larger Atlantic-facing area has higher temperatures, with greater temperature ranges and rainfall totals of between 22 inches (550 millimeters) and 40 inches (1,000 millimeters).

History, Politics, and Economy

Nomadic hunter-gatherers roamed the Americas at least ten thousand years ago. They probably came to South America from the north, and their ancient tools have been found in Venezuela, Ecuador, and Argentina. It is estimated that humans first reached the southern tip of South America about 7000 B.C.

Before the arrival of Europeans, various Indian peoples inhabited South America. Among these were the Incas, whose sophisticated civilization flourished in the areas of present-day Ecuador, Peru, and Bolivia.

The discovery of an American continent by a European was accomplished in 1498, when Christopher Columbus landed at the Peninsula of Paria, Venezuela. Ferdinand Magellan was the first to realize the immensity of South America when he sailed down its coast and rounded its southern tip in 1520. Francisco Pizarro conquered the mighty Inca Empire in the early 1530s.

The first major wave of Europeans came in the wake of the conquistadors, with Spanish and Portuguese settlements. The resistance offered by most Indian groups was ineffectual, and for the most part, Indian lands fell quickly to the invaders. Lima, Peru, was founded in 1535; Santiago, Chile, in 1541; and Rio de Janeiro, Brazil, in 1565.

Many of the early settlers were drawn to South America by the promise of wealth. As word of the continent's natural riches spread back to Europe, fortune-seeking colonists flocked to the region. Oftentimes the promise of gold and silver remained unfulfilled, but most settlers stayed on, establishing large plantations that laid the basis for much of South America's present economy. The colonists took the conquered Indians as slaves to work their farmlands, and soon a thriving agriculture was established.

Top : The second largest city in Brazil and one of the most populous in the world, Rio de Janeiro is a popular tourist destination.

Right: These Indians are descendants of the Incas, rulers of the largest native empire in the Americas. The Inca realm included twelve million people in Peru, Ecuador, Chile, Bolivia, and Argentina.

Far right: La Paz is Bolivia's most populous city and its commercial center. Situated at the edge of the altiplano, its elevation is 12,001 feet (3,658 meters) above sea level.

Below: Rugged Mount Fitzroy towers above the surrounding Andean peaks in Patagonia, at the border of Chile and Argentina. Fitzroy is known for its shark-fin-like spires and the remarkable climbs they have inspired.

Much of the indigenous population disappeared during the colonial period. Wars with the settlers, labor-intensive plantations, and exposure to European diseases claimed thousands of Indian lives. In addition, many Indians who managed to survive intermarried with the Europeans. Modern South America's large mestizo population, of mixed Spanish and Indian blood, is a result of these liaisons.

As the Indians died out, blacks were brought from Africa to continue slave labor on the plantations. Development increased, and the descendants of the early settlers soon established a uniquely South American culture, combining influences of both their Spanish ancestors and the indigenous peoples into a life-style evolved from the plantation economy. Many of the Indians continued their traditional ways of life, however, and remained far from the centers of development, unaffected by the waves of change.

Prosperity continued, and in time the large-estate holders, many of them mestizos, found themselves wielding economic influence by enjoying few of the benefits of their profits. Native-born South Americans of Spanish descent were equally dissatisfied with colonial status. Political power remained in the hands of the mother country, whose people and government now had little in common with South American life. Resentment toward the ruling powers grew, along with the colonies' demands for a voice in a government that did not always consider their welfare.

The struggle for independence began in the late eighteenth century. Two prominent men emerged as leaders of the fight for freedom in the Spanish colonies: the Venezuelan Simón Bolívar and the Argentine José de San Martín. Bolívar helped liberate Venezuela (1821), Colombia (1813), Ecuador (1822), and Peru (1821); San Martín had a hand in Peru's independence and helped Chile to freedom in 1818. Brazil, Portugal's South American stronghold, became an independent country in 1822.

Politically, South America remained unstable after independence. For instance, following a military coup in 1889, Brazil became a republic. Economic problems resulted in a 1930 military coup and a dictatorship lasting until 1945, plus military takeovers in 1954 and 1964.

The nineteenth century saw political instability and revolutionary fervor in Venezuela, followed by a succession of dictatorships in the twentieth century. In

Top: Some of the Indians of the Brazilian Amazon Basin still exist by the slash-and-burn method of agriculture, in which patches of jungle are cut down, farmed and lived upon for a few years, and then allowed to return to forest. Groups of these people, who make up a fraction of the population, have been uprooted as the rain forest has been cleared.

Right: The altiplano of Peru and Bolivia is a flat area between two ranges of the Andes. The plateau is rich in minerals, but, because of poor soil and low precipitation, supports little vegetation. Some agriculture takes place, however, evidenced by these chilies drying in the sun.

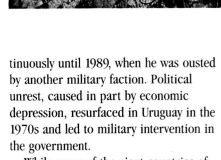

Colombia, Conservative-Liberal conflict led to civil war (1899-1902) and to La Violencia, a civil disorder that continued from the 1940s to the 1960s and resulted in about 200,000 deaths. From 1925 to 1948, no Ecuadoran leader was able to complete a full term in office.

Economically, however, the newly independent nations continued to develop, concentrating the wealth more solidly in the hands of the few. In many cases, this unevenly distributed prosperity led to more unrest. For example, by the 1920s, dissent arising from unequal power and land distribution in Chile united the middle and working classes, and eventually led to military intervention and a new constitution. Resultant social-welfare, education, and economic programs, however, were unable to eliminate inequalities rooted in the past.

Continued unrest has led to military control for several South American nations. In Paraguay, after years of turmoil, General Alfredo Stroessner came to power in 1954 and ruled con-

tinuously until 1989, when he was ousted by another military faction. Political unrest, caused in part by economic depression, resurfaced in Uruguay in the 1970s and led to military intervention in the government.

While some of the giant countries of South America struggled independently, the small nations of northeastern South America long remained under foreign rule. Guyana, for example, became British Guiana in 1831 and remained under British control until 1966. Suriname changed hands among the British, Dutch, and French until 1815, when the Netherlands gained control; independence did not come until 1975. And French Guiana, famous for its penal colonies, remains an overseas department of France, which has controlled the region since the 1600s.

Today, agriculture continues its important role in South America's economy, with large commercial plantations producing crops for export and domestic consumption. Mining is a major

contributor in some countries, and manufacturing is growing. Yet many South Americans are isolated from twentieth-century development, living much as their ancestors did and practicing subsistence agriculture according to ancient methods.

The destruction of South America's rain forest, one of the continent's most urgent issues, has economic considerations. In Amazonia, land is being cleared and burned for farms, cattle ranches, dams, and roads. In Brazil alone, fifty-one million acres were burned in 1987, leaving bare areas that, added together, just about equal the size of Kansas. This destruction not only threatens the millions of species that live in the jungle, but it also may contribute to global warming. Conservation efforts require cash, however, and recession-stricken Brazil's international debt is already among the world's highest. Unless Brazil experiences some economic relief, environmentalists fear the rain forest will continue to burn.

Countries

Argentina

The second largest nation in South America, Argentina stretches from the Tropic of Capricorn to the southern tip of the continent. The nation has a varied terrain, with northern lowlands, the east-central pampas, the Andes in the west, and the southern Patagonian steppe. The climate likewise varies. An indigenous Indian population, Spanish settlement, and a turn-of-the-century influx of immigrants have made Argentina an ethnically diverse nation. Today, most Argentines are descendants of Spanish and Italian immigrants. Political difficulties beginning in the 1930s have resulted in economic problems and have kept this one-time economic giant from realizing its potential. High inflation rates have exacerbated the situation in the 1980s. Elections in 1983 resulted in a new government that is trying to resolve continued economic problems, deal with human-rights transgressions, and institute other reforms.

Bolivia

This is a landlocked nation in central South America. The terrain includes the western altiplano, or high plain; the eastern llano, or low plain; and the central yungas, formed from hills and valleys. The climate varies with altitude. Indians compose the majority of Bolivia's population. Minorities include mestizos of Spanish-Indian descent and Europeans. Bolivia is underdeveloped and among South America's poorest nations. Farming is the main activity, although mining makes the largest contribution to the gross national product. Instability and social unrest have continued since a 1964 coup, but the nation is now controlled by its elected congress. Cocaine trafficking is a current problem.

Brazil

The largest South American nation, Brazil is also the most populous. It takes up a huge region in east-central South America and faces the Atlantic Ocean. Forests cover about half the country; the other regions range from plains to mountains. The climate is semitropical to tropical. The mixed population was shaped by indigenous Indians, Portuguese colonists, black African slaves, and European and Japanese immigrants. Brazil is the only Portuguese-speaking nation in the Americas. The economy is a diversified mix of agriculture, mining, and industry. In 1985, an election ended twenty-one years of military rule. Severe economic recession grips the nation, and its foreign debt is among the largest in the world.

Chile

Chile is a long, narrow nation on South America's southwestern Pacific coast. Chile's land barriers – the eastern Andes, western coastal range, and northern desert – have resulted in a mostly urban population concentrated in a central valley. The climate varies but is generally mild. Chile's land provides the natural resources necessary for a successful economy, but longtime instability has taken its toll. A repressive military junta seized power from an elected Socialist government in 1973 and has remained in control ever since.

Colombia

This nation sits at the extreme northwestern corner of South America and links the continent to Central America. The terrain is characterized by a flat coastal region, central highlands, and wide eastern llanos, or plains. The climate is tropical except in the highlands. Colombia's mixed population traces its roots to indigenous Indians, Spanish colonists, and black African slaves. Industry now keeps pace with traditional agriculture in economic contributions, and mining is also important. Coffee is a traditional crop, and emeralds are an important mineral. Although Colombia has the strongest tradition of democracy in South America, political unrest exists. As cocaine has become the nation's most profitable agricultural product, the government has had problems with corruption of its officials and with controlling drug traffic in and out of the country.

Ecuador

The equator runs through this smallish nation in northwestern South America. The nation is largely mountainous, and climate varies with altitude. Ecuador's ethnicity was established by an indigenous Indian population and Spanish colonists. Despite an oil boom in the 1970s, Ecuador remains underdeveloped. The nation is a member of the Organization of Petroleum Exporting Countries (OPEC), but agriculture remains important for much of the population. Following military rule, a new constitution was established in 1978. Declining oil exports have caused economic recession in the 1980s, a situation that was worsened by a 1987 earthquake that left twenty thousand homeless and destroyed part of a key pipeline.

Right: Machu Picchu, an ancient Inca town, is situated 7,875 feet (2,400 meters) above sea level in the Andes, about fifty miles (eighty kilometers) northwest of Cuzco, Peru. The story behind the once-fortified city is not clear, but certain structures and artifacts suggest religious significance. Machu Picchu was never found by Spanish conquistadors and remained unknown until its discovery in 1911.

Falkland Islands

These South Atlantic islands east of Argentina are a dependent territory of the United Kingdom. The population is mainly of British descent. Sheep raising is the main activity, supplemented by fishing. Although the islands have been under British rule since the 1800s, continued Argentine claims resulted in a 1982 Argentine invasion and occupation. The British won the subsequent battle and continue to govern the Falklands.

French Guiana

Sitting on the Atlantic Ocean in northeastern South America, French Guiana is an overseas department of France. Fertile coastal plains in the north give way to hills and mountains along the Brazilian border. Rain forests cover much of the landscape. The majority population is of African and mixed African-European descent. Shrimp production and a growing timber industry are French Guiana's economic mainstays. The land remains largely undeveloped, however, and reliance on French aid continues. The region has been administered by France since the 1600s.

Guyana

Just north of the equator in northeastern South America lies Guyana. Inland forests give way to savanna and a coastal plain. The climate is tropical. The population includes descendants of black African slaves and East Indian, Chinese, and Portuguese laborers brought to work sugar plantations. Agriculture and mining compose the backbone of the Guyanese economy. Guyana became a republic in 1970 and has pursued Socialist policies. The mostly nationalized economy remains severely depressed.

Paraguay

The Tropic of Capricorn passes through Paraguay, a landlocked nation in south-central South America. There are semi-arid plains in the west; the east is fertile and more temperate. Paraguay's population displays a homogeneity unusual in South America: most people are a mix of Spanish and Guarani Indian ancestry. Agriculture forms the keystone of the economy. The lack of direct access to the sea, unskilled labor, and a history of war and instability have resulted in an underdeveloped economy; manufacturing in particular has suffered. A repressive military regime was in power from 1954 to 1989, when it was overthrown in a military coup. It is doubtful that reforms will be made.

Peru

Peru lies just south of the equator on South America's Pacific coast. Climate varies from arid and mild in the coastal desert to temperate but cool in the Andean highlands and hot and humid in the eastern jungles and plains. The Indian population constitutes the nation's largest ethnic group and the largest Indian concentration in North or South America. Considerable natural resources have made Peru a leader in the production of minerals and in fishing. Productivity has been slowed, however, by a mountainous terrain that impedes transport and communication, earthquakes and other natural disasters, a largely unskilled work force, and years of stringent military rule. Peru had been under military rule before 1980, when it returned to democratic leadership. Police and labor strikes, a border dispute with Ecuador, and terrorist activities by Maoist groups have recently plagued the nation.

Suriname

A small nation in northeastern South America, Suriname borders on the Atlantic Ocean. The terrain is marked by a narrow coastal swamp, central forests and savanna, and southern jungle-covered hills. The climate is tropical. Suriname contains a portion of the vast Amazonian rain forest that is currently being cleared despite international protests and environmental ramifications. Suriname's diverse ethnicity was shaped by the importation of black African slaves and contract laborers from the East. The economy is based on mining and metal processing, but agriculture plays an important role as well. In 1980, the military seized power, and a joint military-civilian government was subsequently established. Instability has continued, with coup attempts.

Uruguay

Uruguay is situated on the Atlantic Ocean in southeastern South America. Most Uruguayans are white descendants of nineteenth- and twentieth-century immigrants from Spain, Italy, and other European countries. Uruguay's soil, plains, and climate provide the basis for agriculture and are especially conducive to livestock raising. Previously under military control, civilian government was restored in 1985. Uruguay's standard of living was once one of the highest in South America. In the 1980s, however, economic deterioration, including inflation, has forced Uruguay to incur a significant international debt.

Venezuela

Venezuela sits at the top of South America on the Caribbean Sea. The varied Venezuelan landscape is dominated by the Andes, a coastal zone, high plateaus, and plains. Temperatures vary with altitude. Spanish colonial rule of the nation is reflected in its predominantly mestizo population. Since the expansion of the petroleum industry in the 1920s, Venezuela has experienced rapid economic growth, but the economy has been hampered by unevenly distributed wealth, a high birthrate, and fluctuations in the price of oil. Venezuela was a founding member of the Organization of Petroleum Exporting Countries (OPEC). Since 1958, Venezuela has tried to achieve a representational form of government and has held a number of democratic elections. Thought to contain the world's largest oil reserves, the Orinoco tar belt is under development.

Below: One of the most famous festivals in the world, Carnival is held annually before and on Shrove Tuesday in Rio de Janeiro, Brazil. Among other sights, Carnival features all-night parades in which the local samba clubs compete for prizes for the best costumes and music.

Top: Montevideo, Uruguay, lies on the Río de la Plata in the southern part of the nation. The port city is the capital as well as the financial, industrial, and cultural center of Uruguay and contains nearly half of the nation's total population.

Right: Inhabited before the eleventh century, Quito, Ecuador, is situated in the Andes, only fifteen miles (twenty-four kilometers) south of the equator. The city is the capital and second largest city in Ecuador, after the more populous Guayaquil.

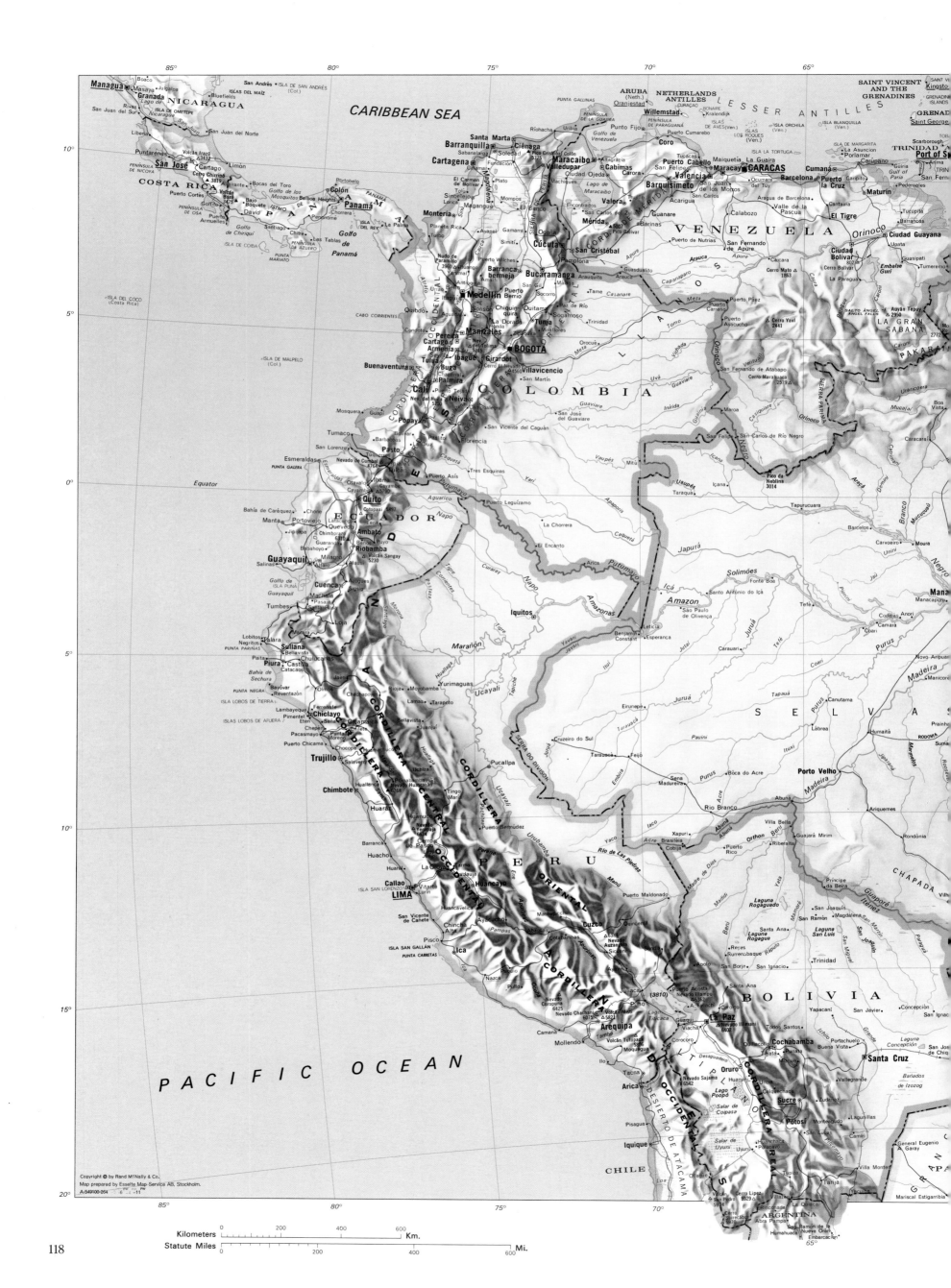

Kilometers
0   200   400   600
                              Km.
Statute Miles
0   200   400   600
                                    Mi.

ATLANTIC OCEAN

BARBADOS
getown

whanna

Charity
Georgetown
Parika
Hyde Park

New Amsterdam
Nieuw Nickerie
Totness

Paramaribo
Nieuw Amsterdam
Moengo
Paranam
Albina
Saint-Laurent-du-Maroni

Cayenne

SURINAME

FRENCH
GUIANA

GUYANA

ACARAI MTS.

TUMUC-HUMAC MTS.

Equator

BRAZIL

AMAZONICA

Amazon

Amazonas

Belém

ILHA DE MARAJÓ

São Luís

Fortaleza

Teresina

Natal

João Pessoa

Recife

Campina Grande

Maceió

Brasília

Goiânia

PLANALTO

CENTRAL

PLANALTO DO

MATO GROSSO

Cuiabá

Corumbá

Salvador

Feira de Santana

Vitória
da Conquista

Ilhéus
Itabuna

SERRA DO ESPINHAÇO

Campo Grande

Montes
Claros

Belo
Horizonte

Governador
Valadares

Vitória
Vila Velha

Uberlândia

Uberaba

Araçatuba

Presidente Prudente

Marília

Juiz de Fora

Campos

Bauru

Piracicaba

Campinas

Volta
Redonda

RIO DE JANEIRO

Niterói

São José
dos Campos

São Paulo

Santos

Tropic of Capricorn

Scale 1:12,000,000
One centimeter represents 120 kilometers.
One inch represents approximately 190 miles.
Oblique Conic Conformal Projection

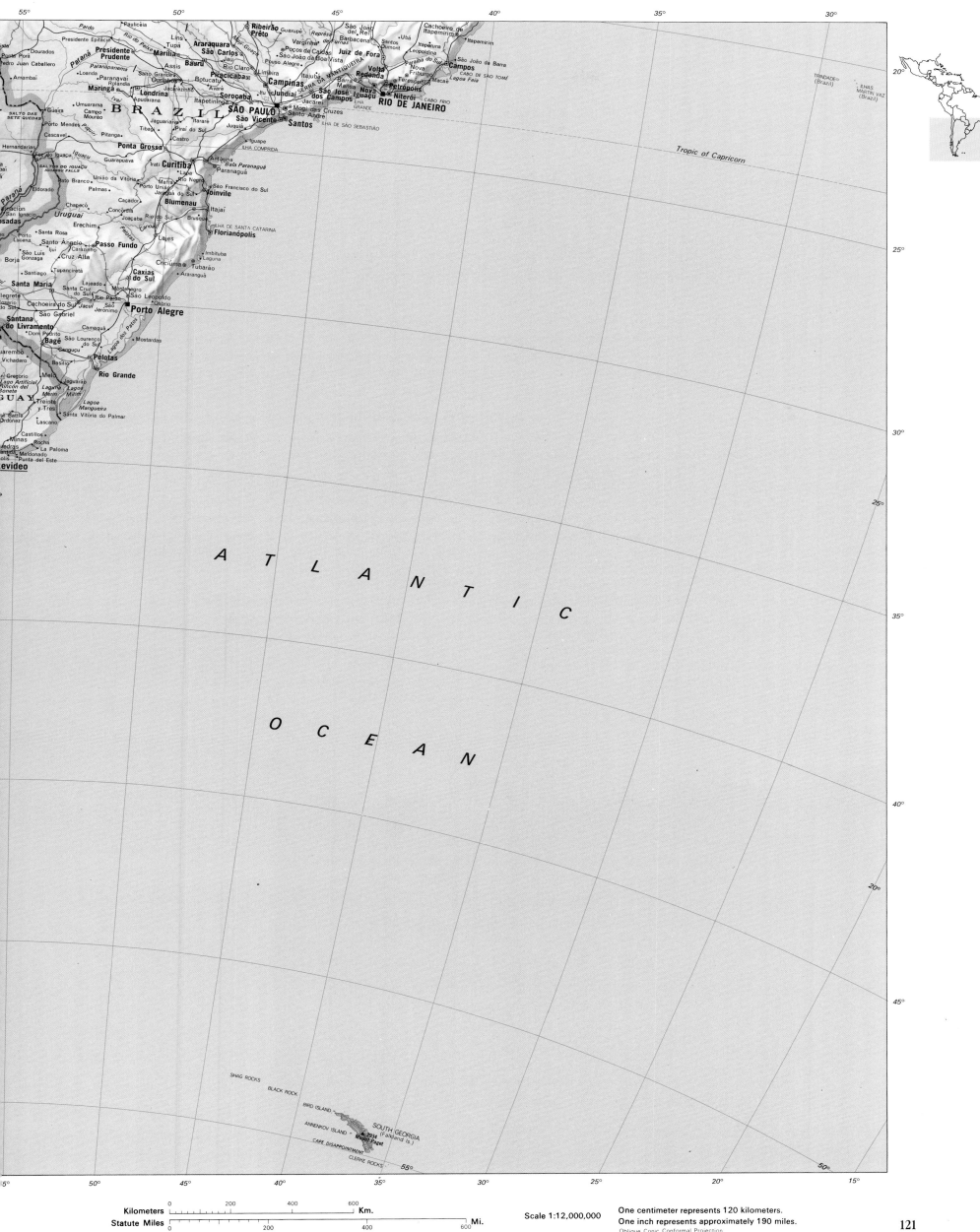

Tropic of Capricorn

BRAZIL

São Paulo

RIO DE JANEIRO

Kilometers
0   200   400   600   Km.

Statute Miles
0   200   400   600   Mi.

Scale 1:12,000,000

One centimeter represents 120 kilometers.
One inch represents approximately 190 miles.
Oblique Conic Conformal Projection

North America
Profile

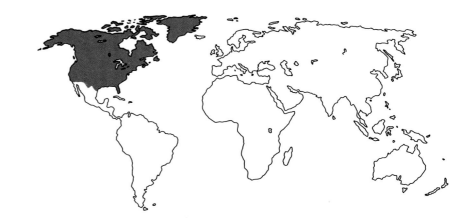

Location and Size

The Americas stretch from well north of the islands of Canada and Greenland to Cape Horn. For the purposes of this atlas, we have departed from the more traditional divisions of South and North America. What we define here as North America extends from the northern tips of the Canadian islands to the Florida Keys – a distance of some 3,900 miles (6,250 kilometers). The most westerly point on the mainland of the continent is the farthest reaches of Alaska. On the Atlantic coast, Newfoundland and Greenland extend farthest to the east.

Mainland North America is compact and essentially rectangular, with appendages in the northwest and southeast. Beyond the mainland lie many islands, especially in the north. Within the main rectangle are hundreds of lakes, with the open sea of Hudson Bay in the north.

The North American coastline shows a number of contrasting features. Some regions, such as British Columbia and Maine, have a complex, fretted outline with a number of offshore islands. Elsewhere, the outline is far more simple, as in Oregon and California. In places such as Texas and Louisiana, the coast is one of bars and lagoons.

Landscape

North America can be broadly divided into four major physical regions. In the north, surrounding Hudson Bay in a great crescent-shaped area, lies the Canadian Shield. It has been stripped of most of its soil during recent glaciations, has hundreds of lakes dotted on its surface, and has little agricultural potential. The main interest lies in the mineral resources of the old rocks and in forestry.

Along the east side of the continent lie ranges of mountains with a maximum height of 6,684 feet (2,037 meters) in the Blue Ridge region of the Appala-chians. Extending from Alabama in the south to the Canadian border in the north, the Appalachians continue into the mainland Maritime Provinces and Newfoundland.

The mountains of the west are far more complex and extensive. The Rocky Mountains are the most easterly of these, while farther west lie the Sierra Nevada, the Cascades, the Coast Ranges, and the Alaska Range. Between and within these lie a number of plateaus; desert basins, including the notorious Death Valley; and such fertile areas as the Central Valley of California and the Willamette Valley-Puget Sound lowlands farther north. These mountains today form the highest areas of the continent, rising 20,320 feet (6,194 meters) at Mount McKinley, Alaska. In this most unstable region of the continent lie the famous geysers of Yellowstone National Park and the much-feared San Andreas Fault, which threatens many of the urban areas of California.

A wide lowland area stretches from the Arctic Ocean in the north to the Gulf of Mexico in the south. Parts of this region are very low, especially the floors of the Mississippi and Mackenzie valleys, but the high plains reach to some 5,000 feet (1,600 meters) above sea level at the front ranges of the Rocky Mountains.

North America is a land of great rivers and river basins, most of which drain toward the Atlantic and Arctic oceans, Hudson Bay, and the Gulf of Mexico. The central lowlands are drained southward by the Mississippi-Missouri river system and northward by the Mackenzie River and the Saskatch-ewan-Nelson system. Rivers flowing to the Pacific are mainly shorter, though a few – especially the Colorado and Snake – have developed impressive scenic courses through the mountains to the coast. The Great Lakes compose another distinctive water feature of the continent, with Lake Superior the largest lake in the Western Hemisphere.

The largest island in the world, Greenland is composed of an inland

Left: The Rocky Mountains form the most extensive mountain system in North America. They are part of the great cordillera that runs down the western regions of North, Middle, and South America. The Teton Range, shown here, is one of the attractions of Grand Teton National Park, Wyoming.

Right: Ancestors of modern Pueblos, a Native American group, inhabited what is now Canyon de Chelly National Monument, Arizona, between the years 350 and 1300. They built villages here and left behind many ruins and artifacts.

Climate

plateau, coastal mountains and fjords, and offshore islands.

Climatically, the North American continent extends from the tropics to the polar reaches and has a full west-east range from one ocean to the other. Parts of mainland Canada, Greenland, and other islands lie well inside the Arctic Circle. In the west of the continent lies the great mountain region, which acts as a major barrier to the movement of air from west to east. In the east, the Appalachians have a similar effect to air movements. Thus the interior of the continent is effectively sealed from oceanic influences, though the unimpeded passage for air moving northward and southward from the Gulf or the Arctic does mean that, at times, warm air may penetrate well north or cold air well south.

In the extreme west, limited areas experience warm and cool temperate climates of an oceanic type. In parts, California enjoys a climate akin to that of some Mediterranean areas, but the Coast Ranges ensure that the Central Valley, for example, has great temperature extremes and, in the south, an acute water shortage. Farther north, in the coastal strip of Oregon, Washington, and British Colombia, the average temperature of the coldest month stays above freezing level, but the summer average monthly temperatures never exceed 72°F (22°C).

East of this coastal area, the climates of the mountain ranges are largely inhospitable. Those of the basins and ranges and into the western Great Plains can be classified as dry; annual precipitation is below ten inches (250 millimeters) and, with the heat of most areas, this moisture has little useful effect. Temperatures are more extreme here than on the coasts, with the monthly average below freezing for parts of the year. Although these regions are largely semiarid, in Arizona, Utah, and New Mexico the more extreme conditions of hot deserts prevail, with July temperatures of 91°F (33°C) and 55°F (13°C) in January.

Except for the tropical tip of Florida, the eastern United States south of Kansas, Kentucky, and Virginia enjoys a subtropical climate with rainfall throughout the year and distinctly warm summers. North of this area are progressively cooler and mainly drier zones. Thus the southern parts of the prairie provinces and the Great Lakes region experience a cool temperate climate, with rainfall increasing in the east.

Still farther north, the climates become less and less inviting. Here there is a broad belt of subarctic climates, which lies between the arctic north and the temperate south. In the tundra margins of northern Canada, an arctic climate prevails, and no month has an average temperature in excess of 50°F (10°C).

More than 80 percent of Greenland is covered by permanent ice. The climate is cold, with warmer temperatures and more precipitation in the southwest. Much of Greenland lies within the Arctic Circle and is considered a polar region.

Below: Hawaii became the fiftieth state of the United States in 1959. The Pacific islands are now among the world's most popular vacation destinations – a position they have earned with their tropical climate and sandy beaches. Shown here is Hanauma Bay, Oahu.

Left: British Columbia is the westernmost province of Canada. It remained isolated from the rest of the nation in its early provincial years because of its largely mountainous terrain. Today it is the site of several national parks, including Yoho National Park, shown here.

Middle, left: The Calgary Stampede, held annually in Calgary, Alberta, is one of the most prestigious rodeos.

Middle, right: Niagara Falls, on the waterway between Lakes Ontario and Erie at the United States-Canada border, attracts thousands of tourists who don waterproof gear to view the torrent up close.

Bottom: Kodiak Island, Alaska, is home to the Kodiak brown bear, which inhabits the wildlife refuge to which three-quarters of the island is dedicated. Also situated on the island off Alaska's southern coast is the city of Kodiak.

125

Below: On the Utah-Arizona border is a scenic region known as Monument Valley. Here are found sandstone buttes, mesas, and arches, some of them rising up to one thousand feet (three hundred meters) above the sandy plain below.

Right: Luring immigrants from around the world, many of the large cities of the United States have ethnic enclaves such as New York's Chinatown.

Below: The United States leads the world in heavy industry. Shown here is an automotive plant in Detroit, Michigan.

History, Politics, and Economy

There is some evidence that humans first entered North America more than twenty thousand years ago. A land bridge at the site of the Bering Strait was probably their access route. While more sophisticated Indian civilizations flourished farther south, with a few exceptions, the Native Americans of North America remained largely hunter-gatherers.

Although the Norse and most likely the Irish knew of North America long before, the flood of European settlement began after Christopher Columbus's discovery in 1492. England established a colony at Jamestown, Virginia, in 1607; subsequent rivalries for power in the northern New World saw Britain eventually gain control of much territory. In the 1763 Treaty of Paris, for example, France lost Canada and other North American territory to Britain.

The United States of America gained its independence when thirteen British colonies won a war waged from 1775 to 1783. Expansion continued westward throughout the nineteenth century. The issues of black slavery and states' rights led to the American Civil War from 1861 to 1865, a struggle that pitted the North against the South and resulted in the end of slavery. Opportunities for prosperity accompanied the industrial revolution in the late nineteenth century and led to a large influx of immigrants. From 1917 to 1918, the country joined the Allies in World War I. A severe economic depression began in 1929, and the United States did not really recover until military spending during World War II stimulated industry and the economy in general. Allied victory came in 1945. Postwar conflicts included the Korean War of the early fifties and the Vietnam War, which involved the United States from the late 1950s to 1973.

To aid in resolving the continued conflict between French and English residents of Canada, the British North America Act of 1867 united the colonies into the Dominion of Canada. In 1926, Canada declared itself an independent member of the British Commonwealth, and in 1931, Britain recognized the declaration. Post World War II years saw an improved economy and the domination of two parties: Liberal and Progressive Conservative.

The United States and Canada – two giants in the world economy – are so bound together economically and agriculturally that they tend to share the same economic problems. When the United States is in an economic downturn, so is Canada, since about half of Canada's manufacturing industry is owned by American firms. When Canada has a bumper crop of wheat and finds it difficult to locate a buyer, it is generally because the United States has harvested a bumper crop the same year. Being neighbors has created both tensions and opportunities for the two countries.

It is estimated that humans migrated from the east to Greenland as early as 4000 B.C. Norwegian Vikings sighted Greenland in the ninth century, and in the tenth century, Erik the Red brought the first settlers from Iceland. Greenland united with Norway in the 1200s, and the two regions came under Danish rule in the 1300s. Denmark retained control of Greenland when Norway left the union in 1814. In 1953, the island became a province of Denmark and in 1979 gained home rule. Although Greenland determines its own fate in international affairs, Denmark continues to handle some international matters.

Below: Sapphire blue Crater Lake, in Crater Lake National Park, Oregon, was formed by the explosion of an ancient volcano. The lake has no outlet or inlet; thus it is maintained solely by precipitation.

Canada

Canada is a huge nation situated north of the United States. It is second in size only to the Soviet Union. Canada was greatly influenced by French and British rule, and its culture reflects this dual nature. Descendants of British and French settlers compose the two main population groups, and languages include both English and French. Minorities include descendants of various European groups, indigenous Native Americans, and Inuit. French-speaking inhabitants, called Québecois, are concentrated in the Province of Québec, where they constitute over 80 percent of the population. These Québecois have strongly resented the anglicization imposed on all of Canada, including Québec, by Canadians of British descent. Historically, that resentment has shown itself in several ways: Québec's insistence that French be the official language of Canada along with English; that the old Canadian flag be replaced by the Maple Leaf flag; and the demand that Québec be allowed to form its own independent republic. Because of the rugged terrain and harsh climate of northern Canada, population is concentrated near the United States border. Rich natural resources – including mineral deposits, fertile land, forests, and lakes – helped shape Canada's economy, which ranks among the world's most prosperous. The economy has shifted from one that is based on production and export of raw agricultural items and natural resources to one that is based on manufacturing those raw materials. Economic problems are those common to most modern industrial nations. Agriculture, mining, and industry are highly developed. Canada is a major wheat producer; mineral output includes asbestos, zinc, silver, and nickel; and crude petroleum in an important export. The service sector is also active. Canada is a self-governing parliamentary state within the Commonwealth of Nations. Canadians recognize Queen Elizabeth II of England as the head of state. The last legislative control Britain had over Canada was severed in 1982 when Canada gained the right to amend its own constitution. In recent years, the

Opposite, top: Some say that football has supplanted baseball as the national pastime of the United States. The sport is played at all levels of age and skill, from peewee to professional.

Opposite, bottom: Pollution now threatens the five Great Lakes, which are glacial in origin and collectively form the world's largest body of fresh water. Shown here is Lake Huron, seen from Bruce Peninsula, Ontario.

Right: The city of Québec is situated in the Canadian province of the same name and is the nation's oldest metropolis. Originally settled in 1608, Québec maintains some of its French heritage and fine old structures.

New Democratic party has challenged the domination of the Liberal and Progressive Conservative parties in politics. In 1987, Canadian leaders agreed on an amendment to the constitution that recognizes Québec as a distinct society within the Canadian Federation.

Greenland
Situated almost entirely within the Arctic Circle, northeast of mainland Canada, is huge Greenland, the largest island in the world. Certain areas of Greenland have twenty-four consecutive hours of daylight in summer and darkness in winter. Most Greenlanders are native-born descendants of mixed Inuit-Danish ancestry. Lutheranism, the predominant religion, reflects Danish ties. Descended from an indigenous Arctic people, pure Inuit are a minority and usually follow traditional life-styles. Because of the harsh northern climate, the population is concentrated along the southern coast. Fishing is Greenland's economic backbone. Despite a difficult arctic environment, mining of zinc and lead continues; but iron, coal, uranium, and molybdenum deposits remain undeveloped. Greenland is a self-governing territory under Danish protection.

St. Pierre and Miquelon
This group of eight islands to the immediate south of Newfoundland is a territorial collectivity of France and the only French-held territory in North America. The islands lie in two distinct sections; the far smaller St. Pierre group contains 90 percent of the total population. The once-plentiful forests have been cut; the islands are now largely bare rock or scrub and do not support much agriculture. Cod fishing is the main occupation, and fish-processing industries are important. Tourism has been increasing.

United States
The United States of America consists of fifty states and extends from the Atlantic to Pacific coasts of North America, directly south of Canada. Two of the states – Alaska and Hawaii – are noncontiguous, and the nation administers several outlying territories. The diverse population of the United States is mostly composed of whites, many descended from eighteenth- and nineteenth-century immigrants; blacks, mainly descended from African slaves; peoples of Spanish and Asian origin; and indigenous Native Americans, Inuit, and Hawaiians. Nearly three-quarters of the population lives in urban areas. Great regional variations in population density exist, with the greatest density in New Jersey and the lowest in Alaska. Religions encompass the world's major faiths; predominating are Protestantism, Roman Catholicism, and Judaism. English is the official language, though Spanish is spoken by many, and other languages are often found in ethnic enclaves. The United States is an international economic power, and all sectors of the economy are highly developed. Fertile soils produce high crop yields, with considerable land under cultivation. Mineral output includes petroleum and natural gas, coal, copper, lead, and zinc, but high consumption makes the United States dependent on foreign oil. The country is a leading manufacturer, and about one-quarter of the work force is engaged in manufacturing. As is the case with other highly developed nations, the service sector employs most of the work force and accounts for the largest percentage of the gross national product. Tourism is also important. The gross national product of the United States is the highest in the world, and the per capita income is among the highest.

The United States is a republic, with the Democratic and Republican parties dominating elections. The more conservative Republican party has held the presidency since the beginning of the 1980s, first with Ronald Reagan and then with George Bush, who took office in 1989. The overwhelming social problem in the United States has historically been racial, particularly the status of blacks, and, more recently, Third World immigrants. Internationally, the United States has begun to reevaluate its foreign policy and its position in the worldwide economic picture. Primary concerns are how to handle the federal budget deficit, increasing military spending, foreign debt, the threat of inflation, and the loss of jobs in manufacturing. Additionally, long-term defense planning is under scrutiny, particularly the development of the Strategic Defense Initiative (SDI) or Star Wars program. By most measures, the United States remains the world's dominant power. Nations in the rest of the world, especially countries in Asia and the Pacific, are becoming increasingly productive, however, and may threaten the United States' stature as world leader.

Kilometers
0   200   400   600   Km.

Statute Miles
0   200   400   600   Mi.

Scale 1:12,000,000

One centimeter represents 120 kilometers.
One inch represents approximately 190 miles.

Lambert Conformal Conic Projection

Kilometers

Statute Miles

Scale 1:12,000,000

One centimeter represents 120 kilometers.
One inch represents approximately 190 miles.

Albers Conical Equal-Area Projection

United States
Northeast

The great natural ports of North America's Atlantic coast have welcomed world travelers since 1620, when the pilgrims anchored at Plymouth, Massachusetts. From Boston, Massachusetts, to Baltimore, Maryland, whalers, traders, and other seafarers sailed into the harbors that became thriving cities during the nation's first decades of independence. You can now trace more than two hundred years of history in the great cities of the Northeast. Boston, Philadelphia, New York, and Washington, D.C., have all played major roles in United States history, and in all, you can visit historic sites.

Beyond the Northeast's major cities, you'll find the calm beauty of fishing towns, farms, and mountain resorts. Additionally, the Northeast offers extensive coastline – from the rocky shores of Maine's Acadia National Park, the only national park in New England, to the sandy shores of Cape Cod National Seashore in Massachusetts to the casinos and boardwalk of Atlantic City, New Jersey.

Right: Washington, D.C., the capital of the United States, is surrounded on three sides by Maryland, with the other side formed by the banks of the Potomac River. The city's many cultural, memorial, and federal buildings include the Capitol, shown here, which houses the legislative branch of the government.

Below: The international metropolis known as New York City is the United States' leading cultural and commercial center as well as its largest city. The Big Apple is central to the eastern megalopolis that extends from New Hampshire to northern Virginia.

Below: The United States Military Academy at West Point, New York, trains officers of the army.

Right: Long a maritime center, New London, Connecticut, has one of the finest deep-water ports on the Atlantic coast.

Bottom, left: Vermont's picturesque towns and mountainous terrain make it a popular tourist destination.

Bottom, right : These lobster pots contribute to Maine's position as the nation's leading lobster producer.

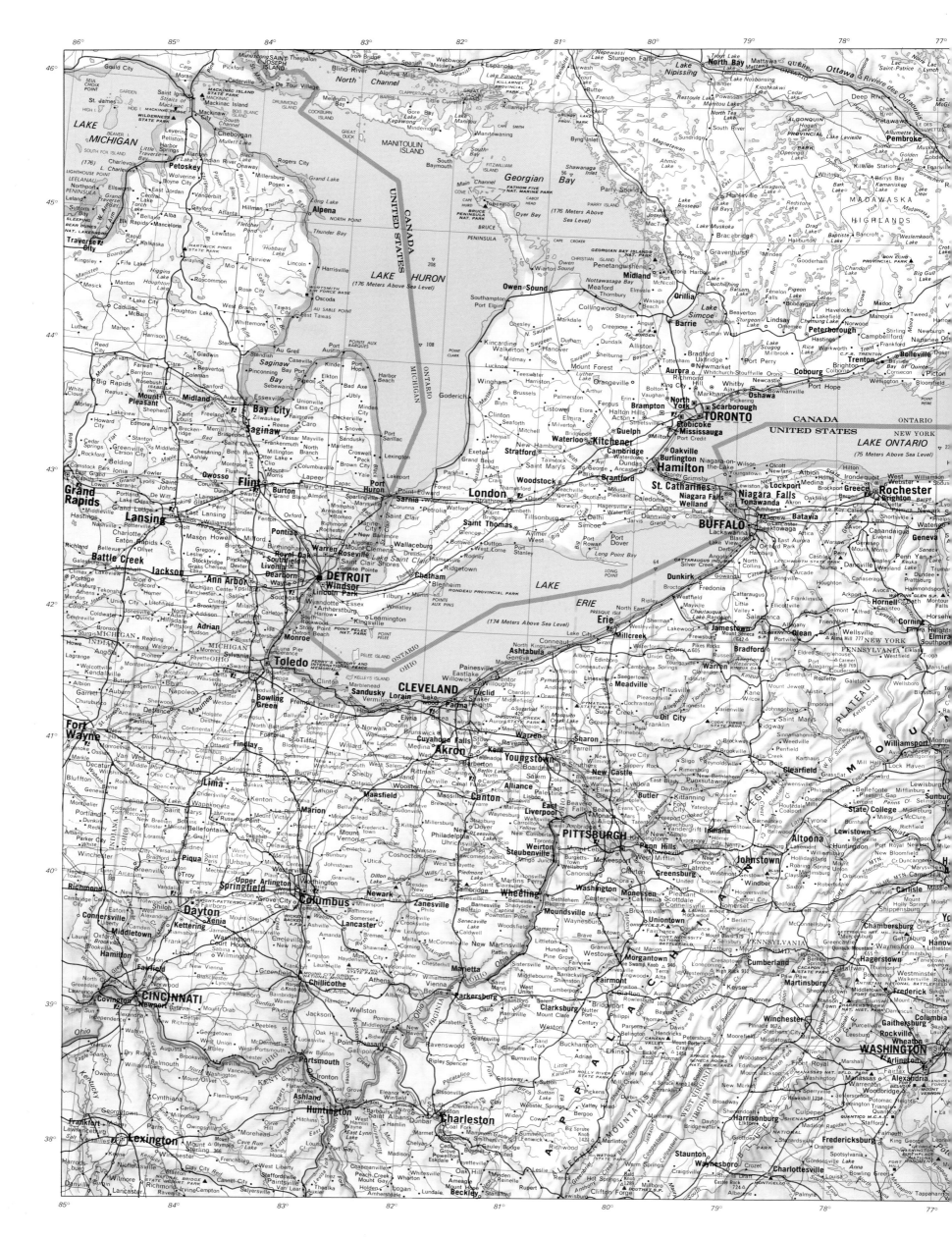

Kilometers
Statute Miles

Scale 1:3,000,000

One centimeter represents 30 kilometers.
One inch represents approximately 47 miles.

Albers Conical Equal-Area Projection

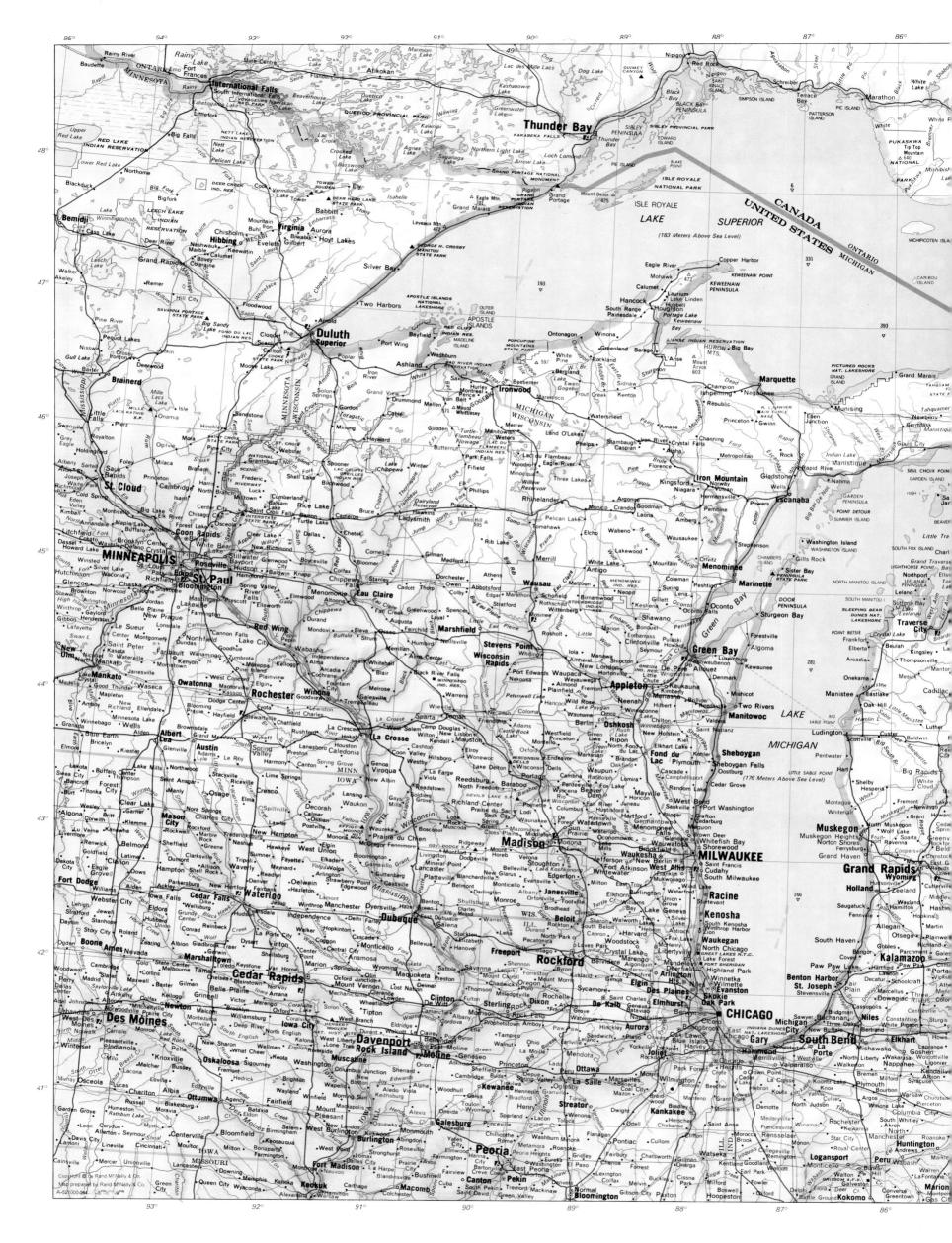

Kilometers
Statute Miles

Scale 1:3,000,000

One centimeter represents 30 kilometers.
One inch represents approximately 47 miles.

Albers Conical Equal Area Projection

Great Lakes Region

The five Great Lakes formed a natural, navigable route for Native Americans and early American explorers long before trains sped across the continent. But once the railroads were built, great cities grew up along the shores of the lakes, each one a connecting point for ship and railroad cargoes. During the nineteenth century, grain and beef from the plains, iron ore from Minnesota, cotton from the South, and manufactured goods from the East all met in Chicago, Illinois. As technology advanced, the raw materials were turned into steel, refined oil, and automobiles and shipped from the mills and factories of Detroit, Michigan; Gary, Indiana; and Cleveland, Ohio. People from around the world found work in the Great Lakes cities.

In addition to their commercial worth, the Great Lakes are a valuable recreation resource. Chicagoans enjoy fine city beaches only blocks away from some of the world's tallest skyscrapers. Nature enthusiasts of all types retreat in all seasons to the wilderness regions of Minnesota, Wisconsin, and Michigan.

The arts, too, have flourished in the Great Lakes region. Chicago's long musical tradition today boasts the world's most highly acclaimed symphony orchestra as well as fine ensembles that specialize in more contemporary genres.

Above: The plains of the southern Great Lakes region form part of the American Midwest. Sophisticated farming techniques and fertile soils help make this region one of the world's most productive.

Right: Much of the northern Great Lakes region consists of forests and small lakes, both of which attract visitors with a variety of recreational interests. Shown is here the Upper Peninsula of Michigan.

Below: Situated on the southwestern shore of Lake Michigan, Chicago, Illinois, has long been a center for transportation, industry, and culture. The Windy City is the nation's third largest.

Sunshine and palm trees, antebellum mansions and Spanish moss, and Southern cooking and hospitality are the traditional hallmarks that draw visitors to the Southeast. Add to these the bustling cities of Atlanta, Georgia, and Miami, Florida, and the picture of today's Southeast begins to take shape.

This region offers a contrast of old and new. Founded by Spanish settlers in 1565, St. Augustine, Florida, is the oldest city in the United States. The restoration at Williamsburg, Virginia, offers tourists a rare opportunity to experience the life-style of colonial Virginians. Savannah's historical seaport and Charleston's lovely gardens recall the serene dignity of another era. Those who enjoy modern playgrounds, however, might head for Florida's Gold Coast or Orlando area, South Carolina's Hilton Head, or North Carolina's Pinehurst.

The Southeast's natural landmarks are varied. They range from Florida's swampy Everglades to the glorious elevations of the Blue Ridge to the spectacular dunes of the Outer Banks.

Left: Cypress trees such as these in Florida thrive in the many swampy regions of the Southeast. Home to a wide variety of wildlife, some of the major swamplands – such as Okefenokee Swamp and the Everglades – have become federally protected.

Bottom, left: The American South was once supported by a thriving plantation economy, which was largely destroyed in the wake of the Civil War. Some of the plantations remain, however, and have been turned into tourist attractions. Shown here is Orton Plantation, near Wilmington, North Carolina.

Below: Among Florida's many vacation destinations are its theme and amusement parks. Shown here is a castle at Walt Disney World, near Orlando.

ATLANTIC

OCEAN

GULF OF MEXICO

GEORGIA

FLORIDA

BAHAMAS

UNITED STATES

NEW PROVIDENCE

GRAND BAHAMA

LITTLE ABACO ISLAND

GREAT ABACO

ANDROS ISLAND

BERRY ISLANDS

BIMINI ISLANDS

ELEUTHERA

Northwest Providence Channel

Providence Channel

Nassau

Freeport

West End

Governors Harbour

Okefenokee Swamp

Lake Okeechobee

Everglades National Park

Big Cypress Swamp

FLORIDA KEYS

Straits of Florida

Cities and places

Brunswick
Waycross
Valdosta
Moultrie
Thomasville
Tallahassee
Jacksonville
Jacksonville Beach
St. Augustine
Gainesville
Ocala
Daytona Beach
New Smyrna Beach
Titusville
Cocoa
Cocoa Beach
Merritt Island
Melbourne
Sanford
Orlando
Winter Park
Winter Haven
Lake Land
Plant City
Tampa
St. Petersburg
Clearwater
Largo
Pinellas Park
Bradenton
Sarasota
Fort Myers
Fort Pierce
Vero Beach
Riviera Beach
West Palm Beach
Palm Beach
Boynton Beach
Delray Beach
Boca Raton
Pompano Beach
Fort Lauderdale
Hollywood
Hialeah
Miami
Miami Beach
North Miami
Coral Gables
Homestead
Key West
Key Largo

JOHN F. KENNEDY SPACE CENTER

CAPE CANAVERAL

DRY TORTUGAS NAT. MON.

FORT JEFFERSON NAT. MON.

KEY WEST N.A.S.

Scale 1:3,000,000

One centimeter represents 30 kilometers.
One inch represents approximately 47 miles.

Albers Conical Equal-Area Projection

Kilometers 0 50 100 150 Km.
Statute Miles 0 50 100 150 Mi.

Copyright © by Rand McNally & Co.
Map prepared by Rand McNally & Co.
A-5011100-264

143

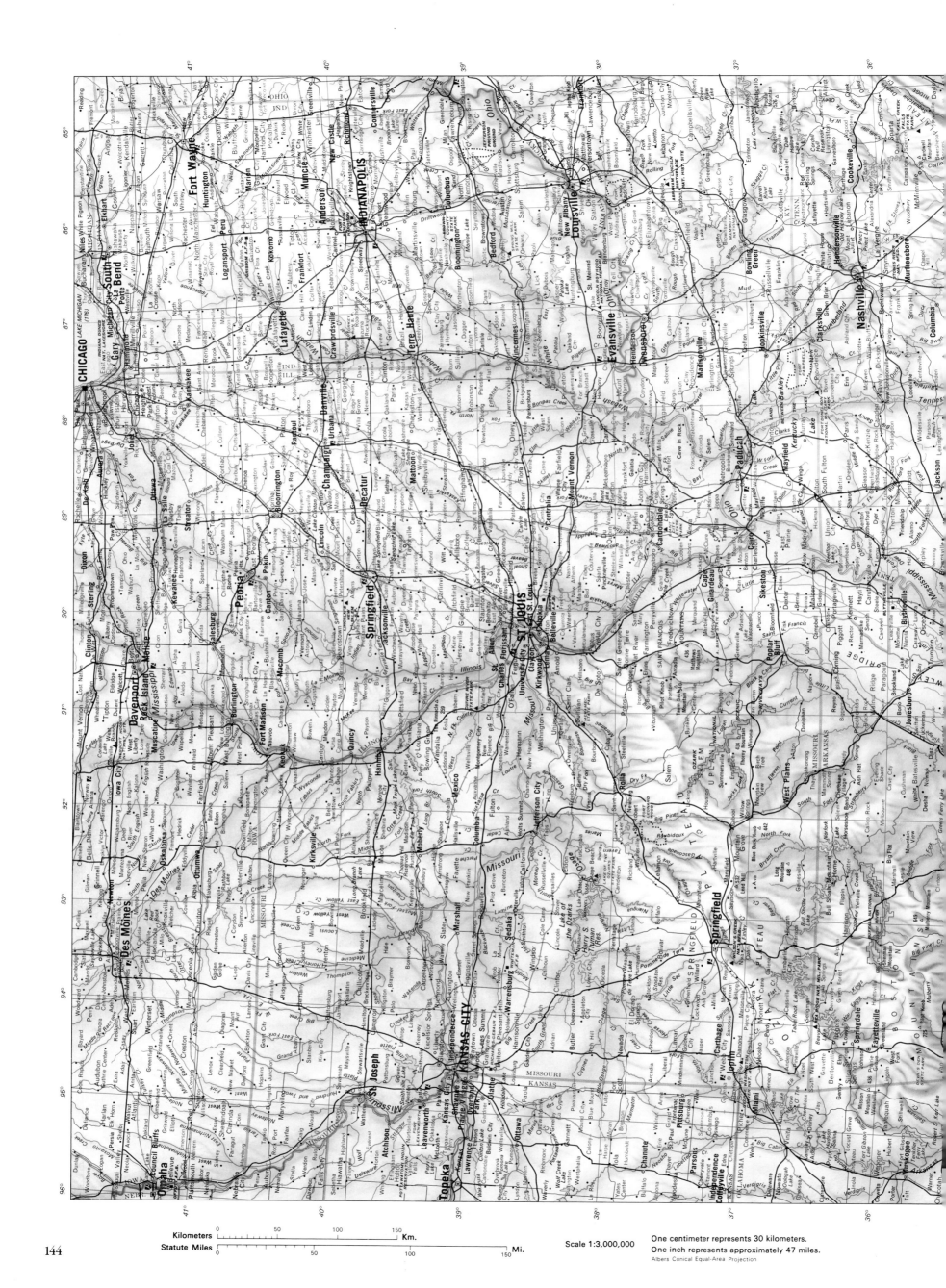

Kilometers

Statute Miles

Scale 1:3,000,000

One centimeter represents 30 kilometers.
One inch represents approximately 47 miles.

Albers Conical Equal-Area Projection

Mississippi Valley

The rousing strains of Dixieland jazz, the foot-stomping twang of bluegrass, and the soulful ballads of country music are as much a part of the Mississippi Valley as the stockyards of Kansas City, Missouri, and the breweries of St. Louis, Missouri. On the farms, in the hills, and in the back quarters of rowdy river towns, some of the United States' native music was born and nurtured. Today, the sounds still beckon listeners to concert halls and nightclubs in cities such as Nashville and New Orleans.

The Mississippi's most famous character is Huckleberry Finn, the raft-roving runaway who has charmed children and provoked literary adults since Mark Twain created him in 1876. If you visit the author's family home in Hannibal, Missouri, you'll find that it remains true to the famous humorist's writings.

But what would Mark Twain make of modern St. Louis, with its towering Gateway Arch? He would undoubtedly recognize the old mansions of Natchez and the thriving commerce of Memphis. And who knows what he would think of the cuisine of today's New Orleans and Louisiana's bayous.

Top: The Mississippi River and its tributaries form the most significant river system in the United States. The mighty Mississippi has played a major role in the settlement of the nation, and many cities have flourished along its banks. The river rises in Minnesota and flows south for more than 2,300 miles (3,700 kilometers) to Louisiana, forming borders for ten states along the way.

Above: Visitors to some cities along the Mississippi can relive the region's past by taking steamboat rides.

Right: One of the United States' greatest contributions to world culture has been jazz, which originated in New Orleans, Louisiana. Visitors and residents alike are still drawn to the city's incomparable jazz bands.

United States
Southern Rocky Mountains

Vistas rise to the heights of Pikes Peak, Colorado, and fall to the depths of the Grand Canyon in Arizona in the breathtakingly beautiful southern Rockies region. Outdoors enthusiasts cherish the ski slopes of Colorado and Utah, the extraordinary rock formations in a variety of national parks and monuments, the open skies of the ranches, and the crystalline splendor of the mountain lakes.

The list of national parks and monuments found in the southern Rockies is impressive. Among them are Colorado's Rocky Mountain and Mesa Verde national parks and Dinosaur National Monument; Utah's Bryce Canyon, Zion, Arches, Canyonlands, and Capitol Reef national parks and six national monuments; Arizona's Grand Canyon and Petrified Forest national parks and six national monuments; and New Mexico's Carlsbad Caverns National Park and ten national monuments.

The human-made attractions of the region span the ages. There are ancient Native American ruins in New Mexico and Arizona, which contrast with the metropolises of the southern Rockies. People come to Salt Lake City, Utah, to gaze on the sparkling white buildings as well as the Great Salt Lake and its surrounding desert. Visitors to Denver, Colorado, enjoy the offerings of a big city along with those of the nearby mountains. Phoenix, Arizona, has become the region's largest city, and travelers are drawn by its sun-drenched climate and unique culture.

Some of North America's oldest settlements – those of the Hopi, Navajo, and Pueblo – flourished beneath the southern Rockies. Sophisticated, agricultural Native American societies were centered mainly south of the Rio Grande, but these were the exceptions. Descendants of these ancient peoples still live in the region and remain culturally active.

Right: Tourists come to Canyonlands National Park, near Moab, Utah, to view spectacular rock formations, canyons, arches, spires, Native American ruins, and desert vegetation.

Above: About 1.5 million Native Americans live in the United States, many of them in the southern Rocky Mountain region. Arizona has more Native Americans than almost any other state.

Left: Havasu Creek flows into the Colorado River in Grand Canyon National Park, Arizona, tumbling over four major falls along the way. The Grand Canyon is one of the most spectacular sights in North America.

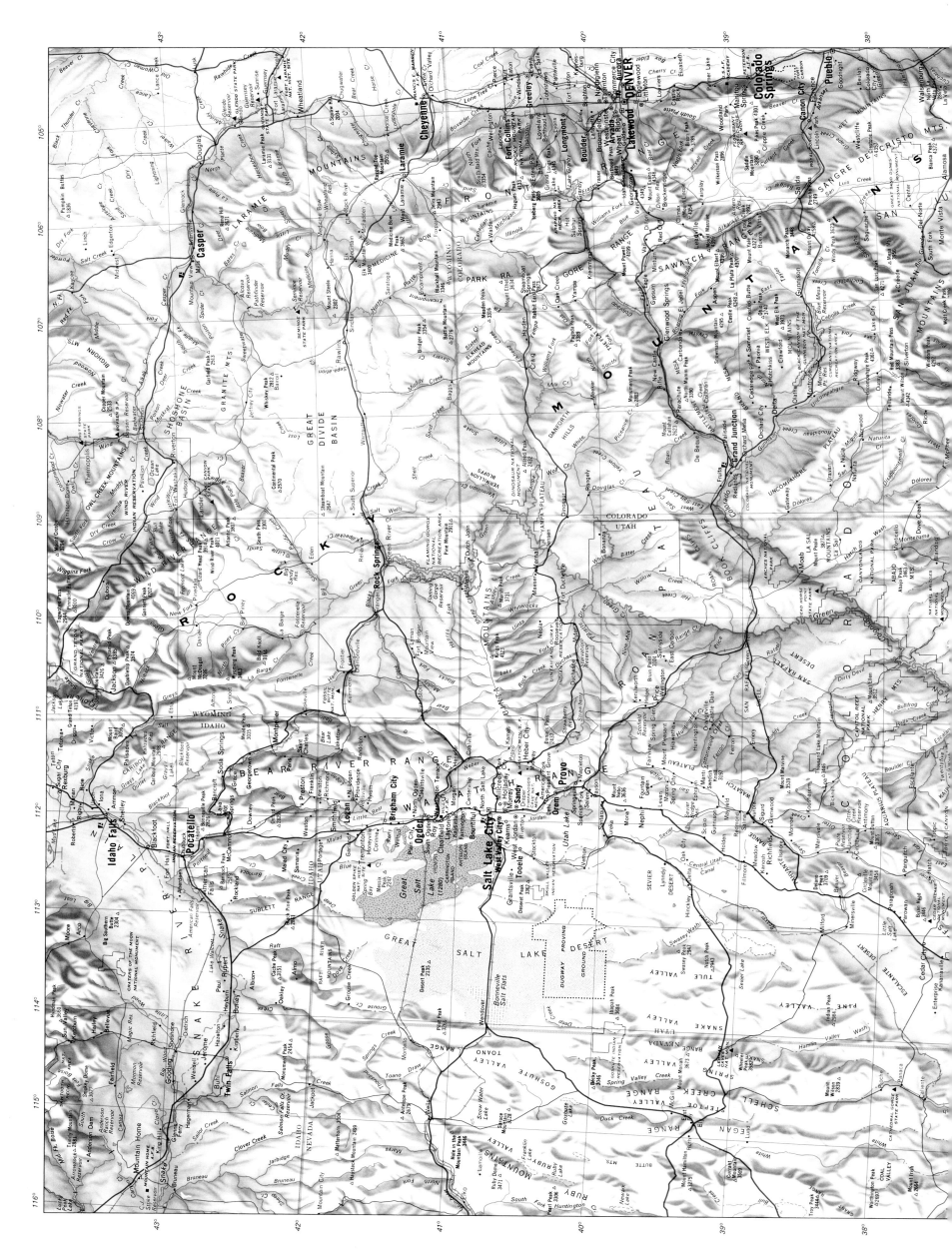

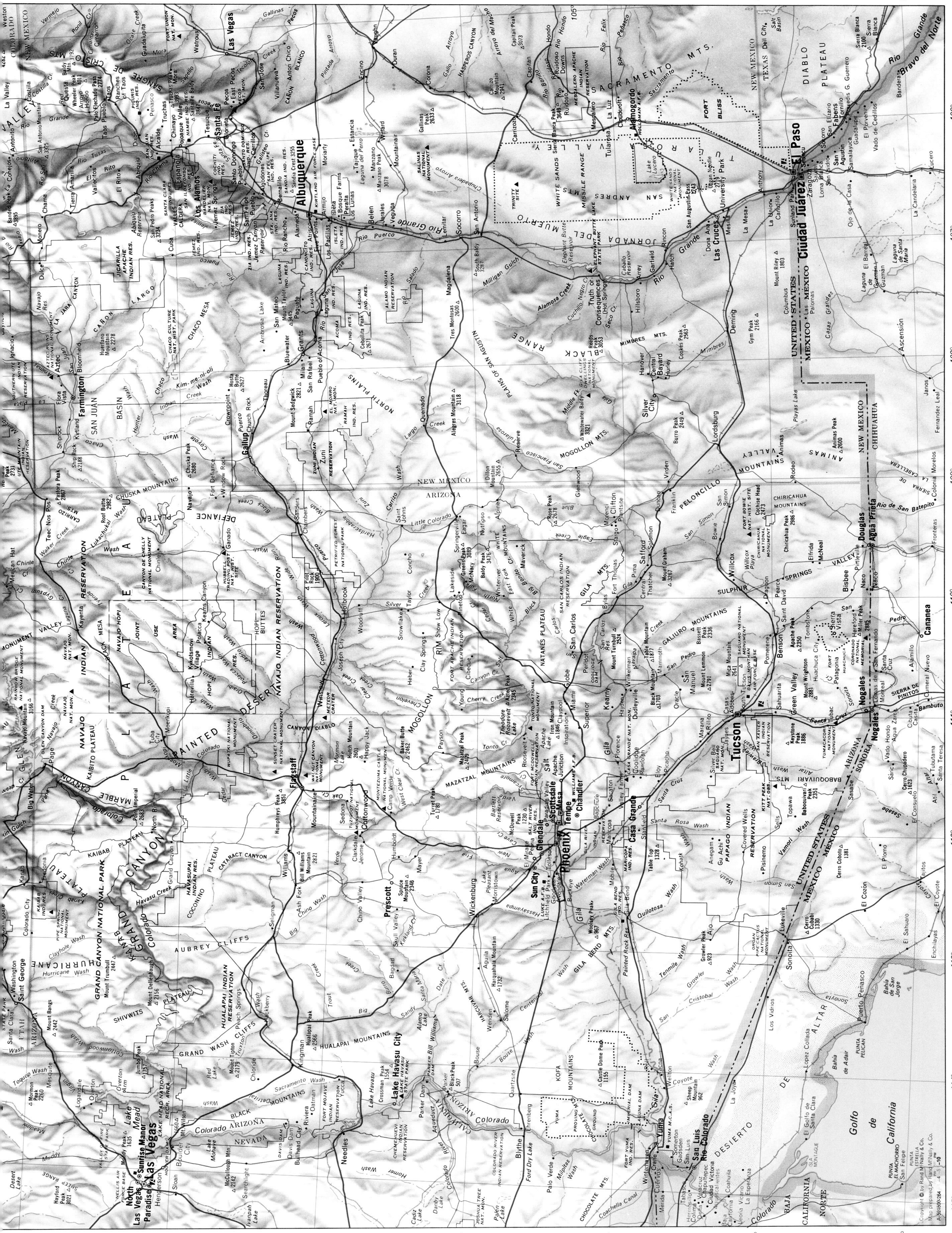

NEW MEXICO

ARIZONA

Albuquerque

Santa Fe

Las Vegas

El Paso

Ciudad Juárez

Las Cruces

Phoenix

Tempe

Glendale

Scottsdale

Chandler

Sun City

Tucson

Nogales

Prescott

Flagstaff

Cottonwood

Farmington

Gallup

Lake Havasu City

Yuma

San Luis Río Colorado

Agua Prieta

Douglas

Cananea

UNITED STATES

MEXICO

TEXAS

CHIHUAHUA

SONORA

COLORADO

NEVADA

CALIFORNIA

NAVAJO INDIAN RESERVATION

HOPI INDIAN RESERVATION

GRAND CANYON NATIONAL PARK

Rio Grande

Colorado

Golfo de California

Kilometers   0   50   100   150   Km.

Statute Miles   0   50   100   150   Mi.

Scale 1:3,000,000

One centimeter represents 30 kilometers.
One inch represents approximately 47 miles.
Albers Conical Equal-Area Projection

149

Scale 1:3,000,000

One centimeter represents 30 kilometers.
One inch represents approximately 47 miles.

Albers Conical Equal-Area Projection

United States
Northwest

The Lewis and Clark Expedition that began in 1804 was the turning point for this corner of the United States. Soon after word of the region returned to the East, the previously unexplored Northwest was crisscrossed by numerous fur traders, missionaries, salmon fishermen, and, finally, settlers.

Today's residents of the Northwest often boast that their region has everything. There's much truth to this claim, for Washington's timberlands, the Willamette valley farms and orchards, the inland cattle ranges, and the coastal fishing industry contribute to a diverse bounty. The cities of Portland, Oregon, and Seattle, Washington, are known for their peaceful prosperity and cultural sophistication.

This is also the land of the Snake River, with its spectacular Hells Canyon at the border of Idaho and Oregon; the geysers, grizzly bears, and jagged Teton Range of Wyoming; the Big Sky country of Montana; the glaciers of North Cascades National Park in Washington; and the marine life and rugged Pacific shoreline of Washington and Oregon.

Top, left: Shown here is Sunshine Peak, one of the more than one thousand mountains in Colorado that rise to 10,000 feet (3,048 meters) or more. Visitors are attracted not only to the peaks themselves but, in the fall, also to the foliage of aspens and other trees.

Above: Seattle's Space Needle dominates the skyline of the city on Washington's Puget Sound. Seattle is now the largest city in the northwestern United States.

Left: Cattle ranching, which is possible between the mountain peaks, is an important economic activity in the Northwest.

Top, left: Livestock that graze on Montana's eastern plains contribute to the state's income, two-thirds of which is agriculturally based.

Above: Abandoned dwellings such as this mill on Colorado's Crystal River speak of the region's past: the gold rush brought waves of settlers, who abandoned some settlements as the rush subsided.

Left: Tourists are drawn to Idaho's mountainous terrain and now contribute substantially to the state's income.

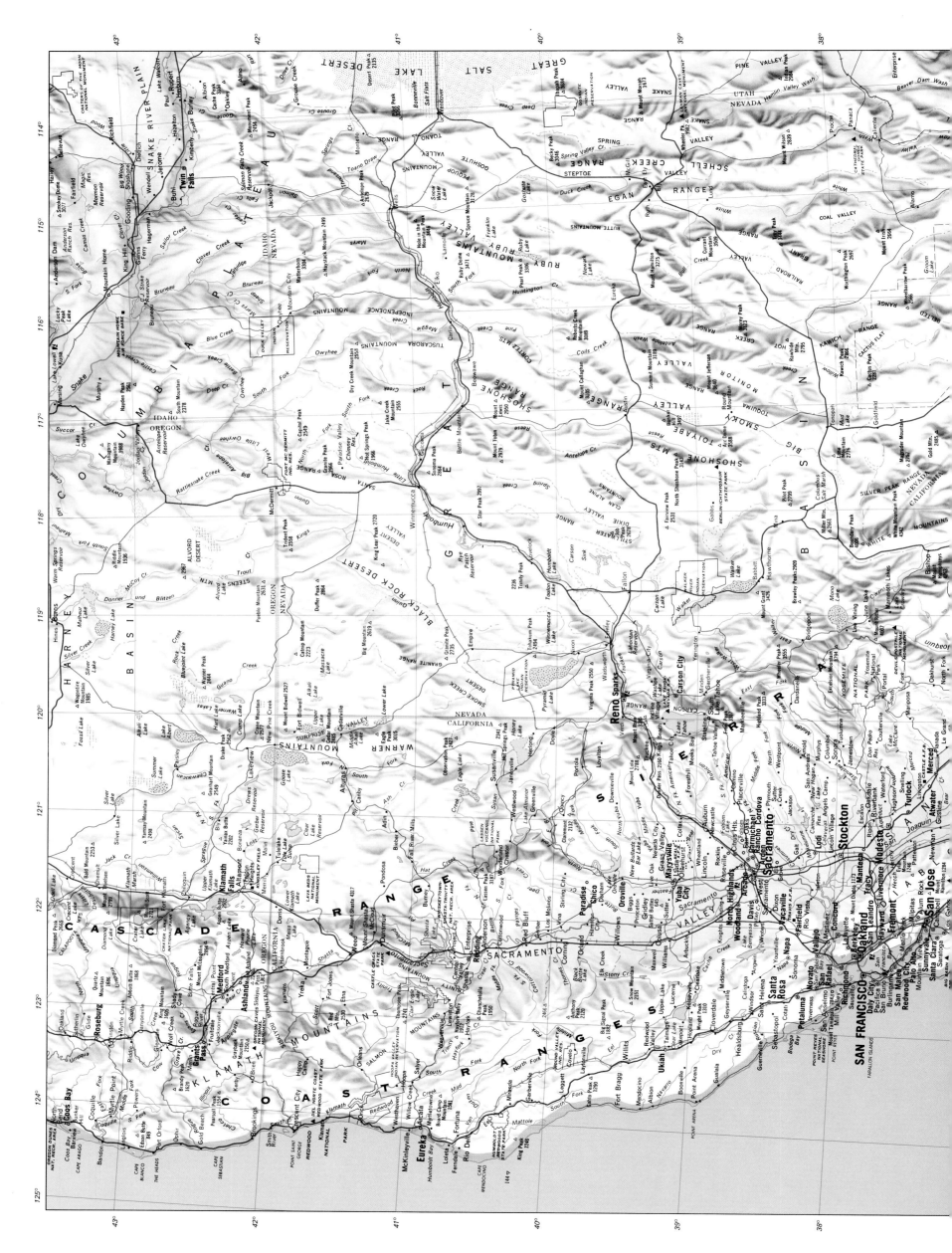

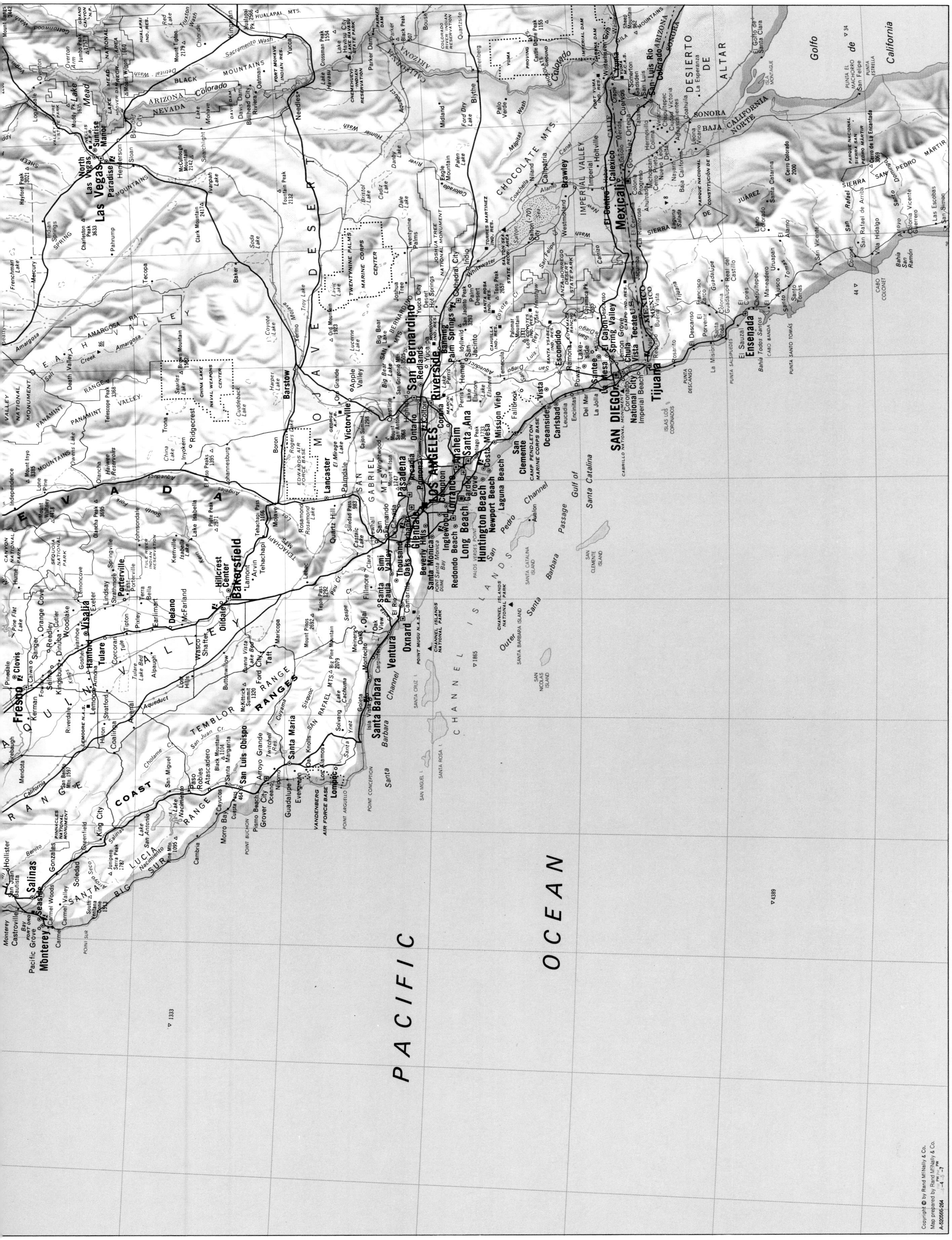

PACIFIC OCEAN

Las Vegas

Fresno

Bakersfield

LOS ANGELES

San Bernardino

Riverside

Santa Ana

Long Beach

Santa Barbara

Ventura

Oxnard

San Diego

Tijuana

Mexicali

Ensenada

DEATH VALLEY NATIONAL MONUMENT

MOJAVE DESERT

Kilometers 0 50 100 150 Km.

Statute Miles 0 50 100 150 Mi.

Scale 1:3,000,000

One centimeter represents 30 kilometers.
One inch represents approximately 47 miles.

Albers Conical Equal-Area Projection

Copyright © by Rand McNally & Co.
Map prepared by Rand McNally & Co.

155

United States
California & Nevada

Dreams of wealth and glamour have lured travelers to California and Nevada ever since miners saw the glint of gold and silver here. After Mormons founded Nevada's first permanent settlement, major lodes of gold and silver were struck in the state, and the population boom was on. Nevada's population increased sixfold in one decade in the late 1800s. California's story is similar, with its gold rush of 1849 and its own population subsequently tripling.

Today, flocks of people still seek to strike gold in the region: aspiring entertainers move to Los Angeles with their sights set on breaking into show business; tourists visit Hollywood and Beverly Hills, hoping to catch a glimpse of movie, television, and rock stars; and gamblers eye the roulette wheels of Las Vegas, Reno, and Lake Tahoe.

But the most fabulous riches of the region are to be found in its near-perfect climate and stunning scenery. The winding road that hugs California's Pacific coastline reveals a treasury of citrus groves, truck farms, and vineyards. The redwood forests, the stark desert, and the Sierra Nevada compete in the grandeur. The sparkling waters of Lake Mead invite boaters and water-skiers; the glacier-cut cliffs of Yosemite thrill hikers and campers; and the breathtaking scenes of Lake Tahoe appeal to almost everyone.

The cities along the West Coast offer their own treasures. From San Francisco in the north, through Monterey, Santa Barbara, Los Angeles, and finally San Diego in the south, these cities share coastline on the Pacific, yet each retains a unique atmosphere.

Opposite, top: Hollywood, home of the entertainment industry, is part of Los Angeles, the largest city in California and the second largest in the United States.

Opposite, bottom: Many factors have drawn enough people to California to make it the most populous state in the nation. Scenic beauty is but one of these factors. Yet many wild regions still exist, often within close proximity to urban areas. Shown here is the stunning Santa Ynez valley, near Santa Barbara.

Above: California has more than 800 miles (1,300 kilometers) of coastline along the Pacific. Southern California features sand beaches, but most of the coast is rocky. Shown here are sandstone forms at Salt Point State Park.

Middle, left: Las Vegas is the largest city in Nevada. Approximately fifteen million tourists annually flock to its hotels, casinos, and nightclubs.

Middle, right: The ancient sequoias, or redwoods, that grow in the Sierra Nevada are among the world's tallest trees. Shown here are redwoods in Yosemite National Park, California.

Right: The lowest elevation in the Western Hemisphere – 282 feet (86 meters) below sea level – is in Death Valley National Monument, in California and Nevada. The desert basin was once a valuable mining region.

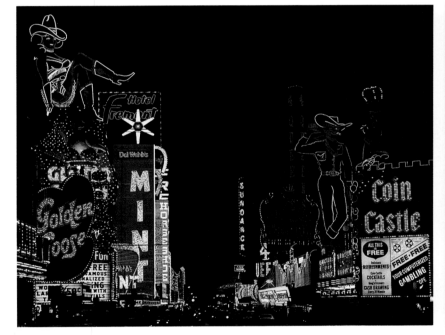

157

Polar Regions
Profile

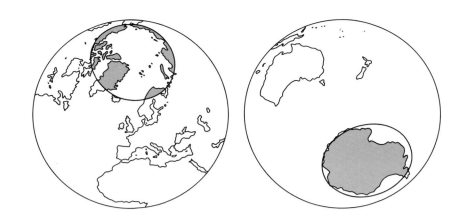

Location and Size

The Arctic is an area of extreme cold surrounding the geographic North Pole. It is usually demarcated by the Arctic Circle, an imaginary line north of which there are periods of twenty-four-hour daylight in summer and darkness in winter. The Arctic comprises the Arctic Ocean, which has an area of roughly 5.4 million square miles (14 million square kilometers), and the northern reaches of the Soviet Union, Alaska, Canada, Iceland, Norway, Sweden, Finland, most of Greenland, and a number of islands.

Antarctica surrounds the South Pole and lies almost entirely within the Antarctic Circle. Larger than either Europe or Australia, Antarctica covers some 5.1 million square miles (13.2 million square kilometers).

At the North Pole, the sun rises above the horizon at the spring equinox, about March 21. It does not set until the autumnal equinox, about September 22, after which it does not rise again until the spring equinox. At the South Pole, the same phenomenon occurs, but in opposite seasons.

Landscape

The Arctic Ocean is covered with ice for much of the year, but it melts in summer months. The region's only permanent ice sheet is in Greenland. Continental Arctic land is mostly low-lying, while the islands are somewhat rugged and mountainous. Four of the world's major rivers flow into the Arctic Ocean.

If all of Antarctica's permanent ice cap were removed, a very rugged landscape would be revealed. Relieved of the weight of ice, the land would rise, and the highest peaks would probably match those of the Himalayas.

Climate

Monthly average temperatures in the Arctic range from −40°F (−40°C) in winter to as high as 59°F (15°C) in summer. Precipitation is low; the region is a cold desert.

The climate of Antarctica is far more severe than that of the Arctic. From the center of this mass representing about 90 percent of the world's permanent ice

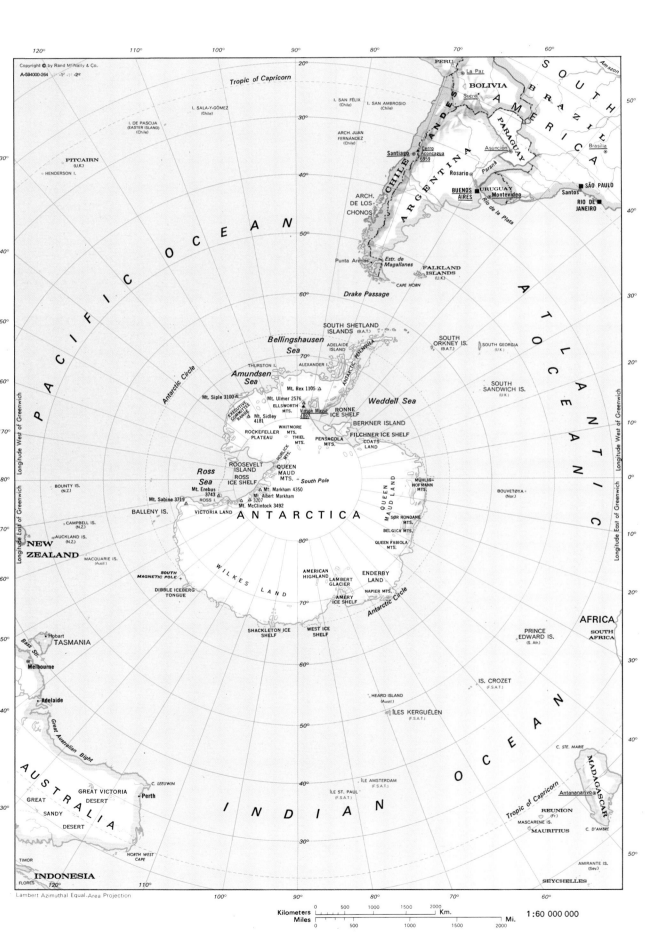

Opposite: The Antarctic Peninsula, shown here, is one of the few points on the continent to extend north of the Antarctic Circle. The tip of the peninsula is only 600 miles (960 kilometers) from South America.

Polar Regions

and snow, bitter winds blow outward.
Winter average temperatures drop as
low as –76°F (–60°C) and in summer
months rise only to –3°F (–20°C) in the
interior. Only along the coasts do
summer monthly temperatures rise
above freezing.

History, Politics, and Economy

The Inuit are believed to have lived in
the Arctic for about ten thousand years.
The Norse settled in Greenland before
1000 A.D., but much of the Arctic
remained uncharted until dreams of a
Northwest Passage to Asia sparked a
flood of exploration in the nineteenth
century. The geographic North Pole was
reached on 1909.

In 1911, the South Pole was reached.
Because of harsh climate and terrain,
Antarctica has no permanent population;
interest in the area remains largely
scientific, though many nations want to
explore the region's vast potential for
mining. The Antarctic Treaty ratified in
1961 froze all territorial claims until
1991 and stated that Antarctica shall be
used for peaceful purposes only.

Below: The frozen wasteland
surrounding the North Pole is
seen here from Point Barrow,
Alaska, the northernmost point
of the United States.

Bottom, right: Penguins are
found in the cold waters of the
Southern Hemisphere. Shown
here are adélie penguins,
one of only two species that
breed in Antarctica.

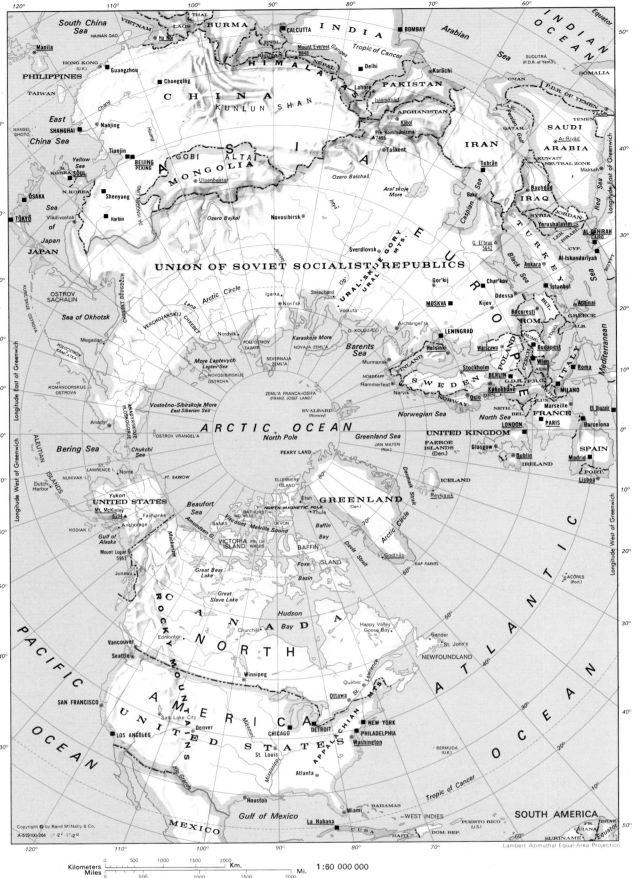

Introduction to the Index

This universal index includes in a single alphabetical list more than 23,000 names of features that appear on the reference maps. Each name is followed by a page reference and geographical coordinates.

Names Local official names are used on the maps and in the index. The names are shown in full, including diacritical marks. Features that extend beyond the boundaries of one country and have no single official name are usually named in English. Many conventional English names and former names are cross-referenced to the official names. Names that appear in shortened versions on the maps due to space limitations are spelled out in full in the index. The portions of these names omitted from the maps are enclosed in brackets—for example, Acapulco [de Juárez].

Transliteration For names in languages not written in the Roman alphabet, the locally official transliteration system has been used where one exists. Thus, names in the Soviet Union and Bulgaria have been transliterated according to the systems adopted by the academies of science of these countries. Similarly, the transliteration for mainland Chinese names follows the Pinyin system, which has been officially adopted in mainland China. For languages with no one locally accepted system, notably Arabic, transliteration closely follows a system adopted by the United States Board on Geographic Names.

Abbreviation and Capitalization Abbreviations of names on the maps have been standardized as much as possible. Names that are abbreviated on the maps are generally spelled out in full in the index. Periods are used after all abbreviations regardless of local practice. The abbreviation "St." is used only for "Saint". "Sankt" and other forms of this term are spelled out.

Most initial letters of names are capitalized, except for generic terms in the Soviet Union and a few Dutch names, such as "'s-Gravenhage". Capitalization of noninitial words in a name follows local practice.

Alphabetization Names are alphabetized in the order of the letters of the English alphabet. Spanish *ll* and *ch*, for example, are not treated as distinct letters. Furthermore, diacritical marks are disregarded in alphabetization—German or Scandinavian *ä* or *ö* are treated as *a* or *o*.

The names of physical features may appear inverted, since they are always alphabetized under the proper, not the generic, part of the name, thus: "Gibraltar, Strait of ꭒ". Otherwise every entry, whether consisting of one word or more, is alphabetized as a single continuous entity. "Lakeland," for example, appears after "La Crosse" and before "La Salle." Names beginning with articles (Le Havre, Den Helder, Al-Qāhirah, As-Suways) are not inverted. Names beginning "Mc" are alphabetized as though spelled "Mac," and names beginning "St.", "Ste." and "Sainte" as though spelled "Saint."

In the case of identical names, towns are listed first, then political divisions, then physical features. Entries that are completely identical (including symbols, discussed below) are distinguished by abbreviations of their official country names. The country abbreviations used for places in the United States, Canada and United Kingdom indicate the state, province or political division in which the feature is located. (See List of Abbreviations below).

Symbols City names are not followed by symbols. The names of all other features are followed by symbols that graphically represent broad categories of features, for example, ▲ for mountain (Everest, Mount ▲). Superior numbers indicate finer distinctions, for example, $\blacktriangle^{1}$ for volcano (Fuji-san $\blacktriangle^{1}$). A complete list of symbols, including those with superior numbers, follows the List of Abbreviations.

All cross-references are indicated by the symbol →.

Page References and Geographical Coordinates The geographical coordinates and page references are found in the last two columns of each entry.

The page number generally refers to the map that shows the feature at the best scale. Countries, mountain ranges and other extensive features are usually indexed to maps that both show the features completely and also show them in their relationship to broad areas. Page references to two-page maps always refer to the left-hand page. If a page contains several maps or insets, a lowercase letter identifies the specific map or inset.

Latitude and longitude coordinates for point features, such as cities and mountain peaks, indicate the locations of the symbols. For extensive areal features, such as countries or mountain ranges, locations are given for the approximate center of the feature. Those for linear features, such as canals and rivers, are given for a terminal point, for example—the mouth of a river, or the point at which the feature reaches the map margin.

List of Abbreviations

	LOCAL NAME	ENGLISH
Ab., Can.	Alberta	Alberta
Afg.	Afghānestān	Afghanistan
Afr.	. . .	Africa
Ak., U.S.	Alaska	Alaska
Al., U.S.	Alabama	Alabama
Alg.	Algérie / Djazaïr	Algeria
Am. Sam.	American Samoa / Amerika Samoa	American Samoa
And.	Andorra	Andorra
Ang.	Angola	Angola
Anguilla	Anguilla	Anguilla
Ant.	. . .	Antarctica
Antig.	Antigua and Barbuda	Antigua and Barbuda
Ar., U.S.	Arkansas	Arkansas
Arc. O.	. . .	Arctic Ocean
Arg.	Argentina	Argentina
Ar. Su.	Al-ʿArabīyah as-Suʿūdīyah	Saudi Arabia
Aruba	Aruba	Aruba
Asia	. . .	Asia
Atl. O.	. . .	Atlantic Ocean
Austl.	Australia	Australia
Az., U.S.	Arizona	Arizona
Ba.	Bahamas	Bahamas
Baḥr.	Al-Baḥrayn	Bahrain
Barb.	Barbados	Barbados
B.A.T.	British Antarctic Territory	British Antarctic Territory
B.C., Can.	British Columbia / Colombie-Britannique	British Columbia
Bdi.	Burundi	Burundi
Bel.	Belgique / België	Belgium
Belize	Belize	Belize
Bénin	Bénin	Benin
Ber.	Bermuda	Bermuda
Ber. S.	. . .	Bering Sea
B.I.O.T.	British Indian Ocean Territory	British Indian Ocean Territory
Blg.	Bâlgarija	Bulgaria
Bngl.	Bangladesh	Bangladesh
Bol.	Bolivia	Bolivia
Boph.	Bophuthatswana	Bophuthatswana
Bots.	Botswana	Botswana
Bra.	Brasil	Brazil
B.R.D.	Bundesrepublik Deutschland	Federal Republic of Germany
Bru.	Brunei	Brunei
Br. Vir. Is.	British Virgin Islands	British Virgin Islands
Burkina	Burkina Faso	Burkina Faso
Ca., U.S.	California	California
Cam.	Cameroun / Cameroon	Cameroon
Can.	Canada	Canada
Carib. S.	. . .	Caribbean Sea
Cay. Is.	Cayman Islands	Cayman Islands
Centraf.	République centrafricaine	Central African Republic
Česko.	Československo	Czechoslovakia
Chile	Chile	Chile
Christ. I.	Christmas Island	Christmas Island
Ciskei	Ciskei	Ciskei
C. Iv.	Côte d'Ivoire	Ivory Coast
C.M.I.K.	Chosŏn-minjujuŭi-inmīn-konghwaguk	North Korea
Co., U.S.	Colorado	Colorado
Cocos Is.	Cocos (Keeling) Islands	Cocos (Keeling) Islands
Col.	Colombia	Colombia
Comores	Comores / Al-Qumur	Comoros
Congo	Congo	Congo
Cook Is.	Cook Islands	Cook Islands
C.R.	Costa Rica	Costa Rica
Ct., U.S.	Connecticut	Connecticut
Cuba	Cuba	Cuba
C.V.	Cabo Verde	Cape Verde
Dan.	Danmark	Denmark
D.C., U.S.	District of Columbia	District of Columbia
D.D.R.	Deutsche Demokratische Republik	German Democratic Republic
De., U.S.	Delaware	Delaware
Dji.	Djibouti	Djibouti
Dom.	Dominica	Dominica
D.Y.	Druk-Yul	Bhutan
Ec.	Ecuador	Ecuador
Ellás	Ellás	Greece
El Sal.	El Salvador	El Salvador
Eng., U.K.	England	England
Esp.	España	Spain
Europe	. . .	Europe
Falk. Is.	Falkland Islands / Islas Malvinas	Falkland Islands
Fiji	Fiji	Fiji
Fl., U.S.	Florida	Florida
Før.	Føroyar	Faeroe Islands
Fr.	France	France
Ga., U.S.	Georgia	Georgia
Gabon	Gabon	Gabon
Gam.	Gambia	Gambia
Ghana	Ghana	Ghana
Gib.	Gibraltar	Gibraltar
Gren.	Grenada	Grenada
Guad.	Guadeloupe	Guadeloupe
Guam	Guam	Guam
Guat.	Guatemala	Guatemala
Guernsey	Guernsey	Guernsey
Gui.-B.	Guiné-Bissau	Guinea-Bissau
Gui. Ecu.	Guinea Ecuatorial	Equatorial Guinea
Guinée	Guinée	Guinea
Guy.	Guyana	Guyana
Guy. fr.	Guyane française	French Guiana
Haï.	Haïti	Haiti
Hi., U.S.	Hawaii	Hawaii
H.K.	Hong Kong	Hong Kong
Hond.	Honduras	Honduras
Ia., U.S.	Iowa	Iowa
Id., U.S.	Idaho	Idaho
I.I.A.	Ittiḥād al-Imārāt al-ʿArabīyah	United Arab Emirates
Il., U.S.	Illinois	Illinois
In., U.S.	Indiana	Indiana
India	India / Bharat	India
Ind. O.	. . .	Indian Ocean
Indon.	Indonesia	Indonesia
I. of Man	Isle of Man	Isle of Man
Īrān	Īrān	Iran
ʿIrāq	Al-ʿIrāq	Iraq
Ire.	Ireland / Éire	Ireland
Ísland	Ísland	Iceland
Isr. Occ.	. . .	Israeli Occupied Areas
It.	Italia	Italy
Ityo.	Ityopiya	Ethiopia
Jam.	Jamaica	Jamaica
Jersey	Jersey	Jersey
Jugo.	Jugoslavija	Yugoslavia
J.Y.D.S.	Jumhūrīyat al-Yaman ad-Dīmuqrāṭīyah ash-Shaʿbīyah	People's Democratic Republic of Yemen
Kal. Nun.	Kalaallit Nunaat / Grønland	Greenland
Kam.	Kâmpŭchéa Prâchéathĭpâtéyy	Kampuchea (Cambodia)
Kenya	Kenya	Kenya
Kıbrıs	Kuzey Kıbrıs	North Cyprus (Turkish Republic of Northern Cyprus)
Kípros	Kípros / Kıbrıs	Cyprus
Kiribati	Kiribati	Kiribati
Ks., U.S.	Kansas	Kansas
Kuwayt	Al-Kuwayt	Kuwait
Ky., U.S.	Kentucky	Kentucky
La., U.S.	Louisiana	Louisiana
Lao	Lao	Laos
Leso.	Lesotho	Lesotho
Liber.	Liberia	Liberia
Lībiyā	Lībiyā	Libya
Liech.	Liechtenstein	Liechtenstein
Lubnān	Al-Lubnān	Lebanon
Lux.	Luxembourg	Luxembourg
Ma., U.S.	Massachusetts	Massachusetts
Macau	Macau	Macau
Madag.	Madagasikara / Madagascar	Madagascar
Magreb	Al-Magreb	Morocco
Magy.	Magyarország	Hungary
Malaŵi	Malaŵi	Malawi
Malay.	Malaysia	Malaysia
Mald.	Maldives	Maldives
Mali	Mali	Mali
Malta	Malta	Malta
Mart.	Martinique	Martinique
Maur.	Mauritanie / Mūrītāniyā	Mauritania
Maus.	Mauritius	Mauritius
Mayotte	Mayotte	Mayotte
Mb., Can.	Manitoba	Manitoba
Md., U.S.	Maryland	Maryland
Me., U.S.	Maine	Maine
Medit. S.	. . .	Mediterranean Sea
Méx.	México	Mexico
Mi., U.S.	Michigan	Michigan
Mid. Is.	Midway Islands	Midway Islands
Miṣr	Miṣr	Egypt
Mn., U.S.	Minnesota	Minnesota
Mo., U.S.	Missouri	Missouri
Moç.	Moçambique	Mozambique
Monaco	Monaco	Monaco
Mong.	Mongol Ard Uls	Mongolia
Monts.	Montserrat	Montserrat
Ms., U.S.	Mississippi	Mississippi
Mt., U.S.	Montana	Montana
Mya.	Myanmā	Burma
N.A.	. . .	North America
Namibia	Namibia	Namibia
Nauru	Nauru / Naoero	Nauru
N.B., Can.	New Brunswick / Nouveau-Brunswick	New Brunswick
N.C., U.S.	North Carolina	North Carolina
N. Cal.	Nouvelle-Calédonie	New Caledonia
N.D., U.S.	North Dakota	North Dakota
Ne., U.S.	Nebraska	Nebraska
Ned.	Nederland	Netherlands
Ned. Ant.	Nederlandse Antillen	Netherlands Antilles
Nepāl	Nepāl	Nepal
Nf., Can.	Newfoundland / Terre-Neuve	Newfoundland
N.H., U.S.	New Hampshire	New Hampshire
Nic.	Nicaragua	Nicaragua
Nig.	Nigeria	Nigeria
Niger	Niger	Niger
Nihon	Nihon	Japan
N. Ire., U.K.	Northern Ireland	Northern Ireland
Niue	Niue	Niue
N.J., U.S.	New Jersey	New Jersey
N.M., U.S.	New Mexico	New Mexico
Nor.	Norge	Norway
Norf. I.	Norfolk Island	Norfolk Island
N.S., Can.	Nova Scotia / Nouvelle-Écosse	Nova Scotia
N.T., Can.	Northwest Territories / Territoires du Nord-Ouest	Northwest Territories
Nv., U.S.	Nevada	Nevada
N.Y., U.S.	New York	New York
N.Z.	New Zealand	New Zealand
Oc.	. . .	Oceania
Oh., U.S.	Ohio	Ohio
Ok., U.S.	Oklahoma	Oklahoma
On., Can.	Ontario	Ontario
Or., U.S.	Oregon	Oregon
Öst.	Österreich	Austria
Pa., U.S.	Pennsylvania	Pennsylvania
Pac. O.	. . .	Pacific Ocean
Pāk.	Pākistān	Pakistan
Pan.	Panamá	Panama
Pap. N. Gui.	Papua New Guinea	Papua New Guinea
Para.	Paraguay	Paraguay
P.E., Can.	Prince Edward Island / Île-du-Prince-Édouard	Prince Edward Island
Perú	Perú	Peru
Pil.	Pilipinas	Philippines
Pit.	Pitcairn	Pitcairn
Pol.	Polska	Poland
Poly. fr.	Polynésie française	French Polynesia
Port.	Portugal	Portugal
P.Q., Can.	Québec	Quebec
P.R.	Puerto Rico	Puerto Rico
P.S.N.Á.	Plazas de Soberanía en el Norte de África	Spanish North Africa
Qaṭar	Qaṭar	Qatar
Rep. Dom.	República Dominicana	Dominican Republic
Réu.	Réunion	Reunion
R.I., U.S.	Rhode Island	Rhode Island
Rom.	România	Romania
Rw.	Rwanda	Rwanda
S.A.	. . .	South America
S. Afr.	South Africa / Suid-Afrika	South Africa
S.C., U.S.	South Carolina	South Carolina
S. Ch. S.	. . .	South China Sea
Schw.	Schweiz / Suisse / Svizzera	Switzerland
Scot., U.K.	Scotland	Scotland
S.D., U.S.	South Dakota	South Dakota
Sén.	Sénégal	Senegal
Sey.	Seychelles	Seychelles
Shq.	Shqipëri	Albania
Sing.	Singapore	Singapore
Sk., Can.	Saskatchewan	Saskatchewan
S.L.	Sierra Leone	Sierra Leone
S. Lan.	Sri Lanka	Sri Lanka
S. Mar.	San Marino	San Marino
Sol. Is.	Solomon Islands	Solomon Islands
Som.	Somaliya	Somalia
S.S.S.R.	Sojuz Sovetskich Socialističeskich Respublik	Union of Soviet Socialist Republics
St. C.-N.	St. Christopher-Nevis	St. Christopher-Nevis
St. Hel.	St. Helena	St. Helena
St. Luc.	St. Lucia	St. Lucia
S. Tom./P.	São Tomé e Príncipe	Sao Tome and Principe
St. P./M.	St.-Pierre-et-Miquelon	St. Pierre and Miquelon
St. Vin.	St. Vincent and the Grenadines	St. Vincent and the Grenadines
Sūd.	As-Sūdān	Sudan
Suomi	Suomi / Finland	Finland
Sur.	Suriname	Suriname
Sūrīy.	As-Sūrīyah	Syria
Sve.	Sverige	Sweden
Swaz.	Swaziland	Swaziland
T.a.a.f.	Terres australes et antarctiques françaises	French Southern and Antarctic Territories
Taehan	Taehan-min'guk	South Korea
T'aiwan	T'aiwan	Taiwan
Tan.	Tanzania	Tanzania
Tchad	Tchad	Chad
T./C. Is.	Turks and Caicos Islands	Turks and Caicos Islands
Thai	Prathet Thai	Thailand
Tn., U.S.	Tennessee	Tennessee
Togo	Togo	Togo
Tok.	Tokelau	Tokelau
Tonga	Tonga	Tonga
Transkei	Transkei	Transkei
Trin.	Trinidad and Tobago	Trinidad and Tobago
T.T.P.I.	Trust Territory of the Pacific Islands	Trust Territory of the Pacific Islands
Tun.	Tunisie / Tunis	Tunisia

List of Abbreviations (continued)

Tür.	Türkiye	Turkey	**Va., U.S.**	Virginia	Virginia	**Wa., U.S.**	Washington	Washington	
Tuvalu	Tuvalu	Tuvalu	**Vanuatu**	Vanuatu	Vanuatu	**Wake I.**	Wake Island	Wake Island	
Tx., U.S.	Texas	Texas	**Vat.**	Città del Vaticano	Vatican City	**Wales,**	Wales	Wales	
Ug.	Uganda	Uganda	**Ven.**	Venezuela	Venezuela	**U.K.**			
U.K.	United Kingdom	United Kingdom	**Venda**	Venda	Venda	**Wal./F.**	Wallis et Futuna	Wallis and Futuna	
'Umān	'Umān	Oman	**Viet.**	Viet-nam	Vietnam	**Wi., U.S.**	Wisconsin	Wisconsin	
Ur.	Uruguay	Uruguay	**Vir. Is.,**	Virgin Islands (U.S.)	Virgin Islands (U.S.)	**W. Sah.**	. . .	Western Sahara	
Urd.	Al-Urdunn	Jordan	**U.S.**			**W. Sam.**	Western Samoa /	Western Samoa	
U.S.	United States	United States	**Vt., U.S.**	Vermont	Vermont		Samoa i Sisifo		
Ut., U.S.	Utah	Utah							

W.V., U.S.	West Virginia	West Virginia
Wy., U.S.	Wyoming	Wyoming
Yaman	Al-Yaman	Yemen
Yis.	Yisra'el / Isrā'īl	Israel
Yk., Can.	Yukon Territory	Yukon
Zaïre	Zaïre	Zaire
Zam.	Zambia	Zambia
Zhg.	Zhongguo	China
Zimb.	Zimbabwe	Zimbabwe

Key to Symbols

ʌ	**Mountain**	⪢¹ Peninsula	±⁴ Cliff	ᴄ **Bay, Gulf**	⊤² Sea
ʌ¹	Volcano	⪢² Spit, Sand Bar	±⁵ Cave, Caves	ᴄ¹ Estuary	⊤³ Anchorage
ʌ²	Hill	I Island	±⁶ Crater	ᴄ² Fjord	⊤⁴ Oasis, Well, Spring
⋋¹	**Mountains**	I¹ Atoll	±⁷ Depression	ᴄ³ Bight	**Submarine**
⋋¹	Plateau	I² Rock	±⁸ Dunes	⊘ **Lake, Lakes**	**Features**
⋋²	Hills	II¹ Rocks	±⁹ Lava Flow	⊘¹ Reservoir	⊤¹ Depression
)(	**Pass**	⊥ **Other Topographic**	≃ **River**	⊞ Swamp	⊤² Reef, Shoal
V	**Valley, Canyon**	**Features**	≃¹ River Channel	⋈ **Ice Features,**	⊤³ Mountain,
⪥	**Plain**	⊥¹ Continent	⊠ Canal	**Glacier**	Mountains
⪥¹	Basin	⊥² Coast, Beach	⊠¹ Aqueduct	⊤ **Other Hydrographic**	⊤⁴ Slope, Shelf
⪥²	Delta	⊥³ Isthmus	∟ **Waterfall, Rapids**	**Features**	
⪢	**Cape**		⋓ **Strait**	⊤¹ Ocean	

□¹ Independent Nation	□⁹ Historical	✦ **Miscellaneous**
□² Dependency	♥¹ **Cultural Institution**	✦¹ Region
□³ State, Canton,	♥¹ Religious Institution	✦² Desert
Republic	♥² Educational	✦³ Forest, Moor
□⁴ Province, Region,	Institution	✦⁴ Reserve,
Oblast	♥³ Scientific, Industrial	Reservation
□⁵ Department, District,	Facility	✦⁵ Transportation
Prefecture	♦ **Historical Site**	✦⁶ Dam
□⁶ County	♦ **Recreational Site**	✦⁷ Mine, Quarry
□⁷ City, Municipality	⊠ **Airport**	✦⁸ Neighborhood
□ **Political Unit**	□⁸ Miscellaneous	■ **Military Installation**	✦⁹ Shopping Center

INDEX

Name	Page	Lat.	Long.
A			
Aachen	30	50.47N	6.05 E
Aaiun			
→ El Aaiún	82	27.09N	13.12W
Aalen	30	48.50N	10.05 E
Aalst	30	50.56N	4.02 E
Aarau	36	47.23N	8.03 E
Aare ≃	36	47.37N	8.13 E
Aarschot	30	50.59N	4.50 E
Aazanén	44	35.13N	3.10W
Aba	82	5.06N	7.21 E
Abacaxis ≃	118	3.54S	58.47W
Ábādān	70	30.20N	48.16 E
Abaj	54	49.38N	72.52 E
Abajo Peak ʌ	148	37.51N	109.28W
Abakan	56	53.43N	91.26 E
Abancay	118	13.35S	72.55W
Abaya, Lake ⊘	84	6.20N	37.55 E
Abbekās	22	55.24N	13.36 E
Abbeville, Fr.	36	50.06N	1.50 E
Abbeville, La., U.S.	144	29.58N	92.08W
Abbeville, Ms., U.S.	144	34.30N	89.30W
Abbeville, S.C., U.S.	142	34.10N	82.22W
Abbiategrasso	40	45.24N	8.54 E
Abbotsford	138	44.56N	90.18W
Abbottābād	70	34.09N	73.13 E
'Abd al-Kūrī I	70	12.12N	52.15 E
Abe, Lake ⊘	84	11.06N	41.50 E
Abéché	84	13.49N	20.49 E
Abéjar	44	41.48N	2.47W
Abengourou	82	6.44N	3.29W
Abenrá	22	55.02N	9.26 E
Abensberg	30	48.49N	11.51 E
Abeokuta	82	7.10N	3.26 E
Aberdare	26	51.43N	3.27W
Aberdeen, Scot., U.K.	26	57.10N	2.04W
Aberdeen, Id., U.S.	150	42.56N	112.50W
Aberdeen, Md., U.S.	136	39.30N	76.09W
Aberdeen, Ms., U.S.	144	33.49N	88.32W
Aberdeen, N.C., U.S.	142	35.07N	79.25W
Aberdeen, S.D., U.S.	132	45.27N	98.29W
Aberdeen, Wa., U.S.	150	46.58N	123.48W
Aberdeen Lake ⊘¹	144	33.55N	88.30W
Abert, Lake ⊘	150	42.38N	120.13W
Aberystwyth	26	52.25N	4.05W
Abetone	40	44.08N	10.40 E
Abhā	70	18.13N	42.30 E
Abidjan	82	5.19N	4.02W
Abilene	132	32.26N	99.43W
Abingdon, Il., U.S.	138	40.48N	90.24W
Abingdon, Va., U.S.	142	36.42N	81.58W
Abiquiu	148	36.12N	106.19W
Abisko	20	68.20N	18.51 E
Abita Springs	144	30.28N	90.02W
Abitau ≃	130	59.53N	109.03W
Abitibi ≃	130	51.03N	80.55W
Abitibi, Lake ⊘	138	48.42N	79.45W
Abiyata, Lake ⊘	84	7.37N	38.36 E
Abomey	82	7.11N	1.59 E
Abongabong, Gunung ʌ	68	4.15N	96.48 E
Abony	30	47.11N	20.01 E
Aborigen, pik ʌ	56	61.59N	149.19 E
Abraham Lincoln Birthplace National Historic Site ♦	144	37.32N	85.44W
Abrantes	44	39.28N	8.12W
Abra Pampa	120	22.43S	65.42W
Abrud	48	46.17N	23.04 E
Absaroka Range ⋋¹	150	44.45N	109.50W
Absarokee	150	45.31N	109.26W
Absecon	136	39.25N	74.29W
Abtenau	30	47.33N	13.21 E
Abū 'Alī I	70	27.20N	49.33 E
Abu Dhabi			
→ Abū Zaby	70	24.28N	54.22 E
Abū Hamad	84	19.32N	33.19 E
Abū Kamāl	70	34.27N	40.55 E
Abū Madd, Ra's ⪢	70	24.50N	37.07 E
Abū Mūsá, Jazīreh-ye I	70	25.52N	55.03 E
Abuná (Abunã) ≃	118	9.41S	65.23W
Abū Shajarah, Ra's ⪢	84	21.04N	37.14 E
Abū Zaby (Abu Dhabi)	70	24.28N	54.22 E
Acadia National Park ♦	136	44.18N	68.15W
Acajutla	108	13.36N	89.50W
Acámbaro	108	20.02N	100.44W
Acapulco [de Juárez]	108	16.51N	99.55W
Acaraí Mountains ⋋¹			
Acarigua	118	9.33N	69.12W
Acay, Nevado de ʌ	120	24.21S	66.12W
Accomac	142	37.43N	75.39W

Name	Page	Lat.	Long.
Accoville	142	37.46N	81.50W
Accra	82	5.33N	0.13W
Acerra	40	40.57N	14.22 E
Achalpur	70	21.16N	77.31 E
Achill Head ⪢	26	53.59N	10.13W
Achill Island I	26	54.00N	10.00W
Achtuba ≃	54	46.42N	48.00 E
Achtubinsk	54	48.17N	46.10 E
Adinsk	56	56.17N	90.30 E
Acipayam	48	37.25N	29.22 E
Acireale	40	37.37N	15.10 E
Ackley	138	42.33N	93.03W
Acklins Island I	108	22.26N	73.58W
Aconcagua, Cerro ʌ	120	32.39S	70.01W
Açores (Azores) II	8	38.30N	28.00W
Acqui Terme	40	44.41N	8.28 E
Acre □³	118	8.45S	67.22W
Acri	40	39.29N	16.23 E
Acworth	142	34.03N	84.40W
Ada, Oh., U.S.	136	40.46N	83.49W
Ada, Ok., U.S.	132	34.46N	96.40W
Adair	144	36.26N	95.16W
Adairsville	142	34.22N	84.56W
Adairville	144	36.40N	86.51W
Adamaoua ⋋¹	82	7.00N	12.00 E
Adamello ʌ	40	46.10N	10.35 E
Adams, Ma., U.S.	136	42.37N	73.07W
Adams, Mn., U.S.	138	43.33N	92.43W
Adams, N.Y., U.S.	136	43.48N	76.01W
Adams, Tn., U.S.	144	36.34N	87.03W
Adams, Wi., U.S.	138	43.57N	89.49W
Adams, Mount ʌ	150	46.12N	121.28W
Adams Bridge ⪢²	70	9.04N	79.37 E
Adams Peak ʌ	70	6.48N	80.30 E
Adamsville	144	35.14N	88.23W
'Adan (Aden)	70	12.45N	45.12 E
Adana	16	37.01N	35.18 E
Adapazarı	16	40.46N	30.24 E
Ad-Dabbah	84	18.03N	30.57 E
Ad-Dahnā' ✦²	70	24.30N	48.10 E
Ad-Dāmir	84	17.35N	33.58 E
Ad-Dammām	70	26.26N	50.07 E
Ad-Dawādimī	70	24.28N	44.18 E
Ad-Dawhah (Doha)	70	25.17N	51.32 E
Addis Abeba	84	30.21N	91.15W
→ Ādīs Ābeba	84	9.02N	38.42 E
Addison	138	41.59N	84.21W
Ad-Dīwānīyah	70	31.59N	44.56 E
Adel, Ga., U.S.	142	31.08N	83.25W
Adel, Ia., U.S.	138	41.36N	94.01W
Adelaide, Austl.	96	34.55S	138.35 E
Adelaide, Ba.	108	25.00N	77.31W
Adelaide Peninsula ⪢¹	130	68.09N	97.45W
Aden → 'Adan	70	12.45N	45.12 E
Aden, Gulf of ᴄ	84	12.30N	48.00 E
Adieu, Cape ⪢	96	31.59S	132.09 E
Adige ≃	40	45.10N	12.20 E
Adigrat	84	14.17N	39.28 E
Adirondack Mountains ⋋¹	136	44.00N	74.00W
Ādīs Ābeba (Addis Ababa)	84	9.02N	38.42 E
Admiralty Inlet ᴄ	130	73.00N	86.00W
Admiralty Islands II	96a	2.10S	147.00 E
Ādoni	70	15.38N	77.17 E
Adour ≃	36	43.32N	1.32W
Adra	44	36.44N	3.01W
Adrano	40	37.40N	14.50 E
Adrār □⁴	82	20.30N	13.30W
Adria	40	45.03N	12.03 E
Adrian, Ga., U.S.	142	32.31N	82.35W
Adrian, Mi., U.S.	138	41.53N	84.02W
Adrian, Mn., U.S.	138	43.38N	95.56W
Adrian, Or., U.S.	150	43.44N	117.04W
Adrian, W.V., U.S.	136	38.54N	80.16W
Adrianople → Edirne	16	41.40N	26.34 E
Adriatic Sea ⊤²	16	42.30N	16.00 E
Advance	144	37.06N	89.54W
Adwa	84	14.10N	38.55 E
Aegean Sea ⊤²	16	38.30N	25.00 E
Aegina → Áiyina I	48	37.45N	23.26 E
Ærø I	22	54.53N	10.20 E
Affton	144	38.33N	90.19W
Afghanistan (Afghānestān) □¹	70	33.00N	65.00 E
Afgooye	84	2.09N	45.07 E
Afikpo	82	5.53N	7.56 E
Africa ±¹	8	10.00N	22.00 E
Afton, Ia., U.S.	138	41.01N	94.11W
Afton, N.Y., U.S.	136	42.13N	75.31W
Afton, Wy., U.S.	150	42.43N	110.55W
Afyon	16	38.45N	30.33 E
Agadez	82	16.58N	7.59 E
Agadir	82	30.26N	9.36W
Agalega Islands II	8	10.25S	56.40 E
Agana	68	13.28N	144.45 E
Agartala	70	23.49N	91.16 E
Agate Beach	150	44.40N	124.03W
Agawa Canyon V	138	47.24N	84.29W
Agboville	82	5.56N	4.13W
Agde	36	43.19N	3.28 E

Name	Page	Lat.	Long.
Agde, Cap d' ⪢	36	43.16N	3.30 E
Agen	36	44.12N	0.37 E
Agency	138	40.59N	92.18W
Agency Lake ⊘	150	42.32N	121.58W
Aggteleki Barlang ±⁵	30	48.30N	20.32 E
Āghā Jārī	70	30.42N	49.50 E
Agly ≃	36	42.47N	3.02 E
Ågra	70	27.11N	78.01 E
Ágreda	44	41.51N	1.56W
Agri ≃	40	40.13N	16.44 E
Agri Bavnehøj ʌ²	22	56.14N	10.33 E
Agrigento	40	37.18N	13.35 E
Agrínion	48	38.37N	21.24 E
Agro Pontino ✦¹	40	41.25N	12.55 E
Agryz	20	56.33N	53.00 E
Aguadas	118	5.37N	75.27W
Agua Fria ≃	148	33.23N	112.21W
Aguarico ≃	118	0.59S	75.11W
Aguascalientes	108	21.53N	102.18W
Águeda ≃	44	41.02N	6.56W
Aguilar	44	37.31N	4.39W
Águilas	44	37.24N	1.35W
Agulhas, Cape ⪢	86	34.52S	20.00 E
Agusan ≃	68	9.00N	125.31 E
Ahaggar ⋋¹	82	23.00N	6.30 E
Ahaggar, Tassili ta-n- ⋋¹	82	21.00N	6.00 E
Ahfir	44	34.57N	2.17W
Ahipara Bay ᴄ	98	35.10S	173.07 E
Ahlen	30	51.46N	7.53 E
Ahmadābād	70	23.02N	72.37 E
Ahmadnagar	70	19.05N	74.44 E
Ahmar Mountains ⋋¹	84	9.15N	41.00 E
Ahoskie	142	36.17N	76.59W
Ahrensburg	30	53.40N	10.14 E
Ahtopol	48	42.06N	27.57 E
Ahväz	70	31.19N	48.42 E
Aigre	36	45.54N	0.01 E
Aiguilles	36	44.47N	6.52 E
Aihui	66	50.16N	127.28 E
Aiken	142	33.33N	81.43W
Ailán Arnat	44	36.11N	5.19 E
Ainaži	22	57.52N	24.21 E
Aïn Berda	44	36.39N	7.35 E
Aïn el Hadjel	44	35.40N	3.53 E
Aïn Touta	44	35.23N	5.54 E
Aïr ⋋¹	82	18.00N	8.30 E
Aire	36	43.42N	0.16W
Aisch ≃	30	49.46N	11.01 E
Aishihik Lake ⊘	130	61.25N	137.06W
Aisne ≃	36	49.26N	2.50 E
Aitkin	138	46.31N	93.42W
Ait Youssef ou Ali	44	35.13N	3.55W
Aix-en-Provence	36	43.32N	5.26 E
Aix-la-Chapelle → Aachen	30	50.47N	6.05 E
Aix-les-Bains	36	45.42N	5.55 E
Aiyina I	48	37.46N	23.26 E
Aíyion	48	38.15N	22.05 E
Aizpute	22	56.43N	21.38 E
Aizu-wakamatsu	66	37.30N	139.56 E
Ajaccio	40	41.55N	8.44 E
Ajaguz	54	47.56N	80.23 E
Ajanta Range ⋋¹	70	20.30N	76.00 E
Ajdābiyā	84	30.48N	20.14 E
Ajdovščina	40	45.53N	13.53 E
Ajjer, Tassili-n-			
Ajka	30	47.07N	17.34 E
Ajmer	70	26.27N	74.38 E
Ajo	148	32.22N	112.51W
Ajo, Cabo de ⪢	44	43.31N	3.35W
Ajtos	48	42.42N	27.15 E
Akademii, zaliv ᴄ	56	54.15N	138.05 E
Akaroa Harbour ᴄ	98	43.50S	172.56 E
'Akasha East	84	21.05N	30.43 E
Akçay ≃	48	37.50N	28.15 E
Aken	30	51.51N	12.02 E
Aketi	84	2.44N	23.46 E
Akharnai	48	38.05N	23.44 E
Akhdar, Al-Jabal al- ⋋¹	70	23.15N	57.20 E
Akhisar	16	38.55N	27.51 E
Akimiski Island I	130	53.00N	81.20W
Akita	66	39.43N	140.07 E
'Akko	70	32.55N	35.05 E
Aklavik	130	68.14N	135.00W
Akobo (Ākūbū) ≃	84	7.47N	33.03 E
Akola	70	20.44N	77.00 E
Akordat	84	15.33N	37.53 E
Akranes	20a	64.18N	22.02W
Akritas, Ákra ⪢	48	36.43N	21.54 E
Akron, In., U.S.	144	41.02N	86.01W
Akron, N.Y., U.S.	136	43.01N	78.29W
Akron, Oh., U.S.	136	41.04N	81.31W
Akron, Pa., U.S.	136	40.09N	76.12W
Aksu	54	50.17N	57.10 E
Akt'ubinsk	54	50.17N	57.10 E
Ākūbū (Akobo) ≃	84	7.47N	33.03 E
Akureyri	20a	65.44N	18.08W
Alabama □³	132	32.50N	87.00W
Alabama ≃	144	31.08N	87.57W
Alabaster	144	33.14N	86.48W
Alaçam Dağları ⋋¹	48	39.45N	28.58 E
Alacant	44	38.21N	0.29W
Alachua	142	29.47N	82.29W

Name	Page	Lat.	Long.
Alagoinhas	118	12.07S	38.26W
Alaior	44	39.56N	4.08 E
Alajskij chrebet ⋋¹	54	39.45N	72.00 E
Al-'Alamayn	84	30.49N	28.57 E
Al-'Amārah	70	31.50N	47.09 E
Alameda, Ca., U.S.	154	37.45N	122.14W
Alameda, N.M., U.S.	148	35.11N	106.37W
Alamein → Al-'Alamayn	84	30.49N	28.57 E
Alamo, Ga., U.S.	142	32.08N	82.46W
Alamo, Nv., U.S.	154	37.21N	115.09W
Alamo, Tn., U.S.	144	35.47N	89.07W
Alamogordo	148	32.53N	105.57W
Alamo Lake ⊘¹	148	34.20N	113.30W
Alamosa	148	37.28N	105.52W
Åland (Ahvenanmaa)	22	60.15N	20.00 E
Ålands hav ⊤²	22	60.00N	19.30 E
Alaotra, Lac ⊘	86	17.30S	48.30 E
Alapaha	142	31.23N	83.13W
Alapaha ≃	142	30.26N	83.06W
Alapajevsk	54	57.52N	61.42 E
Al-'Aqabah	70	29.31N	35.00 E
Alarcón, Embalse de ⊘¹	44	39.36N	2.10W
Al-'Arīsh	84	31.08N	33.48 E
Alaşehir	48	38.21N	28.32 E
Alaska □³	132a	65.00N	153.00W
Alaska, Gulf of ᴄ	132a	58.00N	146.00W
Alaska Peninsula ⪢¹	132a	57.00N	158.00W
Alaska Range ⋋	132a	62.30N	150.00W
Alatri	40	41.43N	13.21 E
Alatyr'	20	54.51N	46.36 E
Alausí	118	2.12S	78.50W
Alava, Cape ⪢	150	48.10N	124.43W
Alavus	22	62.35N	23.37 E
Alba, It.	40	44.42N	8.02 E
Albacete	44	38.59N	1.51W
Alba Iulia	48	46.04N	23.35 E
Alban	36	43.54N	2.28 E
Albanel, Lac ⊘	130	50.55N	73.12W
Albania (Shqipëri) □¹	16	41.00N	20.00 E
Albano Laziale	40	41.44N	12.39 E
Albany, Austl.	96	35.02S	117.53 E
Albany, Ga., U.S.	142	31.34N	84.09W
Albany, In., U.S.	144	40.18N	85.14W
Albany, Mn., U.S.	138	45.37N	94.34W
Albany, Mo., U.S.	144	40.14N	94.19W
Albany, N.Y., U.S.	136	42.39N	73.45W
Albany, Oh., U.S.	136	39.13N	82.12W
Albany, Or., U.S.	150	44.38N	123.06W
Albany, Wi., U.S.	138	42.42N	89.26W
Albany ≃	130	52.17N	81.31W
Albarracín	44	40.25N	1.26W
Al-Başrah	70	30.30N	47.47 E
Albatross Point ⪢	98	38.06S	174.41 E
Al-Bawītī	84	28.21N	28.52 E
Al-Baydā'	84	32.46N	21.43 E
Albemarle	142	35.20N	80.13W
Albemarle Sound ⋓	142	36.03N	76.12W
Albenga	40	44.03N	8.13 E
Alberga Creek ≃	96	27.06S	135.33 E
Albert, Fr.	36	50.00N	2.39 E
Albert, Lake ⊘	86	1.40N	31.00 E
Alberta □⁴	144	32.13N	87.24W
Alberta □⁴	130	54.00N	113.00W
Albertirsa	30	47.15N	19.38 E
Albert Lea	138	43.38N	93.22W
Albert Nile ≃	86	3.36N	32.02 E
Albertville, Fr.	36	45.41N	6.23 E
Albertville, Al., U.S.	144	34.16N	86.12W
Albertville → Kalemie, Zaïre	86	5.56S	29.12 E
Albi	36	43.56N	2.09 E
Albia	138	41.01N	92.48W
Albina	118	5.30N	54.03W
Albino	40	45.46N	9.47 E
Albion, In., U.S.	144	41.23N	85.25W
Albion, Mi., U.S.	138	42.06N	92.59W
Albion, Ne., U.S.	138	41.41N	98.00W
Albion, N.Y., U.S.	136	43.14N	78.11W
Albion, Pa., U.S.	136	41.53N	80.22W
Ålborg	22	57.03N	9.56 E
Ålborg Bugt ᴄ	22	56.45N	10.30 E
Alborz, Reshteh-ye Kūhhā-ye ⋋¹	70	36.00N	53.00 E
Albuquerque	148	35.05N	106.39W
Alburg	136	44.59N	73.18W
Alburquerque	44	39.13N	7.00W
Alcalá de Guadaira	44	37.20N	5.50W
Alcalá de Henares	44	40.29N	3.22W
Alcamo	40	37.59N	12.58 E
Alcanar	44	40.33N	0.28 E
Alcántara, Embalse de ⊘¹	44	39.45N	6.25W
Alcantarilla	44	37.58N	1.13W
Alcaraz	44	38.40N	2.29W

Name	Page	Lat.	Long.
Alcázar de San Juan	44	39.24N	3.12W
Alcoa	142	35.47N	83.58W
Alcobendas	44	40.32N	3.38W
Alcoi	44	38.42N	0.28W
Alconchel	142	33.45N	80.12W
Alcorn	144	31.52N	91.09W
Alcoutim	44	37.28N	7.28W
Alcúdia, Badia d' ᴄ	44	39.48N	3.13 E
Aldabra Island I	86	9.25S	46.22 E
Aldan	56	58.37N	125.24 E
Aldan ≃	56	63.28N	129.35 E
Aldanskoje nagorje ⋋¹	56	57.00N	127.00 E
Alde ≃	26	52.03N	1.28 E
Alderney I	26	49.43N	2.12W
Aldershot	26	51.15N	0.47W
Aledo	138	41.11N	90.44W
Aleg	82	17.03N	13.55W
Alegrete	120	29.46S	55.46W
Alejandro Selkirk, Isla (Isla Más Afuera) I	120	33.45S	80.46W
Aleksandrov	20	56.24N	38.43 E
Aleksandrovsk-Sachalinskij	56	50.54N	142.10 E
Aleksin	54	54.31N	37.05 E
Aleksinac	48	43.32N	21.43 E
Alençon	36	48.26N	0.05 E
Alentejo □⁹	44	38.00N	8.00W
Alès	36	44.08N	4.05 E
Alessandria	40	44.54N	8.37 E
Alessano	40	39.53N	18.20 E
Ålesund	22	62.28N	6.09 E
Aleutian Islands II	132a	53.00N	166.00 E
Alevina, mys ⪢	56	58.50N	151.20 E
Alexander, Cape ⪢	54	6.35S	156.30 E
Alexander City	144	32.56N	85.57W
Alexandra	98	45.15S	169.24 E
Alexandra Falls ∟	130	60.29N	116.18W
Alexandretta, Gulf of → İskenderun Körfezi ᴄ	16	36.30N	35.40 E
Alexandria, On., Can.	136	45.19N	74.38W
Alexandria → Al-Iskandarīyah, Misr	84	31.12N	29.54 E
Alexandria, Rom.	48	43.58N	25.20 E
Alexandria, In., U.S.	144	40.14N	94.19W
Alexandria, Ky., U.S.	136	38.57N	84.23W
Alexandria, La., U.S.	144	31.18N	92.26W
Alexandria, Mo., U.S.	144	40.21N	91.27W
Alexandria, Tn., U.S.	144	36.04N	86.02W
Al-Iskandarīyah (Alexandria)	84	31.12N	29.54 E
Alexandria Bay	136	44.20N	75.55W
Alexandrina, Lake ⊘	96	35.26S	139.10 E
Alexandroúpolis	48	40.50N	25.52 E
Alfaro, Ec.	118	2.12S	79.50W
Alfaro, Esp.	44	42.11N	1.45W
Al-Fāshir	84	13.38N	25.21 E
Al-Fayyūm	84	29.19N	30.50 E
Alfeld	30	51.59N	9.50 E
Alfold ±	30	47.00N	20.00 E
Alfred, Me., U.S.	136	43.28N	70.43W
Alfred, N.Y., U.S.	136	42.15N	77.47W
Al-Fuhayhil	70	29.05N	48.08 E
Algeciras	44	36.08N	5.30W
Algemesi	44	39.11N	0.26W
Alger	108	40.42N	83.50W
Alger, Baie d' ᴄ	44	36.50N	3.15 E
Algeria (Algérie) □¹	82	28.00N	3.00 E
Al-Ghaydah	70	16.12N	52.15 E
Alghero	40	40.34N	8.19 E
Algiers → El Djazaïr	82	36.47N	3.03 E
Algoma	138	44.36N	87.25W
Algona, Ia., U.S.	138	43.04N	94.13W
Algona, Wa., U.S.	150	47.16N	122.15W
Algonac	138	42.37N	82.31W
Algonquin	138	42.10N	88.17W
Alhama de Murcia	44	37.51N	1.25W
Al-Harūj al-Aswad ⋋²	84	27.00N	17.10 E
Al-Hillah	70	32.29N	44.25 E
Al-Hoceïma	44	35.15N	3.55W
Al-Hoceïma, Baie d' ᴄ	44	35.23N	3.50W
Alhucemas, Peñón de ⪢	44	35.13N	3.53W
Al-Hufūf	70	25.22N	49.34 E

Name	Page	Lat.	Long.
Aliákmon ≃	48	40.30N	22.36 E
Alicante → Alacant	44	38.21N	0.29W
Alice	132	27.45N	98.04W
Alice, Punta ⪢	40	39.24N	17.10 E
Alice Springs	96	23.42S	133.53 E
Alice Town	142	25.44N	79.17W
Aliceville	144	33.07N	88.09W
Alīcudi, Isola I	40	38.32N	14.21 E
Aligarh	70	27.53N	78.05 E
Al-Ikhwān II	70	12.09N	53.12 E
Alima ≃	86	1.36S	16.36 E
Alingsås	22	57.56N	12.31 E
Aliquippa	136	40.38N	80.14W
Al-Iskandarīyah (Alexandria)	84	31.12N	29.54 E
Al-Ismā'īlīyah	84	30.35N	32.16 E
Al-Jaghbūb	84	29.45N	24.31 E
Al-Jawf, Ar. Su.	70	29.50N	39.52 E
Al-Jawf, Lībiyā	84	24.11N	23.19 E
Al-Jazīrah ✦¹	84	14.25N	33.00 E
Al-Jīzah	84	30.01N	31.13 E
Al-Junaynah	84	13.27N	22.27 E
Al-Khābūrah	70	31.32N	35.06 E
Al-Khandaq	84	18.36N	30.34 E
Al-Khartūm (Khartoum)	84	15.36N	32.32 E
Al-Khasab	70	26.11N	56.15 E
Al-Khubar	70	26.17N	50.12 E
Al-Khums	84	32.39N	14.16 E
Alkmaar	30	52.37N	4.44 E
Al-Kuwayt	70	29.20N	47.59 E
Al-Lādhiqīyah	70	35.31N	35.47 E
Allāhābād	70	25.27N	81.51 E
Allariz	44	42.11N	7.48W
Allatoona Lake ⊘¹	142	34.08N	84.38W
Allegan	138	42.31N	85.51W
Allegany	136	42.05N	78.29W
Allegheny ≃	136	40.27N	80.00W
Allegheny Mountains ⋋¹	136	38.30N	80.00W
Allegheny Plateau ⋋¹	136	41.30N	78.00W
Allegheny Reservoir ⊘¹	136	41.50N	78.56W
Allemands, Lac Des ⊘	144	29.55N	90.35W
Allen, Lough ⊘	26	54.08N	8.08W
Allendale	142	33.00N	81.18W
Allenstein → Olsztyn	30	53.48N	20.29 E
Allentown	136	40.36N	75.28W
Alleppey	70	9.29N	76.20 E
Aller ≃	30	52.57N	9.11 E
Allevard	36	45.24N	6.04 E
Allgäu ⪥¹	30	47.35N	10.10 E
Allgäuer Alpen ⋋	36	47.20N	10.25 E
Alliance, Ne., U.S.	132	42.12N	102.58W
Alliance, Oh., U.S.	136	40.54N	81.06W
Al-Lidām	70	20.29N	44.50 E
Allier ≃	36	46.58N	3.04 E
Al-Līth	70	20.09N	40.16 E
Allouez	138	46.07N	3.49W
Al-Luhayyah	70	15.42N	42.42 E
Allumettes, Île des I	136	45.50N	77.05W
Allyn	150	47.23N	122.49W
Alma, P.Q., Can.	142	31.32N	82.27W
Alma, Mi., U.S.	138	43.22N	84.39W
Alma-Ata	54	43.15N	76.57 E
Almada	44	38.41N	9.09W
Almadén	44	38.46N	4.50W
Al-Madīnah (Medina)	70	24.28N	39.36 E
Al-Mahallah al-Kubrā	84	30.58N	31.10 E
Almalyk	54	40.50N	69.35 E
Al-Manāmah	70	26.13N	50.35 E
Almansa	44	38.52N	1.05W
Almanor, Lake ⊘	154	40.15N	121.08W
Almansora ≃	44	36.50N	2.00W
Al-Marj	84	32.30N	20.54 E
Almas ≃	48	47.14N	23.10 E
Almas, Pico das ʌ	118	13.33S	41.56W
Al-Maşirah I	70	20.25N	58.50 E
Almassora	44	39.57N	0.03W
Al-Mawşil	70	36.20N	43.08 E
Almelo	30	52.21N	6.39 E
Almendra, Embalse de ⊘¹	44	41.15N	6.10W
Almendralejo	44	38.41N	6.24W
Almería	44	36.50N	2.27W
Almería, Golfo de ᴄ	44	36.46N	2.30W
Al'metjevsk	20	54.53N	52.20 E
Almina, Punta ⪢	44	35.53N	5.15W
Al-Minyā	84	28.06N	30.45 E
Almira	150	47.42N	118.56W
Almirante	108	9.18N	82.24W
Almiroú, Kólpos ᴄ			
Almodóvar del Campo	44	38.43N	4.10W
Almonte	44	37.15N	6.31W
Al-Mubarraz	70	25.25N	49.35 E
Al-Muglad	84	11.02N	27.44 E
Al-Mubarraq	70	26.16N	50.37 E
Al-Mukallā	70	14.32N	49.08 E

Name	Page	Lat.	Long.
Aurora, N.Y., U.S.	136	42.45N	76.42W
Aurora, N.C., U.S.	142	35.18N	76.47W
Aurora, Oh., U.S.	136	41.19N	81.20W
Aurora, Ut., U.S.	148	38.55N	111.56W
Aus	86	26.40S	16.15 E
Au Sable ≐	138	44.25N	83.20W
Auschwitz → Oświęcim	30	50.03N	19.12 E
Austin, In., U.S.	144	38.45N	85.48W
Austin, Mn., U.S.	138	43.40N	92.58W
Austin, Pa., U.S.	136	41.37N	78.05W
Austin, Tx., U.S.	132	30.16N	97.44W
Austin, Lake @	96	27.40S	118.00 E
Australia □1	96	25.00S	135.00 E
Australian Capital Territory □8	96	35.30S	149.00 E
Austria (Österreich) □1	30	47.20N	13.20 E
Austvågøya I	20	68.20N	14.36 E
Authie ≐	36	50.21N	1.38 E
Autun	36	46.57N	4.18 E
Auvergne □9	36	45.25N	2.30 E
Auvézère ≐	36	45.12N	0.51 E
Auxerre	36	47.48N	3.34 E
Auxier	142	37.44N	82.45W
Auxi-le-Château	36	50.14N	2.07 E
Auxvasse	144	39.01N	91.53W
Auyán Tepuy ▲	118	5.55N	62.32W
Auzangate, Nevado ▲	118	13.48S	71.14W
Ava, Il., U.S.	144	37.53N	89.29W
Ava, Mo., U.S.	144	36.57N	92.39W
Avaloirs, Les ▲2	36	48.28N	0.07W
Avalon	154	33.20N	118.19W
Avana ≐	94	21.14S	159.43W
Avarua	94	21.12S	159.46W
Avatiu	94	21.12S	159.47W
Avatiu Harbour c	94	21.11S	159.47W
Ave ≐	44	41.20N	8.45W
Aveiro	44	40.38N	8.39W
Avellaneda	120	34.39S	58.23W
Avellino	40	40.54N	14.47 E
Aven Armand ⊥5	36	44.15N	3.22 E
Aversa	40	40.58N	14.12 E
Avery Island	144	29.54N	91.54W
Aves, Islas de II	118	12.00N	67.30W
Avesnes	36	50.07N	3.56 E
Avesta	22	60.09N	16.12 E
Aveyron ≐	36	44.05N	1.16 E
Avezzano	40	42.02N	13.25 E
Avigliano	40	40.44N	15.44 E
Avignon	36	43.57N	4.49 E
Ávila	44	40.39N	4.42W
Avilés	44	43.33N	5.55W
Avis	136	41.11N	77.18W
Avoca	136	42.24N	77.25W
Avola	40	36.54N	15.08 E
Avon, Mn., U.S.	138	45.36N	94.27W
Avon, N.Y., U.S.	136	42.54N	77.44W
Avon, N.C., U.S.	142	35.21N	75.30W
Avon □6	26	51.30N	2.40W
Avon ≐	26	50.43N	1.46W
Avondale	148	33.26N	112.20W
Avonmore	136	40.31N	79.27W
Avon Park	142	27.35N	81.30W
Avranches	36	48.41N	1.22W
Awash	84	8.59N	40.10 E
Awash ≐	84	11.45N	41.05 E
Awbārī	84	26.35N	12.46 E
Awe, Loch @	26	56.15N	5.17W
Awlef	82	26.58N	1.05 E
Axim	82	4.52N	2.14W
Axiós (Vardar) ≐	48	40.35N	22.50 E
Axis	144	30.55N	88.01W
Ayacucho	118	13.07S	74.13W
Ayamonte	44	37.13N	7.24W
Ayaviri	118	14.52S	70.35W
Ayden	142	35.28N	77.24W
Aydın	48	37.51N	27.51 E
Aydın Dağları ⋏	48	38.00N	28.00 E
Ayer	136	42.33N	71.35W
Ayers Rock ▲	96	25.23S	131.05 E
Áyion Óros ≻1	48	40.15N	24.15 E
Áyios Nikólaos	48	35.11N	25.42 E
Áyiou Órous, Kólpos c	48	40.12N	24.03 E
Aynor	142	33.59N	79.11W
'Ayoûn el 'Atroûs	82	16.40N	9.37W
Ayr	26	55.28N	4.38W
Ayre, Point of ≻	26	54.26N	4.22W
Ayvalık	48	39.18N	26.41 E
Azaila	44	41.17N	0.29W
Azalea Park	142	28.32N	81.18W
Azaouagh, Vallée de l' V	82	15.30N	3.18 E
Azare	82	11.40N	10.11 E
Azazga	44	36.44N	4.22 E
Azerbaijan → Azerbajdžanskaja Sovetskaja Socialističeskaja Respublika □3	54	40.30N	47.30 E
Azerbajdžanskaja Sovetskaja Socialističeskaja Respublika □3	54	40.30N	47.30 E
Azores → Açores II	8	38.30N	28.00W
Azov, Sea of → Azovskoje more ∓2	54	46.00N	36.00 E
Azovskoje more (Sea of Azov) ∓2	54	46.00N	36.00 E
Aztec	148	36.49N	107.59W
Aztec Peak ▲	148	33.48N	110.55W
Aztec Ruins National Monument ♦	148	36.50N	108.10W
Azuaga	44	38.16N	5.41W
Azuer ≐	44	39.08N	3.36W
Azuero, Peninsula de ≻1	108	7.40N	80.35W
Azul	120	36.47S	59.51W
Azur, Côte d' ≛2	36	43.30N	7.00 E
Az-Zahrān (Dhahran)	70	26.18N	50.08 E
Az-Zaqāzīq	84	30.35N	31.31 E
Az-Zarqā'	70	32.05N	36.06 E
Azzel Matti, Sebkha ≐	82	25.55N	0.56 E
Az-Zilfī	70	26.18N	44.48 E
B			
Ba ≐	68	13.02N	109.03 E
Baarn	30	52.13N	5.16 E
Baba Burnu ≻	48	39.29N	26.04 E
Babaeski	48	41.26N	27.06 E
Babahoyo	118	1.49S	79.31W
Babbitt, Mn., U.S.	138	47.43N	91.57W
Babbitt, Nv., U.S.	154	38.32N	118.38W
Babelthuap I	68	7.30N	134.36 E
Babimost	30	52.10N	15.51 E
Babina Greda	48	45.07N	18.33 E
Babine Lake @	130	54.45N	126.00W
Bābol	70	36.34N	52.42 E
Baboquivari Peak ▲	148	31.46N	111.35W
Babor, Djebel ▲	44	36.30N	5.28 E
Bab-Taza	44	35.03N	5.14W
Babuyan Islands II	68	19.15N	121.40 E
Bacabal	118	4.14S	44.47W
Bacău	48	46.34N	26.55 E
Baccarat	36	48.27N	6.45 E
Bačka ◆1	48	45.50N	19.30 E
Bačka Palanka	48	45.15N	19.24 E
Bačka Topola	48	45.49N	19.38 E
Backnang	30	48.56N	9.25 E
Bac-lieu (Vinh-loi)	68	9.17N	105.44 E
Bacolod	68	10.40N	122.57 E
Baconton	142	31.22N	84.09W
Badajoz	44	38.53N	6.58W
Badalona	44	41.27N	2.15 E
Bad Aussee	30	47.36N	13.47 E
Bad Axe	138	43.48N	83.00W
Bad Doberan	30	54.06N	11.53 E
Bad Dürkheim	30	49.28N	8.10 E
Bad Ems	30	50.20N	7.43 E
Baden, Öst.	30	48.00N	16.14 E
Baden, Schw.	36	47.29N	8.18 E
Baden-Baden	30	48.46N	8.14 E
Baden-Württemberg □3	30	48.30N	9.00 E
Bad Freienwalde	30	52.47N	14.01 E
Badgastein	30	47.07N	13.08 E
Bad Hall	30	48.02N	14.13 E
Bad Harzburg	30	51.53N	10.33 E
Bad Hersfeld	30	50.52N	9.42 E
Bad Homburg [vor der Höhe]	30	50.13N	8.37 E
Bad Honnef	30	50.39N	7.13 E
Bad Ischl	30	47.43N	13.37 E
Bad Kissingen	30	50.12N	10.04 E
Bad Kreuznach	30	49.52N	7.51 E
Bad Langensalza	30	51.06N	10.38 E
Bad Lauterberg	30	51.38N	10.28 E
Bad Leonfelden	30	48.33N	14.19 E
Bad Mergentheim	30	49.30N	9.46 E
Bad Nauheim	30	50.22N	8.44 E
Bad Neustadt an der Saale	30	50.19N	10.13 E
Bad Oeynhausen	30	52.12N	8.48 E
Bad Oldesloe	30	53.48N	10.22 E
Bad Pyrmont	30	51.59N	9.15 E
Bad Ragaz	36	47.00N	9.30 E
Bad Reichenhall	30	47.43N	12.52 E
Bad Sachsa	30	51.36N	10.32 E
Bad Salzuflen	30	52.05N	8.44 E
Bad Salzungen	30	50.48N	10.13 E
Bad Sankt Leonhard im Lavanttal	30	46.58N	14.48 E
Bad Schwartau	30	53.55N	10.40 E
Bad Segeberg	30	53.56N	10.17 E
Bad Tölz	30	47.46N	11.34 E
Bad Vöslau	30	47.57N	16.16 E
Bad Waldsee	30	47.55N	9.45 E
Baena	44	37.37N	4.19W
Baeza	44	37.59N	3.28W
Bafatá	82	12.10N	14.40W
Baffin Bay c	130	73.00N	66.00W
Baffin Island I	130	68.00N	70.00W
Bafing ≐	82	13.49N	10.50W
Bafoulabé	82	13.48N	10.50W
Bafoussam	82	5.29N	10.24 E
Bagamoyo	86	6.26S	38.54 E
Bagansiapi-api	68	2.09N	100.49 E
Bağarası	48	37.42N	27.33 E
Bagdad	148	34.34N	113.12W
Bagé	120	31.20S	54.06W
Bages et de Sigean, Étang de c	36	43.05N	3.03 E
Baghdād	70	33.21N	44.25 E
Bagheria	40	38.05N	13.30 E
Baghlān	70	36.13N	68.46 E
Bagnères-de-Bigorre	36	43.04N	0.09 E
Bagnols-sur-Cèze	36	44.10N	4.37 E
Baguio	68	16.25N	120.36 E
Bagzane ▲	82	17.43N	8.45 E
Bahamas □1	108	24.15N	76.00W
Bahāwalpur	70	29.24N	71.41 E
Bahía, Islas de la II	108	16.20N	86.30W
Bahía Blanca	120	38.43S	62.17W
Bahir Dar	84	11.35N	37.28 E
Bahraich	70	27.35N	81.36 E
Bahrain (Al-Bahrayn) □1	70	26.00N	50.30 E
Bahrīyah, Al-Wāḥāt al- ∓4	84	28.15N	28.57 E
Baia-de-Aramă	48	45.00N	22.49 E
Baia Mare	48	47.40N	23.35 E
Baicheng	66	45.38N	122.46 E
Baie-Comeau	130	49.13N	68.10W
Baie-Saint-Paul	130	47.27N	70.30W
Baikal, Lake → Bajkal, ozero @	56	53.00N	107.40 E
Băile Herculane	48	44.54N	22.25 E
Bailén	44	38.06N	3.46W
Băile Olănești	48	45.11N	24.16 E
Băilești	48	44.02N	23.21 E
Bailey	142	35.46N	78.07W
Bailleul	36	50.44N	2.44 E
Bainbridge, Ga., U.S.	142	30.54N	84.34W
Bainbridge, Oh., U.S.	136	39.13N	83.16W
Bains-les-Bains	36	48.00N	6.16 E
Baird, Mount ▲	150	43.22N	111.06W
Bairnsdale	96	37.50S	147.38 E
Bais	36	48.15N	0.22W
Baïse ≐	36	44.17N	0.18 E
Baiyin	66	36.47N	104.07 E
Baja	30	46.11N	18.57 E
Baja California ≻1	108	28.00N	113.30W
Bajanchongor	66	46.08N	100.43 E
Bajdarackaja guba c	54	69.00N	67.30 E
Bajkal, ozero (Lake Baikal) @	56	53.00N	107.40 E
Bajmok	48	45.58N	19.25 E
Bajo Boquete	108	8.47N	82.26W
Baker, La., U.S.	144	30.35N	91.10W
Baker, Mt., U.S.	132	46.22N	104.17W
Baker, Or., U.S.	150	44.46N	117.49W
Baker, Mount ▲	150	48.47N	121.49W
Baker Butte ▲	148	34.27N	111.22W
Baker Lake	130	64.15N	96.00W
Baker Lake @	130	64.10N	95.30W
Bakersfield	154	35.22N	119.01W
Bakhtarān	70	34.19N	47.04 E
Bakony ⋏	30	47.15N	17.50 E
Bakoy ≐	82	13.49N	10.50W
Baku	54	40.23N	49.51 E
Balabac Strait ⊻	68	7.35N	117.00 E
Balakovo	54	52.02N	47.47 E
Balambangan, Pulau I	68	7.15N	116.55 E
Balašov	54	51.32N	43.08 E
Balassagyarmat	30	48.05N	19.18 E
Balaton @	30	46.50N	17.45 E
Balazote	44	38.53N	2.08W
Balboa Heights	108	8.57N	79.33W
Balchaš	54	46.49N	74.59 E
Balchaš, ozero (Lake Balkhash) @	54	46.00N	74.00 E
Balclutha	98	46.14S	169.44 E
Bald Knob	144	35.18N	91.34W
Bald Knob ▲	142	37.56N	79.51W
Baldwin, La., U.S.	144	29.50N	91.32W
Baldwin, Wi., U.S.	138	44.58N	92.22W
Baldwinsville	136	43.09N	76.19W
Baldwinville	136	42.36N	72.04W
Baldwyn	144	34.31N	88.38W
Baldy Mountain ▲	148	36.38N	105.13W
Baldy Peak ▲	148	33.55N	109.35W
Balearic Islands → Balears, Illes II	44	39.30N	3.00 E
Balears □4	44	39.30N	3.00 E
Balears, Illes (Balearic Islands) II	44	39.30N	3.00 E
Baleine, Grande rivière de la ≐	130	55.16N	77.47W
Baleine, Petite rivière de la ≐	130	56.00N	76.45W
Balen	30	51.10N	5.09 E
Balfate	108	15.48N	86.25W
Balfour	142	35.20N	82.28W
Bali I	68	8.20S	115.00 E
Bali, Laut (Bali Sea) ∓2	68	7.45S	115.30 E
Bali, Selat ⊻	68	8.18S	114.25 E
Balıkesir	48	39.39N	27.53 E
Balikpapan	68	1.17S	116.50 E
Balingen	30	48.16N	8.51 E
Balintang Channel ⊻	68	19.49N	121.40 E
Balkan Mountains → Stara Planina ⋏	48	42.45N	25.00 E
Balkh	70	36.46N	66.54 E
Balkhash, Lake → Balchaš, ozero @	54	46.00N	74.00 E
Ball	144	31.24N	92.24W
Ballarat	96	37.34S	143.52 E
Ballina	96	28.52S	153.33 E
Ballsh	48	40.36N	19.44 E
Ballston Spa	136	43.00N	73.50W
Ballymena	26	54.52N	6.17W
Ballymoney	26	55.04N	6.31W
Balmoral Castle ⊥	26	57.02N	3.15W
Balsas ≐	108	17.55N	102.10W
Balsas, Rio das ≐	118	7.14S	44.33W
Bålsta	22	59.35N	17.30 E
Baltic Sea ∓2	20	57.00N	19.00 E
Baltijsk	20	54.39N	19.55 E
Baltijskaja kosa ≻2	30	54.25N	19.35 E
Baltimore, Ire.	26	51.29N	9.22W
Baltimore, Md., U.S.	136	39.17N	76.36W
Baltimore, Oh., U.S.	136	39.50N	82.36W
Baluchistan □9	70	28.00N	63.00 E
Bam	70	29.06N	58.21 E
Bamako	82	12.39N	8.00W
Bambari	84	5.45N	20.40 E
Bamberg, B.R.D.	30	49.53N	10.53 E
Bamberg, S.C., U.S.	142	33.17N	81.02W
Bamenda	82	5.56N	10.10 E
Bāmīān	70	34.50N	67.50 E
Bamingui ≐	84	8.33N	19.05 E
Banana	86	6.01S	12.24 E
Bananal, Ilha do I	118	11.30S	50.15W
Banana River c	142	28.25N	80.38W
Banās, Ra's ≻	84	23.54N	35.48 E
Banat ◆1	48	45.20N	20.40 E
Banbury	26	52.04N	1.20W
Bancroft	130	45.03N	77.51W
Banda, Laut (Banda Sea) ∓2	68	5.00S	128.00 E
Banda Aceh	68	5.34N	95.20 E
Bandak @	22	59.24N	8.15 E
Bandama ≐	82	5.10N	5.00W
Bandama Blanc ≐	82	6.54N	5.31W
Bandama Rouge ≐	82	6.54N	5.31W
Bandar-e 'Abbās	70	27.11N	56.17 E
Bandar-e Anzalī (Bandar-e Pahlavī)	70	37.28N	49.27 E
Bandar Seri Begawan	68	4.56N	114.55 E
Banded Peak ▲	148	37.06N	106.38W
Bandeira, Pico da ▲	118	20.26S	41.47W
Bandera	120	28.54S	62.16W
Bandırma	48	40.20N	27.58 E
Bandundu	86	3.18S	17.20 E
Bandung	68	6.54S	107.36 E
Banes	108	20.58N	75.43W
Banff	130	51.10N	115.34W
Bangalore	70	12.58N	77.36 E
Bangassou	84	4.50N	23.07 E
Banggai, Kepulauan II	68	1.30S	123.15 E
Banggi, Pulau I	68	7.17N	117.12 E
Banghāzī	84	32.07N	20.04 E
Bangka I	68	2.15S	106.00 E
Bangkok → Krung Thep	68	13.45N	100.31 E
Bangladesh □1	70	24.00N	90.00 E
Bangor, N. Ire., U.K.	26	54.40N	5.40W
Bangor, Wales, U.K.	26	53.13N	4.08W
Bangor, Me., U.S.	136	44.48N	68.46W
Bangor, Mi., U.S.	138	42.18N	86.06W
Bangor, Pa., U.S.	136	40.51N	75.12W
Bangs, Mount ▲	148	36.48N	113.51W
Bangui	84	4.22N	18.35 E
Bangweulu, Lake @	86	11.05S	29.45 E
Bani	108	18.17N	70.20W
Bani ≐	82	14.30N	4.12W
Banie	30	53.08N	14.38 E
Banī Mazār	84	28.30N	30.48 E
Banī Suwayf	84	29.05N	31.05 E
Banī Walīd	84	31.45N	14.01 E
Banja Luka	48	44.46N	17.11 E
Banjarmasin	68	3.20S	114.35 E
Banjul	82	13.28N	16.39W
Banks, Îles II	92	13.50S	167.30 E
Banks Island I, B.C., Can.	130	53.25N	130.10W
Banks Island I, N.T., Can.	130	73.15N	121.30W
Banks Lake @1	150	47.45N	119.15W
Banks Peninsula ≻1	98	43.45S	173.00 E
Banks Strait ⊻	96	40.40S	148.07 E
Bānkura	70	23.15N	87.04 E
Bann ≐	26	55.10N	6.46W
Banner Elk	142	36.09N	81.52W
Banning	154	33.55N	116.52W
Bannu	70	32.59N	70.36 E
Baños	118	1.24S	78.25W
Banská Bystrica	30	48.44N	19.07 E
Banská Štiavnica	30	48.28N	18.56 E
Bansko	48	41.50N	23.29 E
Bantry Bay c	26	51.38N	9.48W
Banyoles	44	42.07N	2.46 E
Banyuwangi	68	8.12S	114.21 E
Baoding	66	38.52N	115.29 E
Baoji	66	34.23N	107.09 E
Bao-loc	68	11.32N	107.48 E
Baoshan	66	25.09N	99.09 E
Baotou	66	40.40N	109.59 E
Bar	48	42.05N	19.05 E
Barabinskaja step' ≐	56	55.00N	79.00 E
Baraboo	138	43.28N	89.44W
Baracaldo	44	43.18N	2.59W
Baracoa	108	20.21N	74.30W
Baraga	138	46.46N	88.29W
Baraka V	84	18.13N	37.35 E
Baram ≐	68	4.36N	113.58 E
Baranoviči	54	53.08N	26.02 E
Baratang Island I	70	12.13N	92.45 E
Barataria	144	29.43N	90.07W
Barataria Bay c	144	29.22N	89.57W
Barat Daya, Kepulauan II	68	7.25S	128.00 E
Barbacena	118	21.14S	43.46W
Barbados □1	108	13.10N	59.32W
Barbagia ◆1	40	40.00N	9.10 E
Barbar	84	18.01N	33.59 E
Barbas, Cap ≻	82	22.18N	16.41W
Barbastro	44	42.02N	0.08 E
Barbate de Franco	44	36.12N	5.55W
Barberton	136	41.00N	81.36W
Barboursville	138	38.24N	82.17W
Barbourville	142	36.51N	83.53W
Barbuda I	108	17.38N	61.48W
Barcău (Berettyó) ≐	48	46.59N	21.07 E
Barcellona Pozzo di Gotto	40	38.09N	15.13 E
Barcelona, Esp.	44	41.23N	2.11 E
Barcelona, Ven.	118	10.08N	64.42W
Barcelos	44	41.32N	8.37W
Barcoo ≐	96	23.30S	142.50 E
Bardejov	30	49.18N	21.16 E
Bardenas Reales ⋏1	44	42.10N	1.25W
Bardo	40	36.50N	10.06 E
Bardsey Island I	26	52.45N	4.45W
Bardstown	144	37.48N	85.28W
Bareilly	70	28.21N	79.25 E
Barents Sea (Barencevo more) ∓2	20	69.00N	40.00 E
Barfleur	36	49.40N	1.15W
Barfleur, Pointe de ≻	36	49.42N	1.16W
Bargas	44	39.56N	4.03W
Barge	40	44.43N	7.20 E
Bar Harbor	136	44.23N	68.12W
Bari	40	41.07N	16.52 E
Barika, Oued ≐	44	35.22N	5.18 E
Barīm I	70	12.40N	43.25 E
Barinas	118	8.38N	70.12W
Barisāl	70	22.42N	90.22 E
Barisan, Pegunungan ⋏	68	3.00S	102.15 E
Barito ≐	68	3.32S	114.29 E
Barkley, Lake @1	144	36.40N	87.55W
Barkley Sound ⊻	130	48.53N	125.20W
Barkly Tableland ⋏1	96	18.00S	136.00 E
Bar-le-Duc	36	48.47N	5.10 E
Barlee, Lake @	96	29.10S	119.30 E
Barletta	40	41.19N	16.17 E
Barlinek	30	53.00N	15.12 E
Barling	144	35.19N	94.18W
Barnaul	56	53.22N	83.45 E
Barnegat	136	39.45N	74.13W
Barnegat Bay c	136	39.52N	74.07W
Barnesville, Ga., U.S.	142	33.03N	84.09W
Barnesville, Oh., U.S.	136	39.59N	81.10W
Barneville-Carteret	36	49.23N	1.47W
Barnsley	26	53.34N	1.28W
Barnstable	136	41.42N	70.18W
Barnstaple	26	51.05N	4.04W
Barnwell	142	33.14N	81.21W
Baro ≐	84	8.26N	33.13 E
Baroda	70	22.18N	73.12 E
Barqah (Cyrenaica) □9	84	31.00N	22.30 E
Barques, Pointe aux ≻	138	44.04N	82.58W
Barquisimeto	118	10.04N	69.19W
Barra, Ponta da ≻	86	23.47S	35.32 E
Barra Falsa, Ponta da ≻	86	22.55S	35.37 E
Barrafranca	40	37.22N	14.12 E
Barra Mansa	118	22.32S	44.11W
Barrancabermeja	118	7.03N	73.52W
Barrancas	118	8.42N	62.11W
Barranquilla	118	10.59N	74.48W
Barre	136	44.11N	72.30W
Barreiro	44	38.40N	9.05W
Barren ≐	144	37.11N	86.37W
Barren River Lake @1	144	36.45N	86.02W
Barretos	118	20.33S	48.33W
Barrie	130	44.24N	79.40W
Barrier Range ⋏	96	31.25S	141.25 E
Barron	138	45.24N	91.50W
Barrow	132a	71.17N	156.34W
Barrow ≐	26	52.15N	7.00W
Barrow, Point ≻	132a	71.23N	156.30W
Barrow-in-Furness	26	54.07N	3.14W
Barrow Island I	96	20.48S	115.23 E
Barrow Strait ⊻	130	74.21N	94.10W
Barry, Wales, U.K.	26	51.24N	3.18W
Barry, Il., U.S.	144	39.41N	91.02W
Bārsi	70	18.14N	75.42 E
Barstow	154	34.53N	117.01W
Bar-sur-Aube	36	48.14N	4.43 E
Bar-sur-Seine	36	48.07N	4.22 E
Barth	30	54.22N	12.43 E
Bartholomew, Bayou ≐	144	32.43N	92.04W
Bartle Frere ▲	96	17.23S	145.49 E
Bartlesville	132	36.44N	95.58W
Bartlett	136	44.04N	71.17W
Barton	136	44.44N	72.10W
Bartonville	138	40.39N	89.39W
Bartoszyce	30	54.16N	20.49 E
Bartow	142	27.53N	81.50W
Barú, Volcán ▲1	108	8.48N	82.33W
Barun Bogd uul ▲	66	44.57N	100.15 E
Barwick	142	30.54N	83.44W
Barwon ≐	96	30.00S	148.05 E
Barycz ≐	30	51.42N	16.15 E
Basarabi	48	44.10N	28.24 E
Basatongwula Shan ▲	66	33.05N	91.30 E
Basco	68	20.27N	121.58 E
Bascuñán, Cabo ≻	120	28.51S	71.30W
Basel (Bâle)	36	47.33N	7.35 E
Basento ≐	40	40.21N	16.50 E
Bașeu ≐	48	47.44N	27.15 E
Bashi Channel ⊻	68	22.00N	121.00 E
Basilan	68	6.42N	121.58 E
Basilan Island I	68	6.34N	122.03 E
Basildon	26	51.35N	0.25 E
Basile	144	30.29N	92.35W
Basin	150	44.22N	108.02W
Basingstoke	26	51.15N	1.05W
Baskatong, Réservoir @1	130	46.48N	75.50W
Basque Lands → Euskal Herriko □4	44	43.00N	2.30W
Basra → Al-Basrah	70	30.30N	47.47 E
Bassano del Grappa	40	45.46N	11.44 E
Bassas da India ◆2	86	21.25S	39.42 E
Bassein	68	16.47N	94.44 E
Basse-Terre, Guad.	108	16.00N	61.44W
Basseterre, St. C.-N.	108	17.18N	62.43W
Bassett	142	36.45N	79.59W
Bassett Peak ▲	148	32.30N	110.17W
Bass Harbor	136	44.14N	68.20W
Bass Strait ⊻	96	39.20S	145.30 E
Basswood Lake @	138	48.06N	91.40W
Bastia	40	42.42N	9.27 E
Bastrop	144	32.46N	91.54W
Basutoland → Lesotho □1	86	29.30S	28.30 E
Bata	82	1.51N	9.45 E
Batabanó, Golfo de c	108	22.15N	82.30W
Batajsk	54	47.10N	39.44 E
Batak, jazovir @1	48	41.59N	24.11 E
Batāla	70	31.48N	75.12 E
Batangas	68	13.45N	121.03 E
Batanghari ≐	68	1.16S	104.05 E
Batan Islands II	68	20.30N	121.50 E
Bátaszék	30	46.12N	18.44 E
Batavia, Il., U.S.	138	41.51N	88.18W
Batavia, Ia., U.S.	138	40.59N	92.10W
Batavia, N.Y., U.S.	136	42.59N	78.11W
Batavia, Oh., U.S.	136	39.04N	84.10W
Bătdâmbâng	68	13.06N	103.12 E
Bates, Mount ▲	93	29.01S	167.56 E
Batesburg	142	33.54N	81.33W
Batesville, Ar., U.S.	144	35.46N	91.38W
Batesville, In., U.S.	144	39.18N	85.13W
Batesville, Ms., U.S.	144	34.18N	89.56W
Bath, Eng., U.K.	26	51.23N	2.22W
Bath, Me., U.S.	136	43.54N	69.49W
Bath, N.Y., U.S.	136	42.20N	77.19W
Bathgate	26	55.55N	3.39W
Bathurst, Austl.	96	33.25S	149.35 E
Bathurst, N.B., Can.	130	47.36N	65.39W
Bathurst → Banjul, Gam.	82	13.28N	16.39W
Bathurst Inlet	130	66.50N	108.01W
Bathurst Island I, Austl.	96	11.37S	130.23 E
Bathurst Island I, N.T., Can.	130	76.00N	100.30W
Batina	48	45.51N	18.51 E
Batna	82	35.34N	6.11 E
Baton Rouge	144	30.27N	91.09W
Batticaloa	70	7.43N	81.42 E
Battle ≐	130	52.43N	108.15W
Battle Creek	138	42.19N	85.10W
Battle Ground, In., U.S.	144	40.30N	86.50W
Battle Ground, Wa., U.S.	150	45.46N	122.31W
Battle Mountain	154	40.38N	116.56W
Batu ▲	84	6.55N	39.46 E
Batu Pahat	68	1.51N	102.56 E
Baubau	68	5.28S	122.38 E
Bauchi	82	10.19N	9.50 E
Bauru	118	22.19S	49.04W
Bautzen	30	51.11N	14.26 E
Bauxite	144	34.33N	92.31W
Bavaria → Bayern □3	30	49.00N	11.30 E
Båven @	22	59.01N	16.56 E
Bawdwin	68	23.06N	97.18 E
Baxley	142	31.46N	82.20W
Baxter, Ia., U.S.	138	41.49N	93.09W
Baxter, Mn., U.S.	138	46.20N	94.17W
Baxter, Tn., U.S.	144	36.09N	85.38W
Baxter State Park ♦	136	46.00N	68.58W
Bay, Laguna de @	68	14.23N	121.15 E
Bayamo	108	20.23N	76.39W
Bayano, Lago @1	108	9.10N	78.40W
Bayard, N.M., U.S.	148	32.45N	108.07W
Bayard, W.V., U.S.	136	39.16N	79.21W
Bayboro	142	35.08N	76.46W
Bay City, Mi., U.S.	138	43.35N	83.53W
Bay City, Tx., U.S.	132	28.58N	95.58W
Baydhabo	84	3.07N	43.39 E
Baye, Cap ≻	92	20.57S	165.25 E
Bayern □3	30	49.00N	11.30 E
Bayeux	36	49.16N	0.42W
Bayfield, Co., U.S.	148	37.13N	107.35W
Bayfield, Wi., U.S.	138	46.48N	90.49W
Bayındır	48	38.13N	27.40 E
Baykonur → Bajkonyr	54	47.50N	66.03 E
Bay Minette	144	30.52N	87.46W
Bayona	44	42.07N	8.51W
Bayonne	36	43.29N	1.29W
Bayou Bodcau Reservoir @1	144	32.45N	93.30W
Bayou Cane	144	29.37N	90.45W
Bayou D'Arbonne Lake @1	144	32.45N	92.25W
Bayou La Batre	144	30.24N	88.14W
Bayóvar	118	5.50S	81.03W
Bay Port, Mi., U.S.	138	43.50N	83.22W
Bayport, Mn., U.S.	138	45.01N	92.46W
Bayreuth	30	49.57N	11.35 E
Bayrischzell	30	47.40N	12.00 E
Bayrūt	70	33.53N	35.30 E
Bay Saint Louis	144	30.18N	89.19W
Bay Shore	136	40.43N	73.14W
Bay Springs	144	31.58N	89.17W
Bay Springs Lake @1	144	34.35N	88.20W
Baytown	144	29.44N	94.58W
Baza	44	37.29N	2.46W
Bazaruto, Ilha do I	86	21.40S	35.28 E
Bazas	36	44.26N	0.13W
Be, Nosy I	86	13.20S	48.15 E
Beach Haven	136	39.33N	74.14W
Beachy Head ≻	26	50.44N	0.16 E
Beacon	136	41.30N	73.58W
Beacon Hill	150	46.08N	122.57W
Beagle Gulf c	96	12.00S	130.20 E
Beanblossom Creek ≐	144	39.20N	86.39W
Bear ≐	148	41.30N	112.08W
Bearden	144	33.43N	92.36W
Beardmore	130	49.36N	87.57W
Beardstown	144	40.01N	90.25W
Bear Lake @	148	42.00N	111.20W
Béarn □9	36	43.20N	0.45W
Bear River Range ⋏	148	41.50N	111.30W
Beartooth Mountains ⋏	150	45.00N	109.30W
Beartooth Pass)(	150	44.58N	109.28W
Beata, Isla I	132	17.35N	71.31W
Beatrice, Al., U.S.	144	31.44N	87.12W
Beatrice, Ne., U.S.	132	40.16N	96.44W
Beatty	154	36.54N	116.45W
Beattyville	142	37.34N	83.42W
Beaucaire	36	43.48N	4.38 E
Beauce ◆1	36	48.22N	1.50 E
Beaufort, Malay.	68	5.20N	115.45 E
Beaufort, N.C., U.S.	142	34.43N	76.39W
Beaufort, S.C., U.S.	142	32.25N	80.40W
Beaufort Sea ∓2	130	72.00N	140.00W
Beaufort West	86	32.18S	22.36 E
Beaugency	36	47.47N	1.38 E
Beaujolais □9	36	46.05N	4.10 E
Beaumaris	26	53.16N	4.05W
Beaumont	144	30.05N	94.06W
Beaune	36	47.02N	4.50 E
Beaupréau	36	47.12N	1.00W
Beauvais	36	49.26N	2.05 E
Beauville	36	44.17N	0.52 E
Beaver	136	40.41N	80.18W
Beaver ≐, Can.	130	59.43N	124.16W
Beaver ≐, Can.	130	55.25N	107.45W
Beaver ≐, U.S.	132	36.35N	99.30W
Beaver Dam, Ky., U.S.	144	37.24N	86.52W
Beaver Dam, Wi., U.S.	138	43.27N	88.50W
Beaver Dam Wash V	148	36.54N	114.55W
Beaver Falls	136	40.45N	80.19W
Beaverhead ≐	150	45.31N	112.21W
Beaverhead Mountains ⋏	150	45.00N	113.20W
Beaver Island I	138	45.40N	85.31W
Beaver Lake @1	144	36.20N	93.55W
Beaverton, Mi., U.S.	138	43.52N	84.29W
Beaverton, Or., U.S.	150	45.29N	122.48W
Beāwar	70	26.06N	74.19 E
Bečej	48	45.37N	20.03 E
Béchar	82	31.37N	2.13W
Bechater	40	37.18N	9.45 E
Bechuanaland → Botswana □1	86	22.00S	24.00 E
Beckley	136	37.46N	81.11W
Beckum	30	51.45N	8.02 E
Bedford, Eng., U.K.	26	52.08N	0.29W
Bedford, In., U.S.	144	38.51N	86.29W
Bedford, Pa., U.S.	136	40.01N	78.30W
Bedford, Va., U.S.	142	37.20N	79.31W
Bedfordshire □6	26	52.05N	0.30W
Bedlington	26	55.08N	1.35W
Beebe	144	35.04N	91.52W
Beecher	138	41.20N	87.37W
Beech Grove	144	39.43N	86.05W
Beersheba → Be'er Sheva'	70	31.14N	34.47 E
Be'er Sheva'	70	31.14N	34.47 E
Beeville	132	28.24N	97.44W
Bega	96	36.40S	149.50 E
Bega (Begej) ≐	48	45.13N	20.19 E
Begej (Bega) ≐	48	45.13N	20.19 E
Begur, Cap de ≻	44	41.57N	3.14 E
Behbehān	70	30.35N	50.14 E
Bei'an	66	48.16N	126.36 E
Beida → Al-Bayḍā'	84	32.46N	21.43 E
Beihai	66	21.29N	109.05 E
Beijing (Peking)	66	39.55N	116.25 E
Beipiao	66	41.49N	120.46 E
Beira	86	19.49S	34.52 E
Beira Baixa □9	44	39.45N	7.30W
Beira Litoral □9	44	40.15N	8.25W
Beirut → Bayrūt	70	33.53N	35.30 E
Beitbridge	86	22.13S	30.00 E
Beja, Port.	44	38.01N	7.52W
Béja, Tun.	82	36.44N	9.11 E
Bejaïa	82	36.45N	5.05 E
Bejaïa, Golfe de c	44	36.45N	5.25 E
Béjar	44	40.23N	5.46W
Békés	30	46.46N	21.08 E
Békéscsaba	30	46.41N	21.06 E
Bekily	86	24.13S	45.19 E
Bekkaria	40	35.22N	8.15 E
Bélâbre	36	46.33N	1.09 E
Bela Crkva	48	44.54N	21.26 E
Bel Air	136	39.32N	76.20W
Belaja ≐	54	55.54N	53.33 E
Belaja Cerkov'	54	49.49N	30.07 E
Belalcázar	44	38.34N	5.10W
Belau (Palau) □2	68	5.00N	137.00 E
Bełchatów	30	51.22N	19.21 E
Belcher Islands II	130	56.20N	79.30W
Bel'cy	54	47.46N	27.56 E
Belding	138	43.05N	85.13W
Beled Weyne	84	4.45N	45.12 E
Belém	118	1.27S	48.29W
Belen	148	34.39N	106.46W
Bélep, Îles II	92	19.45S	163.40 E
Belesar, Embalse de @1	44	42.45N	7.40W
Belfast, S. Afr.	86	25.43S	30.03 E
Belfast, N. Ire., U.K.	26	54.35N	5.55W
Belfast, Me., U.S.	136	44.25N	69.00W
Belfast Lough c	26	54.40N	5.50W
Belfort	36	47.38N	6.52 E
Belgaum	70	15.52N	74.31 E
Belgium □1	30	50.50N	4.00 E
Belgorod	54	50.36N	36.35 E
Belgrade → Beograd	48	44.50N	20.30 E
Belhaven	142	35.32N	76.37W
Beli Drim ≐	48	42.06N	20.25 E
Beli Manastir	48	45.46N	18.36 E
Belington	136	39.01N	79.56W
Belitung I	68	2.50S	107.55 E
Belize □1	108	17.15N	88.45W
Belize City	108	17.30N	88.12W
Bell ≐	130	49.48N	77.38W
Bellac	36	46.07N	1.02 E
Bellaire, Mi., U.S.	138	44.58N	85.12W
Bellaire, Oh., U.S.	136	40.00N	80.45W
Bellamy	144	32.26N	88.08W
Bellaria	40	44.09N	12.28 E
Bellary	70	15.09N	76.56 E
Belle	144	38.17N	91.43W
Belledonne, Chaîne de ⋏	36	45.18N	6.08 E
Bellefontaine	136	40.21N	83.45W
Bellefonte	136	40.54N	77.46W
Belle Fourche	132	44.40N	103.51W
Belle Glade	142	26.41N	80.40W
Belle-Île I	36	47.20N	3.10W
Belle Isle I	130	51.55N	55.20W
Belle Isle, Strait of ⊻	130	51.35N	56.30W
Belle Plaine, Ia., U.S.	138	41.53N	92.16W
Belle Plaine, Mn., U.S.	138	44.37N	93.46W
Belleview	142	29.03N	82.03W
Belleville, On., Can.	130	44.10N	77.23W
Belleville, Il., U.S.	144	38.31N	89.59W
Bellevue, Ia., U.S.	138	42.15N	90.25W
Bellevue, Ne., U.S.	144	41.08N	95.53W
Bellevue, Oh., U.S.	136	41.16N	82.50W
Bellevue, Wa., U.S.	150	47.36N	122.11W
Bellingham	150	48.45N	122.29W
Bellingshausen Sea ∓2	8	71.00S	85.00W
Bellinzona	36	46.11N	9.02 E
Bello	118	6.20N	75.33W
Bellows Falls	136	43.08N	72.26W
Bells	144	35.43N	89.05W
Belluno	40	46.09N	12.13 E
Bellwood	136	40.36N	78.19W
Belmond	138	42.50N	93.36W
Belmont, N.H., U.S.	136	43.26N	71.28W
Belmont, N.Y., U.S.	136	42.13N	78.02W
Belmont, S.C., U.S.	142	34.02N	81.01W
Belmonte	44	40.21N	7.21W
Belmopan	108	17.15N	88.46W
Belogradčik	48	43.38N	22.41 E
Belo Horizonte	118	19.55S	43.56W
Beloit	138	42.30N	89.01W
Beloje, ozero @	54	60.11N	37.37 E
Beloje more (White Sea) ∓2	54	65.30N	38.00 E
Belomorsko-Baltijskij kanal ≖	20	62.48N	34.48 E
Belorado	44	42.25N	3.11W
Beloreck	54	53.58N	58.24 E
Belorussia → Belorusskaja Sovetskaja Socialističeskaja Respublika □3	54	53.50N	28.00 E
Belorusskaja Sovetskaja Socialističeskaja Respublika (Belorussia) □3	54	53.50N	28.00 E
Belovo	56	54.25N	86.18 E
Belper	26	53.01N	1.29W
Belpre	136	39.16N	81.34W
Belton, Mo., U.S.	144	38.48N	94.31W
Belton, S.C., U.S.	142	34.31N	82.29W
Belucha, gora ▲	56	49.48N	86.40 E
Belvidere	138	42.15N	88.50W
Belyando ≐	96	21.38S	146.50 E
Belzoni	144	33.11N	90.29W
Bełżyce	30	51.11N	22.18 E
Bement	144	39.55N	88.34W
Bemidji	138	47.28N	94.52W
Benares → Vārānasi	70	25.20N	83.00 E
Benavente	44	42.00N	5.41W
Benbecula I	26	57.26N	7.21W
Ben-Chicao, Col de)(	44	36.12N	2.45 E
Bend	150	44.03N	121.18W
Bendery	54	46.49N	29.29 E
Bendigo	96	36.46S	144.17 E
Bendorf	30	50.25N	7.34 E
Benešov	30	49.47N	14.43 E
Benevento	40	41.08N	14.45 E
Bengal, Bay of c	70	15.00N	90.00 E

Symbols in the index entries are identified on page 162.

Symbols in the index entries are identified on page 162.

Name	Page	Lat.	Long.
Čardžou	54	39.06N	63.34 E
Carei	48	47.42N	22.28 E
Carencro	144	30.19N	92.02W
Carentan	36	49.18N	1.14W
Cares ≃	44	43.19N	4.36W
Carey	136	40.57N	83.22W
Carey, Lake ⊜	96	29.05S	122.15 E
Caribbean Sea ≂²	108	15.00N	73.00W
Caribou	132	46.51N	68.00W
Caribou ≃	130	59.20N	94.44W
Caribou Mountain ∧, Id., U.S.	150	43.06N	111.18W
Caribou Mountain ∧, Me., U.S.	136	45.26N	70.38W
Caribou Mountains ⩘	130	59.12N	115.40W
Carini	40	38.08N	13.11 E
Caripito	118	10.08N	63.06W
Carleton, Mount ∧	130	47.23N	66.53W
Carlin	154	40.42N	116.06W
Carlinville	144	39.16N	89.52W
Carlisle, Eng., U.K.	26	54.54N	2.55W
Carlisle, Ar., U.S.	144	34.46N	91.44W
Carlisle, In., U.S.	144	38.58N	87.24W
Carlisle, Ia., U.S.	138	41.30N	93.29W
Carlisle, Ky., U.S.	136	38.18N	84.01W
Carlisle, Pa., U.S.	136	40.12N	77.11W
Carl Junction	144	37.10N	94.33W
Carloforte	40	39.08N	8.18 E
Carlow □⁶	26	52.40N	6.50W
Carlsbad → Karlovy Vary, Česko.	30	50.11N	12.52 E
Carlsbad, Ca., U.S.	154	33.09N	117.20W
Carlsbad, N.M., U.S.	132	32.25N	104.13W
Carlton	138	46.39N	92.25W
Carlyle	144	38.36N	89.22W
Carlyle Lake ⊜¹	144	38.40N	89.18W
Carmacks	130	62.05N	136.18W
Carmagnola	40	44.51N	7.43 E
Carmarthen	26	51.52N	4.19W
Carmel, Ca., U.S.	154	36.33N	121.55W
Carmel, In., U.S.	144	39.58N	86.07W
Carmel, N.Y., U.S.	136	41.26N	73.41W
Carmel Head >	26	53.24N	4.34W
Carmel Valley	154	36.29N	121.43W
Carmel Woods	154	36.34N	121.54W
Carmer Hill ⩘²	136	41.54N	77.58W
Carmi	144	38.05N	88.09W
Carmichael	154	38.37N	121.19W
Carmona	44	37.28N	5.38W
Carnarvon	96	24.53S	113.40 E
Carnatic ◄►¹	70	12.30N	78.15 E
Carnegie, Lake ⊜	96	26.10S	122.30 E
Carniche, Alpi ⩘	40	46.40N	13.00 E
Carnsore Point >	26	52.10N	6.22W
Caro	138	43.29N	83.23W
Carol City	142	25.56N	80.14W
Caroleen	142	35.16N	81.47W
Caroline Islands ıı, T.T.P.I.	8	8.00N	147.00 E
Caroní ≃	118	8.21N	62.43W
Carora	118	10.11N	70.05W
Carpathian Mountains ⩘	16	48.00N	24.00 E
Carpaţii Meridionali ⩘	48	45.30N	24.15 E
Carpentaria, Gulf of c	96	14.00S	139.00 E
Carpentersville	138	42.07N	88.15W
Carpentras	36	44.03N	5.03 E
Carpi	40	44.47N	10.53 E
Carpinteria	154	34.23N	119.31W
Carquefou	36	47.18N	1.30W
Carranza, Cabo >	120	35.36S	72.38W
Carrara	40	44.05N	10.06 E
Carrauntoohil ∧	26	51.59N	9.45W
Carrboro	142	35.54N	79.04W
Carretas, Punta >	118	14.13S	76.18W
Carrickfergus	26	54.43N	5.49W
Carrick on Shannon	26	53.57N	8.05W
Carrick on Suir	26	52.21N	7.25W
Carrington	132	47.26N	99.07W
Carrington Island ı	148	41.00N	112.37W
Carrión ≃	44	41.53N	4.32W
Carrizozo	148	33.38N	105.52W
Carrollton, Al., U.S.	144	33.10N	88.06W
Carrollton, Ga., U.S.	142	33.35N	85.05W
Carrollton, Il., U.S.	144	39.18N	90.24W
Carrollton, Ky., U.S.	144	38.40N	85.10W
Carrollton, Mi., U.S.	138	43.27N	83.55W
Carrollton, Mo., U.S.	144	39.21N	93.29W
Carson	150	45.43N	121.49W
Carson ≃	154	39.45N	118.40W
Carson City, Mi., U.S.	138	43.10N	84.50W
Carson City, Nv., U.S.	154	39.10N	119.46W
Carson Lake ⊜	154	39.19N	118.43W
Carson Range ⩘	154	39.15N	120.20W
Carson Sink ⊜	154	39.45N	118.30W
Cartagena, Col.	118	10.25N	75.32W
Cartagena, Esp.	44	37.36N	0.59W
Cartago, Col.	118	4.45N	75.55W
Cartago, C.R.	108	9.52N	83.55W
Cartaya	44	37.17N	7.09W
Carter Mountain ∧	150	44.12N	109.25W
Cartersville	142	34.09N	84.48W
Carterton	98	41.02S	175.31 E
Carterville	144	37.45N	89.04W
Carthage, Ar., U.S.	144	34.04N	92.33W
Carthage, Il., U.S.	138	40.24N	91.08W
Carthage, In., U.S.	144	39.44N	85.34W
Carthage, Ms., U.S.	144	32.43N	89.32W
Carthage, Mo., U.S.	144	37.10N	94.18W
Carthage, N.Y., U.S.	136	43.58N	75.36W
Carthage, N.C., U.S.	142	35.20N	79.25W
Carthage, Tn., U.S.	144	36.15N	85.57W
Carthage, Tx., U.S.	144	32.09N	94.20W
Carthage ⊥	40	36.52N	10.20 E
Caruaru	118	8.17S	35.58W
Carúpano	118	10.40N	63.14W
Caruthersville	144	36.11N	89.39W
Carvin	36	50.29N	2.58 E
Carvoeiro, Cabo >	44	39.21N	9.24W
Cary, Ms., U.S.	144	32.48N	90.55W
Cary, N.C., U.S.	142	35.47N	78.46W
Casablanca (Dar-el-Beida)	82	33.39N	7.35W
Casa Grande	148	32.52N	111.45W
Casalbordino	40	42.09N	14.35 E
Casale Monferrato	40	45.08N	8.27 E
Casanare ≃	118	6.02N	69.51W
Casarano	40	40.00N	18.10 E
Casas Adobes	148	32.19N	110.59W
Cascade	138	42.17N	91.00W
Cascade Bay c	93	29.01S	167.58 E
Cascade Locks	150	45.40N	121.53W
Cascade Range ⩘	132	45.00N	121.30W
Cascade Reservoir ⊜¹	150	44.35N	116.06W
Cascais	44	38.42N	9.25W
Cascina	40	43.41N	10.33 E
Casco Bay c	136	43.40N	70.00W
Caserta	40	41.04N	14.20 E
Casey	144	39.17N	87.59W
Caseyr >	84	11.49N	51.15 E
Cashiers	142	35.06N	83.05W
Cashmere	150	47.31N	120.28W
Cashton	138	43.44N	90.46W
Casimcea	48	44.43N	28.23 E
Casino	96	28.52S	153.03 E
Casiquiare ≃	118	2.01N	67.07W
Čáslav	30	49.54N	15.23 E
Caspe	44	41.14N	0.02W
Casper	150	42.52N	106.18W
Caspian Sea ≂²	54	42.00N	50.30 E
Cassai (Kasai) ≃	86	3.02S	16.57 E
Cassano allo Ionio	40	39.47N	16.20 E
Cass City	138	43.36N	83.10W
Cassiar	130	59.16N	129.40W
Cassiar Mountains ⩘	130	59.00N	129.00W
Cassino	40	41.30N	13.49 E
Cass Lake	138	47.22N	94.36W
Cass Lake ⊜	138	47.25N	94.32W
Cassville, Mo., U.S.	144	36.40N	93.52W
Cassville, Wi., U.S.	138	42.42N	90.59W
Castelfranco Veneto	40	45.40N	11.55 E
Castellammare, Golfo di c	40	38.08N	12.54 E
Castellammare del Golfo	40	38.01N	12.53 E
Castellammare [di Stabia]	40	40.42N	14.29 E
Castellane	36	43.51N	6.31 E
Castellaneta	40	40.37N	16.57 E
Castell'Arquato	40	44.51N	9.52 E
Castelló □⁴	44	40.10N	0.10W
Castelló de la Plana	44	39.59N	0.02W
Castelo Branco	44	39.49N	7.30W
Castel San Giovanni	40	45.04N	9.26 E
Castelsarrasin	36	44.02N	1.06 E
Castelvetrano	40	37.41N	12.47 E
Castets	36	43.53N	1.09W
Castile	136	42.37N	78.03W
Castilla	118	5.12S	80.38W
Castilla, Playa de ⊥²	44	37.00N	6.33W
Castilla-La Mancha □⁴	44	39.30N	3.00W
Castilla la Nueva □⁹	44	40.00N	3.45W
Castilla la Vieja □⁹	44	41.30N	4.00W
Castilla-León □⁴	44	41.30N	5.00W
Castillo de San Marcos National Monument ✦	142	29.44N	81.20W
Castine	136	44.23N	68.48W
Castlebar	26	53.52N	9.17W
Castlecliff	98	39.57S	174.59 E
Castle Dome Peak ∧	148	33.05N	114.08W
Castlegar	130	49.19N	117.40W
Castlemaine	96	37.04S	144.13 E
Castle Mountain ∧	130	64.32N	135.27W
Castle Peak ∧, Co., U.S.	148	39.01N	106.52W
Castle Peak ∧, Id., U.S.	150	44.02N	114.35W
Castle Rock	150	46.16N	122.54W
Castle Rock Lake ⊜¹	138	43.56N	89.58W
Castletown	26	54.04N	4.40W
Castres	36	43.36N	2.15 E
Castries	108	14.01N	61.00W
Castro	120	42.29S	73.46W
Castro del Río	44	37.41N	4.28W
Castronuño	44	41.23N	5.16W
Castro Verde	44	37.42N	8.05W
Castrovillari	40	39.49N	16.13 E
Castroville	154	36.45N	121.45W
Castuera	44	38.43N	5.33W
Catahoula Lake ⊜	144	31.30N	92.06W
Catalonia → Catalunya □⁴	44	42.00N	2.00 E
Catalunya □⁴	44	41.40N	1.30 E
Catamarca	120	28.28S	65.47W
Catanduanes Island ı	68	13.45N	124.15 E
Catanduva	118	21.08S	48.58W
Catania	40	37.30N	15.06 E
Catania, Golfo di c	40	37.24N	15.09 E
Catanzaro	40	38.54N	16.36 E
Catarman	68	12.30N	124.38 E
Catarroja	44	39.24N	0.24W
Catawba ≃	142	34.36N	80.54W
Catbalogan	68	11.46N	124.53 E
Cathlamet	150	46.12N	123.22W
Cat Island ı, Ba.	108	24.27N	75.30W
Cat Island ı, Ms., U.S.	144	30.13N	89.06W
Catlettsburg	136	38.24N	82.36W
Catoche, Cabo >	108	21.35N	87.05W
Catonsville	136	39.16N	76.43W
Catskill	136	42.13N	73.51W
Catskill Mountains ⩘	136	42.10N	74.30W
Cattaraugus	136	42.19N	78.52W
Cattolica	40	43.58N	12.44 E
Caubvick, Mount (Mont d'Iberville) ∧	130	58.53N	63.43W
Cauca ≃	118	8.54N	74.28W
Caucasus → Bol'šoj Kavkaz ⩘	54	42.30N	45.00 E
Čaunskaja guba c	56	69.20N	170.00 E
Caura ≃	118	7.38N	64.53W
Cauvery ≃	70	11.09N	79.52 E
Caux, Pays de ◄►¹	36	49.40N	0.40 E
Cavaillon	36	43.50N	5.02 E
Cavalese	40	46.17N	11.27 E
Cavalleria, Cap de >	44	40.05N	4.05 E
Cavan	26	54.00N	7.21W
Cavan □⁶	26	53.55N	7.15W
Cave City	144	37.08N	85.57W
Cave In Rock	144	37.29N	88.10W
Cave Run Lake ⊜¹	136	38.03N	83.30W
Cave Spring	142	34.14N	85.20W
Caviana, Ilha ı	118	0.10N	50.10W
Cavite	68	14.29N	120.55 E
Caxias	118	4.50S	43.21W
Caxias do Sul	120	29.10S	51.11W
Caxito	86	8.33S	13.36 E
Cayambe ∧¹	118	0.02N	77.59W
Cayce	142	33.57N	81.04W
Cayenne	118	4.56N	52.20W
Caylus	36	44.14N	1.46 E
Cayman Brac ı	108	19.43N	79.49W
Cayman Islands □²	108	19.30N	80.40W
Cayuga	144	39.56N	87.27W
Cayuga Heights	136	42.27N	76.29W
Cayuga Lake ⊜	136	42.45N	76.45W
Cazalla de la Sierra	44	37.56N	5.45W
Cazaux et de Sanguinet, Lac de c	36	44.30N	1.10W
Cazenovia	136	42.55N	75.51W
Čazma	40	45.45N	16.37 E
Čeboksarskoje vodochranilišče ⊜¹	20	56.10N	46.00 E
Čeboksary	20	56.09N	47.15 E
Cebu	68	10.18N	123.54 E
Cebu ı	68	10.20N	123.45 E
Čechy □⁹	30	49.50N	14.00 E
Cecil	142	31.02N	83.23W
Cecina	40	43.19N	10.31 E
Cedar ≃, U.S.	138	41.17N	91.21W
Cedar ≃, N.Y., U.S.	136	43.51N	74.11W
Cedar Breaks National Monument ✦	148	37.29N	112.53W
Cedarburg	138	43.17N	87.59W
Cedar City, Mo., U.S.	144	38.35N	92.10W
Cedar City, Ut., U.S.	148	37.40N	113.03W
Cedar Falls	138	42.31N	92.26W
Cedar Lake	144	41.21N	87.26W
Cedar Lake ⊜¹	130	53.20N	100.10W
Cedar Mountain ∧	154	41.36N	120.16W
Cedar Rapids	138	41.59N	91.40W
Cedartown	142	34.03N	85.15W
Cedillo, Embalse de ⊜¹	44	39.40N	7.25W
Cedrino ≃	40	40.23N	9.44 E
Cedros, Isla ı	108	28.12N	115.15W
Cedynia	30	52.50N	14.14 E
Cefalonia → Kefallinía ı	48	38.15N	20.35 E
Cefalù	40	38.02N	14.01 E
Cegléd	30	47.10N	19.48 E
Cehegín	44	38.06N	1.48W
Čel'abinsk	56	55.10N	61.24 E
Celaya	108	20.31N	100.49W
Celebes → Sulawesi ı	68	2.00S	121.00 E
Celebes Sea ≂²	68	3.00N	122.00 E
Celina, Oh., U.S.	136	40.32N	84.34W
Celina, Tn., U.S.	144	36.33N	85.30W
Celinograd	54	51.10N	71.30 E
Celje	40	46.14N	15.16 E
Celle	30	52.37N	10.05 E
Celtic Sea ≂²	26	51.00N	6.30W
Čel'uskin, mys >	56	77.45N	104.20 E
Čemerno	40	43.11N	18.37 E
Čemerno)(	40	43.14N	18.37 E
Cenderawasih, Teluk c	68	2.30S	135.20 E
Ceno ≃	40	44.41N	10.05 E
Centennial Mountains ⩘	150	44.35N	111.55W
Centennial Wash V	148	33.14N	112.46W
Center, Mo., U.S.	144	39.30N	91.31W
Center, Tx., U.S.	144	31.47N	94.10W
Centerburg	136	40.18N	82.41W
Center City	138	45.23N	92.48W
Center Hill Lake ⊜¹	144	36.00N	85.45W
Center Moriches	136	40.48N	72.47W
Center Point, Al., U.S.	144	33.37N	86.41W
Center Point, Ia., U.S.	138	42.11N	91.47W
Centerville, In., U.S.	144	39.49N	84.59W
Centerville, Ia., U.S.	138	40.43N	92.52W
Centerville, Mo., U.S.	144	37.26N	90.57W
Centerville, Pa., U.S.	136	40.02N	79.58W
Centerville, Tn., U.S.	144	35.46N	87.28W
Centerville, Ut., U.S.	148	40.55N	111.52W
Cento	40	44.43N	11.17 E
Central, N.M., U.S.	148	32.46N	108.08W
Central, S.C., U.S.	142	34.43N	82.46W
Central, Cordillera ⩘, Col.	118	5.00N	75.00W
Central, Cordillera ⩘, Perú	118	8.00S	77.00W
Central, Massif ⩘	36	45.00N	3.10 E
Central, Planalto ⩘¹	118	18.00S	47.00W
Central, Sistema ⩘	44	40.30N	5.00W
Central African Republic □¹	84	7.00N	21.00 E
Central City, Ia., U.S.	138	42.12N	91.31W
Central City, Ky., U.S.	144	37.17N	87.07W
Central City, Pa., U.S.	136	40.06N	78.48W
Centralia, Il., U.S.	144	38.31N	89.08W
Centralia, Mo., U.S.	144	39.12N	92.08W
Centralia, Wa., U.S.	150	46.42N	122.57W
Central Makrān Range ⩘	70	26.40N	64.30 E
Central Point	150	42.22N	122.54W
Centre	144	34.09N	85.40W
Centre, Canal du ≍	36	46.27N	4.07 E
Centreville, Al., U.S.	144	32.56N	87.08W
Centreville, Md., U.S.	136	39.02N	76.04W
Centreville, Ms., U.S.	144	31.05N	91.04W
Century, Fl., U.S.	144	30.58N	87.15W
Century, W.V., U.S.	136	39.05N	80.11W
Čepelare	48	41.44N	24.41 E
Ceram → Seram ı	68	3.00S	129.00 E
Ceram Sea → Seram, Laut ≂²	68	2.30S	128.00 E
Čerčany	30	49.51N	14.43 E
Cère ≃	36	44.55N	1.53 E
Čeremchovo	56	53.09N	103.05 E
Čerepovec	20	59.08N	37.54 E
Cerf Island ı	86	9.32S	50.59 E
Cerignola	40	41.16N	15.54 E
Čerkassy	54	49.26N	32.04 E
Cermei	48	46.33N	21.51 E
Čern'achovsk	20	54.38N	21.49 E
Černá hora ∧	30	48.58N	13.48 E
Cernavodă	48	44.21N	28.01 E
Cernay	36	47.49N	7.10 E
Cernei, Munţii ⩘	48	45.02N	22.31 E
Černigov	54	51.30N	31.18 E
Černi vrăh ∧	48	42.34N	23.17 E
Černovcy	48	48.18N	25.56 E
Cërrik	48	41.02N	19.57 E
Cerro de Pasco	118	10.41S	76.16W
Cerro Gordo	144	39.53N	88.43W
Čerskogo, chrebet ⩘	56	65.00N	144.00 E
Cervati, Monte ∧	40	40.17N	15.29 E
Červen Brjag	48	43.16N	24.06 E
Cervera de Pisuerga	44	42.52N	4.30W
Cervia	40	44.15N	12.22 E
Cesena	40	44.08N	12.15 E
Cesenatico	40	44.12N	12.24 E
Česká Kamenice	30	50.47N	14.26 E
Česká Lípa	30	50.42N	14.32 E
Česká Třebová	30	49.54N	16.27 E
České Budějovice	30	48.59N	14.28 E
Českomoravská vrchovina ⩘¹	30	49.20N	15.30 E
Český Krumlov	30	48.49N	14.19 E
Češskaja guba c	54	67.30N	46.30 E
Cessnock	96	32.50S	151.21 E
Cestos ≃	82	5.40N	9.10W
Cetinje	48	42.23N	18.55 E
Ceuta	82	35.53N	5.19W
Cévennes ⩘¹	36	44.00N	3.30 E
Chabarovsk	56	48.27N	135.06 E
Chablais ◄►¹	36	46.18N	6.39 E
Chablis	36	47.49N	3.48 E
Chachani, Nevado ∧	118	16.12S	71.33W
Chaco ≃	148	36.46N	108.39W
Chaco Culture National Historical Park ✦	148	36.06N	108.00W
Chad (Tchad) □¹	84	15.00N	19.00 E
Chad, Lake (Lac Tchad) ⊜	84	13.20N	14.00 E
Chadbourn	142	34.19N	78.49W
Chadron	132	42.49N	103.00W
Chafarinas, Islas ıı	44	35.11N	2.26W
Chaffee	144	37.10N	89.39W
Chagos Archipelago ıı	8	6.00S	72.00 E
Chalais	36	45.16N	0.02 E
Chalbi Desert ◄►²	84	3.00N	37.20 E
Chalcis → Khalkís	48	38.28N	23.36 E
Chalmette	144	29.56N	89.57W
Châlons-sur-Marne	36	48.57N	4.22 E
Chalon-sur-Saône	36	46.47N	4.51 E
Chalosse ◄►¹	36	43.45N	0.30W
Chaltel, Cerro (Monte Fitzroy) ∧	120	49.17S	73.05W
Cham	30	49.13N	12.41 E
Chama	148	36.54N	106.34W
Chama, Rio ≃	148	36.03N	106.05W
Chambal ≃	70	26.30N	79.15 E
Chamberlain	132	43.48N	99.19W
Chamberlain Lake ⊜	136	46.17N	69.20W
Chambersburg	136	39.56N	77.39W
Chambers Island ı	138	45.11N	87.21W
Chambéry	36	45.34N	5.56 E
Chambi, Jebel ∧	82	35.11N	8.42 E
Chamblee	142	33.53N	84.17W
Chambon-sur-Voueize	36	46.11N	2.25 E
Chamo, Lake ⊜	84	5.50N	37.33 E
Chamois	144	38.40N	91.46W
Chamonix-Mont-Blanc	36	45.55N	6.52 E
Champagne □⁹	36	49.00N	4.30 E
Champaign	144	40.06N	88.14W
Champaquí, Cerro ∧	120	31.59S	64.56W
Champeix	36	45.36N	3.08 E
Champéry	36	46.10N	6.52 E
Champion, Mi., U.S.	138	46.30N	87.57W
Champion, Oh., U.S.	136	41.17N	80.51W
Champlain	136	44.59N	73.26W
Champlain, Lake ⊜	132	44.45N	73.15W
Chañaral	120	26.21S	70.37W
Chandeleur Islands ıı	144	29.48N	88.51W
Chandeleur Sound ⊔	144	29.55N	89.10W
Chandīgarh	70	30.44N	76.55 E
Chandler, Az., U.S.	148	33.18N	111.50W
Chandler, In., U.S.	144	38.02N	87.22W
Chandrapur	70	19.57N	79.18 E
Chang (Yangtze) ≃	66	31.48N	121.10 E
Chang, Ko ı	68	12.05N	102.20 E
Changajn nuruu ⩘	66	47.30N	100.00 E
Changane ≃	86	24.43S	33.32 E
Changchun	66	43.53N	125.19 E
Changde	66	29.02N	111.41 E
Changhua	66	24.05N	120.32 E
Changli	66	39.43N	119.11 E
Changsha	66	28.12N	112.58 E
Changshu	66	31.39N	120.45 E
Changting	66	25.52N	116.20 E
Changzhi	66	36.11N	113.08 E
Changzhou	66	31.47N	119.57 E
Chanka, ozero (Xingkai Hu) ⊜	66	45.00N	132.24 E
Channel Islands ıı, Europe	26	49.20N	2.20W
Channel Islands ıı, Ca., U.S.	154	33.30N	119.15W
Channel Islands National Park ✦	154	33.28N	119.02W
Channel-Port-aux-Basques	130	47.34N	59.09W
Channelview	144	29.46N	95.06W
Channing	138	46.08N	88.05W
Chantilly	36	49.12N	2.28 E
Chanute	144	37.40N	95.27W
Chao'an	66	23.41N	116.38 E
Chao Phraya ≃	68	13.32N	100.36 E
Chaouen	44	35.10N	5.16W
Chaoyang	66	41.35N	120.28 E
Chapala, Lago de ⊜	108	20.15N	103.00W
Chaparral	118	3.43N	75.28W
Chapel Hill	142	35.54N	79.03W
Chapleau	130	47.50N	83.24W
Chapmanville	142	37.58N	82.01W
Chāpra	70	25.46N	84.45 E
Chardon	136	41.34N	81.12W
Charente ≃	36	45.57N	1.05W
Chari ≃	84	12.58N	14.31 E
Chārīkār	70	35.01N	69.11 E
Chariton	138	41.00N	93.18W
Chariton ≃	144	39.19N	92.57W
Charity	118	7.24N	58.36W
Char'kov	54	50.00N	36.15 E
Charleroi	30	50.25N	4.26 E
Charles, Cape >	142	37.08N	75.58W
Charles City, Ia., U.S.	138	43.03N	92.40W
Charles City, Va., U.S.	142	37.20N	77.04W
Charles Mound ∧²	138	42.30N	90.14W
Charleston, Ar., U.S.	144	35.17N	94.02W
Charleston, Il., U.S.	144	39.29N	88.10W
Charleston, Ms., U.S.	144	34.00N	90.03W
Charleston, Mo., U.S.	144	36.55N	89.21W
Charleston, S.C., U.S.	142	32.46N	79.55W
Charleston, W.V., U.S.	136	38.20N	81.37W
Charleston Peak ∧	154	36.16N	115.42W
Charlestown, In., U.S.	144	38.27N	85.40W
Charlestown, N.H., U.S.	136	43.14N	72.25W
Charles Town, W.V., U.S.	136	39.17N	77.51W
Charleville	96	26.24S	146.15 E
Charleville-Mézières	36	49.46N	4.43 E
Charlevoix	138	45.19N	85.15W
Charlevoix, Lake ⊜	138	45.15N	85.08W
Charlotte, Mi., U.S.	138	42.33N	84.50W
Charlotte, N.C., U.S.	142	35.13N	80.50W
Charlotte, Tn., U.S.	144	36.10N	87.20W
Charlotte Amalie	108	18.21N	64.56W
Charlotte Harbor c	142	26.45N	82.12W
Charlottesville	142	38.01N	78.28W
Charlottetown	130	46.14N	63.08W
Charly-sur-Marne	36	48.58N	3.17 E
Charters Towers	96	20.05S	146.16 E
Chartres	36	48.27N	1.30 E
Char Us nuur ⊜	66	48.00N	92.10 E
Chase City	142	36.47N	78.27W
Chaska	138	44.47N	93.36W
Chatanga ≃	56	72.55N	106.00 E
Chatangskij zaliv c	54	73.30N	109.00 E
Châteaubriant	36	47.43N	1.23W
Château d'Oex	36	46.28N	7.08 E
Château-du-Loir	36	47.42N	0.25 E
Châteaudun	36	48.05N	1.20 E
Chateaugay	136	44.55N	74.04W
Châteauguay ≃	136	45.24N	73.45W
Château-Landon	36	48.09N	2.42 E
Châteauneuf-sur-Sarthe	36	47.41N	0.30W
Châteauroux	36	46.49N	1.42 E
Château-Thierry	36	49.03N	3.24 E
Châtellerault	36	46.49N	0.33 E
Châtel-sur-Moselle	36	48.18N	6.24 E
Chatfield	138	43.50N	92.11W
Chatgal	66	50.26N	100.09 E
Chatham, N.B., Can.	130	47.02N	65.28W
Chatham, On., Can.	130	42.24N	82.11W
Chatham, Eng., U.K.	26	51.23N	0.32 E
Chatham, Ma., U.S.	136	41.40N	69.57W
Chatham, N.Y., U.S.	136	42.21N	73.35W
Chatham Islands ıı	8	43.55S	176.30W
Châtillon	40	45.45N	7.37 E
Châtillon-sur-Seine	36	47.51N	4.33 E
Chatsworth	142	34.45N	84.46W
Chattahoochee	142	30.42N	84.50W
Chattahoochee ≃	142	30.52N	84.57W
Chattanooga	144	35.02N	85.18W
Chauk	68	20.54N	94.50 E
Chaumont	36	48.07N	5.08 E
Chauncey	136	39.23N	82.07W
Chauny	36	49.37N	3.13 E
Chaussin	36	46.58N	5.25 E
Chautauqua Lake ⊜	136	42.12N	79.27W
Chauvin	144	29.26N	90.35W
Chaves	44	41.44N	7.28W
Chazy	136	44.53N	73.26W
Cheaha Mountain ∧	144	33.30N	85.47W
Cheat ≃	136	39.45N	79.54W
Cheb	30	50.01N	12.25 E
Chebanse	138	41.00N	87.54W
Cheboksary → Čeboksary	20	56.09N	47.15 E
Cheboygan	138	45.38N	84.28W
Chech, Erg ◄►²	82	25.00N	2.15W
Cheddar	26	51.17N	2.46W
Cheduba Island ı	68	18.48N	93.38 E
Cheektowaga	136	42.55N	78.46W
Chefoo → Yantai	66	37.33N	121.20 E
Chehalis	150	46.39N	122.57W
Chehalis ≃	150	46.57N	123.50W
Cheju	66	33.31N	126.32 E
Cheju-do ı	66	33.20N	126.30 E
Chelan	150	47.50N	120.00W
Chelan, Lake ⊜	150	48.05N	120.30W
Chelghoum el Aïd	44	36.10N	6.10 E
Chelif, Oued ≃	44	36.01N	0.07 E
Chełm	30	51.10N	23.28 E
Chełmno	30	53.22N	18.26 E
Chelmsford	26	51.44N	0.28 E
Chełmża	30	53.12N	18.37 E
Chelsea, Ia., U.S.	138	41.55N	92.23W
Chelsea, Mi., U.S.	138	42.19N	84.01W
Cheltenham	26	51.54N	2.04W
Chelyabinsk → Čel'abinsk	54	55.10N	61.24 E
Chelyan	136	38.11N	81.29W
Chemnitz → Karl-Marx-Stadt	30	50.50N	12.55 E
Chemult	150	43.13N	121.46W
Chenāb ≃	70	29.23N	71.02 E
Chenango Bridge	136	42.10N	75.51W
Cheney	150	47.29N	117.34W
Chengde	66	40.58N	117.53 E
Chengdu	66	30.39N	104.04 E
Chengshan Jiao >	66	37.24N	122.42 E
Chengtu → Chengdu	66	30.39N	104.04 E
Chenoa	144	40.44N	88.43W
Chenxian	66	25.48N	112.59 E
Chepén	118	7.13S	79.27W
Chépénéhé	92	20.47S	167.09 E
Cher ≃	36	47.21N	0.29 E
Cheraw	142	34.41N	79.53W
Cherbourg	36	49.39N	1.39W
Cherchell	44	36.36N	2.12 E
Cherepovets → Čerepovec	20	59.08N	37.54 E
Chergui, Chott ech ⊜	82	34.21N	0.30 E
Chernovtsy → Černovcy	48	48.18N	25.56 E
Cherokee	144	34.45N	87.58W
Cherokee Lake ⊜¹	142	36.16N	83.20W
Cherokees, Lake O' The ⊜¹	144	36.39N	94.49W
Cherry Hill	136	39.56N	75.01W
Cherryville	142	35.22N	81.22W
Cherson	54	46.38N	32.35 E
Chesaning	138	43.11N	84.06W
Chesapeake	142	36.49N	76.16W
Chesapeake Bay c	132	38.40N	76.25W
Chesapeake Beach	136	38.41N	76.32W
Chesapeake City	136	39.31N	75.48W
Chesdin, Lake ⊜¹	142	37.15N	77.33W
Cheshire	136	42.33N	73.09W
Cheshire □⁶	26	53.23N	2.30W
Chesnee	142	35.08N	81.51W
Chester, Eng., U.K.	26	53.12N	2.54W
Chester, Il., U.S.	144	37.54N	89.49W
Chester, Pa., U.S.	136	39.50N	75.21W
Chester, S.C., U.S.	142	34.42N	81.12W
Chester, Vt., U.S.	136	43.15N	72.35W
Chester, Va., U.S.	142	37.21N	77.26W
Chesterfield, Eng., U.K.	26	53.15N	1.25W
Chesterfield, Va., U.S.	142	37.22N	77.30W
Chesterfield, Île ı	86	16.20S	43.58 E
Chesterfield, Îles ıı	96	19.30S	158.00 E
Chester-le-Street	26	54.52N	1.34W
Chesterton	144	41.36N	87.03W
Chestertown	136	39.12N	76.04W
Chesuncook Lake ⊜	136	46.00N	69.20W
Chetaïbi	40	37.04N	7.23 E
Chetek	138	45.18N	91.39W
Cheviot	136	39.09N	84.36W
Chew Bahir (Lake Stefanie) ⊜	84	4.40N	36.50 E
Chewelah	150	48.16N	117.42W
Cheyenne	148	41.08N	104.49W
Cheyenne ≃	132	44.40N	101.15W
Chi ≃	68	15.11N	104.43 E
Chiai	66	23.29N	120.27 E
Chianciano Terme	40	43.03N	11.50 E
Chiang Mai	68	18.47N	98.59 E
Chiang Rai	68	19.54N	99.50 E
Chiari	40	45.32N	9.56 E
Chiavari	40	44.19N	9.19 E
Chiba	66	35.36N	140.07 E
Chibougamau	130	49.55N	74.22W
Chicago	138	41.51N	87.39W
Chicago Heights	138	41.30N	87.38W
Chicapa ≃	86	6.26S	20.47 E
Chichester	26	50.50N	0.48W
Chickamauga	142	34.52N	85.17W
Chickamauga Lake ⊜¹	142	35.22N	85.02W
Chickasaw	144	30.45N	88.04W
Chickasawhay ≃	144	31.00N	88.45W
Chickasha	132	35.03N	97.56W
Chiclana de la Frontera	44	36.25N	6.08W
Chiclayo	118	6.46S	79.51W
Chico	154	39.43N	121.50W
Chico ≃, Arg.	120	49.56S	68.32W
Chico ≃, Arg.	120	43.48S	66.25W
Chicopee, Ga., U.S.	142	34.15N	83.50W
Chicopee, Ma., U.S.	136	42.08N	72.36W
Chicoutimi	130	48.26N	71.04W
Chiemsee ⊜	30	47.54N	12.29 E
Chieri	40	45.01N	7.49 E
Chieti	40	42.21N	14.10 E
Chifeng	66	42.18N	119.00 E
Chihli, Gulf of → Bo Hai c	66	38.30N	120.00 E
Chihuahua	108	28.38N	106.05W
Childersburg	144	33.16N	86.21W
Childress	132	34.25N	100.12W
Chile □¹	120	30.00S	71.00W
Chilhowie	142	36.47N	81.40W
Chilia, Braţul ≃¹	48	45.18N	29.40 E
Chililabombwe (Bancroft)	86	12.18S	27.43 E
Chilin → Jilin	66	43.51N	126.33 E
Chilka Lake ⊜	70	19.45N	85.25 E
Chillán	120	36.36S	72.07W
Chillicothe, Il., U.S.	138	40.55N	89.29W
Chillicothe, Mo., U.S.	144	39.47N	93.33W
Chillicothe, Oh., U.S.	136	39.19N	82.58W
Chilliwack	130	49.10N	121.57W
Chillon, Château de ⊥	36	46.25N	6.56 E
Chiloé, Isla de ı	120	42.30S	73.55W
Chilpancingo	108	17.33N	99.30W
Chilton	138	44.01N	88.09W
Chilung	66	25.08N	121.44 E
Chilwa, Lake ⊜	86	15.12S	35.50 E
Chimayo	148	36.00N	105.55W
Chimborazo ∧¹	118	1.28S	78.48W
Chimbote	118	9.05S	78.36W
Chimkent → Čimkent	54	42.18N	69.36 E
Chimney Reservoir ⊜¹	154	41.25N	117.10W
Chimoio	86	19.08S	33.29 E
China (Zhongguo) □¹	66	35.00N	105.00 E
China Grove	142	35.34N	80.34W
China Lake ⊜	154	35.46N	117.39W
Chinandega	108	12.37N	87.09W
Chincha Alta	118	13.27S	76.08W
Chinchorro, Banco ◆⁴	108	18.35N	87.22W
Chincoteague	142	37.55N	75.22W
Chinde	86	18.37S	36.24 E
Chindwin ≃	68	21.26N	95.15 E
Chingola	86	12.32S	27.52 E
Chinhae	66	35.09N	128.40 E
Chin Hills ⩘²	68	22.30N	93.30 E
Chinju	66	35.11N	128.05 E
Chinko ≃	84	4.50N	23.53 E
Chino	154	34.00N	117.41W
Chinon	36	47.10N	0.15 E
Chinook	150	48.35N	109.13W
Chinquapin	142	34.49N	77.49W
Chioggia	40	45.13N	12.17 E
Chios → Khíos	48	38.22N	26.08 E
Chios → Khíos ı	48	38.22N	26.00 E
Chipata	86	13.39S	32.40 E
Chippenham	26	51.28N	2.07W
Chippewa ≃	138	44.25N	92.10W
Chippewa, Lake ⊜	138	45.56N	91.13W
Chippewa Falls	138	44.56N	91.23W
Chiquimula	108	14.48N	89.33W
Chiquinquirá	118	5.37N	73.50W
Chirfa	82	20.57N	12.21 E
Chiricahua Peak ∧	148	31.52N	109.20W
Chiriquí, Golfo de c	108	8.00N	82.20W
Chirripó, Cerro ∧	108	9.29N	83.30W
Chisago City	138	45.22N	92.53W
Chisasibi	130	53.50N	79.00W
Chisholm, Al., U.S.	144	32.25N	86.15W
Chisholm, Mn., U.S.	138	47.29N	92.53W
Chisone ≃	40	44.49N	7.25 E
Chitipa	86	9.43S	33.16 E
Chitrāl	70	35.51N	71.47 E
Chitré	108	7.58N	80.26W
Chittagong	70	22.20N	91.50 E
Chiumbe ≃	86	7.00S	21.12 E
Chiuta, Lake ⊜	86	14.55S	35.50 E
Chivasso	40	45.11N	7.53 E
Chjargas nuur ⊜	66	49.12N	93.24 E
Chmel'nickij	54	49.25N	27.00 E
Chochis, Cerro ∧	118	18.04S	60.03W
Chociwel	30	53.28N	15.19 E
Chocolate Mountains ⩘	154	33.20N	115.15W
Choctawhatchee Bay c	144	30.25N	86.21W
Chodzież	30	52.59N	16.56 E
Choele-Choel	120	39.16S	65.41W
Choiseul ı	94	7.05S	157.00 E
Chojnice	30	53.42N	17.34 E
Chojnów	30	51.17N	15.56 E
Cholet	36	47.04N	0.53W
Choluteca	108	13.18N	87.12W
Choma	86	16.48S	26.59 E
Chomo Lhāri ∧	70	27.50N	89.15 E
Chomutov	30	50.28N	13.26 E
Ch'ŏnan	66	36.48N	127.09 E
Chon Buri	68	13.22N	100.59 E
Chone	118	0.41S	80.06W
Ch'ŏngjin	66	41.47N	129.50 E
Ch'ŏngju	66	36.39N	127.31 E
Chongqing	66	29.34N	106.35 E
Chŏnju	66	35.49N	127.08 E
Chonos, Archipiélago de los ıı	120	45.00S	74.00W
Chop'or ≃	54	49.36N	42.19 E
Ch'ŏrwŏn	66	38.16N	127.12 E
Chorzele	30	53.16N	20.55 E
Choszczno	30	53.10N	15.26 E
Choteau	150	47.48N	112.10W
Chovd	66	48.01N	91.38 E
Chovd ≃	66	48.06N	92.11 E
Chövsgöl Nuur ⊜	66	51.00N	100.30 E
Chowan ≃	142	36.00N	76.40W
Chowchilla	154	37.07N	120.15W
Christianshåb (Qasigiannguit)	130	68.50N	51.12W
Christchurch, N.Z.	98	43.32S	172.38 E
Christchurch, Eng., U.K.	26	50.44N	1.45W
Christiansburg	142	37.07N	80.24W
Christina ≃	130	56.40N	111.03W
Christmas Island □²	68	10.30S	105.40 E
Christopher	144	37.58N	89.03W
Chrudim	30	49.57N	15.48 E
Chrzanów	30	50.09N	19.24 E
Chu ≃	68	19.53N	105.45 E
Chubbuck	150	42.55N	112.27W
Chubut ≃	120	43.20S	65.03W

Symbols in the index entries are identified on page 162.

Chuk—Culy

Name	Page	Lat.	Long.
Chukchi Sea ▾[2]	56	69.00N	175.00W
Chula Vista	154	32.38N	117.05W
Chulucanas	118	5.06S	80.10W
Chumphon	68	10.30N	99.10 E
Ch'unch'ŏn	66	37.52N	127.43 E
Ch'ungju	66	36.58N	127.58 E
Chungking → Chongqing	66	29.34N	106.35 E
Chuquicamata	120	22.19S	68.56W
Chur	36	46.51N	9.32 E
Church Hill	142	36.31N	82.42W
Churchill	130	58.46N	94.10W
Churchill ≃, Can.	130	58.47N	94.12W
Churchill ≃, Nf., Can.	130	53.30N	60.10W
Churchill, Cape ›	130	58.46N	93.12W
Churchill Falls ↳	130	53.35N	64.27W
Churchill Lake ⊜	130	55.55N	108.20W
Church Point	144	30.24N	92.12W
Churubusco	144	41.13N	85.19W
Chuxiong	66	25.02N	101.30 E
Cianjur	68	6.49S	107.08 E
Cicero, Il., U.S.	138	41.50N	87.45W
Cicero, In., U.S.	144	40.07N	86.00W
Ciechanów	30	52.53N	20.38 E
Ciego de Avila	108	21.51N	78.46W
Ciempozuelos	44	40.10N	3.37W
Ciénaga	118	11.01N	74.15W
Cienfuegos	108	22.09N	80.27W
Čierna [nad Tisou]	30	48.25N	22.05 E
Cieszanów	30	50.16N	23.08 E
Cieszyn	30	49.45N	18.38 E
Cieza	44	38.14N	1.25W
Cigüela ≃	44	39.08N	3.44W
Cijara, Embalse de ⊜[1]	44	39.18N	4.52W
Čikoj ≃	56	51.02N	106.39 E
Cilacap	68	7.44S	109.00 E
Cilento ◆[1]	40	40.15N	15.10 E
Cimarron ≃	132	36.10N	96.17W
Čimkent	54	42.18N	69.36 E
Ciml'anskoje vodochranilišče ⊜[1]	54	48.00N	43.00 E
Cimone, Monte ∧	40	44.12N	10.42 E
Cîmpia Turzii	48	46.33N	23.54 E
Cîmpina	48	45.08N	25.44 E
Cîmpulung	48	45.16N	25.03 E
Cîmpulung Moldovenesc	48	47.31N	25.34 E
Cina, Tanjung ›	68	5.56S	104.45 E
Cincar ∧	40	43.54N	17.04 E
Cincinnati, Ia., U.S.	138	40.37N	92.55W
Cincinnati, Oh., U.S.	136	39.09N	84.27W
Çine	48	37.36N	28.04 E
Ciney	30	50.18N	5.06 E
Cingoli	40	43.22N	13.13 E
Cinto, Monte ∧	40	42.23N	8.56 E
Ciociaria ◆[1]	40	41.45N	13.15 E
Cipolletti	120	38.56S	67.59W
Čirčik	54	41.29N	69.35 E
Circle	150	47.20N	105.35W
Circleville, Oh., U.S.	136	39.36N	82.56W
Circleville, Ut,. U.S.	148	38.10N	112.16W
Circleville Mountain ∧	148	38.12N	112.24W
Cirebon	68	6.44S	108.34 E
Ciremay, Gunung ∧	68	6.54S	108.24 E
Cirencester	26	51.44N	1.59W
Ciriè	40	45.14N	7.36 E
Cîrlibaba	48	47.35N	25.07 E
Cirpan	48	42.12N	25.20 E
Ciskei □[1]	86	32.50S	27.00 E
Cisnădie	48	45.43N	24.09 E
Cistierna	44	42.48N	5.07W
Čistopol'	20	55.21N	50.37 E
Čita	56	52.03N	113.30 E
Citronelle	144	31.05N	88.13W
Citrus Heights	154	38.42N	121.16W
Città di Castello	40	43.27N	12.14 E
Cittanova	40	38.21N	16.05 E
City of Sunrise	142	26.08N	80.06W
City Point	142	28.24N	80.45W
Ciucaş, Vîrful ∧	48	45.31N	25.55 E
Ciudad Bolívar	118	8.08N	63.33W
Ciudad del Carmen	108	18.38N	91.50W
Ciudad de México (Mexico City)	108	19.24N	99.09W
Ciudad Guayana	118	8.22N	62.40W
Ciudad Guzmán	108	19.41N	103.29W
Ciudad Juárez	108	31.44N	106.29W
Ciudad Mante	108	22.44N	98.57W
Ciudad Obregón	108	27.29N	109.56W
Ciudad Ojeda	118	10.12N	71.19W
Ciudad Real	44	38.59N	3.56W
Ciudad Rodrigo	44	40.36N	6.32W
Ciudad Valles	108	21.59N	99.01W
Ciudad Victoria	108	23.44N	99.08W
Ciutadella	44	40.02N	3.50 E
Civita Castellana	40	42.17N	12.25 E
Civitanova Marche	40	43.18N	13.44 E
Civitavecchia	40	42.06N	11.48 E
Civray	36	46.09N	0.18 E
C.J. Strike Reservoir ⊜[1]	150	42.57N	115.53W
Clacton-on-Sea	26	51.48N	1.09 E
Clain ≃	36	46.47N	0.32 E
Claire, Lake ⊜	130	58.35N	112.05W
Clair Engle Lake ⊜[1]	154	40.52N	122.43W
Clairton	136	40.17N	79.52W
Clanton	144	32.50N	86.37W
Clare	138	43.49N	84.46W
Clare □[6]	26	52.50N	9.00W
Clare Island I	26	53.48N	10.00W
Claremont, Ca., U.S.	154	34.05N	117.43W
Claremont, N.H., U.S.	136	43.22N	72.20W
Claremont ∧	154	39.53N	120.57W
Clarence Strait ʮ	96	12.00S	131.00 E
Clarendon, Ar., U.S.	144	34.41N	91.18W
Clarendon, Pa., U.S.	136	41.46N	79.05W
Claresholm	130	50.02N	113.35W
Clarion, Ia., U.S.	138	42.43N	93.43W
Clarion, Pa., U.S.	136	41.12N	79.23W
Clarion ≃	136	41.07N	79.41W
Clark Canyon Reservoir ⊜[1]	150	44.58N	112.51W
Clark Fork ≃	150	48.09N	116.15W
Clark Mountain ∧	154	35.32N	115.35W
Clarks	144	32.01N	92.08W
Clarks ≃	144	37.03N	88.33W
Clarksburg	136	39.16N	80.20W
Clarksdale	144	34.12N	90.34W
Clarks Hill	144	40.14N	86.43W
Clarks Hill Lake ⊜[1]	142	33.50N	82.20W
Clarks Summit	136	41.29N	75.42W
Clarkston	150	46.24N	117.02W
Clarksville, Ar., U.S.	144	35.28N	93.27W
Clarksville, In., U.S.	144	38.15N	85.47W
Clarksville, Tn., U.S.	144	36.31N	87.21W
Clarksville, Tx., U.S.	144	33.36N	95.03W
Clarkton	142	34.29N	78.39W
Clatskanie	150	46.06N	123.12W
Clausthal-Zellerfeld	30	51.48N	10.20 E
Claxton	142	32.09N	81.54W
Clay	136	38.27N	81.05W
Clay City	142	37.51N	83.55W
Claymont	136	39.48N	75.27W
Claypool	148	33.24N	110.50W
Claysburg	136	40.17N	78.27W
Clayton, Al., U.S.	144	31.52N	85.26W
Clayton, De., U.S.	136	39.17N	75.38W
Clayton, La., U.S.	144	31.43N	91.32W
Clayton, Mo., U.S.	144	38.38N	90.19W
Clayton, N.M., U.S.	132	36.27N	103.11W
Clayton, N.Y., U.S.	136	44.14N	76.05W
Clayton, N.C., U.S.	142	35.39N	78.27W
Clearfield, Pa., U.S.	136	41.01N	78.26W
Clearfield, Ut,. U.S.	148	41.06N	112.01W
Clear Island I	26	51.26N	9.30W
Clear Lake	138	43.08N	93.22W
Clear Lake ⊜[1]	154	39.02N	122.50W
Clear Lake Reservoir ⊜[1]	154	41.52N	121.08W
Clearwater, Fl., U.S.	142	27.57N	82.48W
Clearwater, S.C., U.S.	142	33.29N	81.53W
Clearwater ≃	150	46.25N	117.02W
Clearwater Mountains ⩘	150	46.00N	115.30W
Cleburne	132	32.20N	97.23W
Cle Elum	150	47.11N	120.56W
Cleethorpes	26	53.34N	0.02W
Clemson	142	34.41N	82.50W
Clerke Rocks II[1]	120	55.01S	34.41W
Clermont, Fr.	36	49.23N	2.24 E
Clermont, Fl., U.S.	142	28.32N	81.46W
Clermont-Ferrand	36	45.47N	3.05 E
Cleveland, Ga., U.S.	142	34.35N	83.45W
Cleveland, Ms., U.S.	144	33.44N	90.43W
Cleveland, N.C., U.S.	142	35.43N	80.40W
Cleveland, Oh., U.S.	136	41.29N	81.41W
Cleveland, Tn., U.S.	144	35.09N	84.52W
Cleveland, Mount ∧	150	48.56N	113.51W
Cleves → Kleve	30	51.48N	6.09 E
Clew Bay ⊂	26	53.50N	9.50W
Clewiston	142	26.45N	80.56W
Clifton, Az., U.S.	148	33.03N	109.17W
Clifton, Il., U.S.	144	40.56N	87.56W
Clifton, Tn., U.S.	144	35.23N	87.59W
Clifton Forge	142	37.48N	79.49W
Climax, Co., U.S.	148	39.22N	106.10W
Climax, Mi., U.S.	138	42.14N	85.20W
Clinch ≃	142	35.53N	84.29W
Clingmans Dome ∧	142	35.35N	83.30W
Clinton, Ar., U.S.	144	35.35N	92.27W
Clinton, Ct., U.S.	136	41.16N	72.31W
Clinton, Il., U.S.	144	40.09N	88.57W
Clinton, In., U.S.	144	39.39N	87.23W
Clinton, Ia., U.S.	138	41.50N	90.11W
Clinton, La., U.S.	144	30.51N	91.00W
Clinton, Me., U.S.	136	44.38N	69.30W
Clinton, Ma., U.S.	136	42.25N	71.41W
Clinton, Mi., U.S.	138	42.04N	83.58W
Clinton, Ms., U.S.	144	32.20N	90.19W
Clinton, Mo., U.S.	144	38.22N	93.46W
Clinton, N.C., U.S.	142	34.59N	78.19W
Clinton, Ok., U.S.	132	35.30N	98.58W
Clinton, S.C., U.S.	142	34.28N	81.52W
Clinton, Tn., U.S.	142	36.06N	84.07W
Clinton, Lake ⊜[1]	144	40.10N	88.50W
Clinton Lake ⊜[1]	144	38.55N	95.25W
Clintonville	138	44.37N	88.45W
Clio, Al., U.S.	144	31.42N	85.36W
Clio, S.C., U.S.	142	34.34N	79.32W
Clipperton, Île I[1]	108	10.17N	109.13W
Cloncurry	96	20.42S	140.30 E
Clonmel	26	52.21N	7.42W
Cloppenburg	30	52.50N	8.02 E
Cloquet	138	46.43N	92.27W
Cloudcroft	148	32.57N	105.44W
Cloud Peak ∧	150	44.25N	107.10W
Cloudy Bay ⊂	98	41.27S	174.10 E
Clover	142	35.06N	81.13W
Clovis, Ca., U.S.	154	36.49N	119.42W
Clovis, N.M., U.S.	132	34.24N	103.12W
Cluj-Napoca	48	46.47N	23.36 E
Clusone	40	45.53N	9.57 E
Clutha ≃	98	46.21S	169.48 E
Clwyd □[6]	26	53.05N	3.20W
Clyde, N.Y., U.S.	136	43.05N	76.52W
Clyde, N.C., U.S.	142	35.32N	82.54W
Clyde, Oh., U.S.	136	41.18N	82.58W
Clyde ≃	26	55.56N	4.29W
Clyde, Firth of ⊂[1]	26	55.42N	5.00W
Clymer	136	40.40N	79.00W
Côa ≃	44	41.05N	7.06W
Coachella	154	33.40N	116.10W
Coachella Canal ≋	154	33.34N	116.00W
Coal City	138	41.17N	88.17W
Coal Fork	136	38.19N	81.32W
Coal Hill	144	35.26N	93.40W
Coalinga	154	36.08N	120.21W
Coalport	136	40.44N	78.32W
Coalville	148	40.55N	111.23W
Coast Mountains ⩘	130	55.00N	129.00W
Coast Ranges ⩘	132	41.00N	123.30W
Coatbridge	26	55.52N	4.01W
Coatesville	136	39.58N	75.49W
Coaticook	130	45.08N	71.48W
Coatzacoalcos	108	18.09N	94.25W
Cobalt	130	47.24N	79.41W
Cobán	108	15.29N	90.19W
Cobh	26	51.51N	8.17W
Coblenz → Koblenz	30	50.21N	7.35 E
Cobleskill	136	42.40N	74.29W
Cobourg	130	43.58N	78.10W
Cobourg Peninsula ›[1]	96	11.20S	132.15 E
Coburg	30	50.15N	10.58 E
Coburn Mountain ∧	136	45.28N	70.06W
Cochabamba	118	17.24S	66.09W
Cochem	30	50.11N	7.09 E
Cochin	70	9.58N	76.14 E
Cochise Head ∧	148	32.03N	109.18W
Cochran	142	32.23N	83.21W
Cochrane	130	49.04N	81.01W
Cochrane ≃	130	57.52N	101.38W
Cochrane, Lago (Lago Pueyrredón) ⊜	120	47.20S	72.00W
Cockburn, Mount ∧	96	25.57S	129.27 E
Cockburn Island I	138	45.55N	83.22W
Cockermouth	26	54.40N	3.21W
Coco ≃	108	15.00N	83.10W
Coco, Isla del I	108	5.32N	87.04W
Cocoa	142	28.23N	80.44W
Cocoa Beach	142	28.19N	80.36W
Coco Channel ʮ	68	13.45N	93.00 E
Coco Islands II	68	14.05N	93.18 E
Cod, Cape ›[1]	136	41.42N	70.15W
Codlea	48	45.42N	25.27 E
Codogno	40	45.09N	9.42 E
Codru-Moma, Munții ⩘	48	46.30N	22.20 E
Cody	150	44.31N	109.03W
Coen	96	13.56S	143.12 E
Coeur d'Alene	150	47.40N	116.46W
Coeur d'Alene Lake ⊜	150	47.32N	116.48W
Coeur d'Alene Mountains ⩘	150	47.50N	116.05W
Coffeen	144	39.05N	89.24W
Coffeyville	132	37.02N	95.36W
Cofrents	44	39.14N	1.04W
Cognac	36	45.42N	0.20W
Cohoes	136	42.46N	73.42W
Coiba, Isla de I	108	7.27N	81.45W
Coimbatore	70	11.00N	76.58 E
Coimbra	44	40.12N	8.25W
Coín, Esp.	44	36.40N	4.45W
Coin, Ia., U.S.	144	40.39N	95.13W
Čojbalsan	66	48.04N	114.30 E
Cokato	138	45.04N	94.11W
Colatina	118	19.32S	40.37W
Colchester, Eng., U.K.	26	51.54N	0.54 E
Colchester, Ct., U.S.	136	41.34N	72.19W
Cold Spring	138	45.27N	94.25W
Coldwater, Mi., U.S.	138	41.56N	85.00W
Coldwater, Ms., U.S.	144	34.41N	89.58W
Coldwater, Oh., U.S.	136	40.28N	84.37W
Coldwater ≃	144	34.11N	90.13W
Colebrook	136	44.53N	71.29W
Coleman, Mi., U.S.	138	43.45N	84.35W
Coleman, Wi., U.S.	138	45.03N	88.02W
Coleraine	26	55.08N	6.40W
Colfax, Ia., U.S.	138	41.40N	93.14W
Colfax, La., U.S.	144	31.31N	92.42W
Colfax, Wa., U.S.	150	46.52N	117.21W
Colhué Huapi, Lago ⊜	120	45.30S	68.48W
Colima	108	19.14N	103.43W
Coll I	26	56.38N	6.34W
Collegedale	144	35.04N	85.03W
College Park	142	33.39N	84.26W
College Place	150	46.02N	118.23W
College Station	144	34.43N	92.13W
Collegeville	144	40.54N	87.09W
Collesalvetti	40	43.35N	10.28 E
Collier Bay ⊂	96	16.10S	124.15 E
Collierville	144	35.02N	89.39W
Collingwood	130	44.29N	80.13W
Collinsville	144	34.15N	85.51W
Collinwood	144	35.10N	87.44W
Collister	150	43.38N	116.15W
Colmar	36	48.05N	7.22 E
Colmars	36	44.11N	6.38 E
Colo	138	42.01N	93.18W
Cologne → Köln, B.R.D.	30	50.56N	6.59 E
Cologne, Mn., U.S.	138	44.46N	93.46W
Colomb-Béchar → Béchar	82	31.37N	2.13W
Colombia □[1]	118	4.00N	72.00W
Colombo	70	6.56N	79.51 E
Colón, Cuba	108	22.43N	80.54W
Colón, Pan.	108	9.22N	79.54W
Colon, Mi., U.S.	138	41.57N	85.19W
Colón, Archipiélago de (Galapagos Islands) II	8	0.30S	90.30W
Colonești	48	46.34N	27.18 E
Colonet, Cabo ›	108	30.58N	116.19W
Colonial Heights	142	37.14N	77.24W
Colonna, Capo ›	40	39.02N	17.11 E
Colorado □[3]	132	39.00N	105.30W
Colorado ≃, Arg.	120	39.50S	62.08W
Colorado ≃, N.A.	132	31.54N	114.57W
Colorado ≃, Tx., U.S.	132	28.36N	95.58W
Colorado National Monument ♦	148	39.04N	108.25W
Colorado River Aqueduct ≋[1]	154	33.50N	117.23W
Colorado Springs	148	38.50N	104.49W
Colquitt	142	31.10N	84.44W
Colt	144	35.07N	90.48W
Colton	154	34.04N	117.18W
Columbia, Il., U.S.	144	38.26N	90.12W
Columbia, Ky., U.S.	144	37.06N	85.18W
Columbia, Md., U.S.	136	39.14N	76.50W
Columbia, Ms., U.S.	144	31.15N	89.50W
Columbia, Mo., U.S.	144	38.57N	92.20W
Columbia, N.C., U.S.	142	35.55N	76.15W
Columbia, Pa., U.S.	136	40.02N	76.30W
Columbia, S.C., U.S.	142	34.00N	81.02W
Columbia, Tn., U.S.	144	35.36N	87.02W
Columbia ≃	130	46.15N	124.05W
Columbia, Mount ∧	130	52.09N	117.25W
Columbia City	144	41.09N	85.29W
Columbia Falls	150	48.22N	114.10W
Columbia Mountains ⩘	130	52.00N	119.00W
Columbiana, Al., U.S.	144	33.10N	86.36W
Columbiana, Oh., U.S.	136	40.53N	80.41W
Columbiaville	138	43.09N	83.24W
Columbus, Ga., U.S.	142	32.29N	84.59W
Columbus, In., U.S.	144	39.12N	85.55W
Columbus, Ms., U.S.	144	33.29N	88.25W
Columbus, Ne., U.S.	132	41.25N	97.22W
Columbus, N.M., U.S.	148	31.49N	107.38W
Columbus, N.C., U.S.	142	35.15N	82.11W
Columbus, Oh., U.S.	136	39.57N	82.59W
Columbus, Wi., U.S.	138	43.20N	89.00W
Colusa	154	39.12N	122.00W
Colville	150	48.32N	117.54W
Colville, Cape ›	98	36.28S	175.21 E
Colwyn Bay	26	53.18N	3.43W
Comacchio	40	44.42N	12.11 E
Comănești	48	46.25N	26.26 E
Comayagua	108	14.25N	87.37W
Combahee ≃	142	32.30N	80.31W
Combarbalá	120	31.11S	71.02W
Combeaufontaine	36	47.43N	5.53 E
Comilla	70	23.27N	91.12 E
Comino → Kemmuna I	40	36.00N	14.20 E
Comino, Capo ›	40	40.32N	9.49 E
Comiso	40	36.56N	14.36 E
Comitán	108	16.15N	92.08W
Comloșu Mare	48	45.54N	20.38 E
Commerce	142	34.12N	83.27W
Commerce City	148	39.49N	104.56W
Commercy	36	48.45N	5.35 E
Comminges ◆[1]	36	43.15N	0.45 E
Como, It.	40	45.47N	9.05 E
Como, Ms., U.S.	144	34.30N	89.56W
Como, Lago di ⊜	40	46.00N	9.20 E
Comodoro Rivadavia	120	45.52S	67.30W
Comores, Archipel des II	86	12.10S	44.15 E
Comorin, Cape ›	70	8.06N	77.33 E
Comoros (Comores) □[1]	86	12.10S	44.15 E
Compiègne	36	49.25N	2.50 E
Compton	154	33.53N	118.13W
Conakry	82	9.31N	13.43W
Concarneau	36	47.52N	3.55W
Concepción, Bol.	118	16.15S	62.04W
Concepción, Chile	120	36.50S	73.03W
Concepción, Para.	120	23.25S	57.17W
Concepción, Laguna ⊜	118	17.29S	61.25W
Concepción del Uruguay	120	32.29S	58.14W
Conception, Point ›	154	34.27N	120.27W
Conception Bay ⊂	130	47.45N	53.00W
Conchos ≃	108	29.35N	104.25W
Concord, Ca., U.S.	154	37.58N	122.01W
Concord, N.H., U.S.	136	43.12N	71.32W
Concord, N.C., U.S.	142	35.24N	80.34W
Concordia, Arg.	120	31.24S	58.02W
Concordia, Mo., U.S.	144	38.59N	93.34W
Concrete	150	48.32N	121.44W
Condé	36	48.51N	0.33W
Condom	36	43.58N	0.22 E
Conecuh ≃	144	30.58N	87.14W
Conegliano	40	45.53N	12.18 E
Confluence	136	39.48N	79.21W
Confuso ≃	120	25.09S	57.34W
Congaree ≃	142	33.45N	80.37W
Congleton	26	53.10N	2.13W
Congo □[1]	86	1.00S	15.00 E
Congo (Zaire) (Zaïre) ≃	86	6.04S	12.24 E
Conn, Lough ⊜	26	54.04N	9.20W
Connaught □[9]	26	53.45N	9.00W
Conneaut	136	41.56N	80.33W
Conneautville	136	41.45N	80.22W
Connecticut □[3]	132	41.45N	72.45W
Connecticut ≃	136	41.17N	72.21W
Connell	150	46.39N	118.51W
Connellsville	136	40.01N	79.35W
Connemara ◆[1]	26	53.25N	9.45W
Connersville	144	39.38N	85.08W
Conover	142	35.42N	81.13W
Conrad, Ia., U.S.	138	42.13N	92.52W
Conrad, Mt., U.S.	150	48.10N	111.56W
Conselheiro Lafaiete	118	20.40S	43.48W
Consett	26	54.51N	1.49W
Con Son II	68	8.43N	106.36 E
Constance → Konstanz	30	47.40N	9.10 E
Constance, Lake → Bodensee ⊜	36	47.35N	9.25 E
Constância	44	39.28N	8.20W
Constanța	48	44.11N	28.39 E
Constantina	44	37.52N	5.37W
Constantine → Qacentina	82	36.22N	6.37 E
Constantinople → İstanbul	48	41.01N	28.58 E
Consuegra	44	39.28N	3.36W
Continental	136	41.06N	84.15W
Contréa	36	47.25N	1.26 E
Conversano	40	40.58N	17.08 E
Converse	144	40.34N	85.52W
Convoy	136	40.55N	84.42W
Conway, Wales, U.K.	26	53.17N	3.50W
Conway, Ar., U.S.	144	35.05N	92.26W
Conway, Mo., U.S.	144	37.30N	92.49W
Conway, N.H., U.S.	136	43.58N	71.07W
Conway, N.C., U.S.	142	36.26N	77.13W
Conway, S.C., U.S.	142	33.50N	79.02W
Conyers	142	33.40N	84.01W
Cook, Cape ›	130	50.08N	127.55W
Cook, Mount ∧	98	43.36S	170.10 E
Cookeville	144	36.09N	85.30W
Cook Islands □[2]	8	20.00S	158.00W
Cookstown	26	54.39N	6.45W
Cook Strait ʮ	98	41.15S	174.30 E
Cooktown	96	15.28S	145.15 E
Cooleemee	142	35.48N	80.33W
Coolgardie	96	30.57S	121.10 E
Coolidge, Az., U.S.	148	32.58N	111.31W
Coolidge, Ga., U.S.	142	31.00N	83.51W
Coonoor	70	11.21N	76.49 E
Coon Rapids, Ia., U.S.	144	41.52N	94.41W
Coon Rapids, Mn., U.S.	138	45.10N	93.19W
Coon Valley	138	43.42N	91.00W
Cooper Creek ≃	96	28.29S	137.46 E
Cooper Road	144	32.26N	93.48W
Cooperstown	136	42.42N	74.55W
Coosa ≃	144	32.30N	86.16W
Coos Bay	150	43.22N	124.12W
Coos Bay ⊂	150	43.23N	124.16W
Copenhagen → København, Dan.	22	55.40N	12.35 E
Copenhagen, N.Y., U.S.	136	43.53N	75.40W
Copertino	40	40.16N	18.03 E
Copiapó	120	27.22S	70.20W
Copparo	40	44.54N	11.49 E
Copper Harbor	138	47.27N	87.53W
Coppermine Point ›	138	46.59N	84.47W
Coquilhatville → Mbandaka	86	0.04N	18.16 E
Coquille	150	43.10N	124.11W
Coquimbo	120	29.58S	71.21W
Corabia	48	43.46N	24.30 E
Coral Gables	142	25.43N	80.16W
Coral Sea ▾[2]	8	20.00S	158.00 E
Coralville	138	41.40N	91.34W
Coralville Lake ⊜[1]	138	41.47N	91.48W
Corantijn (Corentyne) ≃	118	5.55N	57.05W
Corato	40	41.09N	16.25 E
Corbeil-Essonnes	36	48.36N	2.29 E
Corbières ⩘	36	42.55N	2.38 E
Corbin	142	36.56N	84.05W
Corbu	48	44.29N	24.43 E
Corby	26	52.29N	0.40W
Corcoran	154	36.05N	119.33W
Corcovado, Golfo ⊂	120	43.30S	73.30W
Corcovado, Volcán ∧[1]	120	43.12S	72.48W
Corcubión	44	42.57N	9.11W
Cordele	142	31.57N	83.46W
Cordell Hull Reservoir ⊜[1]	144	36.25N	85.40W
Corder	144	39.05N	93.38W
Cordes	36	44.04N	1.57 E
Córdoba, Arg.	120	31.24S	64.11W
Córdoba, Esp.	44	37.53N	4.46W
Córdoba, Méx.	108	18.53N	96.56W
Cordova → Córdoba, Esp.	44	37.53N	4.46W
Cordova, Al., U.S.	144	33.45N	87.11W
Corentyne (Corantijn) ≃	118	5.55N	57.05W
Corfu → Kérkira	48	39.36N	19.56 E
Corfu → Kérkira I	48	39.40N	19.42 E
Coria del Río	44	37.16N	6.03W
Corigliano Calabro	40	39.36N	16.31 E
Corinth → Kórinthos, Ellás	48	37.56N	22.56 E
Corinth, Ms., U.S.	144	34.56N	88.31W
Corinth, N.Y., U.S.	136	43.14N	73.49W
Corinth, Gulf of → Korinthiakós Kólpos ⊂	48	38.19N	22.04 E
Corinth Canal → Korínthou, Dhiórix ≋	48	37.57N	22.56 E
Cork	26	51.54N	8.28W
Cork □[6]	26	51.58N	8.35W
Cork Harbour ⊂	26	51.45N	8.15W
Corleone	40	37.49N	13.18 E
Çorlu	48	41.09N	27.48 E
Cormons	40	45.58N	13.28 E
Cornelia	142	34.30N	83.31W
Cornell	138	45.10N	91.08W
Corner Brook	130	48.57N	57.57W
Corning, Ar., U.S.	144	36.24N	90.34W
Corning, N.Y., U.S.	136	42.08N	77.03W
Corning, Oh., U.S.	136	39.36N	82.05W
Corno Grande ∧	40	42.28N	13.34 E
Cornwall	130	45.02N	74.44W
Cornwall □[6]	26	50.30N	4.40W
Cornwallis Island I	130	75.15N	94.30W
Coro	118	11.25N	69.41W
Corocoro	118	17.12S	68.29W
Coromandel Coast ⊥[2]	70	13.30N	80.30 E
Coromandel Peninsula ›[1]	98	36.50S	175.35 E
Coromandel Range ⩘	98	37.00S	175.40 E
Corona	154	33.52N	117.33W
Coronado	154	32.41N	117.10W
Coronation Gulf ⊂	130	68.25N	110.00W
Coronel	120	37.01S	73.08W
Coronel Oviedo	120	25.25S	56.27W
Coropuna, Nevado ∧	118	15.31S	72.42W
Corozal	108	18.24N	88.24W
Corpus Christi	132	27.48N	97.23W
Correggio	40	44.46N	10.47 E
Correnti, Isola delle I	40	36.38N	15.05 E
Corrib, Lough ⊜	26	53.26N	9.14W
Corrientes	120	27.28S	58.50W
Corrientes ≃	118	3.43S	74.35W
Corrientes, Cabo ›, Col.	118	5.30N	77.34W
Corrientes, Cabo ›, Méx.	108	20.25N	105.42W
Corry	136	41.55N	79.38W
Corse (Corsica) I	40	42.00N	9.00 E
Corse, Cap ›	40	43.00N	9.25 E
Corsica → Corse I	40	42.00N	9.00 E
Corsicana	132	32.05N	96.28W
Cort Adelaer, Kap ›	130	62.00N	42.00W
Corte	40	42.18N	9.08 E
Cortegana	44	37.55N	6.49W
Cortemilia	40	44.35N	8.12 E
Cortez	148	37.20N	108.35W
Cortina d'Ampezzo	40	46.32N	12.08 E
Cortland	136	42.36N	76.10W
Cortona	40	43.16N	11.59 E
Corubal ≃	82	11.57N	15.06W
Çoruh ≃	16	41.36N	41.35 E
Çorum	48	39.14N	28.27 E
Corumbá	118	19.01S	57.39W
Corunna	138	42.58N	84.07W
Corvallis	150	44.33N	123.15W
Corydon, In., U.S.	144	38.12N	86.07W
Corydon, Ia., U.S.	138	40.45N	93.19W
Corydon, Ky., U.S.	144	37.44N	87.42W
Cos → Kos I	48	36.50N	27.10 E
Cosenza	40	39.17N	16.15 E
Coshocton	136	40.16N	81.51W
Cosmoledo Island I	86	9.43S	47.35 E
Cosne-Cours-sur-Loire	36	47.24N	2.55 E
Costa, Cayo I	142	26.41N	82.15W
Costa Mesa	154	33.38N	117.55W
Costa Rica □[1]	108	10.00N	84.00W
Costiera, Catena ⩘	40	39.20N	16.05 E
Cosumnes ≃	154	38.16N	121.26W
Coswig	30	51.53N	12.26 E
Cotabato	68	7.13N	124.15 E
Cotentin ›[1]	36	49.30N	1.30W
Cotmeana ≃	48	44.24N	24.45 E
Cotonou	82	6.21N	2.26 E
Cotopaxi ∧[1]	118	0.40S	78.26W
Cotswold Hills ⩘[2]	26	51.45N	2.10W
Cottage Grove	150	43.47N	123.03W
Cottageville	142	32.56N	80.28W
Cottbus	30	51.45N	14.19 E
Cottiennes, Alpes (Alpi Cozie) ⩘	40	44.45N	7.00 E
Cottondale, Al., U.S.	144	33.11N	87.27W
Cottondale, Fl., U.S.	142	30.47N	85.22W
Cotton Plant	144	35.00N	91.15W
Cottonport	144	30.59N	92.03W
Cotton Valley	144	32.49N	93.25W
Cottonwood, Az., U.S.	148	34.44N	112.00W
Cottonwood, Id., U.S.	150	46.02N	116.20W
Coubre, Pointe de la ›	36	45.41N	1.13W
Coudersport	136	41.46N	78.01W
Coulee City	150	47.36N	119.17W
Coulee Dam	150	47.57N	118.58W
Coulee Dam National Recreation Area ♦	150	48.10N	118.15W
Coulommiers	36	48.49N	3.05 E
Coulterville, Ca., U.S.	154	37.42N	120.11W
Coulterville, Il., U.S.	144	38.11N	89.36W
Counce	144	35.02N	88.16W
Council Bluffs	144	41.15N	95.51W
Country Homes	150	47.44N	117.24W
Courcelles	30	50.28N	4.22 E
Courtalain	36	48.05N	1.09 E
Courtenay	130	49.41N	125.00W
Courtland	144	34.40N	87.18W
Coushatta	144	32.00N	93.20W
Covelo	154	39.47N	123.14W
Coventry	26	52.25N	1.30W
Covilhã	44	40.17N	7.30W
Covington, Ga., U.S.	142	33.35N	83.51W
Covington, In., U.S.	144	40.08N	87.23W
Covington, Ky., U.S.	136	39.05N	84.30W
Covington, La., U.S.	144	30.28N	90.06W
Covington, Tn., U.S.	144	35.33N	89.38W
Covington, Va., U.S.	142	37.47N	79.59W
Cowan	144	35.09N	86.00W
Coward	142	33.58N	79.44W
Cowdenbeath	26	56.07N	3.21W
Cowen, Mount ∧	150	45.23N	110.29W
Cowes	26	50.45N	1.18W
Cowlitz ≃	150	46.05N	122.53W
Cowpens	142	35.01N	81.48W
Cowpens National Battlefield ♦	142	35.06N	81.46W
Coxsackie	136	42.21N	73.48W
Cox's Bāzār	70	21.26N	91.59 E
Cozie, Alpi (Alpes Cottiennes) ⩘	40	44.45N	7.00 E
Cozumel, Isla de I	108	20.25N	86.55W
Crab Orchard, Ky., U.S.	142	37.27N	84.30W
Crab Orchard, Tn., U.S.	142	35.54N	84.52W
Crab Orchard Lake ⊜[1]	144	37.43N	89.05W
Cradock	86	32.08S	25.36 E
Craig, Co., U.S.	148	40.30N	107.32W
Craig, Mo., U.S.	144	40.11N	95.22W
Craignure	26	56.28N	5.42W
Crailsheim	30	49.08N	10.04 E
Craiova	48	44.19N	23.48 E
Cranbrook	130	49.31N	115.46W
Crandon	138	45.34N	88.54W
Crane, Az., U.S.	148	32.42N	114.40W
Crane, In., U.S.	144	38.53N	86.54W
Crane, Mo., U.S.	144	36.54N	93.34W
Crane Mountain ∧	150	42.04N	120.13W
Cranston	136	41.46N	71.26W
Craon	36	47.51N	0.57W
Crasna	48	46.31N	27.51 E
Crasna (Kraszna) ≃	48	48.09N	22.20 E
Crater Lake ⊜	150	42.56N	122.06W
Crater Lake National Park ♦	150	42.49N	122.08W
Craters of the Moon National Monument ♦	150	43.20N	113.35W
Crateús	118	5.10S	40.40W
Crato	118	7.14S	39.23W
Crauford, Cape ›	130	73.43N	84.50W
Crawford Notch State Park ♦	136	44.13N	71.25W
Crawfordsville	144	40.02N	86.52W
Crawley	26	51.07N	0.12W
Crazy Peak ∧	150	46.01N	110.16W
Cree ≃	130	59.00N	105.47W
Cree Lake ⊜	130	57.30N	106.30W
Creil	36	49.16N	2.29 E
Crema	40	45.22N	9.41 E
Cremona	40	45.07N	10.02 E
Crépy-en-Valois	36	49.14N	2.54 E
Cres, Otok I	40	44.50N	14.25 E
Cresaptown	136	39.35N	78.50W
Crescent Lake ⊜	142	29.28N	81.30W
Cresco	138	43.22N	92.06W
Cresson	136	40.27N	78.35W
Crest	36	44.44N	5.02 E
Crestline	136	40.47N	82.44W
Creston	130	49.06N	116.31W
Crestone Peak ∧	148	37.58N	105.36W
Crestview	144	30.45N	86.34W
Crete	138	41.27N	87.38W
Crete → Kríti I	48	35.29N	24.42 E
Crete, Sea of → Kritikón Pélagos ▾[2]	48	35.46N	23.54 E
Creus, Cap de ›	44	42.19N	3.19 E
Creuse ≃	36	47.00N	0.34 E
Creve Coeur	138	40.38N	89.35W
Crevillent	44	38.15N	0.48W
Crewe	26	53.05N	2.27W
Criciúma	120	28.40S	49.23W
Cricket	142	36.10N	81.11W
Crimea → Krymskij poluostrov ›[1]	54	45.00N	34.00 E
Crimmitschau	30	50.49N	12.23 E
Cripple Creek	148	38.44N	105.10W
Crisfield	136	37.59N	75.51W
Cristóbal Colón, Pico ∧	118	10.50N	73.41W
Crișul Alb ≃	48	46.42N	21.17 E
Crișul Negru ≃	48	46.42N	21.16 E
Crișul Repede (Sebes Körös) ≃	48	46.55N	20.59 E
Crivitz	138	45.13N	88.00W
Crna Gora □[3]	48	42.30N	19.18 E
Croatia → Hrvatska □[3]	40	45.10N	15.30 E
Croghan	136	43.53N	75.23W
Croix, Lac la ⊜	138	48.21N	92.05W
Croker, Cape ›	96	10.58S	132.35 E
Croker Island I	96	11.12S	132.32 E
Crooked ≃	150	44.34N	121.16W
Crooked Island I	108	22.45N	74.13W
Crooked Lake ⊜	138	48.13N	91.50W
Crookston	132	47.46N	96.36W
Crooksville	136	39.46N	82.05W
Crosby	138	46.28N	93.57W
Crosby, Mount ∧	150	43.53N	109.20W
Crossett	144	33.07N	91.57W
Cross Fell ∧	26	54.42N	2.29W
Cross Plains	138	43.06N	89.39W
Crossville	144	35.56N	85.01W
Crotone	40	39.05N	17.07 E
Crow ≃	138	45.15N	93.31W
Crow Agency	150	45.36N	107.27W
Crowley	144	30.12N	92.22W
Crowleys Ridge ∧	144	35.45N	90.45W
Crown Point	144	41.25N	87.21W
Crowsnest Pass	130	49.36N	114.26W
Crow Wing ≃	138	46.19N	94.20W
Croydon	96	18.12S	142.14 E
Crump Lake ⊜	150	42.17N	119.50W
Cruz, Cabo ›	108	19.51N	77.44W
Cruz Alta	120	28.39S	53.36W
Cruz del Eje	120	30.44S	64.48W
Crvenka	48	45.39N	19.28 E
Crystal	138	45.01N	93.21W
Crystal City, Mo., U.S.	144	38.13N	90.22W
Crystal City, Tx., U.S.	132	28.40N	99.49W
Crystal Falls	138	46.05N	88.20W
Crystal Lake	138	42.14N	88.18W
Crystal Lake ⊜	138	44.40N	86.10W
Crystal Springs	144	31.59N	90.21W
Csepel-sziget I	30	47.15N	18.57 E
Cserhát ⩘	30	47.55N	19.30 E
Csongrád	30	46.43N	20.09 E
Csorna	30	47.37N	17.16 E
Ču ≃	54	45.00N	67.44 E
Cuamba	86	14.49S	36.33 E
Cuando (Kwando) ≃	86	18.27S	23.32 E
Cuango (Kwango) ≃	86	3.14S	17.23 E
Cuanza ≃	86	9.19S	13.08 E
Cuba, Il., U.S.	144	40.29N	90.11W
Cuba, Mo., U.S.	144	38.03N	91.24W
Cuba, N.M., U.S.	148	36.01N	106.57W
Cuba, N.Y., U.S.	136	42.13N	78.16W
Cuba □[1]	108	21.30N	80.00W
Cubango (Okavango) ≃	86	18.50S	22.25 E
Cúcuta	118	7.54N	72.31W
Cudahy	138	42.57N	87.51W
Cuddalore	70	11.45N	79.45 E
Cuddapah	70	14.28N	78.49 E
Čudskoje ozero ⊜	54	58.45N	27.25 E
Cuenca, Ec.	118	2.53S	78.59W
Cuenca, Esp.	44	40.04N	2.08W
Cuernavaca	108	18.55N	99.15W
Cuevas del Almanzora	44	37.18N	1.53W
Cugir	48	45.50N	23.22 E
Cuiabá	118	15.35S	56.05W
Cuilo (Kwilu) ≃	86	3.22S	17.22 E
Cuíto ≃	86	18.01S	20.48 E
Cuitzeo, Lago de ⊜	108	19.55N	101.05W
Čukotskij poluostrov ›[1]	56	66.00N	175.00W
Culebra, Sierra de la ⩘	44	41.54N	6.20W
Culebra Peak ∧	148	37.07N	105.11W
Culgoa ≃	96	29.56S	146.20 E
Culiacán	108	24.48N	107.24W
Culleoka	144	35.28N	86.58W
Cullera	44	39.10N	0.15W
Cullman	144	34.10N	86.50W
Cullowhee	142	35.18N	83.10W
Culpeper	136	38.28N	77.59W
Culver	144	41.13N	86.25W
Čulym ≃	54	57.43N	83.51 E

Symbols in the index entries are identified on page 162.

Name Page Lat. Long.
Cumalı 48 36.42N 27.27E
Cumaná 118 10.28N 64.10W
Cumbal, Nevado de ∧ 118 0.57N 77.52W
Cumberland, Ky., U.S. 142 36.58N 82.59W
Cumberland, Md., U.S. 136 39.39N 78.45W
Cumberland, Wi., U.S. 138 45.31N 92.01W
Cumberland ≃ 132 37.09N 88.25W
Cumberland, Lake ⊜[1] 142 36.57N 84.55W
Cumberland Gap)(142 36.36N 83.41W
Cumberland Gap National Historical Park ♦ 142 36.36N 83.40W
Cumberland Island National Seashore ♦ 142 30.50N 81.27W
Cumberland Islands II 96 20.40S 149.09E
Cumberland Plateau ⩘[1] 142 36.20N 84.30W
Cumberland Sound ⊔ 130 65.10N 65.30W
Cumbria □[6] 26 54.30N 3.00W
Cumming 142 34.12N 84.08W
Cunco 120 38.55S 72.02W
Cunene (Kunene) ≃ 86 17.20S 11.50E
Cuneo 40 44.23N 7.32E
Curaçao I 108 12.11N 69.00W
Curacó ≃ 120 38.49S 64.57W
Curanilahue 120 37.28S 73.21W
Curaray ≃ 118 2.20S 74.05W
Curcani 48 44.12N 26.35E
Curepipe 86 20.19S 57.31E
Čureški prohod)(48 42.47N 23.49E
Curicó 120 34.59S 71.14W
Curitiba 120 25.25S 49.15W
Currant Mountain ∧ 154 38.55N 115.25W
Current ≃ 144 36.16N 90.57W
Currituck Sound ⊔ 142 36.20N 75.52W
Curtea de Argeş 48 45.08N 24.41E
Curtis Island I 96 23.38S 151.09E
Curuá ≃ 118 5.23S 54.22W
Curvelo 118 18.45S 44.25W
Curwensville 136 40.58N 78.31W
Cushman 144 35.52N 91.45W
Cusick 150 48.20N 117.17W
Cusseta 142 32.18N 84.46W
Custer Battlefield National Monument ♦ 150 45.32N 107.20W
Cut Bank 150 48.37N 112.19W
Cuthbert 142 31.46N 84.47W
Cutler 136 44.39N 67.12W
Cutlerville 138 42.50N 85.39W
Cutro 40 39.02N 16.59E
Cuttack 70 20.30N 85.50E
Cuxhaven 30 53.52N 8.42E
Cuyahoga Falls 136 41.08N 81.29W
Cuyuni ≃ 118 6.23N 58.41W
Cuzco 118 13.31S 71.59W
Cyangugu 86 2.29S 28.54E
Cyclades → Kikládhes II 48 37.30N 25.00E
Cynthiana 136 38.23N 84.17W
Cyprus □[1] 16 35.00N 33.00E
Cyprus, North □[1] 16 35.15N 33.40E
Cyrenaica → Barqah □[9] 84 31.00N 22.30E
Cythera → Kíthira I 48 36.20N 22.58E
Czechoslovakia (Českoslo-vensko) □[1] 30 49.30N 17.00E
Czerniejewo 30 52.26N 17.30E
Częstochowa 30 50.49N 19.06E
Czudec 30 49.57N 21.50E

D

Dabola 82 10.45N 11.07W
Dacca → Dhaka 70 23.43N 90.25E
Dachau 30 48.15N 11.27E
Dade City 142 28.21N 82.11W
Dadeville 144 32.49N 85.45W
Daet 68 14.05N 122.55E
Dagana 82 16.31N 15.30W
Dagupan 68 16.03N 120.20E
Da Hinggan Ling ⩘ 66 49.00N 122.00E
Dahlak Archipelago II 84 15.45N 40.30E
Dahlonega 142 34.31N 83.59W
Dahra ⩘ 44 36.25N 1.00E
Dahy, Nafūd ad- ◆[2] 70 22.20N 45.35E
Daimiel 44 39.04N 3.37W
Daingerfield 144 33.01N 94.43W
Dairen → Dalian 66 38.53N 121.35E
Dajarra 96 21.41S 139.31E
Dajian Shan ∧ 66 26.42N 103.34E
Dakar 82 14.40N 17.26W
Dākhilah, Al-Wāḥāt ad- [4] 84 25.30N 29.05E
Dakhla 82 23.43N 15.57W
Dakota City 138 42.43N 94.12W
Dakovica 48 42.23N 20.25E
Dalälven ≃ 22 60.38N 17.27E
Dalan Dzadgad 66 43.37N 104.29E
Dalarö 22 59.08N 18.24E
Da-lat 68 11.56N 108.25E
Dālbandin 70 28.53N 64.25E
Dalby 96 27.11S 151.16E
Dale 22 61.22N 5.25E
Dale Hollow Lake ⊜[1] 144 36.36N 85.19W
Daleville, Al., U.S. 144 31.18N 85.42W
Daleville, In., U.S. 144 40.07N 85.33W
Dalhart 132 36.03N 102.30W
Dalhousie 130 48.04N 66.23W
Dalian (Dairen) 66 38.53N 121.35E
Dalias 44 36.49N 2.52W
Dallas, Al., U.S. 144 33.50N 86.39W
Dallas, Ga., U.S. 142 33.55N 84.50W
Dallas, N.C., U.S. 142 35.18N 81.10W
Dallas, Or., U.S. 150 44.55N 123.18W
Dallas, Pa., U.S. 136 41.20N 75.57W
Dallas, Tx., U.S. 132 32.46N 96.47W
Dallas City 144 40.38N 91.10W
Dalmacija □[9] 40 43.00N 17.00E
Dalmatia → Dalmacija □[9] 40 43.00N 17.00E
Daloa 82 6.53N 6.27W
Dalton, Ga., U.S. 142 34.47N 84.58W
Dalton, Ma., U.S. 136 42.28N 73.10W
Dalton, Pa., U.S. 136 41.32N 75.44W
Dalwallinu 96 30.17S 116.40E
Daly ≃ 96 13.20S 130.19E
Daly City 154 37.43N 122.31W
Daly Waters 96 16.15S 133.22E
Damanhūr 84 31.02N 30.28E
Damascus → Dimashq, Sūriy. 70 33.30N 36.18E
Damascus, Ga., U.S. 142 34.33N 84.56W
Damascus, Md., U.S. 136 39.17N 77.12W
Damāvand, Qolleh-ye ∧ 70 35.56N 52.08E
Damietta → Dumyāṭ 84 31.25N 31.48E
Dampier 96 20.39S 116.45E
Dampier Archipelago II 96 20.35S 116.35E
Dan ≃ 142 36.42N 78.45W
Dana 144 39.48N 87.29W
Da-nang 68 16.04N 108.13E

Symbols in the index entries are identified on page 162.

Name Page Lat. Long.
Danbury, Ct., U.S. 136 41.23N 73.27W
Danbury, N.C., U.S. 142 36.24N 80.12W
Danby Lake ⊜, Ca., U.S. 148 34.14N 115.07W
Danby Lake ⊜, Ca., U.S. 154 34.14N 115.07W
Dandong 66 40.08N 124.20E
Danielson 136 41.48N 71.53W
Daniels Pass)(148 40.18N 111.15W
Danielsville 142 34.07N 83.13W
Dannemora 136 44.43N 73.43W
Dannenberg 30 53.06N 11.05E
Dannevirke 98 40.12S 176.07E
Dansville 136 42.33N 77.41W
Danube ≃ 16 45.20N 29.40E
Danube, Mouths of the ≃[1] 48 45.10N 29.50E
Danvers 144 40.31N 89.10W
Danville, Ga., U.S. 142 32.36N 83.14W
Danville, Il., U.S. 144 40.07N 87.37W
Danville, In., U.S. 144 39.45N 86.31W
Danville, Ky., U.S. 144 37.42N 84.46W
Danville, Pa., U.S. 136 40.57N 76.36W
Danville, Va., U.S. 142 36.35N 79.23W
Danzig → Gdańsk 30 54.23N 18.40E
Dão ≃ 44 40.20N 8.11W
Daoulas 36 48.22N 4.15W
Dapango 82 10.52N 0.12E
Daphne 144 30.36N 87.54W
Darabani 48 48.11N 26.35E
Darbhanga 70 26.10N 85.54E
Darchan 66 49.29N 105.55E
D'Archiac, Mount ∧ 98 43.28S 170.35E
Dardanelle 144 35.13N 93.09W
Dardanelle Lake ⊜[1] 144 35.25N 93.20W
Dardanelles → Çanakkale Boğazı ⊔ 48 40.15N 26.25E
Dardara 44 35.08N 5.15W
Dar es Salaam 86 6.48S 39.17E
Dargaville 98 35.56S 173.53E
Darica 48 40.45N 29.23E
Darjeeling 70 27.02N 88.16E
Darling ≃ 96 34.07S 141.55E
Darling Range ⩘ 96 31.25S 116.00E
Darlington, Eng., U.K. 26 54.31N 1.34W
Darlington, S.C., U.S. 142 34.17N 79.52W
Darlington, Wi., U.S. 138 42.40N 90.07W
Darlowo 30 54.26N 16.23E
Darmstadt 30 49.53N 8.40E
Darnah 84 32.46N 22.39E
Darnétal 36 49.27N 1.09E
Darrington 150 48.15N 121.36W
Darsser Ort › 30 54.29N 12.31E
Dartmoor ◆[3] 26 50.35N 3.55W
Dartmouth, N.S., Can. 130 44.40N 63.34W
Dartmouth, Eng., U.K. 26 50.21N 3.35W
Daruvar 40 45.36N 17.13E
Darwin 96 12.28S 130.50E
Dasht ≃ 70 25.10N 61.40E
Datong 66 40.05N 113.18E
Datong ≃ 66 36.20N 102.55E
Datu, Tanjung › 66 2.06N 109.39E
Datu Piang 68 7.01N 124.30E
Daugava (Zapadnaja Dvina) ≃ 54 57.04N 24.03E
Daugavpils 20 55.53N 26.32E
Daule ≃ 118 2.10S 79.52W
Dauphin 130 51.09N 100.03W
Dauphin Island 144 30.15N 88.07W
Dauphin Island I 144 30.14N 88.12W
Dauphin Lake ⊜ 130 51.17N 99.48W
Dāvangere 70 14.28N 75.55E
Davant 144 29.37N 89.51W
Davao 68 7.04N 125.36E
Davao Gulf c 68 6.40N 125.55E
Davenport, Ia., U.S. 138 41.31N 90.34W
Davenport, Wa., U.S. 150 47.39N 118.08W
David 108 8.26N 82.26W
Davidson 142 35.29N 80.50W
Davie 142 26.03N 80.13W
Davis, Ca., U.S. 154 38.32N 121.44W
Davis, N.C., U.S. 142 34.47N 76.27W
Davis, Mount ∧ 136 39.47N 79.10W
Davis City 138 40.38N 93.48W
Davis Strait ⊔ 130 67.00N 57.00W
Davos 36 46.48N 9.50E
Davy 142 37.28N 81.39W
Dawa (Daua) ≃ 84 4.11N 42.06E
Dawlish 26 50.35N 3.28W
Dawna Range ⩘ 68 16.50N 98.15E
Dawson, Yk., Can. 130 64.04N 139.25W
Dawson, Ga., U.S. 142 31.46N 84.26W
Dawson ≃ 96 23.38S 149.46E
Dawson, Isla I 120 53.55S 70.45W
Dawson Creek 130 55.46N 120.14W
Dawson Range ⩘ 130 62.40N 139.00W
Dawson Springs 144 37.10N 87.41W
Dax 36 43.43N 1.03W
Daxian 66 31.18N 107.30E
Dayr az-Zawr 70 35.20N 40.09E
Dayrūṭ 84 27.33N 30.49E
Dayton, Oh., U.S. 136 39.45N 84.11W
Dayton, Pa., U.S. 136 40.52N 79.14W
Dayton, Tn., U.S. 144 35.29N 85.00W
Dayton, Wa., U.S. 150 46.19N 117.58W
Daytona Beach 142 29.12N 81.01W
Da Yunhe (Grand Canal) ≊ 66 32.12N 119.31E
De Aar 86 30.39S 24.00E
Dead Sea ⊜ 70 31.30N 35.30E
Deadwood 132 44.22N 103.43W
Deal 26 51.14N 1.24E
Deale 136 38.46N 76.33W
Deal Island 136 38.09N 75.56W
Dearborn 138 42.18N 83.10W
Dearg, Beinn ∧ 26 57.47N 4.56W
Dease ≃ 130 59.54N 128.30W
Death Valley 154 36.18N 116.25W
Death Valley ∨ 154 36.30N 117.00W
Death Valley National Monument ♦ 154 36.30N 117.00W
De Bary 142 28.52N 81.18W
Dębica 30 50.04N 21.24E
Dęblin 30 51.35N 21.50E
Debrecen 30 47.32N 21.38E
Debre Markos 84 10.20N 37.45E
Debre Tabor 84 11.50N 38.05E
Decatur, Al., U.S. 144 34.36N 86.59W
Decatur, Ga., U.S. 142 33.46N 84.17W
Decatur, Il., U.S. 144 39.50N 88.57W
Decatur, In., U.S. 144 40.50N 84.56W
Decatur, Ms., U.S. 144 32.26N 89.06W
Decatur, Tn., U.S. 142 35.30N 84.47W
Decazeville 36 44.34N 2.15E
Deccan ⩘[1] 70 17.00N 78.00E
Deception, Mount ∧ 150 47.49N 123.14W
Decherd 144 35.12N 86.04W
Děčín 30 50.48N 14.13E
Decize 36 46.50N 3.27E
Decorah 138 43.18N 91.47W
Dédougou 82 12.28N 3.28W
Dee ≃, U.K. 26 53.20N 3.12W
Dee ≃, Scot., U.K. 26 57.09N 2.07W

Name Page Lat. Long.
Deep River, On., Can. 130 46.06N 77.30W
Deep River, Ct., U.S. 136 41.23N 72.26W
Deep River, Ia., U.S. 138 41.34N 92.22W
Deerfield 138 42.10N 87.50W
Deerfield Beach 142 26.19N 80.06W
Deer Isle 136 44.13N 68.40W
Deer Lake 130 49.10N 57.26W
Deer Lodge 150 46.23N 112.44W
Deer Mountain ∧ 136 45.01N 70.56W
Deer Park 150 47.57N 117.28W
Defiance 136 41.17N 84.21W
De Forest 138 43.14N 89.20W
De Funiak Springs 144 30.43N 86.06W
Deggendorf 30 48.51N 12.59E
De Graff 136 40.18N 83.54W
De Gray Lake ⊜[1] 144 34.15N 93.15W
De Grey ≃ 96 20.12S 119.11E
Dehalak Deset I 84 15.40N 40.05E
Dehiwala-Mount Lavinia 70 6.51N 79.52E
Dehra Dūn, India 66 30.19N 78.02E
Dehra Dūn, India 70 30.19N 78.02E
Deinze 30 50.59N 3.32E
Dej 48 47.09N 23.52E
De Kalb 138 41.55N 88.45W
De Land 142 29.01N 81.18W
Delano, Ca., U.S. 154 35.46N 119.14W
Delano, Mn., U.S. 138 45.02N 93.47W
Delano Peak ∧ 148 38.22N 112.23W
Delaware 136 40.17N 83.04W
Delaware □[3] 132 39.10N 75.30W
Delaware ≃ 136 39.20N 75.25W
Delaware Bay c 136 39.05N 75.15W
Delaware City 136 39.34N 75.35W
Delcambre 144 29.57N 91.59W
Delémont 36 47.22N 7.21E
De Leon Springs 142 29.07N 81.21W
Delft 30 52.00N 4.21E
Delfzijl 30 53.19N 6.46E
Delgado, Cabo › 86 10.40S 40.35E
Delhi, India 70 28.40N 77.13E
Delhi, La., U.S. 144 32.27N 91.29W
Delhi, N.Y., U.S. 136 42.16N 74.54W
Delicias 108 28.13N 105.28W
Delight 144 34.01N 93.30W
Delitzsch 30 51.31N 12.20E
Delle 36 47.30N 7.00E
Dellenbaugh, Mount ∧ 148 36.07N 113.32W
Dellensjöarna ⊜ 22 61.54N 16.41E
Delles 44 36.55N 3.55E
Del Mar, Ca., U.S. 154 32.57N 117.15W
Delmar, De., U.S. 136 38.27N 75.34W
Delmar, Md., U.S. 136 38.27N 75.34W
Delmarva Peninsula ›[1] 132 38.30N 75.30W
Delmenhorst 30 53.03N 8.38E
Del Norte Coast Redwood State Park ♦ 154 41.38N 124.05W
De-Longa, ostrova II 56 76.30N 153.00E
Delphi 144 40.35N 86.40W
Delphi → Dhelfoí ⊥ 48 38.30N 22.29E
Delphos 136 40.50N 84.20W
Delray Beach 142 26.27N 80.04W
Del Rio 132 29.21N 100.53W
Delta, Co., U.S. 148 38.44N 108.04W
Delta, Mo., U.S. 144 37.11N 89.44W
Delta, Oh., U.S. 136 41.34N 84.00W
Delta, Ut., U.S. 148 39.21N 112.34W
Delta □[9] 144 33.30N 90.45W
Demavend, Mount → Damāvand, Qolleh-ye ∧ 70 35.56N 52.08E
Deming 148 32.16N 107.45W
Demirci 48 39.03N 28.40E
Demircidere 48 37.33N 27.50E
Demir Kapija ∨ 48 41.24N 22.15E
Demmin 30 53.54N 13.02E
Demonte 40 44.19N 7.17E
Demopolis 144 32.31N 87.50W
Demorest 142 34.33N 83.32W
Demotte 144 41.12N 87.12W
Dempo, Gunung ∧ 68 4.02S 103.09E
Denain 36 50.20N 3.23E
Denakil ◆[1] 84 13.00N 41.00E
Dendermonde 30 51.02N 4.07E
Denham, Mount ∧ 108 18.13N 77.32W
Denham Springs 144 30.29N 90.57W
Den Helder 30 52.54N 4.45E
Denison 132 33.45N 96.32W
Denizli 48 37.46N 29.06E
Denmark, S.C., U.S. 142 33.19N 81.08W
Denmark, Wi., U.S. 138 44.20N 87.49W
Denmark (Danmark) □[1] 22 56.00N 10.00E
Denmark Strait ⊔ 20a 67.00N 25.00W
Dennison 136 40.23N 81.20W
Dennis Port 136 41.39N 70.07W
Denpasar 68 8.39S 115.13E
Denton, Md., U.S. 136 38.53N 75.49W
Denton, Mt., U.S. 150 47.19N 109.56W
Denton, Tx., U.S. 132 33.12N 97.07W
D'Entrecasteaux, Point › 96 34.50S 116.00E
Denver, Co., U.S. 148 39.44N 104.59W
Denver, Ia., U.S. 138 42.40N 92.20W
Denver, Pa., U.S. 136 40.13N 76.08W
De Pere 138 44.26N 88.03W
Depew 136 42.54N 78.41W
Deposit 136 42.03N 75.25W
Depue 138 41.19N 89.18W
De Queen 144 34.02N 94.20W
De Quincy 144 30.27N 93.25W
Dera Ghāzi Khān 70 30.03N 70.38E
Dera Ismāīl Khān 70 31.50N 70.54E
Derbent 54 42.03N 48.18E
Derby, Eng., U.K. 26 52.55N 1.29W
Derby, Ks., U.S. 132 37.32N 97.16W
Derby Line 136 45.00N 72.05W
Derbyshire □[6] 26 53.00N 1.33W
Derg, Lough ⊜ 26 52.57N 8.19W
De Ridder 144 30.50N 93.17W
Dermott 144 33.31N 91.26W
Dernieres, Isles II 144 29.02N 90.47W
Déroute, Passage de la ⊔ 26 49.25N 2.00W
Derry → Londonderry, N. Ire., U.K. 26 54.59N 7.20W
Derry, N.H., U.S. 136 42.52N 71.19W
Derventa 48 44.59N 17.55E
Derwent ≃ 26 53.45N 0.57W
Desaguadero ≃, Arg. 120 34.13S 66.47W
Desaguadero ≃, Bol. 118 18.24S 67.05W
Des Allemands 144 29.49N 90.28W
Des Arc 144 34.58N 91.29W
Descartes 36 46.58N 0.42E
Deschambault Lake ⊜ 130 54.40N 103.35W
Deschutes ≃ 150 45.38N 120.54W
Dese 84 11.05N 39.41E
Deseado ≃ 120 47.45S 65.54W
Desengaño, Punta › 120 49.15S 67.37W
Desenzano del Garda 40 45.28N 10.32E
Deseret Peak ∧ 148 40.28N 112.38W
Desert Hot Springs 154 33.57N 116.30W
Desha 144 35.44N 91.40W
Desloge 144 37.52N 90.31W

Name Page Lat. Long.
Des Moines 138 41.36N 93.36W
Des Moines ≃ 132 40.22N 91.26W
Desna ≃ 54 50.33N 30.32E
Desolación, Isla I 120 53.00S 74.10W
De Soto, Il., U.S. 144 37.49N 89.13W
De Soto, Mo., U.S. 144 38.08N 90.33W
Despeñaperros, Desfiladero de)(44 38.24N 3.30W
Des Plaines 138 42.02N 87.53W
Desroches, Île I 86 5.41S 53.41E
Dessau 30 51.50N 12.14E
Destin 144 30.23N 86.29W
Destruction Bay 130 61.15N 138.48W
Detmold 30 51.56N 8.52E
Detour, Point › 138 45.36N 86.37W
De Tour Village 138 46.00N 83.54W
Detroit 138 42.20N 83.03W
Detva 30 48.31N 19.28E
Deutsche Bucht c 30 54.30N 7.30E
Deva 48 45.53N 22.55E
Dévaványa 30 47.02N 20.58E
Devecser 30 47.06N 17.26E
Deventer 30 52.15N 6.10E
Devès, Monts du ⩘ 36 45.00N 3.45E
De View, Bayou ≃ 144 34.48N 91.18W
Devil's Island → Diable, Île du I 118 5.17N 52.35W
Devils Lake 138 48.06N 98.51W
Devils Lake State Park ♦ 138 43.24N 89.44W
Devils Postpile National Monument ♦ 154 37.37N 119.05W
Devin 48 41.45N 24.24E
Devoll ≃ 48 40.49N 19.51E
Devon □[6] 26 50.45N 3.50W
Devon Island I 130 75.00N 87.00W
Devonport, Austl. 96 41.11S 146.21E
Devonport, N.Z. 98 36.49S 174.48E
De Witt, Ar., U.S. 144 34.17N 91.20W
De Witt, Ia., U.S. 138 41.49N 90.32W
De Witt, Mi., U.S. 138 42.50N 84.34W
De Witt, N.Y., U.S. 136 43.02N 76.03W
Dewsbury 26 53.42N 1.37W
Dexter, Me., U.S. 136 45.01N 69.17W
Dexter, Mo., U.S. 144 36.47N 89.57W
Dexter, N.Y., U.S. 136 44.00N 76.02W
Dezfūl 70 32.23N 48.24E
Dezhou 66 37.27N 116.18E
Dežneva, mys › 56 66.06N 169.45W
Dhahran → Az-Zahrān 70 26.18N 50.08E
Dhaka 70 23.43N 90.25E
Dhamār 70 14.46N 44.23E
Dhānbād 70 23.48N 86.27E
Dhangarhi 70 28.41N 80.36E
Dhārwār 70 15.28N 75.01E
Dhaulāgiri ∧ 70 28.42N 83.30E
Dhelfoí ⊥ 48 38.30N 22.29E
Dhíkti ∧ 48 35.08N 25.22E
Dhodhekánisos (Dodecanese) II 48 36.30N 27.00E
Dhule 70 20.54N 74.47E
Diable, Île du I 118 5.17N 52.35W
Diablo, Mount ∧ 154 37.53N 121.55W
Diablo Range ⩘ 154 37.00N 121.20W
Diagonal 144 40.48N 94.20W
Diaka ≃[1] 82 15.13N 4.14W
Diamante 120 32.04S 60.39W
Diamantina 118 18.15S 43.36W
Diamantina ≃ 96 26.45S 139.10E
Diamond 144 37.00N 94.19W
Diamond Peak ∧, Id., U.S. 150 44.09N 113.05W
Diamond Peak ∧, Or., U.S. 150 43.33N 122.09W
Diaz 144 35.38N 91.15W
Dibaya 86 6.30S 22.57E
D'Iberville 144 30.25N 88.53W
Dibrugarh 70 27.29N 94.54E
Dickinson 132 46.52N 102.47W
Dickson 144 36.04N 87.23W
Diego Ramírez, Islas II 120 56.30S 68.44W
Dien-bien-phu 68 21.23N 103.01E
Diepholz 30 52.35N 8.21E
Dieppe 36 49.56N 1.05E
Diest 30 50.59N 5.03E
Dieuze 36 48.49N 6.43E
Digne 36 44.06N 6.14E
Digoin 36 46.29N 3.59E
Digul ≃ 68 7.07S 138.42E
Dijon 36 47.19N 5.01E
Dikhil 84 11.06N 42.22E
Diksmuide 30 51.02N 2.52E
Dikson 54 73.30N 80.35E
Dikwa 82 12.02N 13.56E
Dili 68 8.33S 125.34E
Dillenburg 30 50.44N 8.17E
Dillon, Mt., U.S. 150 45.12N 112.38W
Dillon, S.C., U.S. 142 34.24N 79.22W
Dillon Cone ∧ 98 42.16S 173.13E
Dillon Lake ⊜[1] 136 40.02N 82.10W
Dilolo 86 10.42S 22.20E
Dimashq (Damascus) 70 33.30N 36.18E
Dimass, Rass › 40 35.37N 11.03E
Dîmbovița ≃ 48 44.14N 26.27E
Dimitrovgrad, Blg. 48 42.03N 25.36E
Dimitrovgrad, S.S.S.R. 20 54.14N 49.39E
Dimlang ∧ 82 8.24N 11.47E
Dinagat Island I 68 10.12N 125.35E
Dinājpur 70 25.38N 88.38E
Dinan 36 48.27N 2.02W
Dinant 30 50.16N 4.55E
Dinara ⩘ 40 43.50N 16.35E
Dinard 36 48.38N 2.04W
Dinaric Alps → Dinara ⩘ 40 43.50N 16.35E
Dindigul 70 10.21N 77.57E
Dingalan Bay c 68 15.18N 121.25E
Dingle Bay c 26 52.05N 10.15W
Dingolfing 30 48.38N 12.31E
Dingxian 66 38.32N 114.59E
Dinkelsbühl 30 49.04N 10.19E
Dinosaur National Monument ♦ 148 40.32N 108.58W
Dinuba 154 36.32N 119.23W
Dinwiddie 142 37.04N 77.35W
Diourbel 82 14.40N 16.15W
Dipolog 68 8.35N 123.20E
Dīr 70 35.12N 71.53E
Dira, Djebel ∧ 44 36.05N 3.38E
Dire Dawa 84 9.37N 41.52E
Dirj 84 30.09N 10.26E
Dirk Hartog Island I 96 25.48S 113.00E
Dirranbandi 96 28.35S 148.14E
Disappointment, Cape ›, Falk. Is. 120 54.53S 36.07W
Disappointment, Cape ›, Wa., U.S. 150 46.18N 124.03W
Disappointment, Lake ⊜ 96 23.30S 122.50E
Disentis 36 46.43N 8.51E
Dishman 150 47.39N 117.16W
Disko I 130 69.50N 53.30W
Disko Bugt c 130 69.15N 52.00W
Disūq 84 31.08N 30.39E
Dithmarschen ◆[1] 30 54.05N 9.00E
Dives ≃ 36 49.19N 0.05W
Divinópolis 118 20.09S 44.54W
Divisor, Serra do ⩘[1] 118 8.20S 73.30W
Dixfield 136 44.32N 70.27W
Dixie Valley ∨ 154 39.50N 117.55W
Dixon, Il., U.S. 138 41.50N 89.28W

Name Page Lat. Long.
Dixon, Mo., U.S. 144 37.59N 92.05W
Dixon Entrance ⊔ 130 54.25N 132.30W
Diyarbakır 16 37.55N 40.14E
Dja ≃ 82 2.02N 15.12E
Djakarta → Jakarta 68 6.10S 106.48E
Djedi, Oued ∨ 82 34.28N 6.05E
Djénné 82 13.54N 4.33W
Djérem ≃ 82 5.20N 13.24E
Djibouti 84 11.36N 43.09E
Djibouti □[1] 84 11.30N 43.00E
Djursholm 22 59.24N 18.05E
Dmitrija Lapteva, proliv ⊔ 56 73.00N 142.00E
Dnepr ≃ 54 46.30N 32.18E
Dneprodzeržinsk 54 48.30N 34.37E
Dnepropetrovsk 54 48.27N 34.59E
Dnestr ≃ 54 46.18N 30.17E
Dnieper → Dnepr ≃ 54 46.30N 32.18E
Dniester → Dnestr ≃ 54 46.18N 30.17E
Doba 84 8.39N 16.51E
Dobczyce 30 49.54N 20.06E
Döbeln 30 51.07N 13.07E
Doberai, Jazirah ›[1] 68 1.30S 132.30E
Doboj 48 44.44N 18.06E
Dobra 30 51.54N 18.37E
Dobříš 30 49.47N 14.11E
Dobrudžansko plato ⩘[1] 48 43.32N 27.50E
Dobruja ◆[1] 48 44.00N 28.00E
Doce ≃ 118 19.37S 39.49W
Dock Junction 142 31.11N 81.31W
Dodecanese → Dhodhekánisos II 48 36.30N 27.00E
Dodge Center 138 44.01N 92.51W
Dodge City 132 37.45N 100.01W
Dodgeville 138 42.57N 90.07W
Dodman Point › 26 50.13N 4.48W
Dodoma 86 6.11S 35.45E
Doerun 142 31.19N 83.55W
Doetinchem 30 51.58N 6.17E
Doğanbey 48 38.04N 26.53E
Dog Island I 142 29.48N 84.35W
Dog Lake ⊜ 138 48.46N 89.32W
Doha → Ad-Dawhah 70 25.17N 51.32E
Doiran, Lake ⊜ 48 41.13N 22.44E
Doksy 30 50.35N 14.38E
Dolbeau 130 48.53N 72.14W
Dol-de-Bretagne 36 48.33N 1.45W
Dole 36 47.06N 5.30E
Dolisie 86 4.12S 12.41E
Dolni Lom 48 43.31N 22.47E
Dolomites → Dolomiti ⩘ 40 46.25N 11.50E
Dolomiti ⩘ 40 46.25N 11.50E
Dolores ≃ 148 38.49N 109.17W
Dolphin and Union Strait ⊔ 130 69.05N 114.45W
Domažlice 30 49.27N 12.56E
Dombes ◆[1] 36 46.00N 5.03E
Dombóvár 30 46.23N 18.08E
Dôme, Puy de ∧ 36 45.47N 2.58E
Domeyko 120 28.57S 70.54W
Domeyko, Cordillera ⩘ 120 24.30S 69.00W
Dominica □[1] 108 15.30N 61.20W
Dominican Republic (República Dominicana) □[1] 108 19.00N 70.40W
Domneşti 48 44.25N 25.56E
Domo 84 7.54N 46.52E
Domodossola 40 46.07N 8.17E
Domuyo, Volcán ∧[1] 120 36.38S 70.26W
Domžale 40 46.08N 14.36E
Don ≃ 54 47.04N 39.18E
Donaldsonville 144 30.06N 90.59W
Donalsonville 142 31.02N 84.52W
Donaueschingen 30 47.57N 8.29E
Donauwörth 30 48.43N 10.46E
Don Benito 44 38.57N 5.52W
Doncaster 26 53.32N 1.07W
Dondo, Ang. 86 9.38S 14.25E
Dondo, Moç. 86 19.36S 34.44E
Dondra Head › 70 5.55N 80.35E
Doneck 54 48.00N 37.48E
Donegal □[6] 26 54.50N 8.00W
Donegal Bay c 26 54.30N 8.30W
Donetsk → Doneck 54 48.00N 37.48E
Donga ≃ 82 8.19N 9.58E
Dongara 96 29.15S 114.56E
Dongchuan 66 26.10N 103.01E
Dongen 30 51.37N 4.56E
Donghai Dao I 66 21.02N 110.25E
Dong-hoi 68 17.29N 106.36E
Dong-nai ≃ 68 10.45N 106.46E
Dongting Hu ⊜ 66 29.20N 112.54E
Doniphan 144 36.37N 90.49W
Donjek ≃ 130 62.35N 140.00W
Donner Pass)(154 39.19N 120.20W
Donner und Blitzen ≃ 150 43.17N 118.49W
Donora 136 40.10N 79.51W
Donostia (San Sebastián) 44 43.19N 1.59W
Don Pedro Reservoir ⊜[1] 154 37.43N 120.23W
Door Peninsula ›[1] 138 44.55N 87.20W
Doraville 142 33.53N 84.17W
Dorcheat, Bayou ≃ 144 32.30N 93.21W
Dorchester 26 50.43N 2.26W
Dordogne ≃ 36 45.02N 0.35W
Dordrecht 30 51.49N 4.40E
Dore, Monts ⩘ 36 45.30N 2.45E
Dorfen 30 48.17N 12.08E
Dornbirn 30 47.25N 9.44E
Dornoch Firth c[2] 26 57.53N 4.00W
Dorohoi 48 47.57N 26.24E
Dorsale ⩘ 40 36.00N 9.50E
Dorset □[6] 26 50.47N 2.20W
Dortmund 30 51.31N 7.28E
Dos Bahías, Cabo › 120 44.55S 65.32W
Dos Hermanas 44 37.17N 5.55W
Dothan 144 31.13N 85.23W
Douai 36 50.22N 3.04E
Douala 82 4.03N 9.42E
Douarnenez 36 48.06N 4.20W
Double Cone ∧ 98 45.04S 168.48E
Double Springs 144 34.08N 87.24W
Doubletop Peak ∧ 150 43.21N 110.17W
Doubs ≃ 36 46.54N 5.02E
Doubtful Sound ⊔ 98 45.17S 166.51E
Doubtless Bay c 98 34.55S 173.25E
Douglas, I. of Man 26 54.09N 4.28W
Douglas, Az., U.S. 148 31.20N 109.32W
Douglas, Ga., U.S. 142 31.30N 82.51W
Douglas, Wy., U.S. 148 42.45N 105.22W
Douglas Channel ⊔ 130 53.30N 129.12W
Douglas Lake ⊜[1] 142 36.00N 83.22W
Douglasville 142 33.45N 84.44W
Doulevant-le-Château 36 48.23N 4.55E
Dourdou ≃ 36 44.00N 2.41E
Douro (Duero) ≃ 44 41.08N 8.40W
Douze ≃ 36 43.54N 0.30W
Dover, Eng., U.K. 26 51.08N 1.19E
Dover, Ar., U.S. 144 35.24N 93.06W
Dover, De., U.S. 136 39.09N 75.31W
Dover, N.H., U.S. 136 43.11N 70.52W
Dover, N.J., U.S. 136 40.53N 74.34W
Dover, N.C., U.S. 142 35.12N 77.26W
Dover, Oh., U.S. 136 40.31N 81.28W

Name Page Lat. Long.
Dover, Tn., U.S. 144 36.29N 87.50W
Dover, Strait of (Pas de Calais) ⊔ 26 51.00N 1.30E
Dover-Foxcroft 136 45.11N 69.13W
Dowagiac 138 41.59N 86.06W
Downieville 154 39.33N 120.49W
Downingtown 136 40.00N 75.42W
Downpatrick 26 54.20N 5.43W
Downs Mountain ∧ 150 43.18N 109.40W
Doylestown 136 40.18N 75.07W
Dozier 144 31.29N 86.21W
Dra'a, Hamada du ◆[2] 82 29.00N 6.45W
Drâa, Oued ∨ 82 28.43N 11.09W
Draa el Mizan 44 36.32N 3.50E
Drachten 30 53.06N 6.05E
Dracut 136 42.40N 71.18W
Dragalina 48 44.26N 27.20E
Drăgăşani 48 44.40N 24.16E
Dragonera I 44 39.35N 2.19E
Draguignan 36 43.32N 6.28E
Drakensberg ⩘ 86 27.00S 30.00E
Drake Passage ⊔ 8 58.00S 70.00W
Drake Peak ∧ 150 42.19N 120.07W
Dráma 48 41.09N 24.08E
Drammen 22 59.44N 10.15E
Dranov, Ostrovul I 48 44.52N 29.15E
Draper 148 40.31N 111.51W
Drau (Drava) (Dráva) ≃ 40 45.33N 18.55E
Drava (Drau) (Dráva) ≃ 40 45.33N 18.55E
Dravinja ≃ 40 46.22N 15.57E
Drawno 30 53.13N 15.45E
Drayton 142 34.58N 81.54W
Drayton Valley 130 53.13N 114.59W
Dresden 30 51.03N 13.44E
Dreux 36 48.44N 1.22E
Drew 144 33.48N 90.31W
Driftwood ≃ 144 39.12N 85.56W
Drin ≃ 48 41.45N 19.34E
Drina ≃ 48 44.53N 19.21E
Drinit, Gjiri i c 48 41.45N 19.28E
Driskill Mountain ∧[2] 144 32.25N 92.54W
Drobeta-Turnu Severin 48 44.38N 22.39E
Drogheda 26 53.43N 6.21W
Dronero 40 44.28N 7.22E
Dronne ≃ 36 45.02N 0.09W
Dr. Petru Groza 30 46.32N 22.28E
Drumheller 130 51.28N 112.42W
Drummond Island I 138 46.00N 83.40W
Drummondville 130 45.53N 72.29W
Družba 54 45.15N 82.26E
Drwęca ≃ 30 53.00N 18.42E
Dryden 130 49.47N 92.50W
Dry Ridge 136 38.40N 84.35W
Drysdale ≃ 96 13.59S 126.51E
Dry Tortugas II 142 24.38N 82.55W
Duarte, Pico ∧ 108 19.02N 70.59W
Dubai → Dubayy 70 25.18N 55.18E
Dubawnt Lake ⊜ 130 63.08N 101.30W
Dubayy (Dubai) 70 25.18N 55.18E
Dubbo 96 32.15S 148.36E
Dublin (Baile Átha Cliath), Ire. 26 53.20N 6.15W
Dublin, Ga., U.S. 142 32.32N 82.54W
Dublin □[6] 26 53.20N 6.15W
Dubois, In., U.S. 144 38.26N 86.48W
Du Bois, Pa., U.S. 136 41.07N 78.45W
Dubossarskoje vodochranilišče ⊜[1] 48 47.35N 29.00E
Dubossary 48 47.16N 29.08E
Dubréka 82 9.48N 13.31W
Dubrovnik 48 42.38N 18.07E
Dubuque 138 42.30N 90.39W
Duchcov 30 50.37N 13.45E
Duchesne ≃ 148 40.05N 109.41W
Duchess 96 21.22S 139.52E
Duck ≃ 144 36.02N 87.52W
Dudelange 30 49.28N 6.05E
Dudley 26 52.30N 2.05W
Duero (Douro) ≃ 44 41.08N 8.40W
Due West 142 34.20N 82.23W
Dufourspitze ∧ 36 45.55N 7.52E
Dugger 144 39.04N 87.16W
Dugi Otok I 40 44.00N 15.04E
Du Gué ≃ 130 57.21N 70.45W
Duisburg 30 51.25N 6.46E
Duitama 118 5.50N 73.02W
Dukhān 70 25.25N 50.48E
Dukla Pass)(30 49.25N 21.43E
Dulce 148 36.56N 106.59W
Dülmen 30 51.51N 7.16E
Dulovo 48 43.49N 27.09E
Duluth, Ga., U.S. 142 34.00N 84.08W
Duluth, Mn., U.S. 138 46.45N 92.07W
Dumaguete 68 9.18N 123.18E
Dumas 144 33.53N 91.29W
Dumbarton 26 55.57N 4.35W
Ďumbier ∧ 30 48.57N 19.37E
Dumfries 26 55.04N 3.37W
Dumyāṭ 84 31.25N 31.48E
Dunaharaszti 30 47.21N 19.05E
Dunajec ≃ 30 50.14N 20.44E
Dunajská Streda 30 48.01N 17.35E
Dunakeszi 30 47.38N 19.08E
Dunărea Veche, Braţul ≃ 48 45.17N 28.02E
Dunaújváros 30 46.58N 18.57E
Duna-Völgyi-főcsatorna ≊ 30 46.12N 18.56E
Dunbar 136 38.21N 81.44W
Duncan 132 34.30N 97.57W
Duncansby Head › 26 58.39N 3.02W
Dundalk, Ire. 26 54.01N 6.25W
Dundalk, Md., U.S. 136 39.15N 76.31W
Dundalk Bay c 26 53.57N 6.17W
Dundas 138 44.25N 93.12W
Dundee, S. Afr. 86 28.12S 30.16E
Dundee, Scot., U.K. 26 56.28N 2.58W
Dundee, Fl., U.S. 142 28.01N 81.37W
Dundee, Mi., U.S. 138 41.57N 83.39W
Dundee, N.Y., U.S. 136 42.31N 76.58W
Dundrum Bay c 26 54.13N 5.45W
Dunedin, N.Z. 98 45.52S 170.30E
Dunedin, Fl., U.S. 142 28.01N 82.46W
Dunfermline 26 56.04N 3.29W
Dungarvan 26 52.05N 7.37W
Dungeness › 26 50.55N 0.58E
Dunkerque 36 51.03N 2.22E
Dunkirk → Dunkerque, Fr. 36 51.03N 2.22E
Dunkirk, In., U.S. 144 40.22N 85.12W
Dunkirk, N.Y., U.S. 136 42.28N 79.20W
Dunkwa 82 5.58N 1.47W
Dún Laoghaire 26 53.17N 6.08W
Dunlap 142 35.22N 85.23W
Dunmore 136 41.25N 75.37W
Dunn 142 35.18N 78.36W
Dunnet Head › 26 58.40N 3.24W
Dunsmuir 154 41.13N 122.16W
Dunstable 26 51.53N 0.32W
Dun-sur-Auron 36 46.53N 2.34E
Du Page ≃ 138 41.25N 88.14W
DuQuoin 144 37.59N 89.15W
Durance ≃ 36 43.55N 4.44E
Durand, Mi., U.S. 138 42.54N 83.59W
Durand, Wi., U.S. 138 44.37N 91.57W
Durango, Esp. 44 43.10N 2.37W
Durango, Méx. 108 24.02N 104.40W
Durango, Co., U.S. 148 37.16N 107.52W
Durant, Ms., U.S. 144 33.04N 89.51W
Durant, Ok., U.S. 132 33.59N 96.22W

Name	Page	Lat.	Long.
Durazno	120	33.22 S	56.31 W
Durban	86	29.55 S	30.56 E
Durbin	136	38.32 N	79.49 W
Đurđevac	40	46.03 N	17.04 E
Düren	30	50.48 N	6.28 E
Durg	70	21.11 N	81.17 E
Durham, Eng., U.K.	26	54.47 N	1.34 W
Durham, N.H., U.S.	136	43.08 N	70.55 W
Durham, N.C., U.S.	142	35.59 N	78.53 W
Durham ◻ 6	26	54.45 N	1.45 W
Durmitor ∧	48	43.08 N	19.01 E
Durón	44	40.38 N	2.43 W
Durrës	48	41.19 N	19.26 E
Dursey Island I	26	51.36 N	10.12 W
Duru Gölü ⊜	48	41.20 N	28.35 E
D'Urville Island I	98	40.50 S	173.52 E
Dušanbe	54	38.35 N	68.48 E
Dushan	66	25.53 N	107.30 E
Dushanbe → Dušanbe	54	38.35 N	68.48 E
Dusky Sound ų	98	45.47 S	166.28 E
Duson	144	30.14 N	92.11 W
Düsseldorf	30	51.12 N	6.47 E
Dutch John	148	40.55 N	109.23 W
Duyun	66	26.12 N	107.31 E
Dvinskaja guba c	20	65.00 N	39.45 E
Dvůr Králové [nad Labem]	30	50.26 N	15.48 E
Dwight	138	41.05 N	88.25 W
Dworshak Reservoir ⊜ 1	150	46.40 N	116.00 W
Dyer	144	36.04 N	88.59 W
Dyer, Cape ≻	130	66.37 N	61.18 W
Dyersburg	144	36.02 N	89.23 W
Dyersville	138	42.29 N	91.07 W
Dyfed ◻ 6	26	52.00 N	4.30 W
Dyje (Thaya) ≃	30	48.37 N	16.56 E
Dynów	30	49.49 N	22.14 E
Dysart	138	42.10 N	92.18 W
Džambul	54	42.54 N	71.22 E
Dzaoudzi	86	12.47 S	45.17 E
Dzavchan ≃	66	48.54 N	93.23 E
Dzerzhinsk → Dzeržinsk	20	56.15 N	43.24 E
Dzeržinsk	20	56.15 N	43.24 E
Džezkazgan	54	47.47 N	67.46 E
Dzhambul → Džambul	54	42.54 N	71.22 E
Dzierżoniów (Reichenbach)	30	50.44 N	16.39 E
Džugdžur, chrebet ⋏	56	58.00 N	136.00 E
Dzungarian Basin → Junggar Pendi ≚ 1	66	45.00 N	88.00 E
E			
Eagle	148	39.39 N	106.49 W
Eagle Grove	138	42.39 N	93.54 W
Eagle Lake ⊜	154	40.39 N	120.44 W
Eagle Mountain ∧ 2	138	47.54 N	90.33 W
Eagle Pass	132	28.42 N	100.29 W
Eagle Peak ∧	154	41.17 N	120.12 W
Eagle River	138	45.55 N	89.14 W
Eagleton Village	142	35.46 N	83.56 W
Earle	144	35.16 N	90.28 W
Earlington	144	37.16 N	87.30 W
Earl Park	144	40.40 N	87.24 W
Earlville	136	42.44 N	75.33 W
Earnslaw, Mount ∧	98	44.37 S	168.24 E
Eas	92	16.22 S	168.12 E
Easley	142	34.49 N	82.36 W
East Alton	144	38.52 N	90.06 W
East Aurora	136	42.46 N	78.36 W
East Bay c, Fl., U.S.	144	30.05 N	85.32 W
East Bay c, Tx., U.S.	144	29.30 N	94.35 W
East-Berlin → Berlin (Ost)	30	52.30 N	13.25 E
Eastbourne	26	50.46 N	0.17 E
East Brady	136	40.59 N	79.36 W
East Brewton	144	31.05 N	87.03 W
East Cape ≻	98	37.41 S	178.33 E
East Carbon	148	39.32 N	110.24 W
East Chicago	144	41.38 N	87.27 W
East China Sea ₸ 2	66	30.00 N	126.00 E
East Coast Bays	98	36.45 S	174.46 E
East Cote Blanche Bay c	144	29.35 N	91.40 W
East Dereham	26	52.41 N	0.56 E
East Dubuque	138	42.29 N	90.38 W
Eastern Ghāts ⋏	70	14.00 N	78.50 E
East Falkland I	120	51.55 S	59.00 W
East Fayetteville	142	35.05 N	78.51 W
East Flat Rock	142	35.16 N	82.25 W
East Frisian Islands → Ostfriesische Inseln II	30	53.44 N	7.25 E
East Gaffney	142	35.04 N	81.37 W
East Germany → German Democratic Republic ◻ 1	30	52.00 N	12.30 E
East Grand Rapids	138	42.56 N	85.36 W
East Greenwich	136	41.39 N	71.27 W
East Grinstead	26	51.08 N	0.01 W
Easthampton	136	42.16 N	72.40 W
East Helena	150	46.35 N	111.54 W
East Kilbride	26	55.46 N	4.10 W
Eastlake	136	41.39 N	81.27 W
East Lansing	138	42.44 N	84.29 W
Eastleigh	26	50.58 N	1.22 W
East Liverpool	136	40.37 N	80.34 W
East London (Oos-Londen)	86	33.00 S	27.55 E
East Lynn Lake ⊜ 1	136	38.05 N	82.20 W
Eastmain	130	52.15 N	78.30 W
Eastmain ≃	130	52.15 N	78.35 W
Eastmain-Opinaca, Réservoir ⊜ 1	130	52.25 N	76.35 W
Eastman	142	32.11 N	83.10 W
East Millinocket	136	45.37 N	68.34 W
East Moline	138	41.30 N	90.26 W
East Naples	142	26.06 N	81.44 W
Easton, Md., U.S.	136	38.46 N	76.04 W
Easton, Pa., U.S.	136	40.41 N	75.13 W
East Pakistan → Bangladesh ◻ 1	70	24.00 N	90.00 E
East Palatka	142	29.39 N	81.35 W
East Palestine	136	40.50 N	80.32 W
East Peoria	138	40.39 N	89.34 W
East Point	142	33.40 N	84.26 W
Eastport, Id., U.S.	150	49.00 N	116.10 W
Eastport, Me., U.S.	136	44.54 N	66.59 W
East Porterville	154	36.04 N	118.56 W
East Prairie	144	36.46 N	89.23 W
East Retford	26	53.19 N	0.56 W
East Rockingham	142	34.55 N	79.45 W
East Saint Louis	144	38.38 N	90.09 W
East Siberian Sea → Vostočno-Sibirskoje more ₸ 2	56	74.00 N	166.00 E
East Spencer	142	35.40 N	80.25 W
East Stroudsburg	136	40.59 N	75.10 W
East Sussex ◻ 6	26	50.55 N	0.15 E
East Troy	138	42.47 N	88.24 W
East Walker ≃	154	38.53 N	119.10 W
Eaton	136	39.44 N	84.38 W
Eaton Rapids	138	42.30 N	84.39 W
Eatonton	142	33.19 N	83.23 W
Eau Claire	138	44.48 N	91.29 W
Eau Claire, Lac à l' ⊜	130	56.10 N	74.25 W
Ebbw Vale	26	51.47 N	3.12 W
Ebensburg	136	40.29 N	78.43 W
Ebensee	30	47.48 N	13.46 E
Eberbach	30	49.28 N	8.59 E
Ebersberg	30	48.05 N	11.58 E
Eberswalde	30	52.50 N	13.49 E
Ebingen	30	48.13 N	9.01 E
Ebinur Hu ⊜	66	44.55 N	82.55 E
Ebola ≃	84	3.20 N	20.57 E
Eboli	40	40.37 N	15.04 E
Ebre, Delta de l' ≚ 2	44	40.43 N	0.54 E
Ebro (Ebre) ≃	44	40.43 N	0.54 E
Ebro, Embalse del ⊜ 1	44	43.00 N	3.58 W
Ech Cheliff	82	36.10 N	1.20 E
Echo Bay	130	66.05 N	118.02 W
Echuca	96	36.08 S	144.46 E
Écija	44	37.32 N	5.05 W
Eckernförde	30	54.28 N	9.50 E
Eckerö I	22	60.14 N	19.35 E
Écrins, Barre des ∧	36	44.55 N	6.22 E
Écrins, Massif des ⋏ 1	36	44.55 N	6.20 E
Ecuador ◻ 1	118	2.00 S	77.30 W
Eddystone Rocks II 1	26	50.12 N	4.15 W
Eddyville	144	37.05 N	88.04 W
Ede, Ned.	30	52.03 N	5.40 E
Ede, Nig.	82	7.44 N	4.27 E
Edelény	30	48.18 N	20.44 E
Eden	144	32.59 N	90.19 W
Eden ≃	26	54.57 N	3.01 W
Edenton	142	36.03 N	76.36 W
Eden Valley	138	45.19 N	94.32 W
Eder ≃	30	51.13 N	9.27 E
Edgard	144	30.03 N	90.34 W
Edgartown	136	41.23 N	70.30 W
Edgefield	142	33.47 N	81.55 W
Edgemont	132	43.18 N	103.49 W
Edgerton	138	42.50 N	89.04 W
Edgewater	144	33.31 N	86.57 W
Edgewood	136	39.25 N	76.17 W
Édhessa	48	40.48 N	22.03 E
Edina, Mn., U.S.	138	44.53 N	93.20 W
Edina, Mo., U.S.	144	40.10 N	92.10 W
Edinboro	136	41.52 N	80.07 W
Edinburg, Il., U.S.	144	39.39 N	89.23 W
Edinburg, In., U.S.	144	39.21 N	85.58 W
Edinburg, Tx., U.S.	132	26.18 N	98.09 W
Edinburgh	26	55.57 N	3.13 W
Edirne	48	41.40 N	26.34 E
Edisto ≃	142	32.39 N	80.24 W
Edisto Island I	142	32.35 N	80.20 W
Edmonds	150	47.48 N	122.22 W
Edmonton	130	53.33 N	113.28 W
Edmundston	130	47.22 N	68.20 W
Edremit	48	39.35 N	27.01 E
Edremit Körfezi c	48	39.30 N	26.45 E
Edsbruk	22	58.02 N	16.28 E
Edson	130	53.35 N	116.26 W
Edward, Lake ⊜	86	0.25 S	29.30 E
Edwards	136	44.19 N	75.15 W
Edwards ≃	138	41.09 N	90.59 W
Edwards Plateau ⋏ 1	132	31.20 N	101.00 W
Edwardsville	144	38.48 N	89.57 W
Eeklo	30	51.11 N	3.34 E
Eel ≃, Ca., U.S.	154	40.40 N	124.20 W
Eel ≃, In., U.S.	144	40.45 N	86.22 W
Éfaté I	92	17.40 S	168.25 E
Effigy Mounds National Monument ♦	138	43.06 N	91.13 W
Effingham	144	39.07 N	88.32 W
Eforie Nord	48	44.06 N	28.38 E
Eforie Sud	48	44.03 N	28.38 E
Egadi, Isole II	40	37.58 N	12.16 E
Egan Range ⋏	154	39.10 N	114.55 W
Egedesminde (Aasiaat)	130	68.42 N	52.45 W
Eger	30	47.54 N	20.23 E
Eggenfelden	30	48.25 N	12.46 E
Egg Harbor City	136	39.31 N	74.38 W
Egina → Aíyina I	48	37.46 N	23.26 E
Égletons	36	45.24 N	2.03 E
Egmont, Cape ≻	98	39.17 S	173.45 E
Egmont, Mount → Taranaki, Mount ∧	98	39.18 S	174.04 E
Eğridir Gölü ⊜	16	38.02 N	30.53 E
Egypt (Mişr) ◻ 1	84	27.00 N	30.00 E
Egypt, Lake of ⊜ 1	144	37.35 N	88.55 W
Ehrhardt	142	33.05 N	81.00 W
Eibar	44	43.11 N	2.28 W
Eibiswald	30	46.41 N	15.15 E
Eichstätt	30	48.54 N	11.12 E
Eifel ⋏	30	50.15 N	6.45 E
Eigg I	26	56.54 N	6.10 W
Eighty Mile Beach ⊻ 2	96	19.45 S	121.00 E
Eilenburg	30	51.27 N	12.37 E
Einbeck	30	51.49 N	9.52 E
Eindhoven	30	51.26 N	5.28 E
Einsiedeln	36	47.08 N	8.45 E
Eisenach	30	50.59 N	10.19 E
Eisenberg	30	50.58 N	11.53 E
Eisenerz	30	47.33 N	14.53 E
Eisenhüttenstadt	30	52.10 N	14.39 E
Eisenstadt	30	47.51 N	16.32 E
Eisleben	30	51.31 N	11.32 E
Eislingen	30	48.42 N	9.42 E
Eitorf	30	50.46 N	7.26 E
Eivissa	44	38.54 N	1.26 E
Eivissa (Ibiza) I	44	39.00 N	1.25 E
Ejea de los Caballeros	44	42.08 N	1.08 W
Ekiatapskij chrebet ⋏	56	68.30 N	179.00 E
El Aaiún	82	27.09 N	13.12 W
El Affroun	44	36.30 N	2.38 E
Elaine	144	34.18 N	90.51 W
El Alia	40	37.10 N	10.03 E
Elan ≃	48	46.07 N	28.04 E
El Arahal	44	37.16 N	5.33 W
Elat	70	29.33 N	34.57 E
Elat, Gulf of → Aqaba, Gulf of c	84	29.00 N	34.40 E
Elâzığ	16	38.41 N	39.14 E
Elba	144	31.24 N	86.04 W
Elba, Isola d' I	40	42.46 N	10.17 E
El Banco	118	9.00 N	73.58 W
El Barco de Avila	44	40.21 N	5.31 W
Elbasan	48	41.06 N	20.05 E
Elbe (Labe) ≃	30	53.50 N	9.00 E
Elbe-Havel-Kanal ≊	30	52.24 N	12.23 E
Elbert, Mount ∧	148	39.07 N	106.27 W
Elberta	138	44.37 N	86.13 W
Elberton	142	34.06 N	82.52 W
Elbeuf	36	49.17 N	1.00 E
Elbląg (Elbing)	30	54.10 N	19.25 E
El-Borj	44	35.43 N	5.40 W
El Boulaïda	82	36.28 N	2.50 E
El'brus, gora ∧	54	43.21 N	42.26 E
Elbrus, Mount → El'brus, gora ∧	54	43.21 N	42.26 E
Elburz Mountains → Alborz, Reshteh-ye Kūhhā-ye ⋏	70	36.00 N	53.00 E
El Cajon	154	32.47 N	116.57 W
El Capitan ∧	150	46.01 N	114.23 W
El Carmen de Bolívar	118	9.43 N	75.08 W
El Centro	154	32.47 N	115.33 W
Elche → Elx	44	38.15 N	0.42 W
Elche de la Sierra	44	38.27 N	2.03 W
Elda	44	38.29 N	0.47 W
El Djazaïr (Algiers)	82	36.47 N	3.03 E
Eldon	144	38.20 N	92.34 W
Eldora	138	42.21 N	93.05 W
El Dorado, Ar., U.S.	144	33.12 N	92.39 W
Eldorado, Il., U.S.	144	37.48 N	88.26 W
Eldorado Peak ∧	150	48.32 N	121.08 W
El Dorado Springs	144	37.52 N	94.01 W
Eldoret	86	0.31 N	35.17 E
Eldred	136	41.57 N	78.23 W
Electric City	150	47.56 N	119.02 W
Elephant Butte Reservoir ⊜ 1	148	33.19 N	107.10 W
Elephant Mountain ∧	136	44.46 N	70.46 W
El Eulma	44	36.08 N	5.40 E
Eleusis → Elevsís	48	38.02 N	23.32 E
Eleuthera I	108	25.10 N	76.14 W
Eleven Point ≃	144	36.09 N	91.05 W
Elevsís	48	38.02 N	23.32 E
El Fahs	40	36.22 N	9.55 E
El Ferrol del Caudillo	44	43.29 N	8.14 W
El Ghazawet	44	35.06 N	1.51 W
Elgin, Scot., U.K.	26	57.39 N	3.20 W
Elgin, Il., U.S.	138	42.02 N	88.16 W
Elgon, Mount ∧	86	1.08 N	34.33 E
El Hank ⊻ 4	82	24.30 N	7.00 W
Elhovo	48	42.10 N	26.34 E
Elila ≃	86	2.45 S	25.53 E
Elin Pelin	48	42.40 N	23.36 E
Eliot	136	43.09 N	70.48 W
Élisabethville → Lubumbashi	86	11.40 S	27.28 E
Elista	54	46.16 N	44.14 E
Elizabeth, Austl.	96	34.43 S	138.40 E
Elizabeth, N.J., U.S.	136	40.39 N	74.12 W
Elizabeth, W.V., U.S.	136	39.03 N	81.23 W
Elizabeth City	142	36.18 N	76.13 W
Elizabethton	142	36.20 N	82.12 W
Elizabethtown	144	37.41 N	85.51 W
El-Jadida	82	33.16 N	8.30 W
El-Jebha	44	35.13 N	4.38 W
El Jem	40	35.18 N	10.43 E
Ełk	30	53.50 N	22.22 E
Ełk ≃, Pol.	30	53.31 N	22.47 E
Elk ≃, U.S.	144	34.46 N	87.16 W
Elk ≃, Mn., U.S.	138	45.18 N	93.34 W
Elk ≃, W.V., U.S.	136	38.21 N	81.38 W
El Kef	82	36.11 N	8.43 E
El Kerma	44	35.36 N	0.35 W
Elk Grove	154	38.24 N	121.22 W
Elkhart	144	41.40 N	85.58 W
Elkhart Lake	138	43.50 N	88.01 W
Elk Horn, Ia., U.S.	144	41.35 N	95.03 W
Elkhorn, Wi., U.S.	138	42.40 N	88.32 W
Elkhorn City	142	37.18 N	82.21 W
Elkin	142	36.14 N	80.50 W
Elkins	136	38.55 N	79.50 W
Elkland	136	41.59 N	77.18 W
Elko	154	40.49 N	115.45 W
Elk Rapids	138	44.53 N	85.24 W
El Krib	40	36.19 N	9.09 E
Elk River	138	45.18 N	93.35 W
Elkton, Md., U.S.	136	39.36 N	75.50 W
Elkton, Va., U.S.	136	38.24 N	78.37 W
Ellen, Mount ∧	148	38.07 N	110.49 W
Ellendale	132	46.00 N	98.31 W
Ellensburg	150	46.59 N	120.32 W
Ellenville	136	41.43 N	74.23 W
Ellice ≃	130	68.02 N	103.26 W
Ellice Islands → Tuvalu ◻ 1	8	8.00 S	178.00 E
Ellicott City	136	39.16 N	76.47 W
Ellijay	142	34.41 N	84.28 W
Ellington	144	37.14 N	90.58 W
Elliot Lake	130	46.23 N	82.39 W
Elliott Key I	142	25.27 N	80.11 W
Ellisville	144	31.36 N	89.11 W
Elloree	142	33.31 N	80.34 W
Ellsworth, Me., U.S.	136	44.32 N	68.25 W
Ellsworth, Wi., U.S.	138	44.43 N	92.29 W
Ellwangen	30	48.57 N	10.07 E
Ellwood City	136	40.51 N	80.17 W
Elma	150	47.00 N	123.24 W
Elm City	142	35.48 N	77.51 W
El Menia	82	30.30 N	2.50 E
Elmer	136	39.35 N	75.10 W
Elmhurst	138	41.53 N	87.56 W
Elmira	136	42.05 N	76.48 W
El Mirage	148	33.36 N	112.19 W
Elmira Heights	136	42.07 N	76.49 W
El Mohammadia	44	35.33 N	0.03 E
El Molinillo	44	39.28 N	4.13 W
Elmore	136	41.28 N	83.17 W
El Mreyyé ◆ 1	82	19.30 N	7.00 W
Elmshorn	30	53.45 N	9.39 E
Elmwood	138	44.46 N	92.08 W
El Nevado, Cerro ∧, Arg.	120	35.35 S	68.30 W
El Nevado, Cerro ∧, Col.	118	3.59 N	74.04 W
Elora	144	35.00 N	86.21 W
Eloy	148	32.45 N	111.33 W
El Paso, Il., U.S.	144	40.44 N	89.00 W
El Paso, Tx., U.S.	148	31.45 N	106.29 W
El Prat de Llobregat	44	41.20 N	2.06 E
El Puerto de Santa María	44	36.36 N	6.13 W
El Qala	40	36.50 N	8.30 E
El Reno	132	35.31 N	97.57 W
El Rio	154	34.13 N	119.10 W
Elroy	138	43.44 N	90.16 W
Elsa	130	63.55 N	135.28 W
El Salvador ◻ 1	108	13.50 N	88.55 W
Elsie	138	43.05 N	84.23 W
Elsinore → Helsingør	22	56.02 N	12.37 E
Elsmere	136	39.44 N	75.35 W
Elsterwerda	30	51.28 N	13.31 E
Eltham	98	39.26 S	174.18 E
El Tigre	118	8.55 N	64.15 W
Eltmann	30	49.58 N	10.40 E
Elton	144	30.28 N	92.41 W
El Turbio	120	51.41 S	72.05 W
Elūru	70	16.42 N	81.06 E
Elvas	44	38.53 N	7.10 W
El Vendrell	44	41.13 N	1.32 E
Elvins	144	37.50 N	90.31 W
El Wad	82	33.20 N	6.58 E
Elwell, Lake ⊜ 1	150	48.22 N	111.17 W
Elwood	144	40.16 N	85.50 W
Elx	44	38.15 N	0.42 W
Ely, Mn., U.S.	138	47.54 N	91.52 W
Ely, Nv., U.S.	154	39.14 N	114.53 W
Elyria	136	41.22 N	82.06 W
Emāmshahr (Shāhrūd)	70	36.25 N	55.01 E
Emba ≃	54	46.38 N	53.14 E
Embarcación	120	23.13 S	64.06 W
Embarras ≃	144	38.39 N	87.37 W
Emden	30	53.22 N	7.12 E
Emerald	96	23.32 S	148.10 E
Emery	148	38.55 N	111.14 W
Emet	48	39.20 N	29.15 E
Emine, nos ≻	48	42.42 N	27.51 E
Eminence	144	38.22 N	85.10 W
Emmaus	136	40.32 N	75.29 W
Emmen	30	52.47 N	6.54 E
Emmendingen	30	48.07 N	7.50 E
Emmerich	30	51.50 N	6.15 E
Emmet	144	33.43 N	93.28 W
Emmett	150	43.52 N	116.29 W
Emmitsburg	136	39.42 N	77.20 W
Empalme	108	27.58 N	110.51 W
Emperor Range ⋏	94	5.45 S	154.55 E
Empire	154	40.34 N	119.20 W
Empoli	40	43.43 N	10.57 E
Emporia, Ks., U.S.	132	38.24 N	96.10 W
Emporia, Va., U.S.	142	36.41 N	77.32 W
Empty Quarter → Ar-Rub'al-Khālī ◆ 2	70	20.00 N	51.00 E
Ems ≃	30	53.30 N	7.00 E
Emsdetten	30	52.10 N	7.31 E
En (Inn) ≃	36	48.35 N	13.28 E
Encarnación	120	27.20 S	55.54 W
Encinitas	154	33.02 N	117.17 W
Encontrados	118	9.03 N	72.14 W
Encounter Bay c	96	35.35 S	138.44 E
Encs	30	48.20 N	21.08 E
Endeavour Strait ų	96	10.50 S	142.15 E
Enderby Land ◆ 1	8	67.30 S	53.00 E
Endicott	136	42.05 N	76.02 W
Enfida	40	36.07 N	10.23 E
Enfield, N.H., U.S.	136	43.38 N	72.08 W
Enfield, N.C., U.S.	142	36.10 N	77.40 W
Engelhard	142	35.30 N	75.59 W
Engel's	54	51.30 N	46.07 E
England	144	34.32 N	91.58 W
England ◻ 8	26	52.30 N	1.30 W
Englehart	130	47.49 N	79.52 W
Englewood, Co., U.S.	148	39.38 N	104.59 W
Englewood, Fl., U.S.	142	26.57 N	82.21 W
Englewood, Tn., U.S.	142	35.25 N	84.29 W
English	144	38.20 N	86.27 W
English ≃, On., Can.	130	50.12 N	95.00 W
English ≃, Ia., U.S.	138	41.29 N	91.30 W
English Channel (La Manche) ų	26	50.20 N	1.00 W
Énguera	44	38.59 N	0.41 W
Enid	132	36.23 N	97.52 W
Enid Lake ⊜ 1	144	34.10 N	89.50 W
eNjesuthi ∧	86	29.09 S	29.23 E
Enka	142	35.32 N	82.39 W
Enkhuizen	30	52.42 N	5.17 E
Enköping	22	59.38 N	17.04 E
Enna	40	37.34 N	14.16 E
Ennedi ⋏ 1	84	17.15 N	22.00 E
Ennis	26	52.50 N	8.59 W
Enniskillen	26	54.21 N	7.38 W
Enns	30	48.13 N	14.29 E
Enns ≃	30	48.14 N	14.32 E
Enon	136	39.53 N	83.56 W
Enosburg Falls	136	44.54 N	72.48 W
Enschede	30	52.12 N	6.53 E
Ensenada	108	31.52 N	116.37 W
Entebbe	86	0.04 N	32.28 E
Enterprise, Al., U.S.	144	31.18 N	85.51 W
Enterprise, Ca., U.S.	154	39.32 N	121.22 W
Entinas, Punta de las ≻	44	36.41 N	2.46 W
Entrepeñas, Embalse de ⊜ 1	44	40.34 N	2.42 W
Enugu	82	6.27 N	7.27 E
Enumclaw	150	47.12 N	121.59 W
Envalira, Port d')(	44	42.35 N	1.45 E
Envermeu	36	49.54 N	1.16 E
Enys, Mount ∧	98	43.14 S	171.38 E
Enza ≃	40	44.54 N	10.31 E
Eo ≃	44	43.28 N	7.03 W
Eolia	144	39.14 N	91.00 W
Eolie, Isole II	40	38.30 N	14.50 E
Épernay	36	49.03 N	3.57 E
Ephesus ⊥	48	37.55 N	27.17 E
Ephraim	148	39.21 N	111.35 W
Ephrata, Pa., U.S.	136	40.10 N	76.10 W
Ephrata, Wa., U.S.	150	47.19 N	119.33 W
Épi I	92	16.43 S	168.15 E
Épinal	36	48.11 N	6.27 E
Epirus → Ípeiros ◻ 9	48	39.40 N	20.50 E
Epping, Eng., U.K.	26	51.43 N	0.07 E
Epping, N.H., U.S.	136	43.02 N	71.04 W
Epsom	26	51.20 N	0.16 W
Epte ≃	36	49.04 N	1.37 E
Equality	144	37.44 N	88.20 W
Equatorial Guinea ◻ 1	82	2.00 N	9.00 E
Erath	144	29.57 N	92.02 W
Erba	40	45.48 N	9.15 E
Erbach	30	49.40 N	8.59 E
Erciyes Dağı ∧	16	38.32 N	35.28 E
Érd	30	47.23 N	18.56 E
Erdek	48	40.24 N	27.48 E
Erding	30	48.18 N	11.54 E
Erechim	120	27.38 S	52.17 W
Ereğli	16	37.31 N	34.04 E
Erft ≃	30	51.11 N	6.44 E
Erfurt	30	50.58 N	11.01 E
Ergene ≃	48	41.01 N	26.22 E
Erges (Erjas) ≃	44	39.40 N	7.01 W
Ergun (Argun') ≃	56	53.20 N	121.28 E
Erice	40	38.02 N	12.35 E
Erie	136	42.07 N	80.05 W
Erie, Lake ⊜	132	42.15 N	81.00 W
Erie Canal → New York State Barge Canal ≊	136	43.05 N	78.43 W
Erímanthos ∧	48	37.59 N	21.51 E
Erin	144	36.19 N	87.41 W
Eritrea ◻ 9	84	15.20 N	39.00 E
Erjas (Erges) ≃	44	39.40 N	7.01 W
Erkelenz	30	51.05 N	6.19 E
Erlangen	30	49.36 N	11.01 E
Ermelo	86	26.34 S	29.58 E
Ermidas	44	38.00 N	8.23 W
Ermoúpolis	48	37.26 N	24.56 E
Ernākulam	70	9.59 N	76.17 E
Erne, Lower Lough ⊜	26	54.26 N	7.46 W
Erne, Upper Lough ⊜	26	54.14 N	7.32 W
Erode	70	11.21 N	77.44 E
Errol Heights	150	45.28 N	122.36 W
Erromango I	92	18.45 S	169.05 E
Ersekë	48	40.20 N	20.41 E
Ertix (Irtyš) ≃	54	61.04 N	68.52 E
Erwin, N.C., U.S.	142	35.19 N	78.40 W
Erwin, Tn., U.S.	142	36.08 N	82.25 W
Erzgebirge (Krušné hory) ⋏	30	50.30 N	13.10 E
Erzincan	16	39.44 N	39.29 E
Erzurum	16	39.55 N	41.17 E
Esbjerg	22	55.28 N	8.27 E
Esca ≃	44	42.37 N	1.03 W
Escalon	154	37.47 N	120.59 W
Escambia ≃	144	30.32 N	87.11 W
Escanaba	138	45.44 N	87.04 W
Escarpada Point ≻	68	18.31 N	122.13 E
Escatawpa ≃	144	30.25 N	88.35 W
Escaut (Schelde) ≃	30	51.22 N	4.15 E
Esch-sur-Alzette	30	49.30 N	5.59 E
Eschwege	30	51.11 N	10.04 E
Eschweiler	30	50.49 N	6.16 E
Escondido	154	33.07 N	117.05 W
Escuintla	108	14.18 N	90.47 W
Escurial, Serra do ∧	118	10.04 S	41.05 W
Eşfahān	70	32.40 N	51.38 E
Eskdale	136	38.05 N	81.26 W
Eskilstuna	22	59.22 N	16.30 E
Eskimo Lakes ⊜	130	69.15 N	132.17 W
Eskişehir	16	39.46 N	30.32 E
Eslöv	22	55.50 N	13.20 E
Eşme	48	38.24 N	28.59 E
Esmeraldas	118	0.59 N	79.42 W
Esmeraldas ≃	118	0.58 N	79.38 W
Espanola, On., Can.	130	46.15 N	81.46 W
Espanola, N.M., U.S.	148	35.59 N	106.04 W
Esperance	96	33.51 S	121.53 E
Espichel, Cabo ≻	44	38.25 N	9.13 W
Espinhaço, Serra do ⋏	118	17.30 S	43.30 W
Espinho	44	41.00 N	8.39 W
Espiritu Santo I	92	15.15 S	166.50 E
Espoo (Esbo)	22	60.13 N	24.40 E
Esquel	120	42.54 S	71.19 W
Esquina	120	30.01 S	59.32 W
Essaouira	82	31.30 N	9.47 W
Essen	30	51.28 N	7.01 E
Essequibo ≃	118	6.59 N	58.23 W
Essex, Md., U.S.	136	39.18 N	76.28 W
Essex, Mo., U.S.	144	36.48 N	89.51 W
Essex ◻ 6	26	51.48 N	0.40 E
Essex Junction	136	44.29 N	73.06 W
Essexville	138	43.36 N	83.50 W
Esslingen	30	48.45 N	9.16 E
Est, Cap ≻	86	15.16 S	50.29 E
Est, Pointe de l' ≻	130	49.08 N	61.41 W
Estaca de Bares, Punta de la ≻	44	43.46 N	7.42 W
Estados, Isla de los I	120	54.47 S	64.15 W
Estats, Pique d' ∧	44	42.40 N	1.24 E
Este	40	45.14 N	11.39 E
Estelí	108	13.05 N	86.23 W
Estepa	44	37.18 N	4.54 W
Estepona	44	36.26 N	5.08 W
Estes Park	148	40.22 N	105.31 W
Estevan	130	49.08 N	102.59 W
Eston	130	51.10 N	108.46 W
Estonia → Estonskaja Sovetskaja Socialističeskaja Respublika ◻ 3	54	59.00 N	26.00 E
Estonskaja Sovetskaja Socialističeskaja Respublika (Estonia) ◻ 3	54	59.00 N	26.00 E
Estoril	44	38.42 N	9.23 W
Estrela ∧	44	40.19 N	7.37 W
Estrela, Serra da ⋏	44	40.20 N	7.38 W
Estremadura ◻ 9	44	39.15 N	9.10 W
Esztergom	30	47.48 N	18.45 E
Étampes	36	48.26 N	2.09 E
Étaples	36	50.31 N	1.39 E
Etāwah	70	26.46 N	79.02 E
Eten	118	6.54 S	79.52 W
Ethel, Mount ∧	148	40.39 N	106.41 W
Ethiopia (Ityopiya) ◻ 1	84	9.00 N	39.00 E
Etna, Monte ∧ 1	40	37.46 N	15.00 E
Etosha Pan ≚	86	18.45 S	16.15 E
Etowah	142	35.19 N	84.31 W
Etowah ≃	142	34.15 N	85.11 W
Étretat	36	49.42 N	0.12 E
Ettelbruck	30	49.52 N	6.05 E
Et Tîdra I	82	19.44 N	16.24 W
Ettlingen	30	48.56 N	8.24 E
Ettrick	142	37.14 N	77.25 W
Eu	36	50.03 N	1.25 E
Euboea → Évvoia I	48	38.34 N	23.50 E
Euclid	136	41.35 N	81.31 W
Eudora	144	33.06 N	91.15 W
Eufaula	144	31.53 N	85.08 W
Eufaula Lake ⊜ 1	144	35.17 N	95.31 W
Eugene	150	44.03 N	123.05 W
Eugenia, Punta ≻	108	27.50 N	115.05 W
Eume ≃	44	43.25 N	8.08 W
Eunice	144	30.29 N	92.25 W
Eupen	30	50.38 N	6.02 E
Euphrates (Al-Furāt) (Fırat) ≃	70	31.00 N	47.25 E
Eure ≃	36	49.18 N	1.12 E
Eureka, Ca., U.S.	154	40.48 N	124.09 W
Eureka, S.C., U.S.	142	34.42 N	81.11 W
Eureka Springs	144	36.24 N	93.44 W
Europa, Île I	86	22.20 S	40.22 E
Europa, Picos de ⋏	44	43.12 N	4.48 W
Europa Point ≻	44	36.10 N	5.22 W
Europe ⊻ 1	8	50.00 N	28.00 E
Europoort ◆ 5	30	51.58 N	4.00 E
Euskal Herriko ◻ 4	44	43.00 N	2.30 W
Euskirchen	30	50.39 N	6.47 E
Eustis	142	28.51 N	81.41 W
Eutaw	144	32.50 N	87.53 W
Eutin	30	54.08 N	10.37 E
Evadale	144	30.21 N	94.04 W
Evans	148	40.22 N	104.41 W
Evans, Mount ∧	148	39.35 N	105.38 W
Evans City	136	40.46 N	80.03 W
Evansdale	138	42.28 N	92.16 W
Evanston, Il., U.S.	138	42.02 N	87.41 W
Evanston, Wy., U.S.	150	41.16 N	110.57 W
Evansville, In., U.S.	144	37.58 N	87.33 W
Evansville, Wi., U.S.	138	42.46 N	89.17 W
Evarts	142	36.51 N	83.11 W
Eveleth	138	47.27 N	92.32 W
Evening Shade	144	36.04 N	91.37 W
Everard, Lake ⊜	96	31.25 S	135.05 E
Everest, Mount (Qomolangma Feng) ∧	70	27.59 N	86.56 E
Everett, Pa., U.S.	136	40.00 N	78.22 W
Everett, Wa., U.S.	150	47.58 N	122.12 W
Everett, Mount ∧	136	42.06 N	73.25 W
Everglades City	142	25.52 N	81.23 W
Everglades National Park ♦	142	25.27 N	80.53 W
Evergreen, Al., U.S.	144	31.26 N	86.57 W
Evergreen, Ca., U.S.	154	35.54 N	120.26 W
Evesham	26	52.06 N	1.56 W
Évian-les-Bains	36	46.23 N	6.35 E
Évora	44	38.34 N	7.54 W
Évreux	36	49.01 N	1.09 E
Évros (Marica) (Meriç) ≃	48	40.52 N	26.12 E
Évry	36	48.38 N	2.27 E
Évvoia I	48	38.34 N	23.50 E
Excelsior Mountain ∧	154	38.02 N	119.18 W
Excelsior Springs	144	39.20 N	94.13 W
Exe ≃	26	50.37 N	3.25 W
Exeter, Eng., U.K.	26	50.43 N	3.31 W
Exeter, Ca., U.S.	154	36.17 N	119.08 W
Exeter, N.H., U.S.	136	42.58 N	70.56 W
Exira	144	41.35 N	94.52 W
Exmoor ⋏ 1	26	51.10 N	3.40 W
Exmouth	26	50.37 N	3.25 W
Exmouth Gulf c	96	22.00 S	114.20 E
Experiment	142	33.15 N	84.16 W
Extremadura ◻ 4	44	39.15 N	6.15 W
Exuma Sound ų	108	24.15 N	76.00 W
Eyasi, Lake ⊜	86	3.40 S	35.05 E
Eyre North, Lake ⊜	96	28.40 S	137.10 E
Eyre Peninsula ≻ 1	96	34.00 S	135.45 E
Eyre South, Lake ⊜	96	29.30 S	137.20 E
Ezine	48	39.47 N	26.20 E
F			
Fabens	148	31.30 N	106.09 W
Fabriano	40	43.20 N	12.54 E
Fada	84	17.14 N	21.33 E
Faddeja, zaliv c	54	76.40 N	107.20 E
Faenza	40	44.17 N	11.53 E
Faeroe Islands ◻ 2	16	62.00 N	7.00 W
Fafen ≃	84	5.59 N	44.25 E
Făgăraş	48	45.51 N	24.58 E
Făgăraşului, Munţii ⋏	48	45.35 N	25.00 E
Fagatogo	93	14.17 S	170.41 W
Fagernes	22	60.59 N	9.15 E
Fagersta	22	60.00 N	15.47 E
Faguibine, Lac ⊜	82	16.45 N	3.54 W
Fairbanks	132a	64.51 N	147.43 W
Fairborn	136	39.49 N	84.01 W
Fairburn	142	33.34 N	84.34 W
Fairbury, Il., U.S.	138	40.44 N	88.30 W
Fairbury, Ne., U.S.	132	40.08 N	97.10 W
Fairfax, Al., U.S.	144	32.47 N	85.11 W
Fairfax, S.C., U.S.	142	32.57 N	81.14 W
Fairfax, Vt., U.S.	136	44.39 N	73.00 W
Fairfax, Va., U.S.	136	38.50 N	77.18 W
Fairfield, Al., U.S.	144	33.33 N	86.47 W
Fairfield, Ca., U.S.	154	38.14 N	122.02 W
Fairfield, Il., U.S.	144	38.22 N	88.21 W
Fairfield, Ia., U.S.	138	41.00 N	91.57 W
Fairfield, Me., U.S.	136	44.35 N	69.35 W
Fairfield, Oh., U.S.	136	39.20 N	84.33 W
Fairhaven, Ma., U.S.	136	41.38 N	70.54 W
Fair Haven, N.Y., U.S.	136	43.18 N	76.42 W
Fair Haven, Vt., U.S.	136	43.35 N	73.15 W
Fair Head ≻	26	55.13 N	6.09 W
Fairhope	144	30.31 N	87.54 W
Fair Isle I	26	59.32 N	1.39 W
Fairlie	98	44.06 S	170.50 E
Fairmont, Mn., U.S.	132	43.39 N	94.27 W
Fairmont, N.C., U.S.	142	34.29 N	79.06 W
Fairmont, W.V., U.S.	136	39.29 N	80.08 W
Fairmount	144	40.24 N	85.39 W
Fair Oaks, Ca., U.S.	154	38.38 N	121.16 W
Fair Oaks, Ga., U.S.	142	33.54 N	84.32 W
Fair Plain	138	42.05 N	86.27 W
Fairview	132	47.51 N	104.02 W
Fairweather Mountain ∧	130	58.54 N	137.32 W
Faisalabad	70	31.25 N	73.05 E
Faison	142	35.06 N	78.08 W
Faizābād	70	26.47 N	82.08 E
Falaise	36	48.54 N	0.12 W
Falam	68	22.55 N	93.40 E
Fălciu	48	46.18 N	28.08 E
Falcon, Cap ≻	44	35.46 N	0.48 W
Falconara Marittima	40	43.37 N	13.24 E
Falcon Reservoir ⊜ 1	108	26.37 N	99.11 W
Falelatai	93	13.55 S	171.59 W
Falémé ≃	82	14.46 N	12.14 W
Falkenberg	22	56.54 N	12.28 E
Falkensee	30	52.33 N	13.04 E
Falkenstein	30	50.29 N	12.22 E
Falkirk	26	56.00 N	3.48 W
Falkland Islands ◻ 2	120	51.45 S	59.00 W
Falkland Sound ų	120	51.45 S	59.25 W
Falköping	22	58.10 N	13.31 E
Fallbrook	154	33.22 N	117.15 W
Fallon	154	39.28 N	118.46 W
Fall River, Ma., U.S.	136	41.42 N	71.09 W
Fall River, Wi., U.S.	138	43.23 N	89.02 W
Falls Lake ⊜ 1	142	36.00 N	78.45 W
Falmouth, Eng., U.K.	26	50.08 N	5.04 W
Falmouth, Ky., U.S.	136	38.40 N	84.19 W
Falmouth, Me., U.S.	136	43.43 N	70.14 W
Falmouth, Ma., U.S.	136	41.33 N	70.36 W
Falmouth, Va., U.S.	136	38.19 N	77.28 W
False Divi Point ≻	70	15.43 N	80.49 E
Falster I	22	54.48 N	11.58 E
Fălticeni	48	47.28 N	26.18 E
Falun	22	60.36 N	15.38 E
Famagusta → Gazi Magosa	16	35.07 N	33.57 E
Famenne ◆ 1	30	50.10 N	5.15 E
Fangak	84	9.04 N	30.53 E
Fannaråki ∧	22	61.31 N	7.55 E
Fano	40	43.50 N	13.01 E
Fanø I	22	55.25 N	8.25 E
Fan-si-pan ∧	68	22.15 N	103.46 E
Faradje	84	3.44 N	29.43 E
Faradofay	86	25.02 S	47.00 E
Farafangana	86	22.49 S	47.50 E
Farāfirah, Al-Wāhat al- ₸ 4	84	27.15 N	28.10 E
Farāh	70	32.22 N	62.07 E
Farah ≃	70	31.29 N	61.24 E
Farallon de Pajaros I	68	20.32 N	144.54 E
Farallon Islands II	154	37.43 N	123.03 W
Farasān, Jazā'ir II	70	16.48 N	41.54 E
Farcău, Vîrful ∧	48	47.56 N	24.27 E
Fareham	26	50.51 N	1.10 W
Farewell, Cape ≻	98	40.30 S	172.41 E
Farewell Spit ≻ 2	98	40.31 S	172.52 E
Färgelanda	22	58.34 N	11.59 E
Fargo	132	46.52 N	96.47 W
Faribault	138	44.17 N	93.16 W
Farilhões II	44	39.28 N	9.34 W
Färjestaden	22	56.39 N	16.27 E
Farmer City	144	40.14 N	88.38 W
Farmersville	144	39.26 N	89.39 W
Farmerville	144	32.46 N	92.24 W
Farmington, Il., U.S.	138	40.41 N	90.00 W
Farmington, Ia., U.S.	138	40.38 N	91.44 W
Farmington, Me., U.S.	136	44.40 N	70.09 W
Farmington, Mn., U.S.	138	44.38 N	93.08 W
Farmington, Mo., U.S.	144	37.47 N	90.25 W
Farmington, N.H., U.S.	136	43.23 N	71.03 W
Farmington, N.M., U.S.	148	36.43 N	108.13 W
Farmington, Ut,. U.S.	148	40.58 N	111.53 W
Farmville, N.C., U.S.	142	35.35 N	77.35 W
Farmville, Va., U.S.	142	37.18 N	78.23 W
Farne Islands II	26	55.38 N	1.38 W
Faro	44	37.01 N	7.56 W
Faro ≃	82	9.21 N	12.55 E
Fårön I	22	57.56 N	19.08 E
Farquhar Group II	86	10.10 S	51.10 E
Farrell	136	41.12 N	80.29 W
Farrukhābād	70	27.24 N	79.34 E
Fartak, Ra's ≻	70	15.38 N	52.15 E
Farvel, Kap ≻	130	59.45 N	44.00 W
Fasano	40	40.50 N	17.22 E
Fathom Five National Marine Park ♦	138	45.15 N	81.40 W
Fátima	44	39.37 N	8.39 W
Faucilles, Monts ⋏	36	48.07 N	6.16 E
Fauro Island I	94	6.55 S	156.04 E
Fauske	20	67.15 N	15.24 E
Favara	40	37.19 N	13.39 E

Symbols in the index entries are identified on page 162.

Name	Page	Lat.	Long.
Faverges	36	45.45N	6.18 E
Favignana, Isola I	40	37.56N	12.19 E
Faxaflói c	20a	64.25N	23.00W
Faxälven ⌐	20	63.13N	17.13 E
Fayette, Al., U.S.	144	33.41N	87.49W
Fayette, Ia., U.S.	138	42.50N	91.48W
Fayette, Ms., U.S.	144	31.42N	91.03W
Fayette, Mo., U.S.	144	39.08N	92.41W
Fayette, Oh., U.S.	136	41.40N	84.19W
Fayetteville, Ar., U.S.	144	36.03N	94.09W
Fayetteville, Ga., U.S.	142	33.26N	84.27W
Fayetteville, N.C., U.S.	142	35.03N	78.52W
Fayetteville, Tn., U.S.	142	35.09N	86.34W
Fazzān (Fezzan) □⁹	84	26.00N	14.00 E
Fdérik	82	22.41N	12.43W
Fear, Cape ⊁	142	33.50N	77.58W
Feather ⌐	154	38.47N	121.36W
Fécamp	36	49.45N	0.22 E
Federalsburg	136	38.41N	75.46W
Fehérgyarmat	30	47.58N	22.32 E
Fehmarn I	30	54.28N	11.08 E
Fehmarn Belt ᵾ	30	54.35N	11.15 E
Feia, Lagoa c	118	22.00S	41.20W
Feijó	118	8.09S	70.21W
Feilding	98	40.13S	175.34 E
Feira	86	15.37S	30.25 E
Feira de Santana	118	12.15S	38.57W
Feistritz ⌐	30	47.01N	16.08 E
Fejaj, Chott ⓔ	82	33.55N	9.10 E
Feldkirch	30	47.14N	9.36 E
Feldkirchen in Kärnten	30	46.43N	14.05 E
Felixstowe	26	51.58N	1.20 E
Fellbach	30	48.48N	9.15 E
Feltre	40	46.01N	11.54 E
Femund ⓔ	22	62.12N	11.52 E
Fen ⌐	66	35.36N	110.42 E
Fengcheng	66	28.00N	115.46 E
Fengzhen	66	40.24N	113.09 E
Fennimore	138	42.59N	90.39W
Feno, Capo di ⊁	40	41.57N	8.36 E
Fenton	138	42.47N	83.42W
Fenyang	66	37.17N	111.48 E
Ferentino	40	41.42N	13.15 E
Fergana	54	40.23N	71.44 E
Fergus Falls	132	46.16N	96.04W
Ferguson	144	38.44N	90.18W
Ferlo, Vallée du V	82	15.42N	15.30W
Fermo	40	43.09N	13.43 E
Fermont	130	52.47N	67.05W
Fernandina Beach	142	30.40N	81.27W
Fernando de Noronha, Ilha I	118	3.51S	32.25W
Fernando Póo → Bioko I	82	3.30N	8.40 E
Fernán-Núñez	44	37.40N	4.43W
Ferndale, Ca., U.S.	154	40.34N	124.15W
Ferndale, Wa., U.S.	150	48.50N	122.35W
Fernie	150	49.30N	115.03W
Fernley	154	39.36N	119.15W
Ferrara	40	44.50N	11.35 E
Ferrat, Cap ⊁	44	35.54N	0.23W
Ferrato, Capo ⊁	40	39.18N	9.38 E
Ferret, Cap ⊁	36	44.37N	1.15W
Ferriday	144	31.37N	91.33W
Fès	82	34.05N	4.57W
Festus	144	38.13N	90.23W
Fethiye	48	36.37N	29.07 E
Feucht	30	49.22N	11.13 E
Feuilles, Rivière aux ⌐	130	58.47N	70.04W
Feurs	36	45.45N	4.14 E
Fez → Fès	82	34.05N	4.57W
Fezzan → Fazzān □⁹	84	26.00N	14.00 E
Ffestiniog	26	52.58N	3.55W
Fhada, Beinn ⌐	26	57.13N	5.18W
Fianarantsoa	86	21.26S	47.05 E
Fichtelberg ⌐	30	50.26N	12.57 E
Fichtelgebirge ⌐	30	50.00N	11.55 E
Fidenza	40	44.52N	10.03 E
Fier	48	40.43N	19.34 E
Fierzës, Liqeni i ⓔ	48	42.10N	20.15 E
Fiesole	40	43.48N	11.17 E
Fife Ness ⊁	26	56.17N	2.36W
Figueira da Foz	44	40.09N	8.52W
Figueres	44	42.16N	2.58 E
Figuig	82	32.10N	1.15W
Fiji □¹	91	18.00S	178.00 E
Filicudi, Isola I	40	38.34N	14.34 E
Fillmore	154	34.23N	118.55W
Fimi ⌐	86	3.01S	16.58 E
Finale Ligure	40	44.10N	8.20 E
Findlay	136	41.02N	83.39W
Finisterre, Cabo de ⊁	44	42.53N	9.16W
Finke	96	26.35S	136.00 E
Finland (Suomi) □¹	20	64.00N	26.00 E
Finland, Gulf of (Suomenlahti) (Finskij zaliv) c	22	60.00N	27.00 E
Finlay ⌐	130	56.54N	124.57W
Finn ⌐	26	54.50N	7.29W
Finspång	22	58.43N	15.47 E
Finsterwalde	30	51.38N	13.42 E
Fiora ⌐	40	42.20N	11.34 E
Fiorenzuola d'Arda	40	44.56N	9.55 E
Fire Island National Seashore ⁴	136	40.38N	73.08W
Firenze (Florence)	40	43.46N	11.15 E
Firminy	36	45.23N	4.18 E
Fīrozābād	70	27.09N	78.25 E
Firozpur	70	30.55N	74.36 E
Fish ⌐	86	28.07S	17.45 E
Fisheating Creek ⌐	142	26.57N	81.07W
Fisher, Ar., U.S.	144	35.29N	90.58W
Fisher, La., U.S.	144	31.29N	93.27W
Fishers Island I	136	41.16N	72.00W
Fisk	144	36.46N	90.12W
Fitchburg	136	42.35N	71.48W
Fitzgerald	142	31.42N	83.15W
Fitz Roy	120	47.02S	67.15W
Fitzroy, Monte (Cerro Chaltel) ⌐	120	49.17S	73.05W
Five Points	148	35.03N	106.39W
Fivizzano	40	44.14N	10.08 E
Flagler Beach	142	29.28N	81.07W
Flagstaff	148	35.11N	111.39W
Flagstaff Lake ⓔ	136	45.10N	70.15W
Flattery, Cape ⊁	150	48.23N	124.43W
Flatwoods	136	38.31N	82.43W
Fleetwood	26	53.56N	3.01W
Flemingsburg	136	38.25N	83.44W
Flensburg	30	54.47N	9.26 E
Fletcher Pond ⓔ¹	138	44.58N	83.52W
Flinders ⌐	96	17.36S	140.36 E
Flinders Island I	96	40.00S	148.00 E
Flin Flon	130	54.46N	101.53W
Flint, Wales, U.K.	26	53.15N	3.07W
Flint, Mi., U.S.	138	43.00N	83.41W
Flint ⌐, Ga., U.S.	142	30.52N	84.38W
Flint ⌐, Mi., U.S.	138	43.21N	84.03W
Flomaton	144	31.00N	87.15W
Flora, Il., U.S.	144	38.40N	88.29W
Flora, In., U.S.	144	40.32N	86.31W
Florala	144	31.00N	86.19W
Florence → Firenze, It.	40	43.46N	11.15 E
Florence, Al., U.S.	144	34.47N	87.40W
Florence, Az., U.S.	148	33.02N	111.23W
Florence, Co., U.S.	148	38.23N	105.07W
Florence, S.C., U.S.	142	34.11N	79.45W
Florence, Wi., U.S.	138	45.55N	88.15W
Florencia	118	1.36N	75.36W
Florenville	30	49.42N	5.18 E
Flores I	68	8.30S	121.00 E
Flores, Laut (Flores Sea) ⌐²	68	8.00S	120.00 E
Flores Sea → Flores, Laut ⌐²	68	8.00S	120.00 E
Floriano	118	6.47S	43.01W
Florianópolis	120	27.35S	48.34W
Florida	120	34.06S	56.13W
Florida □³	132	28.00N	82.00W
Florida, Straits of ᵾ	108	25.00N	79.45W
Florida Bay c	142	25.00N	80.45W
Florida City	142	25.26N	80.28W
Florida Islands II	94	9.00S	160.10 E
Florida Keys II	142	24.45N	81.00W
Floridia	40	37.05N	15.09 E
Flórina	48	40.47N	21.24 E
Florissant	144	38.47N	90.19W
Florissant Fossil Beds National Monument ⁴	148	38.54N	105.16W
Flotte, Cap de ⊁	96a	21.35S	167.25 E
Flumen ⌐	44	41.43N	0.09W
Flumendosa ⌐	40	39.26N	9.37 E
Flushing → Vlissingen, Ned.	30	51.26N	3.35 E
Flushing, Mi., U.S.	138	43.03N	83.51W
Fluvià ⌐	44	42.12N	3.07 E
Foča	48	43.31N	18.46 E
Focșani	48	45.41N	27.11 E
Foeni	48	45.30N	20.53 E
Foggia	40	41.27N	15.34 E
Fogo I	82	14.55N	24.25W
Fogo Island I	130	49.40N	54.13W
Fohnsdorf	30	47.13N	14.41 E
Föhr I	30	54.43N	8.30 E
Foia ⌐	44	37.19N	8.36W
Foix	36	43.00N	1.40 E
Fojnica	40	43.58N	17.54 E
Folarskardnuten ⌐	22	60.37N	7.45 E
Folda c²	20	67.36N	14.50 E
Foley	144	30.24N	87.41W
Foligno	40	42.57N	12.42 E
Folkestone	26	51.05N	1.11 E
Folkston	142	30.49N	82.00W
Follonica, Golfo di c	40	42.54N	10.43 E
Folsom	154	38.40N	121.10W
Folsom Lake ⓔ¹	154	38.42N	121.08W
Fomboni	86	12.16S	43.45 E
Fonda	136	42.57N	74.22W
Fond du Lac, Sk., Can.	130	59.19N	107.10W
Fond du Lac, Wi., U.S.	138	43.46N	88.26W
Fondi	40	41.21N	13.25 E
Fondouk el Aouareb	40	35.34N	9.46 E
Fonseca, Golfo de c	108	13.10N	87.40W
Fontainebleau	36	48.24N	2.42 E
Fontana	154	34.05N	117.26W
Fontana Lake ⓔ¹	142	35.26N	83.38W
Fontanelle	144	41.17N	94.33W
Fontenay-le-Comte	36	46.28N	0.48W
Fontenelle Reservoir ⓔ¹	150	42.05N	110.06W
Foochow → Fuzhou	66	26.06N	119.17 E
Forari	92	17.39S	168.32 E
Forbach, B.R.D.	30	48.41N	8.21 E
Forbach, Fr.	36	49.11N	6.54 E
Forcalquier	36	43.58N	5.47 E
Forchheim	30	49.43N	11.04 E
Ford City	136	40.46N	79.31W
Ford Dry Lake ⓔ	154	33.48N	115.00W
Ferdelfjorden c²	22	61.28N	5.39 E
Fordyce	144	33.48N	92.24W
Forel, Mont ⌐	130	67.00N	37.00W
Foreman	144	33.43N	94.23W
Forest, Ms., U.S.	144	32.21N	89.28W
Forest, Oh., U.S.	136	40.48N	83.30W
Forest Acres	142	34.01N	80.59W
Forest City, Ia., U.S.	138	43.15N	93.38W
Forest City, N.C., U.S.	142	35.20N	81.51W
Forest City, Pa., U.S.	136	41.39N	75.28W
Forest Lake	138	45.16N	92.59W
Forest Park	142	33.37N	84.22W
Forestville	138	44.41N	87.28W
Forez, Monts du ⌐	36	45.35N	3.48 E
Forks	150	47.57N	124.23W
Forlì	40	44.13N	12.03 E
Formby Point ⊁	26	53.33N	3.06W
Formentera I	44	38.42N	1.28 E
Formentor, Cap de ⊁	44	39.58N	3.12 E
Formia	40	41.15N	13.37 E
Formosa	120	26.11S	58.11W
Formosa Strait → Taiwan Strait ᵾ	66	24.00N	119.00 E
Fornovo di Taro	40	44.42N	10.06 E
Forrest City	144	35.00N	90.47W
Forsayth	96	18.35S	143.36 E
Forst	30	51.44N	14.39 E
Forsyth, Ga., U.S.	142	33.02N	83.56W
Forsyth, Mo., U.S.	144	36.41N	93.07W
Forsyth, Mt., U.S.	150	46.15N	106.40W
Fort Adams	144	31.05N	91.32W
Fort Albany	130	52.15N	81.37W
Fortaleza	118	3.43S	38.30W
Fort-Archambault → Sarh	84	9.09N	18.23 E
Fort Atkinson	138	42.55N	88.50W
Fort Beaufort	86	32.46S	26.40 E
Fort Benton	150	47.49N	110.40W
Fort Branch	144	38.15N	87.34W
Fort Chambly National Historic Park ⁴	138	45.27N	73.17W
Fort Collins	148	40.35N	105.05W
Fort Covington	136	44.59N	74.29W
Fort-de-France	108	14.36N	61.05W
Fort Dodge	138	42.29N	94.10W
Fort Edward	136	43.16N	73.35W
Fortescue ⌐	96	21.00S	116.06 E
Fort Frances	130	48.36N	93.24W
Fort Gaines	142	31.36N	85.02W
Fort Garland	148	37.25N	105.26W
Fort Gibson Lake ⓔ¹	144	36.00N	95.18W
Fort Jefferson National Monument ⁴	142	24.37N	82.54W
Fort Klamath	150	42.42N	121.59W
Fort Knox	144	37.54N	85.57W
Fort-Lamy → N'Djamena	84	12.07N	15.03 E
Fort Laramie	148	42.12N	104.31W
Fort Laramie National Historic Site ⊥	148	42.09N	104.41W
Fort Lauderdale	142	26.07N	80.08W
Fort Leavenworth ⦿	144	39.21N	94.55W
Fort Lennox National Historic Park ⁴	138	45.06N	73.16W
Fort Liard	130	60.15N	123.28W
Fort Loudoun Lake ⓔ¹	142	35.45N	84.10W
Fort Lupton	148	40.05N	104.48W
Fort Macleod	130	49.43N	113.25W
Fort Madison	138	40.37N	91.18W
Fort McMurray	130	56.44N	111.23W
Fort McPherson	130	67.27N	134.53W
Fort Meade	142	27.45N	81.48W
Fort Mill	142	35.00N	80.56W
Fort Myers	142	26.38N	81.52W
Fort Myers Beach	142	26.27N	81.56W
Fort Necessity National Battlefield ⊥	136	39.47N	79.39W
Fort Nelson	130	58.49N	122.43W
Fort Ogden	142	27.05N	81.57W
Fort Payne	144	34.26N	85.43W
Fort Peck Lake ⓔ¹	150	47.45N	106.50W
Fort Pierce	142	27.26N	80.19W
Fort Plain	136	42.55N	74.37W
Fort Portal	86	0.40N	30.17 E
Fort Pulaski National Monument ⁴	142	32.01N	80.59W
Fort Qu'Appelle	130	50.46N	103.48W
Fort Recovery	136	40.24N	84.46W
Fortress Mountain ⌐	150	44.20N	109.47W
Fort Sandeman	70	31.20N	69.27 E
Fort Scott	144	37.50N	94.42W
Fort Ševčenko	54	44.31N	50.16 E
Fort Severn	130	56.00N	87.38W
Fort Simpson	130	61.52N	121.23W
Fort Smith, N.T., Can.	130	60.00N	111.53W
Fort Smith, Ar., U.S.	144	35.23N	94.23W
Fort Stockton	132	30.53N	102.52W
Fort Sumter National Monument ⁴	142	32.44N	79.46W
Fort Valley	142	32.33N	83.53W
Fortville	144	39.55N	85.50W
Fort Walton Beach	144	30.24N	86.37W
Fort Wayne	144	41.07N	85.07W
Fort Wellington National Historic Park ⁴	136	44.44N	75.31W
Fort William → Thunder Bay, On., Can.	130	48.23N	89.15W
Fort William, Scot., U.K.	26	56.49N	5.07W
Fort Worth	132	32.43N	97.19W
Foshan	66	23.03N	113.09 E
Fosna ⊁¹	22	64.00N	10.30 E
Fossano	40	44.33N	7.43 E
Fossil Butte National Monument ⁴	150	41.50N	110.40W
Fostoria	136	41.09N	83.25W
Fougères	36	48.21N	1.12W
Foulness Island I	26	51.36N	0.55 E
Foulwind, Cape ⊁	98	41.45S	171.28 E
Fountain	82	5.43N	10.55 E
Fountain City	138	44.07N	91.43W
Fountain Inn	142	34.41N	82.11W
Fountain Peak ⌐	154	34.57N	115.32W
Fountain Place	144	30.31N	91.09W
Fourche LaFave ⌐	144	34.58N	92.35W
Four Corners	150	44.55N	122.58W
Fourmies	36	50.00N	4.03 E
Fouta Djalon ⌐¹	82	11.30N	12.30W
Foveaux Strait ᵾ	98	46.35S	168.00 E
Fowler	144	40.37N	87.19W
Fox ⌐, Il., U.S.	138	41.21N	88.50W
Fox ⌐, Wi., U.S.	138	44.18N	91.30W
Fox ⌐, Wi., U.S.	138	44.32N	88.01W
Foxe Basin c	130	68.25N	77.00W
Foxe Channel ᵾ	130	64.30N	80.00W
Foxen ⓔ	22	59.23N	11.52 E
Fox Peninsula ⊁¹	130	76.00N	77.00W
Fox Lake	138	42.23N	88.11W
Foyle, Lough c	26	55.06N	7.08W
Foz do Cunene	86	17.16S	11.50 E
Foz do Iguaçu	120	25.33S	54.35W
Fraga	44	41.31N	0.21 E
Fraijn, Chott el ⓔ	44	35.57N	5.38 E
Framingham	136	42.16N	71.25W
Franca	118	20.32S	47.24W
Francavilla al Mare	40	42.25N	14.17 E
Francavilla Fontana	40	40.31N	17.35 E
France □¹	36	46.00N	2.00 E
Frances Lake ⓔ	130	61.25N	129.30W
Franceville	86	1.38S	13.35 E
Franche-Comté □⁹	36	47.00N	6.00 E
Francis Case, Lake ⓔ¹	132	43.15N	99.00W
Francistown	86	21.11S	27.32 E
Francofonte	40	37.14N	14.53 E
Franconia Notch State Park ⁴	136	44.06N	71.43W
Francs Peak ⌐	150	43.58N	109.20W
Frankenberg	30	50.54N	13.01 E
Frankenmuth	138	43.19N	83.44W
Frankfort, In., U.S.	144	40.17N	86.30W
Frankfort, Ky., U.S.	144	38.12N	84.52W
Frankfort, Mi., U.S.	138	44.38N	86.14W
Frankfort, N.Y., U.S.	136	43.02N	75.04W
Frankfort, Oh., U.S.	136	39.24N	83.10W
Frankfurt am Main	30	50.07N	8.40 E
Frankfurt an der Oder	30	52.20N	14.33 E
Franklin, Ga., U.S.	142	33.17N	85.05W
Franklin, In., U.S.	144	39.28N	86.03W
Franklin, Ky., U.S.	144	36.43N	86.34W
Franklin, La., U.S.	144	29.47N	91.30W
Franklin, Me., U.S.	136	44.35N	68.14W
Franklin, Ma., U.S.	136	42.05N	71.23W
Franklin, N.H., U.S.	136	43.26N	71.38W
Franklin, N.J., U.S.	136	41.07N	74.34W
Franklin, N.C., U.S.	142	35.10N	83.22W
Franklin, Oh., U.S.	136	39.33N	84.18W
Franklin, Pa., U.S.	136	41.24N	79.50W
Franklin, Tn., U.S.	144	35.55N	86.52W
Franklin, Va., U.S.	142	36.40N	76.55W
Franklin, Wi., U.S.	138	42.54N	88.03W
Franklin ⌐	130	72.00N	100.00W
Franklin Delano Roosevelt National Historic Site ⊥	136	41.46N	73.56W
Franklin D. Roosevelt Lake ⓔ¹	150	48.20N	118.10W
Franklinton	144	30.50N	90.09W
Frankville	144	31.38N	88.08W
Fränsta	22	62.30N	16.09 E
Franz Josef Land → Zeml'A Franca-Iosifa II	8	81.00N	55.00 E
Frascati	40	41.48N	12.41 E
Fraser ⌐	130	49.09N	123.12W
Fraserburg	86	31.55S	21.31 E
Fraserburgh	26	57.42N	2.00W
Fraser Island I	96	25.15S	153.10 E
Frauenfeld	30	47.34N	8.54 E
Fray Bentos	120	33.08S	58.18W
Frederica	136	39.00N	75.27W
Fredericia	22	55.35N	9.46 E
Frederick	136	39.24N	77.24W
Fredericksburg	136	38.18N	77.27W
Fredericktown	144	37.33N	90.17W
Fredericton	144	45.58N	66.39W
Frederik Hendrik-Eiland → Yos Sudarsa, Pulau I	68	7.50S	138.30 E
Frederikshåb (Paamiut)	130	62.00N	49.43W
Frederikshavn	22	57.26N	10.32 E
Frederiksværk	22	55.58N	12.02 E
Fredonia, Az., U.S.	148	36.03N	112.08W
Fredonia, N.Y., U.S.	136	42.26N	79.19W
Freehold	136	40.15N	74.16W
Freeland	136	41.01N	75.53W
Freel Peak ⌐	154	38.52N	119.54W
Freels, Cape ⊁	130	49.15N	53.28W
Freeport, Ba.	108	26.30N	78.45W
Freeport, Il., U.S.	138	42.17N	89.37W
Freeport, Me., U.S.	136	43.51N	70.06W
Freeport, N.Y., U.S.	136	40.39N	73.35W
Freeport, Pa., U.S.	136	40.40N	79.41W
Freeport, Tx., U.S.	144	28.57N	95.21W
Freetown	82	8.30N	13.15W
Fregenal de la Sierra	44	38.10N	6.39W
Freiberg	30	50.54N	13.20 E
Freiburg [im Breisgau]	30	47.59N	7.51 E
Freising	30	48.23N	11.44 E
Freital	30	51.00N	13.39 E
Fréjus	36	43.26N	6.44 E
Fremantle	96	32.03S	115.45 E
Fremont, Ca., U.S.	154	37.32N	121.59W
Fremont, In., U.S.	144	41.43N	84.55W
Fremont, Mi., U.S.	138	43.28N	85.56W
Fremont, Ne., U.S.	132	41.26N	96.29W
Fremont, Oh., U.S.	136	41.21N	83.07W
Fremont ⌐	148	41.09N	112.20W
Fremont Island I	148	41.09N	112.20W
French Broad ⌐	142	35.57N	83.51W
Frenchburg	142	37.57N	83.37W
French Guiana (Guyane française) □²	118	4.00N	53.00W
French Lick	144	38.32N	86.37W
Frenchman Bay c	136	44.25N	68.10W
French Polynesia □²	8	15.00S	140.00W
French Somaliland → Djibouti □¹	84	11.30N	43.00 E
French Southern and Antarctic Territories □²	8	49.30S	69.30 E
Fresnillo	108	23.10N	102.53W
Fresno	154	36.44N	119.46W
Fresno Reservoir ⓔ¹	150	48.41N	109.57W
Freudenstadt	30	48.28N	8.25 E
Frewsburg	136	42.03N	79.09W
Fria, Cape ⊁	86	18.30S	12.01 E
Friant	154	36.59N	119.42W
Fribourg (Freiburg)	30	46.48N	7.09 E
Friday Harbor	150	48.32N	123.00W
Fridley	138	45.05N	93.15W
Friedberg, B.R.D.	30	50.20N	8.45 E
Friedberg, B.R.D.	30	48.21N	10.58 E
Friedrichshafen	30	47.39N	9.28 E
Friedrichstadt	30	54.22N	9.05 E
Friendship, Tn., U.S.	144	35.54N	89.14W
Friendship, Wi., U.S.	138	43.58N	89.49W
Fries	142	36.42N	80.59W
Friesach	30	46.57N	14.24 E
Friesland □⁹	30	53.00N	5.40 E
Frio, Cabo ⊁	118	22.53S	42.00W
Frisian Islands II	16	53.35N	6.40 E
Friza, proliv ᵾ	56	45.30N	149.10 E
Frobisher Bay c	130	62.30N	66.00W
Frohavet c	22	63.52N	9.26 E
Frolovo	54	49.48N	43.40 E
Frome, Lake ⓔ	96	30.48S	139.48 E
Front Range ⌐	148	40.25N	105.45W
Front Royal	136	38.55N	78.11W
Frosinone	40	41.38N	13.19 E
Frostburg	136	39.39N	78.55W
Frostproof	142	27.44N	81.31W
Frøya I	20	63.43N	8.42 E
Fruita	148	39.09N	108.43W
Fruitdale	144	31.20N	88.24W
Fruitland	150	36.13N	108.24W
Fruitport	138	43.07N	86.09W
Fruitvale	148	39.04N	108.34W
Frunze	54	42.54N	74.36 E
Frutigen	30	46.35N	7.39 E
Frýdek-Místek	30	49.41N	18.22 E
Fryeburg	136	44.00N	70.58W
Fryingpan ⌐	148	39.22N	107.02W
Fucino, Conca del ⌐	40	42.01N	13.31 E
Fuente-obejuna	44	38.16N	5.25W
Fuerte ⌐	108	25.54N	109.22W
Fuerteventura I	82	28.20N	14.00W
Fugløysund ᵾ	20	70.12N	20.20 E
Fuji	66	35.09N	138.39 E
Fuji, Mount → Fuji-san ⌐	66	35.22N	138.44 E
Fujin	66	47.14N	132.00 E
Fuji-san ⌐	66	35.22N	138.44 E
Fujiyama → Fuji-san ⌐	66	35.22N	138.44 E
Fukui	66	36.04N	136.13 E
Fukuoka	66	33.35N	130.24 E
Fukushima	66	37.45N	140.28 E
Fülädi, Küh-e ⌐	70	34.38N	67.32 E
Fulda	30	50.33N	9.41 E
Fulda ⌐	30	51.25N	9.39 E
Fuling	66	29.42N	107.21 E
Fullerton	154	33.52N	117.55W
Fulton, Ar., U.S.	144	33.36N	93.48W
Fulton, Il., U.S.	138	41.52N	90.09W
Fulton, Ky., U.S.	144	36.30N	88.52W
Fulton, Mo., U.S.	144	38.50N	91.56W
Fulton, N.Y., U.S.	136	43.19N	76.25W
Fultondale	144	33.36N	86.47W
Funchal	82	32.38N	16.54W
Fundy, Bay of c	130	45.00N	66.00W
Fuquay-Varina	142	35.35N	78.48W
Furnas, Reprêsa de ⓔ¹	118	20.45S	46.00W
Furneaux Group II	96	40.10S	148.05 E
Fürstenfeldbruck	30	48.10N	11.15 E
Fürstenwalde	30	52.21N	14.04 E
Furth	30	49.28N	10.59 E
Furth im Wald	30	49.18N	12.51 E
Fury and Hecla Strait ᵾ	130	69.56N	84.00W
Fushun	66	41.52N	123.53 E
Füssen	30	47.34N	10.42 E
Fuxian	66	39.37N	122.01 E
Fuxin	66	42.03N	121.46 E
Fuyang	66	32.54N	115.49 E
Fuyu	66	45.10N	124.50 E
Fuzhou, Zhg.	66	28.01N	116.20 E
Fuzhou, Zhg.	66	26.06N	119.17 E
Fyn I	22	55.20N	10.30 E
Fyresvatn ⓔ	22	59.06N	8.12 E

G

Name	Page	Lat.	Long.
Gaalkacyo	84	6.47N	47.26 E
Gabas ⌐	36	43.46N	0.42W
Gabbs	154	38.52N	117.55W
Gabès	82	33.53N	10.07 E
Gabès, Golfe de c	82	34.00N	10.25 E
Gabin	30	52.25N	19.44 E
Gabon □¹	86	1.00S	11.45 E
Gaborone	86	24.45S	25.55 E
Gabriel y Galán, Embalse de ⓔ¹	44	40.15N	6.15W
Gabrovo	48	42.52N	25.19 E
Gäddede	22	64.30N	14.09 E
Gadsden	144	34.00N	86.00W
Gaeta	40	41.12N	13.35 E
Gaeta, Golfo di c	40	41.05N	13.30 E
Gaffney	142	35.04N	81.39W
Gafsa	82	34.25N	8.48 E
Gagarin	22	55.33N	35.00 E
Gaggenau	30	48.48N	8.19 E
Gagnoa	82	6.08N	5.56W
Gagnon	130	51.53N	68.10W
Gaillac	36	43.54N	1.54 E
Gaillater Alpen ⌐	30	46.42N	13.00 E
Gainesboro	144	36.21N	85.39W
Gainesville, Fl., U.S.	142	29.39N	82.19W
Gainesville, Ga., U.S.	142	34.17N	83.49W
Gainesville, Tx., U.S.	132	33.37N	97.07W
Gainsborough	26	53.24N	0.46W
Gairdner, Lake ⓔ	96	31.35S	136.00 E
Gaithersburg	136	39.08N	77.12W
Galán, Cerro ⌐	120	25.55S	66.52W
Galana ⌐	86	3.09S	40.08 E
Galashiels	26	55.37N	2.49W
Galați	48	45.26N	28.03 E
Galatia	144	37.50N	88.36W
Galatina	40	40.10N	18.10 E
Galax	142	36.39N	80.55W
Galdhøpiggen ⌐	22	61.37N	8.17 E
Galeana	108	24.50N	100.04W
Galena, Il., U.S.	138	42.25N	90.25W
Galena, Mo., U.S.	144	36.48N	93.27W
Galera, Punta ⊁, Chile	120	39.59S	73.43W
Galera, Punta ⊁, Ec.	118	0.49N	80.03W
Galesburg	138	40.56N	90.22W
Galeton	136	41.43N	77.38W
Galicia □⁴	44	42.45N	8.00W
Galicia □⁹	16	49.00N	22.00 E
Galion	136	40.44N	82.47W
Galite, Canal de la ᵾ	40	37.20N	9.00 E
Gallarate	40	45.40N	8.47 E
Gallatin, Mo., U.S.	144	39.54N	93.57W
Gallatin, Tn., U.S.	144	36.23N	86.26W
Gallatin ⌐	150	45.56N	111.29W
Galle	70	6.02N	80.13 E
Galliano	144	29.26N	90.17W
Gallinas, Punta ⊁	118	12.28N	71.40W
Gallipoli, It.	40	40.03N	17.58 E
Gallipoli → Gelibolu, Tür.	48	40.24N	26.40 E
Gallipoli Peninsula → Gelibolu Yarımadası ⊁¹	48	40.20N	26.30 E
Gallipolis	136	38.48N	82.12W
Gällivare	20	67.07N	20.45 E
Gallo, Capo ⊁	40	38.13N	13.19 E
Galloo Island I	136	43.54N	76.25W
Galloway, Mull of ⊁	26	54.38N	4.50W
Gallup	148	35.31N	108.44W
Gallur	44	41.52N	1.19W
Gallura ⌐¹	44	41.00N	9.13 E
Galtür	30	46.58N	10.11 E
Galva	138	41.10N	90.02W
Galveston, In., U.S.	144	40.34N	86.11W
Galveston, Tx., U.S.	144	29.17N	94.47W
Galveston Bay c	144	29.36N	94.57W
Galveston Island I	144	29.13N	94.55W
Galway	26	53.16N	9.03W
Galway □⁶	26	53.20N	9.00W
Galway Bay c	26	53.10N	9.15W
Gamarra	118	8.20N	73.45W
Gambia □¹	82	13.30N	15.30W
Gambia (Gambie) ⌐	82	13.28N	16.34W
Gananoque	130	44.20N	76.10W
Gandak ⌐	70	25.39N	85.13 E
Ganderkesee	30	53.02N	8.32 E
Gandia	44	38.58N	0.11W
Gangaw	70	22.11N	94.07 E
Gangdisê Shan ⌐	70	31.00N	82.00 E
Ganges (Ganga) (Padma) ⌐	70	23.22N	90.32 E
Gangi	40	37.48N	14.13 E
Gangtok	70	27.20N	88.37 E
Gannat	36	46.06N	3.12 E
Gannett Peak ⌐	150	43.10N	109.39W
Ganzhou	66	25.54N	114.55 E
Gao	82	16.16N	0.03W
Gap	36	44.34N	6.05 E
Garanhuns	118	8.54S	36.29W
García de Sola, Embalse de ⓔ¹	44	39.15N	5.05W
Garda, Lago di ⓔ	40	45.40N	10.41 E
Gardelegen	30	52.31N	11.23 E
Garden City, Ga., U.S.	142	32.06N	81.09W
Garden City, Ks., U.S.	132	37.58N	100.52W
Garden City, Mi., U.S.	138	42.20N	83.20W
Garden Grove, Ca., U.S.	154	33.46N	117.56W
Garden Grove, Ia., U.S.	138	40.50N	93.36W
Garden Lakes	144	34.17N	85.16W
Garden Peninsula ⊁¹	138	45.45N	86.35W
Gardīz	70	33.37N	69.07 E
Gardiner, Me., U.S.	136	44.13N	69.46W
Gardiner, Mt., U.S.	150	45.01N	110.42W
Gardiners Bay c	136	41.08N	72.10W
Gardner	136	42.34N	71.59W
Gardnerville	154	38.56N	119.44W
Gardone Val Trompia	40	45.41N	10.11 E
Garet, Mont ⌐¹	92	14.16S	167.30 E
Garfield Mountain ⌐	150	44.31N	112.37W
Gargano, Testa del ⊁	40	41.49N	16.12 E
Gargantua, Cape ⊁	138	47.36N	85.02W
Garies	86	30.30S	18.00 E
Garmisch-Partenkirchen	30	47.29N	11.05 E
Garnavillo	138	42.52N	91.14W
Garner, Ia., U.S.	138	43.06N	93.36W
Garner, N.C., U.S.	142	35.42N	78.36W
Garonne ⌐	36	45.02N	0.36W
Garoua	82	9.18N	13.24 E
Garrel	30	52.57N	8.01 E
Garrett, In., U.S.	144	41.21N	85.08W
Garrett, Ky., U.S.	142	37.28N	82.49W
Gartempe ⌐	36	46.48N	0.50 E
Garut	68	7.13S	107.54 E
Garwolin	30	51.54N	21.37 E
Gary, In., U.S.	144	41.35N	87.20W
Gary, W.V., U.S.	142	37.21N	81.33W
Gas City	144	40.29N	85.36W
Gascogne □⁹	36	44.00N	0.05 E
Gasconade ⌐	144	38.40N	91.33W
Gascoyne ⌐	96	24.52S	113.37 E
Gash (Nahr al-Qāsh) ⌐	84	16.48N	35.51 E
Gashaka	82	7.21N	11.27 E
Gasparilla Island I	142	26.46N	82.16W
Gaspé	130	48.50N	64.29W
Gaston	142	36.30N	77.38W
Gaston, Lake ⓔ¹	142	36.35N	78.00W
Gastonia	142	35.15N	81.11W
Gata, Cabo de ⊁	44	36.43N	2.12W
Gatčina	20	59.34N	30.08 E
Gateshead	26	54.58N	1.37W
Gâtine, Hauteurs de ⌐²	36	46.40N	0.50W
Gatineau ⌐	130	45.27N	75.40W
Gatlinburg	142	35.42N	83.30W
Gauhāti	70	26.10N	91.45 E
Gauley ⌐	136	38.10N	81.12W
Gauley Bridge	136	38.10N	81.11W
Gausta ⌐	22	59.50N	8.35 E
Gauting	30	48.04N	11.23 E
Gavà	44	41.18N	2.01 E
Gávdhos I	48	34.50N	24.06 E
Gävle	22	60.40N	17.10 E
Gavorrano	40	42.55N	10.54 E
Gawler	96	34.37S	138.44 E
Gaya	70	24.47N	85.00 E
Gaylord, Mi., U.S.	138	45.01N	84.40W
Gaylord, Mn., U.S.	138	44.33N	94.13W
Gayndah	96	25.37S	151.36 E
Gays Mills	138	43.19N	90.50W
Gaza	16	31.30N	34.28 E
→ Ghazzah	70	31.30N	34.28 E
Gaziantep	16	37.05N	37.22 E
Gazi Magosa	16	35.07N	33.57 E
Gazivoda Jezero ⓔ¹	48	42.55N	20.40 E
Gdańsk (Danzig)	30	54.23N	18.40 E
Gdansk, Gulf of c	30	54.40N	19.15 E
Gdynia	30	54.32N	18.33 E
Gearhart Mountain ⌐	150	42.30N	120.53W
Geba ⌐	82	11.46N	15.36W
Gebeler	48	39.26N	29.00 E
Gebze	48	40.48N	29.26 E
Gediz ⌐	48	38.35N	26.48 E
Gedser	22	54.35N	11.57 E
Geel	30	51.10N	5.00 E
Geelong	96	38.08S	144.21 E
Ge'ermu	66	36.23N	94.50 E
Geesthacht	30	53.26N	10.22 E
Geisenfeld	30	48.41N	11.37 E
Geislingen	30	48.36N	9.50 E
Geistown	136	40.17N	78.52W
Geita	86	2.52S	32.10 E
Gejiu	66	23.22N	103.06 E
Gela	40	37.04N	14.15 E
Gela, Golfo di c	40	37.00N	14.15 E
Gelasa, Selat ᵾ	68	2.40S	107.15 E
Geleen	30	50.58N	5.52 E
Gelibolu	48	40.24N	26.40 E
Gelibolu Yarımadası (Gallipoli Peninsula) ⊁¹	48	40.20N	26.30 E
Gêlise ⌐	36	44.11N	0.17 E
Gelsenkirchen	30	51.31N	7.07 E
Gemla	22	56.52N	14.38 E
Gemlik	48	40.26N	29.09 E
Gemlik Körfezi c	48	40.25N	28.55 E
Gemünden	30	50.03N	9.41 E
Genale (Jubba) ⌐	84	0.40N	42.45 E
General Carrera, Lago (Lago Buenos Aires) ⓔ	120	46.35S	72.00W
General Manuel Belgrano, Cerro ⌐	120	29.01S	67.49W
General Roca	120	39.02S	67.35W
Genesee ⌐	138	43.16N	77.36W
Geneseo, Il., U.S.	138	41.26N	90.09W
Geneseo, N.Y., U.S.	136	42.47N	77.49W
Geneva → Genève, Schw.	36	46.12N	6.09 E
Geneva, Al., U.S.	144	31.01N	85.51W
Geneva, Il., U.S.	138	41.53N	88.18W
Geneva, N.Y., U.S.	144	40.35N	84.57W
Geneva, Oh., U.S.	136	41.48N	80.56W
Geneva, Lake → Léman, Lac ⓔ	30	46.25N	6.30 E
Genève (Geneva)	36	46.12N	6.09 E
Genil ⌐	44	37.42N	5.19W
Genk	30	50.58N	5.30 E
Gennargentu, Monti del ⌐	40	40.01N	9.19 E
Gennes	36	47.20N	0.14W
Genoa → Genova, It.	40	44.25N	8.57 E
Genoa, Il., U.S.	138	42.06N	88.41W
Genoa, Oh., U.S.	136	41.31N	83.21W
Genova (Genoa)	40	44.25N	8.57 E
Genova, Golfo di c	40	44.10N	8.57 E
Genrijetty, ostrov I	56	77.06N	156.30 E
Genthin	30	52.24N	12.09 E
Geographe Bay c	96	33.35S	115.15 E
Geographe Channel ᵾ	96	24.40S	113.20 E
George ⌐	130	58.49N	66.10W
George, Lake ⓔ, Ug.	86	0.02N	30.12 E
George, Lake ⓔ, Fl., U.S.	142	29.17N	81.36W
George, Lake ⓔ, N.Y., U.S.	136	43.35N	73.35W
Georgetown, Cay. Is.	108	19.18N	81.23W

Symbols in the index entries are identified on page 162.

Symbols in the index entries are identified on page 162.

Name	Page	Lat.	Long.
Humahuaca	120	23.12S	65.21W
Humbe	86	16.40S	14.55E
Humber ≃	26	53.40N	0.10W
Humberside ☐6	26	53.55N	0.40W
Humboldt, Sk., Can.	130	52.12N	105.07W
Humboldt, Tn., U.S.	144	35.49N	88.54W
Humboldt ▲	92	21.53S	166.25E
Humboldt ≃	154	40.02N	118.31W
Humboldt Bay c	154	40.47N	124.11W
Humboldt Redwoods State Park ◆	154	40.19N	124.00W
Humboldt Salt Marsh ≡	154	39.50N	117.55W
Humenné	30	48.56N	21.55E
Humeston	138	40.51N	93.29W
Humphrey	144	34.25N	91.42W
Humphreys, Mount ▲	154	37.17N	118.40W
Humphreys Peak ▲	148	35.20N	111.40W
Humpty Doo	96	12.38S	131.15E
Húnaflói c	20a	65.50N	20.50W
Hunedoara	48	45.45N	22.54E
Hünfeld	30	50.40N	9.46E
Hungary (Magyarország) ☐1	30	47.00N	20.00E
Hŭngnam	66	39.50N	127.38E
Hungry Horse Reservoir ⊜1	150	48.15N	113.50W
Hunsberge ✗	86	27.45S	17.12E
Hunsrück ✗	30	49.50N	6.40E
Hunte ≃	30	52.30N	8.19E
Hunter Mountain ▲	136	42.10N	74.14W
Huntingburg	144	38.17N	86.57W
Huntingdon, Eng., U.K.	26	52.20N	0.12W
Huntingdon, Pa., U.S.	136	40.29N	78.00W
Huntingdon, Tn., U.S.	144	36.00N	88.25W
Huntington, In., U.S.	136	40.52N	85.29W
Huntington, N.Y., U.S.	136	40.51N	73.25W
Huntington, W.V., U.S.	136	38.25N	82.26W
Huntington Beach	154	33.39N	117.59W
Huntly	98	37.33S	175.10E
Huntsville, Al., U.S.	144	34.43N	86.35W
Huntsville, Tx., U.S.	132	30.43N	95.33W
Hunyani ≃	86	15.37S	30.39E
Hunyuan	66	39.48N	113.41E
Huon Gulf c	96a	7.10S	147.25E
Hurd, Cape ≻	138	45.13N	81.44W
Hurley, Ms., U.S.	144	30.39N	88.29W
Hurley, N.M., U.S.	148	32.41N	108.07W
Hurley, Wi., U.S.	138	46.26N	90.11W
Hurlock	136	38.37N	75.51W
Huron, Oh., U.S.	136	41.22N	82.33W
Huron, S.D., U.S.	132	44.21N	98.12W
Huron ≃	138	42.03N	83.14W
Huron, Lake ⊜	132	44.30N	82.15W
Huron Mountains ✗2	138	46.50N	87.55W
Hurricane	136	38.25N	82.01W
Hurtsboro	144	32.14N	85.24W
Huşi	48	46.40N	28.04E
Huskvarna	22	57.48N	14.16E
Husum	30	54.28N	9.03E
Hutchinson, Ks., U.S.	132	38.03N	97.55W
Hutchinson, Mn., U.S.	138	44.53N	94.22W
Hutchinson Island I	142	27.25N	80.17W
Hutch Mountain ▲	148	34.47N	111.22W
Hutsonville	144	39.06N	87.39W
Huxford	144	31.13N	87.28W
Huy	30	50.31N	5.14E
Huzhou	66	30.52N	120.06E
Hvannadalshnúkur ▲	20a	64.01N	16.41W
Hvar, Otok I	40	43.09N	16.45E
Hvarski Kanal ⅃	40	43.15N	16.37E
Hwange	86	18.22S	26.29E
Hwang Ho → Huang ≃	66	37.32N	118.19E
Hyannis	136	41.39N	70.17W
Hyco Lake ⊜1	142	36.30N	79.05W
Hyde Park	136	41.47N	73.56W
Hyderābād, India	70	17.23N	78.29E
Hyderābād, Pāk.	70	25.22N	68.22E
Hydra → Ídhra I	48	37.20N	23.32E
Hyères	36	43.07N	6.07E
Hyltebruk	22	57.00N	13.14E
Hymera	144	39.11N	87.18W
Hyndman	136	39.49N	78.43W
Hyndman Peak ▲	150	43.45N	114.08W
Hyrum	148	41.38N	111.51W
Hyvinkää	22	60.38N	24.52E
I			
Iaco (Yaco) ≃	118	9.03S	68.34W
Iaeger	142	37.27N	81.48W
Ialomiţa ≃	48	44.42N	27.51E
Ialomiţei, Balta ≡	48	44.30N	28.00E
Iaşi	48	47.10N	27.35E
Ibadan	82	7.17N	3.30E
Ibagué	118	4.27N	75.14W
Ibapah Peak ▲	148	39.50N	113.55W
Ibar ≃	48	43.44N	20.45E
Ibarra	118	0.21N	78.07W
Ibb	70	14.01N	44.10E
Ibbenbüren	30	52.16N	7.43E
Iberia	144	38.05N	92.17W
Ibérico, Sistema ✗	44	41.00N	2.30W
Iberville, Mont d' (Mount Caubvick) ▲	130	58.53N	63.43W
Ibicuí ≃	120	29.25S	56.47W
Ibiza → Eivissa I	44	39.00N	1.25E
Ibo	86	12.20S	40.35E
Ica	118	14.04S	75.42W
Ica ≃, Perú	118	14.54S	75.34W
Içá (Putumayo) ≃, S.A.	118	3.07S	67.58W
Içana ≃	118	0.26N	67.19W
Iceberg Pass ✕	148	40.25N	105.45W
Iceland (Ísland) ☐1	20a	65.00N	18.00W
Ichalkaranji	70	16.42N	74.28E
Ichilo ≃	118	15.57S	64.42W
Ichkeul, Lac ⊜	40	37.10N	9.40E
Ich Ovoo uul ▲	66	44.40N	95.08E
Ičinskaja Sopka, vulkan ▲1	56	55.42N	157.35E
Ida	138	41.54N	83.34W
Idabel	144	33.53N	94.49W
Idaho ☐3	152	45.00N	115.00W
Idaho Falls	150	43.28N	112.02W
Idaho Springs	148	39.44N	105.00W
Idar-Oberstein	30	49.42N	7.19E
Iderijn ≃	66	49.16N	100.41E
Idfū	84	24.58N	32.52E
Ídhi Óros ▲	48	35.18N	24.43E
Ídhra I	48	37.20N	23.32E
Idlib	70	35.55N	36.38E
Ieper	30	50.51N	2.53E
Iesolo	40	45.32N	12.38E
Ife	82	7.30N	4.30E
Ifni ☐9	82	29.15N	10.08W
Ifôghas, Adrar des ✗	82	20.00N	2.00E
Igal	30	46.31N	17.55E
Iglesias	40	39.19N	8.32E
Iglesiente ✦1	40	39.18N	8.40E
İğneada	48	41.52N	27.58E
İğneada Burnu ≻	48	41.54N	28.03E
Igombe ≃	86	4.38S	31.40E
Iguaçu ≃	120	25.36S	54.36W
Iguaçu, Saltos do (Iguassu Falls) ↳	120	25.41S	54.26W
Iguala	108	18.21N	99.32W
Igualada	44	41.35N	1.38E
Iguassu Falls → Iguaçu, Saltos do ↳	120	25.41S	54.26W
Iguatu	118	6.22S	39.18W
Iguîdi, 'Erg ⚬8	82	26.35N	5.40W
Ihosy	86	22.24S	46.08E
Iijoki ≃	22	65.20N	25.17E
Iisalmi	22	63.34N	27.11E
Iivaara ▲2	22	65.47N	29.40E
Ijāfene ✦2	82	20.30N	8.00W
IJmuiden	30	52.27N	4.36E
IJsselmeer (Zuiderzee) ▼2	30	52.45N	5.25E
Ikaría I	48	37.41N	26.20E
Ikela	86	1.11S	23.16E
Ilan	66	24.46N	121.45E
Iława	30	53.37N	19.33E
Île-à-la-Crosse	130	55.27N	107.53W
Île-à-la-Crosse, Lac ⊜	130	55.40N	107.45W
Ilebo	86	4.19S	20.35E
Île-de-France ☐9	36	49.00N	2.20E
Ilesha	82	7.38N	4.45E
Ilhéus	118	14.49S	39.02W
Ili ≃	54	45.24N	74.02E
Ilia	48	45.56N	22.39E
Iligan	68	8.14N	124.14E
Ilion	136	43.00N	75.02W
Illampu, Nevado ▲	118	15.50S	68.34W
Illéla	82	14.28N	5.15E
Iller ≃	30	48.23N	9.58E
Illescas	44	40.07N	3.50W
Illimani, Nevado ▲	118	16.39S	67.48W
Illinois ☐3	132	40.00N	89.00W
Illinois ≃, U.S.	144	35.30N	95.06W
Illinois ≃, Il., U.S.	144	38.58N	90.27W
Illiopolis	144	39.51N	89.14W
Il'men', ozero ⊜	54	58.17N	31.20E
Ilmenau	30	50.41N	10.55E
Ilo	118	17.38S	71.20W
Iloilo	68	10.42N	122.34E
Ilorin	82	8.30N	4.32E
Iłowa	30	51.30N	15.12E
Imandra, ozero ⊜	54	67.30N	33.00E
Imatra	22	61.10N	28.46E
Immenstadt	30	47.33N	10.13E
Immokalee	142	26.25N	81.25W
Imnaha ≃	150	45.49N	116.46W
Imola	40	44.21N	11.42E
Imperia	40	43.53N	8.03E
Imperial	154	32.50N	115.34W
Imperial Beach	154	32.35N	117.06W
Imperial de Aragón, Canal ≡	44	42.02N	1.33W
Imperial Valley V	154	32.50N	115.30W
Impfondo	86	1.37N	18.04E
Imphāl, India	66	24.49N	93.57E
Imphāl, India	70	24.49N	93.57E
In Amnas	82	28.05N	9.30E
In'aptuk, gora ▲	56	56.22N	110.11E
Inari	20	68.54N	27.01E
Inarijärvi ⊜	20	69.00N	28.00E
Inca	44	39.43N	2.54E
Inca de Oro	120	26.45S	69.54W
Inch'ŏn	66	37.28N	126.38E
Incline Village	154	39.16N	119.56W
Indalsälven ≃	20	62.31N	17.27E
Independence, Ia., U.S.	138	42.28N	91.53W
Independence, Ks., U.S.	144	37.13N	95.42W
Independence, La., U.S.	144	30.38N	90.30W
Independence, Mo., U.S.	144	39.05N	94.24W
India (Bhārat) ☐1	70	20.00N	77.00E
Indialantic	142	28.05N	80.34W
Indiana	136	40.37N	79.09W
Indiana ☐3	132	40.00N	86.15W
Indiana Dunes National Lakeshore ◆	144	41.40N	87.00W
Indianapolis	144	39.46N	86.09W
Indian Grave Mountain ▲2	142	32.59N	84.21W
Indian Head	130	50.32N	103.40W
Indian Ocean ▼1	8	10.00S	70.00E
Indianola, Ia., U.S.	138	41.21N	93.33W
Indianola, Ms., U.S.	144	33.27N	90.39W
Indian River c	142	28.00N	80.30W
Indiantown	142	27.01N	80.29W
Indigirka ≃	56	70.48N	148.54E
Indio	154	33.43N	116.12W
Indispensable Strait ⅃	94	9.00S	160.30E
Indonesia ☐1	68	5.00S	120.00E
Indore	70	22.43N	75.50E
Indrāvati ≃	70	18.44N	80.16E
Indre ≃	36	47.16N	0.19E
Indus ≃	70	24.20N	67.47E
Industry	144	40.20N	90.36W
İnegöl	48	40.05N	29.31E
Infiernillo, Presa del ⊜1	108	18.35N	101.45W
Ingelheim	30	49.59N	8.05E
Inglewood, N.Z.	98	39.09S	174.12E
Inglewood, Ca., U.S.	154	33.57N	118.21W
Ingolstadt	30	48.46N	11.27E
In Guezzam	82	19.32N	5.42E
Ingwiller	36	48.52N	7.29E
Inhaca, Ilha da I	86	26.03S	32.57E
Inhambane	86	23.51S	35.29E
Inhaminga	86	18.24S	35.00E
Inharrime	86	24.29S	35.01E
Inírida ≃	118	3.55N	67.52W
Inishbofin I	26	53.37N	10.15W
Inisheer I	26	53.03N	9.26W
Inishmaan I	26	53.05N	9.32W
Inishmore I	26	53.07N	9.45W
Inishtrahull I	26	55.26N	7.14W
Inishturk I	26	53.43N	10.08W
Inle Lake ⊜	68	20.32N	96.55E
Inman	142	35.02N	82.05W
Inn (En) ≃	30	48.35N	13.28E
Inner Hebrides II	26	56.30N	6.00W
Inner Sound ⅃	26	57.25N	5.56W
Innsbruck	30	47.16N	11.24E
Innviertel ✦1	30	48.10N	13.15E
Inowrocław	30	52.48N	18.15E
In Salah	82	27.12N	2.28E
Inta	20	66.02N	60.08E
Interlaken	36	46.41N	7.51E
International Falls	138	48.36N	93.24W
Inthanon, Doi ▲	68	18.35N	98.29E
Intracoastal Waterway ≡, U.S.	136	38.10N	76.20W
Intracoastal Waterway ≡, U.S.	142	24.33N	81.46W
Intracoastal Waterway ≡, U.S.	144	28.55N	95.25W
Inukjuak	130	58.27N	78.06W
Inuvik	130	68.25N	133.30W
Invercargill	98	46.24S	168.21E
Inverness, Scot., U.K.	26	57.27N	4.15W
Inverness, Ca., U.S.	154	38.06N	122.51W
Investigator Strait ⅃	96	35.25S	137.10E
Inyangani ▲	86	18.20S	32.50E
Inyo, Mount ▲	154	36.44N	117.59W
Inyokern	154	35.38N	117.48W
Ioánnina	48	39.40N	20.50E
Iola, Ks., U.S.	144	37.55N	95.23W
Iola, Wi., U.S.	138	44.30N	89.07W
Iona	150	43.31N	111.55W
Ione, Ca., U.S.	154	38.21N	120.55W
Ione, Or., U.S.	150	45.30N	119.50W
Ione, Wa., U.S.	150	48.44N	117.24W
Ionia	138	42.59N	85.04W
Ionian Islands → Iónioi Nísoi II	48	38.30N	20.30E
Ionian Sea ▼2	16	39.00N	19.00E
Iónioi Nísoi II	48	38.30N	20.30E
Íos I	48	36.42N	25.24E
Iota	144	30.19N	92.29W
Iowa	144	30.14N	93.00W
Iowa ☐3	132	42.15N	93.15W
Iowa ≃	138	41.10N	91.02W
Iowa City	138	41.39N	91.31W
Iowa Falls	138	42.31N	93.15W
Ipava	144	40.21N	90.19W
Ipeiros ☐9	48	39.40N	20.50E
Ipel' (Ipoly) ≃	30	47.49N	18.52E
Ipiales	118	0.50N	77.37W
Ipin → Yibin	66	28.47N	104.38E
Ipoh	68	4.35N	101.05E
Ipoly (Ipel') ≃	30	47.49N	18.52E
Ipswich, Austl.	96	27.36S	152.46E
Ipswich, Eng., U.K.	26	52.04N	1.10E
Ipswich, Ma., U.S.	136	42.40N	70.50W
Ipu	118	4.20S	40.42W
Iqaluit	130	63.44N	68.28W
Iquique	118	20.13S	70.10W
Iquitos	118	3.46S	73.15W
Iráklion	48	35.20N	25.09E
Iran (Īrān) ☐1	70	32.00N	53.00E
Iran, Pegunungan ✗	68	2.05N	114.55E
Irapuato	108	20.41N	101.21W
Iraq (Al-'Irāq) ☐1	70	33.00N	44.00E
Irazú, Volcán ▲1	108	9.58N	83.53W
Irbenskij proliv ⅃	22	57.48N	22.05E
Irbid	70	32.33N	35.51E
Irbīl	70	36.11N	44.01E
Ire, Mount ▲	94	9.10S	161.05E
Ireland ☐1	26	53.00N	8.00W
Iri	66	35.56N	126.57E
Iringa	86	7.46S	35.42E
Iriri ≃	118	3.52S	52.37W
Irish Sea ▼2	26	53.30N	5.20W
Irkutsk	56	52.16N	104.20E
Iroise c	36	48.15N	4.55W
Iron Bottom Sound ⅃	94	9.15S	160.00E
Iron City	144	35.01N	87.34W
Irondale	144	33.32N	86.42W
Irondequoit	136	43.12N	77.36W
Iron Gate V	48	44.41N	22.31E
Iron Gate Reservoir ⊜1	48	44.30N	22.00E
Iron Mountain	138	45.49N	88.03W
Iron Mountains ✗	142	36.30N	81.50W
Iron River, Mi., U.S.	138	46.05N	88.38W
Iron River, Wi., U.S.	138	46.33N	91.24W
Ironton, Mn., U.S.	138	46.28N	93.58W
Ironton, Mo., U.S.	144	37.35N	90.37W
Ironton, Oh., U.S.	136	38.32N	82.40W
Ironwood	138	46.27N	90.10W
Iroquois ≃	138	41.05N	87.49W
Iroquois Falls	130	48.46N	80.41W
Irrawaddy ≃	68	15.50N	95.06E
Irtyš (Ertix) ≃	54	61.04N	68.52E
Irtysh → Irtyš ≃	54	61.04N	68.52E
Irún	44	43.21N	1.47W
Irurzun	44	42.55N	1.50W
Irvine, Scot., U.K.	26	55.37N	4.40W
Irvine, Ky., U.S.	142	37.42N	83.58W
Ísafjördur	20a	66.08N	23.13W
Işalniţa	48	44.24N	23.44E
Isangel	92	19.32S	169.16E
Isar ≃	30	48.49N	12.58E
Ischia	40	40.44N	13.57E
Ischia, Isola d' I	40	40.43N	13.54E
Ise	66	34.29N	136.42E
Isefjord c	22	55.52N	11.49E
Iseo, Lago d' ⊜	40	45.43N	10.04E
Isère ≃	36	45.59N	4.51E
Iserlohn	30	51.22N	7.41E
Isernia	40	41.36N	14.14E
Iseyin	82	7.58N	3.36E
Isfahan → Eşfahān	70	32.40N	51.38E
Ishikari ≃	66	43.15N	141.23E
Ishinomaki	66	38.25N	141.18E
Ishpeming	138	46.29N	87.40W
Išim ≃	54	57.45N	71.12E
Išimskaja step' ≡	54	55.00N	70.00E
Isiolo	86	0.21N	37.35E
Isiro	86	2.47N	27.37E
Iskăr ≃	48	43.44N	24.27E
Iskăr, jazovir ⊜1	48	42.28N	23.35E
Iskenderun	16	36.37N	36.07E
Iskenderun Körfezi c	16	36.30N	35.40E
Islāmābād	70	33.42N	73.10E
Island Lake ⊜	130	53.47N	94.25W
Island Park Reservoir ⊜1	150	44.25N	111.29W
Island Pond	136	44.48N	71.52W
Islands, Bay of c, Nf., Can.	130	49.10N	58.15W
Islands, Bay of c, N.Z.	98	35.12S	174.10E
Isla Vista	154	34.25N	119.50W
Islay I	26	55.46N	6.10W
Isle ≃	36	44.55N	0.15W
Isle of Hope	142	31.58N	81.05W
Isle of Man ☐2	26	54.15N	4.30W
Isle of Palms	142	32.47N	79.48W
Isle of Wight	142	36.54N	76.42W
Isle of Wight ☐6	26	50.40N	1.20W
Isle Royale National Park ◆	138	48.00N	89.00W
Islesboro Island I	136	44.20N	68.53W
Isleta	148	34.54N	106.41W
Ismailia → Al-Ismā'īlīyah	84	30.35N	32.16E
Isny	30	47.41N	10.02E
Isola	144	33.15N	90.35W
Isola della Scala	40	45.16N	11.00E
Isola del Liri	40	41.41N	13.34E
Isola di Capo Rizzuto	40	38.58N	17.06E
Iso-Syöte ▲2	22	65.37N	27.35E
Isparta	16	37.46N	30.33E
Israel (Yisra'el) ☐1	70	31.30N	35.00E
Isser, Oued ≃	44	36.52N	3.40E
Issoire	36	45.33N	3.15E
Issoudun	36	46.57N	2.00E
Issyk-Kul', ozero ⊜	54	42.25N	77.15E
İstanbul	48	41.01N	28.58E
İstanbul Boğazı (Bosporus) ⅃	48	41.06N	29.04E
Istokpoga, Lake ⊜	142	27.22N	81.17W
Istra ≻1	40	45.15N	14.00E
Istranca Dağları ✗	48	41.50N	27.30E
Istria → Istra ≻1	40	45.15N	14.00E
Itabuna	118	14.48S	39.16W
Itagüí	118	6.10N	75.36W
Itajaí	120	26.53S	48.39W
Itajubá	118	22.26S	45.27W
Italy (Italia) ☐1	40	42.50N	12.50E
Itapecuru ≃	118	2.52S	44.12W
Itapetininga	118	23.36S	48.03W
Iténez (Guaporé) ≃	118	11.54S	65.01W
Ithaca, Mi., U.S.	138	43.17N	84.36W
Ithaca, N.Y., U.S.	136	42.26N	76.29W
Itháki I	48	38.24N	20.42E
Itta Bena	144	33.29N	90.19W
Ituango	118	7.04N	75.45W
Ituiutaba	118	18.58S	49.28W
Ituri ≃	86	1.40N	27.01E
Iturup, ostrov (Etorofu-tō) I	56	44.54N	147.30E
Ituxi ≃	118	7.18S	64.51W
Itzehoe	30	53.55N	9.31E
Iuka	144	34.48N	88.11W
Iva	142	34.18N	82.39W
Ivaí ≃	120	23.18S	53.42W
Ivajlovgrad	48	41.32N	26.08E
Ivanec	40	46.13N	16.08E
Ivangrad	48	42.50N	19.52E
Ivanhoe	154	36.23N	119.13W
Ivano-Frankovsk	54	48.55N	24.43E
Ivanovo	20	57.00N	40.59E
Ivanpah Lake ⊜	154	35.35N	115.25W
Ivigtut	130	61.12N	48.10W
Ivory Coast (Côte d'Ivoire) ☐1	82	8.00N	5.00W
Ivösjön ⊜	22	56.06N	14.27E
Ivrea	40	45.28N	7.52E
Ivujivik	130	62.24N	77.55W
Iwaki	66	37.03N	140.55E
Iwo	82	7.38N	4.11E
Izbica	30	54.42N	17.26E
Izegem	30	50.55N	3.12E
Iževsk	20	56.51N	53.14E
Ižma ≃	54	65.19N	52.54E
Izmail	54	45.21N	28.50E
İzmir (Smyrna)	48	38.25N	27.09E
İzmir Körfezi c	48	38.30N	26.50E
İzmit	16	40.46N	29.55E
İzmit Körfezi c	48	40.45N	29.35E
Iznajar, Embalse de ⊜1	44	37.15N	4.30W
Iznalloz	44	37.23N	3.31W
İznik Gölü ⊜	48	40.26N	29.30E
Izozog, Bañados de ≡	118	18.48S	62.10W
Izsák	30	46.48N	19.22E
Izu-shotō II	66	32.00N	140.00E
J			
Jabal al-Awliyā'	84	15.14N	32.30E
Jabalambre ▲	44	40.06N	1.03W
Jabalón ≃	44	38.53N	4.05W
Jabalpur	70	23.10N	79.57E
Jablanica ≃	48	43.07N	21.57E
Jablonec nad Nisou	30	50.44N	15.10E
Jablonovyj chrebet ✗	56	53.30N	115.00E
Jablunkov	30	49.35N	18.47E
Jaboatão	118	8.07S	35.01W
Jacareí	118	23.19S	45.58W
Jaceel V	84	10.25N	51.01E
Jack Mountain ▲	150	48.47N	120.57W
Jackpot	154	41.59N	114.40W
Jackson, Al., U.S.	144	31.30N	87.53W
Jackson, Ca., U.S.	154	38.20N	120.46W
Jackson, Ga., U.S.	142	33.17N	83.57W
Jackson, Ky., U.S.	142	37.33N	83.23W
Jackson, La., U.S.	144	30.50N	91.13W
Jackson, Mi., U.S.	138	42.14N	84.24W
Jackson, Ms., U.S.	144	32.17N	90.11W
Jackson, Mo., U.S.	144	37.22N	89.39W
Jackson, N.C., U.S.	142	36.23N	77.25W
Jackson, Oh., U.S.	136	39.03N	82.38W
Jackson, S.C., U.S.	142	33.19N	81.47W
Jackson, Tn., U.S.	144	35.36N	88.48W
Jackson, Wy., U.S.	150	43.28N	110.45W
Jackson, Cape ≻	98	41.00S	174.18E
Jackson, Lake ⊜	142	30.30N	84.17W
Jackson Head ≻	98	43.58S	168.37E
Jackson Lake ⊜	150	43.55N	110.40W
Jackson Lake ⊜1	142	33.22N	83.52W
Jackson Mountain ▲	136	44.46N	70.32W
Jacksonville, Al., U.S.	144	33.48N	85.45W
Jacksonville, Ar., U.S.	144	34.51N	92.06W
Jacksonville, Fl., U.S.	142	30.19N	81.39W
Jacksonville, Il., U.S.	144	39.44N	90.13W
Jacksonville, N.C., U.S.	142	34.45N	77.25W
Jacksonville, Tx., U.S.	144	31.57N	95.16W
Jacksonville Beach	142	30.17N	81.23W
Jacmel	108	18.14N	72.32W
Jacobābād	70	28.17N	68.26E
Jacques-Cartier, Détroit de ⅃	130	50.00N	63.30W
Jacques-Cartier, Mont ▲	130	48.59N	65.57W
Jadebusen c	30	53.30N	8.10E
J.A.D. Jensens Nunatakker ▲	130	62.45N	48.00W
Jadotville → Likasi	86	10.59S	26.44E
Jaén	44	37.46N	3.47W
Jaffa, Cape ≻	96	36.58S	139.40E
Jaffna	70	9.40N	80.00E
Jaffrey	136	42.48N	72.01W
Jagādhri	70	30.10N	77.18E
Jagst ≃	30	49.14N	9.11E
Jaguaribe ≃	118	4.25S	37.45W
Jahrom	70	28.31N	53.33E
Jaipur	70	26.55N	75.49E
Jajce	40	44.21N	17.16E
Jakarta	68	6.10S	106.48E
Jakobshavn (Ilulissat)	130	69.13N	51.06W
Jakobstad (Pietarsaari)	22	63.40N	22.42E
Jakupica ✗	48	41.43N	21.26E
Jakutsk	56	62.00N	129.40E
Jalālābād	70	34.26N	70.28E
Jalapa	108	19.32N	96.55W
Jalgaon	70	21.01N	75.34E
Jālna	70	19.50N	75.53E
Jalón ≃	44	41.47N	1.04W
Jalpaiguri	70	26.31N	88.44E
Jalta	54	44.30N	34.10E
Jamaica ☐1	108	18.15N	77.30W
Jamal, poluostrov ≻1	56	70.00N	70.00E
Jamālpur	70	25.18N	86.30E
Jamantau, gora ▲	54	54.15N	58.06E
Jambes	30	50.28N	4.52E
Jambi	68	1.36S	103.37E
Jambol	48	42.29N	26.30E
Jambongan, Pulau I	68	6.40N	117.27E
James ≃, U.S.	132	42.52N	97.18W
James ≃, Mo., U.S.	144	36.45N	93.30W
James ≃, Va., U.S.	142	36.57N	76.26W
James, Lake ⊜1	142	35.45N	81.55W
James Bay c	130	53.30N	80.30W
James Island	142	32.44N	79.57W
Jamestown, N.Y., U.S.	136	42.05N	79.14W
Jamestown, N.D., U.S.	132	46.54N	98.42W
Jamestown, Oh., U.S.	136	39.39N	83.44W
Jamestown, Tn., U.S.	142	36.25N	84.55W
Jamestown ⊥	142	37.12N	76.46W
Jammerbugten c	22	57.20N	9.30E
Jammu	70	32.42N	74.52E
Jammu and Kashmir ☐2	70	34.00N	76.00E
Jāmnagar	70	22.28N	70.04E
Jamshedpur	70	22.48N	86.11E
Jamuna ≃	70	23.51N	89.45E
Jana ≃	56	71.31N	136.32E
Janda, Laguna de la ⊜	44	36.15N	5.51W
Jane Peak ▲	98	45.20S	168.19E
Janesville	138	42.40N	89.01W
Janja	48	44.40N	19.15E
Janów Lubelski	30	50.43N	22.24E
Janskij zaliv c	56	71.50N	136.00E
Jantra ≃	48	43.38N	25.34E
Japan (Nihon) ☐1	66	36.00N	138.00E
Japan, Sea of ▼2	66	40.00N	135.00E
Japurá (Caquetá) ≃	118	3.08S	64.46W
Jarama ≃	44	40.02N	3.39W
Jarandilla	44	40.08N	5.39W
Jargeau	36	47.52N	2.07E
Jari ≃	118	1.09S	51.54W
Jarocin	30	51.59N	17.31E
Jaroměř	30	50.21N	15.55E
Jaroslavl'	20	57.37N	39.52E
Jarosław	30	50.02N	22.42E
Jarreau	144	30.39N	91.29W
Järvenpää	22	60.28N	25.06E
Jasło	30	49.45N	21.29E
Jason Islands II	120	51.05S	61.00W
Jasonville	144	39.09N	87.11W
Jasper, Ab., Can.	130	52.53N	118.05W
Jasper, Al., U.S.	144	33.49N	87.16W
Jasper, In., U.S.	144	38.23N	86.55W
Jasper, Mo., U.S.	144	37.20N	94.18W
Jasper, Tn., U.S.	144	35.04N	85.37W
Jasper, Tx., U.S.	144	30.55N	93.59W
Jászapáti	30	47.31N	20.09E
Jászberény	30	47.30N	19.55E
Jataí	118	17.53S	51.43W
Jaú	118	22.18S	48.33W
Jauja	118	11.48S	75.30W
Jaunpur	70	25.44N	82.41E
Java → Jawa I	68	7.30S	110.00E
Javari (Yavarí) ≃	118	4.21S	70.02W
Java Sea → Jawa, Laut ▼2	68	5.00S	110.00E
Javor ✗	48	44.05N	18.55E
Jawa (Java) I	68	7.30S	110.00E
Jawa, Laut (Java Sea) ▼2	68	5.00S	110.00E
Jawor	30	51.03N	16.11E
Jaworzno	30	50.13N	19.15E
Jaya, Puncak ▲	68	4.05S	137.11E
Jayapura (Sukarnapura)	68	2.32S	140.42E
Jay Cooke State Park ◆	138	46.41N	92.23W
Jay Peak ▲	136	44.55N	72.32W
Jaz Mūrīān, Hāmūn-e ⊜	70	27.20N	58.55E
Jeanerette	144	29.54N	91.39W
Jebba	82	9.08N	4.50E
Jebel	48	45.33N	21.14E
Jędrzejów	30	50.39N	20.18E
Jefferson, N.C., U.S.	142	36.25N	81.28W
Jefferson, Oh., U.S.	136	41.44N	80.46W
Jefferson, S.C., U.S.	142	34.39N	80.23W
Jefferson, Wi., U.S.	138	43.00N	88.48W
Jefferson ≃	150	45.56N	111.30W
Jefferson, Mount ▲, U.S.	150	44.34N	111.30W
Jefferson, Mount ▲, Nv., U.S.	154	38.46N	116.55W
Jefferson, Mount ▲, Or., U.S.	150	44.40N	121.47W
Jefferson City, Mo., U.S.	144	38.34N	92.10W
Jefferson City, Tn., U.S.	142	36.07N	83.29W
Jeffersontown	144	38.11N	85.33W
Jeffersonville, Ga., U.S.	142	32.41N	83.20W
Jeffersonville, In., U.S.	144	38.16N	85.44W
Jegorjevsk	20	55.23N	39.02E
Jejsk	54	46.42N	38.16E
Jekateriny, proliv ⅃	56	44.30N	146.45E
Jekyll Island I	142	31.04N	81.25W
Jelec	54	52.37N	38.30E
Jelenia Góra (Hirschberg)	30	50.55N	15.46E
Jelgava	20	56.39N	23.42E
Jelizavety, mys ≻	56	54.26N	142.42E
Jellico	142	36.35N	84.07W
Jeloguj ≃	56	63.13N	87.45E
Jember	68	8.10S	113.42E
Jemez Springs	148	35.46N	106.41W
Jemmal	40	35.38N	10.46E
Jemnice	30	49.01N	15.35E
Jena, D.D.R.	30	50.56N	11.35E
Jena, La., U.S.	144	31.40N	92.08W
Jenbach	30	47.24N	11.47E
Jendouba (Souk el Arba)	40	36.30N	8.47E
Jenisej (Yenisey) ≃	54	71.50N	82.40E
Jenisejskij kr'až ✗	54	59.00N	93.00E
Jenisejskij zaliv c	54	72.30N	80.00E
Jenkins	142	37.10N	82.37W
Jenkinsville	142	34.16N	81.17W
Jenkintown	136	40.05N	75.07W
Jennings	144	30.13N	92.39W
Jequié	118	13.51S	40.05W
Jerba, Île de I	82	33.48N	10.54E
Jérémie	108	18.39N	74.07W
Jerevan	54	40.11N	44.30E
Jerez de la Frontera	44	36.41N	6.08W
Jerez de los Caballeros	44	38.19N	6.46W
Jergeni ✗2	54	47.00N	44.00E
Jerid, Chott ≡	82	33.42N	8.26E
Jerimoth Hill ▲2	136	41.52N	71.47W
Jerome	150	42.43N	114.31W
Jersey ☐2	26	49.15N	2.10W
Jersey City	136	40.43N	74.04W
Jersey Shore	136	41.12N	77.16W
Jerseyville	144	39.07N	90.19W
Jerte ≃	44	39.58N	6.17W
Jerusalem → Yerushalayim	70	31.46N	35.14E
Jervis Bay c	96	35.05S	150.44E
Jesenice	30	50.04N	13.29E
Jesi	40	43.31N	13.14E
Jesselton → Kota Kinabalu	68	5.59N	116.04E
Jessore	70	23.10N	89.13E
Jessup	136	41.28N	75.33W
Jesup, Ga., U.S.	142	31.36N	81.53W
Jesup, Ia., U.S.	138	42.28N	92.03W
Jevpatorija	54	45.12N	33.22E
Jewett City	136	41.36N	71.58W
Jezerce ▲	48	42.26N	19.49E
Jeziorany	30	53.58N	20.46E
Jhang Maghiāna	70	31.16N	72.19E
Jhānsi	70	25.26N	78.35E
Jhelum	70	32.56N	73.44E
Jhelum ≃	70	31.12N	72.08E
Jialing ≃	66	29.34N	106.35E
Jiamusi	66	46.50N	130.21E
Ji'an	66	27.07N	114.58E
Jiangmen	66	22.35N	113.05E
Jian'ou	66	27.03N	118.19E
Jianshui	66	23.38N	102.49E
Jiaohe	66	43.42N	127.19E
Jiaoxian	66	36.18N	119.58E
Jiaozuo	66	35.15N	113.13E
Jiaxing	66	30.46N	120.45E
Jičín	30	50.26N	15.21E
Jiddah	70	21.30N	39.12E
Jieyang	66	23.35N	116.21E
Jigel	44	36.48N	5.46E
Jihlava	30	49.24N	15.36E
Jihlava ≃	30	48.55N	16.37E
Jijia ≃	48	46.54N	28.05E
Jilib	86	0.29N	42.46E
Jilin	66	43.51N	126.33E
Jill, Kediet ej ▲	82	22.38N	12.33W
Jīma	84	7.36N	36.50E
Jimbolia	48	45.47N	20.43E
Jim Thorpe	136	40.52N	75.43W
Jinan (Tsinan)	66	36.40N	116.57E
Jincheng	66	35.30N	112.50E
Jindřichův Hradec	30	49.09N	15.00E
Jingdezhen	66	29.16N	117.11E
Jinhua	66	29.07N	119.39E
Jining, Zhg.	66	40.57N	113.02E
Jining, Zhg.	66	35.25N	116.36E
Jinja	86	0.26N	33.12E
Jinsha ≃	66	28.50N	104.36E
Jinshi	66	29.39N	111.52E
Jinxian	66	39.04N	121.40E
Jinzhou	66	41.07N	121.08E
Jiparaná ≃	118	8.03S	62.52W
Jipijapa	118	1.20S	80.35W
Jirjā	84	26.20N	31.53E
Jirkov	30	50.30N	13.27E
Jiu ≃	48	43.47N	23.48E
Jiuquan	66	39.45N	98.34E
Jixi	66	45.17N	130.59E
Jizera ≃	30	50.10N	14.43E
Joanna	142	34.24N	81.48W
João Pessoa	118	7.07S	34.52W
Jódar	44	37.50N	3.21W
Jodhpur	70	26.17N	73.02E
Joensuu	22	62.36N	29.46E
Joetsu	66	37.06N	138.15E
Johannesburg	86	26.12S	28.05E
John Day	150	44.24N	118.57W
John Day ≃	150	45.44N	120.39W
John Day Fossil Beds National Monument ◆	150	44.34N	119.39W
John F. Kennedy Space Center ✈3	142	28.40N	80.40W
John H. Kerr Reservoir ⊜1	142	36.35N	78.35W
Johns Island I	142	32.40N	80.05W
Johnson	136	44.38N	72.40W
Johnsonburg	136	41.29N	78.40W
Johnson City, N.Y., U.S.	136	42.06N	75.57W
Johnson City, Tn., U.S.	142	36.18N	82.21W
Johnston	142	33.49N	81.48W
Johnston Atoll I1	8	16.45N	169.32W
Johnston City	144	37.49N	88.55W
Johnstown, N.Y., U.S.	136	43.00N	74.22W
Johnstown, Pa., U.S.	136	40.19N	78.55W
Johor Baharu	68	1.28N	103.45E
Joiner	144	35.30N	90.08W
Joinville	120	26.18S	48.50W
Joinville	36	48.27N	5.08E
Jokkmokk	20	66.37N	19.50E
Joliet	138	41.31N	88.04W
Jolo	68	6.03N	121.00E
Jolo Island I	68	5.58N	121.06E
Jonesboro, Ar., U.S.	144	35.50N	90.42W
Jonesboro, Ga., U.S.	142	33.31N	84.21W
Jonesboro, Il., U.S.	144	37.27N	89.16W
Jonesboro, In., U.S.	144	40.28N	85.37W
Jonesboro, La., U.S.	144	32.14N	92.42W
Jonesboro, Tn., U.S.	142	36.17N	82.28W
Jonesport	136	44.31N	67.35W
Jonesville, La., U.S.	144	31.37N	91.49W
Jonesville, Mi., U.S.	144	41.59N	84.40W
Jonesville, S.C., U.S.	142	34.50N	81.40W
Jönköping	22	57.47N	14.11E
Jonquière	130	48.24N	71.15W
Joplin	144	37.05N	94.30W
Jordan, Mn., U.S.	138	44.40N	93.37W
Jordan, Mt., U.S.	150	47.19N	106.54W
Jordan (Al-Urdunn) ☐1	70	31.00N	36.00E
Jordan ≃	148	40.49N	112.08W
Jordan Valley	150	42.58N	117.03W
Jornado del Muerto ✦2	148	33.20N	106.50W
Jos	82	9.55N	8.53E
Joseph, Lake ⊜	138	45.10N	79.44W
Joseph Bonaparte Gulf c	96	14.15S	128.30E
Joshua Tree	154	34.08N	116.18W
Joshua Tree National Monument ◆	154	33.55N	116.00W
Joškar-Ola	20	56.38N	47.52E
Jostedalsbreen ⊠	22	61.40N	7.00E
Jotunheimen ✗	22	61.38N	8.18E
Joutsijärvi	20	66.40N	28.00E
J. Percy Priest Lake ⊜1	144	36.05N	86.30W
Juan de Fuca, Strait of ⅃	132	48.18N	124.00W
Juan de Nova, Île I	86	17.03S	42.45E
Juan Fernández, Archipiélago II	120	33.00S	80.00W
Juárez → Ciudad Juárez	108	31.44N	106.29W
Juàzeiro	118	9.25S	40.30W
Juàzeiro do Norte	118	7.12S	39.20W
Jūbā	84	4.51N	31.37E
Jubba ≃	86	0.15S	42.38E
Juby, Cap ≻	82	27.58N	12.55W
Júcar (Xúquer) ≃	44	39.09N	0.14W
Juchitán	108	16.26N	95.01W
Juddah → Jiddah	70	21.30N	39.12E
Judenburg	30	47.10N	14.40E
Judith ≃	150	47.44N	109.38W
Judith Peak ▲	150	47.13N	109.13W
Judson	142	34.50N	82.27W
Judsonia	144	35.16N	91.38W
Juigalpa	108	12.05N	85.24W
Juist I	30	53.40N	7.00E
Juiz de Fora	118	21.45S	43.20W
Jukagirskoje ploskogorje ✗1	56	66.00N	155.00E
Juliaca	118	15.30S	70.08W
Julian Alps ✗	40	46.00N	14.00E
Juliana Top ▲	118	3.41N	56.32W
Julianehåb (Qaqortoq)	130	60.43N	46.01W
Jülich	30	50.55N	6.21E
Juliette, Lake ⊜1	142	33.05N	83.50W
Jullundur	70	31.19N	75.34E
Jumboo	86	0.15S	42.38E
Jumilla	44	38.29N	1.17W
Junāgadh	70	21.31N	70.28E
Junction City, Ks., U.S.	132	39.01N	96.49W
Junction City, Ky., U.S.	142	37.35N	84.47W
Jundiaí	118	23.11S	46.52W
Juneau, Ak., U.S.	132a	58.20N	134.27W

Symbols in the index entries are identified on page 162.

Name	Page	Lat.	Long.
Juneau, Wi., U.S.	138	43.24N	88.42W
Junee	96	34.52S	147.35 E
Jungfrau ∧	36	46.32N	7.58 E
Junggar Pendi ≚[1]	66	45.00N	88.00 E
Juniata ≃	136	40.24N	77.01W
Junín	120	34.35S	60.57W
Junín, Lago ◎	118	11.02S	76.06W
Junín de los Andes	120	39.56S	71.05W
Jupiter	142	26.56N	80.05W
Jur	30	48.15N	17.13 E
Jur ≃	84	8.39N	29.18 E
Jura ⋏	36	46.45N	6.30 E
Jura I	26	56.00N	5.50W
Jura, Sound of ʊ	26	55.57N	5.48W
Jūrmala	20	56.58N	23.42 E
Juruá ≃	118	2.37S	65.44W
Juruena ≃	118	7.20S	58.03W
Jurva	22	62.41N	21.59 E
Jutaí ≃	118	2.43S	66.57W
Jüterbog	30	51.59N	13.04 E
Jutiapa	108	14.17N	89.54W
Juticalpa	108	14.42N	86.15W
Jutland → Jylland ◆[1]	22	56.00N	9.15 E
Juventud, Isla de la I	108	21.40N	82.50W
Južno-Sachalinsk	56	46.58N	142.42 E
Južnyj, mys ›	56	57.45N	156.45 E
Južnyj Bug ≃	54	46.59N	31.58 E
Jylland (Jutland) ◆[1]	22	56.00N	9.15 E
Jyväskylä	22	62.14N	25.44 E
K			
K2 (Godwin Austen) ∧	70	35.53N	76.30 E
Kabale	86	1.15S	29.59 E
Kabalega Falls ∟	84	2.17N	31.41 E
Kabalo	86	6.03S	26.55 E
Kabetogama Lake ◎	138	48.28N	92.59W
Kab-hegy ∧	30	47.03N	17.39 E
Kabinakagami Lake ◎	138	48.54N	84.25W
Kabinda	86	6.08S	24.29 E
Kabīr Kūh ⋏	70	33.25N	46.45 E
Kābol	70	34.30N	69.11 E
Kabompo ≃	86	14.10S	23.11 E
Kābul → Kābol	70	34.30N	69.11 E
Kābul ≃	70	33.55N	72.14 E
Kabwe (Broken Hill)	86	14.27S	28.27 E
Kabylie ◆[1]	44	36.30N	4.30 E
Kachovskoje vodochranilišče ◎[1]	54	47.25N	34.10 E
Kadan Kyun I	68	12.30N	98.22 E
Kade	82	6.05N	0.50W
Kadéï ≃	84	3.31N	16.05 E
Kadoma	86	18.21S	29.55 E
Kaduna	82	10.33N	7.27 E
Kaduna ≃	82	8.45N	5.45 E
Kaédi	82	16.09N	13.30W
Kaesŏng	66	37.59N	126.33 E
Kafirévs, Ákra ›	48	38.09N	24.36 E
Kafo ≃	86	1.08N	31.05 E
Kafue ≃	86	15.56S	28.55 E
Kagera ≃	86	0.57S	31.47 E
Kagoshima	66	31.36N	130.33 E
Kagul	54	45.54N	28.11 E
Kahayan ≃	68	3.20S	114.04 E
Kahler Asten ∧	30	51.11N	8.29 E
Kahoka	144	40.25N	91.43W
Kai, Kepulauan II	68	5.35S	132.45 E
Kaiapoi	98	43.23S	172.40 E
Kaieteur Fall ∟	118	5.10N	59.28W
Kaifeng	66	34.51N	114.21 E
Kaikohe	98	35.25S	173.48 E
Kaikoura	98	42.25S	173.41 E
Kailua	132b	21.24N	157.44W
Kaimai Range ⋏	98	37.45S	175.55 E
Kaïmaktsalán ∧	48	40.58N	21.48 E
Kaipara Harbour c	98	36.25S	174.13 E
Kairouan	82	35.41N	10.07 E
Kaiserslautern	30	49.26N	7.46 E
Kaitaia	98	35.07S	173.16 E
Kaitangata	98	46.18S	169.51 E
Kajaani	22	64.14N	27.41 E
Kakamas	86	28.45S	20.33 E
Kākināda	70	16.56N	82.13 E
Kalaa Kebira	40	35.52N	10.32 E
Kalaallit Nunaat → Greenland □[2]	130	67.30N	45.00W
Ka Lae ›	132b	18.55N	155.41W
Kalahari Desert ◆[2]	86	24.00S	21.30 E
Kalama	150	46.00N	122.50W
Kalámai	48	37.04N	22.07 E
Kalamariá	48	40.35N	22.58 E
Kalamazoo	138	42.17N	85.35W
Kalamazoo ≃	138	42.40N	86.10W
Kalb, Ra's al- ›	70	14.02N	48.40 E
Kalemie (Albertville)	86	5.56S	29.12 E
Kalewa	68	23.12N	94.17 E
Kalgan → Zhangjiakou	66	40.50N	114.53 E
Kalgoorlie	96	30.45S	121.28 E
Kaliakra, nos ›	48	43.21N	28.27 E
Kálimnos	48	36.57N	26.59 E
Kálimnos I	48	37.00N	27.00 E
Kalinin	20	56.52N	35.55 E
Kaliningrad (Königsberg)	20	54.43N	20.30 E
Kalispell	150	48.11N	114.18W
Kalisz	30	51.46N	18.06 E
Kalisz Pomorski	30	53.19N	15.54 E
Kalix	22	65.51N	23.08 E
Kalixälven ≃	20	65.50N	23.11 E
Kalkaska	138	44.44N	85.10W
Kallavesi ◎	22	62.50N	27.45 E
Kallsjön ◎	22	63.37N	13.00 E
Kalmar	22	56.40N	16.22 E
Kalmarsund ʊ	22	56.40N	16.25 E
Kalničko Gorje ⋏	40	46.10N	16.30 E
Kalocsa	30	46.32N	18.59 E
Kalomo	86	17.02S	26.30 E
Kalona	138	41.28N	91.42W
Kalpeni Island I	70	10.05N	73.38 E
Kalsūbai ∧	70	19.36N	73.43 E
Kaluga	20	54.31N	36.16 E
Kalundborg	22	55.41N	11.06 E
Kalyān	70	19.15N	73.09 E
Kama ≃	54	55.45N	52.00 E
Kamaishi	66	39.16N	141.53 E
Kamarān I	70	15.21N	42.34 E
Kamčatka, poluostrov (Kamchatka) ›[1]	56	56.00N	160.00 E
Kamčatskij zaliv c	56	55.35N	162.21 E
Kamchatka → Kamčatka, poluostrov ›[1]	56	56.00N	160.00 E
Kamčija ≃	48	43.02N	27.53 E
Kamenec-Podol'skij	54	48.41N	26.36 E
Kamenjak, Rt ›	40	44.46N	13.55 E
Kamensk-Ural'skij	54	56.28N	61.54 E
Kamenz	30	51.16N	14.06 E
Kāmet ∧	70	30.54N	79.37 E
Kamienna ≃	30	51.06N	21.47 E
Kamienna Góra	30	50.47N	16.01 E
Kamieńsk	30	51.12N	19.30 E
Kamina	86	8.44S	25.00 E
Kamloops	130	50.40N	120.20W
Kampala	86	0.19N	32.25 E
Kampar ≃	68	0.32N	103.08 E
Kampen	30	52.33N	5.54 E
Kâmpóng Cham	68	12.00N	105.27 E
Kâmpóng Chhnăng	68	12.15N	104.40 E
Kâmpóng Saôm	68	10.38N	103.30 E
Kâmpóng Saôm, Chhâk c	68	10.50N	103.32 E
Kâmpóng Thum	68	12.42N	104.54 E
Kâmpôt	68	10.37N	104.11 E
Kampuchea (Cambodia) □[1]	68	13.00N	105.00 E
Kamsack	130	51.34N	101.54W
Kamskoje vodochranilišče ◎[1]	54	58.52N	56.15 E
Kamyšin	54	50.06N	45.24 E
Kanaaupscow ≃	130	53.39N	77.09W
Kananga (Luluabourg)	86	5.54S	22.25 E
Kanawha ≃	136	38.50N	82.08W
Kanazawa	66	36.34N	136.39 E
Kānchenjunga ∧	70	27.42N	88.08 E
Kānchipuram	70	12.50N	79.43 E
Kandalakša	20	67.09N	32.21 E
Kandalakšskaja guba c	20	66.55N	32.45 E
Kandangan	68	2.47S	115.16 E
Kandavu Island I	91	19.03S	178.13 E
Kandavu Passage ʊ	91	18.45S	178.00 E
Kandel	30	49.05N	8.11 E
Kandy	70	7.18N	80.38 E
Kane	136	41.39N	78.48W
Kaneohe	132b	21.25N	157.48W
Kangar	68	6.26N	100.12 E
Kangaroo Island I	96	35.50S	137.06 E
Kangding	66	30.03N	102.02 E
Kanggye	66	40.58N	126.34 E
Kangiqsualujjuaq	130	58.41N	65.57W
Kangiqsujuaq	130	61.36N	71.58W
Kangirsuk	130	60.01N	70.01W
Kangnŭng	66	37.45N	128.54 E
Kango	86	0.09N	10.08 E
Kangto ∧	70	27.52N	92.30 E
Kanin, poluostrov ›[1]	54	68.00N	45.00 E
Kanin Nos, mys ›	54	68.39N	43.16 E
Kanjiža	48	46.04N	20.04 E
Kankaanpää	20	61.48N	22.25 E
Kankakee	138	41.07N	87.51W
Kankakee ≃	138	41.23N	88.16W
Kankan	82	10.23N	9.18W
Kanmaw Kyun I	68	11.40N	98.28 E
Kannapolis	142	35.29N	80.37W
Kano	82	12.00N	8.30 E
Kānpur	70	26.28N	80.21 E
Kansas	144	39.33N	87.56W
Kansas □[3]	132	38.45N	98.15W
Kansas ≃	144	39.07N	94.36W
Kansas City, Ks., U.S.	144	39.06N	94.37W
Kansas City, Mo., U.S.	144	39.05N	94.34W
Kansk	54	56.13N	95.41 E
Kantang	68	7.25N	99.31 E
Kanye	86	24.59S	25.19 E
Kaohsiung	66	22.38N	120.17 E
Kaoka Bay c	94	9.42S	160.40 E
Kaoko Veld ⋏[1]	86	20.00S	14.00 E
Kaolack	82	14.09N	16.04W
Kapaonik ⋏	48	43.20N	20.50 E
Kapčagajskoje vodochranilišče ◎[1]	54	43.50N	78.00 E
Kapfenberg	30	47.26N	15.18 E
Kapıdağ Yarımadası ›[1]	48	40.28N	27.50 E
Kaplan	144	29.59N	92.17W
Kaplice	30	48.45N	14.30 E
Kapos ≃	30	46.44N	18.30 E
Kaposvár	30	46.22N	17.47 E
Kapsukas	20	54.33N	23.21 E
Kapuas ≃	68	0.25S	109.40 E
Kapuas Hulu, Pegunungan ⋏	68	1.25N	113.30 E
Kapuskasing	130	49.25N	82.26W
Kapuskasing ≃	130	49.49N	82.00W
Kapuvár	30	47.36N	17.02 E
Karabiğa	48	40.24N	27.18 E
Kara-Bogaz-Gol, zaliv c	54	41.00N	53.15 E
Karabük	16	41.12N	32.37 E
Karacabey	48	40.13N	28.21 E
Karāchi	70	24.52N	67.03 E
Karaganda	54	49.50N	73.10 E
Karaginskij zaliv c	56	58.50N	164.00 E
Karagoš, gora ∧	56	51.44N	89.24 E
Karakoram Range ⋏	70	35.30N	77.00 E
Karakumskij kanal ≡	54	37.35N	61.50 E
Karakumy ◆[2]	54	39.00N	60.00 E
Karamay	66	45.30N	84.55 E
Karamea Bight c[3]	98	41.30S	171.40 E
Karamürsel	48	40.42N	29.36 E
Karanti	48	40.15N	27.07 E
Karasburg	86	28.00S	18.43 E
Kara Sea → Karskoje more ▿[2]	54	76.00N	80.00 E
Karašjåkka ≃	20	69.26N	25.49 E
Karatau, chrebet ⋏	54	43.50N	68.30 E
Karawanken ⋏	40	46.30N	14.25 E
Karbalā'	70	32.36N	44.02 E
Karcag	30	47.19N	20.56 E
Kardhítsa	48	39.21N	21.55 E
Kărdžali	48	41.39N	25.22 E
Karelia □[9]	20	63.00N	32.00 E
Karesuando	20	68.25N	22.30 E
Karhula	22	60.31N	26.57 E
Kariba, Lake ◎[1]	86	17.00S	28.00 E
Karibib	86	21.58S	15.51 E
Karimata, Selat (Karimata Strait) ʊ	68	2.05S	108.40 E
Karl-Marx-Stadt (Chemnitz)	30	50.50N	12.55 E
Karlovac	40	45.29N	15.34 E
Karlovo	48	42.38N	24.48 E
Karlovy Vary	30	50.11N	12.52 E
Karlsbad → Karlovy Vary	30	50.11N	12.52 E
Karlshamn	22	56.10N	14.51 E
Karlskoga	22	59.20N	14.31 E
Karlskrona	22	56.10N	15.35 E
Karlsöarna II	22	57.17N	17.58 E
Karlsruhe	30	49.03N	8.24 E
Karlstad	22	59.22N	13.30 E
Karlstadt	30	49.57N	9.45 E
Karnak	144	37.17N	88.58W
Karnāl	70	29.41N	76.59 E
Karnāli ≃	70	28.45N	81.16 E
Karnobat	48	42.39N	26.59 E
Kárpathos I	48	35.40N	27.10 E
Karpenísion	48	38.55N	21.40 E
Karpogory	54	64.00N	44.24 E
Karrats Fjord c[2]	130	71.20N	54.00W
Kars	16	40.36N	43.05 E
Karši	54	38.53N	65.48 E
Karskije Vorota, proliv ʊ	54	70.30N	58.00 E
Karskoje more (Kara Sea) ▿[2]	54	76.00N	80.00 E
Kartuzy	30	54.20N	18.12 E
Karviná	30	49.50N	18.30 E
Kasai (Cassai) ≃	86	3.02S	16.57 E
Kasaji	86	10.22S	23.27 E
Kasama	86	10.13S	31.12 E
Kåseberga	22	55.23N	14.04 E
Kasese	86	0.10N	30.05 E
Kāshān	70	33.59N	51.29 E
Kashgar → Kashi	66	39.29N	75.59 E
Kashi	66	39.29N	75.59 E
Kashmir → Jammu and Kashmir □[2]	70	34.00N	76.00 E
Kaskaskia ≃	144	37.59N	89.56W
Kaskö (Kaskinen)	22	62.23N	21.13 E
Kásos I	48	35.22N	26.56 E
Kasr, Ra's ›	84	18.02N	38.35 E
Kassalā	84	15.28N	36.24 E
Kassándra ›[1]	48	40.06N	23.22 E
Kassándras, Kólpos c	48	40.06N	23.30 E
Kassel	30	51.19N	9.29 E
Kasserine	82	35.11N	8.48 E
Kasson	138	44.01N	92.45W
Kastoría	48	40.31N	21.15 E
Kastrávion, Tekhnití Límni ◎[1]	48	38.50N	21.20 E
Kasūr	70	31.07N	74.27 E
Kaszuby ◆[1]	30	54.10N	18.15 E
Katahdin, Mount ∧	136	45.55N	68.55W
Katanga □[9]	86	10.00S	26.00 E
Kateríni	48	40.16N	22.30 E
Katherine	96	14.28S	132.16 E
Kāthiāwār ›[1]	70	22.00N	71.00 E
Kathmandu	70	27.43N	85.19 E
Katihār	70	25.32N	87.35 E
Katiola	82	8.08N	5.06W
Kātmāndu → Kathmandu	70	27.43N	85.19 E
Katowice	30	50.16N	19.00 E
Kātrīnā, Jabal ∧	84	28.31N	33.57 E
Katrineholm	22	59.00N	16.12 E
Katsina	82	13.00N	7.32 E
Katsina Ala ≃	82	7.48N	8.52 E
Kattegat ʊ	22	57.00N	11.00 E
Katwijk aan Zee	30	52.13N	4.24 E
Katzenbuckel ∧	30	49.28N	9.02 E
Kauai I	132c	22.00N	159.30W
Kaufbeuren	30	47.53N	10.37 E
Kaukauna	138	44.16N	88.16W
Kaukau Veld ⋏[1]	86	19.30S	20.30 E
Kaunas	20	54.54N	23.54 E
Kaura Namoda	82	12.35N	6.35 E
Kavajë	48	41.11N	19.33 E
Kavála	48	40.56N	24.25 E
Kavīr, Dasht-e ◆[2]	70	34.40N	54.30 E
Kawasaki	66	35.32N	139.43 E
Kawerau	98	38.03S	176.43 E
Kawhia Harbour c	98	38.05S	174.50 E
Kawm Umbū	84	24.28N	32.57 E
Kawthaung	68	9.59N	98.33 E
Kayan ≃	68	2.55N	117.35 E
Kayes, Congo	86	4.25S	11.41 E
Kayes, Mali	82	14.27N	11.26W
Kayseri	16	38.43N	35.30 E
Kaysville	148	41.02N	111.56W
Kazachskaja Sovetskaja Socialističeskaja Respublika (Kazakhstan) □[3]	54	48.00N	68.00 E
Kazachskij melkosopočnik ⋏[2]	54	49.00N	72.00 E
Kazakhstan → Kazachskaja Sovetskaja Socialističeskaja Respublika □[3]	54	48.00N	68.00 E
Kazan'	20	55.49N	49.08 E
Kazanlăk	48	42.38N	25.21 E
Kazbek, gora ∧	54	42.42N	44.31 E
Kāzerūn	70	29.37N	51.38 E
Kazincbarcika	30	48.16N	20.37 E
Kazungula	86	17.45S	25.20 E
Kcynia	30	53.00N	17.30 E
Kdyně	30	49.23N	13.02 E
Kéa I	48	37.34N	24.22 E
Kearney, Mo., U.S.	144	39.22N	94.21W
Kearney, Ne., U.S.	132	40.41N	99.04W
Kearns	148	40.39N	111.59W
Kearny	148	33.03N	110.54W
Keban Barajı ◎[1]	16	38.50N	39.15 E
Kebîr, Oued el ≃	44	36.50N	6.07 E
Kebnekaise ∧	20	67.53N	18.33 E
Kecel	30	46.32N	19.16 E
Kech ≃	70	26.00N	62.44 E
Kecskemét	30	46.54N	19.42 E
Kediri	68	7.49S	112.01 E
Kędzierzyn Kozle	30	50.20N	18.12 E
Keele Peak ∧	130	63.26N	130.19W
Keene, Ky., U.S.	142	37.56N	84.38W
Keene, N.H., U.S.	136	42.56N	72.16W
Keeseville	136	44.30N	73.28W
Keetmanshoop	86	26.36S	18.08 E
Keewatin □[5]	130	65.00N	95.00W
Kefallinía I	48	38.15N	20.35 E
Keffi	82	8.51N	7.52 E
Keflavík	20a	64.02N	22.36W
Keiser	144	35.40N	90.05W
Keith	26	57.32N	2.57W
Keithsburg	138	41.05N	90.56W
Keizer	150	44.59N	123.01W
Kékes ∧	30	47.55N	20.02 E
Kelang	68	3.02N	101.27 E
Kelantan ≃	68	6.11N	102.15 E
Kelbia, Sebkhet ◎	40	35.51N	10.16 E
Keleti-főcsatorna ≡	30	48.01N	21.20 E
Kelheim	30	48.55N	11.52 E
Kelibia	40	36.51N	11.06 E
Kelleys Island I	136	41.36N	82.42W
Kellogg, Id., U.S.	150	47.32N	116.07W
Kellogg, Ia., U.S.	138	41.43N	92.54W
Kelowna	130	49.53N	119.29W
Kelso	150	46.08N	122.54W
Keluang	68	2.02N	103.19 E
Kem'	20	64.57N	34.36 E
Kemerovo	56	55.20N	86.05 E
Kemi	22	65.49N	24.32 E
Kemijärvi	20	66.40N	27.25 E
Kemijärvi ◎	20	66.36N	27.24 E
Kemijoki ≃	20	65.47N	24.30 E
Kemmerer	150	41.47N	110.32W
Kemmuna (Comino) I	40	36.00N	14.20 E
Kemnath	30	49.52N	11.54 E
Kempen	30	51.22N	6.25 E
Kempten [Allgäu]	30	47.43N	10.19 E
Kemul, Kong ∧	68	1.52N	116.11 E
Kenbridge	142	36.57N	78.07W
Kendal	26	54.20N	2.45W
Kendall	142	25.40N	80.19W
Kendallville	144	41.26N	85.15W
Kenema	82	7.52N	11.12W
Kenhardt	86	29.19S	21.12 E
Kenitra	82	34.16N	6.40W
Kenly	142	35.35N	78.07W
Kennebec ≃	136	44.00N	69.50W
Kennebunk	136	43.23N	70.32W
Kennedy, Mount ∧	130	60.30N	139.00W
Kenner	144	29.59N	90.14W
Kennett	144	36.14N	90.03W
Kennett Square	136	39.50N	75.42W
Kennewick	150	46.12N	119.08W
Kenogami ≃	130	51.06N	84.28W
Keno Hill	130	63.55N	135.18W
Kenora	130	49.47N	94.29W
Kenosha	138	42.35N	87.49W
Kenova	136	38.23N	82.34W
Kent, Oh., U.S.	136	41.09N	81.21W
Kent, Wa., U.S.	150	47.22N	122.14W
Kent □[6]	26	51.15N	0.40 E
Kentland	144	40.46N	87.26W
Kenton, Oh., U.S.	136	40.38N	83.36W
Kenton, Tn., U.S.	144	36.12N	89.00W
Kentucky □[3]	132	37.30N	85.15W
Kentucky ≃	144	38.41N	85.11W
Kentucky Lake ◎[1]	144	36.25N	88.05W
Kentville	130	45.05N	64.30W
Kentwood	144	30.56N	90.30W
Kenya □[1]	86	1.00N	38.00 E
Kenya, Mount → Kirinyaga ∧	86	0.10S	37.20 E
Kenyon	138	44.16N	92.59W
Keokuk	138	40.23N	91.23W
Keosauqua	138	40.43N	91.57W
Keota	138	41.21N	91.57W
Keowee, Lake ◎[1]	142	34.45N	82.55W
Kępno	30	51.17N	17.59 E
Kerava	22	60.24N	25.07 E
Kerč'	54	45.22N	36.27 E
Kerch → Kerč'	54	45.22N	36.27 E
Keren	84	15.46N	38.28 E
Kerguélen, Îles II	8	49.15S	69.10 E
Kericho	86	0.22S	35.17 E
Kerinci, Gunung ∧	68	1.42S	101.16 E
Kerkenna, Îles II	82	34.44N	11.12 E
Kérkira (Corfu)	48	39.36N	19.56 E
Kérkira I	48	39.40N	19.42 E
Kerkrade	30	50.52N	6.04 E
Kerkrade [-Holz]	30	50.52N	6.04 E
Kermān, Īrān	70	30.17N	57.05 E
Kerman, Ca., U.S.	154	36.43N	120.04W
Kern ≃	154	35.13N	119.17W
Kernersville	142	36.07N	80.04W
Kernville	154	35.45N	118.25W
Kerrobert	130	51.55N	109.08W
Kerrville	132	30.02N	99.08W
Kerry □[6]	26	52.10N	9.30W
Kerry Head ›	26	52.25N	9.57W
Kershaw	142	34.33N	80.35W
Kert, Oued ≃	44	35.15N	3.15W
Kerulen (Cherlen) (Herlen) ≃	66	48.48N	117.00 E
Keşan	48	40.51N	26.37 E
Keshena	138	44.53N	88.38W
Keşirlik	48	41.58N	27.12 E
Kesra	40	35.49N	9.22 E
Keszthely	30	46.46N	17.15 E
Keta	82	5.55N	1.00 E
Ketama	44	34.50N	4.37W
Kete Krachi	82	7.46N	0.03W
Kętrzyn (Rastenburg)	30	54.06N	21.23 E
Kettering, Eng., U.K.	26	52.24N	0.44W
Kettering, Oh., U.S.	136	39.41N	84.10W
Kettle ≃	150	48.42N	118.07W
Kettle Falls	150	48.36N	118.03W
Kęty	30	49.53N	19.13 E
Keuka Lake ◎	136	42.27N	77.10W
Kevelaer	30	51.35N	6.15 E
Kewanee	138	41.14N	89.55W
Kewanna	144	41.01N	86.25W
Kewaunee	138	44.27N	87.30W
Keweenaw Bay c	138	46.56N	88.23W
Keweenaw Peninsula ›[1]	138	47.12N	88.25W
Keweenaw Point ›	138	47.30N	87.50W
Key Largo	142	25.04N	80.28W
Key Largo I	142	25.16N	80.19W
Keyser	136	39.26N	78.58W
Key West	142	24.33N	81.46W
Kežmarok	30	49.08N	20.25 E
Khadki	70	18.34N	73.52 E
Khairpur	70	27.32N	68.46 E
Khakhea	86	24.51S	23.20 E
Khalkís	48	38.28N	23.36 E
Khambhāt, Gulf of c	70	21.00N	72.30 E
Khānābād	70	36.41N	69.07 E
Khandwa	70	21.50N	76.20 E
Khānewāl	70	30.18N	71.56 E
Khanh-hung	68	9.36N	105.58 E
Khaniá	48	35.31N	24.02 E
Khānpur	70	28.39N	70.39 E
Kharagpur	70	22.20N	87.20 E
Kharg Island → Khārk, Jazīreh-ye I	70	29.15N	50.20 E
Khārijah, Al-Wāḥāt al- ▿[4]	84	25.20N	30.35 E
Khārk, Jazīreh-ye I	70	29.15N	50.20 E
Kharkov → Char'kov	54	50.00N	36.15 E
Khartoum → Al-Kharṭūm	84	15.36N	32.32 E
Khāsh ≃	70	31.11N	62.05 E
Khashm al-Qirbah	84	14.58N	35.55 E
Khatt, Oued al V	82	26.45N	13.03W
Khemis el Khechna	44	36.39N	3.20 E
Khersan ≃	70	31.33N	50.22 E
Kherson → Cherson	54	46.38N	32.35 E
Khíos	48	38.22N	26.08 E
Khíos I	48	38.22N	26.00 E
Kholm	70	36.42N	67.41 E
Khon Kaen	68	16.26N	102.50 E
Khorramābād	70	33.30N	48.20 E
Khorramshahr	70	30.25N	48.11 E
Khouribga	82	32.54N	6.57W
Khulna	70	22.48N	89.33 E
Khunjerab Pass)(	70	36.52N	75.27 E
Khūryān Mūryān (Kuria Muria Islands) II	70	17.30N	56.00 E
Khvoy	70	38.33N	44.58 E
Khyber Pass)(	70	34.05N	71.10 E
Kiamichi ≃	144	33.57N	95.14W
Kiamusze → Jiamusi	66	46.50N	130.21 E
Kiangarow, Mount ∧	96	26.49S	151.33 E
Kibombo	86	3.54S	25.55 E
Kibondo	86	3.35S	30.42 E
Kičevo	48	41.31N	20.57 E
Kicking Horse Pass)(	130	51.27N	116.18W
Kidira	82	14.28N	12.13W
Kidnappers, Cape ›	98	39.39S	177.07 E
Kiefersfelden	30	47.37N	12.11 E
Kiel, B.R.D.	30	54.20N	10.08 E
Kiel, Wi., U.S.	138	43.54N	88.02W
Kielce	30	50.52N	20.37 E
Kieler Bucht c	30	54.35N	10.35 E
Kieta	94	6.13S	155.38 E
Kiev → Kijev	54	50.26N	30.31 E
Kiffa	82	16.37N	11.24W
Kifisiá	48	38.04N	23.48 E
Kifisós ≃	48	38.26N	23.15 E
Kigali	86	1.57S	30.04 E
Kigoma	86	4.52S	29.38 E
Kii-suidō ʊ	66	33.55N	134.55 E
Kijev (Kiev)	54	50.26N	30.31 E
Kijevskoje vodochranilišče ◎[1]	54	51.00N	30.25 E
Kikinda	48	45.50N	20.28 E
Kikládhes II	48	37.30N	25.00 E
Kikwit	86	5.02S	18.49 E
Kilauea Crater ∧[1]	132b	19.25N	155.17W
Kilbrannan Sound ʊ	26	55.40N	5.25W
Kildare □[6]	26	53.15N	6.45W
Kilgore	144	32.23N	94.52W
Kilija	48	45.27N	29.16 E
Kilimanjaro ∧	86	3.04S	37.22 E
Kilindoni	86	7.55S	39.39 E
Kilis	16	36.44N	37.05 E
Kilkenny	26	52.39N	7.15W
Kilkenny □[6]	26	52.40N	7.20W
Kilkís	48	41.00N	22.53 E
Killarney	26	52.03N	9.30W
Killarney, Lakes of ◎	26	52.01N	9.30W
Killbuck	136	40.29N	81.59W
Killeen	132	31.07N	97.43W
Killen	144	34.51N	87.32W
Killington Peak ∧	136	43.36N	72.49W
Killíni ∧	48	37.57N	22.23 E
Kilmarnock	26	55.36N	4.30W
Kilombero ≃	86	8.31S	37.22 E
Kilosa	86	6.50S	36.59 E
Kiltān I	70	11.29N	73.00 E
Kilwa Kivinje	86	8.45S	39.24 E
Kim ≃	82	5.28N	11.07 E
Kimberley	86	28.43S	24.46 E
Kimberley Plateau ⋏[1]	96	17.00S	127.00 E
Kimberly	138	44.16N	88.20W
Kimch'aek	66	40.41N	129.12 E
Kimch'ŏn	66	36.07N	128.05 E
Kimito I	22	60.07N	22.40 E
Kimry	20	56.52N	37.21 E
Kinabalu, Gunong ∧	68	6.05N	116.33 E
Kincaid	144	39.35N	89.24W
Kincardine	130	44.11N	81.38W
Kinder	144	30.29N	92.51W
Kindersley	130	51.27N	109.10W
Kindia	82	10.04N	12.51W
Kindu	86	2.57S	25.56 E
Kinel'	20	53.14N	50.39 E
Kinešma	20	57.26N	42.09 E
King City, Ca., U.S.	154	36.12N	121.07W
King City, Mo., U.S.	144	40.03N	94.31W
King George	136	38.16N	77.11W
King Island I	96	39.50S	144.00 E
King Leopold Ranges ⋏	96	17.30S	125.45 E
Kingman	148	35.11N	114.03W
Kings ≃	154	36.03N	119.49W
Kings Beach	154	39.14N	120.01W
Kingsburg	154	36.30N	119.33W
Kings Canyon National Park ♦	154	36.48N	118.30W
Kingsford	138	45.47N	88.04W
King's Lynn	26	52.45N	0.24 E
Kings Mountain	142	35.14N	81.20W
Kings Mountain National Military Park ♦	142	35.07N	81.33W
King Sound ʊ	96	17.00S	123.30 E
Kings Peak ∧	148	40.46N	110.22W
Kingsport	142	36.32N	82.33W
Kingston, On., Can.	130	44.14N	76.30W
Kingston, Jam.	108	18.00N	76.48W
Kingston, Norf. I.	93	29.03S	167.58 E
Kingston, Ma., U.S.	136	41.59N	70.43W
Kingston, N.Y., U.S.	136	41.55N	73.59W
Kingston, Oh., U.S.	136	39.28N	82.54W
Kingston, Pa., U.S.	136	41.15N	75.53W
Kingston, Tn., U.S.	142	35.52N	84.30W
Kingston upon Hull	26	53.45N	0.20W
Kingstown	108	13.09N	61.14W
Kingstree	142	33.40N	79.49W
Kingsville	132	27.30N	97.51W
Kingtechen → Jingdezhen	66	29.16N	117.11 E
King William	142	37.41N	77.00W
King William Island I	130	69.00N	97.30W
King William's Town	86	32.51S	27.22 E
Kingwood	136	39.28N	79.41W
Kinkony, Lac ◎	86	16.08S	45.50 E
Kinnaird Head ›	26	57.42N	2.00W
Kinsale, Old Head of ›	26	51.36N	8.32W
Kinshasa (Léopoldville)	86	4.18S	15.18 E
Kinsman	136	41.27N	80.36W
Kinston, Al., U.S.	144	31.12N	86.10W
Kinston, N.C., U.S.	142	35.15N	77.34W
Kintyre ›[1]	26	55.32N	5.35W
Kintyre, Mull of ›	26	55.17N	5.55W
Kinyeti ∧	84	3.57N	32.54 E
Kiparissiakós Kólpos c	48	37.37N	21.24 E
Kipawa, Lac ◎	130	46.55N	79.00W
Kipengere Range ⋏	86	9.10S	34.15 E
Kipushi	86	11.46S	27.14 E
Kirakira	94	10.27S	161.55 E
Kirchberg	30	49.12N	9.58 E
Kirchheim	30	48.10N	10.30 E
Kireç	48	39.33N	28.22 E
Kirgizskaja Sovetskaja Socialističeskaja Respublika □[3]	54	41.30N	75.00 E
Kirgizskij chrebet ⋏	54	42.30N	74.00 E
Kiribati □[1]	8	5.00S	170.00W
Kırıkkale	16	39.50N	33.31 E
Kirin → Jilin	66	43.51N	126.33 E
Kirinyaga ∧	86	0.10S	37.20 E
Kırkağaç	48	39.06N	27.40 E
Kirkcaldy	26	56.07N	3.10W
Kirkenes	20	69.40N	30.03 E
Kirkland	150	47.40N	122.12W
Kirkland Lake	130	48.09N	80.02W
Kırklareli	48	41.44N	27.12 E
Kirksville	144	40.11N	92.34W
Kirkūk	70	35.28N	44.28 E
Kirkwall	26	58.59N	2.58W
Kirkwood, Il., U.S.	144	40.51N	90.44W
Kirkwood, Mo., U.S.	144	38.35N	90.24W
Kirov	20	58.38N	49.42 E
Kirovabad	54	40.40N	46.22 E
Kirovakan	54	40.48N	44.30 E
Kirovo-Čepeck	20	58.33N	50.01 E
Kirovograd	54	48.30N	32.18 E
Kirovsk	20	67.37N	33.35 E
Kīrthar Range ⋏	70	27.00N	67.10 E
Kirtland	148	36.44N	108.21W
Kiruna	20	67.51N	20.16 E
Kisangani (Stanleyville)	86	0.30N	25.12 E
Kisbér	30	47.30N	18.02 E
Kisel'ovsk	56	54.00N	86.39 E
Kishinev → Kišin'ov	54	47.00N	28.50 E
Kishwaukee ≃	138	42.11N	89.08W
Kišin'ov	54	47.00N	28.50 E
Kiskörei-víztároló ◎[1]	30	47.35N	20.40 E
Kiskőrös	30	46.38N	19.17 E
Kiskunfélegyháza	30	46.43N	19.52 E
Kiskunhalas	30	46.26N	19.30 E
Kiskunmajsa	30	46.30N	19.45 E
Kislovodsk	54	43.55N	42.44 E
Kismaayo	86	0.22S	42.32 E
Kissidougou	82	9.11N	10.06W
Kissimmee	142	28.17N	81.24W
Kissimmee ≃	142	27.10N	80.53W
Kissimmee, Lake ◎	142	27.55N	81.16W
Kistanje	40	43.59N	15.58 E
Kisújszállás	30	47.13N	20.46 E
Kisumu	86	0.06S	34.45 E
Kisvárda	30	48.13N	22.05 E
Kita	82	13.03N	9.29W
Kitakyūshū	66	33.53N	130.50 E
Kitami	66	43.48N	143.54 E
Kitchener	130	43.27N	80.29W
Kíthira I	48	36.20N	22.58 E
Kíthnos I	48	37.25N	24.28 E
Kitimat	130	54.03N	128.33W
Kittanning	136	40.48N	79.31W
Kittery	136	43.05N	70.44W
Kitt Peak National Observatory ⊙[3]	148	31.58N	111.36W
Kitwe	86	12.49S	28.13 E
Kitzbühel	30	47.27N	12.23 E
Kitzingen	30	49.44N	10.09 E
Kivijärvi ◎	22	63.10N	25.09 E
Kivu, Lac ◎	86	2.00S	29.10 E
Kızıl Adalar II	48	40.52N	29.05 E
Kızılırmak ≃	16	41.44N	35.58 E
Kjustendil	48	42.17N	22.41 E
Kladno	30	50.08N	14.05 E
Klagenfurt	30	46.37N	14.18 E
Klaipėda (Memel)	20	55.43N	21.07 E
Klamath	154	41.31N	124.02W
Klamath ≃	154	41.33N	124.04W
Klamath Falls	150	42.13N	121.46W
Klamath Marsh ≡≡	150	42.54N	121.44W
Klamath Mountains ⋏	150	41.40N	123.20W
Klarälven (Trysilelva) ≃	22	59.23N	13.32 E
Klatovy	30	49.24N	13.18 E
Kłecko	30	52.38N	17.26 E
Klerksdorp	86	26.58S	26.39 E
Klet' ∧	30	48.52N	14.17 E
Kleve	30	51.48N	6.09 E
Klickitat	150	45.49N	121.09W
Klin	20	56.20N	36.44 E
Klingenthal	30	50.21N	12.28 E
Klínovec ∧	30	50.24N	12.58 E
Klipplaat	86	33.02S	24.21 E
Kłobuck	30	50.55N	18.57 E
Kłodzko	30	50.27N	16.39 E
Klondike □[9]	130	63.30N	139.00W
Klosterneuburg	30	48.18N	16.20 E
Klosters	36	46.54N	9.53 E
Kloten	36	47.27N	8.35 E
Kluane Lake ◎	130	61.15N	138.40W
Kl'učevskaja Sopka, vulkan ∧[1]	56	56.04N	160.38 E
Kluczbork	30	50.59N	18.13 E
Knaresborough	26	54.00N	1.27W
Kneža	48	43.30N	24.05 E
Knightstown	144	39.47N	85.31W
Knin	40	44.02N	16.12 E
Knittelfeld	30	47.14N	14.50 E
Knjaževac	48	43.34N	22.16 E
Knob Noster	144	38.45N	93.33W
Knokke	30	51.21N	3.17 E
Knox, In., U.S.	144	41.17N	86.37W
Knox, Pa., U.S.	136	41.14N	79.32W
Knox, Cape ›	130	54.11N	133.04W
Knoxville, Ga., U.S.	142	32.43N	83.59W
Knoxville, Il., U.S.	138	40.54N	90.17W
Knoxville, Ia., U.S.	138	41.19N	93.06W
Knoxville, Tn., U.S.	142	35.57N	83.55W
Kobar Sink ≛[7]	84	13.35N	40.50 E
Kōbe	66	34.41N	135.10 E
København (Copenhagen)	22	55.40N	12.35 E
Koblenz	30	50.21N	7.35 E
Kočani	48	41.55N	22.25 E
Kocher ≃	30	49.14N	9.12 E
Kōchi	66	33.33N	133.33 E
Koch Peak ∧	150	45.02N	111.28W
Kodiak Island I	132a	57.30N	153.30W
Köflach	30	47.04N	15.05 E
Koforidua	82	6.03N	0.17W
Kōfu	66	35.39N	138.35 E
Kogaluc ≃	130	59.40N	77.35W
Kogaluc, Baie c	130	59.20N	77.50W
Køge	22	55.27N	12.11 E
Køge Bugt c, Dan.	22	55.30N	12.20 E
Køge Bugt c, Kal. Nun.	130	65.00N	40.30W
Kohāt	70	33.35N	71.26 E
Kohler	138	43.44N	87.46W
Kohtla-Järve	20	59.24N	27.15 E
Kokand	54	40.33N	70.57 E
Kokčetav	54	53.17N	69.25 E
Kokemäenjoki ≃	22	61.33N	21.42 E
Kokiu → Gejiu	66	23.22N	103.06 E
Kokkola (Karleby)	22	63.50N	23.07 E
Kokomo	144	40.29N	86.08W
Kokšaalatau, chrebet ⋏	54	41.00N	78.00 E
Koksoak ≃	130	58.32N	68.10W
Kokstad	86	30.32S	29.29 E
Kola Peninsula → Kol'skij poluostrov ›[1]	54	67.30N	37.00 E
Kolār Gold Fields	70	12.55N	78.17 E
Kolárovo	30	47.52N	18.02 E
Kolding	22	55.31N	9.29 E
Kolea	44	36.38N	2.46 E
Kolgujev, ostrov I	54	69.05N	49.15 E
Kolhāpur	70	16.42N	74.13 E
Kolima ◎	22	63.16N	25.50 E
Kolín	30	50.01N	15.13 E
Kolkas rags ›	22	57.47N	22.36 E
Köln (Cologne)	30	50.56N	6.59 E
Kolno	30	53.25N	21.56 E
Koło	30	52.12N	18.38 E
Kołobrzeg	30	54.12N	15.33 E
Kolombangara Island I	94	8.00S	157.05 E
Kolomna	20	55.05N	38.49 E
Kolomyja	54	48.32N	25.04 E
Kolpino	20	59.45N	30.36 E
Kol'skij poluostrov (Kola Peninsula) ›[1]	54	67.30N	37.00 E
Kolubara ≃	48	44.40N	20.15 E
Kolwezi	86	10.43S	25.28 E
Kolyma ≃	56	69.30N	161.00 E
Kolymskaja nizmennost' ≚	56	68.30N	154.00 E
Kom ∧	48	43.10N	23.03 E
Komadugu Gana ≃	82	13.05N	12.24 E
Komadugu Yobe ≃	82	13.43N	13.20 E
Komandorskije ostrova II	56	55.00N	167.00 E
Komárno	30	47.45N	18.09 E
Komárom	30	47.44N	18.08 E
Komatipoort	86	25.25S	31.55 E
Komló	30	46.12N	18.16 E
Kommunarsk	54	48.30N	38.47 E
Kommunizma, pik ∧	54	38.57N	72.01 E
Komoé ≃	82	5.12N	3.44W
Komotiní	48	41.08N	25.25 E
Kompasberg ∧	86	31.45S	24.32 E
Komsomolec, ostrov I	56	80.30N	95.00 E
Komsomolec, zaliv c	54	45.30N	52.45 E
Komsomol'sk-na-Amure	56	50.35N	137.02 E
Komsomol'skoj Pravdy, ostrova II	56	77.20N	107.40 E
Kondopoga	54	62.12N	34.17 E
Koné	92	21.04S	164.52 E
Kông ≃	68	13.32N	105.58 E
Kongolo	86	5.23S	27.00 E
Kongur Shan ∧	66	38.37N	75.20 E
Konice	30	49.35N	16.53 E
Koniecpol	30	50.48N	19.41 E
Königsberg → Kaliningrad	20	54.43N	20.30 E
Konin	30	52.13N	18.16 E
Konjic	40	43.39N	17.57 E
Könkämäälven ≃	20	68.29N	22.17 E
Konkouré ≃	82	9.58N	13.42W
Końskie	30	51.12N	20.26 E
Konstantinovka	20	56.41N	50.53 E
Konstanz	30	47.40N	9.10 E
Kontagora	82	10.24N	5.28 E
Kontum	68	14.21N	108.00 E
Konya	16	37.52N	32.31 E
Konz	30	49.42N	6.34 E
Konza	86	1.45S	37.07 E
Konžakovskij Kamen', gora ∧	54	59.38N	59.08 E
Koontz Lake	144	41.25N	86.29W
Kootenai (Kootenay) ≃	150	49.15N	117.39W

Symbols in the index entries are identified on page 162.

Symbols in the index entries are identified on page 162.

Name	Page	Lat.	Long.
Leizhou Bandao ›[1]	66	21.15N	110.09 E
Leland	144	33.24N	90.53W
Leli Shan ∧	66	33.26N	81.42 E
Le Locle	36	47.03N	6.45 E
Le Madonie ⋏	40	37.52N	13.58 E
Le Maire, Estrecho de ʯ	120	54.50S	65.00W
Le Mans	36	48.00N	0.12 E
Lemay	144	38.32N	90.17W
Lemberg ∧	30	48.09N	8.45 E
Lemdiyya	44	36.12N	2.50 E
Lemesós	16	34.40N	33.02 E
Lemgo	30	52.02N	8.54 E
Lemhi Pass)(	150	44.58N	113.27W
Lemhi Range ⋏	150	44.30N	113.25W
Lemmon	132	45.56N	102.09W
Lemmon, Mount ∧	148	32.26N	110.47W
Lemnos → Límnos I	48	39.54N	25.21 E
Lemon Grove	154	32.44N	117.01W
Lemont	136	40.49N	77.49W
Le Mont-Saint-Michel ♦[1]	36	48.38N	1.32W
Lemoore	154	36.18N	119.46W
Le Murge ⋏[1]	40	40.52N	16.42 E
Lena	138	44.57N	88.02W
Lena ≃	56	72.25N	126.40 E
Lencloître	36	46.49N	0.20 E
Lendinara	40	45.05N	11.36 E
Lenina, pik ∧	54	39.20N	72.55 E
Leninabad	54	40.17N	69.37 E
Leninakan	54	40.48N	43.50 E
Leningrad	20	59.55N	30.15 E
Leninogorsk	20	54.36N	52.30 E
Leninsk-Kuzneckij	56	54.38N	86.10 E
Lenk	36	46.28N	7.27 E
Lennox, Isla I	120	55.18S	66.50W
Lenoir	142	35.54N	81.32W
Lenoir City	142	35.47N	84.15W
Lenox	136	42.22N	73.17W
Lens	36	50.26N	2.50 E
Lenti	30	46.37N	16.33 E
Lentini	40	37.17N	15.00 E
Léo	82	11.06N	2.06W
Leoben	30	47.23N	15.06 E
Leola	144	34.10N	92.35W
Leominster, Eng., U.K.	26	52.14N	2.45W
Leominster, Ma., U.S.	136	42.31N	71.45W
León, Esp.	44	42.36N	5.34W
León, Méx.	108	21.07N	101.40W
León, Nic.	108	12.26N	86.53W
Leon, Ia., U.S.	138	40.44N	93.44W
León □[9]	44	42.00N	6.00W
León, Montes de ⋏	44	42.30N	6.18W
Leonardtown	136	38.17N	76.38W
Leonberg	30	48.48N	9.01 E
Leonforte	40	37.38N	14.23 E
Leonora	96	28.53S	121.20 E
Leonville	144	30.28N	91.58W
Léopold II, Lac → Mai-Ndombe, Lac ⊜	86	2.00S	18.20 E
Léopoldville → Kinshasa	86	4.18S	15.18 E
Lepe	44	37.15N	7.12W
Le Pont-de-Beauvoisin	36	45.32N	5.40 E
Lepontine, Alpi ⋏	36	46.25N	8.40 E
Le Port	86	20.55S	55.18 E
Le Puy	36	45.02N	3.53 E
Lerici	40	44.04N	9.55 E
Lerma	44	42.02N	3.45W
Léros I	48	37.08N	26.52 E
Le Roy, Il., U.S.	144	40.21N	88.45W
Le Roy, N.Y., U.S.	136	42.58N	77.59W
Lerwick	26	60.09N	1.09W
Lesbos → Lésvos I	48	39.10N	26.20 E
Les Cayes	108	18.12N	73.45W
Leshan	66	29.34N	103.45 E
Lesko	30	49.29N	22.21 E
Leskovac	48	42.59N	21.57 E
Lesosibirsk	56	58.16N	92.29 E
Lesotho □[1]	86	29.30S	28.30 E
Les Posets ∧	44	42.39N	0.25 E
Les Riceys	36	47.59N	4.22 E
Les Sables-d'Olonne	36	46.30N	1.47W
Lesser Antilles II	108	15.00N	61.00W
Lesser Khingan Range → Xiao Hinggan Ling ⋏	66	48.45N	127.00 E
Lesser Slave Lake ⊜	130	55.25N	115.30W
Lesser Sunda Islands → Nusa Tenggara II	68	9.00S	120.00 E
Le Sueur	138	44.30N	93.52W
Lésvos I	48	39.10N	26.20 E
Leszno	30	51.51N	16.35 E
Letea, Ostrovul I	48	45.20N	29.20 E
Lethbridge	130	49.42N	112.50W
Leticia	118	4.09S	69.57W
Le Trayas	36	43.28N	6.55 E
Letsôk-aw Kyun I	68	11.37N	98.15 E
Leucadia	154	33.04N	117.18W
Leucate, Étang de ⊂	36	42.51N	3.00 E
Leuk	36	46.19N	7.38 E
Leulumoega	93	13.49S	171.55W
Leuna	30	51.19N	12.01 E
Leutkirch	30	47.49N	10.01 E
Leuven	30	50.53N	4.42 E
Levádhia	48	38.25N	22.54 E
Levante, Riviera di ≗[2]	40	44.15N	9.30 E
Leveque, Cape ›	96	16.24S	122.56 E
Levering	138	45.38N	84.47W
Leverkusen	30	51.03N	6.59 E
Levice	30	48.13N	18.37 E
Levin	98	40.37S	175.17 E
Lévis	130	46.48N	71.11W
Levisa Fork ≃	136	38.06N	82.36W
Levítha I	48	37.00N	26.28 E
Levittown, N.Y., U.S.	136	40.43N	73.30W
Levittown, Pa., U.S.	136	40.09N	74.49W
Lévka Óri ∧	48	35.18N	24.01 E
Levkás	48	38.50N	20.41 E
Levkás I	48	38.39N	20.27 E
Levski	48	43.22N	25.08 E
Levuka	91	17.41S	178.50 E
Lewes, Eng., U.K.	26	50.52N	0.01 E
Lewes, De., U.S.	136	38.46N	75.08W
Lewis, Butt of ›	26	58.31N	6.16W
Lewis, Isle of I	26	58.10N	6.40W
Lewis and Clark Range ⋏	150	47.30N	113.00W
Lewisburg, Pa., U.S.	136	40.57N	76.53W
Lewisburg, Tn., U.S.	144	35.26N	86.47W
Lewisburg, W.V., U.S.	136	37.48N	80.26W
Lewis Range ⋏	150	48.35N	113.40W
Lewis Run	136	41.52N	78.39W
Lewis Smith Lake ⊜[1]	144	34.05N	87.07W
Lewiston, Id., U.S.	150	46.25N	117.01W
Lewiston, Me., U.S.	136	44.06N	70.12W
Lewiston, N.Y., U.S.	136	43.10N	79.02W
Lewiston, Ut,. U.S.	148	41.58N	111.51W
Lewistown, Il., U.S.	144	40.23N	90.09W
Lewistown, Mt., U.S.	150	47.03N	109.25W
Lewistown, Pa., U.S.	136	40.35N	77.34W
Lexington, Il., U.S.	144	40.38N	88.47W
Lexington, Ky., U.S.	142	38.02N	84.30W
Lexington, Ma., U.S.	136	42.26N	71.13W
Lexington, Ms., U.S.	144	33.06N	90.03W
Lexington, Mo., U.S.	144	39.11N	93.52W
Lexington, N.C., U.S.	142	35.49N	80.15W
Lexington, Or., U.S.	150	45.26N	119.41W
Lexington, Tn., U.S.	144	35.39N	88.23W
Lexington, Va., U.S.	142	37.47N	79.26W
Lexington Park	136	38.16N	76.27W
Leyre ≃	36	44.39N	1.01W
Leyte I	68	10.50N	124.50 E
Leyte Gulf ⊂	68	10.50N	125.25 E
Lezhë	48	41.47N	19.39 E
Lhasa	66	29.40N	91.09 E
Lhokseumawe	68	5.10N	97.08 E
L'Hospitalet de Llobregat	44	41.22N	2.08 E
Lianxian	66	24.48N	112.25 E
Lianyungang	66	34.39N	119.16 E
Liao ≃	66	40.50N	121.48 E
Liaocheng	66	36.30N	115.59 E
Liaodong Bandao ›[1]	66	40.00N	122.20 E
Liaodong Wan ⊂	66	40.30N	121.30 E
Liaotung, Gulf of → Liaodong Wan ⊂	66	40.30N	121.30 E
Liaotung Peninsula → Liaodong Bandao ›[1]	66	40.00N	122.20 E
Liaoyang	66	41.17N	123.11 E
Liaoyuan	66	42.54N	125.07 E
Liard ≃	130	61.52N	121.18W
Libby	150	48.23N	115.33W
Libenge	84	3.39N	18.38 E
Liberal, Ks., U.S.	132	37.02N	100.55W
Liberal, Mo., U.S.	144	37.33N	94.31W
Liberec	30	50.46N	15.03 E
Liberia	108	10.38N	85.27W
Liberia □[1]	82	6.30N	9.30W
Liberty, In., U.S.	144	39.38N	84.55W
Liberty, Ky., U.S.	144	37.19N	84.56W
Liberty, Ms., U.S.	144	31.09N	90.48W
Liberty, Mo., U.S.	144	39.14N	94.25W
Liberty, N.Y., U.S.	136	41.48N	74.44W
Liberty, N.C., U.S.	142	35.51N	79.34W
Liberty, S.C., U.S.	142	34.47N	82.41W
Libertyville	138	42.16N	87.57W
Lībīyah, Aṣ-Ṣaḥrā' al- (Libyan Desert) ◆[2]	84	24.00N	25.00 E
Libourne	36	44.55N	0.14W
Libramont	30	49.55N	5.23 E
Libreville	86	0.23N	9.27 E
Libya (Lībiyā) □[1]	84	27.00N	17.00 E
Libyan Desert → Lībīyah, Aṣ-Ṣaḥrā' al- ◆[2]	84	24.00N	25.00 E
Licata	40	37.06N	13.56 E
Lichfield	26	52.42N	1.48W
Lichtenfels	30	50.09N	11.04 E
Licking	144	37.29N	91.51W
Licking ≃	136	39.06N	84.30W
Lidingö	22	59.22N	18.08 E
Lidköping	22	58.30N	13.10 E
Lido di Ostia	40	41.44N	12.14 E
Lidzbark	30	53.17N	19.49 E
Lidzbark Warmiński	30	54.09N	20.35 E
Liebig, Mount ∧	96	23.18S	131.22 E
Liechtenstein □[1]	36	47.09N	9.35 E
Liège	30	50.38N	5.34 E
Lienz	30	46.50N	12.47 E
Liepāja	20	56.31N	21.01 E
Lier	30	51.08N	4.34 E
Liestal	36	47.29N	7.44 E
Liești	48	45.38N	27.32 E
Liévin	36	50.25N	2.46 E
Lifford	26	54.50N	7.29W
Lifou I	92	20.53S	167.13 E
Lighthouse Point	142	26.16N	80.05W
Lighthouse Point ›	138	45.13N	85.32W
Ligny-en-Barrois	36	48.41N	5.20 E
Ligonier, In., U.S.	144	41.27N	85.35W
Ligonier, Pa., U.S.	136	40.14N	79.14W
Ligurian Sea ⊤[2]	40	43.30N	9.00 E
Lihue	132c	21.58N	159.22W
Likasi (Jadotville)	86	10.59S	26.44 E
Likoma Island I	86	12.05S	34.45 E
Likouala ≃	86	1.13S	16.48 E
Lilbourn	144	36.35N	89.36W
L'Île-Rousse	40	42.38N	8.56 E
Lilienfeld	30	48.03N	15.36 E
Lille	36	50.38N	3.04 E
Lillebælt ʯ	22	55.20N	9.45 E
Lillehammer	22	61.08N	10.30 E
Lillers	36	50.34N	2.29 E
Lillestrøm	22	59.57N	11.05 E
Lilongwe	86	13.59S	33.44 E
Lily	142	37.01N	84.04W
Lim ≃	48	43.45N	19.13 E
Lima, Perú	118	12.03S	77.03W
Lima, N.Y., U.S.	136	42.54N	77.36W
Lima, Oh., U.S.	136	40.44N	84.06W
Lima (Limia) ≃	44	41.41N	8.50W
Limassol → Lemesós	16	34.40N	33.02 E
Limay ≃	120	38.59S	68.00W
Limburg an der Lahn	30	50.23N	8.04 E
Limeira	118	22.34S	47.24W
Limerick	26	52.40N	8.38W
Limerick □[6]	26	52.30N	8.45W
Lime Springs	138	43.27N	92.17W
Limfjorden ʯ	22	56.55N	9.10 E
Limia (Lima) ≃	44	41.41N	8.50W
Limmen Bight ⊂[3]	96	14.45S	135.40 E
Límnos I	48	39.54N	25.21 E
Limoges	36	45.50N	1.16 E
Limón	108	10.00N	83.02W
Limousin, Plateaux du ⋏[1]	36	45.30N	1.15 E
Limoux	36	43.04N	2.14 E
Limpopo ≃	86	25.15S	33.30 E
Linares, Chile	120	35.51S	71.36W
Linares, Esp.	44	38.05N	3.38W
Lincoln, Arg.	120	34.52S	61.32W
Lincoln, Eng., U.K.	26	53.14N	0.33W
Lincoln, Ar., U.S.	144	35.56N	94.25W
Lincoln, Il., U.S.	144	40.08N	89.21W
Lincoln, Me., U.S.	136	45.21N	68.30W
Lincoln, Mo., U.S.	144	38.23N	93.20W
Lincoln, Ne., U.S.	132	40.48N	96.40W
Lincoln, N.H., U.S.	136	44.02N	71.40W
Lincoln, Mount ∧	148	39.21N	106.07W
Lincoln City	150	44.57N	124.00W
Lincoln Park, Co., U.S.	148	38.25N	105.13W
Lincoln Park, Ga., U.S.	142	32.52N	84.19W
Lincoln Park, Mi., U.S.	138	42.15N	83.10W
Lincolnshire □[6]	26	52.55N	0.22W
Lincoln's New Salem State Park ♦	144	39.58N	89.52W
Lincolnton	142	35.28N	81.15W
Lincoln Village	154	38.00N	121.19W
Lind	150	46.58N	118.36W
Linda	154	39.07N	121.32W
Lindale	142	34.11N	85.10W
Lindau	30	47.33N	9.41 E
Linden, Al., U.S.	144	32.18N	87.47W
Linden, Tn., U.S.	144	35.37N	87.50W
Linderödsåsen ⋏[2]	22	55.53N	13.56 E
Lindesnes ›	22	58.00N	7.02 E
Lindi	86	10.00S	39.43 E
Lindi ≃	86	0.33N	25.05 E
Lindlar	30	51.01N	7.23 E
Lindsay	130	44.21N	78.44W
Line Islands II	8	0.05N	157.00W
Linesville	136	41.39N	80.25W
Linfen	66	36.05N	111.32 E
Lingayen	68	16.01N	120.14 E
Lingayen Gulf ⊂	68	16.15N	120.14 E
Lingbo	22	61.03N	16.41 E
Lingen	30	52.31N	7.19 E
Lingga, Kepulauan II	68	0.05S	104.35 E
Lingling	66	26.13N	111.37 E
Linh, Ngoc ∧	68	15.04N	107.59 E
Linhai	66	28.51N	121.07 E
Linjiang	66	41.44N	126.55 E
Linköping	22	58.25N	15.37 E
Linkou	66	45.15N	130.16 E
Linlithgow	26	55.59N	3.37W
Linn	144	38.29N	91.51W
Linnhe, Loch ⊂	26	56.39N	5.21W
Linosa, Isola di I	40	35.51N	12.52 E
Linqing	66	36.53N	115.41 E
Linru	66	34.11N	112.49 E
Lins	118	21.40S	49.45W
Lintao	66	35.27N	103.46 E
Linton	144	39.02N	87.09W
Linville	142	36.03N	81.52W
Linxia	66	35.35N	103.13 E
Linyanti ≃	86	17.58S	24.16 E
Linyi	66	35.04N	118.22 E
Linz	30	48.18N	14.18 E
Lion, Golfe du ⊂	36	43.00N	4.00 E
Lipa	68	13.57N	121.10 E
Lipany	30	49.10N	20.58 E
Lipari, Isola I	40	38.29N	14.56 E
Lipeck	54	52.37N	39.35 E
Lipetsk → Lipeck	54	52.37N	39.35 E
Lipez, Cerro ∧	118	21.53S	66.52W
Lipno	30	52.51N	19.10 E
Lipno, údolní nádrž ⊜[1]	30	48.43N	14.04 E
Lipova	48	46.05N	21.40 E
Lippe ≃	30	51.39N	6.38 E
Lippstadt	30	51.40N	8.19 E
Liptovská Teplička	30	48.59N	20.06 E
Liptovský Mikuláš	30	49.06N	19.37 E
Lira	84	2.15N	32.54 E
Liro	92	16.27S	168.13 E
Lisala	86	2.09N	21.31 E
Lisboa (Lisbon)	44	38.43N	9.08W
Lisbon → Lisboa, Port.	44	38.43N	9.08W
Lisbon, N.H., U.S.	136	44.12N	71.54W
Lisbon, Oh., U.S.	136	40.46N	80.46W
Lisbon Falls	136	43.59N	70.03W
Lisburn	26	54.31N	6.03W
Liscia ≃	40	41.11N	9.19 E
Lishui	66	28.27N	119.54 E
Lisičansk	54	48.55N	38.26 E
Lisieux	36	49.09N	0.14 E
Lismore	96	28.48S	153.17 E
Lismore Island I	26	56.29N	5.33W
Lista ›[1]	22	58.07N	6.40 E
Litchfield, Il., U.S.	144	39.10N	89.39W
Litchfield, Mn., U.S.	138	45.07N	94.31W
Litchfield Park	148	33.29N	112.21W
Lithgow	96	33.29S	150.09 E
Líthinon, Ákra ›	48	34.55N	24.44 E
Lithonia	142	33.42N	84.06W
Lithuanian Soviet Socialist Republic → Litovskaja Sovetskaja Socialističeskaja Respublika □[3]	54	56.00N	24.00 E
Litija	40	46.03N	14.50 E
Lititz	136	40.09N	76.18W
Litoměřice	30	50.35N	14.09 E
Litomyšl	30	49.52N	16.19 E
Litovskaja Sovetskaja Socialističeskaja Respublika (Lithuania) □[3]	54	56.00N	24.00 E
Little ≃, U.S.	144	35.32N	90.25W
Little ≃, U.S.	144	33.37N	93.52W
Little Abaco Island I	142	26.53N	77.43W
Little Andaman I	70	10.45N	92.30 E
Little Barrier Island I	98	36.12S	175.05 E
Little Belt Mountains ⋏	150	46.45N	110.35W
Little Bighorn ≃	150	45.44N	107.34W
Little Cayman I	108	19.41N	80.03W
Little Chute	138	44.16N	88.19W
Little Colorado ≃	148	36.11N	111.48W
Little Current	130	45.58N	81.56W
Little Falls, Mn., U.S.	138	45.58N	94.21W
Little Falls, N.Y., U.S.	136	43.02N	74.51W
Littlefork	138	48.23N	93.33W
Little Inagua I	108	21.30N	73.00W
Little Juniata ≃	136	40.34N	78.03W
Little Kanawha ≃	136	39.16N	81.34W
Little Karroo ⋏[1]	86	33.45S	21.30 E
Little Lake ⊜	144	29.30N	90.10W
Little Laramie ≃	148	41.28N	105.44W
Little Lost ≃	150	43.46N	112.58W
Little Missouri ≃	132	47.30N	102.25W
Little Ouse ≃	26	52.30N	0.22 E
Little Platte ≃	144	39.24N	94.41W
Little Rock	144	34.44N	92.17W
Little Sable Point ›	138	43.38N	86.32W
Little Saint Bernard Pass → Petit-Saint-Bernard, Col du)(	36	45.41N	6.53 E
Little Scarcies ≃	82	8.51N	13.09W
Little Smoky ≃	130	55.42N	117.38W
Little Snake ≃	148	40.27N	108.26W
Littlestown	136	39.44N	77.05W
Little Tennessee ≃	142	35.47N	84.15W
Littleton, Co., U.S.	148	39.36N	105.00W
Littleton, N.H., U.S.	136	44.18N	71.46W
Little Traverse Bay ⊂	138	45.24N	85.03W
Little Valley	136	42.15N	78.48W
Little Wabash ≃	144	37.54N	88.05W
Litvínov	30	50.37N	13.36 E
Liuzhou	66	24.19N	109.24 E
Livanjsko Polje ≚	40	43.55N	16.45 E
Live Oak	142	30.17N	82.59W
Livermore	154	37.40N	121.46W
Livermore Falls	136	44.28N	70.11W
Liverpool, Eng., U.K.	26	53.25N	2.55W
Liverpool, Pa., U.S.	136	40.34N	76.59W
Liverpool, Cape ›	130	73.38N	78.06W
Lívingston, Guat.	108	15.50N	88.45W
Livingston, Al., U.S.	144	32.35N	88.11W
Livingston, Mt., U.S.	150	45.39N	110.33W
Livingston, Tn., U.S.	144	36.23N	85.19W
Livingstone	86	17.50S	25.53 E
Livingstone, Chutes de ⌊	86	4.50S	14.30 E
Livingstone, Lake ⊜[1]	144	30.50N	95.30W
Livingstone Falls → Livingstone, Chutes de ⌊	86	4.50S	14.30 E
Livojoki ≃	20	65.24N	26.48 E
Livonia, La., U.S.	144	30.33N	91.33W
Livonia, Mi., U.S.	138	42.22N	83.21W
Livonia, N.Y., U.S.	136	42.49N	77.40W
Livorno (Leghorn)	40	43.33N	10.19 E
Liwale	86	9.46S	37.56 E
Lizard Head Peak ∧	150	42.47N	109.11W
Lizard Point ›	26	49.56N	5.13W
Ljubljana	40	46.03N	14.31 E
Ljubovija	48	44.11N	19.22 E
Ljungan ≃	22	62.19N	17.23 E
Ljungby	22	56.50N	13.56 E
Ljusdal	22	61.50N	16.05 E
Ljusnan ≃	22	61.12N	17.08 E
Ljusterö I	22	59.31N	18.37 E
Llançà	44	42.22N	3.09 E
Llandrindod Wells	26	52.15N	3.23W
Llandudno	26	53.19N	3.49W
Llanelli	26	51.42N	4.10W
Llanos ≚	118	5.00N	70.00W
Lleida	44	41.37N	0.37 E
Llerena	44	38.14N	6.01W
Llobregat ≃	44	41.19N	2.09 E
Lloydminster	130	53.17N	110.00W
Llucmajor	44	39.29N	2.54 E
Llullaillaco, Volcán ∧[1]	120	24.43S	68.33W
Loa ≃	120	21.26S	70.04W
Loami	144	39.40N	89.51W
Loange (Luangue) ≃	86	4.17S	20.02 E
Lobatse	86	25.11S	25.40 E
Löbau	30	51.05N	14.40 E
Lobaye ≃	84	3.41N	18.35 E
Lobelville	144	35.46N	87.47W
Łobez	30	53.39N	15.36 E
Lobito	86	12.20S	13.34 E
Lobos de Afuera, Islas II	118	6.57S	80.42W
Lobos de Tierra, Isla I	118	6.27S	80.52W
Locarno	36	46.10N	8.48 E
Lochaline	26	56.32N	5.47W
Lochboisdale	26	57.09N	7.19W
Lochmaddy	26	57.36N	7.11W
Lock Haven	136	41.08N	77.26W
Lockport, Il., U.S.	138	41.35N	88.03W
Lockport, La., U.S.	144	29.39N	90.32W
Lockport, N.Y., U.S.	136	43.10N	78.41W
Loc-ninh	68	11.51N	106.36 E
Locri	40	38.14N	16.16 E
Locust Fork ≃	144	33.33N	87.11W
Lodi, It.	40	45.19N	9.30 E
Lodi, Ca., U.S.	154	38.07N	121.16W
Lodi, Oh., U.S.	136	41.02N	82.00W
Lodi, Wi., U.S.	138	43.18N	89.31W
Łódź	30	51.46N	19.30 E
Lofa ≃	82	6.36N	11.08W
Lofer	30	47.35N	12.41 E
Lofoten II	20	68.30N	15.00 E
Logan, Oh., U.S.	136	39.32N	82.24W
Logan, Ut,. U.S.	148	41.44N	111.50W
Logan, W.V., U.S.	136	37.50N	81.59W
Logan, Mount ∧, Yk., Can.	130	60.34N	140.24W
Logan, Mount ∧, Wa., U.S.	150	48.32N	120.57W
Logan Martin Lake ⊜[1]	144	33.40N	86.15W
Logan Pass)(	150	48.42N	113.43W
Logansport, In., U.S.	144	40.45N	86.21W
Logansport, La., U.S.	144	31.58N	93.59W
Logone ≃	84	12.06N	15.02 E
Logroño	44	42.28N	2.27W
Logrosán	44	39.20N	5.29W
Logudoro ◆[1]	40	40.35N	8.40 E
Lohjanjärvi ⊜	22	60.15N	23.55 E
Lohne	30	52.42N	8.12 E
Lohr	30	50.00N	9.34 E
Loi-kaw	68	19.41N	97.13 E
Loir ≃	36	47.33N	0.32W
Loire ≃	36	47.16N	2.11W
Loja, Ec.	118	4.00S	79.13W
Loja, Esp.	44	37.10N	4.09W
Lokan tekojärvi ⊜[1]	20	67.55N	27.40 E
Løken	22	59.48N	11.29 E
Lokeren	30	51.06N	4.00 E
Loket	30	50.09N	12.43 E
Lokoro ≃	86	1.43S	18.23 E
Lol ≃	84	9.13N	28.59 E
Lola, Mount ∧	154	39.26N	120.22W
Lolland I	22	54.46N	11.30 E
Lolo	150	46.45N	114.04W
Lolo Pass)(	150	46.38N	114.35W
Lolowai	92	15.18S	168.00 E
Loltong	92	15.33S	168.08 E
Lom	48	43.49N	23.14 E
Lom ≃	82	5.20N	13.24 E
Lomaloma	91	17.17S	178.59W
Lomami ≃	86	0.46N	24.16 E
Lomax	144	40.41N	91.04W
Łomazy	30	51.55N	23.10 E
Lombok I	68	8.45S	116.30 E
Lomé	82	6.08N	1.13 E
Lomela	86	2.18S	23.17 E
Lomela ≃	86	0.14S	20.42 E
Lomira	138	43.35N	88.26W
Lommel	30	51.14N	5.18 E
Lomond, Loch ⊜	26	56.08N	4.38W
Lomonosov	54	59.55N	29.46 E
Lompoc	154	34.38N	120.27W
Łomża	30	53.11N	22.05 E
Lonaconing	136	39.33N	78.58W
London, On., Can.	130	42.59N	81.14W
London, Eng., U.K.	26	51.30N	0.10W
London, Ky., U.S.	142	37.07N	84.05W
London, Oh., U.S.	136	39.53N	83.26W
Londonderry	26	54.59N	7.20W
Londonderry, Cape ›	96	13.45S	126.55 E
Londrina	120	23.18S	51.09W
Lone Oak	144	37.02N	88.39W
Lone Pine	154	36.36N	118.03W
Lone Rock	138	43.11N	90.11W
Lone Tree	138	41.29N	91.25W
Longa ≃	86	10.15S	13.30 E
Longa, proliv ʯ	56	70.20N	178.00 E
Longana	92	15.20S	167.55 E
Long Bay ⊂	142	33.35N	78.45W
Long Beach, Ca., U.S.	154	33.46N	118.11W
Long Beach, Ms., U.S.	144	30.21N	89.09W
Long Beach, N.Y., U.S.	136	40.35N	73.39W
Long Beach ≗[2]	136	39.39N	74.11W
Longboat Key	142	27.24N	82.39W
Long Branch	136	40.18N	73.59W
Long Eaton	26	52.54N	1.15W
Longeau	36	47.46N	5.18 E
Longford	26	53.44N	7.47W
Longford □[6]	26	53.40N	7.40W
Long Island I, Ba.	108	23.15N	75.07W
Long Island I, N.Y., U.S.	136	40.50N	73.00W
Long Island Sound ʯ	136	41.05N	72.58W
Longjiang	66	47.19N	123.12 E
Long Lake ⊜, Mi., U.S.	138	45.12N	83.30W
Long Lake ⊜, N.Y., U.S.	136	44.04N	74.20W
Longli	66	26.26N	106.58 E
Longmeadow	136	42.03N	72.35W
Longmont	148	40.10N	105.06W
Long Range Mountains ⋏	130	49.20N	57.30W
Longs Peak ∧	148	40.15N	105.37W
Longueuil	130	45.32N	73.30W
Longview, N.C., U.S.	142	35.43N	81.23W
Longview, Tx., U.S.	144	32.30N	94.44W
Longview, Wa., U.S.	150	46.08N	122.56W
Longwy	36	49.31N	5.46 E
Long-xuyen	68	10.23N	105.25 E
Lonoke	144	34.47N	91.53W
Lons-le-Saunier	36	46.40N	5.33 E
Loogootee	144	38.40N	86.54W
Lookout, Cape ›	142	34.35N	76.32W
Lookout Mountain ∧	144	34.25N	85.40W
Lookout Pass)(	150	47.27N	115.42W
Loop Head ›	26	52.34N	9.56W
Lopatka, mys ›	56	50.52N	156.40 E
Lop Buri	68	14.48N	100.37 E
Lopez, Cap ›	86	0.37S	8.43 E
Lop Nur (Lop Nor) ⊜	66	40.20N	90.15 E
Lora, Hāmūn-i- ⊜	70	29.20N	64.50 E
Lora del Río	44	37.39N	5.32W
Lorain	136	41.27N	82.10W
Lorca	44	37.40N	1.42W
Lord Howe Island I	96	31.33S	159.05 E
Lordsburg	148	32.21N	108.42W
Loreauville	144	30.03N	91.44W
Loreley ♦	30	50.08N	7.44 E
Lorica	118	9.14N	75.49W
Lorient	36	47.45N	3.22W
Loriol	36	44.45N	4.49 E
Lorn, Firth of ⊂[1]	26	56.20N	5.45W
Lörrach	30	47.37N	7.40 E
Lorraine □[9]	36	49.00N	6.00 E
Los Alamos	148	35.53N	106.19W
Los Ángeles, Chile	120	37.28S	72.21W
Los Angeles, Ca., U.S.	154	34.03N	118.14W
Los Angeles Aqueduct ≡[1]	154	35.22N	118.05W
Los Banos	154	37.03N	120.50W
Los Gatos	154	37.13N	121.58W
Lošinj, Otok I	40	44.36N	14.24 E
Los Mochis	108	25.45N	108.57W
Los Navalmorales	44	39.43N	4.38W
Losolava	92	14.11S	167.34 E
Los Padillas	148	34.58N	106.41W
Los Palacios y Villafranca	44	37.10N	5.56W
Los Roques, Islas II	118	11.50N	66.45W
Losser	30	52.15N	7.00 E
Lost ≃	144	38.33N	86.49W
Lost Hills	154	35.36N	119.41W
Lost Nation	138	41.57N	90.49W
Lost River Range ⋏	150	44.10N	113.35W
Lost Trail Pass)(	150	45.41N	113.57W
Lot ≃	36	44.18N	0.20 E
Lota	120	37.05S	73.10W
Lotrului, Munții ⋏	48	45.30N	23.52 E
Lotsane ≃	86	22.41S	28.11 E
Lotta ≃	20	68.36N	31.06 E
Louangphrabang	68	19.52N	102.08 E
L'Ouarsenis, Massif de ⋏	44	35.40N	1.50 E
Loudon	142	35.43N	84.20W
Loudonville	136	40.38N	82.14W
Louga	82	15.37N	16.13W
Louge ≃	36	43.27N	1.20 E
Loughborough	26	52.47N	1.11W
Louhans	36	46.38N	5.13 E
Louin	144	32.04N	89.15W
Louisa	142	38.06N	82.36W
Louisburg	142	36.05N	78.18W
Louisiana	144	39.26N	91.03W
Louisiana □[3]	132	31.15N	92.15W
Louis Trichardt	86	23.01S	29.43 E
Louisville, Al., U.S.	144	31.47N	85.33W
Louisville, Ga., U.S.	142	33.00N	82.24W
Louisville, Ky., U.S.	144	38.15N	85.45W
Louisville, Ms., U.S.	144	33.07N	89.03W
Louisville, Oh., U.S.	136	40.50N	81.15W
Louis-XIV, Pointe ›	130	54.37N	79.45W
Loukkos, Oued ≃	44	35.12N	6.09W
Louny	30	50.19N	13.46 E
Lourdes	36	43.06N	0.03W
Lourenço Marques → Maputo	86	25.58S	32.35 E
Loures	44	38.50N	9.10W
Louth	26	53.22N	0.01W
Louth □[6]	26	53.55N	6.30W
Louvain → Leuven	30	50.53N	4.42 E
Louviers	36	49.13N	1.10 E
Lovat' ≃	54	58.14N	31.28 E
Loveč	48	43.08N	24.43 E
Loveland	148	40.23N	105.04W
Lovell	150	44.50N	108.23W
Lovelock	154	40.10N	118.28W
Lovely	142	37.49N	82.24W
Loves Park	138	42.19N	89.03W
Lovingston	142	37.45N	78.52W
Lovisa (Loviisa)	22	60.27N	26.14 E
Lovosice	30	50.31N	14.03 E
Lövstabruk	22	60.24N	17.53 E
Low, Cape ›	130	63.07N	85.18W
Lowell, In., U.S.	144	41.17N	87.25W
Lowell, Ma., U.S.	136	42.38N	71.19W
Lowell, Mi., U.S.	138	42.56N	85.20W
Lowell, Lake ⊜[1]	150	43.33N	116.40W
Lower Hutt	98	41.13S	174.55 E
Lower Klamath Lake ⊜	154	41.55N	121.42W
Lower Lake ⊜	154	41.15N	120.02W
Lower Red Lake ⊜	132	48.00N	94.50W
Lowestoft	26	52.29N	1.45 E
Łowicz	30	52.07N	19.56 E
Lowville	136	43.47N	75.29W
Loyalty Islands → Loyauté, Îles II	92	21.00S	167.00 E
Loyauté, Îles (Loyalty Islands) II	92	21.00S	167.00 E
Loznica	48	44.32N	19.13 E
Lua ≃	84	2.46N	18.26 E
Lualaba ≃	86	0.26N	25.20 E
Lu'an	66	31.44N	116.31 E
Luanda	86	8.48S	13.14 E
Luando ≃	86	10.19S	16.40 E
Luang Prabang → Louangphrabang	68	19.52N	102.08 E
Luangue (Loange) ≃	86	4.17S	20.02 E
Luanguinga ≃	86	15.11S	22.56 E
Luangwa ≃	86	15.36S	30.25 E
Luanshya	86	13.08S	28.24 E
Luapula ≃	86	9.26S	28.33 E
Luarca	44	43.32N	6.32W
Luba	82	3.27N	8.33 E
Lubaczów	30	50.10N	23.07 E
Lubań	30	51.08N	15.18 E
Lubango	86	14.55S	13.30 E
Lübben	30	51.56N	13.53 E
Lübbenau	30	51.52N	13.57 E
Lubbock	132	33.34N	101.51W
Lubec	136	44.51N	66.59W
Lübeck	30	53.52N	10.40 E
Lubelska, Wyżyna ⋏[2]	30	51.00N	23.00 E
L'ubercy	20	55.41N	37.53 E
Lubilash ≃	86	6.02S	23.45 E
Lubin	30	51.24N	16.13 E
Lublin	30	51.15N	22.35 E
Lubliniec	30	50.40N	18.41 E
Lubomierz	30	51.01N	15.30 E
Lubsko	30	51.46N	14.59 E
Lubudi	86	9.57S	25.58 E
Lubudi ≃	86	9.13S	25.38 E
Lubumbashi (Élisabethville)	86	11.40S	27.28 E
Lucania □[9]	40	40.30N	16.00 E
Lucania, Mount ∧	130	61.01N	140.28W
Lucasville	136	38.52N	82.59W
Lucca	40	43.50N	10.29 E
Luce Bay ⊂	26	54.47N	4.50W
Lucedale	144	30.55N	88.35W
Lucena, Esp.	44	37.24N	4.29W
Lucena, Pil.	68	13.56N	121.37 E
Lučenec	30	48.20N	19.40 E
Lucera	40	41.30N	15.20 E
Lucerne → Luzern	36	47.03N	8.18 E
Lucerne, Lake → Vierwaldstätter See ⊜	36	47.00N	8.28 E
Lüchow	30	52.58N	11.10 E
Luck	54	50.44N	25.20 E
Luckenwalde	30	52.05N	13.10 E
Lucknow	70	26.51N	80.55 E
Luçon	36	46.27N	1.10W
Luda Kamčija ≃	48	43.03N	27.29 E
Lüdenscheid	30	51.13N	7.38 E
Lüderitz	86	26.38S	15.10 E
Ludhiāna	70	30.54N	75.51 E
Ludington	138	43.57N	86.27W
Ludlow, Ma., U.S.	136	42.09N	72.28W
Ludlow, Vt., U.S.	136	43.23N	72.42W
Ludogorie ◆[1]	48	43.46N	26.56 E
Ludowici	142	31.42N	81.44W
Ludvika	22	60.09N	15.11 E
Ludwigsburg	30	48.53N	9.11 E
Ludwigsfelde	30	52.17N	13.16 E
Ludwigshafen	30	49.29N	8.26 E
Ludwigslust	30	53.19N	11.30 E
Luena	86	11.47S	19.52 E
Luena ≃	86	12.31S	22.34 E
Lufeng	66	22.57N	115.38 E
Lufkin	144	31.20N	94.43W
Luga	54	58.44N	29.52 E
Lugano	36	46.01N	8.58 E
Lugano, Lago di ⊜	40	46.00N	9.00 E
Luganville	92	15.32S	167.10 E
Lugenda ≃	86	11.25S	38.33 E
Lugnaquillia Mountain ∧	26	52.58N	6.27W
Lugo, Esp.	44	43.00N	7.34W
Lugo, It.	40	44.25N	11.54 E
Lugoj	48	45.41N	21.54 E
Luilaka ≃	86	0.52S	20.12 E
Luino	40	46.00N	8.44 E
Lukanga Swamp ≡	86	14.25S	27.45 E
Lukenie ≃	86	2.44S	18.09 E
Łuków	30	51.56N	22.23 E
Lukuga ≃	86	5.40S	26.55 E
Lula	144	34.27N	90.28W
Luleå	22	65.34N	22.10 E
Luleälven ≃	20	65.35N	22.03 E
Lüleburgaz	48	41.24N	27.21 E
Lulonga ≃	86	0.43N	18.23 E
Lulua ≃	86	5.02S	21.07 E
Luluabourg → Kananga	86	5.54S	22.25 E
Lumber ≃	142	34.12N	79.10W
Lumber City	142	31.55N	82.40W
Lumberton, Ms., U.S.	144	31.00N	89.27W
Lumberton, N.C., U.S.	142	34.37N	79.00W
Lumbres	36	50.42N	2.08 E
Luna Pier	138	41.48N	83.26W
Lund, Sve.	22	55.42N	13.11 E
Lund, Nv., U.S.	154	38.51N	115.00W
Lundi ≃	86	21.43S	32.34 E
Lundy I	26	51.10N	4.40W
Lune ≃	26	54.02N	2.50W
Lüneburg	30	53.15N	10.23 E
Lüneburger Heide ◆[1]	30	53.10N	10.20 E
Lünen	30	51.36N	7.32 E
Lunenburg	142	36.57N	78.15W
Lunéville	36	48.36N	6.30 E
Lunga ≃	86	14.34S	26.25 E
Lungi	82	8.38N	13.13W
Lungué-Bungo ≃	86	14.19S	23.14 E
Lūni ≃	70	24.41N	71.15 E
Lunndörrsfjällen ∧	22	63.00N	13.00 E
Luogosanto	40	41.03N	9.13 E
Luohe	66	33.35N	114.01 E
Luoyang	66	34.41N	112.28 E
Lupeni	48	45.22N	23.13 E
Luque	44	37.33N	4.16W
Luray	136	38.39N	78.27W
Lurgan	26	54.28N	6.20W
Lurín	118	12.17S	76.52W
Lúrio ≃	86	13.35S	40.32 E
Lusaka	86	15.25S	28.17 E
Lusambo	86	4.58S	23.27 E
Lushnje	48	40.56N	19.42 E
Lüshun (Port Arthur)	66	38.48N	121.16 E
Lusk	148	42.45N	104.27W
Lūt, Dasht-e ◆[2]	70	33.00N	57.00 E
Lutcher	144	30.02N	90.41W
Luther	138	44.02N	85.40W
Luton	26	51.53N	0.25W
Lutong	68	4.28N	114.00 E
Lutz	142	28.09N	82.27W
Luverne, Al., U.S.	144	31.42N	86.15W
Lu Verne, Ia., U.S.	138	42.54N	94.04W
Luvua ≃	86	6.46S	26.58 E
Luwegu ≃	86	8.31S	37.23 E
Luxembourg	36	49.36N	6.09 E
Luxembourg □[1]	30	49.45N	6.05 E
Luxemburg	138	44.32N	87.42W
Luxor → Al-Uqṣur	84	25.41N	32.39 E
Luy ≃	36	43.39N	1.08W
Luzern	36	47.03N	8.18 E
Luzhou	66	28.54N	105.27 E
Luziânia	118	16.15S	47.56W
Lužnice ≃	30	49.14N	14.23 E
Luzon I	68	16.00N	121.00 E
Luzon Strait ʯ	68	20.30N	121.00 E
Luzy	36	46.48N	3.58 E
L'vov	54	49.50N	24.00 E
Lwówek	30	52.28N	16.10 E
Lycksele	22	64.36N	18.40 E
Lydia □[9]	48	38.40N	27.30 E
Lydia Mills	142	34.28N	81.55W
Lyle	138	43.30N	92.56W
Lyles	144	35.55N	87.20W
Lyme Bay ⊂	26	50.38N	3.00W
Lyme Regis	26	50.44N	2.57W
Łyna (Lava) ≃	30	54.37N	21.14 E
Lynchburg	142	37.24N	79.08W
Lynches ≃	142	33.50N	79.22W
Lynden	150	48.56N	122.27W
Lyndonville	136	44.32N	72.00W
Lyngen ⊂[2]	20	69.58N	20.30 E
Lynn, In., U.S.	144	40.02N	84.56W
Lynn, Ma., U.S.	136	42.28N	70.57W
Lynn Garden	142	36.34N	82.34W

Symbols in the index entries are identified on page 162.

Name	Page	Lat.	Long.
Lynn Haven	144	30.14N	85.38W
Lynn Lake	130	56.51N	101.03W
Lyon	36	45.45N	4.51 E
Lyon Mountain	136	44.43N	73.54W
Lyonnais, Monts du ⋏	36	45.40N	4.30 E
Lyons, Ga., U.S.	142	32.12N	82.19W
Lyons, N.Y., U.S.	136	43.03N	76.59W
Lys (Leie) ≃	36	51.03N	3.43 E
Łysica ∧	30	50.54N	20.55 E
Lys'va	54	58.07N	57.47 E
Lytham Saint Anne's	26	53.45N	2.57W
Lyttelton	98	43.35S	172.42 E
M			
Ma ≃	66	19.47N	105.56 E
Ma'anshan	66	31.42N	118.30 E
Maas (Meuse) ≃	30	51.49N	5.01 E
Maastricht	30	50.52N	5.43 E
Mababe Depression ⩡[7]	86	18.50S	24.15 E
Mabeul	40	36.27N	10.46 E
Mableton	142	33.49N	84.34W
Mabton	150	46.12N	119.59W
McAdoo	136	40.54N	75.59W
McAlester	132	34.56N	95.46W
McAllen	132	26.12N	98.13W
Macao → Macau □[2]	66	22.10N	113.33 E
Macapá	118	0.02N	51.03W
Macau (Aomen)	66	22.14N	113.35 E
Macau □[2]	66	22.10N	113.33 E
McBee	142	34.28N	80.15W
McCaysville	142	34.59N	84.22W
McCleary	150	47.03N	123.15W
Macclesfield	26	53.16N	2.07W
McCloud	154	41.15N	122.08W
McCloud ≃	154	40.46N	122.18W
McColl	142	34.40N	79.32W
McComas	142	37.23N	81.17W
McComb, Ms., U.S.	144	31.14N	90.27W
McComb, Oh., U.S.	136	41.06N	83.47W
McConnellsburg	136	39.55N	77.59W
McCook	132	40.12N	100.37W
McCormick	142	33.54N	82.17W
McCrory	144	35.15N	91.12W
MacDonald Pass)(	150	46.34N	112.18W
Macdonnell Ranges ⋏	96	23.45S	133.20 E
McDonough	142	33.26N	84.08W
Macdui, Ben ∧	26	57.05N	3.38W
Macedonia → Makedonija □[3]	48	41.50N	22.00 E
Macedonia □[9]	48	41.00N	23.00 E
Maceió	118	9.40S	35.43W
Mcensk	54	53.17N	36.35 E
Macerata	40	43.18N	13.27 E
McFarland	138	43.00N	89.17W
MacFarlane ≃	130	59.12N	107.58W
Macfarlane, Mount ∧	98	43.56S	169.23 E
McGehee	144	33.37N	91.23W
McGill	154	39.24N	114.46W
McGraw	136	42.35N	76.05W
McGuire, Mount ∧	150	45.10N	114.36W
Machačkala	54	42.58N	47.30 E
Machakos	86	1.31S	37.16 E
Machala	118	3.16S	79.58W
McHenry	138	42.20N	88.16W
Machias	136	44.42N	67.27W
Machichaco, Cabo ›	44	43.27N	2.45W
Machilīpatnam	70	16.10N	81.08 E
Mchinji	86	13.41S	32.55 E
Machiques	118	10.04N	72.34W
Macintyre ≃	96	29.25S	148.45 E
Mackay	96	21.09S	149.11 E
Mackay, Lake ⊜	96	22.30S	129.00 E
McKeesport	136	40.20N	79.51W
McKenzie	144	36.07N	88.31W
Mackenzie □[5]	130	65.00N	115.00W
Mackenzie ≃	130	69.15N	134.08W
Mackenzie Bay ⊂	130	69.00N	136.30W
Mackenzie Mountains ⋏	130	64.00N	130.00W
Mackinac, Straits of Ʉ	138	45.49N	84.42W
Mackinac Bridge ◆[5]	138	45.50N	84.45W
Mackinac Island	138	45.50N	84.37W
Mackinac Island I	138	45.51N	84.38W
Mackinaw	144	40.32N	89.21W
Mackinaw ≃	144	40.33N	89.44W
Mackinaw City	138	45.47N	84.43W
McLeansboro	144	38.05N	88.32W
McLeod ≃	130	54.08N	115.42W
McLoughlin, Mount ∧	150	42.27N	122.19W
Macmillan ≃	130	62.52N	135.55W
McMinnville, Or., U.S.	150	45.12N	123.11W
McMinnville, Tn., U.S.	144	35.41N	85.46W
Macomb	138	40.27N	90.40W
Macomer	40	40.16N	8.47 E
Mâcon, Fr.	36	46.18N	4.50 E
Macon, Ga., U.S.	142	32.50N	83.37W
Macon, Il., U.S.	144	39.42N	88.59W
Macon, Ms., U.S.	144	33.06N	88.33W
Macon, Mo., U.S.	144	39.44N	92.28W
McPherson	132	38.22N	97.39W
McRae	142	32.04N	82.54W
Mad ≃, Ca., U.S.	154	40.57N	124.07W
Mad ≃, Oh., U.S.	136	39.46N	84.11W
Mada ≃	82	7.59N	7.55 E
Madagascar (Madagasikara) □[1]	86	19.00S	46.00 E
Madang	96a	5.15S	145.50 E
Madawaska ≃	130	45.27N	76.21W
Maddalena, Isola I	40	41.14N	9.25 E
Maddaloni	40	41.02N	14.23 E
Madeira I	82	32.44N	17.00W
Madeira ≃	118	3.22S	58.45W
Madeira, Arquipélago da (Madeira Islands) II	82	32.40N	16.45W
Mädelegabel ∧	36	47.18N	10.18 E
Madeleine, Îles de la II	130	47.30N	61.45W
Madelia	138	44.03N	94.25W
Madeline Island I	138	46.50N	90.40W
Madera	154	36.57N	120.03W
Madidi ≃	118	12.32S	66.52W
Madīnat ash-Sha'b	70	12.50N	44.56 E
Madison, Al., U.S.	144	34.41N	86.44W
Madison, Fl., U.S.	142	30.28N	83.24W
Madison, Ga., U.S.	142	33.35N	83.28W
Madison, In., U.S.	144	38.44N	85.22W
Madison, Me., U.S.	136	44.47N	69.52W
Madison, N.C., U.S.	142	36.23N	79.57W
Madison, Oh., U.S.	136	41.46N	81.03W
Madison, S.D., U.S.	132	44.00N	97.06W
Madison, W.V., U.S.	136	38.04N	81.49W
Madison, Wi., U.S.	138	43.04N	89.24W
Madison ≃	150	45.56N	111.30W
Madison Heights	142	37.25N	79.07W
Madison Range ⋏	150	45.15N	111.20W
Madisonville, Ky., U.S.	144	37.19N	87.29W
Madisonville, Tn., U.S.	142	35.31N	84.21W
Madiun	68	7.37S	111.31 E
Madrakah, Ra's al- ›	70	19.00N	57.50 E
Madras	70	13.05N	80.17 E
Madre, Laguna ⊂, Méx.	108	25.00N	97.40W
Madre, Laguna ⊂, Tx., U.S.	132	27.00N	97.35W
Madre, Sierra ⋏	68	16.20N	122.00 E
Madre de Dios ≃	118	10.59S	66.08W
Madre del Sur, Sierra ⋏	108	17.00N	100.00W
Madre Occidental, Sierra ⋏	108	25.00N	105.00W
Madre Oriental, Sierra ⋏	108	22.00N	99.30W
Madrid, Esp.	44	40.24N	3.41W
Madrid, Al., U.S.	144	31.02N	85.23W
Madrid, Ia., U.S.	138	41.52N	93.49W
Madrid □[4]	44	40.30N	3.40W
Madura I	68	7.00S	113.20 E
Madurai	70	9.56N	78.07 E
Maebashi	66	36.23N	139.04 E
Mae Hong Son	68	19.16N	97.56 E
Mae Klong ≃	68	13.21N	100.00 E
Maeser	148	40.28N	109.35W
Mae Sot	68	16.43N	98.34 E
Maesteg	26	51.37N	3.40W
Maestra, Sierra ⋏	108	20.00N	76.45W
Maevatanana	86	16.56S	46.49 E
Maéwo I	92	15.10S	168.10 E
Mafia Island I	86	7.50S	39.50 E
Mafikeng	86	25.53S	25.39 E
Magadan	56	59.34N	150.48 E
Magallanes, Estrecho de (Strait of Magellan) Ʉ	120	54.00S	71.00W
Magangué	118	9.14N	74.45W
Magazine Mountain ∧	144	35.10N	93.38W
Magdalena ≃	118	11.06N	74.51W
Magdalena, Isla I	120	44.40S	73.10W
Magdeburg	30	52.07N	11.38 E
Magee	144	31.52N	89.44W
Magelang	68	7.28S	110.13 E
Magellan, Strait of → Magallanes, Estrecho de Ʉ	120	54.00S	71.00W
Magenta	40	45.28N	8.53 E
Magerøy I	20	71.03N	25.45 E
Maggiore, Lago ⊜	40	46.00N	8.40 E
Mágina ∧	44	37.43N	3.28W
Magione	40	43.08N	12.12 E
Magnitogorsk	54	53.27N	59.04 E
Magnolia, Ar., U.S.	144	33.16N	93.14W
Magnolia, Ms., U.S.	144	31.08N	90.27W
Maguari, Cabo ›	118	0.18S	48.22W
Magwe	68	20.09N	94.55 E
Mahābhārat Range ⋏	70	27.40N	84.30 E
Mahajamba, Helodranon' i ⊂	86	15.24S	47.05 E
Mahajanga	86	15.43S	46.19 E
Mahakam ≃	68	0.35S	117.17 E
Mahalatswe	86	23.05S	26.51 E
Mahānadi ≃	70	20.19N	86.45 E
Mahanoy City	136	40.48N	76.08W
Maha Sarakham	68	16.11N	103.18 E
Mahdia	40	35.30N	11.04 E
Mahébourg	86	20.24S	57.42 E
Mahé Island I	86	4.40S	55.28 E
Mahia Peninsula ›[1]	98	39.10S	177.53 E
Mahomet	144	40.11N	88.24W
Mahora	44	39.13N	1.44W
Maia	44	41.14N	8.37W
Maiden	142	35.34N	81.12W
Maidenhead	26	51.32N	0.44W
Maidstone	26	51.17N	0.32 E
Maiduguri	82	11.51N	13.10 E
Maignelay	36	49.33N	2.31 E
Main ≃	30	50.00N	8.18 E
Mainburg	30	48.38N	11.47 E
Main Channel Ʉ	138	45.22N	81.50W
Mai-Ndombe, Lac ⊜	86	2.00S	18.20 E
Maine □[9]	36	48.15N	0.05W
Maine □[3]	132	45.15N	69.15W
Maine, Gulf of ⊂	132	43.00N	68.00W
Mainland I, Scot., U.K.	26	59.00N	3.15W
Mainland I, Scot., U.K.	26	60.16N	1.16W
Mainz	30	50.01N	8.16 E
Maio I	82	15.15N	23.10W
Maipo, Volcán ∧[1]	120	34.10S	69.50W
Maipú	120	36.52S	57.52W
Maiquetía	118	10.36N	66.57W
Maitland	96	32.44S	151.33 E
Maíz, Islas del II	108	12.15N	83.00W
Maizuru	66	35.28N	135.24 E
Majene	68	3.33S	118.57 E
Majkop	54	44.35N	40.07 E
Majorca → Mallorca I	44	39.30N	3.00 E
Makale	68	3.06S	119.51 E
Makarakomburu, Mount ∧	94	9.43S	160.02 E
Makasar, Selat (Makassar Strait) Ʉ	68	2.00S	117.30 E
Makassar Strait → Makasar, Selat Ʉ	68	2.00S	117.30 E
Makedonija □[3]	48	41.50N	22.00 E
Makejevka	54	48.02N	37.58 E
Makeni	82	8.53N	12.03W
Makgadikgadi ≃	86	20.45S	25.30 E
Makkah (Mecca)	70	21.27N	39.49 E
Makó	30	46.13N	20.29 E
Makthar	40	35.51N	9.12 E
Makung	66	23.34N	119.34 E
Makurdi	82	7.45N	8.32 E
Malabang	68	7.38N	124.03 E
Malabar Coast ⩡[2]	70	11.00N	75.00 E
Malabo	82	3.45N	8.47 E
Malacca, Strait of Ʉ	68	2.30N	101.20 E
Malacky	30	48.27N	17.00 E
Malad ≃	150	41.35N	112.07W
Málaga	44	36.43N	4.25W
Malaimbandy	86	20.20S	45.36 E
Malaita I	94	9.00S	161.00 E
Malaja Kuril'skaja Gr'ada (Habomai-shotō) II	56	43.30N	146.10 E
Malakāl	84	9.31N	31.39 E
Mala Kapela ⋏	40	44.50N	15.30 E
Malakula I	92	16.15S	167.30 E
Malang	68	7.59S	112.37 E
Malanje	86	9.32S	16.20 E
Malanville	82	11.52N	3.23 E
Mała Panew ≃	30	50.44N	17.52 E
Mälaren ⊜	22	59.30N	17.12 E
Malartic	130	48.08N	78.08W
Malatya	16	38.21N	38.19 E
Malau	92	15.10S	166.48 E
Malawi □[1]	86	13.30S	34.00 E
Malawi, Lake → Nyasa, Lake ⊜	86	12.00S	34.30 E
Malaya □[9]	68	4.00N	102.00 E
Malay Peninsula ›[1]	68	6.00N	101.00 E
Malaysia □[1]	68	2.30N	112.30 E
Malbork	30	54.02N	19.01 E
Malcolm	96	28.56S	121.30 E
Malczyce	30	51.14N	16.29 E
Maldegem	30	51.13N	3.27 E
Malden	144	36.33N	89.57W
Maldives □[1]	8	3.15N	73.00 E
Maléa, Ákra ›	48	36.26N	23.12 E
Mālegaon	70	20.33N	74.32 E
Malé Karpaty ⋏	30	48.30N	17.20 E
Malema	86	14.57S	37.20 E
Malheur ≃	150	44.03N	116.59W
Malheur Lake ⊜	150	43.20N	118.45W
Mali □[1]	82	17.00N	4.00W
Mali ≃	66	25.43N	97.29 E
Malik, Wādī al- V	84	18.02N	30.58 E
Malin Head ›	26	55.23N	7.24W
Malkara	48	40.53N	26.54 E
Malko Târnovo	48	41.59N	27.32 E
Mallawī	84	27.44N	30.50 E
Mallersdorf	30	48.47N	12.16 E
Mallorca I	44	39.30N	3.00 E
Malmberget	20	67.10N	20.40 E
Malmédy	30	50.25N	6.02 E
Malmesbury	86	33.28S	18.44 E
Malmö	22	55.36N	13.00 E
Malmslätt	22	58.25N	15.30 E
Maloja	36	46.24N	9.41 E
Malone	136	44.50N	74.17W
Małopolska ◆[1]	30	50.10N	21.30 E
Malpelo, Isla de I	118	3.59N	81.35W
Målselva ≃	20	69.14N	18.30 E
Malta, Mt., U.S.	150	48.21N	107.52W
Malta, Oh., U.S.	136	39.38N	81.51W
Malta □[1]	40	35.50N	14.35 E
Malta I	40	35.53N	14.27 E
Malta Channel Ʉ	40	36.20N	15.00 E
Malte Brun ∧	98	43.34S	170.18 E
Maluku (Moluccas) II	68	2.00S	128.00 E
Maluku, Laut (Molucca Sea) ⊤[2]	68	0.00	125.00 E
Malvern	144	34.21N	92.48W
Malý Dunaj ≃	30	47.45N	18.09 E
Malyj Kavkaz ⋏	54	41.00N	44.35 E
Malyj Uzen' ≃	54	48.50N	49.39 E
Mamberamo ≃	68	1.26S	137.53 E
Mambéré ≃	84	3.31N	16.03 E
Mamie	142	36.07N	75.50W
Mammoth	136	38.15N	81.22W
Mammoth Cave National Park ♠	144	37.08N	86.13W
Mammoth Lakes	154	37.38N	118.58W
Mammoth Spring	144	36.29N	91.32W
Mamoré ≃	118	10.23S	65.23W
Mamou, Guinée	82	10.23N	12.05W
Mamou, La., U.S.	144	30.38N	92.25W
Mamry, Jezioro ⊜	30	54.08N	21.42 E
Man	82	7.24N	7.33W
Mana ≃	118	5.44N	53.54W
Manacor	44	39.34N	3.12 E
Manado	68	1.29N	124.51 E
Managua	108	12.09N	86.17W
Managua, Lago de ⊜	108	12.20N	86.20W
Manakara	86	22.08S	48.01 E
Manakau ∧	98	42.14S	173.37 E
Manama → Al-Manāmah	70	26.13N	50.35 E
Mananara	86	16.10S	49.46 E
Mananjary	86	21.13S	48.20 E
Manapouri, Lake ⊜	98	45.30S	167.30 E
Manās ≃	70	26.13N	90.38 E
Manas Hu ⊜	66	45.45N	85.55 E
Manasquan	136	40.07N	74.02W
Manassas	136	38.45N	77.28W
Manassas National Battlefield Park ♠	136	38.50N	77.32W
Manatee ≃	142	27.32N	82.38W
Manaus	118	3.08S	60.01W
Manawa	138	44.27N	88.55W
Mancha Real	44	37.47N	3.37W
Manchester, Eng., U.K.	26	53.28N	2.15W
Manchester, Ct., U.S.	136	41.46N	72.31W
Manchester, Ga., U.S.	142	32.51N	84.37W
Manchester, Ia., U.S.	138	42.29N	91.27W
Manchester, Ky., U.S.	142	37.09N	83.45W
Manchester, Ma., U.S.	136	42.34N	70.46W
Manchester, N.H., U.S.	136	42.59N	71.27W
Manchester, Tn., U.S.	144	35.28N	86.05W
Manchester, Vt., U.S.	136	43.09N	73.04W
Manchuria □[9]	66	47.00N	125.00 E
Mand ≃	70	28.11N	51.17 E
Manda	86	10.28S	34.35 E
Mandala, Puncak ∧	68	4.44S	140.20 E
Mandalay	68	22.00N	96.05 E
Mandan	132	46.49N	100.53W
Mandara Mountains ⋏	82	10.45N	13.40 E
Mandeb, Bab el Ʉ	84	12.40N	43.20 E
Mandeville	144	30.21N	90.03W
Manduria	40	40.24N	17.38 E
Måne ≃	22	59.00N	9.40 E
Manfalūṭ	84	27.19N	30.58 E
Manfredonia	40	41.38N	15.55 E
Manfredonia, Golfo di ⊂	40	41.35N	16.05 E
Mangabeiras, Chapada das ⋏[2]	118	10.00S	46.30W
Mangakino	98	38.22S	175.47 E
Mangalore	70	12.52N	74.53 E
Mangham	144	32.18N	91.46W
Mangkalihat, Tanjung ›	68	1.02N	118.59 E
Mangoky ≃	86	21.29S	43.41 E
Mangole, Pulau I	68	1.53S	125.50 E
Manhattan	132	39.11N	96.34W
Manicouagan ≃	130	49.11N	68.13W
Manicouagan, Réservoir ⊜[1]	130	51.30N	68.19W
Manila, Pil.	68	14.35N	121.00 E
Manila, Ar., U.S.	144	35.52N	90.10W
Manila Bay ⊂	68	14.30N	120.45 E
Manisa	48	38.36N	27.26 E
Manistee	138	44.14N	86.19W
Manistee ≃	138	44.15N	86.21W
Manistique	138	45.57N	86.14W
Manito	144	40.25N	89.46W
Manitoba □[4]	130	54.00N	97.00W
Manitoba, Lake ⊜	130	51.00N	98.45W
Manitou, Lake ⊜	138	45.48N	82.00W
Manitoulin Island I	130	45.50N	82.20W
Manitou Springs	148	38.51N	104.55W
Manitowish Waters	138	46.09N	89.53W
Manitowoc	138	44.05N	87.39W
Maniwaki	130	46.23N	75.58W
Manizales	118	5.05N	75.32W
Manja	86	21.26S	44.20 E
Mankato	138	44.09N	93.59W
Mannar, Gulf of ⊂	70	8.30N	79.00 E
Mannheim	30	49.29N	8.29 E
Manning	142	33.41N	80.12W
Manning Strait Ʉ	94	7.24S	158.00 E
Mannington	136	39.31N	80.20W
Mannu ≃	40	40.50N	8.23 E
Manono	86	7.18S	27.25 E
Manresa	44	41.44N	1.50 E
Mansfield, Eng., U.K.	26	53.09N	1.11W
Mansfield, Ga., U.S.	142	33.31N	83.44W
Mansfield, La., U.S.	144	32.02N	93.42W
Mansfield, Ma., U.S.	136	42.02N	71.13W
Mansfield, Oh., U.S.	136	40.45N	82.30W
Mansfield, Pa., U.S.	136	41.48N	77.04W
Mansfield, Mount ∧	136	44.33N	72.49W
Manta	118	0.57S	80.44W
Manteca	154	37.47N	121.12W
Manteno	138	41.15N	87.49W
Manteo	142	35.54N	75.40W
Mantes-la-Jolie	36	48.59N	1.43 E
Manti	148	39.16N	111.38W
Mantiqueira, Serra da ⋏	120	22.00S	44.45W
Mantova	40	45.09N	10.48 E
Mantua → Mantova, It.	40	45.09N	10.48 E
Mantua, Oh., U.S.	136	41.17N	81.13W
Mäntyluoto	22	61.35N	21.29 E
Manú ≃	118	12.16S	70.51W
Manua Islands II	93	14.13S	169.35W
Manukau	98	37.02S	174.54 E
Manukau Harbour ⊂	98	37.01S	174.44 E
Manus Island I	96a	2.05S	147.00 E
Many	144	31.34N	93.29W
Manyara, Lake ⊜	86	3.35S	35.50 E
Manyč ≃	54	47.15N	40.00 E
Manyoni	86	5.45S	34.50 E
Manzanares	44	39.00N	3.22W
Manzanares ≃	44	40.19N	3.32W
Manzanillo, Cuba	108	20.21N	77.07W
Manzanillo, Méx.	108	19.03N	104.20W
Manzhouli	66	49.35N	117.22 E
Manzini	86	26.30S	31.25 E
Maó	44	39.53N	4.15 E
Maoke, Pegunungan ⋏	68	4.00S	138.00 E
Maoming	66	21.39N	110.54 E
Maouri, Dallol V	82	12.05N	3.32 E
Maple Creek	130	49.55N	109.27W
Maple Lake	138	45.13N	94.00W
Mapleton, Mn., U.S.	138	43.55N	93.57W
Mapleton, Ut., U.S.	148	40.07N	111.34W
Maputo	86	25.58S	32.35 E
Maqueda	44	40.04N	4.22W
Maquoketa	138	42.04N	90.39W
Maquoketa ≃	138	42.11N	90.19W
Mara ≃	86	1.31S	33.56 E
Marabá	118	5.21S	49.07W
Maracá, Ilha de I	118	2.05N	50.25W
Maracaibo	118	10.40N	71.37W
Maracaibo, Lago de ⊜	118	9.50N	71.30W
Maracay	118	10.15N	67.36W
Maradi	82	13.29N	7.06 E
Marāgheh	70	37.23N	46.13 E
Marahuaca, Cerro ∧	118	3.34N	65.27W
Marais des Cygnes ≃	144	38.02N	94.14W
Marajó, Baía de ⊂	118	1.00S	48.30W
Marajó, Ilha de I	118	1.00S	49.30W
Marañón ≃	118	4.30S	73.27W
Maraş	16	37.36N	36.55 E
Marathon, On., Can.	130	48.43N	86.23W
Marathon, Wi., U.S.	138	44.55N	89.50W
Marble Canyon V	148	36.30N	111.50W
Marburg	30	50.49N	8.46 E
Marca, Ponta da ›	86	16.31S	11.42 E
Marcal ≃	30	47.41N	17.32 E
Marcaria	40	45.07N	10.32 E
Marceline	144	39.42N	92.56W
March	26	52.33N	0.06 E
March (Morava) ≃	30	48.10N	16.59 E
Marche □[9]	36	46.05N	2.10 E
Marchena	44	37.20N	5.24W
Mar Chiquita, Laguna ⊜	120	30.42S	62.36W
Marcigny	36	46.17N	4.02 E
Marcy, Mount ∧	136	44.07N	73.56W
Mardān	70	34.12N	72.02 E
Mar del Plata	120	38.00S	57.33W
Maré I	92	21.30S	168.00 E
Mare a Brăilei, Insula I	48	45.00N	28.00 E
Maree, Loch ⊜	26	57.42N	5.30W
Mareeba	96	17.00S	145.26 E
Maremma ◆[1]	40	42.30N	11.30 E
Marengo, Il., U.S.	138	42.14N	88.36W
Marengo, In., U.S.	144	38.22N	86.20W
Marengo, Ia., U.S.	138	41.47N	92.04W
Marettimo, Isola I	40	37.58N	12.03 E
Margarita, Isla de I	118	11.00N	64.00W
Margate, Eng., U.K.	26	51.24N	1.24 E
Margate, Fl., U.S.	142	26.14N	80.12W
Margate City	136	39.19N	74.30W
Margecany	30	48.54N	21.01 E
Margeride, Monts de la ⋏	36	44.50N	3.30 E
Margherita Peak ∧	86	0.22N	29.51 E
Marghita	48	47.21N	22.21 E
Margilan	54	40.28N	71.44 E
Māṛgow, Dasht-e ◆[2]	70	30.45N	63.10 E
María Elena	120	22.21S	69.40W
Maria Gail	30	46.36N	13.52 E
Mariana Islands II	68	16.00N	145.30 E
Marianna, Ar., U.S.	144	34.46N	90.45W
Marianna, Fl., U.S.	142	30.46N	85.13W
Mariánské Lázně	30	49.59N	12.43 E
Marias ≃	150	47.56N	110.30W
Marías, Islas II	108	21.25N	106.28W
Marias Pass)(	150	48.19N	113.21W
Mariato, Punta ›	108	7.13N	80.53W
Maribor	40	46.33N	15.39 E
Marica (Évros) (Meriç) ≃	48	40.52N	26.12 E
Maricopa	154	35.03N	119.24W
Marie Byrd Land ◆[1]	8	80.00S	120.00W
Marie-Galante I	108	15.56N	61.16W
Mariehamn	22	60.06N	19.57 E
Marienbad → Mariánské Lázně	30	49.59N	12.43 E
Mariental	86	24.36S	17.59 E
Mariestad	22	58.43N	13.51 E
Marietta, Ga., U.S.	142	33.57N	84.33W
Marietta, Oh., U.S.	136	39.24N	81.27W
Mariga ≃	82	9.40N	5.55 E
Marignane	36	43.25N	5.13 E
Marília	118	22.13S	49.56W
Marín	44	42.23N	8.42W
Marinduque Island I	68	13.24N	121.58 E
Marine City	138	42.43N	82.29W
Marinette	138	45.06N	87.37W
Maringá	120	23.25S	51.55W
Marino, It.	40	41.46N	12.39 E
Marino, Vanuatu	92	15.00S	168.09 E
Marion, Al., U.S.	144	32.37N	87.19W
Marion, Il., U.S.	144	37.43N	88.55W
Marion, In., U.S.	144	40.33N	85.39W
Marion, Ia., U.S.	138	42.02N	91.35W
Marion, Ky., U.S.	144	37.19N	88.04W
Marion, La., U.S.	144	32.54N	92.14W
Marion, N.C., U.S.	142	35.41N	82.00W
Marion, Oh., U.S.	136	40.35N	83.07W
Marion, S.C., U.S.	142	34.10N	79.24W
Marion, Va., U.S.	142	36.50N	81.30W
Marion, Wi., U.S.	138	44.40N	88.53W
Marion, Lake ⊜[1]	142	33.30N	80.25W
Marionville	144	37.00N	93.38W
Mariposa	154	37.29N	119.57W
Maritime Alps ⋏	36	44.15N	7.10 E
Marka	84	1.43N	44.53 E
Marked Tree	144	35.31N	90.25W
Markermeer ⊜	30	52.33N	5.15 E
Markle	144	40.50N	85.20W
Marks	144	34.15N	90.16W
Marksville	144	31.07N	92.03W
Marktheidenfeld	30	49.50N	9.36 E
Marktredwitz	30	50.00N	12.06 E
Mark Twain Lake ⊜[1]	144	39.30N	91.45W
Marlborough	136	42.20N	71.33W
Marmande	36	44.30N	0.10 E
Marmara, Sea of → Marmara Denizi ⊤[2]	48	40.40N	28.15 E
Marmara Adası I	48	40.38N	27.37 E
Marmara Denizi (Sea of Marmara) ⊤[2]	48	40.40N	28.15 E
Marmara Ereğlisi	48	40.58N	27.57 E
Marmaton ≃	144	38.00N	94.19W
Marmet	136	38.14N	81.34W
Marmolada ∧	30	46.26N	11.51 E
Marne ≃	36	48.49N	2.24 E
Marne au Rhin, Canal de la ≋	36	48.35N	7.47 E
Maroa	118	2.43N	67.33W
Maromokotro ∧	86	14.01S	48.59 E
Marondera	86	18.10S	31.36 E
Maroni ≃	118	5.45N	53.58W
Maros (Mureş) ≃	48	46.15N	20.13 E
Maroua	82	10.36N	14.20 E
Marovoay	86	16.06S	46.39 E
Marquesas Keys II	142	24.34N	82.08W
Marquette	138	46.32N	87.23W
Marquise	36	50.49N	1.42 E
Marquises, Îles II	8	9.00S	139.30W
Marradi	40	44.04N	11.37 E
Marrah, Jabal ∧	84	13.04N	24.21 E
Marrakech	82	31.38N	8.00W
Marree	96	29.39S	138.04 E
Marrero	144	29.53N	90.06W
Marromeu	86	18.20S	35.56 E
Mars	136	40.41N	80.00W
Marsā al-Burayqah	84	30.25N	19.34 E
Marsabit	84	2.20N	37.59 E
Marsala	40	37.48N	12.26 E
Marsā Maṭrūḥ	84	31.21N	27.14 E
Marseille	36	43.18N	5.24 E
Marseilles	138	41.19N	88.42W
Marsfjället ∧	20	65.05N	15.28 E
Marshall, Liber.	82	6.10N	10.23W
Marshall, Ar., U.S.	144	35.54N	92.37W
Marshall, Il., U.S.	144	39.23N	87.41W
Marshall, Mi., U.S.	138	42.16N	84.57W
Marshall, Mo., U.S.	144	39.07N	93.11W
Marshall, Tx., U.S.	144	32.32N	94.22W
Marshall Islands II	8	9.00N	168.00 E
Marshalltown	138	42.02N	92.54W
Marshallville	142	32.27N	83.56W
Marshfield, Mo., U.S.	144	37.20N	92.54W
Marshfield, Wi., U.S.	138	44.40N	90.10W
Mars Hill	142	35.49N	82.32W
Marsh Island I	144	29.35N	91.53W
Marsh Peak ∧	148	40.43N	109.50W
Märsta	22	59.37N	17.51 E
Martaban	68	16.32N	97.37 E
Martaban, Gulf of ⊂	68	16.30N	97.00 E
Martapura	68	3.25S	114.51 E
Martha's Vineyard I	136	41.25N	70.40W
Martigny	36	46.06N	7.04 E
Martigues	36	43.24N	5.03 E
Martil	44	35.37N	5.17W
Martin, Česko.	30	49.05N	18.55 E
Martin, Tn., U.S.	144	36.20N	88.51W
Martín ≃	44	41.18N	0.19W
Martina Franca	40	40.42N	17.21 E
Martinez, Ca., U.S.	154	38.01N	122.07W
Martinez, Ga., U.S.	142	33.31N	82.04W
Martinique □[2]	108	14.40N	61.00W
Martin Lake ⊜[1]	144	32.50N	85.55W
Martinsburg	136	39.27N	77.57W
Martins Ferry	136	40.05N	80.43W
Martinsville, In., U.S.	144	39.25N	86.25W
Martinsville, Va., U.S.	142	36.41N	79.52W
Martin Vaz, Ilhas II	120	20.30S	28.51W
Marton	98	40.05S	175.23 E
Martos	44	37.43N	3.58W
Marum, Mont ∧	92	16.15S	168.07 E
Marungu ⋏	86	7.42S	30.00 E
Marvell	144	34.33N	90.54W
Marvine, Mount ∧	148	38.40N	111.39W
Mary	54	37.36N	61.50 E
Maryborough	96	37.03S	143.45 E
Maryland □[3]	132	39.00N	76.45W
Maryport	26	54.43N	3.30W
Marys ≃	154	41.04N	115.16W
Marysville, Ca., U.S.	154	39.08N	121.35W
Marysville, Mi., U.S.	138	42.54N	82.29W
Marysville, Oh., U.S.	136	40.14N	83.22W
Marysville, Wa., U.S.	150	48.03N	122.10W
Maryville, Mo., U.S.	144	40.20N	94.52W
Maryville, Tn., U.S.	142	35.45N	83.58W
Marzūq	84	25.55N	13.55 E
Marzūq, Ṣaḥrā' ◆[2]	84	24.30N	13.00 E
Masai Steppe ⋏[1]	86	4.45S	37.00 E
Masaka	86	0.20S	31.44 E
Masan	66	35.11N	128.32 E
Masaya	108	11.58N	86.06W
Masbate	68	12.22N	123.36 E
Masbate Island I	68	12.15N	123.30 E
Mascarene Islands II	86	21.00S	57.00 E
Mascoutah	144	38.29N	89.47W
Maseru	86	29.28S	27.30 E
Mashābih I	70	25.37N	36.29 E
Mashhad	70	36.18N	59.36 E
Māshkel, Hāmūn-i- ⊜	70	28.15N	63.00 E
Mashra'ur-Raqq	84	8.25N	29.16 E
Masindi	86	1.41N	31.43 E
Maṣīrah, Khalīj al- ⊂	70	20.10N	58.15 E
Masjed Soleymān	70	31.58N	49.18 E
Mask, Lough ⊜	26	53.35N	9.20W
Masoala, Presqu'île de ›[1]	86	15.40S	50.12 E
Mason, Mi., U.S.	138	42.34N	84.26W
Mason, Oh., U.S.	136	39.21N	84.18W
Mason, Tn., U.S.	144	35.24N	89.31W
Mason City, Il., U.S.	144	40.12N	89.41W
Mason City, Ia., U.S.	138	43.09N	93.12W
Masqaṭ (Muscat)	70	23.37N	58.35 E
Massa	40	44.01N	10.09 E
Massachusetts □[3]	132	42.15N	71.50W
Massachusetts Bay ⊂	136	42.20N	70.50W
Massafra	40	40.35N	17.07 E
Massa Marittima	40	43.03N	10.53 E
Massarosa	40	43.52N	10.20 E
Massawa → Mitsiwa	84	15.38N	39.28 E
Massena	136	44.55N	74.53W
Massiac	36	45.15N	3.12 E
Massillon	136	40.48N	81.32W
Massina ◆[1]	82	14.30N	5.00W
Massive, Mount ∧	148	39.12N	106.28W
Masterton	98	40.57S	175.40 E
Masvingo	86	20.05S	30.50 E
Mat ≃	48	41.39N	19.34 E
Matachel ≃	44	38.50N	6.17W
Matadi	86	5.49S	13.27 E
Matagalpa	108	12.55N	85.55W
Matagami	130	49.45N	77.38W
Matamata	98	37.49S	175.47 E
Matamoros	108	25.53N	97.30W
Matandu ≃	86	8.45S	39.19 E
Matane	130	48.51N	67.32W
Matanzas	108	23.03N	81.35W
Mataram	68	8.35S	116.07 E
Mataró	44	41.32N	2.27 E
Matatula, Cape ›	93	14.15S	170.34W
Mataura ≃	98	46.34S	168.43 E
Matāutu	93	13.57S	171.56W
Matavera	94	21.13S	159.44W
Matehuala	108	23.39N	100.39W
Matelica	40	43.15N	13.00 E
Matera	40	40.40N	16.37 E
Mateur	40	37.03N	9.40 E
Matewan	142	37.37N	82.09W
Mather	136	39.56N	80.04W
Mathura	70	27.30N	77.41 E
Matlock	26	53.08N	1.32W
Mato, Cerro ∧	118	7.15N	65.14W
Matočkin Šar, proliv Ʉ	54	73.20N	55.21 E
Mato Grosso, Planalto do ⋏[1]	118	15.30S	56.00W
Matosinhos	44	41.11N	8.42W
Matoury	118	4.51N	52.20W
Mátra ⋏	30	47.55N	20.00 E
Maṭraḥ	70	23.38N	58.34 E
Matsu → Matsu Tao I	66	26.09N	119.56 E
Matsue	66	35.28N	133.04 E
Matsumoto	66	36.14N	137.58 E
Matsu Tao I	66	26.09N	119.56 E
Matsuyama	66	33.50N	132.45 E
Mattagami ≃	130	50.43N	81.29W
Mattawa	130	46.19N	78.42W
Matterhorn ∧, Europe	36	45.59N	7.43 E
Matterhorn ∧, Nv., U.S.	154	41.49N	115.23W
Mattoon, Il., U.S.	144	39.28N	88.22W
Mattoon, Wi., U.S.	138	45.00N	89.02W
Mattydale	136	43.05N	76.08W
Maturín	118	9.45N	63.11W
Maubeuge	36	50.17N	3.58 E
Ma-ubin	68	16.44N	95.39 E
Mauga Silisili ∧	93	13.35S	172.27W
Maui I	132b	20.45N	156.15W
Mauldin	142	34.46N	82.18W
Maumee	136	41.33N	83.39W
Maumee ≃	136	41.42N	83.28W
Maun	86	20.00S	23.25 E
Mauna Kea ∧[1]	132b	19.50N	155.28W
Mauna Loa ∧[1]	132b	19.29N	155.36W
Maurepas, Lake ⊜	144	30.15N	90.30W
Maures ⋏	36	43.16N	6.23 E
Mauriac	36	45.13N	2.20 E
Mauritania (Mauritanie) □[1]	82	20.00N	12.00W
Mauritius □[1]	86	20.17S	57.33 E
Mauston	138	43.47N	90.04W
Mauthausen	30	48.14N	14.32 E
Maxwell	154	39.16N	122.11W
May, Cape ›[1]	136	38.58N	74.55W
Mayaguana I	108	22.23N	72.57W
Mayagüez	108	18.12N	67.09W
Mayen	30	50.19N	7.13 E
Mayenne	36	48.18N	0.37W
Mayenne ≃	36	47.30N	0.33W
Mayfield	144	36.44N	88.38W
Maymyo	68	22.02N	96.28 E
Maynard	138	42.46N	91.52W
Mayo, Yk., Can.	130	63.35N	135.54W
Mayo, Fl., U.S.	142	30.03N	83.10W
Mayo □[6]	26	53.54N	9.15W
Mayodan	142	36.24N	79.58W
Mayon Volcano ∧[1]	68	13.15N	123.41 E
Mayor Island I	98	37.18S	176.16 E
Mayotte □[2]	86	12.50S	45.10 E
Mays Landing	136	39.27N	74.43W
Maysville	136	38.38N	83.44W
Mayville, N.D., U.S.	132	47.29N	97.19W
Mayville, Wi., U.S.	138	43.29N	88.32W
Mazabuka	86	15.51S	27.46 E
Mazamet	36	43.30N	2.24 E
Mazara, Val di ◆[1]	40	37.50N	13.00 E
Mazara del Vallo	40	37.39N	12.35 E
Mazār-e Sharīf	70	36.42N	67.06 E
Mazaruni ≃	118	6.25N	58.38W
Mazatenango	108	14.32N	91.30W
Mazatlán	108	23.13N	106.25W
Mazatzal Peak ∧	148	34.03N	111.28W
Mazoe ≃	86	16.32S	33.25 E
Mazon	138	41.14N	88.25W
Mazury ◆[1]	30	53.45N	21.00 E
Mba	91	17.33S	177.41 E
Mbabane	86	26.18S	31.06 E
Mbaïki	84	3.53N	18.00 E
Mbala	86	8.50S	31.22 E
Mbale	86	1.05N	34.10 E
Mbamba Bay	86	11.17S	34.46 E
Mbandaka (Coquilhatville)	86	0.04N	18.16 E
Mbanza-Ngungu	86	5.15S	14.52 E
Mbarara	86	0.37S	30.39 E
Mbari ≃	84	4.34N	22.43 E
Mbeya	86	8.54S	33.27 E
Mbini	82	1.35N	9.37 E
Mbomou (Bomu) ≃	84	4.08N	22.26 E
Mbout	82	16.02N	12.35W
Mbuji-Mayi (Bakwanga)	86	6.09S	23.38 E
M'Clintock Channel Ʉ	130	72.00N	102.00W
M'Clure Strait Ʉ	130	74.30N	116.00W
Mead, Lake ⊜[1]	148	36.05N	114.25W
Meaden Peak ∧	148	40.46N	107.03W
Meade Peak ∧	150	42.30N	111.15W
Meadow Valley Wash V	154	36.39N	114.35W
Meadville	136	41.38N	80.09W
Meath □[6]	26	53.35N	6.40W
Meath □[9]	26	53.40N	7.00W
Meaux	36	48.57N	2.52 E
Mebane	142	36.05N	79.16W
Mecca → Makkah	70	21.27N	39.49 E
Mechanic Falls	136	44.06N	70.23W
Mechanicsburg	136	40.04N	83.33W
Mechanicsville	142	37.36N	77.22W
Mechanicville	136	42.54N	73.41W
Mechelen	30	51.02N	4.28 E
Mechra Safsaf	44	34.52N	2.36W
Mecklenburg □[9]	30	53.30N	13.00 E
Mecklenburger Bucht ⊂	30	54.20N	11.40 E
Mecsek ⋏	30	46.15N	18.05 E
Medan	68	3.35N	98.40 E
Medanosa, Punta ›	120	48.06S	65.55W
Medaryville	144	41.04N	86.53W
Medellín	118	6.15N	75.35W
Médenine	82	33.21N	10.30 E

Symbols in the index entries are identified on page 162.

Name	Page	Lat.	Long.
Medford, Or., U.S.	150	42.19N	122.52W
Medford, Wi., U.S.	138	45.08N	90.20W
Medgidia	48	44.15N	28.16 E
Mediapolis	138	41.00N	91.09W
Mediaș	48	46.10N	24.21 E
Medical Lake	150	47.34N	117.40W
Medicina	40	44.28N	11.38 E
Medicine Bow ≐	148	42.00N	106.40W
Medicine Bow Mountains ⋏	148	41.10N	106.10W
Medicine Bow Peak ʌ	148	41.21N	106.19W
Medicine Hat	130	50.03N	110.40W
Medina, N.Y., U.S.	136	43.13N	78.23W
Medina, Oh., U.S.	136	41.08N	81.51W
Medina del Campo	44	41.18N	4.55W
Medina de Rioseco	44	41.53N	5.02W
Mediterranean Sea ᵹ2	16	36.00N	15.00 E
Medjerda, Monts de la ⋏	40	36.35N	8.15 E
Medkovec	48	43.37N	23.10 E
Médoc ◆1	36	45.20N	1.00W
Medvedica ≐	54	49.35N	42.41 E
Medvežji ostrova II	56	70.52N	161.26 E
Medway ≐	26	51.27N	0.44 E
Medynskij Zavorot, mys ⟩	20	68.58N	59.17 E
Medzilaborce	30	49.16N	21.55 E
Meekatharra	96	26.36S	118.29 E
Meerane	30	50.51N	12.28 E
Meerut	70	28.59N	77.42 E
Mégara	48	38.01N	23.21 E
Meghna ≐	70	22.50N	90.50 E
Meharry, Mount ʌ	96	22.59S	118.35 E
Meiktila	68	20.52N	95.52 E
Meiningen	30	50.34N	10.25 E
Meiringen	36	46.43N	8.12 E
Meissen	30	51.10N	13.28 E
Meixian	66	24.21N	116.08 E
Mejerda, Oued (Oued Medjerda) ≐	40	37.07N	10.13 E
Mejez el Bab	40	36.39N	9.37 E
Mekele	84	13.33N	39.30 E
Meknès	82	33.53N	5.37W
Mekong ≐	68	10.33N	105.24 E
Mékrou ≐	82	12.24N	2.49 E
Melaka (Malacca)	68	2.12N	102.15 E
Melanesia II	8	13.00S	164.00 E
Melbourne, Austl.	96	37.49S	144.58 E
Melbourne, Fl., U.S.	142	28.04N	80.36W
Melegnano	40	45.21N	9.19 E
Melfi	40	41.00N	15.39 E
Melfort	130	52.52N	104.36W
Melghir, Chott ◎	82	34.20N	6.20 E
Meliane, Oued ≐	40	36.46N	10.18 E
Melilla	82	35.19N	2.58W
Melitopol'	54	46.50N	35.22 E
Mellègue, Oued ≐	40	36.32N	8.51 E
Mělník	30	50.20N	14.29 E
Melo	120	32.22S	54.11W
Melos → Mílos I	48	36.41N	24.15 E
Melton Hill Lake ◎1	142	36.00N	84.15W
Melton Mowbray	26	52.46N	0.53W
Melun	36	48.32N	2.40 E
Melville, Sk., Can.	130	50.55N	102.48W
Melville, La., U.S.	144	30.41N	91.44W
Melville, Cape ⟩	96	14.11S	144.30 E
Melville, Lake ◎	130	53.45N	59.30W
Melville Island I, Austl.	96	11.40S	131.00 E
Melville Island I, N.T., Can.	130	75.15N	110.00W
Melville Peninsula ⟩1	130	68.00N	84.00W
Melville Sound ␣	130	68.05N	107.30W
Melvin	142	37.21N	82.41W
Melvin, Lough ◎	26	54.26N	8.10W
Mélykút	30	46.13N	19.24 E
Melzo	40	45.30N	9.25 E
Memel → Klaipėda	20	55.43N	21.07 E
Memel → Nemunas ≐	54	55.18N	21.23 E
Memmingen	30	47.59N	10.11 E
Memphis, Fl., U.S.	142	27.32N	82.33W
Memphis, Mi., U.S.	138	42.54N	82.46W
Memphis, Mo., U.S.	144	40.27N	92.10W
Memphis, Tn., U.S.	144	35.08N	90.02W
Memphremagog, Lake ◎	136	45.05N	72.15W
Mena	144	34.35N	94.14W
Menai Bridge	26	53.14N	4.10W
Ménaka	82	15.55N	2.24 E
Menasha	138	44.12N	88.26W
Mende	36	44.30N	3.30 E
Menden	30	51.26N	7.47 E
Mendenhall	144	31.57N	89.52W
Mendip Hills ⋏2	26	51.15N	2.40W
Mendocino	154	39.18N	123.47W
Mendocino, Cape ⟩	154	40.25N	124.25W
Mendota, Ca., U.S.	154	36.45N	120.22W
Mendota, Il., U.S.	138	41.32N	89.07W
Mendoza	120	32.53S	68.49W
Ménéac	36	48.09N	2.28W
Menemen	48	38.36N	27.04 E
Menén	30	50.48N	3.07 E
Menfi	40	37.36N	12.58 E
Menggala	68	4.28S	105.17 E
Mengzi	66	23.22N	103.20 E
Menlo Park	154	37.27N	122.10W
Menominee	138	45.06N	87.36W
Menominee ≐	138	45.05N	87.36W
Menomonee Falls	138	43.10N	88.07W
Menomonie	138	44.52N	91.55W
Menongue	86	14.36S	17.48 E
Menor, Mar ⊂	44	37.43N	0.48W
Menorca I	44	40.00N	4.00 E
Mentawai, Kepulauan II	68	2.00S	99.30 E
Mentawai, Selat ␣	68	1.56S	100.12 E
Menton	36	43.47N	7.30 E
Mentor	136	41.39N	81.20W
Menzel Bourguiba	82	37.10N	9.48 E
Menzel Bou Zelfa	40	36.41N	10.36 E
Menzel Temime	40	36.47N	10.59 E
Menzies	96	29.41S	121.02 E
Meppel	30	52.42N	6.11 E
Meppen	30	52.41N	7.17 E
Meqerghane, Sebkha ≐	82	26.19N	1.20 E
Mequinenza, Embalse de ◎1	44	41.20N	0.05 E
Mequon	138	43.13N	87.59W
Meramec ≐	144	38.23N	90.21W
Merano (Meran)	40	46.40N	11.09 E
Mercato Saraceno	40	43.57N	12.12 E
Merced	154	37.18N	120.28W
Merced ≐	154	37.21N	120.58W
Mercedes, Arg.	120	33.40S	65.28W
Mercedes, Ur.	120	33.16S	58.01W
Mercer, Mo., U.S.	144	40.30N	93.31W
Mercer, Pa., U.S.	136	41.13N	80.14W
Mercer, Wi., U.S.	138	46.09N	90.03W
Mercury Islands II	98	36.35S	175.55 E
Mercy, Cape ⟩	130	64.53N	63.32W
Meredith	136	43.39N	71.30W
Meredosia	144	39.50N	90.34W
Merenkurkku (Norra Kvarken) ␣	22	63.36N	20.43 E
Mergui	68	12.26N	98.36 E
Mergui Archipelago II	68	12.00N	98.00 E
Meriç (Marica) (Évros) ≐	48	40.52N	26.12 E
Mérida, Esp.	44	38.55N	6.20W
Mérida, Méx.	108	20.58N	89.37W
Mérida, Ven.	118	8.36N	71.08W
Mérida, Cordillera de ⋏	118	8.40N	71.00W
Meriden	136	41.32N	72.48W
Meridian, Ga., U.S.	142	31.27N	81.22W
Meridian, Id., U.S.	150	43.36N	116.23W
Meridian, Ms., U.S.	144	32.21N	88.42W
Meridianville	144	34.51N	86.34W
Mérignac	36	44.50N	0.42W
Merkendorf	30	49.12N	10.42 E
Merrill	138	45.10N	89.41W
Merrillville	144	41.28N	87.19W
Merrimack ≐	136	42.49N	70.49W
Merritt	130	50.07N	120.47W
Merritt Island	142	28.21N	80.42W
Mer Rouge	144	32.46N	91.47W
Mersea Island I	26	51.47N	0.55 E
Merseburg	30	51.21N	11.59 E
Mersin	16	36.48N	34.38 E
Merthyr Tydfil	26	51.46N	3.23W
Mértola	44	37.38N	7.40W
Meru, Mount ʌ	86	3.14S	36.45 E
Méry	36	48.30N	3.53 E
Merzig	30	49.27N	6.36 E
Mesa	148	33.25N	111.49W
Mesa ≐	44	41.15N	1.48W
Mesabi Range ⋏2	138	47.30N	92.50W
Mesagne	40	40.33N	17.49 E
Mesa Mountain ʌ	148	37.55N	106.38W
Mesa Verde National Park ♦	148	37.13N	108.30W
Meschede	30	51.20N	8.17 E
Mesilla	148	32.16N	106.48W
Mesolóngion	48	38.21N	21.17 E
Mesopotamia ◻9	70	34.00N	44.00 E
Messalo ≐	86	11.40S	40.26 E
Messina, It.	40	38.11N	15.33 E
Messina, S. Afr.	86	22.23S	30.00 E
Messina, Stretto di ␣	40	38.15N	15.35 E
Messini	48	37.04N	22.00 E
Mesta (Néstos) ≐	48	40.41N	24.44 E
Mestghanem	82	35.51N	0.07 E
Mestre	40	45.29N	12.15 E
Meta ≐	118	6.12N	67.28W
Metairie	144	29.59N	90.09W
Metallifere, Colline ⋏	40	43.15N	11.00 E
Meteor Crater ◆6	148	35.02N	111.02W
Methven	98	43.38S	171.39 E
Metković	48	43.03N	17.39 E
Meto, Bayou ≐	144	34.05N	91.26W
Metropolis	144	37.09N	88.43W
Metter	142	32.23N	82.03W
Mettmann	30	51.15N	6.58 E
Metz	36	49.08N	6.10 E
Metzingen	30	48.32N	9.17 E
Meurthe ≐	36	48.47N	6.09 E
Meuse (Maas) ≐	30	51.49N	5.01 E
Mexiana, Ilha I	118	0.02S	49.35W
Mexicali	108	32.40N	115.29W
Mexican Hat	148	37.09N	109.52W
Mexico, Me., U.S.	136	44.33N	70.32W
Mexico, Mo., U.S.	144	39.10N	91.52W
Mexico, N.Y., U.S.	136	43.27N	76.13W
Mexico (México) ◻1	108	23.00N	102.00W
Mexico, Gulf of ⊂	108	25.00N	90.00W
Mexico Bay ⊂	136	43.31N	76.17W
Mexico Beach	142	29.58N	85.24W
Mexico City → Ciudad de México	108	19.24N	99.09W
Meymaneh	70	35.55N	64.47 E
Mèze	36	43.25N	3.36 E
Mezen' ≐	54	66.11N	43.59 E
Mezenskaja guba ⊂	20	66.40N	43.45 E
Mezőberény	30	46.50N	21.02 E
Mezőkövesd	30	47.50N	20.34 E
Mezőtúr	30	47.00N	20.38 E
Mezzolombardo	40	46.13N	11.05 E
M'goun, Irhil ʌ	82	31.31N	6.25W
Miajadas	44	39.09N	5.54W
Miami, Az., U.S.	148	33.23N	110.52W
Miami, Fl., U.S.	142	25.46N	80.11W
Miami, Ok., U.S.	144	36.52N	94.52W
Miami Beach	142	25.47N	80.07W
Miami Canal ⩧	142	25.47N	80.15W
Miamisburg	136	39.38N	84.17W
Miami Springs	142	25.49N	80.17W
Miandrivazo	86	19.31S	45.28 E
Mianyang	66	30.23N	113.25 E
Miass	54	54.59N	60.06 E
Miastko	30	54.01N	17.00 E
Mica Mountain ʌ	148	32.13N	110.33W
Michalovce	30	48.45N	21.55 E
Michigamme ≐	138	46.04N	88.13W
Michigan ◻3	132	44.00N	85.00W
Michigan, Lake ◎	138	44.00N	87.00W
Michigan Center	138	42.13N	84.19W
Michigan City	144	41.42N	86.53W
Michipicoten Island I	130	47.45N	85.45W
Micronesia II	8	11.00N	159.00 E
Micronesia, Federated States of ◻2	68	8.30N	142.00 E
Mičurinsk	54	52.54N	40.30 E
Midar	44	34.58N	3.30W
Middelburg	30	51.30N	3.37 E
Middelfart	22	55.30N	9.45 E
Middle Alkali Lake ◎	154	41.28N	120.04W
Middle Andaman I	70	12.30N	92.50 E
Middleboro	136	41.53N	70.54W
Middlebury	136	44.00N	73.10W
Middlefield	136	41.27N	81.04W
Middle Point	136	40.51N	84.27W
Middlesboro	142	36.36N	83.43W
Middlesbrough	26	54.35N	1.14W
Middleton, Tn., U.S.	144	35.03N	88.53W
Middleton, Wi., U.S.	138	43.05N	89.30W
Middletown, Ct., U.S.	136	41.33N	72.39W
Middletown, De., U.S.	136	39.26N	75.43W
Middletown, In., U.S.	144	40.03N	85.32W
Middletown, Ky., U.S.	144	38.14N	85.32W
Middletown, Md., U.S.	136	39.26N	77.32W
Middletown, N.Y., U.S.	136	41.26N	74.25W
Middletown, Oh., U.S.	136	39.30N	84.23W
Middletown, R.I., U.S.	136	41.32N	71.17W
Middleville	138	42.42N	85.27W
Mid Glamorgan ◻6	26	51.40N	3.30W
Midi, Canal du ⩧	36	43.36N	1.58 E
Midi de Bigorre, Pic du ʌ	36	42.56N	0.08 E
Midland, On., Can.	130	44.45N	79.53W
Midland, Mi., U.S.	138	43.36N	84.14W
Midland, N.C., U.S.	142	35.13N	80.30W
Midland, Tx., U.S.	132	31.59N	102.04W
Midnapore	70	22.26N	87.20 E
Midou ≐	36	43.54N	0.30W
Midville	142	32.49N	82.14W
Midway, Al., U.S.	144	32.04N	85.31W
Midway, Ky., U.S.	136	38.09N	84.41W
Midway Islands ◻2	8	28.13N	177.22W
Międzylesie	30	50.10N	16.40 E
Międzyrzec Podlaski	30	52.00N	22.47 E
Międzyrzecz	30	52.28N	15.35 E
Mielec	30	50.18N	21.25 E
Mielno	30	54.16N	16.01 E
Miercurea-Ciuc	48	46.22N	25.48 E
Mieres	44	43.15N	5.46W
Mifflinburg	136	40.55N	77.02W
Miguel Alemán, Presa ◎1	108	18.13N	96.32W
Mihăești	48	45.07N	25.00 E
Mihai Viteazu	48	44.39N	28.41 E
Mihajlovgrad	48	43.25N	23.13 E
Mikindani	86	10.17S	40.07 E
Mikkeli	22	61.41N	27.15 E
Mikkwa ≐	130	58.25N	114.45W
Mikołów	30	50.11N	18.55 E
Míkonos I	48	37.29N	25.25 E
Mikulov	30	48.49N	16.39 E
Mikumi	86	7.24S	36.59 E
Milagro	118	2.07S	79.36W
Milan → Milano, It.	40	45.28N	9.12 E
Milan, In., U.S.	144	39.07N	85.07W
Milan, Mi., U.S.	138	42.05N	83.40W
Milan, Mo., U.S.	144	40.12N	93.07W
Milan, N.M., U.S.	148	35.10N	107.53W
Milan, Tn., U.S.	144	35.55N	88.45W
Milano (Milan)	40	45.28N	9.12 E
Milâs	48	37.19N	27.47 E
Milazzo	40	38.13N	15.14 E
Milbank	132	45.13N	96.38W
Miles City	150	46.24N	105.50W
Miletto, Monte ʌ	40	41.27N	14.22 E
Milford, Ct., U.S.	136	41.13N	73.04W
Milford, De., U.S.	136	38.54N	75.25W
Milford, In., U.S.	144	41.24N	85.50W
Milford, Me., U.S.	136	44.56N	68.38W
Milford, Ma., U.S.	136	42.08N	71.31W
Milford, Mi., U.S.	138	42.35N	83.35W
Milford, N.H., U.S.	136	42.50N	71.38W
Milford, N.J., U.S.	136	40.34N	75.05W
Milford, Pa., U.S.	136	41.19N	74.48W
Milford Haven	26	51.40N	5.02W
Milford Sound ␣	98	44.35S	167.47 E
Milk ≐	132	48.05N	106.15W
Millau	36	44.06N	3.05 E
Millcreek, Pa., U.S.	136	42.05N	80.10W
Millcreek, Ut., U.S.	148	40.27N	111.54W
Milledgeville	142	33.04N	83.13W
Mille Lacs, Lac des ◎	130	48.50N	90.30W
Mille Lacs Lake ◎	138	46.15N	93.40W
Millen	142	32.48N	81.56W
Miller, Mo., U.S.	144	37.13N	93.50W
Miller, S.D., U.S.	132	44.31N	98.59W
Miller Peak ʌ	148	31.23N	110.17W
Millersburg, Ky., U.S.	136	38.18N	84.08W
Millersburg, Pa., U.S.	136	40.32N	76.57W
Millersville	136	39.59N	76.21W
Millevaches, Plateau de ⋏1	36	45.30N	2.10 E
Mill Hall	136	41.06N	77.29W
Milligan	144	30.45N	86.38W
Millington	144	35.20N	89.53W
Millinocket	136	45.39N	68.42W
Mills	150	42.50N	106.21W
Mill Valley	154	37.54N	122.32W
Millville	136	39.24N	75.02W
Millwood Lake ◎1	144	33.45N	94.00W
Milo, Ia., U.S.	138	41.17N	93.26W
Milo, Me., U.S.	136	45.15N	68.59W
Mílos I	48	36.41N	24.15 E
Milpitas	154	37.25N	121.54W
Milroy	136	40.42N	77.35W
Milton, N.Z.	98	46.07S	169.58 E
Milton, De., U.S.	136	38.46N	75.18W
Milton, Fl., U.S.	144	30.37N	87.02W
Milton, Pa., U.S.	136	41.00N	76.50W
Milton, Vt., U.S.	136	44.38N	73.06W
Milton, Wi., U.S.	138	42.46N	88.56W
Milton-Freewater	150	45.55N	118.23W
Milwaukee	138	43.02N	87.54W
Milwaukie	150	45.26N	122.38W
Mimbres Mountains ⋏	148	32.45N	107.45W
Mimizan	36	44.12N	1.14W
Mims	142	28.39N	80.50W
Minahasa ⟩1	68	1.00N	124.35 E
Minas	120	34.23S	55.14W
Minatitlán	108	17.59N	94.31W
Minčol ʌ	30	49.15N	20.59 E
Mindanao I	68	8.00N	125.00 E
Mindanao Sea ᵹ2	68	9.10N	124.25 E
Mindelo	82	16.53N	25.00W
Minden, B.R.D.	30	52.17N	8.55 E
Minden, La., U.S.	144	32.36N	93.17W
Minden, Nv., U.S.	154	38.57N	119.45W
Minden, W.V., U.S.	142	37.58N	81.07W
Mindoro I	68	12.50N	121.05 E
Mindoro Strait ␣	68	12.20N	120.40 E
Mineral	150	46.43N	122.10W
Mineral'nyje Vody	54	44.12N	43.08 E
Mineral Point	138	42.51N	90.10W
Mineral Springs	144	33.52N	93.54W
Mineral Wells	132	32.48N	98.06W
Minersville	136	40.41N	76.16W
Minerva	136	40.43N	81.06W
Minervino Murge	40	41.05N	16.05 E
Mingo Junction	136	40.19N	80.36W
Minho ◻9	44	41.40N	8.30W
Minho (Miño) ≐	44	41.52N	8.51W
Minna	82	9.37N	6.33 E
Minneapolis	138	44.58N	93.15W
Minnehaha	150	45.39N	122.37W
Minnesota ◻3	132	46.00N	94.15W
Minnesota ≐	138	44.54N	93.10W
Miño (Minho) ≐	44	41.52N	8.51W
Minocqua	138	45.52N	89.42W
Minonk	144	40.54N	89.02W
Minorca → Menorca I	44	40.00N	4.00 E
Minot	132	48.13N	101.17W
Minquiers, Plateau des II	36	48.57N	2.09W
Minsk	54	53.54N	27.34 E
Mińsk Mazowiecki	30	52.11N	21.34 E
Minster	136	40.24N	84.22W
Minto, Lac ◎	130	57.13N	75.00W
Minturno	40	41.15N	13.45 E
Minxian	66	34.26N	104.02 E
Minya Konka → Gongga Shan ʌ	66	29.35N	101.51 E
Mio	138	44.39N	84.07W
Mira ≐	44	37.43N	8.47W
Miraflores	118	5.12N	73.12W
Miraj	70	16.50N	74.38 E
Miramar	120	38.16S	57.51W
Miramichi Bay ⊂	130	47.08N	65.08W
Miranda de Ebro	44	42.41N	2.57W
Mirandola	40	44.53N	11.04 E
Mira Taglio	40	45.26N	12.08 E
Miravete, Puerto de)(	44	39.43N	5.43W
Miri	68	4.23N	113.59 E
Mirim, Lagoa (Laguna Merín) ⊂	120	32.45S	52.50W
Miroslav	30	48.57N	16.18 E
Mīrpur Khās	70	25.32N	69.00 E
Mirtóön Pélagos ᵹ2	48	36.51N	23.18 E
Mirzāpur	70	25.09N	82.35 E
Misāhah, Bi'r ᵹ4	84	22.12N	27.57 E
Misenheimer	142	35.29N	80.17W
Mishawaka	144	41.39N	86.09W
Mishicot	138	44.14N	87.38W
Mishmi Hills ⋏2	70	29.00N	96.00 E
Misilmeri	40	38.02N	13.27 E
Miskitos, Cayos II	108	14.23N	82.46W
Miskolc	30	48.06N	20.47 E
Misool, Pulau I	68	1.52S	130.10 E
Misrātah	84	32.23N	15.06 E
Misserghin	44	35.37N	0.45W
Missinaibi ≐	130	50.44N	81.29W
Mission Viejo	154	33.36N	117.40W
Mississinewa ≐	144	40.46N	86.02W
Mississippi ◻3	132	32.50N	89.30W
Mississippi ≐, On., Can.	138	45.26N	76.16W
Mississippi ≐, U.S.	132	29.00N	89.15W
Mississippi Delta ≐2	144	29.10N	89.15W
Mississippi Sound ␣	144	30.15N	88.40W
Mississippi State	144	33.26N	88.47W
Missoula	150	46.52N	113.59W
Missouri ◻3	132	38.30N	93.30W
Missouri ≐	132	38.50N	90.08W
Missouri City	144	29.37N	95.32W
Missouri Valley	144	41.33N	95.53W
Mistassini	130	50.25N	73.52W
Mistassini, Lac ◎	130	51.00N	73.37W
Misterbianco	40	37.31N	15.00 E
Misti, Volcán ʌ1	118	16.18S	71.24W
Mistretta	40	37.56N	14.22 E
Mita, Punta ⟩	108	20.47N	105.33W
Mitchell, In., U.S.	144	38.43N	86.28W
Mitchell, S.D., U.S.	132	43.42N	98.01W
Mitchell ≐	96	15.12S	141.35 E
Mitchell, Mount ʌ	142	35.46N	82.16W
Mitidja, Plaine de la ≐	44	36.45N	3.00 E
Mitilíni	48	39.06N	26.32 E
Mito	66	36.22N	140.28 E
Mitsio, Nosy I	86	12.54S	48.36 E
Mitsiwa	84	15.38N	39.28 E
Mittellandkanal ⩧	30	52.16N	11.41 E
Mittweida	30	50.59N	12.59 E
Mitumba, Monts ⋏	86	6.00S	29.00 E
Miyako	66	39.38N	141.57 E
Miyakonojō	66	31.44N	131.04 E
Miyazaki	66	31.54N	131.26 E
Mize	144	31.52N	89.33W
Mizen Head ⟩	26	51.27N	9.49W
Mizque	118	17.56S	65.19W
Mjölby	22	58.19N	15.08 E
Mjøsa ◎	22	60.40N	11.00 E
Mkalama	86	4.07S	34.38 E
Mladá Boleslav	30	50.23N	14.59 E
Mlanje Peak → Sapitwa ʌ	86	15.57S	35.36 E
Mława	30	53.06N	20.23 E
Mljet, Otok I	40	42.45N	17.30 E
Mljetski Kanal ␣	40	42.48N	17.35 E
Mmabatho	86	25.51S	25.38 E
Mo	20	66.15N	14.08 E
Moa ≐	82	6.59N	11.36W
Moab	148	38.34N	109.32W
Moala Island I	91	18.36S	179.53 E
Mobaye	84	4.19N	21.11 E
Moberly	144	39.25N	92.26W
Mobile	144	30.41N	88.02W
Mobile ≐	144	30.29N	88.01W
Mobile Bay ⊂	144	30.25N	88.00W
Mobridge	132	45.32N	100.25W
Moçambique	86	15.03S	40.45 E
Moçambique → Mozambique ◻1	86	18.15S	35.00 E
Mocha → Al-Mukhā	70	13.19N	43.15 E
Mochudi	86	24.28S	26.05 E
Möckeln ◎	22	56.40N	14.10 E
Mocksville	142	35.53N	80.33W
Môco, Serra ʌ	86	12.28S	15.10 E
Močurica ≐	48	42.31N	26.32 E
Modder ≐	86	29.02S	24.37 E
Modena	40	44.40N	10.55 E
Modesto	154	37.38N	120.59W
Modica	40	36.52N	14.46 E
Mödling	30	48.05N	16.17 E
Modra	30	48.21N	17.17 E
Modra Špilja ◆5	40	43.00N	16.02 E
Modriča	48	44.57N	18.18 E
Moe	96	38.10S	146.15 E
Moerewa	98	35.23S	174.02 E
Moers	30	51.27N	6.37 E
Moffat Peak ʌ	98	45.02S	168.07 E
Mogadiscio → Muqdisho	84	2.04N	45.22 E
Mogadishu → Muqdisho	84	2.04N	45.22 E
Mogi das Cruzes	118	23.31S	46.11W
Mogielnica	30	51.42N	20.43 E
Mogilev → Mogil'ov	54	53.54N	30.21 E
Mogil'ov	54	53.54N	30.21 E
Mogil'ov-Podol'skij	54	48.27N	27.48 E
Mogliano Veneto	40	45.33N	12.14 E
Mogollon Rim ≐4	148	34.25N	110.50W
Mogotón, Pico ʌ	108	13.45N	86.23W
Moguer	44	37.16N	6.50W
Mohács	30	45.59N	18.42 E
Mohammedia	82	33.44N	7.24W
Mohave, Lake ◎1	154	35.25N	114.38W
Mohawk ≐	136	42.47N	73.42W
Mohawk Mountain ʌ	136	41.49N	73.17W
Moinești	48	46.28N	26.29 E
Mojave	154	35.03N	118.10W
Mojave ≐	154	35.06N	116.04W
Mojave Desert ◆2	154	35.00N	117.00W
Moji-Guaçu ≐	118	20.53S	48.10W
Mokelumne ≐	154	38.13N	121.28W
Moknine	40	35.38N	10.54 E
Mokp'o	66	34.48N	126.22 E
Mokrisset	44	35.29N	5.20W
Mokša ≐	54	54.44N	41.53 E
Mol	30	51.11N	5.06 E
Mola di Bari	40	41.04N	17.05 E
Molat, Otok I	40	44.15N	14.49 E
Moldau → Vltava ≐	30	50.21N	14.30 E
Moldavia → Moldavskaja Sovetskaja Socialističeskaja Respublika ◻3	54	47.00N	29.00 E
Moldavia ◻9	48	47.00N	27.15 E
Moldavskaja Sovetskaja Socialističeskaja Respublika ◻3	54	47.00N	29.00 E
Molde	22	62.44N	7.11 E
Moldova ≐	48	46.54N	26.58 E
Moldova Nouă	48	44.44N	21.40 E
Moldoveanu, Vîrful ʌ	48	45.36N	24.44 E
Molepolole	86	24.25S	25.30 E
Molfetta	40	41.12N	16.36 E
Molina de Segura	44	38.03N	1.12W
Moline	138	41.30N	90.30W
Molinella	40	44.37N	11.40 E
Molins de Rei	44	41.25N	2.01 E
Molkom	22	59.36N	13.43 E
Mollendo	118	17.02S	72.01W
Mölln	30	53.37N	10.41 E
Mölndal	22	57.39N	12.01 E
Molokai I	132b	21.07N	157.00W
Molopo ≐	86	28.30S	20.13 E
Moluccas → Maluku II	68	2.00S	128.00 E
Molucca Sea → Maluku, Laut ᵹ2	68	0.00	125.00 E
Mombasa	86	4.03S	39.40 E
Mombuey	44	42.02N	6.20W
Momence	138	41.10N	87.39W
Momskij chrebet ⋏	56	66.00N	146.00 E
Møn I	22	55.00N	12.20 E
Mona	148	39.48N	111.51W
Mona, Canal de la ␣	108	18.30N	67.45W
Mona, Isla de I	108	18.05N	67.54W
Monaca	136	40.41N	80.16W
Monaco	36	43.42N	7.23 E
Monaco ◻1	36	43.45N	7.25 E
Monadhliath Mountains ⋏	26	57.10N	4.00W
Monadnock Mountain ʌ	136	42.52N	72.07W
Monaghan	26	54.15N	6.58W
Monaghan ◻6	26	54.10N	7.00W
Monarch Pass)(	148	38.30N	106.19W
Monastir	40	35.47N	10.50 E
Moncalieri	40	45.00N	7.41 E
Mončegorsk	20	67.54N	32.58 E
Mönchengladbach	30	51.12N	6.28 E
Monclova	108	26.54N	101.25W
Moncontour	36	48.21N	2.39W
Moncton	130	46.06N	64.47W
Mondego ≐	44	40.09N	8.52W
Mondovi	138	44.34N	91.40W
Mondragone	40	41.07N	13.53 E
Monero	148	36.54N	106.52W
Monessen	136	40.08N	79.53W
Monett	144	36.55N	93.55W
Monfalcone	40	45.49N	13.32 E
Monferrato ◻9	40	44.55N	8.05 E
Monforte de Lemos	44	42.31N	7.30W
Mongala ≐	84	1.53N	19.46 E
Möng Hsat	68	20.32N	99.15 E
Monghyr	70	25.23N	86.28 E
Mongol Altajn nuruu ⋏	66	46.30N	93.00 E
Mongolia (Mongol Ard Uls) ◻1	66	46.00N	105.00 E
Mongu	86	15.15S	23.09 E
Monheim	30	48.50N	10.51 E
Monico	138	45.34N	89.09W
Monida Pass)(	150	44.33N	112.18W
Monitor Range ⋏	154	38.45N	116.30W
Monitor Valley V	154	39.00N	116.40W
Monmouth, Wales, U.K.	26	51.50N	2.43W
Monmouth, Il., U.S.	138	40.54N	90.38W
Monmouth, Or., U.S.	150	44.50N	123.13W
Mono ≐	82	6.17N	1.51 E
Mono Lake ◎	154	38.00N	119.00W
Monon	144	40.52N	86.52W
Monona	138	43.03N	89.20W
Monongahela ≐	136	40.27N	80.00W
Monopoli	40	40.57N	17.19 E
Monor	30	47.21N	19.27 E
Monreale	40	38.05N	13.17 E
Monroe, Ga., U.S.	142	33.47N	83.42W
Monroe, La., U.S.	144	32.30N	92.07W
Monroe, Mi., U.S.	138	41.54N	83.23W
Monroe, N.Y., U.S.	136	41.19N	74.11W
Monroe, N.C., U.S.	142	34.59N	80.32W
Monroe, Wa., U.S.	150	47.51N	121.58W
Monroe, Wi., U.S.	138	42.36N	89.38W
Monroe, Lake ◎	142	28.52N	81.16W
Monroe City	144	39.39N	91.44W
Monroe Lake ◎1	144	39.05N	86.25W
Monroeville, Al., U.S.	144	31.31N	87.19W
Monroeville, In., U.S.	144	40.58N	84.52W
Monroeville, Pa., U.S.	136	40.26N	79.47W
Monrovia	82	6.18N	10.47W
Mons	30	50.27N	3.56 E
Monserrato	40	39.15N	9.08 E
Montalto ʌ	40	38.10N	15.55 E
Montana ◻3	132	47.00N	110.00W
Montánchez	44	39.13N	6.09W
Montargil	44	39.05N	8.10W
Montargis	36	48.00N	2.45 E
Montauban	36	44.01N	1.21 E
Montauk	136	41.02N	71.57W
Montauk Point ⟩	136	41.04N	71.52W
Montbard	36	47.37N	4.20 E
Montbéliard	36	47.31N	6.48 E
Montbrison	36	45.36N	4.03 E
Montceau [-les-Mines]	36	46.40N	4.22 E
Montchanin	36	46.45N	4.27 E
Montclair, Ca., U.S.	154	34.06N	117.41W
Montclair, N.J., U.S.	136	40.49N	74.12W
Mont-de-Marsan	36	43.53N	0.30W
Montecassino, Abbazia di ◆1	40	41.29N	13.48 E
Montecatini-Terme	40	43.53N	10.46 E
Montecito	154	34.26N	119.37W
Monte Cristo, Cerro ʌ	108	14.25N	89.21W
Montecristo, Isola di I	40	42.20N	10.19 E
Montefalco	40	42.54N	12.39 E
Montego Bay	108	18.28N	77.55W
Montélimar	36	44.34N	4.45 E
Montelindo ≐	120	23.56S	57.12W
Montemuro ʌ	44	40.58N	7.56W
Montenegro → Crna Gora ◻3	48	42.30N	19.18 E
Montereau-Faut-Yonne	36	48.23N	2.57 E
Monterey, Ca., U.S.	154	36.36N	121.53W
Monterey, Tn., U.S.	144	36.08N	85.16W
Monterey Bay ⊂	154	36.45N	121.55W
Montería	118	8.46N	75.53W
Monteros	120	27.10S	65.30W
Monterotondo	40	42.03N	12.37 E
Monterrey	108	25.40N	100.19W
Montesano, It.	40	40.16N	15.43 E
Montesano, Wa., U.S.	150	46.58N	123.36W
Monte Sant'Angelo	40	41.42N	15.57 E
Monte Santu, Capo di ⟩	40	40.05N	9.44 E
Montes Claros	118	16.43S	43.52W
Montevallo	144	33.06N	86.51W
Montevarchi	40	43.31N	11.34 E
Montevideo	120	34.53S	56.11W
Monte Vista	148	37.34N	106.08W
Montezuma, Ga., U.S.	142	32.18N	84.01W
Montezuma, In., U.S.	144	39.47N	87.22W
Montgomery, Al., U.S.	144	32.23N	86.18W
Montgomery, Mn., U.S.	138	44.26N	93.34W
Montgomery, Pa., U.S.	136	41.10N	76.52W
Montgomery, W.V., U.S.	136	38.11N	81.19W
Montgomery City	144	38.58N	91.30W
Montguyon	36	45.13N	0.11W
Monticello, Ar., U.S.	144	33.37N	91.47W
Monticello, Ga., U.S.	142	33.18N	83.41W
Monticello, Il., U.S.	144	40.01N	88.34W
Monticello, In., U.S.	144	40.44N	86.45W
Monticello, Ia., U.S.	138	42.14N	91.11W
Monticello, Ky., U.S.	136	36.49N	84.50W
Monticello, N.Y., U.S.	136	41.39N	74.41W
Monticello ⊥	136	38.00N	78.30W
Montichiari	40	45.25N	10.23 E
Montiel, Campo de ≐	44	38.46N	2.44W
Montijo, Esp.	44	38.55N	6.37W
Montijo, Port.	44	38.42N	8.58W
Montilla	44	37.35N	4.38W
Mont-Joli	130	48.35N	68.11W
Mont-Laurier	130	46.33N	75.30W
Mont-Louis	36	42.31N	2.07 E
Montluçon	36	46.21N	2.36 E
Montmagny	130	46.59N	70.33W
Montmorillon	36	46.26N	0.52 E
Monto	96	24.52S	151.07 E
Montoro	44	38.01N	4.23W
Montour Falls	136	42.20N	76.50W
Montoursville	136	41.15N	76.55W
Montpelier, Id., U.S.	150	42.19N	111.17W
Montpelier, In., U.S.	144	40.33N	85.16W
Montpelier, Oh., U.S.	136	41.35N	84.36W
Montpelier, Vt., U.S.	136	44.15N	72.34W
Montpellier	36	43.36N	3.53 E
Montréal, P.Q., Can.	130	45.31N	73.34W
Montreal, Wi., U.S.	138	46.25N	90.14W
Montreal ≐	138	47.08N	79.27W
Montreal Lake ◎	130	54.20N	105.40W
Montreux	36	46.26N	6.55 E
Montrose, Scot., U.K.	26	56.43N	2.29W
Montrose, Co., U.S.	148	38.28N	107.52W
Mont-Saint-Michel → Le Mont-Saint-Michel ◆1	36	48.38N	1.32W
Montserrat ◻2	108	16.45N	62.12W
Montuenga	44	41.03N	4.37W
Monument Peak ʌ	150	42.07N	114.14W
Monument Valley V	148	37.05N	110.20W
Monywa	68	22.05N	95.08 E
Monza	40	45.35N	9.16 E
Moora	96	30.39S	116.00 E
Moore, Lake ◎	96	29.50S	117.35 E
Moorefield	136	39.03N	78.58W
Moore Reservoir ◎1	136	44.25N	71.50W
Mooresville, In., U.S.	144	39.36N	86.22W
Mooresville, N.C., U.S.	142	35.35N	80.48W
Moorhead	132	46.52N	96.46W
Moosburg	30	48.29N	11.57 E
Moosehead Lake ◎	136	45.40N	69.40W
Moose Jaw	130	50.23N	105.32W
Mooselookmeguntic Lake ◎	136	44.53N	70.48W
Moosomin	130	50.07N	101.40W
Moosonee	130	51.17N	80.39W
Mopti	82	14.30N	4.12W
Mór	30	47.23N	18.12 E
Mora, Esp.	44	39.41N	3.46W
Mora, Sve.	22	61.00N	14.33 E
Mora, Mn., U.S.	138	45.52N	93.17W
Morādābād	70	28.50N	78.47 E
Mórahalom	30	46.13N	19.54 E
Moraleda, Canal de ␣	120	44.30S	73.30W
Morant Cays II	108	17.24N	75.59W
Moratalla	44	38.12N	1.53W
Moratuwa	70	6.46N	79.53 E
Morava ◻9	30	49.30N	17.00 E
Morava (March) ≐	30	48.10N	16.59 E
Moravia	136	42.42N	76.25W
Moravia → Morava ◻9	30	49.20N	17.00 E
Moravské Budějovice	30	49.03N	15.49 E
Morawhanna	118	8.16N	59.45W
Moray Firth ⊂1	26	57.50N	3.30W
Morden	130	49.11N	98.05W
More, Ben ʌ	26	56.21N	4.35W
Moreau ≐	132	45.18N	100.43W
Morecambe	26	54.04N	2.53W
Moree	96	29.28S	149.51 E
Morehead	136	38.11N	83.25W
Morehead City	142	34.43N	76.43W
Moreland	142	37.30N	84.48W
Morelia	108	19.42N	101.07W
Morella	44	40.37N	0.06W
Morena, Sierra ⋏	44	38.00N	5.00W
Morenci, Az., U.S.	148	33.04N	109.21W
Morenci, Mi., U.S.	138	41.43N	84.13W
Moresby Island I	130	52.50N	131.55W
Morestel	36	45.40N	5.28 E
Moreton Island I	96	27.10S	153.25 E
Morgan City, Al., U.S.	144	34.28N	86.34W
Morgan City, La., U.S.	144	29.41N	91.12W
Morganfield	144	37.41N	87.55W
Morganton	142	35.44N	81.41W
Morgantown, Ky., U.S.	144	37.13N	86.41W
Morgantown, W.V., U.S.	136	39.37N	79.57W
Morganza	144	30.44N	91.35W
Morghāb (Murgab) ≐	70	38.18N	61.12 E
Moriah, Mount ʌ	154	39.17N	114.12W
Morioka	66	39.42N	141.09 E
Morlaix	36	48.35N	3.50W
Mornington Island I	96	16.33S	139.24 E
Morocco	144	40.56N	87.27W
Morocco (Al-Magreb) ◻1	82	32.00N	5.00W
Morogoro	86	6.49S	37.40 E
Moro Gulf ⊂	68	6.51N	123.00 E
Morombe	86	21.45S	43.22 E
Morón	108	22.06N	78.38W
Morondava	86	20.17S	44.17 E
Morón de la Frontera	44	37.08N	5.27W
Moroni	86	11.41S	43.16 E
Morpeth	26	55.10N	1.41W
Morrilton	144	35.09N	92.44W
Morrinsville	98	37.39S	175.32 E
Morris	138	41.21N	88.25W
Morrison	138	41.48N	89.57W
Morristown	142	36.12N	83.17W
Morrisville, Pa., U.S.	136	40.12N	74.47W
Morrisville, Vt., U.S.	136	44.33N	72.35W
Morro, Punta ⟩	120	27.07S	70.57W
Morro Bay	154	35.21N	120.50W
Mors I	22	56.50N	8.45 E
Mortain	36	48.39N	0.56W
Mortara	40	45.15N	8.44 E
Mortes, Rio das ≐	118	11.45S	50.44W
Morton, Il., U.S.	138	40.36N	89.27W
Morton, Ms., U.S.	144	32.21N	89.39W

Symbols in the index entries are identified on page 162.

Mort—Newt

Name	Page	Lat.	Long.
Morton, Wa., U.S.	150	46.33N	122.16W
Morua	92	16.54S	168.32E
Morvan ✱	36	47.05N	4.00E
Morven	142	30.56N	83.29W
Morvi	70	22.49N	70.50E
Moryń	30	52.49N	14.13E
Mosbach	30	49.21N	9.08E
Moscow → Moskva, S.S.S.R.	20	55.45N	37.35E
Moscow, Id., U.S.	150	46.43N	116.59W
Mosel (Moselle) ≐	30	50.22N	7.36E
Moselle (Mosel) ≐	30	50.22N	7.36E
Moses Lake	150	47.07N	119.16W
Mosgiel	98	45.53S	170.21E
Mosheim	142	36.11N	82.57W
Moshi	86	3.21S	37.20E
Mosinee	138	44.47N	89.42W
Moskenesøya I	20	67.59N	13.00E
Moskva (Moscow)	20	55.45N	37.35E
Moskva ≐	20	55.05N	38.50E
Mosonmagyaróvár	30	47.51N	17.17E
Mosquera	118	2.30N	78.29W
Mosquito Creek Lake ◎[1]	136	41.22N	80.45W
Mosquitos, Golfo de los ⊂	108	9.00N	81.15W
Moss	22	59.26N	10.42E
Mossaka	86	1.13S	16.48E
Mosselbaai	86	34.11S	22.08E
Mossoró	118	5.11S	37.20W
Moss Point	144	30.24N	88.32W
Most	30	50.32N	13.39E
Mostar	40	43.20N	17.49E
Møsting, Kap ➤	130	64.00N	41.00W
Mostiştea ≐	48	44.15N	27.10E
Mosul → Al-Mawṣil	70	36.20N	43.08E
Møsvatnet ◎	22	59.52N	8.05E
Mota del Marqués	44	41.38N	5.10W
Motagua ≐	108	15.44N	88.14W
Motala	22	58.33N	15.03E
Motherwell	26	55.48N	4.00W
Motril	44	36.45N	3.31W
Motru	48	44.50N	23.00E
Mottola	40	40.38N	17.03E
Motueka	98	41.07S	173.00E
Motutapu I	94	21.14S	159.43W
Mou	92	21.05S	165.26E
Mouaskar	82	35.45N	0.01E
Moulay-bou-Selham	44	34.53N	6.15W
Moulay-Idriss	82	34.02N	5.27W
Moulins	36	46.34N	3.20E
Moulmein	68	16.30N	97.38E
Moulouya, Oued ≐	82	35.05N	2.25W
Moulton	144	34.28N	87.17W
Moultrie	142	31.10N	83.47W
Moultrie, Lake ◎[1]	142	33.20N	80.05W
Mound Bayou	144	33.52N	90.43W
Mound City, Il., U.S.	144	37.05N	89.09W
Mound City, Mo., U.S.	144	40.07N	95.13W
Mound City Group National Monument ♦	136	39.23N	83.00W
Moundou	84	8.34N	16.05E
Moundsville	136	39.55N	80.44W
Mountainair	148	34.31N	106.14W
Mountain Brook	144	33.30N	86.45W
Mountain City	142	34.55N	83.23W
Mountain Grove	144	37.07N	92.15W
Mountain Home, Ar., U.S.	144	36.20N	92.23W
Mountain Home, Id., U.S.	150	43.07N	115.41W
Mountain Nile (Baḥr al-Jabal) ≐	84	9.30N	30.30E
Mountain View, Ar., U.S.	144	35.52N	92.07W
Mountain View, Ca., U.S.	154	37.23N	122.04W
Mountain View, Wy., U.S.	150	42.51N	106.23W
Mount Airy, Md., U.S.	136	39.22N	77.09W
Mount Airy, N.C., U.S.	142	36.29N	80.36W
Mount Carmel, Il., U.S.	144	38.24N	87.45W
Mount Carmel, Pa., U.S.	136	40.47N	76.24W
Mount Carroll	138	42.05N	89.58W
Mount Clemens	138	42.35N	82.52W
Mount Cook	98	43.44S	170.06E
Mount Desert Island I	136	44.20N	68.20W
Mount Dora	142	28.48N	81.38W
Mount Gambier	96	37.50S	140.46E
Mount Gilead	136	40.32N	82.49W
Mount Holly	142	35.17N	81.00W
Mount Horeb	138	43.00N	89.44W
Mount Isa	96	20.44S	139.30E
Mount Jewett	136	41.43N	78.38W
Mount Kisco	136	41.12N	73.43W
Mount Lebanon	136	40.21N	80.02W
Mount Magnet	96	28.04S	117.49E
Mount Maunganui	98	37.37S	176.11E
Mount Morgan	96	23.39S	150.23E
Mount Morris, Il., U.S.	138	42.03N	89.25W
Mount Morris, Mi., U.S.	138	43.07N	83.41W
Mount Morris, N.Y., U.S.	136	42.43N	77.52W
Mount Olive	142	35.11N	78.04W
Mount Olivet	136	38.31N	84.02W
Mount Orab	136	39.01N	83.55W
Mount Pleasant, Ia., U.S.	138	40.57N	91.33W
Mount Pleasant, Mi., U.S.	138	43.35N	84.46W
Mount Pleasant, Pa., U.S.	136	40.08N	79.32W
Mount Pleasant, S.C., U.S.	142	32.47N	79.51W
Mount Pleasant, Tn., U.S.	144	35.32N	87.12W
Mount Pleasant, Tx., U.S.	144	33.09N	94.58W
Mount Rainier National Park ♦	150	46.52N	121.43W
Mount Roskill	98	36.55S	174.45E
Mount Saint Helens National Volcanic Monument ♦	150	46.12N	122.11W
Mount Savage	136	39.41N	78.52W
Mount's Bay ⊂	26	50.03N	5.25W
Mount Shasta	154	41.18N	122.18W
Mount Sterling, Ky., U.S.	142	38.03N	83.56W
Mount Sterling, Oh., U.S.	136	39.43N	83.15W
Mount Union	136	40.23N	77.52W
Mount Vernon, Al., U.S.	144	31.05N	88.00W
Mount Vernon, Ga., U.S.	142	32.10N	82.35W
Mount Vernon, Il., U.S.	144	38.19N	88.54W
Mount Vernon, In., U.S.	144	37.55N	87.53W
Mount Vernon, Ia., U.S.	138	41.55N	91.25W
Mount Vernon, Ky., U.S.	142	37.21N	84.20W
Mount Vernon, Mo., U.S.	144	37.06N	93.49W
Mount Vernon, Oh., U.S.	136	40.23N	82.29W
Mount Vernon, Wa., U.S.	150	48.25N	122.19W
Mount Vernon ⊥	136	38.47N	77.06W
Mount Wellington	98	36.54S	174.51E
Mount Wolf	136	40.03N	76.42W
Mourdi, Dépression du ⊥[7]	84	18.10N	23.00E
Mourne Mountains ▲	26	54.10N	6.04W
Mouscron	30	50.44N	3.13E
Moutier	36	47.17N	7.23E
Moy ≐	26	54.12N	9.08W
Moyamba	82	8.10N	11.26W
Moyen Atlas ✱	82	33.30N	5.00W
Moyeuvre-Grande	36	49.15N	6.02E
Mozambique → Moçambique	86	15.03S	40.42E
Mozambique (Moçambique) □[1]	86	18.15S	35.00E
Mozambique Channel ⊔	86	19.00S	41.00E
Možga	20	56.23N	52.17E
Mozyr'	54	52.03N	29.14E
Mpika	86	11.54S	31.26E
Mpraeso	82	6.35N	0.44W
Mpwapwa	86	6.21S	36.29E
Mrągowo	30	53.52N	21.19E
Mrhila, Jebel ▲	40	35.25N	9.14E
Mrkopalj	40	45.19N	14.51E
M'Saken	40	35.44N	10.35E
M'Sila	44	35.46N	4.31E
Mtwara	86	10.16S	40.11E
Muanda	86	5.56S	12.21E
Muang Ngoy	68	20.43N	102.41E
Muang Pakxan	68	18.22N	103.39E
Muang Sing	68	21.11N	101.09E
Muang Xépôn	68	16.41N	106.14E
Muar	68	2.02N	102.34E
Muchinga Mountains ✱	86	12.20S	31.00E
Mudanjiang	66	44.35N	129.36E
Mufulira	86	12.33S	28.14E
Muğla	48	37.12N	28.22E
Muhammad, Ra's ➤	84	27.44N	34.15E
Mühlacker	30	48.57N	8.50E
Mühldorf	30	48.15N	12.32E
Mühlhausen	30	51.12N	10.27E
Mühlviertel ✤[1]	30	48.25N	14.10E
Muhu I	20	58.38N	23.15E
Muhu väin ⊔	22	58.45N	23.20E
Mui Ca-mau ➤	68	8.38N	104.44E
Mui Ke-ga ➤	68	12.53N	109.28E
Muiron Islands II	96	21.35S	114.20E
Mui Ron-ma ➤	68	18.07N	106.22E
Mukačevo	48	48.27N	22.45E
Mukden → Shenyang	66	41.48N	123.27E
Mukilteo	150	47.56N	122.18W
Mukwonago	138	42.51N	88.19W
Mulanje	86	16.03S	35.31E
Mulberry	144	35.30N	94.03W
Mulberry Fork ≐	144	33.33N	87.11W
Mulde ≐	30	51.52N	12.15E
Muldraugh	144	37.56N	85.59W
Muldrow	144	35.24N	94.35W
Mulhacén ▲	44	37.03N	3.19W
Mulhouse	36	47.45N	7.20E
Mulinu'u, Cape ➤	93	13.26S	172.43W
Mull, Island of I	26	56.27N	6.00W
Mullan	150	47.28N	115.48W
Mullens	142	37.34N	81.22W
Mullett Lake ◎	138	45.30N	84.30W
Mullewa	96	28.33S	115.31E
Mullica ≐	136	39.33N	74.25W
Mullingar	26	53.32N	7.20W
Mullins	142	34.12N	79.15W
Multān	70	30.11N	71.29E
Mun ≐	68	15.19N	105.30E
Muna, Pulau I	68	5.00S	122.30E
Münchberg	30	50.11N	11.47E
München (Munich)	30	48.08N	11.34E
Muncie	144	40.11N	85.23W
Muncy	136	41.12N	76.47W
Mundelein	138	42.15N	88.00W
Münden	30	51.25N	9.39E
Mundo ≐	44	38.19N	1.40W
Munford	144	35.26N	89.48W
Munich → München	30	48.08N	11.34E
Muniesa	44	41.02N	0.48W
Munising	138	46.24N	86.38W
Münsingen	30	48.25N	9.29E
Münster, B.R.D.	30	52.59N	10.05E
Münster, B.R.D.	30	51.57N	7.37E
Münster, Fr.	36	48.03N	7.08E
Munster □[9]	26	52.25N	8.20W
Muntele Mare, Vîrful ▲	48	46.29N	23.14E
Muonio	20	67.57N	23.42E
Muoro	40	40.20N	9.20E
Muqayshiṭ I	70	24.12N	53.42E
Muqdisho (Mogadishu)	84	2.04N	45.22E
Mur (Mura) ≐	30	46.18N	16.53E
Mura (Mur) ≐	30	46.18N	16.53E
Muradiye	48	38.39N	27.21E
Murat ≐	16	38.39N	39.50E
Muratlı	48	41.10N	27.30E
Murau	30	47.07N	14.10E
Murča	44	41.24N	7.27W
Murchison ≐	96	27.42S	114.09E
Murchison, Mount ▲	98	43.01S	171.22E
Murchison Falls → Kabalega Falls ↘	84	2.17N	31.41E
Murcia	44	37.59N	1.07W
Murcia □[4]	44	38.00N	1.30W
Mureş (Maros) ≐	48	46.15N	20.13E
Murfreesboro, Ar., U.S.	144	34.03N	93.41W
Murfreesboro, N.C., U.S.	142	36.26N	77.05W
Murfreesboro, Tn., U.S.	144	35.50N	86.23W
Murgab (Morghāb) ≐	70	38.18N	61.12E
Muri	94	21.14S	159.43W
Müritz ◎	30	53.25N	12.43E
Murmansk	20	68.58N	33.05E
Murnau	30	47.40N	11.12E
Murom	20	55.34N	42.02E
Muroran	66	42.18N	140.59E
Muros	44	42.47N	9.02W
Murphy	142	35.05N	84.02W
Murphysboro	144	37.45N	89.20W
Murray, Ky., U.S.	144	36.36N	88.18W
Murray, Ut., U.S.	148	40.40N	111.53W
Murray ≐	96	35.22S	139.22E
Murray, Lake ◎[1]	142	34.04N	81.23W
Murray Bridge	96	35.07S	139.17E
Murray City	136	39.30N	82.09W
Murraysburg	86	31.58S	23.47E
Murree	70	33.54N	73.24E
Murrumbidgee ≐	96	34.43S	143.12E
Murten	36	46.56N	7.07E
Murter, Otok I	40	43.48N	15.37E
Muru, Capu di ➤	40	41.44N	8.40E
Murud, Gunong ▲	68	3.52N	115.30E
Murwāra	70	23.51N	80.24E
Mürzzuschlag	30	47.36N	15.41E
Musala ▲	48	42.11N	23.34E
Musay'īd	70	24.59N	51.32E
Muscat → Masqaṭ	70	23.37N	58.35E
Muscat and Oman → Oman □[1]	70	22.00N	58.00E
Muscatatuck ≐	144	38.46N	86.10W
Muscatine	144	41.25N	91.03W
Mus-Chaja, gora ▲	56	62.35N	140.50E
Muscle Shoals	144	34.44N	87.40W
Musgrave, Mount ▲	98	43.48S	170.43E
Mushin	82	6.32N	3.22E
Muskegon	138	43.14N	86.14W
Muskegon ≐	138	43.14N	86.20W
Muskegon Heights	138	43.12N	86.14W
Muskingum ≐	136	39.27N	81.30W
Muskogee	132	35.44N	95.22W
Muskoka, Lake ◎	138	45.00N	79.25W
Musselshell ≐	150	47.21N	107.58W
Mussomeli	40	37.35N	13.45E
Mustafakemalpaşa	48	40.02N	28.24E
Mustafa Kemal Paşa ≐	48	40.07N	28.33E
Muszyna	30	49.21N	20.54E
Mutare	86	18.58S	32.40E
Mutsamudu	86	12.09S	44.25E
Muttonbird Islands II	98	47.15S	167.24E
Muzaffarnagar	70	29.28N	77.41E
Muzaffarpur	70	26.07N	85.24E
Muztag ▲, Zhg.	66	36.25N	87.25E
Muztag ▲, Zhg.	66	36.03N	80.07E
Mwali I	86	12.15S	43.45E
Mwanza	86	2.31S	32.54E
Mwenezi	86	21.22S	30.45E
Mweru, Lake ◎	86	9.00S	28.45E
Myakka ≐	142	26.56N	82.11W
Myanaung	68	18.17N	95.19E
Myaungmya	68	16.36N	94.56E
Myerstown	136	40.22N	76.19W
Myingyan	68	21.28N	95.23E
Myitkyinā	66	25.23N	97.24E
Myjava	30	48.45N	17.34E
Mymensingh	70	24.45N	90.24E
Myrtle Beach	142	33.41N	78.53W
Myrtle Grove	144	30.25N	87.18W
Mysia □[9]	48	39.15N	28.00E
Myślenice	30	49.51N	19.56E
Mysłowice	30	50.15N	19.07E
Mysore	70	12.18N	76.39E
Mystic	136	41.21N	71.58W
Myszków	30	50.36N	19.20E
My-tho	68	10.21N	106.21E
Mytilene → Mitilíni	48	39.06N	26.32E
Mytišči	20	55.55N	37.46E
Mzuzu	86	11.27S	33.55E
N			
Naab ≐	30	49.01N	12.02E
Naach, Jbel ▲	44	34.53N	3.22W
Nabadwīp	70	23.25N	88.22E
Naberežnyje Čelny	54	55.42N	52.19E
Nabeul	82	36.27N	10.44E
Nabī Shu'ayb, Jabal an- ▲, Yaman	70	15.18N	43.59E
Nabī Shu'ayb, Jabal an- ▲, Yaman	84	15.18N	43.59E
Nābulus	70	32.13N	35.16E
Nacala-Velha	86	14.32S	40.37E
Nachingwea	86	10.23S	38.46E
Náchod	30	50.25N	16.10E
Nachodka	56	42.48N	132.52E
Nacimiento ≐	154	35.49N	120.45W
Nacimiento, Lake ◎[1]	154	35.45N	121.00W
Nacka	22	59.18N	18.10E
Nacogdoches	144	31.36N	94.39W
Nadiād	70	22.42N	72.52E
Nădlac	48	46.10N	20.45E
Nador	44	35.12N	2.55W
Næstved	22	55.14N	11.46E
Naga	68	13.37N	123.11E
Nagano	66	36.39N	138.11E
Nagaoka	66	37.27N	138.51E
Nāgappattinam	70	10.46N	79.50E
Nagasaki	66	32.48N	129.55E
Nāgercoil	70	8.10N	77.26E
Nagoya	66	35.10N	136.55E
Nāgpur	70	21.09N	79.06E
Nagu I	22	60.10N	21.48E
Nagyatád	30	46.14N	17.22E
Nagybajom	30	46.23N	17.31E
Nagykanizsa	30	46.27N	17.00E
Nagykáta	30	47.25N	19.45E
Nagykőrös	30	47.02N	19.43E
Naha	66	26.13N	127.40E
Nahe ≐	30	49.58N	7.57E
Nahma	138	45.50N	86.39W
Nahoï, Cap ➤	92	14.39S	166.37E
Nahr Ouassel, Oued ≐	44	35.42N	2.33E
Nahuel Huapi, Lago ◎	120	40.58S	71.30W
Nahunta	142	31.12N	81.58W
Nairn	144	29.27N	89.38W
Nairobi	86	1.17S	36.49E
Naivasha	86	0.43S	36.26E
Najac	36	44.13N	1.59E
Najafābād	70	32.37N	51.21E
Najin	66	42.15N	130.18E
Nakhon Pathom	68	13.49N	100.03E
Nakhon Ratchasima	68	14.58N	102.07E
Nakhon Sawan	68	15.41N	100.07E
Nakhon Si Thammarat	68	8.26N	99.58E
Nakina	130	50.10N	86.42W
Nakło nad Notecią	30	53.08N	17.35E
Nakskov	22	54.50N	11.09E
Näkten ◎	22	62.52N	14.38E
Nakuru	86	0.17S	36.04E
Nal'čik	54	43.29N	43.37E
Namak, Daryācheh-ye ◎	70	34.45N	51.36E
Namakan Lake ◎	138	48.27N	92.35W
Namangan	54	41.00N	71.40E
Namcha Barwa → Namjagbarwa Feng ▲	66	29.38N	95.04E
Nam Co ◎	66	30.42N	90.30E
Nam-dinh	68	20.25N	106.10E
Namib Desert ✤[2]	86	23.00S	15.00E
Namibe	86	15.10S	12.09E
Namibia (South West Africa) □[2]	86	22.00S	17.00E
Namjagbarwa Feng ▲	66	29.38N	95.04E
Nampa	150	43.32N	116.33W
Namp'o	66	38.45N	125.23E
Nampula	86	15.07S	39.15E
Namsang	68	20.53N	97.43E
Namsen ≐	20	64.27N	11.28E
Namsos	20	64.29N	11.30E
Namur	30	50.28N	4.52E
Namysłów	30	51.05N	17.42E
Nan	68	18.47N	100.47E
Nan ≐	68	15.42N	100.09E
Nanaimo	130	49.10N	123.56W
Nanchang	66	28.41N	115.53E
Nanchong	66	30.48N	106.04E
Nancy	36	48.41N	6.12E
Nanda Devi ▲	70	30.23N	79.59E
Nānded	70	19.09N	77.20E
Nandi	91	17.48S	177.25E
Nandi Bay ⊂	91	17.44S	177.25E
N'andoma	20	61.40N	40.12E
Nanga Parbat ▲	70	35.15N	74.36E
Nanjing	66	32.03N	118.47E
Nanking → Nanjing	66	32.03N	118.47E
Nan Ling ✱	66	25.00N	112.00E
Nanning	66	22.48N	108.20E
Nansa ≐	44	43.22N	4.29W
Nansei-shotō (Ryukyu Islands) II	66	26.30N	128.00E
Nantes	36	47.13N	1.33W
Nanticoke	136	41.12N	76.00W
Nantong	66	32.02N	120.53E
Nantua	36	46.09N	5.37E
Nantucket	136	41.17N	70.06W
Nantucket Island I	136	41.16N	70.03W
Nantucket Sound ⊔	136	41.30N	70.15W
Nanty Glo	136	40.28N	78.50W
Nanuque	118	17.50S	40.21W
Nanxiong	66	25.10N	114.20E
Nanyang	66	33.00N	112.32E
Nanyuki	86	0.01N	37.04E
Náousa	48	40.37N	22.05E
Napa	154	38.17N	122.17W
Napa ≐	154	38.07N	122.18W
Naperville	138	41.47N	88.08W
Napier	98	39.29S	176.55E
Naples → Napoli, It.	40	40.51N	14.17E
Naples, Fl., U.S.	142	26.08N	81.47W
Naples, N.Y., U.S.	136	42.36N	77.24W
Napo ≐	118	3.20S	72.40W
Napoleon	136	41.23N	84.07W
Napoleonville	144	29.56N	91.01W
Napoli (Naples)	40	40.51N	14.17E
Nappanee	144	41.26N	86.00W
Nara	66	34.41N	135.50E
Nārāyanganj	70	23.37N	90.30E
Narbonne	36	43.11N	3.00E
Nardò	40	40.11N	18.02E
Narew ≐	30	52.26N	20.42E
Narinda, Baie de ⊂	86	14.55S	47.30E
Narmada ≐	70	21.38N	72.36E
Narni	40	42.31N	12.31E
Naro	40	37.18N	13.47E
Narodnaja, gora ▲	54	65.04N	60.09E
Narol	30	50.22N	23.21E
Narrabri	96	30.19S	149.47E
Narromine	96	32.14S	148.15E
Narssaq	130	60.54N	46.00W
Narva	20	59.23N	28.12E
Narva ≐	22	59.27N	28.02E
Narvik	20	68.26N	17.25E
Narvskij zaliv (Narva laht) ⊂	22	59.30N	27.40E
Narvskoje vodochranilišče ◎[1]	22	59.18N	28.14E
Näsåker	22	63.26N	16.54E
Nasawa	92	15.13S	168.09E
Nashua, Ia., U.S.	138	42.57N	92.32W
Nashua, N.H., U.S.	136	42.45N	71.28W
Nashville, Ar., U.S.	144	33.56N	93.50W
Nashville, Ga., U.S.	142	31.12N	83.15W
Nashville, Il., U.S.	144	38.20N	89.22W
Nashville, In., U.S.	144	39.12N	86.15W
Nashville, N.C., U.S.	142	35.58N	77.57W
Nashville, Tn., U.S.	144	36.09N	86.47W
Näsijärvi ◎	22	61.37N	23.42E
Nāsik	70	19.59N	73.48E
Nāṣir, Buḥayrat ◎[1]	84	22.40N	32.00E
Nasorolevu ▲	91	16.38S	178.42E
Nassau, Ba.	108	25.05N	77.21W
Nassau, N.Y., U.S.	136	42.30N	73.36W
Nasser, Lake → Nāṣir, Buḥayrat ◎[1]	84	22.40N	32.00E
Nässjö	22	57.39N	14.41E
Natal	118	5.47S	35.13W
Natchez	144	31.33N	91.24W
Natchitoches	144	31.45N	93.05W
Natewa Bay ⊂	91	16.35S	179.40E
National City	154	32.40N	117.05W
Natron, Lake ◎	86	2.25S	36.00E
Nattaset ▲	20	68.12N	27.20E
Natuna Besar I	68	4.00N	108.15E
Natural Bridges National Monument ♦	148	37.30N	110.08W
Naturaliste, Cape ➤	96	33.32S	115.01E
Naturaliste Channel ⊔	96	25.25S	113.00E
Naturita	148	38.13N	108.34W
Nau, Cap de la ➤	44	38.44N	0.14E
Nauen	30	52.36N	12.52E
Naugatuck	136	41.30N	73.03W
Naumburg	30	51.09N	11.48E
Nauru □[1]	8	0.32S	166.55E
Nausori	91	18.02S	178.32E
Nauvoo	144	40.33N	91.23W
Nava del Rey	44	41.20N	5.05W
Navajo Mountain ▲	148	37.02N	110.52W
Navajo Reservoir ◎[1]	148	36.55N	107.30W
Navan	26	53.39N	6.41W
Navarin, mys ➤	56	62.16N	179.10E
Navarino, Isla I	120	55.05S	67.40W
Navarra □[4]	44	42.40N	1.30W
Navarre	136	40.43N	81.31W
Navia ≐	44	43.33N	6.44W
Năvodari	48	44.19N	28.36E
Navoi	54	40.15N	65.15E
Navojoa	108	27.06N	109.26W
Návpaktos	48	38.23N	21.50E
Návplion	48	37.34N	22.48E
Navsāri	70	20.51N	72.55E
Nawābshāh	70	26.15N	68.25E
Náxos I	48	37.02N	25.35E
Naylor	144	36.34N	90.36W
Nazareth, Pa., U.S.	136	40.44N	75.18W
Nazareth, Vanuatu	92	15.29S	168.10E
Nazareth, Vanuatu	92	15.21S	167.50E
Nazca	118	14.50S	74.57W
Naze	66	28.23N	129.30E
Nazilli	48	37.55N	28.21E
Nazret	84	8.33N	39.16E
N'dalatando	86	9.18S	14.54E
N'Djamena	84	12.07N	15.03E
Ndjolé	86	0.11S	10.45E
Ndola	86	12.58S	28.38E
Nduindui	92	15.24S	167.46E
Neagh, Lough ◎	26	54.38N	6.24W
Neah Bay	150	48.22N	124.37W
Neajlov ≐	48	44.11N	26.12E
Neath	26	51.40N	3.48W
Neblina, Pico da ▲	118	0.48N	66.02W
Nebo	144	39.27N	90.47W
Nebo, Mount ▲	148	39.49N	111.46W
Nebraska □[3]	132	41.30N	100.00W
Nebraska City	132	40.40N	95.51W
Nebrodi ✱	40	37.54N	14.35E
Necedah	138	44.01N	90.04W
Nechako Reservoir ◎[1]	130	53.25N	125.10W
Neches ≐	144	29.55N	93.52W
Neckar ≐	30	49.31N	8.26E
Neckarsulm	30	49.12N	9.13E
Necochea	120	38.33S	58.45W
Nedalsjön ◎	22	62.56N	12.11E
Nederland	144	29.58N	93.59W
Nédroma	44	35.01N	1.45W
Neebish Island I	138	46.16N	84.09W
Needle Mountain ▲	150	44.05N	109.37W
Needles	154	34.50N	114.36W
Neenah	138	44.11N	88.27W
Neepawa	130	50.13N	99.29W
Nefza	40	36.58N	9.05E
Negage	86	7.45S	15.16E
Negaunee	138	46.29N	87.36W
Negombo	70	7.13N	79.50E
Negra, Punta ➤	118	6.06S	81.09W
Negreira	44	42.54N	8.44W
Negreşti	48	46.50N	27.27E
Negro ≐, Arg.	120	41.02S	62.47W
Negro ≐, S.A.	118	3.08S	59.55W
Negros I	68	10.00N	123.00E
Néhoué, Baie de ⊂	92	20.21S	164.09E
Neijiang	66	29.35N	105.03E
Neillsville	138	44.33N	90.35W
Neisse (Nysa Łużycka) (Nisa) ≐	30	52.04N	14.46E
Neiva	118	2.56N	75.18W
Nejdek	30	50.17N	12.42E
Nekoosa	138	44.18N	89.54W
Nellore	70	14.26N	79.58E
Nelson, B.C., Can.	130	49.29N	117.17W
Nelson, N.Z.	98	41.17S	173.17E
Nelson ≐	130	57.04N	92.30W
Nelson, Cape ➤	96	38.26S	141.33E
Nelsonville	136	39.27N	82.14W
Nelspruit	86	25.30S	30.58E
Néma	82	16.37N	7.15W
Neman (Nemunas) ≐	54	55.18N	21.23E
Nemuna, Bjeshkët e ✱	48	42.27N	19.47E
Nemunas (Neman) ≐	54	55.18N	21.23E
Nemuro	66	43.20N	145.35E
Nen ≐	66	45.25N	124.40E
Neopit	138	44.58N	88.49W
Neosho	144	36.52N	94.22W
Neosho ≐	144	35.48N	95.18W
Nepal (Nepāl) □[1]	70	28.00N	84.00E
Nepālganj	70	28.03N	81.37E
Nephi	148	39.42N	111.50W
Nepomuk	30	49.29N	13.36E
Neptune	136	40.12N	74.02W
Neptune Beach	142	30.18N	81.23W
Nera ≐	40	42.26N	12.24E
Neretva ≐	48	43.40N	17.59E
Nerva	44	37.42N	6.32W
Nesebăr	48	42.39N	27.44E
Nesjøen ◎[1]	22	63.02N	12.01E
Ness, Loch ◎	26	57.15N	4.30W
Nesselwang	30	47.37N	10.30E
Néstos (Mesta) ≐	48	40.41N	24.44E
Netanya	70	32.20N	34.51E
Netherdale	96	21.08S	148.32E
Netherlands (Nederland) □[1]	30	52.15N	5.30E
Netherlands Antilles (Nederlandse Antillen) □[2]	108	12.15N	68.45W
Netherlands Guiana → Suriname □[1]	118	4.00N	56.00W
Neto ≐	40	39.13N	17.08E
Nettilling Lake ◎	130	66.30N	70.40W
Nettleton	144	34.05N	88.37W
Nettuno	40	41.27N	12.39E
Neubrandenburg	30	53.33N	13.15E
Neuburg an der Donau	30	48.44N	11.11E
Neuchâtel	36	46.59N	6.56E
Neuchâtel, Lac de ◎	36	46.52N	6.50E
Neufchâteau, Bel.	30	49.50N	5.26E
Neufchâteau, Fr.	36	48.21N	5.42E
Neu-Isenburg	30	50.03N	8.41E
Neumarkt in der Oberpfalz	30	49.16N	11.28E
Neumarkt-Sankt Veit	30	48.22N	12.30E
Neumünster	30	54.04N	9.59E
Neunkirchen	30	47.43N	16.05E
Neunkirchen/Saar	30	49.20N	7.10E
Neuquén	120	38.57S	68.04W
Neuruppin	30	52.55N	12.48E
Neuse ≐	142	35.06N	76.30W
Neusiedl am See	30	47.57N	16.51E
Neusiedler See ◎	30	47.50N	16.45E
Neuss	30	51.12N	6.41E
Neustadt an der Waldnaab	30	49.44N	12.11E
Neustadt an der Weinstrasse	30	49.21N	8.08E
Neustadt bei Coburg	30	50.19N	11.07E
Neustadt in Holstein	30	54.06N	10.48E
Neustettin → Szczecinek	30	53.43N	16.42E
Neustrelitz	30	53.21N	13.04E
Neutral Zone □[2]	70	29.10N	45.30E
Neu-Ulm	30	48.23N	10.01E
Neuwied	30	50.25N	7.27E
Nevada, Ia., U.S.	138	42.01N	93.27W
Nevada, Mo., U.S.	144	37.50N	94.21W
Nevada, Oh., U.S.	136	40.49N	83.07W
Nevada □[3]	132	39.00N	117.00W
Nevada, Sierra ✱, Esp.	44	37.05N	3.10W
Nevada, Sierra ✱, Ca., U.S.	154	38.00N	119.15W
Nevers	36	47.00N	3.09E
Nevinnomyssk	54	44.38N	41.56E
Nevis I	108	17.10N	62.34W
Nevis, Ben ▲	26	56.48N	5.01W
New ≐, N.A.	154	33.08N	115.44W
New ≐, U.S.	136	38.10N	81.12W
New Albany, In., U.S.	144	38.17N	85.49W
New Albany, Ms., U.S.	144	34.29N	89.00W
New Amsterdam	118	6.15N	57.31W
Newark, De., U.S.	136	39.41N	75.45W
Newark, N.J., U.S.	136	40.44N	74.10W
Newark, N.Y., U.S.	136	43.02N	77.05W
Newark, Oh., U.S.	136	40.04N	82.24W
Newark Lake ◎	154	39.41N	115.44W
Newark-on-Trent	26	53.05N	0.49W
Newark Valley	136	42.13N	76.11W
New Baltimore	138	42.40N	82.44W
New Bedford	136	41.38N	70.56W
Newberg	150	45.18N	122.58W
New Berlin, Il., U.S.	144	39.43N	89.54W
New Berlin, Wi., U.S.	138	42.58N	88.06W
New Bern, N.C., U.S.	142	35.06N	77.02W
Newbern, Tn., U.S.	144	36.06N	89.15W
Newberry, Mi., U.S.	138	46.21N	85.30W
Newberry, S.C., U.S.	142	34.16N	81.37W
New Bethlehem	136	41.00N	79.19W
New Boston, Oh., U.S.	136	38.45N	82.56W
New Boston, Tx., U.S.	144	33.27N	94.24W
New Brighton	98	43.31S	172.44E
New Britain	136	41.39N	72.46W
New Britain I	96a	6.00S	150.00E
New Brunswick	136	40.29N	74.27W
New Brunswick □[4]	130	46.30N	66.15W
New Buffalo	138	41.47N	86.44W
Newburgh, In., U.S.	144	37.56N	87.24W
Newburgh, N.Y., U.S.	136	41.30N	74.00W
Newbury	26	51.25N	1.20W
Newburyport	136	42.48N	70.52W
New Caledonia (Nouvelle-Calédonie) □[2]	92	21.30S	165.30E
New-Carlisle, P.Q., Can.	130	48.01N	65.20W
New Carlisle, Oh., U.S.	136	39.56N	84.01W
Newcastle, Austl.	96	32.56S	151.46E
Newcastle, N.B., Can.	130	47.00N	65.34W
Newcastle, S. Afr.	86	27.49S	29.55E
Newcastle, N. Ire., U.K.	26	54.12N	5.54W
New Castle, De., U.S.	136	39.39N	75.34W
New Castle, In., U.S.	144	39.55N	85.22W
New Castle, Pa., U.S.	136	41.00N	80.20W
Newcastle Emlyn	26	52.02N	4.28W
Newcastle-under-Lyme	26	53.00N	2.14W
Newcastle upon Tyne	26	54.59N	1.35W
Newcastle Waters	96	17.24S	133.24E
New City	136	41.08N	73.59W
Newcomerstown	136	40.16N	81.36W
New Concord	136	39.59N	81.44W
Newdegate	96	33.06S	119.01E
New Delhi	70	28.36N	77.12E
New Edinburg	144	33.45N	92.14W
New Egypt	136	40.04N	74.31W
New Ellenton	142	33.25N	81.41W
New Florence	136	40.22N	79.04W
Newfound Gap ✕	142	35.37N	83.25W
Newfoundland □[4]	130	52.00N	56.00W
Newfoundland I	130	48.30N	56.00W
New Georgia I	94	8.15S	157.30E
New Georgia Group II	94	8.30S	157.20E
New Georgia Sound ⊔	94	8.00S	158.10E
New Glarus	138	42.48N	89.38W
New Glasgow	130	45.35N	62.39W
New Guinea I	96a	5.00S	140.00E
Newhall	154	34.23N	118.31W
New Hampshire □[3]	132	43.35N	71.40W
New Hampton	138	43.03N	92.19W
New Hanover I	96a	2.30S	150.15E
New Harmony	144	38.07N	87.56W
New Hartford	136	41.52N	72.58W
Newhaven, Eng., U.K.	26	50.47N	0.03E
New Haven, Ct., U.S.	136	41.18N	72.56W
New Haven, In., U.S.	136	41.04N	85.00W
New Haven, In., U.S.	144	41.04N	85.00W
New Haven, Ky., U.S.	144	37.39N	85.35W
New Haven, Mo., U.S.	144	38.36N	91.13W
New Hebrides → Vanuatu □[1]	92	16.00S	167.00E
New Hebrides II	92	16.00S	167.00E
Newhebron	144	31.44N	89.58W
New Holland, Oh., U.S.	136	39.33N	83.15W
New Holland, Pa., U.S.	136	40.06N	76.05W
New Holstein	138	43.57N	88.05W
New Iberia	144	30.00N	91.49W
New Ireland I	96a	3.20S	152.00E
New Jersey □[3]	132	40.15N	74.30W
New Kensington	136	40.34N	79.45W
Newlands	96	21.11S	147.54E
New Lexington	136	39.42N	82.12W
New Lisbon	138	43.52N	90.09W
New Liskeard	130	47.30N	79.40W
Newllano	144	31.06N	93.16W
New London, Ct., U.S.	136	41.21N	72.07W
New London, Ia., U.S.	138	40.55N	91.23W
New London, Mo., U.S.	144	39.35N	91.24W
New London, N.H., U.S.	136	43.24N	71.59W
New London, Oh., U.S.	136	41.05N	82.24W
New London, Wi., U.S.	138	44.23N	88.44W
New Madrid	144	36.35N	89.31W
Newman	96	23.20S	119.46E
Newmarket, On., Can.	130	44.03N	79.28W
Newmarket, Eng., U.K.	26	52.15N	0.25E
New Market, Al., U.S.	144	34.54N	86.25W
Newmarket, N.H., U.S.	136	43.04N	70.56W
New Market, Va., U.S.	136	38.39N	78.40W
New Martinsville	136	39.38N	80.51W
New Mexico □[3]	132	34.30N	106.00W
New Milford, Ct., U.S.	136	41.34N	73.24W
New Milford, Pa., U.S.	136	41.52N	75.43W
Newnan	142	33.22N	84.47W
Newnans Lake ◎	142	29.39N	82.13W
New Orleans	144	29.57N	90.04W
New Paltz	136	41.44N	74.05W
New Paris	136	39.51N	84.47W
New Philadelphia	136	40.30N	81.27W
New Plymouth	98	39.04S	174.05E
Newport, Eng., U.K.	26	50.42N	1.18W
Newport, Wales, U.K.	26	52.01N	4.51W
Newport, Ar., U.S.	144	35.36N	91.16W
Newport, Ky., U.S.	136	39.05N	84.29W
Newport, Me., U.S.	136	44.50N	69.16W
Newport, N.H., U.S.	136	43.21N	72.10W
Newport, Or., U.S.	150	44.38N	124.03W
Newport, R.I., U.S.	136	41.29N	71.18W
Newport, Tn., U.S.	142	35.58N	83.11W
Newport, Vt., U.S.	136	44.56N	72.12W
Newport, Wa., U.S.	150	48.11N	117.02W
Newport Beach	154	33.37N	117.55W
Newport News	142	36.58N	76.25W
New Port Richey	142	28.14N	82.43W
New Prague	138	44.32N	93.34W
New Providence I	108	25.02N	77.24W
Newquay	26	50.25N	5.05W
New Richmond	138	45.07N	92.32W
New Roads	144	30.42N	91.26W
New Rochelle	136	40.54N	73.46W
Newry, N. Ire., U.K.	26	54.11N	6.20W
Newry, S.C., U.S.	142	34.43N	82.54W
New Smyrna Beach	142	29.01N	80.55W
New South Wales □[3]	96	33.00S	146.00E
Newton, Il., U.S.	144	38.59N	88.09W
Newton, Ia., U.S.	138	41.41N	93.02W
Newton, Ma., U.S.	136	42.20N	71.12W
Newton, Ms., U.S.	144	32.19N	89.09W
Newton, N.J., U.S.	136	41.03N	74.45W

Symbols in the index entries are identified on page 162.

Newt—Ordz

Name	Page	Lat.	Long.
Newton, N.C., U.S.	142	35.40N	81.13W
Newton, Tx., U.S.	144	30.50N	93.45W
Newton Abbot	26	50.32N	3.36W
Newtownabbey	26	54.42N	5.54W
Newtownards	26	54.36N	5.41W
Newtown Saint Boswells	26	55.34N	2.40W
New Ulm	138	44.18N	94.27W
New Vienna	136	39.19N	83.41W
New Vineyard	136	44.48N	70.07W
New Waterford	130	46.15N	60.05W
New Westminster	130	49.12N	122.55W
New Whiteland	144	39.33N	86.05W
New Wilmington	136	41.07N	80.19W
New York	136	40.43N	74.01W
New York □3	132	43.00N	75.00W
New York State Barge Canal ☰	136	43.05N	78.43W
New Zealand □1	98	41.00S	174.00 E
Nezahualcóyotl, Presa ⊜1	108	17.10N	93.40W
Nežin	54	51.03N	31.54 E
Ngami, Lake ⊜	86	20.37S	22.40 E
Ngaoundéré	82	7.19N	13.35 E
Ngaruawahia	98	37.40S	175.09 E
Ngatangiia	94	21.14S	159.43W
Ngau I	91	18.02S	179.18 E
Ngauruhoe, Mount ∧	98	39.09S	175.38 E
Ngela Sule I	94	9.05S	160.15 E
Nggatokae Island I	94	8.46S	158.11 E
Nggela Pile I	94	9.05S	160.15 E
Ng'iro, Ewaso ≐	86	0.28N	39.55 E
Ngoko ≐	86	1.40N	16.03 E
Nguigmi	82	14.15N	13.07 E
Nguru	82	12.52N	10.27 E
Nha-trang	68	12.15N	109.11 E
Niafounké	82	15.56N	4.00W
Niagara	138	45.46N	87.59W
Niagara Falls, On., Can.	130	43.06N	79.04W
Niagara Falls, N.Y., U.S.	136	43.05N	79.03W
Niah	68	3.52N	113.44 E
Niamey	82	13.31N	2.07 E
Niantic	144	39.51N	89.10W
Nias, Pulau I	68	1.05N	97.35 E
Nicaragua □1	108	13.00N	85.00W
Nicaragua, Lago de ⊜	108	11.30N	85.30W
Nicastro	40	38.59N	16.20 E
Nice	36	43.42N	7.15 E
Niceville	144	30.31N	86.28W
Nicholasville	142	37.52N	84.34W
Nicholson ≐	96	17.31S	139.36 E
Nicobar Islands II	68	8.00N	93.30 E
Nicolet, Lake ⊜	138	46.20N	84.15W
Nicollet	138	44.16N	94.11W
Nicosia, It.	40	37.45N	14.24 E
Nicosia (Levkosía), Kípros	16	35.10N	33.22 E
Nicotera	40	38.34N	15.57 E
Nicoya, Península de ≻1	108	10.00N	85.25W
Nida ≐	30	50.18N	20.52 E
Nidd ≐	26	54.01N	1.12W
Nidzica	30	53.22N	20.26 E
Niedere Tauern ∧	30	47.18N	14.00 E
Niedermarsberg	30	51.28N	8.50 E
Niedersachsen □3	30	52.40N	9.00 E
Niemodlin	30	50.39N	17.37 E
Nienburg	30	52.38N	9.13 E
Nieuw Amsterdam	118	5.53N	55.05W
Nieuw Nickerie	118	5.57N	56.59W
Nieuwpoort	30	51.08N	2.45 E
Niğde	16	37.59N	34.42 E
Niger □1	82	16.00N	8.00 E
Niger ≐	82	5.33N	6.33 E
Nigeria □1	82	10.00N	8.00 E
Nigrita	48	40.55N	23.30 E
Niigata	66	37.55N	139.03 E
Nijmegen	30	51.50N	5.50 E
Nikel'	20	69.24N	30.12 E
Nikolajev	54	46.58N	32.00 E
Nikolayev → Nikolajev	54	46.58N	32.00 E
Nikopol'	54	47.35N	34.25 E
Nikšić	48	42.46N	18.56 E
Nilakka ⊜	22	63.07N	26.33 E
Nile (Nahr an-Nīl) ≐	84	30.10N	31.06 E
Niles, Il., U.S.	138	42.01N	87.48W
Niles, Mi., U.S.	138	41.49N	86.15W
Niles, Oh., U.S.	136	41.10N	80.45W
Nimba, Mont ∧	82	7.37N	8.25W
Nimba Range ∧	82	7.30N	8.30W
Nîmes	36	43.50N	4.21 E
Nimule	84	3.36N	32.03 E
Nine Degree Channel ⊔	70	9.00N	73.00 E
Ninety Mile Beach ⩡2, Austl.	96	38.13S	147.23 E
Ninety Mile Beach ⩡2, N.Z.	98	34.48S	173.00 E
Ninety Six	142	34.10N	82.01W
Ningbo	66	29.52N	121.31 E
Ninh-binh	68	20.15N	105.59 E
Niobrara ≐	132	42.45N	98.00W
Niono	82	14.15N	6.00W
Nioro du Sahel	82	15.15N	9.35W
Niort	36	46.19N	0.27W
Nipawin	130	53.22N	104.00W
Nipigon	130	49.01N	88.16W
Nipigon, Lake ⊜	130	49.50N	88.30W
Nipissing, Lake ⊜	130	46.17N	80.00W
Nipomo	154	35.02N	120.28W
Niš	48	43.19N	21.54 E
Nisa (Neisse) (Nysa Łużycka) ≐	30	52.04N	14.46 E
Nišava ≐	48	43.22N	21.46 E
Niscemi	40	37.09N	14.23 E
Nisling ≐	130	62.27N	139.30W
Nissan ≐	22	56.40N	12.51 E
Nisser ⊜	22	59.10N	8.30 E
Nissum Bredning ᴄ	22	56.38N	8.22 E
Niterói	118	22.53S	43.07W
Nith ≐	26	55.00N	3.35W
Nitra	30	48.20N	18.05 E
Nitra ≐	30	47.46N	18.10 E
Nitro	136	38.24N	81.50W
Niue □2	8	19.02S	169.52W
Nive ≐	36	43.30N	1.29W
Nivelles	30	50.36N	4.20 E
Nixa	144	37.02N	93.17W
Nizāmābād	70	18.40N	78.07 E
Nízke Tatry ∧	30	48.54N	19.40 E
Nižn'aja Tunguska ≐	54	65.48N	88.04 E
Nižnekamsk	20	55.32N	51.58 E
Nižnij Tagil	54	57.55N	59.57 E
Njazidja I	86	11.35S	43.20 E
Njombe ≐	86	6.56S	35.06 E
Nkongsamba	82	4.57N	9.56 E
Nmai ≐	66	25.42N	97.30 E
Nobeoka	66	32.35N	131.40 E
Noblesville	144	40.02N	86.00W
Nocatee	142	27.09N	81.52W
Noce ≐	40	46.09N	11.04 E
Nocera [Inferiore]	40	40.44N	14.38 E
Nodaway ≐	144	39.54N	94.58W
Noel	144	36.32N	94.29W
Nogales, Méx.	108	31.20N	110.56W
Nogales, Az., U.S.	148	31.20N	110.56W
Nogara	40	45.11N	11.04 E
Nogaro	36	43.46N	0.02W
Nogent-le-Rotrou	36	48.19N	0.50 E
Noginsk	20	55.51N	38.27 E
Noir, Causse ∧1	36	44.10N	3.15 E
Noirmoutier, Île de I	36	47.00N	2.15W
Nokia	22	61.28N	23.30 E
Nokomis, Fl., U.S.	142	27.07N	82.26W
Nokomis, Il., U.S.	144	39.18N	89.17W
Nokuku	92	14.53S	166.35 E
Nola	40	40.55N	14.33 E
Nolichucky ≐	142	36.07N	83.14W
Nolin ≐	144	37.13N	86.15W
Nolin Lake ⊜1	144	37.20N	86.10W
Nome	132a	64.30N	165.24W
Nong'an	66	44.25N	125.10 E
Nong Khai	68	17.52N	102.44 E
Nooksack ≐	150	48.46N	122.35W
Noordoost Polder ◆1	30	52.42N	5.45 E
Nóqui	86	5.51S	13.25 E
Nora Islands II	84	16.02N	40.03 E
Noranda	130	48.15N	79.02W
Nora Springs	138	43.08N	93.00W
Norcross	142	33.56N	84.12W
Norden	30	53.36N	7.12 E
Nordenham	30	53.29N	8.28 E
Nordenšel'da, archipelag II	56	76.45N	96.00 E
Norderney I	30	53.42N	7.10 E
Nordfjord ᴄ2	22	61.54N	5.12 E
Nordhausen	30	51.30N	10.47 E
Nordhorn	30	52.27N	7.05 E
Nordkapp ≻	20	71.11N	25.48 E
Nordkinnhalvøya ≻1	20	70.55N	27.45 E
Nördlingen	30	48.51N	10.30 E
Nord-Ostsee-Kanal ☰	30	53.53N	9.08 E
Nordre Strømfjord ᴄ2	130	67.50N	52.00W
Nordrhein-Westfalen □3	30	51.30N	7.30 E
Nordstrand I	30	54.30N	8.53 E
Norfolk, Ne., U.S.	132	42.02N	97.25W
Norfolk, Va., U.S.	142	36.50N	76.17W
Norfolk □6	26	52.35N	1.00 E
Norfolk Island □2	93	29.02S	167.57 E
Norfork Lake ⊜1	144	36.25N	92.10W
Noril'sk	56	69.20N	88.06 E
Norlina	142	36.26N	78.11W
Normal, Al., U.S.	144	34.47N	86.34W
Normal, Il., U.S.	138	40.30N	88.59W
Norman	132	35.13N	97.26W
Norman ≐	96	17.28S	140.49 E
Norman, Lake ⊜1	142	35.35N	80.55W
Normandie □9	36	49.00N	0.05W
Normandie, Collines de ∧2	36	48.40N	0.30W
Normandy → Normandie □9	36	49.00N	0.05W
Norman Park	142	31.16N	83.41W
Normanton	96	17.40S	141.05 E
Norman Wells	130	65.17N	126.51W
Norra Kvarken (Merenkurkku) ⊔	22	63.36N	20.43 E
Norra Storfjället ∧	20	65.52N	15.18 E
Nørresundby	22	57.04N	9.55 E
Norris Lake ⊜1	142	36.20N	83.55W
Norristown	136	40.07N	75.20W
Norrköping	22	58.36N	16.11 E
Norrtälje	22	59.46N	18.42 E
Norseman	96	32.12S	121.46 E
Norsup	92	16.05S	167.23 E
Norte, Canal do ⊔	118	0.30N	50.30W
North	142	33.36N	81.06W
North, Cape ≻	130	47.02N	60.25W
North Adams, Ma., U.S.	136	42.42N	73.06W
North Adams, Mi., U.S.	138	41.58N	84.32W
Northam	96	31.39S	116.40 E
North America ⩡1	8	45.00N	100.00W
Northampton, Eng., U.K.	26	52.14N	0.54W
Northampton, Ma., U.S.	136	42.19N	72.38W
Northampton, Pa., U.S.	136	40.41N	75.29W
Northamptonshire □6	26	52.20N	0.50W
North Andaman I	70	13.15N	92.55 E
North Atlanta	142	33.51N	84.20W
North Augusta	142	33.30N	81.57W
North Baltimore	136	41.10N	83.40W
North Battleford	130	52.47N	108.17W
North Bay	130	46.19N	79.28W
North Bend	150	43.24N	124.13W
North Canton	136	40.52N	81.24W
North Cape ≻, N.Z.	98	34.25S	173.02 E
North Cape → Nordkapp ≻, Nor.	20	71.11N	25.48 E
North Carolina □3	132	35.30N	80.00W
North Cascades National Park ◆	150	48.30N	121.00W
North Channel ⊔, On., Can.	130	46.02N	82.50W
North Channel ⊔, U.K.	26	55.10N	5.40W
North Charleston	142	32.51N	79.58W
North Chicago	138	42.19N	87.50W
North College Hill	136	39.13N	84.33W
North Conway	136	44.03N	71.07W
North Crossett	144	33.09N	91.56W
North Dakota □3	132	47.30N	100.15W
North Downs ∧1	26	51.20N	0.10 E
North East, Md., U.S.	136	39.36N	75.56W
North East, Pa., U.S.	136	42.12N	79.50W
Northeim	30	51.42N	10.00 E
Northern Dvina → Severnaja Dvina ≐	54	64.32N	40.30 E
Northern Indian Lake ⊜	130	57.20N	97.20W
Northern Ireland □8	26	54.40N	6.45W
Northern Mariana Islands □2	68	18.00N	146.00 E
Northern Territory □8	96	20.00S	134.00 E
Northfield, Ma., U.S.	136	42.41N	72.27W
Northfield, Mn., U.S.	138	44.27N	93.09W
Northfield, Vt., U.S.	136	44.09N	72.39W
North Flinders Range ∧	96	31.00S	139.00 E
North Fond du Lac	138	43.48N	88.29W
North Foreland ≻	26	51.23N	1.27 E
North Fork ≐	144	36.13N	92.17W
North Fort Myers	142	26.40N	81.52W
North Freedom	138	43.27N	89.52W
North Frisian Islands II	20	54.50N	8.12 E
Northglenn	148	39.53N	104.59W
North Gulfport	144	30.24N	89.06W
North Head ≻	98	36.25S	174.03 E
North Henderson	142	36.21N	78.22W
North Hero	136	44.49N	73.17W
North Highlands	154	38.41N	121.22W
North Island I	98	39.00S	176.00 E
North Judson	144	41.12N	86.46W
North Laramie ≐	148	42.08N	104.56W
North Las Vegas	154	36.11N	115.07W
North La Veta Pass ⌅	148	37.37N	105.11W
North Liberty	144	41.32N	86.25W
North Little Rock	144	34.46N	92.16W
North Mamm Peak ∧	148	39.23N	107.52W
North Manchester	144	41.00N	85.46W
North Manitou Island I	138	45.06N	86.01W
North Mankato	138	44.10N	94.02W
North Miami	142	25.53N	80.11W
North Miami Beach	142	25.55N	80.09W
North Muskegon	138	43.15N	86.16W
North Myrtle Beach	142	33.49N	78.40W
North New River Canal ☰	142	26.05N	80.12W
North Ogden	148	41.18N	111.57W
North Palisade ∧	154	37.06N	118.31W
North Palm Beach	142	26.49N	80.04W
North Park	138	42.20N	89.03W
North Platte	132	41.07N	100.45W
North Platte ≐	132	41.07N	100.42W
North Point ≻	138	45.02N	83.16W
Northport	144	33.13N	87.34W
North Salt Lake	148	40.50N	111.54W
North Saskatchewan ≐	130	53.15N	105.05W
North Sea ᴛ2	16	56.00N	3.00 E
North Siberian Lowland → Severo-Sibirskaja nizmennost' ≚	54	73.00N	100.00 E
North Stradbroke Island I	96	27.35S	153.28 E
North Terre Haute	144	39.31N	87.21W
North Thompson ≐	130	50.41N	120.21W
North Uist I	26	57.36N	7.18W
Northumberland □6	26	55.15N	2.05W
Northumberland Strait ⊔	130	46.00N	63.30W
North Vernon	144	39.00N	85.37W
North West Cape ≻	96	21.45S	114.10 E
Northwest Territories □4	130	70.00N	100.00W
North Wilkesboro	142	36.09N	81.08W
Northwood	138	43.26N	93.13W
North Yorkshire □6	26	54.15N	1.30W
Norton	142	36.56N	82.37W
Norton Shores	138	43.10N	86.15W
Nort-sur-Erdre	36	47.26N	1.30W
Norwalk, Ct., U.S.	136	41.07N	73.24W
Norwalk, Ia., U.S.	138	41.28N	93.40W
Norwalk, Oh., U.S.	136	41.14N	82.36W
Norway, Ia., U.S.	138	41.54N	91.55W
Norway, Ia., U.S.	144	41.54N	91.55W
Norway, Me., U.S.	136	44.12N	70.32W
Norway, Mi., U.S.	138	45.47N	87.54W
Norway (Norge) □1	20	62.00N	10.00 E
Norwegian Sea ᴛ2	20	69.00N	12.00 E
Norwich, Eng., U.K.	26	52.38N	1.18 E
Norwich, Ct., U.S.	136	41.32N	72.05W
Norwich, N.Y., U.S.	136	42.31N	75.31W
Norwood, Ma., U.S.	136	42.11N	71.12W
Norwood, N.C., U.S.	142	35.13N	80.07W
Norwood, Oh., U.S.	136	39.10N	84.27W
Norwoodville	138	41.39N	93.33W
Noshiro	66	40.12N	140.02 E
Nossob (Nosop) ≐	86	26.55S	20.37 E
Noteć ≐	30	52.44N	15.26 E
Notikewin ≐	130	57.15N	117.05W
Noto	40	36.53N	15.04 E
Noto, Golfo di ᴄ	40	36.50N	15.12 E
Noto-hantō ≻1	66	37.20N	137.00 E
Notre-Dame, Monts ∧	130	48.10N	68.00W
Nottingham	26	52.58N	1.10W
Nottinghamshire □6	26	53.00N	1.00W
Nottoway ≐	142	36.33N	76.55W
Nouâdhibou	82	20.54N	17.04W
Nouâdhibou, Râs ≻	82	20.46N	17.03W
Nouakchott	82	18.06N	15.57W
Nouâmghâr	82	19.22N	16.31W
Nouméa	92	22.16S	166.27 E
Noupoort	86	31.10S	24.57 E
Nouveau-Québec, Cratère du ≛6	130	61.17N	73.40W
Nouvelle-Calédonie (New Caledonia) I	92	21.30S	165.30 E
Nouvelle-France, Cap de ≻	130	62.27N	73.42W
Nova Friburgo	118	22.16S	42.32W
Nova Gradiška	48	45.16N	17.23 E
Nova Iguaçu	118	22.45S	43.27W
Novaja Sibir', ostrov I	56	75.00N	149.00 E
Novaja Zeml'a II	54	74.00N	57.00 E
Nováky	30	48.43N	18.34 E
Nova Lisboa → Huambo	86	12.44S	15.47 E
Novara	40	45.28N	8.38 E
Nova Scotia □4	130	45.00N	63.00W
Novato	154	38.06N	122.34W
Nova Zagora	48	42.29N	26.01 E
Novelda	44	38.23N	0.46W
Nové Město nad Váhom	30	48.46N	17.49 E
Nové Zámky	30	47.59N	18.11 E
Novgorod	20	58.31N	31.17 E
Novi Bečej	48	45.36N	20.08 E
Novi Beograd	48	44.49N	20.27 E
Novigrad	48	44.11N	15.33 E
Novi Ligure	40	44.46N	8.47 E
Novi Pazar, Blg.	48	43.21N	27.12 E
Novi Pazar, Jugo.	48	43.08N	20.31 E
Novi Sad	48	45.15N	19.50 E
Novi Vinodolski	48	45.08N	14.48 E
Novo Aripuanã	118	5.08S	60.22W
Novočerkassk	54	47.25N	40.06 E
Novodvinsk	54	64.26N	40.47 E
Novokujbyševsk	20	53.07N	49.58 E
Novokuzneck	56	53.45N	87.06 E
Novokuznetsk → Novokuzneck	56	53.45N	87.06 E
Novomoskovsk, S.S.S.R.	54	48.37N	35.12 E
Novomoskovsk, S.S.S.R.	54	54.05N	38.13 E
Novorossijsk	54	44.45N	37.45 E
Novošachtinsk	54	47.47N	39.56 E
Novosibirsk	56	55.02N	82.55 E
Novosibirskije ostrova II	56	75.00N	142.00 E
Novosibirskoje vodochranilišče ⊜1	54	54.35N	82.35 E
Novotroick	54	51.12N	58.20 E
Novov'atsk	54	58.29N	49.44 E
Nový Bohumín	30	49.56N	18.20 E
Nový Bor	30	50.45N	14.33 E
Nový Jičín	30	49.36N	18.00 E
Nowa Dęba	30	50.26N	21.46 E
Nowa Ruda	30	50.35N	16.31 E
Nowa Sól (Neusalz)	30	51.48N	15.44 E
Nowe	30	53.40N	18.43 E
Nowgong	70	26.20N	92.42 E
Nowogard	30	53.40N	15.08 E
Nowshāk ∧	70	36.26N	71.50 E
Nowshera	70	34.01N	71.59 E
Nowy Dwór Mazowiecki	30	52.26N	20.43 E
Nowy Sącz	30	49.38N	20.42 E
Nowy Staw	30	54.09N	19.00 E
Nowy Targ	30	49.29N	20.02 E
Noxapater	144	32.59N	89.03W
Noxen	136	41.25N	76.03W
Noxon	150	48.00N	115.47W
Noxubee ≐	144	32.50N	88.10W
Noyon	36	49.35N	3.00 E
Nsanje	86	16.55S	35.12 E
Nsawam	82	5.50N	0.20W
Nsukka	82	6.52N	7.24 E
Ntem ≐	82	2.15N	9.45 E
Nūbah, Jibāl an- ∧	84	11.00N	30.45 E
Nubian Desert ◆2	84	20.30N	33.00 E
Nueva, Isla I	120	55.13S	66.30W
Nueva Gerona	108	21.53N	82.48W
Nueva Imperial	120	38.44S	72.57W
Nueva Rosita	108	27.57N	101.13W
Nuevitas	108	21.33N	77.16W
Nuevo Laredo	108	27.30N	99.31W
Nûgssuaq ≻1	130	70.25N	52.30W
Nukus	54	42.50N	59.29 E
Nul	92	16.49S	168.24 E
Nullarbor Plain ≚	96	31.00S	129.00 E
Nunda	136	42.34N	77.56W
Nuneaton	26	52.32N	1.28W
Nuoro	40	40.19N	9.20 E
Nuremberg → Nürnberg	30	49.27N	11.04 E
Nurmes	22	63.33N	29.07 E
Nürnberg (Nuremberg)	30	49.27N	11.04 E
Nurri	40	39.43N	9.14 E
Nürtingen	30	48.38N	9.20 E
Nusa Tenggara (Lesser Sunda Islands) II	68	9.00S	120.00 E
Nu Shan ∧	66	27.00N	99.00 E
Nushki	70	29.33N	66.01 E
Nutter Fort	136	39.15N	80.19W
Nuweveldberge ∧	86	32.15S	21.50 E
Nyack	136	41.05N	73.55W
Nyala	84	12.03N	24.53 E
Nyanza	86	2.21S	29.45 E
Nyasa, Lake (Lake Malawi) ⊜	86	12.00S	34.30 E
Nyborg	22	55.19N	10.48 E
Nybro	22	56.45N	15.54 E
Nyíradony	30	47.41N	21.55 E
Nyírbátor	30	47.50N	22.08 E
Nyíregyháza	30	47.59N	21.43 E
Nykøbing, Dan.	22	56.48N	8.52 E
Nykøbing, Dan.	22	54.46N	11.53 E
Nyköping	22	58.45N	17.00 E
Nykroppa	22	59.38N	14.18 E
Nymburk	30	50.11N	15.03 E
Nynäshamn	22	58.54N	17.57 E
Nyngan	96	31.34S	147.11 E
Nyon	36	46.23N	6.14 E
Nyong ≐	82	3.17N	9.54 E
Nýrsko	30	49.18N	13.09 E
Nysa	30	50.29N	17.20 E
Nysa Kłodzka ≐	30	50.49N	17.50 E
Nysa Łużycka (Neisse) (Nisa) ≐	30	52.04N	14.46 E
Nzérékoré	82	7.45N	8.49W
Nzi ≐	82	5.57N	4.50W
Nzwani I	86	12.15S	44.25 E
O			
Oahe, Lake ⊜1	132	45.30N	100.25W
Oahu I	132b	21.30N	158.00W
Oak Bluffs	136	41.27N	70.33W
Oakboro	142	35.13N	80.19W
Oak Creek ≐	148	34.41N	111.56W
Oakdale	144	30.48N	92.39W
Oakesdale	150	47.07N	117.14W
Oakfield	138	43.41N	88.32W
Oak Grove	144	32.51N	91.23W
Oak Harbor	150	48.17N	122.38W
Oak Hill	136	37.58N	81.08W
Oak Knolls	154	34.51N	120.27W
Oakland, Ca., U.S.	154	37.48N	122.16W
Oakland, Ia., U.S.	144	41.18N	95.23W
Oakland, Me., U.S.	136	44.32N	69.43W
Oakland, Md., U.S.	136	39.24N	79.24W
Oakland City	144	38.20N	87.20W
Oakland Park	142	26.10N	80.07W
Oak Lawn	138	41.43N	87.45W
Oak Park	138	41.53N	87.47W
Oakridge, Or., U.S.	150	43.44N	122.27W
Oak Ridge, Tn., U.S.	142	36.00N	84.16W
Oak Ridge National Laboratory ⊛3	142	36.00N	84.15W
Oamaru	98	45.06S	170.58 E
Oancea	48	45.55N	28.06 E
Oaxaca	108	17.03N	96.43W
Ob' ≐	54	66.45N	69.30 E
Oban	26	56.25N	5.29W
Oberhausen	30	51.28N	6.50 E
Oberlin	136	41.17N	82.13W
Obernburg am Main	30	49.50N	9.08 E
Oberursel	30	50.11N	8.35 E
Obihiro	66	42.55N	143.12 E
Obing	30	48.00N	12.24 E
Obion	144	36.15N	89.11W
Obion ≐	144	35.55N	89.39W
Obock	84	11.59N	43.16 E
Obra ≐	30	52.36N	15.28 E
Obščij Syrt ∧	54	52.00N	51.30 E
Observation Peak ∧	154	40.46N	120.10W
Obskaja guba ᴄ	54	69.00N	73.00 E
Obuasi	82	6.14N	1.39W
Ocala	142	29.11N	82.08W
Ocaña	118	8.15N	73.20W
Occidental, Cordillera ∧, Col.	118	5.00N	76.00W
Occidental, Cordillera ∧, Perú	118	10.00S	77.00W
Oceana	142	37.41N	81.37W
Ocean City, Md., U.S.	136	38.20N	75.05W
Ocean City, N.J., U.S.	136	39.16N	74.34W
Ocean Falls	130	52.21N	127.40W
Oceanside	154	33.11N	117.22W
Ocean Springs	144	30.24N	88.49W
Ochlocknee	142	30.58N	84.03W
Ochlockonee ≐	142	29.58N	84.21W
Ochotsk	56	59.23N	143.18 E
Ochtrup	30	52.13N	7.11 E
Ocilla	142	31.35N	83.15W
Ocklawaha, Lake ⊜1	142	29.30N	81.50W
Ocmulgee ≐	142	31.58N	82.32W
Ocoee	142	28.34N	81.32W
Ocoee (Toccoa) ≐	142	35.12N	84.40W
Ocoña ≐	118	16.28S	73.07W
Oconee ≐	142	31.58N	82.32W
Oconee, Lake ⊜1	142	33.30N	83.15W
Oconomowoc	138	43.06N	88.29W
Oconto	138	44.53N	87.51W
Oconto Falls	138	44.52N	88.08W
Ocotal	108	13.38N	86.29W
Ocotlán	108	20.21N	102.46W
Ocracoke Island I	142	35.09N	75.53W
Ocumare del Tuy	118	10.07N	66.46W
Oda	82	5.55N	0.59W
Oda, Jabal ∧	84	20.21N	36.39 E
Odell	138	41.00N	88.31W
Ödemiş	48	38.13N	27.59 E
Odendaalsrus	86	27.48S	26.45 E
Odense	22	55.24N	10.23 E
Odenwald ∧	30	49.40N	9.00 E
Oder (Odra) ≐	30	53.32N	14.38 E
Oderhaff (Zalew Szczeciński) ᴄ	30	53.46N	14.14 E
Odessa, S.S.S.R.	54	46.28N	30.44 E
Odessa, Mo., U.S.	144	38.59N	93.57W
Odessa, Tx., U.S.	132	31.50N	102.22W
Odessa, Wa., U.S.	150	47.20N	118.41W
Odienné	82	9.30N	7.34W
Odobeşti	48	45.45N	27.04 E
Odon	144	38.50N	86.59W
Odorheiu Secuiesc	48	46.18N	25.18 E
Odžaci	48	45.30N	19.16 E
Oelde	30	51.49N	8.08 E
Oelsnitz	30	50.24N	12.10 E
Oelwein	138	42.40N	91.54W
O'Fallon	144	38.48N	90.41W
Ofanto ≐	40	41.22N	16.13 E
Offaly □6	26	53.20N	7.30W
Offenbach	30	50.08N	8.47 E
Offenburg	30	48.28N	7.57 E
Ofotfjorden ᴄ2	20	68.23N	16.12 E
Ofu	93	14.10S	169.42W
Ogaden ◆1	84	8.00N	44.00 E
Ogallala	132	41.07N	101.43W
Ogasawara-guntō II	8	27.00N	142.10 E
Ogbomosho	82	8.08N	4.15 E
Ogden, Ia., U.S.	138	42.02N	94.01W
Ogden, Ut., U.S.	148	41.13N	111.58W
Ogdensburg	136	44.41N	75.29W
Ogeechee ≐	142	31.51N	81.06W
Ogilvie Mountains ∧	130	65.00N	139.30W
Oglesby	138	41.17N	89.03W
Oglethorpe	142	32.17N	84.03W
Ogliastra ◆1	40	39.56N	9.37 E
Oglio ≐	40	45.02N	10.39 E
Ognon ≐	36	47.20N	5.29 E
Ogoja	82	6.40N	8.48 E
Ogooué ≐	86	0.49S	9.00 E
Ogunquit	136	43.14N	70.35W
Ohakune	98	39.25S	175.24 E
Ohau, Lake ⊜	98	44.15S	169.51 E
O'Higgins, Lago (Lago San Martín) ⊜	120	49.00S	72.40W
Ohio	138	41.34N	89.28W
Ohio □3	132	40.15N	82.45W
Ohio ≐	132	36.59N	89.08W
Ohio City	136	40.46N	84.36W
Ohio Peak ∧	148	38.49N	107.07W
Ohoopee ≐	142	31.54N	82.07W
Ohře ≐	30	50.32N	14.08 E
Ohrid	48	41.07N	20.47 E
Ohrid, Lake ⊜	48	41.02N	20.43 E
Öhringen	30	49.12N	9.29 E
Oiapoque (Oyapock) ≐	118	4.08N	51.40W
Oil City, La., U.S.	144	32.44N	93.58W
Oil City, Pa., U.S.	136	41.26N	79.42W
Oil Creek ≐	136	41.26N	79.42W
Oildale	154	35.25N	119.01W
Oil Trough	144	35.37N	91.27W
Oise ≐	36	49.00N	2.04 E
Oisemont	36	49.57N	1.46 E
Ōita	66	33.14N	131.36 E
Ojai	154	34.26N	119.14W
Ojinaga	108	29.34N	104.25W
Ojos del Salado, Nevado ∧	120	27.06S	68.32W
Oka ≐	54	56.20N	43.59 E
Okahandja	86	21.59S	16.58 E
Okanogan	150	48.21N	119.34W
Okanogan ≐	150	48.06N	119.43W
Okāra	70	30.49N	73.27 E
Okavango (Cubango) ≐	86	18.50S	22.25 E
Okavango Delta ≛2	86	18.45S	22.45 E
Okayama	66	34.39N	133.55 E
Okeechobee	142	27.14N	80.49W
Okeechobee, Lake ⊜	142	26.55N	80.45W
Okefenokee Swamp ≡	142	30.42N	82.20W
Okemos	138	42.43N	84.25W
Okene	82	7.33N	6.15 E
Okhotsk, Sea of (Ochotskoje more) ᴛ2	56	53.00N	150.00 E
Okinawa-jima I	66	26.30N	128.00 E
Okinawa-shotō II	66	25.00N	126.00 E
Okino-Tori-shima (Parece Vela) I	66	20.25N	136.00 E
Oki-shotō II	66	36.15N	133.15 E
Oklahoma □3	132	35.30N	98.00W
Oklahoma City	132	35.28N	97.30W
Oklawaha ≐	142	29.28N	81.41W
Okmulgee	132	35.37N	95.57W
Okolona, Ky., U.S.	144	38.08N	85.41W
Okolona, Ms., U.S.	144	34.00N	88.45W
Oksskolten ∧	20	65.59N	14.15 E
Okt'abr'skoj Revol'ucii, ostrov I	56	79.30N	97.00 E
Olancha	154	36.16N	118.00W
Olancha Peak ∧	154	36.16N	118.07W
Olanchito	108	15.30N	86.35W
Öland I	22	56.45N	16.38 E
Olanta	142	33.56N	79.55W
Olar	142	33.10N	81.11W
Olathe	144	38.52N	94.49W
Olavarría	120	36.54S	60.17W
Oława	30	50.57N	17.17 E
Olbia	40	40.55N	9.31 E
Ol'chon, ostrov I	56	53.09N	107.24 E
Olcott	136	43.20N	78.42W
Old Crow	130	67.35N	139.50W
Old Crow ≐	130	67.35N	139.50W
Oldenburg	30	53.08N	8.13 E
Oldenburg [in Holstein]	30	54.17N	10.52 E
Oldenzaal	30	52.19N	6.56 E
Old Faithful Geyser ᴛ4	150	44.30N	110.45W
Old Forge, N.Y., U.S.	136	43.42N	74.58W
Old Forge, Pa., U.S.	136	41.22N	75.44W
Oldham	26	53.33N	2.07W
Old Hickory Lake ⊜1	144	36.18N	86.30W
Old Orchard Beach	136	43.31N	70.22W
Olds	130	51.47N	114.06W
Old Saybrook	136	41.17N	72.22W
Old Speck Mountain ∧	136	44.34N	70.57W
Old Town	136	44.56N	68.38W
Old Trap	142	36.15N	76.02W
Old Wives Lake ⊜	130	50.06N	106.00W
Olean	136	42.04N	78.25W
Olekma → Ol'okma ≐	56	60.22N	120.42 E
Olen'ok ≐	56	73.00N	119.55 E
Olen'okskij zaliv ᴄ	56	73.20N	121.00 E
Oléron, Île d' I	36	45.56N	1.15W
Oleśnica	30	51.13N	17.23 E
Olesno	30	50.53N	18.25 E
Olga, Mount ∧	96	25.19S	130.46 E
Olhão	44	37.02N	7.50W
Olib, Otok I	40	44.22N	14.48 E
Olifants ≐	86	24.10S	32.40 E
Olimbia ⊥	48	37.38N	21.41 E
Ólimbos ∧, Ellás	48	40.05N	22.21 E
Ólimbos ∧, Kípros	16	34.56N	32.52 E
Olinda	118	8.01S	34.51W
Oliva	44	38.55N	0.07W
Oliva de la Frontera	44	38.16N	6.55W
Olive Hill	136	38.18N	83.10W
Olivehurst	154	39.05N	121.33W
Olivenza	44	38.41N	7.06W
Oliver Springs	142	36.02N	84.20W
Olla	144	31.54N	92.14W
Ollagüe	118	21.14S	68.16W
Olmos	118	5.59S	79.46W
Olney	144	38.43N	88.05W
Ol'okma ≐	56	60.22N	120.42 E
Olomouc	30	49.36N	17.16 E
Olongapo	68	14.50N	120.16 E
Oloron, Gave d' ≐	36	43.33N	1.05W
Oloron-Sainte-Marie	36	43.12N	0.36W
Olot	44	42.11N	2.29 E
Olpe	30	51.02N	7.52 E
Olsztyn (Allenstein)	30	53.48N	20.29 E
Olsztynek	30	53.36N	20.17 E
Olt ≐	48	43.43N	24.51 E
Olten	36	47.21N	7.54 E
Olteniţa	48	44.05N	26.39 E
Olteţ ≐	48	44.14N	24.27 E
Oluan Pi ≻	66	21.54N	120.51 E
Ol'utorskij, mys ≻	56	59.55N	170.27 E
Ol'utorskij zaliv ᴄ	56	60.15N	168.30 E
Olympia	150	47.02N	122.53W
Olympia → Olimbia ⊥	48	37.38N	21.41 E
Olympic Mountains ∧	150	47.50N	123.45W
Olympic National Park ◆	150	47.48N	123.30W
Olympus, Mount → Ólimbos ∧	48	40.05N	22.21 E
Olympus, Mount ∧	150	47.48N	123.43W
Omagh	26	54.36N	7.18W
Omaha	132	41.15N	95.56W
Omak	150	48.24N	119.31W
Omak Lake ⊜	150	48.16N	119.23W
Oman ('Umān) □1	70	22.00N	58.00 E
Oman, Gulf of ᴄ	70	24.30N	58.30 E
Omatako ≐	86	17.59S	20.30 E
Omdurman → Umm Durmān	84	15.38N	32.30 E
Omegna	40	45.53N	8.24 E
Ometepe, Isla de I	108	11.30N	85.35W
Omineca ≐	130	56.05N	124.30W
Omo ≐	84	4.31N	35.59 E
Omodeo, Lago ⊜	40	40.08N	8.55 E
Omro	138	44.02N	88.44W
Omsk	56	55.00N	73.24 E
Omul, Vîrful ∧	48	45.26N	25.26 E
Omulew ≐	30	53.05N	21.32 E
Omurtag	48	43.06N	26.25 E
Ōmuta	66	33.02N	130.27 E
Omutninsk	54	58.40N	52.12 E
Onda	44	39.58N	0.15W
Ondava ≐	30	48.27N	21.48 E
Ondjiva	86	17.03S	15.47 E
Ondo	82	7.04N	4.47 E
Oneco	142	27.26N	82.32W
Onega	54	63.55N	38.05 E
Onega ≐	54	63.58N	37.55 E
Onega, Lake → Onežskoje ozero ⊜	54	61.30N	35.45 E
One Hundred and Two ≐	144	39.44N	94.43W
Oneida, Il., U.S.	138	41.04N	90.13W
Oneida, Ky., U.S.	142	37.16N	83.38W
Oneida, N.Y., U.S.	136	43.05N	75.39W
Oneida, Tn., U.S.	142	36.29N	84.30W
Oneida Lake ⊜	136	43.13N	76.00W
O'Neill	132	42.27N	98.38W
Oneonta, Al., U.S.	144	33.56N	86.28W
Oneonta, N.Y., U.S.	136	42.27N	75.03W
Onežskaja guba ᴄ	20	64.20N	36.30 E
Onežskij poluostrov ≻1	20	64.35N	38.00 E
Onežskoje ozero ⊜	54	61.30N	35.45 E
Onitsha	82	6.09N	6.47 E
Onon ≐	66	51.42N	115.50 E
Onset	136	41.44N	70.39W
Onslow	96	21.39S	115.06 E
Onslow Bay ᴄ	142	34.20N	77.20W
Ontario, Ca., U.S.	154	34.03N	117.39W
Ontario, Oh., U.S.	136	40.45N	82.35W
Ontario, Or., U.S.	150	44.01N	116.57W
Ontario □4	130	51.00N	85.00W
Ontario, Lake ⊜	132	43.45N	78.00W
Ontinyent (Onteniente)	44	38.49N	0.37W
Ontonagon	138	46.52N	89.18W
Oolitic	144	38.54N	86.31W
Oologah Lake ⊜1	144	36.33N	95.36W
Oostburg	138	43.37N	87.47W
Oostelijk Flevoland ◆1	30	52.30N	5.45 E
Oostende (Ostende)	30	51.13N	2.55 E
Oosterhout	30	51.38N	4.51 E
Ootacamund	70	11.24N	76.42 E
Opava	30	49.56N	17.54 E
Opava ≐	30	49.50N	18.13 E
Opelika	144	32.38N	85.22W
Opelousas	144	30.32N	92.04W
Ophir	150	42.33N	124.22W
Opoczno	30	51.23N	20.17 E
Opole (Oppeln)	30	50.41N	17.55 E
Oporto → Porto	44	41.11N	8.36W
Opotiki	98	38.00S	177.17 E
Opp	144	31.16N	86.15W
Opportunity	150	47.39N	117.14W
Opunake	98	39.27S	173.51 E
Oquawka	144	40.55N	90.56W
Ora	40	46.21N	11.18 E
Oracle	148	32.36N	110.46W
Oradea	48	47.03N	21.57 E
Oran → Wahran	82	35.43N	0.43W
Oran	144	37.05N	89.39W
Oran, Sebkha d' ⊜	44	35.32N	0.48W
Orange, Austl.	96	33.17S	149.06 E
Orange, Fr.	36	44.08N	4.48 E
Orange, Ma., U.S.	136	42.35N	72.18W
Orange, Tx., U.S.	144	30.05N	93.44W
Orange, Va., U.S.	136	38.14N	78.06W
Orange (Oranje) ≐	86	28.41S	16.28 E
Orange, Cabo ≻	118	4.24N	51.33W
Orangeburg	142	33.29N	80.51W
Orange City	142	28.57N	81.17W
Orange Lake	142	29.25N	82.13W
Orange Park	142	30.09N	81.42W
Oranienburg	30	52.45N	13.14 E
Oranjemund	86	28.38S	16.24 E
Oranjestad	108	12.33N	70.06W
Orăştie	48	45.50N	23.12 E
Oravita	48	45.02N	21.41 E
Orb ≐	36	43.15N	3.18 E
Orbetello	40	42.27N	11.13 E
Orbieu ≐	36	43.14N	2.54 E
Orbost	96	37.42S	148.27 E
Orcera	44	38.19N	2.39W
Orchard Homes	150	46.51N	114.02W
Orchard Mesa	148	39.02N	108.33W
Orchard Park	136	42.46N	78.44W
Orchard Valley	148	41.05N	104.48W
Orchila, Isla I	118	11.48N	66.09W
Orchon ≐	66	50.21N	106.05 E
Ord ≐	96	15.30S	128.21 E
Ordžonikidze	54	43.03N	44.40 E

Symbols in the index entries are identified on page 162.

Symbols in the index entries are identified on page 162.

Name	Page	Lat.	Long.
Pforzheim	30	48.54N	8.42 E
Pfronten	30	47.34N	10.33 E
Pfunds	30	46.58N	10.33 E
Pfungstadt	30	49.48N	8.36 E
Phangan, Ko I	68	9.45N	100.04 E
Phanom Dongrak, Thiu Khao ⋏	68	14.25N	103.30 E
Phan-rang	68	11.34N	108.59 E
Phan-thiet	68	10.56N	108.06 E
Pheba	144	33.35N	88.56W
Phelps, N.Y., U.S.	136	42.57N	77.03W
Phelps, Wi., U.S.	138	46.03N	89.05W
Phenix City	142	32.28N	85.00W
Phetchabun, Thiu Khao ⋏	68	16.20N	100.55 E
Philadelphia, Ms., U.S.	144	32.46N	89.07W
Philadelphia, N.Y., U.S.	136	44.09N	75.42W
Philadelphia, Pa., U.S.	136	39.57N	75.09W
Phil Campbell	144	34.21N	87.42W
Philippeville → Skikda	82	36.50N	6.58 E
Philippi	136	39.09N	80.02W
Philippines (Pilipinas) □ [1]	68	13.00N	122.00 E
Philippine Sea ⩡ [2]	8	20.00N	135.00 E
Philipsburg	136	40.53N	78.13W
Phillips	138	45.41N	90.24W
Phillipsburg, Ga., U.S.	142	31.34N	83.31W
Phillipsburg, N.J., U.S.	136	40.41N	75.11W
Philo, Il., U.S.	144	40.01N	88.09W
Philo, Oh., U.S.	136	39.51N	81.54W
Phimai	68	15.13N	102.30 E
Phitsanulok	68	16.50N	100.15 E
Phnom Penh → Phnum Pénh	68	11.33N	104.55 E
Phnum Pénh	68	11.33N	104.55 E
Phoenix, Az., U.S.	148	33.26N	112.04W
Phoenix, N.Y., U.S.	136	43.13N	76.18W
Phoenix Islands II	8	4.00S	172.00W
Phoenixville	136	40.07N	75.30W
Phrae	68	18.09N	100.08 E
Phra Nakhon Si Ayutthaya	68	14.21N	100.33 E
Phuket	68	7.53N	98.24 E
Phuket, Ko I	68	8.00N	98.22 E
Phu-ly	68	20.32N	105.56 E
Phu-quoc, Dao I	68	10.12N	104.00 E
Piacenza	40	45.01N	9.40 E
Pianella	40	42.24N	14.02 E
Pianosa, Isola I	40	42.35N	10.04 E
Piaseczno	30	52.05N	21.01 E
Piatra-Neamț	48	46.56N	26.22 E
Piatra Olt	48	44.24N	24.16 E
Piave ≃	40	45.32N	12.44 E
Piazza Armerina	40	37.23N	14.22 E
Pibor ≃	84	8.26N	33.13 E
Pibor Post	84	6.48N	33.08 E
Picardie □ [9]	36	49.45N	2.50 E
Picayune	144	30.31N	89.40W
Pichanal	120	23.19S	64.13W
Picher	144	36.59N	94.49W
Pickens	142	34.53N	82.42W
Pickle Crow	130	51.30N	90.04W
Pickwick Lake ⊜ [1]	144	34.55N	88.10W
Picton	98	41.18S	174.01 E
Picton, Isla I	120	55.02S	66.57W
Pictou	130	45.41N	62.43W
Pictured Rocks National Lakeshore ♦	138	46.35N	86.20W
Pidurutalagala ∧	70	7.00N	80.46 E
Piedmont, Al., U.S.	144	33.55N	85.36W
Piedmont, Mo., U.S.	144	37.09N	90.41W
Piedras Negras	108	28.42N	100.31W
Pieksämäki	22	62.18N	27.08 E
Pielinen ⊜	22	63.15N	29.40 E
Pierre	132	44.22N	100.21W
Pierre Part	144	29.57N	91.12W
Pierson	142	29.14N	81.27W
Pierz	138	45.58N	94.06W
Piešt'any	30	48.36N	17.50 E
Pietermaritzburg	86	29.37S	30.16 E
Pietersburg	86	23.54S	29.25 E
Pietrasanta	40	43.57N	10.14 E
Pietrosu, Vîrful ∧, Rom.	48	47.08N	25.11 E
Pietrosu, Vîrful ∧, Rom.	48	47.36N	24.38 E
Pieve di Cadore	40	46.26N	12.22 E
Pigeon	138	43.49N	83.16W
Pigeon Forge	142	35.47N	83.33W
Piggott	144	36.22N	90.11W
Pihlava	22	61.33N	21.36 E
Pikes Peak ∧	148	38.51N	105.03W
Pikesville	136	39.22N	76.43W
Piketon	136	39.04N	83.00W
Pikeville	142	37.28N	82.31W
Piła (Schneidemühl)	30	53.10N	16.44 E
Pilcomayo ≃	120	25.21S	57.42W
Pīlībhīt	70	28.38N	79.48 E
Pilica ≃	30	51.52N	21.17 E
Pilot Knob	144	37.37N	90.38W
Pilot Mountain	142	36.23N	80.28W
Pilot Peak ∧	150	44.58N	109.53W
Pilsen → Plzeň	30	49.45N	13.23 E
Pinang → George Town	68	5.25N	100.20 E
Pinang, Pulau I	68	5.23N	100.15 E
Pinar del Río	108	22.25N	83.42W
Pinardville	136	42.59N	71.30W
Pinckney	138	42.27N	83.56W
Pinckneyville	144	38.04N	89.22W
Pińczów	30	50.32N	20.35 E
Píndhos Óros ⋏	48	39.49N	21.14 E
Pindus Mountains → Píndhos Óros ⋏	48	39.49N	21.14 E
Pine Barrens ◆ [1]	136	39.48N	74.35W
Pine Bluff	144	34.13N	92.00W
Pine Castle	142	28.28N	81.22W
Pine City	138	45.49N	92.58W
Pine Creek	96	13.49S	131.49 E
Pine Creek ≃	136	41.10N	77.16W
Pine Creek Lake ⊜ [1]	144	34.05N	95.05W
Pinedale	154	36.50N	119.48W
Pinega ≃	54	64.08N	41.54 E
Pine Grove	136	40.32N	76.23W
Pine Hills	142	28.33N	81.27W
Pinehouse Lake ⊜	130	55.32N	106.35W
Pinehurst	150	45.15N	116.20W
Pine Island I	142	26.35N	82.06W
Pinellas Park	142	27.50N	82.41W
Pine Mountain ∧	142	32.51N	84.47W
Pine Point	130	61.01N	114.15W
Pinerolo	40	44.53N	7.21 E
Pinetops	142	35.47N	77.38W
Pineville, Ky., U.S.	142	36.45N	83.41W
Pineville, La., U.S.	144	31.19N	92.26W
Pineville, N.C., U.S.	142	35.04N	80.53W
Ping ≃	68	15.42N	100.09 E
Pingdingshan	66	33.45N	113.17 E
Pingliang	66	35.32N	106.41 E
P'ingtung	66	22.40N	120.29 E
Pingxiang	66	22.09N	106.43 E
Pingyao	66	37.16N	112.09 E
Piniós ≃	48	39.54N	22.45 E
Pinjarra	96	32.37S	115.53 E
Pinnacle ∧	98	41.49S	173.17 E
Pinnacle Buttes ∧	150	43.44N	109.57W
Pinneberg	30	53.40N	9.47 E
Pinos, Mount ∧	154	34.50N	119.09W
Pinrang	68	3.48S	119.38 E
Pins, Île des I	92	22.37S	167.30 E
Pinsk	54	52.07N	26.04 E
Piombino	40	42.55N	10.32 E
Pionki	30	51.30N	21.27 E
Piotrków Trybunalski	30	51.25N	19.42 E
Pipestone ≃	130	52.53N	89.23W
Pipmuacan, Réservoir ⊜ [1]	130	49.35N	70.30W
Piqua	136	40.08N	84.14W
Piracicaba	118	22.43S	47.38W
Piraeus → Piraiévs	48	37.57N	23.38 E
Piraiévs (Piraeus)	48	37.57N	23.38 E
Pirapora	118	17.21S	44.56W
Pirdop	48	42.42N	24.11 E
Pires do Rio	118	17.18S	48.17W
Pírgos	48	37.41N	21.28 E
Pirin ⋏	48	41.40N	23.30 E
Pirmasens	30	49.12N	7.36 E
Pirna	30	50.58N	13.56 E
Pirón ≃	44	41.23N	4.31W
Pirot	48	43.09N	22.35 E
Pīr Panjāl Range ⋏	70	33.37N	74.32 E
Pisa	40	43.43N	10.23 E
Pisa ≃	30	53.15N	21.52 E
Pisco	118	13.42S	76.13W
Pișcolt	48	47.35N	22.18 E
Písek	30	49.19N	14.10 E
Pismo Beach	154	35.08N	120.38W
Pisticci	40	40.23N	16.34 E
Pistoia	40	43.55N	10.54 E
Pisz	30	53.38N	21.49 E
Pit ≃	154	40.45N	122.22W
Pitcairn □ [2]	8	25.04S	130.05W
Piteå	22	65.20N	21.30 E
Piteälven ≃	20	65.14N	21.32 E
Pitești	48	44.52N	24.52 E
Pitigliano	40	42.38N	11.40 E
Pitt, Mount ∧	93	29.01S	167.56 E
Pittsboro, Ms., U.S.	144	33.56N	89.20W
Pittsboro, N.C., U.S.	142	35.43N	79.10W
Pittsburg, Ks., U.S.	144	37.24N	94.42W
Pittsburg, Tx., U.S.	144	32.59N	94.57W
Pittsburgh	136	40.26N	79.59W
Pittsfield, Il., U.S.	144	39.36N	90.48W
Pittsfield, Me., U.S.	136	44.46N	69.23W
Pittsfield, Ma., U.S.	136	42.27N	73.14W
Pittsfield, N.H., U.S.	136	43.18N	71.19W
Pittston	136	41.19N	75.47W
Piura	118	5.12S	80.38W
Piute Peak ∧	154	35.27N	118.24W
Piva ≃	48	43.21N	18.51 E
Piwniczna	30	49.27N	20.42 E
Placentia Bay ⊂	130	47.15N	54.30W
Placerville	154	38.43N	120.47W
Placetas	108	22.19N	79.40W
Plačkovica ⋏	48	41.45N	22.35 E
Plainfield, Ct., U.S.	136	41.40N	71.54W
Plainfield, In., U.S.	144	39.42N	86.23W
Plainfield, N.J., U.S.	136	40.37N	74.26W
Plains	142	32.02N	84.23W
Plainview, Mn., U.S.	138	44.09N	92.10W
Plainview, Tx., U.S.	132	34.11N	101.42W
Plainwell	138	42.26N	85.38W
Plaistow	136	42.50N	71.05W
Planeta Rica	118	8.25N	75.36W
Plano	138	41.39N	88.32W
Plantation	142	26.07N	80.14W
Plant City	142	28.01N	82.06W
Plantersville	144	32.39N	86.55W
Plaquemine	144	30.17N	91.14W
Plasencia	44	40.02N	6.05W
Plasy	30	49.56N	13.24 E
Plata, Río de la ⊂ [1]	120	35.00S	57.00W
Platani ≃	40	37.24N	13.16 E
Platte ≃, U.S.	144	39.16N	94.50W
Platte ≃, Ne., U.S.	132	41.04N	95.53W
Platte City	144	39.22N	94.46W
Platteville	138	42.44N	90.28W
Plattsburg	144	39.33N	94.26W
Plattsburgh	136	44.41N	73.27W
Plattsmouth	144	41.00N	95.52W
Plauen	30	50.30N	12.08 E
Pleasant, Mount ∧	142	37.44N	79.10W
Pleasant Gap	136	40.52N	77.44W
Pleasant Grove	148	40.21N	111.44W
Pleasant Hill	144	38.47N	94.16W
Pleasantville	136	39.23N	74.31W
Pleiku	68	13.59N	108.00 E
Plenty, Bay of ⊂	98	37.40S	177.00 E
Plessisville	130	46.14N	71.47W
Pleszew	30	51.54N	17.48 E
Pleven	48	43.25N	24.37 E
Plješevica ⋏	40	44.40N	15.45 E
Pljevlja	48	43.21N	19.21 E
Ploaghe	40	40.40N	8.45 E
Ploče	40	43.04N	17.26 E
Płock	30	52.33N	19.43 E
Plöckenpass)(	30	46.36N	12.58 E
Pločno ∧	40	43.23N	17.57 E
Ploiești	48	44.56N	26.02 E
Plomb du Cantal ∧	36	45.03N	2.46 E
Plön	30	54.09N	10.25 E
Płońsk	30	52.38N	20.23 E
Płoty	30	53.49N	15.16 E
Ploudalmézeau	36	48.32N	4.39W
Plovdiv	48	42.09N	24.45 E
Plumtree	86	20.30S	27.50 E
Plymouth, Monts.	108	16.42N	62.13W
Plymouth, Eng., U.K.	26	50.23N	4.10W
Plymouth, In., U.S.	144	41.20N	86.18W
Plymouth, Ma., U.S.	136	41.57N	70.40W
Plymouth, N.H., U.S.	136	43.45N	71.41W
Plymouth, N.C., U.S.	142	35.52N	76.44W
Plymouth, Oh., U.S.	136	41.00N	82.40W
Plymouth, Pa., U.S.	136	41.14N	75.56W
Plymouth, Wi., U.S.	138	43.44N	87.58W
Plzeň	30	49.45N	13.23 E
Po ≃	40	44.57N	12.04 E
Poarta Orientală, Pasul)(	48	45.06N	22.18 E
Pobeda, gora ∧	56	65.12N	146.12 E
Pobedy, pik ∧	54	42.02N	80.05 E
Pocahontas	144	36.15N	90.58W
Pocatello	150	42.52N	112.26W
Pocola	144	35.13N	94.28W
Pocomoke City	136	38.04N	75.34W
Pocono Mountains ⋏ [2]	136	41.10N	75.20W
Pocono Summit	136	41.07N	75.25W
Poços de Caldas	118	21.48S	46.34W
Poděbrady	30	50.08N	15.07 E
Podkamennaja Tunguska ≃	54	61.36N	90.18 E
Podlasie ◆ [1]	30	52.30N	23.00 E
Podol'sk	20	55.26N	37.33 E
Podravina ◆ [1]	48	45.40N	17.40 E
Podu Turcului	48	46.12N	27.23 E
Poel I	30	54.00N	11.26 E
Pogăniș ≃	48	45.41N	21.22 E
Poggibonsi	40	43.28N	11.09 E
P'ohang	66	36.03N	129.20 E
Point Au Fer Island I	144	29.15N	91.15W
Pointe-à-Pitre	108	16.14N	61.32W
Pointe-Noire	86	4.48S	11.51 E
Point Imperial ∧	148	36.16N	111.58W
Point Pelee National Park ♦	138	41.57N	82.30W
Point Pleasant, N.J., U.S.	136	40.04N	74.04W
Point Pleasant, W.V., U.S.	136	38.50N	82.08W
Point Reyes National Seashore ♦	154	38.00N	122.58W
Poissy	36	48.56N	2.03 E
Poitiers	36	46.35N	0.20 E
Pola de Laviana	44	43.15N	5.34W
Poland (Polska) □ [1]	30	52.00N	19.00 E
Polesje ◆ [1]	54	52.00N	27.00 E
Polgár	30	47.52N	21.08 E
Policastro, Golfo di ⊂	40	40.00N	15.30 E
Police	30	53.35N	14.33 E
Polillo Islands II	68	14.50N	122.05 E
Polistena	40	38.25N	16.05 E
Polk	136	41.22N	79.55W
Polkton	142	35.00N	80.12W
Pollino, Monte ∧	40	39.55N	16.11 E
Pollock	144	31.31N	92.24W
Pollux ∧	98	44.14S	168.53 E
Polo, Il., U.S.	138	41.59N	89.34W
Polo, Mo., U.S.	144	39.33N	94.02W
Polock	20	55.31N	28.46 E
Polson	150	47.41N	114.09W
Poltava	54	49.35N	34.34 E
Polynesia II	8	4.00S	156.00W
Pomabamba	118	8.50S	77.28W
Pomahaka ≃	98	46.09S	169.34 E
Pomerania □ [9]	30	54.00N	16.00 E
Pomeranian Bay ⊂	30	54.00N	14.15 E
Pomeroy	150	46.28N	117.36W
Pomme de Terre ≃	144	38.11N	93.24W
Pomme de Terre Lake ⊜ [1]	144	37.51N	93.19W
Pomona	154	34.03N	117.45W
Pomona Park	142	29.30N	81.35W
Pomorie	48	42.33N	27.39 E
Pomorskij proliv ʉ	20	68.30N	50.00 E
Pompano Beach	142	26.14N	80.07W
Pompei	40	40.45N	14.30 E
Pompei ⊥	40	40.45N	14.30 E
Pompton Lakes	136	41.00N	74.17W
Ponca City	132	36.42N	97.05W
Ponce	108	18.01N	66.37W
Ponce de Leon	144	30.43N	85.56W
Ponce de Leon Inlet ⊂	142	29.04N	80.55W
Poncha Pass)(	148	38.25N	106.05W
Ponchatoula	144	30.26N	90.26W
Pondicherry	70	11.56N	79.53 E
Ponente, Riviera di ⩤ [2]	40	44.10N	8.20 E
Ponferrada	44	42.33N	6.35W
Pongolo ≃	86	26.57S	32.17 E
Ponoj ≃	54	66.59N	41.17 E
Ponoka	130	52.42N	113.35W
Ponta Grossa	120	25.05S	50.09W
Pontão	44	39.55N	8.22W
Pontarlier	36	46.54N	6.22 E
Pontassieve	40	43.46N	11.26 E
Pont Canavese	40	45.25N	7.36 E
Pontchartrain, Lake ⊜	144	30.10N	90.10W
Pont-de-Vaux	36	46.26N	4.56 E
Ponte Caldelas	44	42.23N	8.30W
Pontedera	40	43.40N	10.38 E
Ponte Nova	118	20.24S	42.54W
Pontevedra	44	42.26N	8.38W
Ponte Vedra Beach	142	30.14N	81.23W
Pontiac, Il., U.S.	138	40.52N	88.37W
Pontiac, Mi., U.S.	138	42.38N	83.17W
Pontianak	68	0.02S	109.20 E
Pontivy	36	48.04N	2.59W
Pontoise	36	49.03N	2.06 E
Pontotoc	144	34.14N	88.59W
Pontremoli	40	44.22N	9.53 E
Pontresina	36	46.28N	9.53 E
Pontypridd	26	51.37N	3.22W
Pony	150	45.39N	111.53W
Ponziane, Isole II	40	40.55N	12.57 E
Poole	26	50.43N	1.59W
Poopó, Lago ⊜	118	18.45S	67.07W
Popayán	118	2.27N	76.36W
Pope	144	34.12N	89.56W
Poperinge	30	50.51N	2.43 E
Popești-Leordeni	48	44.23N	26.10 E
Poplar Bluff	144	36.45N	90.23W
Poplarville	144	30.50N	89.32W
Popocatépetl, Volcán ∧ [1]	108	19.02N	98.38W
Popovo	48	43.21N	26.13 E
Poprad	30	49.03N	20.18 E
Poprad ≃	30	49.38N	20.42 E
Poquoson	142	37.07N	76.21W
Porbandar	70	21.38N	69.36 E
Porcuna	44	37.52N	4.11W
Porcupine ≃	130	66.35N	145.15W
Porcupine Mountains State Park ♦	138	46.47N	89.50W
Pordenone	40	45.57N	12.39 E
Poreč	40	45.13N	13.37 E
Pori	22	61.29N	21.47 E
Porirua	98	41.08S	174.51 E
Porkkala	22	59.59N	24.26 E
Porlamar	118	10.57N	63.51W
Porretta Terme	40	44.09N	10.59 E
Porsangen ⊂ [2]	20	70.58N	27.00 E
Porsangerhalvøya › [1]	20	70.50N	25.00 E
Porsgrunn	22	59.09N	9.40 E
Portadown	26	54.26N	6.27W
Portage, Mi., U.S.	138	42.12N	85.34W
Portage, Wi., U.S.	138	43.32N	89.27W
Portage-la-Prairie	130	48.59N	98.18W
Portageville	144	36.25N	89.41W
Port Alberni	130	49.14N	124.48W
Portalegre	44	39.17N	7.26W
Portales	132	34.11N	103.20W
Port Alfred	86	33.36S	26.55 E
Port Allegany	136	41.48N	78.16W
Port Allen	144	30.27N	91.12W
Port Angeles	150	48.07N	123.25W
Port Antonio	108	18.11N	76.28W
Port Arthur, Austl.	96	43.09S	147.51 E
Port Arthur → Thunder Bay, On., Can.	130	48.23N	89.15W
Port Arthur, Tx., U.S.	144	29.53N	93.55W
Port Arthur → Lüshun, Zhg.	66	38.48N	121.16 E
Port Askaig	26	55.51N	6.07W
Port Augusta	96	32.30S	137.46 E
Port-au-Prince	108	18.32N	72.20W
Port Barre	144	30.33N	91.57W
Port Blair	70	11.40N	92.45 E
Port Byron	138	41.36N	90.20W
Port-Cartier	130	50.01N	66.52W
Port Chalmers	98	45.49S	170.37 E
Port Charlotte	142	26.58N	82.05W
Port Chester	136	41.00N	73.39W
Port Clinton	136	41.30N	82.56W
Port Clyde	136	43.55N	69.15W
Port Coquitlam	150	49.16N	122.46W
Port Dickson	68	2.31N	101.48 E
Port Edward	86	31.02S	30.13 E
Port Edwards	138	44.21N	89.51W
Port Elizabeth	86	33.58S	25.40 E
Porterville	154	36.03N	119.00W
Port-Étienne → Nouâdhibou	82	20.54N	17.04W
Port Gamble	150	47.51N	122.34W
Port Gentil	86	0.43S	8.47 E
Port Gibson	144	31.57N	90.59W
Port Harcourt	82	4.43N	7.05 E
Port Hedland	96	20.19S	118.34 E
Port Henry	136	44.02N	73.27W
Port Hope	138	43.56N	82.42W
Port Huron	138	42.58N	82.25W
Portimão	44	37.08N	8.32W
Port Jervis	136	41.22N	74.41W
Portland, Austl.	96	38.21S	141.36 E
Portland, In., U.S.	144	40.26N	84.58W
Portland, Me., U.S.	136	43.39N	70.15W
Portland, Mi., U.S.	138	42.52N	84.54W
Portland, Or., U.S.	150	45.31N	122.40W
Portland, Tn., U.S.	144	36.34N	86.30W
Portland, Bill of ›	26	50.31N	2.27W
Port Laoise	26	53.02N	7.17W
Port Leyden	136	43.35N	75.21W
Port Lincoln	96	34.44S	135.52 E
Port Loko	82	8.46N	12.47W
Port Louis	86	20.10S	57.30 E
Port Moresby	96a	9.30S	147.10 E
Port Neches	144	29.59N	93.57W
Port Nolloth	86	29.17S	16.51 E
Port Norris	136	39.14N	75.02W
Porto	44	41.11N	8.36W
Porto Alegre	120	30.04S	51.11W
Portobelo	108	9.33N	79.39W
Pôrto de Mós	44	39.36N	8.39W
Porto Empedocle	40	37.17N	13.32 E
Porto Esperança	118	19.37S	57.27W
Porto Esperidião	118	15.51S	58.28W
Porto Farina	40	37.10N	10.12 E
Port of Spain	108	10.39N	61.31W
Portogruaro	40	45.47N	12.50 E
Porto Lucena	120	27.51S	55.01W
Portomaggiore	40	44.42N	11.48 E
Porto Mendes	120	24.30S	54.20W
Porto Murtinho	118	21.42S	57.52W
Porto-Novo	82	6.29N	2.37 E
Port Orange	142	29.06N	80.59W
Port Orchard	150	47.32N	122.38W
Porto San Giorgio	40	43.11N	13.48 E
Porto Sant'Elpidio	40	43.15N	13.45 E
Porto Torres	40	40.50N	8.24 E
Porto-Vecchio	40	41.35N	9.16 E
Porto Velho	118	8.46S	63.54W
Portoviejo	118	1.03S	80.27W
Port Patrick	92	20.08S	169.47 E
Port Phillip Bay ⊂	96	38.07S	144.48 E
Port Pirie	96	33.11S	138.01 E
Port Richey	142	28.16N	82.43W
Port Royal, Pa., U.S.	136	40.32N	77.23W
Port Royal, S.C., U.S.	142	32.22N	80.41W
Portrush	26	55.12N	6.40W
Port Said → Būr Sa'īd	84	31.16N	32.18 E
Port Saint Joe	142	29.49N	85.18W
Port Saint Johns	86	31.38S	29.33 E
Port Saint Lucie	142	27.20N	80.20W
Port Sanilac	138	43.25N	82.32W
Portsmouth, Eng., U.K.	26	50.48N	1.05W
Portsmouth, N.H., U.S.	136	43.04N	70.45W
Portsmouth, Oh., U.S.	136	38.43N	82.59W
Portsmouth, Va., U.S.	142	36.50N	76.17W
Port Sudan → Būr Sūdān	84	19.37N	37.14 E
Port Sulphur	144	29.28N	89.41W
Port Talbot	26	51.36N	3.47W
Porttipahdan tekojärvi ⊜ [1]	20	68.08N	26.40 E
Port Townsend	150	48.07N	122.45W
Portugal □ [1]	44	39.30N	8.00W
Portugalete	44	43.19N	3.01W
Portuguese Guinea → Guinea-Bissau □ [1]	82	12.00N	15.00W
Port Vila	92	17.44S	168.19 E
Port Washington	138	43.23N	87.52W
Port Wentworth	142	32.08N	81.09W
Porvenir	120	53.18S	70.22W
Porvoo (Borgå)	22	60.24N	25.40 E
Porz	30	50.53N	7.03 E
Porzuna	44	39.09N	4.09W
Posada ≃	40	40.39N	9.45 E
Posadas, Arg.	120	27.23S	55.53W
Posadas, Esp.	44	37.48N	5.06W
Posavina V	48	45.00N	19.00 E
Posen → Poznań, Pol.	30	52.25N	16.55 E
Posen, Mi., U.S.	138	45.15N	83.41W
Poso, Danau ⊜	68	1.52S	120.35 E
Pössneck	30	50.42N	11.37 E
Poste-de-la-Baleine	130	55.17N	77.45W
Post Falls	150	47.43N	116.57W
Postojna	40	45.47N	14.13 E
Potchefstroom	86	26.46S	27.01 E
Poteau	144	35.03N	94.37W
Poteau ≃	144	35.23N	94.26W
Potenza	40	40.38N	15.49 E
Poteriteri, Lake ⊜	98	46.06S	167.08 E
Potholes Reservoir ⊜ [1]	150	47.01N	119.19W
Potiskum	82	11.43N	11.05 E
Potomac	144	40.18N	87.48W
Potomac ≃	136	38.00N	76.18W
Potomac Heights	136	38.36N	77.08W
Potosí, Bol.	118	19.35S	65.45W
Potosi, Mo., U.S.	144	37.56N	90.47W
Potsdam, D.D.R.	30	52.24N	13.04 E
Potsdam, N.Y., U.S.	136	44.40N	74.58W
Pottstown	136	40.14N	75.39W
Pottsville	136	40.41N	76.11W
Poughkeepsie	136	41.42N	73.55W
Poulan	142	31.30N	83.47W
Poulaphouca Reservoir ⊜ [1]	26	53.08N	6.31W
Poulsbo	150	47.44N	122.38W
Poultney	136	43.31N	73.14W
Pound	142	37.07N	82.36W
Poutasi	93	14.01S	171.41W
Poŭthisăt	68	12.32N	103.55 E
Považská Bystrica	30	49.08N	18.27 E
Povljen ⋏	48	43.55N	19.30 E
Póvoa de Varzim	44	41.23N	8.46W
Povungnituk	130	60.02N	77.10W
Poway	154	32.57N	117.02W
Powder ≃, U.S.	132	46.44N	105.26W
Powder ≃, Or., U.S.	150	44.45N	117.03W
Powderly	144	37.09N	87.10W
Powell	150	44.45N	108.45W
Powell ≃	142	36.29N	83.42W
Powell, Lake ⊜ [1]	148	37.25N	110.45W
Powell, Mount ∧	148	39.46N	106.20W
Powellhurst	150	45.30N	122.32W
Powell River	130	49.52N	124.33W
Powellton	136	38.05N	81.19W
Powers	138	45.41N	87.31W
Powhatan, La., U.S.	144	31.52N	93.12W
Powhatan, Va., U.S.	142	37.32N	77.55W
Powys □ [6]	26	52.17N	3.20W
Poyang Hu ⊜	66	29.00N	116.25 E
Poygan, Lake ⊜	138	44.09N	88.50W
Poynette	138	43.23N	89.24W
Požarevac	48	44.37N	21.11 E
Poznań	30	52.25N	16.55 E
Pozoblanco	44	38.22N	4.51W
Pozo-Cañada	44	38.48N	1.45W
Pozzuoli	40	40.49N	14.07 E
Prabuty	30	53.46N	19.10 E
Prachatice	30	49.01N	14.00 E
Prachin Buri	68	14.03N	101.22 E
Prades	36	42.37N	2.26 E
Prague → Praha	30	50.05N	14.26 E
Praha (Prague)	30	50.05N	14.26 E
Praha ∧	30	49.40N	13.49 E
Prahova ≃	48	44.43N	26.27 E
Praia	82	14.55N	23.31W
Prairie City, Il., U.S.	144	40.37N	90.28W
Prairie City, Ia., U.S.	138	41.35N	93.14W
Prairie du Chien	138	43.03N	91.08W
Prairie du Sac	138	43.17N	89.43W
Prairie Grove	144	35.58N	94.19W
Prairie Village	144	38.59N	94.38W
Praslin Island I	86	4.19S	55.44 E
Prasonísi, Ákra ›	48	35.42N	27.46 E
Praszka	30	51.04N	18.26 E
Pratas Island → Tungsha Tao I	66	20.42N	116.43 E
Prato	40	43.53N	11.06 E
Prattsburg	136	42.31N	77.17W
Prattville	144	32.27N	86.27W
Praya	68	8.42S	116.17 E
Preetz	30	54.14N	10.16 E
Přelouč	30	50.02N	15.34 E
Premnitz	30	52.32N	12.19 E
Premuda, Otok I	40	44.20N	14.37 E
Prentice	138	45.32N	90.17W
Prentiss	144	31.35N	89.52W
Prenzlau	30	53.19N	13.52 E
Preparis Island I	68	14.52N	93.41 E
Preparis North Channel ʉ	68	15.27N	94.05 E
Preparis South Channel ʉ	68	14.40N	94.00 E
Přerov	30	49.27N	17.27 E
Prescott, On., Can.	130	44.43N	75.31W
Prescott, Az., U.S.	148	34.32N	112.28W
Prescott, Ar., U.S.	144	33.48N	93.22W
Prescott, Wi., U.S.	138	44.44N	92.48W
Presidencia Roque Sáenz Peña	120	26.47S	60.27W
Presidente Prudente	118	22.07S	51.22W
Prešov	30	49.00N	21.15 E
Prespa, Lake ⊜	48	40.55N	21.00 E
Presque Isle	132	46.40N	68.00W
Presque Isle › [1]	136	42.09N	80.06W
Přeštice	30	49.34N	13.20 E
Preston, Eng., U.K.	26	53.46N	2.42W
Preston, Id., U.S.	150	42.05N	111.52W
Preston Peak ∧	154	41.50N	123.37W
Prestonsburg	142	37.39N	82.46W
Prestwick	26	55.29N	4.37W
Pretoria	86	25.45S	28.10 E
Préveza	48	38.57N	20.44 E
Priboj	48	43.35N	19.31 E
Příbram	30	49.42N	14.01 E
Price	148	39.35N	110.48W
Price ≃	148	39.10N	110.06W
Prichard	144	30.44N	88.04W
Priego de Córdoba	44	37.26N	4.11W
Prien	30	47.51N	12.20 E
Prieska	86	29.40S	22.42 E
Priest Lake ⊜	150	48.34N	116.52W
Priest River	150	48.10N	116.54W
Prieta, Peña ∧	44	43.01N	4.44W
Prievidza	30	48.47N	18.37 E
Prijedor	40	44.59N	16.43 E
Prikaspijskaja nizmennost' ≚	54	48.00N	52.00 E
Prilep	48	41.20N	21.33 E
Prince Albert	130	53.12N	105.46W
Prince Charles Island I	130	67.50N	76.00W
Prince Edward Island □ [4]	130	46.20N	63.20W
Prince Frederick	136	38.32N	76.35W
Prince George	130	53.55N	122.45W
Prince of Wales Island I, Austl.	96	10.40S	142.10 E
Prince of Wales Island I, N.T., Can.	130	72.40N	99.00W
Prince of Wales Strait ʉ	130	73.00N	117.00W
Prince Regent Inlet ⊂	130	73.00N	90.30W
Prince Rupert	130	54.19N	130.19W
Princess Anne	136	38.12N	75.41W
Princeton, Il., U.S.	138	41.22N	89.27W
Princeton, In., U.S.	144	38.21N	87.34W
Princeton, Ky., U.S.	144	37.06N	87.52W
Princeton, Mn., U.S.	138	45.34N	93.34W
Princeton, N.J., U.S.	136	40.20N	74.39W
Princeton, W.V., U.S.	142	37.21N	81.06W
Princeton, Wi., U.S.	138	43.51N	89.07W
Príncipe I	86	1.37N	7.25 E
Prineville	150	44.18N	120.51W
Prip'at' ≃	54	51.21N	30.09 E
Pripet → Prip'at' ≃	54	51.21N	30.09 E
Pripet Marshes → Polesje ◆ [1]	54	52.00N	27.00 E
Priština	48	42.39N	21.10 E
Pritzwalk	30	53.09N	12.10 E
Privolžskaja vozvyšennost' ⋏ [1]	54	52.00N	46.00 E
Prizren	48	42.12N	20.44 E
Prizzi	40	37.43N	13.26 E
Probolinggo	68	7.45S	113.13 E
Prochowice	30	51.17N	16.22 E
Proctor, Mn., U.S.	138	46.44N	92.13W
Proctor, Vt., U.S.	136	43.39N	73.02W
Proddatūr	70	14.44N	78.33 E
Progreso	108	21.17N	89.40W
Prokopjevsk	56	53.53N	86.45 E
Prokopyevsk → Prokopjevsk	56	53.53N	86.45 E
Prokuplje	48	43.14N	21.36 E
Prome (Pyè)	68	18.49N	95.13 E
Prophetstown	138	41.40N	89.56W
Prosna ≃	30	52.10N	17.39 E
Prosser	150	46.12N	119.46W
Prostějov	30	49.29N	17.07 E
Provadija	48	43.11N	27.26 E
Provencal	144	31.39N	93.12W
Provence □ [9]	36	44.00N	6.00 E
Providence, Ky., U.S.	144	37.23N	87.45W
Providence, R.I., U.S.	136	41.49N	71.24W
Providence, Ut., U.S.	148	41.42N	111.48W
Providence Island I	86	9.14S	51.02 E
Providencia, Isla de I	108	13.21N	81.22W
Provincetown	136	42.03N	70.10W
Provins	36	48.33N	3.18 E
Provo	148	40.14N	111.39W
Provo ≃	148	40.14N	111.44W
Prudnik	30	50.19N	17.34 E
Pruszków	30	52.11N	20.48 E
Prut ≃	48	45.30N	28.12 E
Pryor	144	36.19N	95.19W
Przasnysz	30	53.01N	20.55 E
Przedbórz	30	51.06N	19.53 E
Przemyśl	30	49.47N	22.47 E
Pskov	20	57.50N	28.20 E
Pskovskoje ozero ⊜	22	58.00N	28.00 E
Pszczyna	30	49.59N	18.57 E
Ptolemaís	48	40.31N	21.41 E
Ptuj	40	46.25N	15.52 E
Pucallpa	118	8.23S	74.32W
Pucheng	66	27.55N	118.31 E
Púchov	30	49.08N	18.20 E
Pudukkottai	70	10.23N	78.49 E
Puebla	108	19.03N	98.12W
Puebla de Don Fadrique	44	37.58N	2.26W
Pueblo	148	38.15N	104.36W
Pueblo Mountain ∧	150	42.06N	118.39W
Puente-Genil	44	37.23N	4.47W
Puente Nuevo, Embalse de ⊜ [1]	44	38.00N	5.00W
Puerco ≃	148	34.53N	110.07W
Puerco, Rio ≃	148	34.22N	106.50W
Puerto Aisén	120	45.24S	72.42W
Puerto Armuelles	108	8.17N	82.52W
Puerto Ayacucho	118	5.40N	67.35W
Puerto Barrios	108	15.43N	88.36W
Puerto Berrío	118	6.29N	74.24W
Puerto Cabello	118	10.28N	68.01W
Puerto Cabezas	108	14.02N	83.23W
Puerto Carreño	118	6.12N	67.22W
Puerto Chicama	118	7.42S	79.27W
Puerto Cortés, C.R.	108	8.58N	83.32W
Puerto Cortés, Hond.	108	15.48N	87.56W
Puerto Cumarebo	118	11.29N	69.21W
Puerto de Nutrias	118	8.05N	69.18W
Puerto de San José	108	13.55N	90.49W
Puerto Deseado	120	47.45S	65.54W
Puerto la Cruz	118	10.13N	64.38W
Puerto Leguízamo	118	0.12S	74.46W
Puertollano	44	38.41N	4.07W
Puerto Madryn	120	42.46S	65.03W
Puerto Maldonado	118	12.36S	69.11W
Puerto Montt	120	41.28S	72.57W
Puerto Morazán	108	12.51N	87.11W
Puerto Natales	120	51.44S	72.31W
Puerto Páez	118	6.13N	67.28W
Puerto Princesa	68	9.44N	118.44 E
Puerto Real	44	36.32N	6.11W
Puerto Rico □ [2]	108	18.15N	66.30W
Puerto Sastre	120	22.06S	57.59W
Puerto Suárez	118	18.57S	57.51W
Puerto Vallarta	108	20.37N	105.15W
Pueyrredón, Lago (Lago Cochrane) ⊜	120	47.20S	72.00W
Puget Sound ʉ	150	47.50N	122.30W
Puigcerdá	44	42.26N	1.56 E
Puigmal ∧	44	42.23N	2.07 E
Pukaki, Lake ⊜	98	44.07S	170.10 E
Pukaskwa National Park ♦	138	48.20N	85.50W
Pukekohe	98	37.12S	174.55 E
Pula	40	44.52N	13.50 E
Pulaski, N.Y., U.S.	136	43.34N	76.07W
Pulaski, Tn., U.S.	144	35.11N	87.01W
Pulaski, Va., U.S.	142	37.02N	80.46W
Pulaski, Wi., U.S.	138	44.40N	88.14W
Puławy	30	51.25N	21.57 E
Pullman	150	46.43N	117.10W
Pullo	118	15.14S	73.50W
Pulog, Mount ∧	68	16.36N	120.54 E
Pułtusk	30	52.43N	21.05 E
Puná, Isla I	118	2.50S	80.08W
Pune (Poona)	70	18.32N	73.52 E
Pungo ≃	142	35.23N	76.33W
Punitaqui	120	30.50S	71.16W
Puno	118	15.50S	70.02W
Punta Alta	120	38.53S	62.05W
Punta Arenas	120	53.09S	70.55W
Punta del Este	120	34.58S	54.57W
Punta Gorda	142	26.55N	82.02W
Puntarenas	108	9.58N	84.50W
Punto Fijo	118	11.42N	70.13W
Punxsutawney	136	40.56N	78.58W
Purdy	144	36.49N	93.55W
Puri	70	19.48N	85.51 E
Purus (Purús) ≃	118	3.42S	61.28W
Purwakarta	68	6.34S	107.26 E
Purwokerto	68	7.25S	109.14 E
Pusan	66	35.06N	129.03 E
Puškin	20	59.43N	30.25 E
Püspökladány	30	47.19N	21.07 E
Putao	66	27.21N	97.24 E
Putaruru	98	38.03S	175.47 E
Puting, Tanjung ›	68	3.31S	111.46 E
Putnam	136	41.54N	71.54W
Putney	136	42.58N	72.31W
Putorana, plato ⋏ [1]	54	69.00N	95.00 E
Puttalam	70	8.02N	79.49 E
Puttgarden	30	54.30N	11.13 E
Putumayo (Içá) ≃	118	3.07S	67.58W
Puula ⊜	22	61.50N	26.42 E
Pu'upu'a	93	13.34S	172.09W
Puyallup	150	47.11N	122.17W
Puymorens, Col de)(	36	42.30N	1.50 E
Puysegur Point ›	98	46.09S	166.36 E
Pwllheli	26	52.53N	4.25W
Pyhäselkä ⊜	22	62.26N	29.58 E
Pyhätunturi ∧	20	67.01N	27.09 E
Pyinmana	68	19.44N	96.13 E
Pymatuning Reservoir ⊜ [1]	136	41.37N	80.30W
P'yŏngyang	66	39.01N	125.45 E
Pyramid Lake ⊜	154	40.00N	119.35W
Pyrenees ⋏	44	42.40N	1.00 E
Pyrzyce	30	53.10N	14.55 E

Q

Name	Page	Lat.	Long.
Qacentina	82	36.22N	6.37 E
Qaidam Pendi ≚ [1]	66	37.00N	95.00 E
Qalāt	70	32.07N	66.54 E
Qal'at Bīshah	70	20.01N	42.36 E
Qamar, Ghubbat al- ⊂	70	16.00N	52.30 E
Qamdo	66	31.11N	97.15 E
Qandahār	70	31.32N	65.30 E
Qārūn, Birkat ⊜	84	29.28N	30.40 E
Qāsh, Nahr al- (Gash) ≃	84	16.48N	35.51 E
Qaṣr al-Farāfirah	84	27.03N	27.58 E
Qasr el-Boukhari	44	35.51N	2.52 E
Qatar (Qaṭar) □ [1]	70	25.00N	51.10 E
Qattara Depression → Qaṭṭārah, Munkhafaḍ al- ⩤ [7]	84	30.00N	27.30 E
Qaṭṭārah, Munkhafaḍ al- ⩤ [7]	84	30.00N	27.30 E
Qazvīn	70	36.16N	50.00 E
Qeqertaq I	130	71.55N	55.30W
Qeshm I	70	26.45N	55.45 E
Qezel Owzan ≃	70	36.45N	49.22 E
Qianyang	66	27.11N	110.04 E
Qijiang	66	29.02N	106.39 E
Qilian Shan ∧	66	39.12N	98.35 E
Qilian Shan ⋏	66	39.06N	98.40 E
Qinā	84	26.10N	32.43 E
Qingdao (Tsingtao)	66	36.06N	120.19 E
Qinghai Hu ⊜	66	36.50N	100.20 E
Qinhuangdao	66	39.56N	119.36 E
Qionglai	66	30.25N	103.27 E
Qiongzhou Haixia ʉ	66	20.10N	110.15 E
Qiqihar (Tsitsihar)	66	47.19N	123.55 E
Qīzān	70	16.54N	42.29 E

Symbols in the index entries are identified on page 162.

Symbols in the index entries are identified on page 162.

Symbols in the index entries are identified on page 162.

Name	Page	Lat.	Long.
Santa Barbara Channel ʯ	154	34.15N	119.55W
Santa Catalina, Gulf of ⊂	154	33.20N	117.45W
Santa Catalina Island I	154	33.23N	118.24W
Santa Clara, Cuba	108	22.24N	79.58W
Santa Clara, Ca., U.S.	154	37.20N	121.56W
Santa Clara ≃	154	34.14N	119.16W
Santa Cruz, Bol.	118	17.48S	63.10W
Santa Cruz, Ca., U.S.	154	36.58N	122.01W
Santa Cruz ≃	148	32.42N	111.33W
Santa Cruz de la Palma	82	28.41N	17.45W
Santa Cruz de la Zarza	44	39.58N	3.10W
Santa Cruz del Sur	108	20.43N	78.00W
Santa Cruz de Tenerife	82	28.27N	16.14W
Santa Cruz Island I	154	34.01N	119.45W
Santa Eulalia	44	40.34N	1.19W
Santa Eulària del Riu	44	38.59N	1.31 E
Santa Fe, Arg.	120	31.38S	60.42W
Santa Fe, N.M., U.S.	148	35.41N	105.56W
Santa Fe Baldy ∧	148	35.50N	105.46W
Santai	66	31.10N	105.02 E
Santa Inés, Isla I	120	53.45S	72.45W
Santa Isabel → Malabo	82	3.45N	8.47 E
Santa Isabel I	94	8.00S	159.00 E
Santa Lucía	120	34.27S	56.24W
Santa Lucia Range ⋏	154	36.00N	121.20W
Santa Margarita	154	35.23N	120.36W
Santa Margherita Ligure	40	44.20N	9.12 E
Santa Maria, Bra.	120	29.41S	53.48W
Santa Maria, Ca., U.S.	154	34.57N	120.26W
Santa Maria I	92	14.15S	167.30 E
Santa Maria, Cabo de ›, Ang.	86	13.25S	12.32 E
Santa Maria, Cabo de ›, Port.	44	36.58N	7.54W
Santa Maria Capua Vetere	40	41.05N	14.15 E
Santa Maria di Leuca, Capo ›	40	39.47N	18.22 E
Santa Marta	118	11.15N	74.13W
Santa Monica	154	34.01N	118.29W
Santa Monica Bay ⊂	154	33.54N	118.25W
Santana do Livramento	120	30.53S	55.31W
Santander, Esp.	44	43.28N	3.48W
Santander, Pil.	68	9.25N	123.20 E
Santanilla, Islas II	108	17.25N	83.55W
Sant'Antioco, Isola di I	40	39.02N	8.25 E
Sant Antoni de Portmany	44	38.58N	1.18 E
Santa Paula	154	34.21N	119.03W
Sant'Arcangelo	40	40.15N	16.17 E
Santarém, Bra.	118	2.26S	54.42W
Santarém, Port.	44	39.14N	8.41W
Santa Rita	108	15.09N	87.53W
Santa Rosa, Arg.	120	32.20S	65.12W
Santa Rosa, Ca., U.S.	154	38.26N	122.42W
Santa Rosa Beach	144	30.23N	86.13W
Santa Rosa de Copán	108	14.47N	88.46W
Santa Rosa Island I, Ca., U.S.	154	33.58N	120.06W
Santa Rosa Island I, Fl., U.S.	144	30.22N	86.55W
Šantarskije ostrova II	56	55.00N	137.36 E
Santa Teresa, Embalse de ⊜[1]	44	40.40N	5.30W
Santa Ynez ≃	154	34.41N	120.36W
Santee	154	32.50N	116.58W
Santee ≃	142	33.14N	79.28W
Sant'Eufemia, Golfo di ⊂	40	38.50N	16.00 E
Sant Feliu de Guíxols	44	41.47N	3.02 E
Santiago, Chile	120	33.27S	70.40W
Santiago, Pan.	108	8.06N	80.59W
Santiago, Rep. Dom.	108	19.27N	70.42W
Santiago I	82	15.05N	23.40W
Santiago de Compostela	44	42.53N	8.33W
Santiago de Cuba	108	20.01N	75.49W
Santiago del Estero	120	27.47S	64.16W
Santiago Peak ∧	154	33.42N	117.32W
Santiam Pass)(	150	44.25N	121.51W
Säntis ∧	36	47.15N	9.21 E
Santisteban del Puerto	44	38.15N	3.12W
Sant Jordi, Golf de ⊂	44	40.53N	1.00 E
Santo	92	15.32S	167.08 E
Santo André	118	23.40S	46.31W
Santo Ângelo	120	28.18S	54.16W
Santo Antão I	82	17.05N	25.10W
Santo António	86	1.39N	7.26 E
Santo Domingo	108	18.28N	69.54W
Santo Domingo Pueblo	148	35.30N	106.21W
Santop, Pic ∧	92	18.39S	169.03 E
Santorini → Thíra I	48	36.24N	25.29 E
Santos	118	23.57S	46.20W
San Valentín, Cerro ∧	120	46.36S	73.20W
San Vicente	108	13.38N	88.48W
San Vicente de Alcántara	44	39.21N	7.08W
San Vito	40	39.26N	9.32 E
San Vito, Capo ›	40	38.11N	12.44 E
San Vito dei Normanni	40	40.39N	17.42 E
São Borja	120	28.39S	56.00W
São Carlos	118	22.01S	47.54W
São Francisco ≃	118	10.30S	36.24W
São Gabriel	120	30.20S	54.19W
São Jerônimo	120	29.58S	51.43W
São João da Boa Vista	118	21.58S	46.47W
São João da Madeira	44	40.54N	8.30W
São João del Rei	118	21.09S	44.16W
São José do Rio Prêto	118	20.48S	49.23W
São José dos Campos	118	23.11S	45.53W
São Leopoldo	120	29.46S	51.09W
São Lourenço ≃	118	17.53S	57.27W
São Lourenço, Pantanal de ≡	118	17.30S	56.30W
São Luís	118	2.31S	44.16W
São Manuel ≃	118	7.21S	58.03W
Saône ≃	36	45.44N	4.50 E
São Nicolau I	82	16.35N	24.15W
São Paulo	118	23.32S	46.37W
São Roque, Cabo de ›	118	5.29S	35.16W
São Sebastião, Ponta ›	86	22.07S	35.30 E
São Tomé	86	0.20N	6.44 E
São Tomé I	86	0.12N	6.39 E
São Tomé, Cabo de ›	118	21.59S	40.59W
Sao Tome and Principe □[1]	86	1.00N	7.00 E
Saoura, Oued V	82	29.00N	0.55W
São Vicente	118	23.58S	46.23W
São Vicente I	82	16.50N	25.00W
São Vicente, Cabo de (Cape Saint Vincent) ›	44	37.01N	9.00W
Sapele	82	5.54N	5.41 E
Sapelo Island I	142	31.28N	81.15W
Sapitwa ∧	86	15.57S	35.36 E
Sapporo	66	43.03N	141.21 E
Sapt Kosi ≃	70	26.31N	86.58 E
Sapulpa	132	35.59N	96.06W
Sarajevo	48	43.52N	18.25 E
Saraland	144	30.49N	88.04W
Saranac	138	42.55N	85.12W
Saranac ≃	136	44.42N	73.27W
Saranac Lake	136	44.19N	74.07W
Saransk	20	54.11N	45.11 E
Sarapul	20	56.28N	53.48 E
Sarasota	142	27.20N	82.31W
Saratoga, Ca., U.S.	154	37.15N	122.01W
Saratoga, Wy., U.S.	148	41.27N	106.48W
Saratoga National Historical Park ♦	136	43.00N	73.38W
Saratoga Springs	136	43.04N	73.47W
Saratov	54	51.34N	46.02 E
Saratovskoje vodochranilišče ⊜[1]	54	52.45N	48.30 E
Sarayköy	48	37.55N	28.58 E
Sarcidano ◆[1]	40	39.55N	9.05 E
Sardegna (Sardinia) I	40	40.00N	9.00 E
Sardinia → Sardegna I	40	40.00N	9.00 E
Sardis, Al., U.S.	144	32.17N	86.59W
Sardis, Ga., U.S.	142	32.58N	81.45W
Sardis, Ms., U.S.	144	34.26N	89.55W
Sardis, Tn., U.S.	144	35.27N	88.18W
Sardis Lake ⊜[1]	144	34.27N	89.43W
Sarek ∧	20	67.25N	17.46 E
Sarepta	144	32.53N	93.26W
Sargans	36	47.03N	9.26 E
Sargent	142	33.25N	84.52W
Sargodha	70	32.05N	72.40 E
Sarh	84	9.09N	18.23 E
Sārī	70	36.34N	53.04 E
Sarina	96	21.26S	149.13 E
Sariwŏn	66	38.31N	125.44 E
Sark I	26	49.26N	2.21W
Sármellék	30	46.44N	17.10 E
Sarmiento, Cerro ∧	120	54.27S	70.50W
Sârnena ⋏	48	42.35N	25.10 E
Sarnia	130	42.58N	82.23W
Sarno	40	40.49N	14.37 E
Saronikós Kólpos ⊂	48	37.54N	23.12 E
Saronno	40	45.38N	9.02 E
Saros Körfezi ⊂	48	40.30N	26.20 E
Sárospatak	30	48.19N	21.34 E
Šar Planina ⋏	48	42.05N	20.50 E
Sarpsborg	22	59.17N	11.07 E
Sarrath, Oued V	40	35.59N	8.23 E
Sarreguemines	36	49.06N	7.03 E
Sarria	44	42.47N	7.24W
Sartène	40	41.36N	8.59 E
Sarthe ≃	36	47.30N	0.32W
Saruhanlı	48	38.44N	27.34 E
Sárvár	30	47.15N	16.57 E
Sárvíz ≃	30	46.24N	18.41 E
Sarzana	40	44.07N	9.58 E
Sasebo	66	33.10N	129.43 E
Saskatchewan □[4]	130	54.00N	105.00W
Saskatchewan ≃	130	53.12N	99.16W
Saskatoon	130	52.07N	106.38W
Sassafras	142	37.14N	83.06W
Sassafras Mountain ∧	142	35.03N	82.48W
Sassandra	82	4.58N	6.05W
Sassandra ≃	82	4.58N	6.05W
Sassari	40	40.44N	8.33 E
Sassnitz	30	54.31N	13.38 E
Sasso Marconi	40	44.24N	11.15 E
Sassuolo	40	44.33N	10.47 E
Sata-misaki ›	66	30.59N	130.40 E
Sātāra	70	17.41N	73.59 E
Satellite Beach	142	28.10N	80.35W
Satilla ≃	142	30.59N	81.28W
Sátoraljaújhely	30	48.24N	21.39 E
Sātpura Range ⋏	70	22.00N	78.00 E
Satsuma	144	30.51N	88.03W
Satsunan-shotō II	66	29.00N	130.00 E
Sattahip	68	12.40N	100.54 E
Satu Mare	48	47.48N	22.53 E
Saucier	144	30.38N	89.08W
Saudi Arabia (Al-'Arabīyah as-Sa'ūdīyah) □[1]	70	25.00N	45.00 E
Sauerland ◆[1]	30	51.10N	8.00 E
Saugatuck	138	42.39N	86.12W
Saugerties	136	42.04N	73.57W
Sauk City	138	43.16N	89.43W
Sauk Rapids	138	45.35N	94.09W
Saukville	138	43.22N	87.56W
Saül	118	3.37N	53.12W
Sault Sainte Marie, On., Can.	130	46.31N	84.20W
Sault Sainte Marie, Mi., U.S.	138	46.29N	84.20W
Saumur	36	47.16N	0.05W
Sauquoit	136	43.00N	75.16W
Sausalito	154	37.51N	122.29W
Sauwald ◆[3]	30	48.28N	13.40 E
Sava	40	40.24N	17.34 E
Sava ≃	16	44.50N	20.26 E
Savage	136	39.08N	76.49W
Savai'i I	93	13.35S	172.25W
Savanna	138	42.05N	90.09W
Savannah, Ga., U.S.	142	32.05N	81.06W
Savannah, Mo., U.S.	144	39.56N	94.49W
Savannah, Tn., U.S.	144	35.13N	88.14W
Savannah ≃	142	32.02N	80.53W
Savannakhét	68	16.33N	104.45 E
Savanna-la-Mar	108	18.13N	78.08W
Save (Sabi) ≃, Afr.	86	21.00S	35.02 E
Save ≃, Fr.	36	43.47N	1.17 E
Savenay	36	47.22N	1.57W
Săveni	48	47.57N	26.52 E
Saverne	36	48.44N	7.22 E
Savigliano	40	44.38N	7.40 E
Šavnik	48	42.57N	19.05 E
Savona	40	44.17N	8.30 E
Savonlinna	22	61.52N	28.53 E
Savusavu	91	16.16S	179.21 E
Savu Sea → Sawu, Laut ▾[2]	68	9.40S	122.00 E
Sawākin	84	19.07N	37.20 E
Sawatch Range ⋏	148	39.10N	106.25W
Sawdā', Jabal as- ⋏[2]	84	28.40N	15.30 E
Sawdā', Qurnat as- ∧	70	34.18N	36.07 E
Sawel Mountain ∧	26	54.49N	7.02W
Sawhāj	84	26.33N	31.42 E
Sawqarah, Dawhat ⊂	70	18.35N	57.15 E
Sawtooth National Recreation Area ♦	150	44.00N	114.55W
Sawu, Laut (Savu Sea) ▾[2]	68	9.40S	122.00 E
Saxony → Sachsen □[9]	30	52.45N	9.30 E
Saxton	136	40.12N	78.14W
Sayan Mountains (Sajany) ⋏	54	52.45N	96.00 E
Şaydā	70	33.33N	35.22 E
Saylorville Lake ⊜[1]	138	41.48N	93.46W
Sayre	136	41.58N	76.30W
Sayreville	136	40.27N	74.21W
Say'ūn	70	15.56N	48.47 E
Sazanit I	48	40.30N	19.16 E
Sazlijka ≃	48	42.02N	25.52 E
Sbeïtla	40	35.14N	9.08 E
Sbiba	40	35.33N	9.05 E
Scafell Pikes ∧	26	54.27N	3.12W
Scalea	40	39.49N	15.48 E
Scapa Flow ⊂	26	58.55N	3.06W
Scarborough, Trin.	108	11.11N	60.44W
Scarborough, Eng., U.K.	26	54.17N	0.24W
Scărişoara	48	44.00N	24.35 E
Schaffhausen	36	47.42N	8.38 E
Schefferville	130	54.48N	66.50W
Schelde (Escaut) ≃	30	51.22N	4.15 E
Schell Creek Range ⋏	154	39.10N	114.40W
Schenectady	136	42.48N	73.56W
Schesslitz	30	49.59N	11.01 E
Schiedam	30	51.55N	4.24 E
Schiermonnikoog I	30	53.28N	6.15 E
Schiltigheim	36	48.36N	7.45 E
Schio	40	45.43N	11.21 E
Schkeuditz	30	51.24N	12.13 E
Schleswig	30	54.31N	9.33 E
Schleswig-Holstein □[3]	30	54.20N	9.40 E
Schlitz	30	50.40N	9.33 E
Schmalkalden	30	50.43N	10.26 E
Schmölln	30	50.53N	12.20 E
Schneeberg	30	50.36N	12.38 E
Schneeberg ∧	36	50.03N	11.51 E
Schofield	138	44.54N	89.36W
Schoharie	136	42.39N	74.18W
Schönebeck	30	52.01N	11.44 E
Schongau	30	47.49N	10.54 E
Schoolcraft	138	42.06N	85.38W
Schorndorf	30	48.48N	9.31 E
Schouwen I	30	51.43N	3.50 E
Schramberg	30	48.13N	8.23 E
Schreiber	130	48.48N	87.15W
Schrobenhausen	30	48.33N	11.17 E
Schuylkill ≃	136	39.53N	75.12W
Schuylkill Haven	136	40.37N	76.10W
Schwabach	30	49.20N	11.01 E
Schwaben □[9]	30	48.10N	9.25 E
Schwäbische Alb ⋏	30	48.25N	9.30 E
Schwäbisch Gmünd	30	48.48N	9.47 E
Schwäbisch Hall	30	49.07N	9.44 E
Schwandorf	30	49.20N	12.08 E
Schwarza ≃	30	47.43N	16.13 E
Schwarzwald (Black Forest) ⋏	30	48.00N	8.15 E
Schwechat	30	48.08N	16.29 E
Schwedt	30	53.03N	14.17 E
Schweinfurt	30	50.03N	10.14 E
Schwerin	30	53.38N	11.25 E
Schweriner See ⊜	30	53.45N	11.28 E
Schwetzingen	30	49.23N	8.34 E
Schwyz	36	47.02N	8.40 E
Sciacca	40	37.31N	13.03 E
Scicli	40	36.47N	14.42 E
Scilly, Isles of II	26	49.55N	6.20W
Ścinawa	30	51.25N	16.27 E
Scio	136	40.23N	81.05W
Scioto ≃	136	38.44N	83.01W
Ščokino	54	54.01N	37.31 E
Scooba	144	32.49N	88.28W
Scordia	40	37.18N	14.51 E
Scotia	136	42.49N	73.57W
Scotland □[8]	26	57.00N	4.00W
Scotland Neck	142	36.07N	77.25W
Scotlandville	144	30.31N	91.10W
Scott, Mount ∧	150	42.56N	122.01W
Scott City	144	37.13N	89.31W
Scottdale	136	40.06N	79.35W
Scott Peak ∧	150	44.21N	112.50W
Scottsbluff	132	41.52N	103.40W
Scottsboro	144	34.40N	86.02W
Scottsburg	144	38.41N	85.46W
Scottsdale	148	33.30N	111.53W
Scottsville	144	36.45N	86.11W
Scranton	136	41.24N	75.39W
Scugog, Lake ⊜	138	44.10N	78.51W
Scunthorpe	26	53.36N	0.38W
Scuol	36	46.48N	10.18 E
Scutari, Lake ⊜	48	42.12N	19.18 E
Seaboard	142	36.29N	77.26W
Seaford	136	38.38N	75.36W
Seaham	26	54.52N	1.21W
Seahorse Point ›	130	63.47N	80.09W
Sea Islands II	142	31.20N	81.20W
Sea Isle City	136	39.09N	74.41W
Seal ≃	130	59.04N	94.48W
Seale	144	32.17N	85.10W
Sealevel	142	34.51N	76.23W
Searcy	144	35.15N	91.44W
Searles Lake ⊜	154	35.43N	117.20W
Searsport	136	44.27N	68.55W
Seaside, Ca., U.S.	154	36.36N	121.51W
Seaside, Or., U.S.	150	45.59N	123.55W
Seaside Park	136	39.55N	74.04W
Seattle	150	47.36N	122.19W
Sebago Lake ⊜	136	43.50N	70.35W
Sebastián Vizcaíno, Bahía ⊂	108	28.00N	114.30W
Sebastopol, Ca., U.S.	154	38.24N	122.49W
Sebastopol, Ms., U.S.	144	32.34N	89.20W
Sebec Lake ⊜	136	45.18N	69.18W
Sebeş	48	45.58N	23.34 E
Sebes Körös (Crişul Repede) ≃	48	46.55N	20.59 E
Sebewaing	138	43.43N	83.27W
Sebnitz	30	50.58N	14.16 E
Sebree	144	37.36N	87.31W
Sebring	142	27.29N	81.26W
Sechura, Bahía de ⊂	118	5.42S	81.00W
Secretary Island I	98	45.15S	166.55 E
Séd ≃	30	47.00N	18.31 E
Sedalia	144	38.42N	93.13W
Sedan	36	49.42N	4.57 E
Sedlčany	30	49.40N	14.26 E
Sedona	148	34.52N	111.45W
Sedova, pik ∧	54	73.29N	54.58 E
Sedro Woolley	150	48.30N	122.14W
Sędziszów	30	50.04N	21.41 E
Seeheim	86	26.50S	17.45 E
Sefton, Mount ∧	98	43.41S	170.03 E
Segama ≃	68	5.27N	118.48 E
Segangane	44	35.09N	3.00W
Şegarcea	48	44.06N	23.45 E
Šegeža	20	63.44N	34.19 E
Segorbe	44	39.51N	0.29W
Ségou	82	13.27N	6.16W
Segovia	44	40.57N	4.07W
Segre ≃	44	41.40N	0.43 E
Segura	44	39.50N	6.59W
Segura ≃	44	38.06N	0.38W
Segura, Sierra de ⋏	44	38.00N	2.43W
Seiland I	20	70.25N	23.15 E
Sein, Île de I	36	48.02N	4.51W
Seinäjoki	22	62.47N	22.50 E
Seine ≃, On., Can.	130	48.40N	92.49W
Seine ≃, Fr.	36	49.26N	0.26 E
Seine, Baie de la ⊂	36	49.30N	0.30W
Sejerø I	22	55.53N	11.09 E
Sejm ≃	54	51.27N	32.34 E
Sejny	30	54.07N	23.20 E
Şekondi-Takoradi	82	4.59N	1.43W
Šelagskij, mys ›	56	70.06N	170.26 E
Selah	150	46.39N	120.31W
Selatan, Tanjung ›	68	4.10S	114.38 E
Selb	30	50.10N	12.08 E
Selbusjøen ⊜	22	63.14N	10.54 E
Selby	26	53.48N	1.04W
Selbyville	136	38.27N	75.13W
Selçuk	48	37.56N	27.22 E
Selenga (Selenge) ≃	56	52.16N	106.16 E
Selenge (Selenga) ≃	56	52.16N	106.16 E
Selenicë	48	40.32N	19.38 E
Sélestat	36	48.16N	7.27 E
Šelichova, zaliv ⊂	56	60.00N	158.00 E
Seliger, ozero ⊜	54	57.13N	33.05 E
Seligman	148	35.19N	112.52W
Selinsgrove	136	40.47N	76.51W
Selkirk	130	50.09N	96.52W
Sellers	142	34.17N	79.28W
Sellersburg	144	38.23N	85.45W
Selm	30	51.42N	7.28 E
Selma, Al., U.S.	144	32.24N	87.01W
Selma, Ca., U.S.	154	36.34N	119.36W
Selma, N.C., U.S.	142	35.32N	78.17W
Selmer	144	35.10N	88.35W
Selmont	144	32.23N	87.01W
Selouane	44	35.04N	2.58W
Selvagens, Ilhas II	82	30.05N	15.55W
Selvas ◆[3]	118	5.00S	68.00W
Selwyn, Passage ʯ	92	16.03S	168.12 E
Selwyn Mountains ⋏	130	63.10N	130.20W
Seman ≃	48	40.56N	19.24 E
Semarang	68	6.58S	110.25 E
Semenicului, Munţii ⋏	48	45.05N	22.05 E
Semeru, Gunung ∧	68	8.06S	112.55 E
Seminoe Reservoir ⊜[1]	148	42.00N	106.50W
Seminole, Lake ⊜[1]	142	30.46N	84.50W
Semipalatinsk	56	50.28N	80.13 E
Semporna	68	4.28N	118.36 E
Semuliki ≃	86	1.14N	30.28 E
Seňa, Česko.	30	48.34N	21.15 E
Sena, Moç.	86	17.27S	35.00 E
Senath	144	36.08N	90.09W
Senatobia	144	34.37N	89.58W
Sendai	66	38.15N	140.53 E
Seneca, Il., U.S.	138	41.18N	88.36W
Seneca, Mo., U.S.	144	36.50N	94.36W
Seneca, S.C., U.S.	142	34.41N	82.57W
Seneca Falls	136	42.54N	76.47W
Seneca Lake ⊜	136	42.40N	76.57W
Senegal (Sénégal) □[1]	82	14.00N	14.00W
Sénégal ≃	82	15.48N	16.32W
Senetosa, Capu di ›	40	41.33N	8.47 E
Senftenberg	30	51.31N	14.00 E
Senica	30	48.41N	17.22 E
Senigallia	40	43.43N	13.13 E
Senj	40	44.59N	14.54 E
Senja I	20	69.20N	17.30 E
Senlis	36	49.12N	2.35 E
Senneterre	130	48.23N	77.15W
Sennori	40	40.48N	8.35 E
Sens	36	48.12N	3.17 E
Senta	48	45.56N	20.04 E
Seo de Urgel	44	42.21N	1.28 E
Seoul → Sŏul	66	37.33N	126.58 E
Separation Point ›	98	40.47S	173.00 E
Sepi	94	8.33S	159.50 E
Sepik ≃	96a	3.51S	144.34 E
Sępólno Krajeńskie	30	53.28N	17.32 E
Sept-Îles (Seven Islands)	130	50.12N	66.23W
Sequatchie ≃	142	35.02N	85.38W
Sequim	150	48.04N	123.06W
Sequoia National Park ♦	154	36.30N	118.30W
Seraing	30	50.36N	5.29 E
Seram (Ceram) I	68	3.00S	129.00 E
Seram, Laut (Ceram Sea) ▾[2]	68	2.30S	128.00 E
Serang	68	6.07S	106.09 E
Serbia → Srbija □[3]	48	44.00N	21.00 E
Séré'ama, Mont ∧	92	13.47S	167.29 E
Sered'	30	48.17N	17.44 E
Seremban	68	2.43N	101.56 E
Serengeti Plain ≚	86	2.50S	35.00 E
Serenje	86	13.15S	30.14 E
Sergeja Kirova, ostrova II	54	77.12N	89.30 E
Seria	68	4.39N	114.23 E
Sérifos I	48	37.11N	24.31 E
Sermilik ⊂[2]	130	65.37N	38.03W
Serov	54	59.29N	60.31 E
Serowe	86	22.25S	26.44 E
Serpuchov	20	54.55N	37.25 E
Sérrai	48	41.05N	23.32 E
Serrat, Cap ›	40	37.14N	9.13 E
Serres	36	44.26N	5.43 E
Servi Burnu ›	48	41.40N	28.06 E
Sesia ≃	40	45.05N	8.37 E
Sessa Aurunca	40	41.14N	13.56 E
Ses Salines, Cap de ›	44	39.16N	3.03 E
Sestao	44	43.18N	3.00W
Sestri Levante	40	44.16N	9.24 E
Sestroreck	20	60.06N	29.58 E
Sète	36	43.24N	3.41 E
Sete Lagoas	118	19.27S	44.14W
Seto-naikai ▾[2]	66	34.20N	133.30 E
Settat	82	33.04N	7.37W
Sette-Daban, chrebet ⋏	56	62.00N	138.00 E
Setúbal	44	38.32N	8.54W
Setúbal, Baía de ⊂	44	38.27N	8.53W
Seui	40	39.50N	9.19 E
Seul, Lac ⊜	130	50.20N	92.30W
Seul Choix Point ›	138	45.56N	85.52W
Sevan, ozero ⊜	54	40.20N	45.20 E
Sevastopol'	54	44.36N	33.32 E
Ševčenko	54	43.35N	51.05 E
Severn ≃, On., Can.	130	56.02N	87.36W
Severn ≃, U.K.	26	51.35N	2.40W
Severnaja Dvina ≃	54	64.32N	40.30 E
Severnaja Zeml'a II	56	79.30N	98.00 E
Severna Park	136	39.04N	76.32W
Severnyje uvaly ⋏[2]	54	59.30N	49.00 E
Severodvinsk	20	64.34N	39.50 E
Severomorsk	20	69.05N	33.24 E
Severo-Sibirskaja nizmennost' ≚	54	73.00N	100.00 E
Severskij Donec ≃	54	47.35N	40.54 E
Sevier ≃	148	39.04N	113.06W
Sevier Lake ⊜	148	38.55N	113.09W
Sevierville	142	35.52N	83.33W
Sevilla, Col.	118	4.16N	75.57W
Sevilla (Seville), Esp.	44	37.23N	5.59W
Seville → Sevilla, Esp.	44	37.23N	5.59W
Seville, Oh., U.S.	136	41.00N	81.51W
Sevlievo	48	43.01N	25.06 E
Sewanee	144	35.04N	85.55W
Seward, Ak., U.S.	132a	60.06N	149.26W
Seward, Ne., U.S.	132	40.54N	97.05W
Seward, Pa., U.S.	136	40.25N	79.01W
Seychelles □[1]	86	4.35S	55.40 E
Seylac	84	11.21N	43.29 E
Seymour, Ct., U.S.	136	41.23N	73.04W
Seymour, In., U.S.	144	38.57N	85.53W
Seymour, Mo., U.S.	144	37.08N	92.46W
Seymour, Wi., U.S.	138	44.30N	88.19W
Seymourville	144	30.27N	91.29W
Sežana	40	45.42N	13.52 E
Sezimovo Ústí	30	49.23N	14.42 E
Sfax	82	34.44N	10.46 E
Sfîntu-Gheorghe	48	45.52N	25.47 E
Sfîntu Gheorghe, Braţul ≃[1]	48	44.53N	29.36 E
Sfîntu Gheorghe, Ostrovul I	48	45.07N	29.22 E
's-Gravenhage (The Hague)	30	52.06N	4.18 E
Shabeelle (Shebele) ≃	84	0.50N	43.10 E
Shache	66	38.25N	77.16 E
Shadyside	136	39.58N	80.45W
Shag ≃	98	45.29S	170.49 E
Shag Rocks II[1]	120	53.33S	42.02W
Shahdād, Namakzār-e ≚	70	30.30N	58.30 E
Shāhjahānpur	70	27.53N	79.55 E
Shakawe	86	18.23S	21.50 E
Shaker Heights	136	41.28N	81.32W
Shakhty → Šachty	54	47.42N	40.13 E
Shaki	82	8.39N	3.25 E
Shakopee	138	44.47N	93.31W
Shala, Lake ⊜	84	7.25N	38.30 E
Shām, Bādiyat ash- ◆[2]	70	32.00N	40.00 E
Shām, Jabal ash- ∧	70	23.13N	57.16 E
Shamokin	136	40.47N	76.33W
Shandī	84	16.42N	33.26 E
Shandong Bandao ›[1]	66	37.00N	121.00 E
Shangani ≃	86	18.41S	27.10 E
Shanghai	66	31.14N	121.28 E
Shangqiu	66	34.27N	115.42 E
Shangrao	66	28.26N	117.58 E
Shangshui	66	33.33N	114.34 E
Shannon	142	34.20N	85.04W
Shannon ≃	26	52.36N	9.41W
Shannontown	142	33.53N	80.21W
Shantou (Swatow)	66	23.23N	116.41 E
Shantung Peninsula → Shandong Bandao ›[1]	66	37.00N	121.00 E
Shanxian	66	34.48N	116.03 E
Shaoguan	66	24.50N	113.37 E
Shaoxing	66	30.00N	120.35 E
Shaoyang	66	27.15N	111.28 E
Sharbatāt, Ra's ash- ›	70	17.52N	56.22 E
Sharjah → Ash-Shāriqah	70	25.22N	55.23 E
Shark Bay ⊂	96	25.30S	113.30 E
Sharon	136	41.13N	80.29W
Sharqīyah, Aş-Şaḥrā' ash- (Arabian Desert) ◆[2]	84	28.00N	32.00 E
Shashe ≃	86	22.14S	29.20 E
Shashi	66	30.19N	112.14 E
Shasta	154	40.36N	122.29W
Shasta ≃	154	41.50N	122.35W
Shasta, Mount ∧[1]	154	41.20N	122.20W
Shasta Lake ⊜[1]	154	40.50N	122.25W
Shaunavon	130	49.40N	108.25W
Shaw	144	33.36N	90.46W
Shawano	138	44.46N	88.36W
Shawinigan	130	46.33N	72.45W
Shawnee, Oh., U.S.	136	39.36N	82.12W
Shawnee, Ok., U.S.	132	35.19N	96.55W
Shawneetown	144	37.42N	88.11W
Shaybārā I	70	25.27N	36.48 E
Shay Gap	96	20.25S	120.03 E
Shaykh, Jabal ash- ∧	70	33.26N	35.51 E
Shaykh 'Uthmān	70	12.52N	44.59 E
Shebele (Shabeelle) ≃	84	0.50N	43.10 E
Sheberghān	70	36.41N	65.45 E
Sheboygan	138	43.45N	87.42W
Sheboygan Falls	138	43.43N	87.48W
Sheep Mountain ∧	150	43.33N	110.32W
Sheffield, Eng., U.K.	26	53.23N	1.30W
Sheffield, Al., U.S.	144	34.45N	87.41W
Sheffield, Pa., U.S.	136	41.42N	79.02W
Shekhūpura	70	31.42N	73.59 E
Shelbina	144	39.41N	92.02W
Shelburn	144	39.11N	87.24W
Shelburne	130	43.46N	65.19W
Shelburne Falls	136	42.36N	72.44W
Shelby, Ms., U.S.	144	33.57N	90.46W
Shelby, Mt., U.S.	150	48.30N	111.51W
Shelby, N.C., U.S.	142	35.17N	81.32W
Shelby, Oh., U.S.	136	40.52N	82.39W
Shelbyville, Il., U.S.	144	39.24N	88.47W
Shelbyville, In., U.S.	144	39.31N	85.46W
Shelbyville, Ky., U.S.	144	38.12N	85.13W
Shelbyville, Tn., U.S.	144	35.29N	86.27W
Shelbyville, Lake ⊜[1]	144	39.30N	88.40W
Sheldon	144	37.39N	94.17W
Shellbrook	130	53.13N	106.24W
Shelley	150	43.22N	112.07W
Shell Rock ≃	138	42.38N	92.30W
Shelton, Ct., U.S.	136	41.18N	73.05W
Shelton, Wa., U.S.	150	47.13N	123.06W
Shenandoah, Pa., U.S.	136	40.49N	76.12W
Shenandoah, Va., U.S.	136	38.29N	78.37W
Shenandoah ≃	136	39.19N	77.44W
Shenandoah National Park ♦	136	38.48N	78.12W
Shenyang (Mukden)	66	41.48N	123.27 E
Shepherd, Îles II	92	16.55S	168.36 E
Shepherdsville	144	37.59N	85.42W
Sheppey, Isle of I	26	51.24N	0.50 E
Sherbro Island I	82	7.45N	12.55W
Sherbrooke	130	45.25N	71.54W
Sheridan, Ar., U.S.	144	34.18N	92.24W
Sheridan, In., U.S.	144	40.08N	86.13W
Sheridan, Wy., U.S.	150	44.47N	106.57W
Sherman	136	42.09N	79.35W
's-Hertogenbosch	30	51.41N	5.19 E
Sherwood	144	34.48N	92.13W
Shetland Islands II	26	60.30N	1.15W
Sheyenne ≃	132	47.05N	96.50W
Shibām	70	15.56N	48.38 E
Shickshinny	136	41.09N	76.09W
Shijiazhuang	66	38.03N	114.28 E
Shikārpur	70	27.57N	68.38 E
Shikoku I	66	33.45N	133.30 E
Shillelagh	26	52.45N	6.32W
Shillington	136	40.18N	75.57W
Shillong	70	25.34N	91.53 E
Shiloh	136	39.49N	84.13W
Shiloh National Military Park ♦	144	35.06N	88.21W
Shimber Berris ∧	84	10.44N	47.15 E
Shimoga	70	13.55N	75.34 E
Shimonoseki	66	33.57N	130.57 E
Shin, Loch ⊜	26	58.06N	4.34W
Shinglehouse	136	41.57N	78.11W
Shinkolobwe	86	11.02S	26.35 E
Shinnston	136	39.23N	80.18W
Shinyanga	86	3.40S	33.26 E
Shiocton	138	44.26N	88.34W
Shiono-misaki ›	66	33.26N	135.45 E
Shippensburg	136	40.03N	77.31W
Shiprock	148	36.47N	108.41W
Ship Rock ∧	148	36.42N	108.50W
Shire ≃	86	17.42S	35.19 E
Shiretoko-misaki ›	66	44.14N	145.17 E
Shirley	144	39.53N	85.34W
Shively	144	38.12N	85.49W
Shizuoka	66	34.58N	138.23 E
Shkodër	48	42.05N	19.30 E
Shkumbin ≃	48	41.01N	19.26 E
Sholāpur	70	17.41N	75.55 E
Shorewood	138	43.05N	87.53W
Shortland Islands II	94	6.55S	155.53 E
Shoshone ≃	150	44.52N	108.11W
Shoshone Lake ⊜	150	44.22N	110.43W
Shoshone Mountains ⋏	154	39.00N	117.30W
Shoshone Range ⋏	154	40.20N	116.50W
Shoshoni	150	43.14N	108.06W
Show Low	148	34.15N	110.01W
Shreve	136	40.40N	82.01W
Shreveport	144	32.30N	93.44W
Shrewsbury, Eng., U.K.	26	52.43N	2.45W
Shrewsbury, Ma., U.S.	136	42.17N	71.42W
Shropshire □[6]	26	52.40N	2.40W
Shuangcheng	66	45.21N	126.17 E
Shuangliao	66	43.31N	123.30 E
Shuangyashan	66	46.37N	131.22 E
Shubrā al-Khaymah	84	30.06N	31.15 E
Shuksan, Mount ∧	150	48.50N	121.36W
Shullsburg	138	42.34N	90.13W
Shuqrah	70	13.21N	45.42 E
Shūshtar	70	32.03N	48.51 E
Shwebo	68	22.34N	95.42 E
Shyok ≃	70	35.13N	75.53 E
Siālkot	70	32.30N	74.31 E
Siam, Gulf of → Thailand, Gulf of ⊂	68	10.00N	101.00 E
Şiasconset	136	41.15N	69.58W
Šiauliai	20	55.56N	23.19 E
Šibenik	40	43.44N	15.54 E
Siberia → Sibir' ◆[1]	56	65.00N	110.00 E
Sibérie Occidental, Dépression de la → Zapadno-Sibirskaja ravnina ≚	54	60.00N	75.00 E
Siberut, Pulau I	68	1.20S	98.55 E
Sibir' (Siberia) ◆[1]	56	65.00N	110.00 E
Sibiu	48	45.48N	24.09 E
Sibley, La., U.S.	144	32.33N	93.18W
Sibley, Ms., U.S.	144	31.22N	91.23W
Sibolga	68	1.45N	98.48 E
Sibu	68	2.18N	111.49 E
Sibuyan Sea ▾[2]	68	12.50N	122.40 E
Sichote-Alin' ⋏	56	48.00N	138.00 E
Sicié, Cap ›	36	43.03N	5.51 E
Sicilia (Sicily) I	40	37.30N	14.00 E
Sicily → Sicilia I	40	37.30N	14.00 E
Sicily, Strait of ʯ	40	37.20N	11.20 E
Sicily Island	144	31.50N	91.39W
Sicuani	118	14.16S	71.13W
Sídheros, Ákra ›	48	35.19N	26.19 E
Sidi Aïch	44	36.37N	4.42 E
Sidi bel Abbès	82	35.13N	0.10W
Sidi Bennour	82	32.30N	8.30W
Sidi el Hani, Sebkhet ⊜	40	35.33N	10.25 E
Sidi Ifni	82	29.24N	10.12W
Sidmouth	26	50.41N	3.15W
Sidnaw	138	46.30N	88.42W
Sidney, Mt., U.S.	132	47.43N	104.09W
Sidney, Ne., U.S.	132	41.08N	102.58W
Sidney, N.Y., U.S.	136	42.18N	75.23W
Sidney, Oh., U.S.	136	40.17N	84.09W
Sidney Lanier, Lake ⊜[1]	142	34.15N	83.57W
Sidra, Gulf of → Surt, Khalīj ⊂	84	31.30N	18.00 E
Siedlce	30	52.11N	22.16 E
Siegburg	30	50.47N	7.12 E
Siegen	30	50.52N	8.02 E
Siemianowice Śląskie	30	50.19N	19.01 E
Siemiatycze	30	52.26N	22.53 E
Siĕmréab	68	13.22N	103.51 E
Siena	40	43.19N	11.21 E
Sieradz	30	51.36N	18.45 E
Sieraków	30	52.39N	16.04 E
Sierpc	30	52.52N	19.41 E
Sierra Blanca	148	31.11N	105.21W
Sierra Blanca Peak ∧	148	33.23N	105.48W
Sierra de Outes	44	42.51N	8.54W
Sierra Leone □[1]	82	8.30N	11.30W
Sierra Vista	148	31.33N	110.18W
Sierre	36	46.18N	7.32 E
Siesta Key	142	27.19N	82.34W
Sífnos I	48	36.59N	24.40 E
Sighetu Marmaţiei	48	47.56N	23.54 E
Sighişoara	48	46.13N	24.48 E
Siglufjörður	20a	66.10N	18.56W
Sigmaringen	30	48.05N	9.13 E
Signal Mountain	144	35.07N	85.20W
Sigourney	138	41.20N	92.12W
Sigsig	118	3.01S	78.45W
Siguiri	82	11.25N	9.10W
Sikanni Chief ≃	130	58.20N	121.50W
Sīkar	70	27.37N	75.09 E
Sikasso	82	11.19N	5.40W
Sikéai	48	36.46N	22.56 E
Sikeston	144	36.52N	89.35W
Sikiang → Xi ≃	66	22.25N	113.23 E
Síkinos I	48	36.39N	25.06 E
Silchar	70	24.49N	92.48 E
Şile	48	41.11N	29.36 E
Šiler City	142	35.43N	79.27W
Silesia □[9]	30	51.00N	16.45 E
Siletz ≃	150	44.54N	124.00W
Siliana, Oued ≃	40	36.33N	9.25 E
Silīguri	70	26.42N	88.26 E
Silistra	48	44.07N	27.16 E
Siljan ⊜	22	60.50N	14.45 E
Šilka ≃	56	53.22N	121.32 E
Silkeborg	22	56.10N	9.34 E
Sillon de Talbert ›[1]	36	48.53N	3.05W
Siloam Springs	144	36.11N	94.32W
Silsbee	144	30.20N	94.10W
Silver Bay	138	47.17N	91.15W

Symbols in the index entries are identified on page 162.

Name	Page	Lat.	Long.
Silver City, N.M., U.S.	148	32.46N	108.16W
Silver City, N.C., U.S.	142	35.00N	79.12W
Silver Creek	136	42.32N	79.10W
Silverdale	150	47.38N	122.41W
Silver Spring	136	38.59N	77.01W
Silver Star Mountain ∧	150	48.33N	120.35W
Silverton, Co., U.S.	148	37.48N	107.39W
Silverton, Or., U.S.	150	45.00N	122.46W
Silves	44	37.11N	8.26W
Simav ≃	48	40.23N	28.31 E
Simbach	30	48.34N	12.45 E
Simcoe, Lake ⊜	138	44.20N	79.20W
Simeria	48	45.51N	23.01 E
Simeto ≃	40	37.24N	15.06 E
Simeulue, Pulau I	68	2.35N	96.00 E
Simferopol'	54	44.57N	34.06 E
Sími I	48	36.35N	27.52 E
Simi Valley	154	34.16N	118.47W
Simla	70	22.47N	88.16 E
Simmesport	144	30.59N	91.48W
Simojoki ≃	20	65.37N	25.03 E
Simon's Town	86	34.14S	18.26 E
Simplon Pass)(	36	46.15N	8.02 E
Simpson	144	31.14N	93.00W
Simpson Desert ⬥²	96	25.00S	137.00 E
Simpsonville	142	34.44N	82.15W
Simrishamn	22	55.33N	14.20 E
Simsbury	136	41.52N	72.48W
Sīnā', Shibh Jazīrat (Sinai Peninsula) ›¹	84	29.30N	34.00 E
Sinaia	48	45.21N	25.33 E
Sinai Peninsula → Sīnā', Shibh Jazīrat ›¹	84	29.30N	34.00 E
Sincelejo	118	9.18N	75.24W
Sinclair	150	41.46N	107.06W
Sinclair, Lake ⊜¹	142	33.11N	83.16W
Sindelfingen	30	48.42N	9.00 E
Sine V	82	14.10N	16.28W
Singapore	68	1.17N	103.51 E
Singapore □¹	68	1.22N	103.48 E
Singaraja	68	8.07S	115.06 E
Singatoka	91	18.08S	177.30 E
Singen [Hohentwiel]	30	47.46N	8.50 E
Singkang	68	4.08S	120.01 E
Singkawang	68	0.54N	109.00 E
Sining → Xining	66	36.38N	101.55 E
Siniscola	40	40.34N	9.41 E
Sinjah	84	13.09N	33.56 E
Sinkāt	84	18.50N	36.50 E
Sinnamahoning	136	41.19N	78.06W
Sinnamary	118	5.23N	52.57W
Sinni ≃	40	40.09N	16.42 E
Sînnicolau Mare	48	46.05N	20.38 E
Sinnūris	84	29.25N	30.52 E
Sinoie, Lacul ⊜	48	44.38N	28.53 E
Sint-Niklaas	30	51.10N	4.08 E
Sint-Truiden	30	50.48N	5.12 E
Sinú ≃	118	9.24N	75.49W
Sinŭiju	66	40.05N	124.24 E
Sió ≃	30	46.20N	18.55 E
Siófok	30	46.54N	18.04 E
Sion	36	46.14N	7.21 E
Sioule ≃	36	46.22N	3.19 E
Sioux City	132	42.30N	96.24W
Sioux Falls	132	43.33N	96.42W
Sioux Lookout	130	50.06N	91.55W
Šipčenski prohod)(	48	42.46N	25.19 E
Siping	66	43.12N	124.20 E
Sipsey ≃	144	33.00N	88.10W
Siracusa	40	37.04N	15.17 E
Sirājganj	70	24.27N	89.43 E
Sirdalsvatn ⊜	22	58.33N	6.41 E
Sir Edward Pellew Group II	96	15.40S	136.48 E
Siret ≃	48	45.24N	28.01 E
Sirḥān, Wādī as- V	70	30.30N	38.00 E
Sirino, Monte ∧	40	40.08N	15.50 E
Sir James MacBrien, Mount ∧	130	62.07N	127.41W
Síros I	48	37.26N	24.54 E
Sirrī, Jazīreh-ye I	70	25.55N	54.32 E
Sirte, Gulf of → Surt, Khalīj c	84	31.30N	18.00 E
Sir Wilfrid Laurier's Birthplace National Historic Site ⊥	136	45.51N	73.45W
Sisaba ∧	86	6.09S	29.48 E
Sisak	40	45.29N	16.23 E
Sisaket	68	15.07N	104.20 E
Sishen	86	27.55S	22.59 E
Siskiyou Mountains ⩘	150	41.55N	123.15W
Siskiyou Pass)(	150	42.03N	122.36W
Sissach	36	47.28N	7.49 E
Sīstān, Daryācheh-ye ⊜	70	31.00N	61.15 E
Sister Bay	138	45.11N	87.07W
Sisters	150	44.17N	121.32W
Sistersville	136	39.33N	80.59W
Sītāpur	70	27.34N	80.41 E
Sithonía ›¹	48	40.10N	23.47 E
Sitna ≃	48	47.37N	27.08 E
Sitnica ≃	48	42.45N	21.01 E
Sittang ≃	68	17.10N	96.58 E
Sittard	30	51.00N	5.53 E
Sittwe (Akyab)	68	20.09N	92.54 E
Sivas	16	39.45N	37.02 E
Siveluč, vulkan ∧¹	56	56.39N	161.18 E
Sjælland I	22	55.30N	11.45 E
Sjællands Odde ›¹	22	55.58N	11.22 E
Sjeništa ∧	48	43.42N	18.37 E
Skagen	22	57.44N	10.36 E
Skagerrak ʊ	22	57.45N	9.00 E
Skagit ≃	150	48.20N	122.25W
Skalbmierz	30	50.19N	20.25 E
Skalka ⊜	20	66.50N	18.46 E
Skamlingsbanke ∧²	22	55.25N	9.34 E
Skåne □⁹	22	55.59N	13.30 E
Skārdu	70	35.18N	75.37 E
Skarżysko-Kamienna	30	51.08N	20.53 E
Skaugum	22	59.51N	10.26 E
Skawina	30	49.59N	19.49 E
Skeena ≃	130	54.09N	130.02W
Skegness	26	53.10N	0.21 E
Skellefteå	22	64.46N	20.57 E
Skellefteälven ≃	20	64.42N	21.06 E
Skiddaw ∧	26	54.38N	3.08W
Skien	22	59.12N	9.36 E
Skierniewice	30	51.58N	20.08 E
Skiftet ʊ	22	60.15N	21.05 E
Skikda	82	36.50N	6.58 E
Skíros I	48	38.53N	24.32 E
Skive	22	56.34N	9.02 E
Skoki	30	52.41N	17.10 E
Skokie	138	42.02N	87.44W
Skópelos I	48	39.10N	23.40 E
Skopje	48	41.59N	21.26 E
Skövde	22	58.24N	13.50 E
Skowhegan	136	44.45N	69.43W
Skunk ≃	138	40.42N	91.07W
Skurup	22	55.28N	13.30 E
Skye, Island of I	26	57.18N	6.15W
Skyland	142	35.29N	82.31W
Skyring, Seno ʊ	120	52.35S	72.00W
Slagelse	22	55.24N	11.22 E
Slamet, Gunung ∧	68	7.14S	109.12 E
Slancy	20	59.06N	28.04 E
Slanské vrchy ⩘	30	48.50N	21.30 E
Slaný	30	50.11N	14.04 E
Slater	144	39.13N	93.04W
Slatina	48	44.26N	24.22 E
Slav'ansk	54	48.52N	37.37 E
Slave ≃	130	61.18N	113.39W
Slavkov u Brna	30	49.09N	16.52 E
Slavonska Požega	40	45.20N	17.41 E
Slavonski Brod	48	45.10N	18.01 E
Sławno	30	54.22N	16.40 E
Sleat, Sound of ʊ	26	57.06N	5.49W
Sledge	144	34.25N	90.13W
Sleeping Bear Dunes National Lakeshore ♦	138	44.50N	86.08W
Slidell	144	30.16N	89.46W
Slide Mountain ∧	136	42.00N	74.23W
Sliedrecht	30	51.49N	4.45 E
Sligo, Ire.	26	54.17N	8.28W
Sligo, Pa., U.S.	136	41.06N	79.29W
Sligo □⁶	26	54.10N	8.40W
Sligo Bay c	26	54.20N	8.40W
Slinger	138	43.20N	88.17W
Slippery Rock	136	41.03N	80.03W
Sliven	48	42.40N	26.19 E
Slobozia, Rom.	48	43.51N	25.54 E
Slobozia, Rom.	48	44.34N	27.23 E
Slocomb	144	31.06N	85.35W
Slovakia → Slovensko □⁹	30	48.50N	20.00 E
Slovenia → Slovenija □³	40	46.15N	15.10 E
Slovenija □³	40	46.15N	15.10 E
Slovenska Bistrica	40	46.23N	15.34 E
Slovenské rudohorie ⩘	30	48.45N	20.00 E
Slovensko □⁹	30	48.50N	20.00 E
Słupia ≃	30	54.35N	16.50 E
Słupsk (Stolp)	30	54.28N	17.01 E
Smackover	144	33.21N	92.43W
Smallwood Reservoir ⊜¹	130	54.05N	64.30W
Smara	82	26.44N	11.41W
Smederevo	48	44.40N	20.56 E
Smethport	136	41.48N	78.26W
Smethwick	26	52.30N	1.58W
Śmigiel	30	52.01N	16.32 E
Smith ≃	154	41.56N	124.12W
Smithers, B.C., Can.	130	54.47N	127.10W
Smithers, W.V., U.S.	136	38.10N	81.18W
Smithfield, N.C., U.S.	142	35.30N	78.20W
Smithfield, Ut., U.S.	148	41.50N	111.49W
Smith Island I	142	33.52N	77.59W
Smithland	144	37.08N	88.24W
Smith Mountain Lake ⊜¹	142	37.10N	79.40W
Smiths Falls	130	44.54N	76.01W
Smiths Fork ≃	150	41.23N	110.12W
Smithton	96	40.51S	145.07 E
Smithville, Mo., U.S.	144	39.23N	94.34W
Smithville, Tn., U.S.	144	35.57N	85.48W
Smithville Lake ⊜¹	144	39.25N	94.30W
Smokey Dome ∧	150	43.29N	114.56W
Smoky ≃	130	56.10N	117.21W
Smøla I	20	63.24N	8.00 E
Smolensk	20	54.47N	32.03 E
Smólikas ∧	48	40.06N	20.52 E
Smoljan	48	41.35N	24.41 E
Smygehuk ›	22	55.21N	13.23 E
Smyrna → İzmir	48	38.25N	27.09 E
Smyrna, De., U.S.	136	39.17N	75.36W
Smyrna, Ga., U.S.	142	33.53N	84.30W
Smyrna, Tn., U.S.	144	35.58N	86.31W
Smythe, Mount ∧	130	57.54N	124.53W
Snaefell ∧	26	54.16N	4.27W
Snag	130	62.24N	140.22W
Snake ≃, Yk., Can.	130	65.58N	134.10W
Snake ≃, U.S.	150	46.12N	119.02W
Snasahögarna ∧	22	63.13N	12.21 E
Sneads	142	30.42N	84.55W
Sneek	30	53.02N	5.40 E
Sněžnik ∧	40	45.35N	14.27 E
Śniardwy, Jezioro ⊜	30	53.46N	21.44 E
Snina	30	48.59N	22.07 E
Snøhetta ∧	22	62.20N	9.17 E
Snohomish	150	47.54N	122.05W
Snoqualmie Pass)(	150	47.25N	121.25W
Snøtinden ∧	20	66.38N	14.00 E
Snowdon ∧	26	53.04N	4.05W
Snow Hill, Md., U.S.	136	38.10N	75.23W
Snow Hill, N.C., U.S.	142	35.27N	77.40W
Snowmass Mountain ∧	148	39.07N	107.04W
Snow Mountain ∧	154	39.23N	122.45W
Snowy Mountain ∧	136	43.42N	74.23W
Snowy Mountains ⩘	96	36.30S	148.20 E
Snowyside Peak ∧	150	43.57N	114.58W
Soalala	86	16.06S	45.20 E
Soap Lake	150	47.23N	119.29W
Sobat ≃	84	9.22N	31.33 E
Sobernheim	30	49.47N	7.38 E
Sobral	118	3.42S	40.21W
Sochaczew	30	52.14N	20.14 E
Sochi → Soči	54	43.35N	39.45 E
Soči	54	43.35N	39.45 E
Société, Îles de la (Society Islands) II	8	17.00S	150.00W
Society Hill	142	34.30N	79.51W
Socorro, N.M., U.S.	148	34.03N	106.53W
Socorro, Tx., U.S.	148	31.39N	106.18W
Socotra → Suquṭrā I	70	12.30N	54.00 E
Socuéllamos	44	39.17N	2.48W
Soda Lake ⊜	154	35.08N	116.04W
Sodankylä	20	67.29N	26.32 E
Soda Springs	150	42.39N	111.36W
Soddy-Daisy	144	35.16N	85.10W
Söderhamn	22	61.18N	17.03 E
Södertälje	22	59.12N	17.37 E
Sodo	84	6.52N	37.47 E
Södra Kvarken ʊ	22	60.15N	19.05 E
Sodražica	40	45.46N	14.38 E
Sodus	136	43.14N	77.03W
Soe	68	9.52S	124.17 E
Soela väin ʊ	22	58.40N	22.35 E
Soest, B.R.D.	30	51.34N	8.07 E
Soest, Ned.	30	52.09N	5.18 E
Sofia → Sofija	48	42.41N	23.19 E
Sofia ≃	86	15.27S	47.23 E
Sofija (Sofia)	48	42.41N	23.19 E
Sogamoso	118	5.43N	72.56W
Sognafjorden c²	22	61.06N	5.10 E
Søgne	22	58.05N	7.49 E
Sogne Fjord → Sognafjorden c²	22	61.06N	5.10 E
Sohano	94	5.27S	154.40 E
Soignies	30	50.35N	4.04 E
Soissons	36	49.22N	3.20 E
Sŏjosŏn-man c	66	39.20N	124.50 E
Šokal'skogo, proliv ʊ	54	79.00N	100.25 E
Sŏkch'o	66	38.12N	128.36 E
Söke	48	37.45N	27.24 E
Sokodé	82	8.59N	1.08 E
Sokol	20	59.28N	40.10 E
Sokółka	30	53.25N	23.31 E
Sokolov	30	50.09N	12.40 E
Sokołów	30	50.14N	22.07 E
Sokołów Podlaski	30	52.25N	22.15 E
Sokoto	82	13.04N	5.16 E
Sokoto ≃	82	11.20N	4.10 E
Sol, Costa del ⩘²	44	36.40N	4.00W
Sola	92	13.53S	167.33 E
Soła ≃	30	50.04N	19.13 E
Solana	142	26.56N	82.01W
Solec Kujawski	30	53.06N	18.14 E
Soledad, Col.	118	10.55N	74.46W
Soledad, Ca., U.S.	154	36.25N	121.19W
Soledad Pass)(	154	34.30N	118.07W
Solihull	26	52.25N	1.45W
Solikamsk	20	59.39N	56.47 E
Solingen	30	51.10N	7.05 E
Sollentuna	22	59.28N	17.54 E
Solna	22	59.22N	18.01 E
Sologne ⬥¹	36	47.50N	2.00 E
Solomon Islands □¹	94	8.00S	159.00 E
Solomon Sea ᴛ²	96	8.00S	155.00 E
Solon	136	44.56N	69.51W
Solon Springs	138	46.21N	91.49W
Solothurn	36	47.13N	7.32 E
Solsona	44	41.59N	1.31 E
Solt	30	46.48N	19.00 E
Šolta, Otok I	40	43.23N	16.15 E
Soltau	30	52.59N	9.49 E
Solvang	154	34.36N	120.08W
Solvay	136	43.03N	76.12W
Solway Firth c¹	26	54.50N	3.35W
Soma	48	39.10N	27.36 E
Somalia (Somaliya) □¹	84	6.00N	48.00 E
Sombor	48	45.46N	19.07 E
Şomcuta-Mare	48	47.31N	23.29 E
Somerset, Ky., U.S.	142	37.05N	84.36W
Somerset, Ma., U.S.	136	41.46N	71.07W
Somerset, Pa., U.S.	136	40.00N	79.04W
Somerset □⁶	26	51.08N	3.00W
Somerset Island I	130	73.15N	93.30W
Somers Point	136	39.19N	74.35W
Somersworth	136	43.15N	70.51W
Somerton	148	32.35N	114.42W
Somerville	136	40.34N	74.36W
Someş (Szamos) ≃	48	48.07N	22.22 E
Someşu Cald ≃	48	46.44N	23.22 E
Someşul Mare ≃	48	47.12N	24.12 E
Someşu Mic ≃	48	47.09N	23.55 E
Somme ≃	36	50.11N	1.39 E
Sommen ⊜	22	58.01N	15.15 E
Sömmerda	30	51.10N	11.07 E
Somosomo Strait ʊ	91	16.47S	179.58 E
Sompolno	30	52.24N	18.31 E
Somport, Puerto de)(	44	42.48N	0.31W
Sønderborg	22	54.55N	9.47 E
Sondershausen	30	51.22N	10.52 E
Søndre Strømfjord	130	66.59N	50.40W
Søndre Strømfjord c²	130	66.30N	52.15W
Sondrio	40	46.10N	9.52 E
Songea	86	10.41S	35.39 E
Songhua ≃	66	47.44N	132.32 E
Songhua Hu ⊜¹	66	43.20N	127.07 E
Songkhla	68	7.12N	100.36 E
Songnim	66	38.44N	125.38 E
Sonmiāni Bay c	70	25.15N	66.30 E
Sonneberg	30	50.22N	11.10 E
Sonoma	154	38.17N	122.27W
Sonora ≃	108	28.48N	111.33W
Sonsón	118	5.42N	75.18W
Sonsonate	108	13.43N	89.44W
Sontag	144	31.39N	90.12W
Son-tay	68	21.08N	105.30 E
Sonthofen	30	47.31N	10.17 E
Soo → Sault Sainte Marie	138	46.29N	84.20W
Sopchoppy	142	30.03N	84.29W
Soperton	142	32.22N	82.35W
Sopot	30	54.28N	18.34 E
Sopron	30	47.41N	16.36 E
Sora	40	41.43N	13.37 E
Söråker	22	62.31N	17.30 E
Sorel	130	46.02N	73.07W
Sorell, Cape ›	96	42.12S	145.10 E
Sorgues	36	44.00N	4.52 E
Soria	44	41.46N	2.28W
Sorocaba	118	23.29S	47.27W
Soroki	48	48.09N	28.17 E
Sorol I¹	68	8.08N	140.23 E
Soroti	86	1.43N	33.37 E
Sørøya I	20	70.36N	22.46 E
Sorraia ≃	44	38.56N	8.53W
Sorrento, It.	40	40.37N	14.22 E
Sorrento, La., U.S.	144	30.11N	90.51W
Sorsatunturi ∧	20	67.24N	29.38 E
Sortavala	20	61.42N	30.41 E
Sos del Rey Católico	44	42.30N	1.13W
Sösjöfjällen ⩘	22	63.53N	13.15 E
Sosnogorsk	20	63.37N	53.51 E
Sosnowiec	30	50.18N	19.08 E
Sotteville	36	49.25N	1.06 E
Souderton	136	40.18N	75.19W
Souk-Khemis-Du-Sahel	44	35.17N	6.05W
Sŏul (Seoul)	66	37.33N	126.58 E
Soummam, Oued ≃	44	36.45N	5.04 E
Souq Ahras	40	36.23N	8.00 E
Souris ≃	130	49.39N	99.34W
Sourland Mountain ∧²	136	40.29N	74.43W
Sousse	82	35.49N	10.38 E
South Africa (Suid-Afrika) □¹	86	30.00S	26.00 E
South America •¹	8	15.00S	60.00W
Southampton, Eng., U.K.	26	50.55N	1.25W
Southampton, N.Y., U.S.	136	40.53N	72.23W
Southampton Island I	130	64.20N	84.40W
South Andaman I	70	11.45N	92.45 E
South Australia □³	96	30.00S	135.00 E
Southaven	144	34.59N	90.02W
South Bay	142	26.39N	80.42W
South Beloit	138	42.29N	89.02W
South Bend, In., U.S.	144	41.41N	86.15W
South Bend, Wa., U.S.	150	46.40N	123.48W
South Boston	142	36.41N	78.54W
Southbridge	136	42.04N	72.02W
South Bruny Island I	96	43.23S	147.17 E
South Burlington	136	44.28N	73.10W
South Carolina □³	132	34.00N	81.00W
South Charleston	136	38.22N	81.41W
South China Sea ᴛ²	68	10.00N	113.00 E
South Dakota □³	132	44.15N	100.00W
South Downs ⩘¹	26	50.55N	0.25W
South East Cape ›	96	43.39S	146.50 E
South East Point ›	96	39.00S	146.20 E
Southend-on-Sea	26	51.33N	0.43 E
Southern Alps ⩘	98	43.30S	170.30 E
Southern Cross	96	31.13S	119.19 E
Southern Indian Lake ⊜	130	57.10N	98.40W
Southern Ocean ᴛ¹	8	50.00S	135.00 E
Southern Pines	142	35.10N	79.23W
Southern Yemen → Yemen, People's Democratic Republic of □¹	70	15.00N	48.00 E
Southfield	138	42.28N	83.13W
South Foreland ›	26	51.09N	1.23 E
South Fulton	144	36.30N	88.52W
Southgate	138	42.12N	83.11W
South Georgia I	120	54.15S	36.45W
South Glamorgan □⁶	26	51.30N	3.25W
South Hadley	136	42.15N	72.34W
South Haven	138	42.24N	86.16W
South Head ›	98	36.26S	174.14 E
South Henderson	142	36.17N	78.25W
South Hero	136	44.38N	73.18W
South Hill	142	36.43N	78.07W
South Holston Lake ⊜¹	142	36.35N	82.00W
Southington	136	41.35N	72.52W
South International Falls	138	48.35N	93.23W
South Island I	98	43.00S	171.00 E
South Kenosha	138	42.32N	87.50W
South Lake Tahoe	154	38.56N	119.58W
South Lyon	138	42.27N	83.39W
South Medford	150	42.18N	122.50W
South Miami	142	25.42N	80.17W
South Milwaukee	138	42.54N	87.51W
South Ogden	148	41.11N	111.58W
South Orkney Islands II	8	60.35S	45.30W
South Paris	136	44.13N	70.30W
South Pass)(	150	42.22N	108.55W
South Pekin	144	40.29N	89.39W
South Pittsburg	144	35.00N	85.42W
South Platte ≃	132	41.07N	100.42W
Southport, Austl.	96	27.58S	153.25 E
Southport, Eng., U.K.	26	53.39N	3.01W
Southport, In., U.S.	144	39.39N	86.07W
Southport, N.Y., U.S.	136	42.03N	76.49W
Southport, N.C., U.S.	142	33.55N	78.01W
South Portland	136	43.38N	70.14W
South River	130	45.50N	79.23W
South Ronaldsay I	26	58.46N	2.58W
South San Francisco	154	37.39N	122.24W
South Saskatchewan ≃	130	53.15N	105.05W
South Shields	26	55.00N	1.25W
South Tucson	148	32.11N	110.58W
South Uist I	26	57.15N	7.21W
South West Africa → Namibia □²	86	22.00S	17.00 E
South West Cape ›, Austl.	96	43.34S	146.02 E
South West Cape ›, N.Z.	98	47.17S	167.28 E
South Whitley	144	41.05N	85.37W
Sovetsk	20	55.05N	21.53 E
Soviet Union → Union of Soviet Socialist Republics □¹	54	60.00N	80.00 E
Spa	30	50.30N	5.52 E
Spain (España) □¹	44	40.00N	4.00W
Spalding	26	52.47N	0.10W
Spanish ≃	138	46.11N	82.19W
Spanish Fork	148	40.06N	111.39W
Spanish North Africa □²	44	35.53N	5.19W
Spanish Sahara → Western Sahara □²	82	24.30N	13.00W
Spanish Town	108	17.59N	76.57W
Sparks, Ga., U.S.	142	31.10N	83.26W
Sparks, Nv., U.S.	154	39.32N	119.45W
Sparrows Point	136	39.13N	76.28W
Sparta → Spárti, Ellás	48	37.05N	22.27 E
Sparta, Ga., U.S.	142	33.16N	82.58W
Sparta, Il., U.S.	144	38.07N	89.42W
Sparta, Ky., U.S.	144	38.40N	84.54W
Sparta, Mi., U.S.	138	43.09N	85.42W
Sparta, N.J., U.S.	136	41.02N	74.38W
Sparta, N.C., U.S.	142	36.30N	81.07W
Sparta, Tn., U.S.	144	35.55N	85.27W
Sparta, Wi., U.S.	138	43.56N	90.48W
Spartanburg	142	34.57N	81.55W
Spartel, Cap ›	44	35.48N	5.56W
Spárti (Sparta)	48	37.05N	22.27 E
Spartivento, Capo ›	40	38.53N	8.50 E
Spátha, Ákra ›	48	35.42N	23.44 E
Spear, Cape ›	130	47.32N	52.32W
Spearfish	132	44.29N	103.51W
Spednic Lake ⊜	136	45.36N	67.35W
Speedway	144	39.48N	86.16W
Spello	40	42.59N	12.40 E
Spencer, In., U.S.	144	39.17N	86.45W
Spencer, Ma., U.S.	136	42.14N	71.59W
Spencer, N.C., U.S.	142	35.41N	80.26W
Spencer, Tn., U.S.	142	35.44N	85.28W
Spencer, W.V., U.S.	136	38.48N	81.21W
Spencer, Wi., U.S.	138	44.45N	90.17W
Spencer, Cape ›	96	35.18S	136.53 E
Spencer Gulf c	96	34.00S	137.00 E
Spey ≃	26	57.40N	3.06W
Speyer	30	49.19N	8.26 E
Spickard	144	40.14N	93.35W
Spiekeroog I	30	53.46N	7.42 E
Spillville	138	43.12N	91.57W
Spindale	142	35.21N	81.55W
Spiro	144	35.14N	94.37W
Spišská Nová Ves	30	48.57N	20.34 E
Spittal an der Drau	30	46.48N	13.30 E
Split	40	43.31N	16.27 E
Spokane	150	47.39N	117.25W
Spokane ≃	150	47.44N	118.20W
Spoleto	40	42.44N	12.44 E
Spoon ≃	144	40.18N	90.04W
Spooner	138	45.49N	91.53W
Spotsylvania	136	38.12N	77.35W
Sprague	150	47.18N	117.58W
Sprague ≃	150	42.34N	121.51W
Spratly Island I	68	8.38N	111.55 E
Spreča ≃	48	44.45N	18.06 E
Spremberg	30	51.34N	14.22 E
Spring ≃	144	36.52N	94.44W
Spring Bay c	148	41.40N	112.50W
Springdale, Nf., Can.	130	49.30N	56.04W
Springdale, Ar., U.S.	144	36.11N	94.07W
Springdale, S.C., U.S.	142	33.57N	81.06W
Springfield, Fl., U.S.	144	30.09N	85.36W
Springfield, Ga., U.S.	142	32.22N	81.18W
Springfield, Il., U.S.	144	39.48N	89.38W
Springfield, Ky., U.S.	144	37.41N	85.13W
Springfield, Ma., U.S.	136	42.06N	72.35W
Springfield, Mo., U.S.	144	37.12N	93.17W
Springfield, Oh., U.S.	136	39.55N	83.48W
Springfield, Or., U.S.	150	44.02N	123.01W
Springfield, S.D., U.S.	132	42.51N	97.53W
Springfield, Tn., U.S.	144	36.30N	86.53W
Springfield, Vt., U.S.	136	43.17N	72.28W
Springfield, Lake ⊜¹	144	39.40N	89.36W
Springfontein	86	30.19S	25.36 E
Spring Green	138	43.10N	90.04W
Springhill, N.S., Can.	130	45.39N	64.03W
Springhill, La., U.S.	144	33.00N	93.28W
Spring Hill, Tn., U.S.	144	35.45N	86.55W
Spring Lake	142	35.10N	78.58W
Springs	86	26.13S	28.25 E
Springvale	136	43.28N	70.47W
Spring Valley, Ca., U.S.	154	32.44N	116.59W
Spring Valley, Il., U.S.	138	41.19N	89.11W
Spring Valley, Mn., U.S.	138	43.41N	92.23W
Spring Valley, N.Y., U.S.	136	41.06N	74.02W
Spring Valley, Wi., U.S.	138	44.50N	92.14W
Spring Valley V	154	39.15N	114.25W
Springville, Ca., U.S.	154	36.08N	118.49W
Springville, N.Y., U.S.	136	42.30N	78.40W
Springville, Ut., U.S.	148	40.09N	111.36W
Spruce Knob ∧	136	38.42N	79.32W
Spruce Knob-Seneca Rocks National Recreation Area ♦	136	38.50N	79.20W
Spruce Mountain ∧	148	34.28N	112.24W
Spruce Pine, Al., U.S.	144	34.23N	87.43W
Spruce Pine, N.C., U.S.	142	35.54N	82.03W
Spulico, Capo ›	40	39.58N	16.39 E
Spurn Head ›	26	53.34N	0.07 E
Squamish	130	49.42N	123.09W
Squillace, Golfo di c	40	38.50N	16.50 E
Squinzano	40	40.26N	18.03 E
Squire	142	37.14N	81.36W
Srbija (Serbia) □³	48	44.00N	21.00 E
Srbobran	48	45.33N	19.48 E
Sredinnyj chrebet ⩘	56	56.00N	158.00 E
Sredna Gora ⩘	48	42.30N	25.00 E
Srednerusskaja vozvyšennost' ⩘¹	54	52.00N	38.00 E
Srednesibirskoje ploskogorje ⩘¹	54	65.00N	105.00 E
Śrem	30	52.08N	17.01 E
Sremska Mitrovica	48	44.58N	19.37 E
Sremski Karlovci	48	45.12N	19.57 E
Sri Gangānagar	70	29.55N	73.53 E
Sri Lanka □¹	70	7.00N	81.00 E
Srīnagar	70	34.05N	74.49 E
Środa Wielkopolski	30	52.14N	17.17 E
Stachanov	54	48.34N	38.40 E
Stade	30	53.36N	9.28 E
Stadskanaal	30	53.00N	6.55 E
Stadtoldendorf	30	51.53N	9.37 E
Stafford	26	52.48N	2.07W
Staffordshire □⁶	26	52.50N	2.00W
Stafford Springs	136	41.57N	72.18W
Staffordsville	142	37.49N	82.50W
Staines	26	51.26N	0.31W
Stalin (Kuçovë)	48	40.48N	19.54 E
Stalingrad → Volgograd	54	48.44N	44.25 E
Stalowa Wola	30	50.35N	22.02 E
Stamford, Eng., U.K.	26	52.39N	0.29W
Stamford, Ct., U.S.	136	41.03N	73.32W
Stamford, N.Y., U.S.	136	42.24N	74.36W
Stamford, Tx., U.S.	132	32.56N	99.48W
Stamps	144	33.21N	93.29W
Stanberry	144	40.13N	94.32W
Standerton	86	26.58S	29.07 E
Standish	138	43.58N	83.57W
Stanfield	148	32.52N	111.57W
Stanford	142	37.31N	84.39W
Stanislaus ≃	154	37.40N	121.14W
Stanke Dimitrov	48	42.16N	23.07 E
Stanley, Falk. Is.	120	51.42S	57.51W
Stanley, N.C., U.S.	142	35.21N	81.05W
Stanley, Wi., U.S.	138	44.57N	90.56W
Stanley Falls ᒪ	86	0.30N	25.12 E
Stanleyville → Kisangani	86	0.30N	25.12 E
Stann Creek	108	16.58N	88.13W
Stanovoj chrebet ⩘	56	56.20N	126.00 E
Stanovoje nagorje (Stanovoy Mountains) ⩘	56	56.00N	114.00 E
Stanovoy Mountains → Stanovoje nagorje ⩘	56	56.00N	114.00 E
Stanton	142	37.50N	83.51W
Stanwood	150	48.14N	122.22W
Star	142	35.24N	79.47W
Stará Boleslav	30	50.12N	14.42 E
Starachowice	30	51.03N	21.04 E
Staraja Russa	20	58.00N	31.23 E
Stara Planina (Balkan Mountains) ⩘	48	42.45N	25.00 E
Stara Zagora	48	42.25N	25.38 E
Star City, Ar., U.S.	144	33.56N	91.50W
Star City, In., U.S.	144	40.58N	86.33W
Stargard Szczeciński (Stargard in Pommern)	30	53.20N	15.02 E
Star Harbour c	94	10.47S	162.18 E
Stari Grad	40	43.11N	16.36 E
Stari Vlah ⬥¹	48	43.35N	20.15 E
Starke	142	29.56N	82.06W
Starkville	144	33.27N	88.49W
Starnberg	30	48.00N	11.20 E
Starnberger See ⊜	30	47.55N	11.18 E
Starogard Gdański	30	53.59N	18.33 E
Start Point ›	26	50.13N	3.38W
Staryj Oskol	54	51.19N	37.51 E
Stassfurt	30	51.51N	11.34 E
State College	136	40.47N	77.51W
State Line, Ms., U.S.	144	31.26N	88.28W
Stateline, Nv., U.S.	154	38.58N	119.56W
Statenville	142	30.42N	83.01W
Statesboro	142	32.26N	81.47W
Statesville	142	35.46N	80.53W
Staunton, Il., U.S.	144	39.00N	89.47W
Staunton, Va., U.S.	136	38.08N	79.04W
Stavanger	22	58.58N	5.45 E
Stavropol'	54	45.02N	41.59 E
Stawiski	30	53.23N	22.09 E
Stawiszyn	30	51.55N	18.07 E
Stayton	150	44.48N	122.47W
Steamboat Springs	148	40.29N	106.49W
Stębark	30	53.30N	20.08 E
Steele	144	36.05N	89.49W
Steels Point ›	93	29.02S	168.00 E
Steenbergen	30	51.35N	4.19 E
Steens Mountain ∧	150	42.35N	118.40W
Steep Point ›	96	26.08S	113.08 E
Steinfurt	30	52.09N	7.21 E
Steinkjer	20	64.01N	11.30 E
Stellarton	130	45.34N	62.40W
Stellenbosch	86	33.58S	18.50 E
Stelvio, Passo dello)(	40	46.32N	10.27 E
Stendal	30	52.36N	11.51 E
Stephens, Cape ›	98	40.42S	173.57 E
Stephenson	138	45.24N	87.36W
Stephenville	130	48.33N	58.35W
Steps Point ›	93	14.22S	170.45W
Sterling, Co., U.S.	132	40.37N	103.12W
Sterling, Il., U.S.	138	41.47N	89.41W
Sterlitamak	54	53.37N	55.58 E
Šternberk	30	49.44N	17.18 E
Steszew	30	52.18N	16.42 E
Stettin → Szczecin	30	53.24N	14.32 E
Steubenville	136	40.22N	80.38W
Stevenage	26	51.55N	0.14W
Stevenson	144	34.52N	85.50W
Stevens Pass)(	150	47.45N	121.04W
Stevens Point	138	44.31N	89.34W
Stewart ≃	130	63.18N	139.25W
Stewart Island I	98	47.00S	167.50 E
Stewartstown	136	39.45N	76.35W
Stewartville	138	43.51N	92.29W
Steyr	30	48.03N	14.25 E
Štiavnické vrchy ⩘	30	48.40N	18.45 E
Stif	82	36.09N	5.26 E
Stikine ≃	130	56.40N	132.30W
Stillmore	142	32.26N	82.12W
Stillwater, Mn., U.S.	138	45.03N	92.48W
Stillwater, Ok., U.S.	132	36.06N	97.03W
Stillwell	144	35.49N	94.38W
Stilo, Punta ›	40	38.28N	16.36 E
Stimson, Mount ∧	150	48.31N	113.36W
Stînişoarei, Munţii ⩘	48	47.10N	26.00 E
Štip	48	41.44N	22.12 E
Stirling	26	56.07N	3.57W
Stockach	30	47.51N	9.00 E
Stockerau	30	48.23N	16.13 E
Stockholm	22	59.20N	18.03 E
Stockport	26	53.25N	2.10W
Stockton, Al., U.S.	144	30.59N	87.51W
Stockton, Ca., U.S.	154	37.57N	121.17W
Stockton, Mo., U.S.	144	37.41N	93.47W
Stockton Reservoir ⊜¹	144	37.40N	93.45W
Stœng Trêng	68	13.31N	105.58 E
Stoke-on-Trent	26	53.00N	2.10W
Stolberg	30	50.46N	6.13 E
Stonefort	144	37.37N	88.42W
Stone Harbor	136	39.03N	74.45W
Stone Mountain	142	33.48N	84.10W
Stone Mountain Memorial State Park ♦	142	33.49N	84.06W
Stonewall	144	32.16N	93.49W
Stony Rapids	130	59.16N	105.50W
Stopnica	30	50.27N	20.57 E
Storå ≃	22	56.19N	8.19 E
Stora Alvaret ≍	22	56.30N	16.30 E
Stora Lulevatten ⊜	20	67.10N	19.16 E
Storavan ⊜	20	65.40N	18.15 E
Storebælt ʊ	22	55.30N	11.00 E
Storfjorden c²	22	62.25N	6.30 E
Storm Bay c	96	43.10S	147.32 E
Stornoway	26	58.12N	6.23W
Storrs	136	41.48N	72.15W
Storsjön ⊜	22	63.12N	14.18 E
Storsteinsfjellet ∧	20	68.14N	17.52 E
Storstrømmen ʊ	22	54.58N	11.55 E
Storuman	20	65.06N	17.06 E
Storvätteshågna ∧	22	62.07N	12.27 E
Storvindeln ⊜	20	65.43N	17.05 E
Story City	138	42.11N	93.35W
Stoughton, Ma., U.S.	136	42.07N	71.06W
Stoughton, Wi., U.S.	138	42.55N	89.13W
Stour ≃	26	50.43N	1.46W
Stover	144	38.26N	92.59W
Stow	136	41.10N	81.27W
Stowe	136	44.27N	72.41W
Strabane	26	54.49N	7.27W
Stradella	40	45.05N	9.18 E
Strakonice	30	49.16N	13.55 E
Stralsund	30	54.19N	13.05 E
Strangford Lough ⊜	26	54.28N	5.35W
Stranraer	26	54.55N	5.02W
Strasbourg	36	48.35N	7.45 E
Strasburg	136	40.35N	81.31W
Stratford, N.Z.	98	39.20S	174.17 E
Stratford, Ct., U.S.	136	41.11N	73.08W
Stratford, Wi., U.S.	138	44.48N	90.04W
Stratford-upon-Avon	26	52.12N	1.41W
Strathy Point ›	26	58.35N	4.02W
Stratton Mountain ∧	136	43.05N	72.56W
Straubing	30	48.53N	12.34 E
Strausberg	30	52.35N	13.53 E
Strawberry ≃	148	40.10N	110.24W
Strawberry Mountain ∧	150	44.19N	118.43W
Strážske	30	48.53N	21.50 E
Streator	144	41.07N	88.50W
Streetsboro	136	41.14N	81.20W
Strehaia	48	44.37N	23.12 E
Stresa	40	45.53N	8.32 E
Strimón (Struma) ≃	48	40.47N	23.51 E
Strjama ≃	48	42.10N	24.56 E
Stromboli, Isola I	40	38.47N	15.13 E
Stromness	26	58.57N	3.18W
Strong	144	33.06N	92.21W
Stronghurst	144	40.44N	90.54W
Strongoli	40	39.15N	17.03 E
Stronsay I	26	59.07N	2.37W
Stroud	26	51.45N	2.12W
Stroudsburg	136	40.59N	75.11W
Strum	138	44.32N	91.23W
Struma (Strimón) ≃	48	40.47N	23.51 E
Strumble Head ›	26	52.02N	5.04W
Strumica	48	41.26N	22.38 E
Struthers	136	41.03N	80.36W
Stryker	136	41.30N	84.24W
Strzegom	30	50.57N	16.21 E
Strzelce Opolskie	30	50.31N	18.19 E
Strzelecki Creek ≃	96	29.37S	139.59 E
Strzelin	30	50.47N	17.03 E
Stuart	142	27.11N	80.15W
Stuarts Draft	136	38.01N	79.02W
Studen Kladenec, jazovir ⊜¹	48	41.37N	25.30 E
Stupino	20	54.53N	38.05 E

Symbols in the index entries are identified on page 162.

Name	Page	Lat.	Long.
Usumbura → Bujumbura	86	3.23 S	29.22 E
Utah □³	132	39.30 N	111.30 W
Utah Lake ⊜	148	40.13 N	111.49 W
Utembo ≃	86	17.06 S	22.01 E
Utersum	30	54.43 N	8.24 E
Utete	86	7.59 S	38.47 E
Utica, Mi., U.S.	138	42.37 N	83.02 W
Utica, N.Y., U.S.	136	43.06 N	75.13 W
Utica, Oh., U.S.	136	40.14 N	82.27 W
Utrecht	30	52.05 N	5.08 E
Utrera	44	37.11 N	5.47 W
Utsunomiya	66	36.33 N	139.52 E
Uttaradit	68	17.38 N	100.06 E
Uusimaa ◆¹	22	60.30 N	25.00 E
Uvá ≃	118	3.57 N	68.24 W
Uvalda	142	33.41 N	83.25 W
Uvalde	132	29.12 N	99.47 W
Uvinza	86	5.06 S	30.22 E
Uvs nuur ⊜	56	50.20 N	92.45 E
Uwajima	66	33.13 N	132.34 E
'Uwaynāt, Jabal al- ▲	84	21.54 N	24.58 E
Uyuni	118	20.28 S	66.50 W
Uyuni, Salar de ≍	118	20.20 S	67.42 W
Už (Uh) ≃	30	48.34 N	22.00 E
Uzbekskaja Sovetskaja Socialističeskaja Respublika □³	54	41.00 N	64.00 E
Užgorod	48	48.37 N	22.18 E
Uzunköprü	48	41.16 N	26.41 E
Uzunkuyu	48	38.17 N	26.33 E
V			
Vaal ≃	86	29.04 S	23.38 E
Vaasa (Vasa)	22	63.06 N	21.36 E
Vác	30	47.47 N	19.08 E
Vacaville	154	38.21 N	121.59 W
Vaccarès, Étang de c	36	43.32 N	4.34 E
Väddö I	22	60.00 N	18.50 E
Vadeni	48	45.22 N	27.56 E
Vadsø	20	70.05 N	29.46 E
Vaduz	36	47.09 N	9.31 E
Værøy I	20	67.40 N	12.39 E
Vaga ≃	54	62.48 N	42.56 E
Váh ≃	30	47.55 N	18.00 E
Vaigat ⊔	16	70.11 N	53.00 W
Vail	148	39.38 N	106.22 W
Vaimali	92	16.34 S	168.11 E
Vajgač, ostrov I	54	70.00 N	59.30 E
Vākhān ◆¹	70	37.00 N	73.00 E
Valašské Meziříčí	30	49.28 N	17.58 E
Valatie	136	42.24 N	73.40 W
Valdagno	40	45.39 N	11.18 E
Valdai Hills → Valdajskaja vozvyšennost' ⋩²	20	57.00 N	33.30 E
Valdajskaja vozvyšennost' ⋩²	54	57.00 N	33.30 E
Valdavia ≃	44	42.24 N	4.16 W
Valdecañas, Embalse de ⊜¹	44	39.45 N	5.30 W
Valdepeñas	44	38.46 N	3.23 W
Valderaduey ≃	44	41.31 N	5.42 W
Valderas	44	42.05 N	5.27 W
Valders	138	44.03 N	87.53 W
Valdés, Península ⊱¹	120	42.30 S	64.00 W
Valdese	142	35.44 N	81.33 W
Valdivia	120	39.48 S	73.14 W
Valdobbiadene	40	45.54 N	12.00 E
Val-d'Or	130	48.07 N	77.47 W
Valdosta	142	30.49 N	83.16 W
Valdoviño	44	43.36 N	8.08 W
Valence	36	44.56 N	4.54 E
València, Esp.	44	39.28 N	0.22 W
Valencia, Ven.	118	10.11 N	68.00 W
València, Golf de c	44	39.50 N	0.30 E
Valencia de Alcántata	44	39.25 N	7.14 W
Valencia de Don Juan	44	42.18 N	5.31 W
Valencia Island I	26	51.52 N	10.20 W
Valenciennes	36	50.21 N	3.32 E
Valentine	132	42.52 N	100.33 W
Valenza	40	45.01 N	8.38 E
Valera	118	9.19 N	70.37 W
Valjevo	48	44.16 N	19.53 E
Valkeakoski	22	61.16 N	24.02 E
Valkenswaard	30	51.21 N	5.28 E
Valladolid	44	41.39 N	4.43 W
Vallecitos	148	36.05 N	106.20 W
Valle de la Pascua	118	9.13 N	66.00 W
Valledolmo	40	37.45 N	13.49 E
Valledupar	118	10.29 N	73.15 W
Vallejo	154	38.06 N	122.15 W
Vallenar	120	28.35 S	70.46 W
Vallentuna	22	59.32 N	18.05 E
Valles Caldera ⩓⁶	148	35.52 N	106.33 W
Valletta	40	35.54 N	14.31 E
Valley City	132	46.55 N	97.59 W
Valley Forge National Historical Park ♦	136	40.06 N	75.27 W
Valley of Fire State Park ♦	154	36.26 N	114.30 W
Valley Station	144	38.06 N	85.52 W
Vallgrund I	22	63.12 N	21.14 E
Valls	44	41.17 N	1.15 E
Valmaseda	44	43.12 N	3.12 W
Valparaíso, Chile	120	33.02 S	71.38 W
Valparaiso, Fl., U.S.	144	30.29 N	86.29 W
Valparaiso, In., U.S.	144	41.28 N	87.03 W
Valpovo	48	45.39 N	18.26 E
Vals, Tanjung ⊱	68	8.26 S	137.38 E
Valsbaai c	86	34.12 S	18.40 E
Valverde del Camino	44	37.34 N	6.45 W
Van	16	38.28 N	43.20 E
Van Buren, Ar., U.S.	144	35.26 N	94.20 W
Van Buren, Mo., U.S.	144	36.59 N	91.00 W
Vancouver, B.C., Can.	130	49.16 N	123.07 W
Vancouver, Wa., U.S.	150	45.38 N	122.39 W
Vancouver, Cape ⊱	96	35.01 S	118.12 E
Vancouver Island I	130	49.45 N	126.00 W
Vandalia, Il., U.S.	144	38.57 N	89.05 W
Vandalia, Mo., U.S.	144	39.18 N	91.29 W
Vandalia, Oh., U.S.	136	39.53 N	84.11 W
Vanderbijlpark	86	26.42 S	27.54 E
Vanderbilt	138	45.08 N	84.39 W
Vandergrift	136	40.36 N	79.33 W
Van Diemen Gulf c	96	11.50 S	132.00 E
Vänern ⊜	22	58.55 N	13.30 E
Vänersborg	22	58.22 N	12.19 E
Van Gölü ⊜	16	38.33 N	42.46 E
Vangunu Island I	94	8.38 S	158.00 E
Vanna I	20	70.09 N	19.51 E
Vännäs	22	63.55 N	19.45 E
Vannes	36	47.39 N	2.46 W
Vanoise, Massif de la ⩓	36	45.20 N	6.40 E
Vanrhynsdorp	86	31.36 S	18.44 E
Vantaa	22	60.13 N	24.59 E
Vanua Lava I	92	13.48 S	167.28 E
Vanua Levu I	91	16.33 S	179.15 E
Vanua Mbalavu Island I	91	17.40 S	178.57 W
Vanuatu □¹	92	16.00 S	167.00 E
Van Wert	136	40.52 N	84.35 W
Vārānasi (Benares)	70	25.20 N	83.00 E
Varangerfjorden c²	20	70.00 N	30.00 E
Varangerhalvøya ⊱¹	20	70.25 N	29.30 E
Varaždin	40	46.19 N	16.20 E
Varazze	40	44.22 N	8.34 E
Varberg	22	57.06 N	12.15 E
Vardar (Axiós) ≃	48	40.35 N	22.50 E
Vardø	20	70.21 N	31.02 E
Varel	30	53.22 N	8.10 E
Vareš	48	44.09 N	18.19 E
Varese	40	45.48 N	8.48 E
Varese Ligure	40	44.22 N	9.37 E
Varginha	118	21.33 S	45.26 W
Varkaus	22	62.19 N	27.55 E
Värmeln ⊜	22	59.32 N	12.54 E
Varna	48	43.13 N	27.55 E
Värnamo	22	57.11 N	14.02 E
Varnenski zaliv c	48	43.11 N	27.56 E
Varnsdorf	30	50.52 N	14.40 E
Varnville	142	32.51 N	81.04 W
Várpalota	30	47.12 N	18.09 E
Varšec	48	43.12 N	23.17 E
Varsinais-Suomi ◆¹	22	60.40 N	22.30 E
Vașcău	48	46.28 N	22.28 E
Vashon Island I	150	47.24 N	122.27 W
Vaslui	48	46.38 N	27.44 E
Vass	142	35.15 N	79.16 W
Vassar	138	43.22 N	83.35 W
Västerås	22	59.37 N	16.33 E
Västerdalälven ≃	22	60.33 N	15.08 E
Västervik	22	57.45 N	16.38 E
Vasto	40	42.07 N	14.42 E
Vas'uganje ⩸	54	58.00 N	77.00 E
Vasvár	30	47.03 N	16.49 E
Vathí	48	37.45 N	26.59 E
Vatican City (Città del Vaticano) □¹	40	41.54 N	12.27 E
Vaticano, Capo ⊱	40	38.38 N	15.50 E
V'atka ≃	54	55.36 N	51.30 E
Vatnajökull ⩎	20a	64.25 N	16.50 W
Vatoa Island I	91	19.50 S	178.13 W
Vatra Dornei	48	47.21 N	25.21 E
Vättern ⊜	22	58.24 N	14.36 E
Vatu Ira Channel ⊔	91	17.17 S	178.31 E
Vatukoula	91	17.31 S	177.51 E
Vaughn	148	34.36 N	105.12 W
Vaupés (Uaupés) ≃	118	0.02 N	67.16 W
Växjö	22	56.52 N	14.49 E
V'az'ma	20	55.13 N	34.18 E
Veazie	136	44.50 N	68.42 W
Vechta	30	52.43 N	8.16 E
Vecsés	30	47.25 N	19.16 E
Veddige	22	57.16 N	12.19 E
Vedea ≃	48	43.43 N	25.32 E
Veedersburg	144	40.06 N	87.15 W
Veendam	30	53.06 N	6.58 E
Veenendaal	30	52.02 N	5.34 E
Vefsna ≃	20	65.50 N	13.12 E
Vega I	20	65.39 N	11.50 E
Vegreville	130	53.30 N	112.03 W
Vejer de la Frontera	44	36.15 N	5.58 W
Vejle	22	55.42 N	9.32 E
Vela Luka	40	42.58 N	16.43 E
Velbert	30	51.20 N	7.02 E
Velebitski Kanal ⊔	40	45.00 N	14.50 E
Velencei-tó ⊜	30	47.12 N	18.35 E
Velez de la Gomera, Peñón de I	44	35.11 N	4.21 W
Vélez-Málaga	44	36.47 N	4.06 W
Vélez Rubio	44	37.39 N	2.04 W
Velikaja ≃	54	57.48 N	28.20 E
Velika Morava ≃	48	44.43 N	21.03 E
Velikije Luki	20	56.20 N	30.32 E
Velikij Ust'ug	20	60.48 N	46.18 E
Veliki kanal ≍	48	45.45 N	18.50 E
Veliki Vitorog ▲	40	44.07 N	17.03 E
Veliko Tărnovo	48	43.04 N	25.39 E
Veli Lošinj	40	44.31 N	14.30 E
Velingrad	48	42.04 N	24.00 E
Velino, Monte ▲	40	42.09 N	13.23 E
Vella Lavella I	94	7.45 S	156.40 E
Velletri	40	41.41 N	12.47 E
Vellore	70	12.56 N	79.08 E
Venado Tuerto	120	33.45 S	61.58 W
Venda □¹	86	23.00 S	30.30 E
Vendéen, Bocage ◆¹	36	46.40 N	1.30 W
Vendôme	36	47.48 N	1.04 E
Venezia (Venice)	40	45.27 N	12.21 E
Venezuela □¹	118	8.00 N	66.00 W
Venezuela, Golfo de c	118	11.30 N	71.00 W
Venice → Venezia, It.	40	45.27 N	12.21 E
Venice, Fl., U.S.	142	27.05 N	82.27 W
Venice, La., U.S.	144	29.16 N	89.21 W
Venice, Gulf of c	40	45.15 N	13.00 E
Vénissieux	36	45.41 N	4.53 E
Venlo	30	51.24 N	6.10 E
Venosa	40	40.57 N	15.49 E
Ventimiglia	40	43.47 N	7.36 E
Ventspils	20	57.24 N	21.36 E
Ventuari ≃	118	3.58 N	67.02 W
Ventura	154	34.16 N	119.17 W
Venus	142	27.04 N	81.21 W
Veracruz	108	19.12 N	96.08 W
Verāval	70	20.54 N	70.22 E
Verbania	40	45.56 N	8.33 E
Vercelli	40	45.19 N	8.25 E
Verchojansk	56	67.35 N	133.27 E
Verchojanskij chrebet ⋩	56	67.00 N	129.00 E
Verde ≃	148	33.33 N	111.40 W
Verden	30	52.55 N	9.13 E
Verdigris ≃	144	35.48 N	95.19 W
Verdon ≃	36	43.43 N	5.46 E
Verdun-sur-Meuse	36	49.10 N	5.23 E
Vereeniging	86	26.38 S	27.57 E
Vergennes	136	44.10 N	73.15 W
Vermilion	136	41.25 N	82.21 W
Vermilion ≃, Il., U.S.	138	41.19 N	89.04 W
Vermilion ≃, La., U.S.	144	29.46 N	92.09 W
Vermilion Bay c	144	29.40 N	92.00 W
Vermilion Lake ⊜	138	47.53 N	92.25 W
Vermillion	132	42.46 N	96.55 W
Vermont	144	40.17 N	90.25 W
Vermont □³	132	43.50 N	72.45 W
Vernal	148	40.27 N	109.31 W
Verneukpan ≍	86	30.00 S	21.10 E
Vernon, B.C., Can.	130	50.16 N	119.16 W
Vernon, Fr.	36	49.05 N	1.29 E
Vernon, Al., U.S.	144	33.45 N	88.06 W
Vernon, Ct., U.S.	136	41.49 N	72.28 W
Vernon, Fl., U.S.	144	30.37 N	85.42 W
Vernon, In., U.S.	144	38.59 N	85.36 W
Vero Beach	142	27.38 N	80.23 W
Véroia	48	40.31 N	22.12 E
Verona, It.	40	45.27 N	11.00 E
Verona, Ms., U.S.	144	34.11 N	88.43 W
Verona, Wi., U.S.	138	42.59 N	89.31 W
Versailles, Fr.	36	48.48 N	2.08 E
Versailles, In., U.S.	144	39.04 N	85.15 W
Versailles, Ky., U.S.	144	38.03 N	84.43 W
Versailles, Mo., U.S.	144	38.25 N	92.50 W
Versailles, Oh., U.S.	136	40.13 N	84.29 W
Vert, Cap ⊱	82	14.43 N	17.30 W
Vertou	36	47.10 N	1.29 W
Verviers	30	50.35 N	5.52 E
Vesoul	36	47.38 N	6.10 E
Vestavia Hills	144	33.26 N	86.46 W
Vesterålen II	20	68.45 N	15.00 E
Vestfjorden c²	20	68.08 N	15.00 E
Vestmannaeyjar	20a	63.26 N	20.12 W
Vestvågøya I	20	68.15 N	13.50 E
Vesuvio ▲¹	40	40.49 N	14.26 E
Vesuvius → Vesuvio ▲¹	40	40.49 N	14.26 E
Veszprém	30	47.06 N	17.55 E
Vésztő	30	46.55 N	21.16 E
Vetlanda	22	57.26 N	15.04 E
Vetren	48	42.16 N	24.03 E
Vettore, Monte ▲	40	42.49 N	13.16 E
Veurne	30	51.04 N	2.40 E
Vevay	144	38.44 N	85.04 W
Vevey	36	46.28 N	6.51 E
Vézère ≃	36	44.53 N	0.53 E
Viacha	118	16.39 S	68.18 W
Viadana	40	44.56 N	10.31 E
Viana del Bollo	44	42.11 N	7.06 W
Viana do Castelo	44	41.42 N	8.50 W
Viangchan (Vientiane)	68	17.58 N	102.36 E
Viareggio	40	43.52 N	10.14 E
Viaur ≃	36	44.08 N	2.23 E
Viborg	22	56.26 N	9.24 E
Vibo Valentia	40	38.40 N	16.06 E
Vic (Vich)	44	41.56 N	2.15 E
Vicco	142	37.12 N	83.03 W
Vicenza	40	45.33 N	11.33 E
Vichada ≃	118	4.55 N	67.50 W
Vichadero	120	31.48 S	54.43 W
Vichy	36	46.08 N	3.26 E
Vicksburg	144	32.21 N	90.52 W
Vicksburg National Military Park ♦	144	32.24 N	90.52 W
Victoria, Cam.	82	4.01 N	9.12 E
Victoria, B.C., Can.	130	48.25 N	123.22 W
Victoria (Xianggang), H.K.	66	22.17 N	114.09 E
Victoria, Malay.	68	5.17 N	115.15 E
Victoria, Sey.	86	4.38 S	55.27 E
Victoria, Tx., U.S.	132	28.48 N	97.00 W
Victoria □³	96	38.00 S	145.00 E
Victoria ≃	96	15.12 S	129.43 E
Victoria, Lake ⊜	86	1.00 S	33.00 E
Victoria, Mount ▲	68	21.14 N	93.55 E
Victoria de las Tunas	108	20.58 N	76.57 W
Victoria Falls ∟	86	17.55 S	25.51 E
Victoria Island I	130	71.00 N	110.00 W
Victoria Nile ≃	84	2.14 N	31.26 E
Victoria Peak ▲	108	16.48 N	88.37 W
Victoriaville	130	46.03 N	71.57 W
Victoria West	86	31.25 S	23.04 E
Victorville	154	34.32 N	117.17 W
Vičuga	20	57.13 N	41.56 E
Vidalia, Ga., U.S.	142	32.13 N	82.24 W
Vidalia, La., U.S.	144	31.33 N	91.25 W
Vidin	48	43.59 N	22.52 E
Vidor	144	30.07 N	94.00 W
Viedma, Lago ⊜	120	49.35 S	72.35 W
Viella	44	42.42 N	0.48 E
Vienna → Wien, Öst.	30	48.13 N	16.20 E
Vienna, Ga., U.S.	142	32.05 N	83.47 W
Vienna, Il., U.S.	144	37.25 N	88.54 W
Vienna, Md., U.S.	136	38.29 N	75.49 W
Vienna, Mo., U.S.	144	38.11 N	91.56 W
Vienna, W.V., U.S.	136	39.19 N	81.32 W
Vienne	36	45.31 N	4.52 E
Vienne ≃	36	47.13 N	0.05 E
Vieques, Isla de I	108	18.08 N	65.25 W
Viersen	30	51.15 N	6.23 E
Vierwaldstätter See ⊜	36	47.00 N	8.28 E
Vierzon	36	47.13 N	2.05 E
Vieste	40	41.53 N	16.10 E
Vietnam □¹	68	16.00 N	108.00 E
Vigan	68	17.34 N	120.23 E
Vigevano	40	45.19 N	8.51 E
Vignola	40	44.29 N	11.00 E
Vigo	44	42.14 N	8.43 W
Vigo, Ría de c¹	44	42.15 N	8.45 W
Vihren ▲	48	41.46 N	23.24 E
Vijayawāda	70	16.31 N	80.37 E
Vila de Manica	86	18.56 S	32.53 E
Vila do Conde	44	41.21 N	8.45 W
Vila Fontes	86	17.50 S	35.21 E
Vilafranca del Penedès	44	41.21 N	1.42 E
Vila Franca de Xira	44	38.57 N	8.59 W
Vilaine ≃	36	47.30 N	2.27 W
Vila Nova de Gaia	44	41.08 N	8.37 W
Vilanova i la Geltrú	44	41.14 N	1.44 E
Vila-real, Esp.	44	39.56 N	0.06 W
Vila Real, Port.	44	41.18 N	7.45 W
Vila Velha	118	20.20 S	40.17 W
Vil'kickogo, proliv ⊔	56	77.55 N	103.00 E
Villa Bella	118	10.23 S	65.24 W
Villablino	44	42.56 N	6.19 W
Villacañas	44	39.38 N	3.20 W
Villacarrillo	44	38.07 N	3.05 W
Villach	30	46.36 N	13.50 E
Villacidro	40	39.27 N	8.44 E
Villada	44	42.15 N	4.58 W
Villafranca de los Barros	44	38.34 N	6.20 W
Villafranca di Verona	40	45.21 N	10.50 E
Villa Grove	144	39.51 N	88.09 W
Villa Hayes	120	25.06 S	57.34 W
Villahermosa	108	17.59 N	92.55 W
Villalba	44	43.18 N	7.41 W
Villa María	120	32.25 S	63.15 W
Villa Montes	118	21.15 S	63.30 W
Villanova Monteleone	40	40.30 N	8.28 E
Villa Nueva	120	32.54 S	68.47 W
Villanueva de Córdoba	44	38.20 N	4.37 W
Villanueva de la Serena	44	38.58 N	5.48 W
Villanueva de la Sierra	44	40.12 N	6.24 W
Villanueva del Río y Minas	44	37.39 N	5.42 W
Villardefrades	44	41.43 N	5.15 W
Villar del Arzobispo	44	39.44 N	0.49 W
Villa Rica	142	33.43 N	84.55 W
Villarrica, Chile	120	39.16 S	72.13 W
Villarrica, Para.	120	25.45 S	56.26 W
Villarrobledo	44	39.16 N	2.36 W
Villas	136	39.01 N	74.56 W
Villasor	40	39.23 N	8.56 E
Villavicencio	118	4.09 N	73.37 W
Villazón	118	22.06 S	65.36 W
Villefranche	36	45.59 N	4.43 E
Villefranche-de-Rouergue	36	44.21 N	2.02 E
Villena	44	38.38 N	0.51 W
Villeneuve-Saint-Georges	36	48.44 N	2.27 E
Villeneuve-sur-Lot	36	44.25 N	0.42 E
Ville Platte	144	30.41 N	92.16 W
Villerupt	36	49.28 N	5.56 E
Villeurbanne	36	45.46 N	4.53 E
Villingen-Schwenningen	30	48.04 N	8.28 E
Vilna → Vilnius	20	54.41 N	25.19 E
Vilnius	20	54.41 N	25.19 E
Vilsbiburg	30	48.27 N	12.12 E
Vil'uj ≃	56	64.24 N	126.26 E
Vil'ujskoje vodochranilišče ⊜¹	56	62.30 N	111.00 E
Vilvoorde	30	50.56 N	4.26 E
Vina ≃	82	7.45 N	15.36 E
Viña del Mar	120	33.02 S	71.34 W
Vinalhaven	136	44.02 N	68.49 W
Vinalhaven Island I	136	44.05 N	68.52 W
Vinaròs	44	40.28 N	0.29 E
Vincennes	144	38.40 N	87.31 W
Vincent	144	33.22 N	86.22 W
Vincent, Point ⊱	93	29.00 S	167.55 E
Vindelälven ≃	20	63.54 N	19.52 E
Vindhya Range ⋩	70	23.00 N	77.00 E
Vinegar Hill ▲	150	44.43 N	118.34 W
Vine Grove	144	37.48 N	85.58 W
Vineland	136	39.29 N	75.01 W
Vineyard Haven	136	41.27 N	70.36 W
Vineyard Sound ⊔	136	41.25 N	70.46 W
Vinh	68	18.40 N	105.40 E
Vinh-long	68	10.15 N	105.58 E
Vinica	48	45.28 N	15.15 E
Vinita	144	36.38 N	95.09 W
Vinkovci	48	45.17 N	18.49 E
Vinnica	54	49.14 N	28.29 E
Vinnitsa → Vinnica	54	49.14 N	28.29 E
Vinson Massif ▲	8	78.35 S	85.25 W
Vinton, Ia., U.S.	138	42.10 N	92.01 W
Vinton, La., U.S.	144	30.11 N	93.34 W
Vinton, Va., U.S.	142	37.16 N	79.53 W
Virden	144	39.30 N	89.46 W
Vire	36	48.50 N	0.53 W
Vire ≃	36	49.20 N	1.07 W
Virgin ≃	148	36.31 N	114.20 W
Virginia, S. Afr.	86	28.12 S	26.49 E
Virginia, Il., U.S.	144	39.57 N	90.12 W
Virginia, Mn., U.S.	138	47.31 N	92.32 W
Virginia □³	132	37.30 N	78.45 W
Virginia Beach	142	36.51 N	75.58 W
Virginia City, Mt., U.S.	150	45.17 N	111.56 W
Virginia City, Nv., U.S.	154	39.18 N	119.38 W
Virginia Falls ∟	130	61.38 N	125.42 W
Virgin Islands □²	108	18.20 N	64.50 W
Virihaure ⊜	20	67.20 N	16.35 E
Virojoki	22	60.35 N	27.42 E
Viroqua	138	43.33 N	90.53 W
Virovitica	40	45.50 N	17.23 E
Virtopu	48	44.12 N	23.21 E
Vis, Otok I	40	43.02 N	16.11 E
Visalia	154	36.19 N	119.17 W
Visayan Sea ⇁²	68	11.35 N	123.51 E
Visby	22	57.38 N	18.18 E
Viseu	44	40.39 N	7.55 W
Vișeu ≃	48	47.55 N	24.09 E
Vishākhapatnam	70	17.42 N	83.18 E
Viskafors	22	57.38 N	12.50 E
Vislinskij zaliv c	30	54.27 N	19.40 E
Viso, Monte ▲	40	44.40 N	7.07 E
Visoko	40	43.59 N	18.11 E
Visp	36	46.18 N	7.53 E
Vista	154	33.12 N	117.14 W
Vistula → Wisła ≃	30	54.22 N	18.55 E
Vitanje	40	46.23 N	15.18 E
Vitarte	118	12.02 S	76.56 W
Vitebsk	20	55.12 N	30.11 E
Viterbo	40	42.25 N	12.06 E
Vitigudino	44	41.01 N	6.26 W
Viti Levu I	91	18.00 S	178.00 E
Vitim ≃	56	59.26 N	112.34 E
Vitória, Bra.	118	20.19 S	40.21 W
Vitória (Gasteiz), Esp.	44	42.51 N	2.40 W
Vitória da Conquista	118	14.51 S	40.51 W
Vitré	36	48.08 N	1.12 W
Vitry-le-François	36	48.44 N	4.35 E
Vittoria	40	36.57 N	14.32 E
Vittorio Veneto	40	45.59 N	12.18 E
Vivero	44	43.40 N	7.35 W
Vivian	144	32.52 N	93.59 W
Viwa I	91	17.08 S	176.54 E
Vizianagaram	70	18.07 N	83.25 E
Vizzini	40	37.10 N	14.53 E
Vlaardingen	30	51.54 N	4.21 E
Vlădeasa, Vîrful ▲	48	46.45 N	22.48 E
Vladičin Han	48	42.42 N	22.04 E
Vladimir	20	56.10 N	40.25 E
Vladivostok	56	43.10 N	131.56 E
Vlieland I	30	53.15 N	5.00 E
Vlissingen (Flushing)	30	51.26 N	3.35 E
Vlorë	48	40.27 N	19.30 E
Vlorës, Gji i c	48	40.25 N	19.25 E
Vltava ≃	30	50.21 N	14.30 E
Vočin	40	45.37 N	17.32 E
Vogelkop → Doberai, Jazirah ⊱¹	68	1.30 S	132.30 E
Vogel Peak → Dimlang ▲	82	8.24 N	11.47 E
Vogelsberg ⋩	30	50.30 N	9.15 E
Voghera	40	44.59 N	9.01 E
Vohibinany	86	18.49 S	49.04 E
Vohimarina	86	13.21 S	50.02 E
Voi	86	3.23 S	38.34 E
Voiron	36	45.22 N	5.35 E
Vojmsjön ⊜	22	64.55 N	16.40 E
Volchov	20	59.55 N	32.20 E
Volchov ≃	54	60.08 N	32.20 E
Volga ≃, S.S.S.R.	54	45.55 N	47.52 E
Volga ≃, Ia., U.S.	138	42.45 N	91.17 W
Volga-Baltic Canal → Volgo-Baltijskij kanal ≍	20	59.00 N	38.00 E
Volgo-Baltijskij kanal ≍	20	59.00 N	38.00 E
Volgograd (Stalingrad)	54	48.44 N	44.25 E
Volgogradskoje vodochranilišče ⊜¹	54	49.20 N	45.00 E
Völklingen	30	49.15 N	6.50 E
Volksrust	86	27.24 S	29.53 E
Vologda	20	59.12 N	39.55 E
Vólos	48	39.21 N	22.56 E
Volta, Lake ⊜¹	82	7.30 N	0.15 E
Volta Blanche (White Volta) ≃	82	9.10 N	1.15 W
Volta Noire (Black Volta) ≃	82	8.41 N	1.33 E
Volta Redonda	118	22.32 S	44.07 W
Volterra	40	43.24 N	10.51 E
Volturno ≃	40	41.01 N	13.55 E
Volyně	30	49.10 N	13.53 E
Volžsk	20	55.53 N	48.21 E
Volžskij	54	48.50 N	44.44 E
Vonavona Island I	94	8.15 S	157.05 E
Vorderrhein ≃	36	46.49 N	9.25 E
Vordingborg	22	55.01 N	11.55 E
Vorioi Sporádhes II	48	39.17 N	23.23 E
Vórios Evvoïkós Kólpos c	48	38.40 N	23.15 E
Vorkuta	20	67.27 N	63.58 E
Voronež	54	51.40 N	39.10 E
Vorošilovgrad	54	48.34 N	39.20 E
Vosges ⋩	36	48.30 N	7.10 E
Voskresensk	20	55.19 N	38.42 E
Voss	22	60.39 N	6.26 E
Vostočno-Sibirskoje more (East Siberian Sea) ⇁²	56	74.00 N	166.00 E
Votkinsk	20	57.03 N	53.59 E
Vouga ≃	44	40.41 N	8.40 W
Voyageurs National Park ♦	138	48.30 N	93.00 W
Vraca	48	43.12 N	23.33 E
Vrancei, Munții ⋩	48	46.00 N	26.30 E
Vrangel'a, ostrov I	56	71.00 N	179.30 W
Vranje	48	42.33 N	21.54 E
Vrbas	48	45.35 N	19.39 E
Vrbas ≃	48	45.06 N	17.31 E
Vrbovsko	40	45.23 N	15.05 E
Vrchlabí	30	50.38 N	15.37 E
Vredenburgh	144	31.49 N	87.19 W
Vršac	48	45.07 N	21.18 E
Vryburg	86	26.55 S	24.45 E
Vsetín	30	49.21 N	17.59 E
Vsevoložsk	20	60.01 N	30.40 E
Vught	30	51.40 N	5.17 E
Vukovar	48	45.21 N	19.00 E
Vulcan, Rom.	48	45.23 N	23.17 E
Vulcan, Mi., U.S.	138	45.46 N	87.51 W
Vulcano, Isola I	40	38.27 N	14.58 E
Vung-tau	68	10.21 N	107.04 E
Vuoksenniska	22	61.13 N	28.49 E
Vyborg	22	60.42 N	28.45 E
Vyborgskij zaliv c	22	60.35 N	28.24 E
Vyčegda ≃	54	61.18 N	46.36 E
Vygozero, ozero ⊜	54	63.35 N	34.42 E
Vyškov	30	49.16 N	17.00 E
Vyšnij Voločok	20	57.35 N	34.34 E
Vysoké Tatry ⋩	30	49.12 N	20.05 E
Vyšší Brod	30	48.37 N	14.19 E
W			
Wa	82	10.04 N	2.29 W
Waal ≃	30	51.49 N	4.58 E
Waalwijk	30	51.42 N	5.04 E
Wabana	130	47.38 N	52.57 W
Wabasca ≃	130	58.22 N	115.20 W
Wabash	144	40.47 N	85.49 W
Wabash ≃	144	37.46 N	88.02 W
Wabasha	138	44.23 N	92.01 W
Wabasso	142	27.44 N	80.26 W
Wabe Gestro ≃	84	4.17 N	42.02 E
Wabeno	138	45.26 N	88.39 W
Wąbrzeźno	30	53.17 N	18.57 E
Waccamaw ≃	142	33.21 N	79.16 W
Waccamaw, Lake ⊜	142	34.17 N	78.30 W
Waccasassa Bay c	142	29.06 N	82.52 W
Wachau ◆¹	30	48.18 N	15.24 E
Wachusett Mountain ▲	136	42.29 N	71.53 W
Wacissa	142	30.21 N	83.59 W
Waco	132	31.32 N	97.08 W
Waconia	138	44.51 N	93.47 W
Waddeneilanden II	30	53.26 N	5.30 E
Waddenzee ⇁²	30	53.15 N	5.15 E
Waddington, Mount ▲	130	51.23 N	125.15 W
Wadena	138	46.26 N	95.08 W
Wädenswil	36	47.14 N	8.40 E
Wadesboro	142	34.58 N	80.04 W
Wadī Halfā'	84	21.56 N	31.20 E
Wadley	142	32.52 N	82.24 W
Wad Madanī	84	14.25 N	33.28 E
Wadsworth, Nv., U.S.	154	39.38 N	119.17 W
Wadsworth, Oh., U.S.	136	41.01 N	81.43 W
Wageningen	30	51.58 N	5.40 E
Wagga Wagga	96	35.07 S	147.22 E
Waging am See	30	47.56 N	12.43 E
Wagoner	144	35.57 N	95.22 W
Wagontire Mountain ▲	150	43.21 N	119.53 W
Wagrien ◆¹	30	54.15 N	10.45 E
Wągrowiec	30	52.49 N	17.11 E
Wahiawa	132b	21.30 N	158.01 W
Wahpeton	132	46.15 N	96.36 W
Wahran (Oran)	82	35.43 N	0.43 W
Waiau ≃	98	42.47 S	173.22 E
Waiblingen	30	48.50 N	9.19 E
Waigeo, Pulau I	68	0.14 S	130.45 E
Waiheke Island I	98	36.48 S	175.06 E
Waihi	98	37.24 S	175.51 E
Waikare, Lake ⊜	98	37.26 S	175.13 E
Waikaremoana, Lake ⊜	98	38.46 S	177.07 E
Waikato ≃	98	37.23 S	174.43 E
Wailuku	132b	20.53 N	156.30 W
Waimakariri ≃	98	43.24 S	172.42 E
Waimate	98	44.44 S	171.02 E
Wainganga ≃	70	18.50 N	79.55 E
Waingapu	68	9.39 S	120.16 E
Wainuiomata	98	41.16 S	174.57 E
Wainwright	130	52.49 N	110.52 W
Waipa ≃	98	37.41 S	175.09 E
Waipukurau	98	40.00 S	176.34 E
Wairau ≃	98	41.30 S	174.04 E
Wairio	98	46.00 S	168.02 E
Wairoa	98	39.02 S	177.25 E
Waitaki ≃	98	44.57 S	171.09 E
Waitara	98	39.00 S	174.13 E
Waitemata	98	36.56 S	174.42 E
Waite Park	138	45.33 N	94.13 W
Wajir	84	1.45 N	40.04 E
Wakarusa	144	41.32 N	86.03 W
Wakatipu, Lake ⊜	98	45.05 S	168.34 E
Wakayama	66	34.13 N	135.11 E
Wakefield, Eng., U.K.	26	53.42 N	1.29 W
Wakefield, R.I., U.S.	136	41.26 N	71.30 W
Wake Forest	142	35.58 N	78.30 W
Wake Island □²	8	19.17 N	166.36 E
Wakhān → Vākhān ◆¹	70	37.00 N	73.00 E
Wakkanai	66	45.25 N	141.40 E
Wałbrzych (Waldenburg)	30	50.46 N	16.17 E
Walcheren I	30	51.33 N	3.35 E
Wałcz	30	53.17 N	16.28 E
Waldbröl	30	50.53 N	7.37 E
Walden	136	41.33 N	74.11 W
Waldenburg → Wałbrzych	30	50.46 N	16.17 E
Walden Ridge ⋩	142	35.30 N	85.15 W
Waldmünchen	30	49.23 N	12.43 E
Waldorf	136	38.37 N	76.56 W
Waldron, Ar., U.S.	144	34.53 N	94.05 W
Waldron, In., U.S.	144	39.27 N	85.40 W
Waldshut	30	47.37 N	8.13 E
Waldviertel ◆¹	30	48.40 N	15.40 E
Wales □⁸	26	52.30 N	3.30 W
Walgett	96	30.01 S	148.07 E
Walhalla, N.D., U.S.	132	48.55 N	97.55 W
Walhalla, S.C., U.S.	142	34.45 N	83.03 W
Walhalla ⊥	30	49.03 N	12.14 E
Walker	138	42.17 N	91.46 W
Walker ≃	154	38.54 N	118.47 W
Walker Lake ⊜	154	38.44 N	118.43 W
Walkerton	144	41.28 N	86.28 W
Walkertown	142	36.10 N	80.09 W
Wallace, Id., U.S.	150	47.28 N	115.55 W
Wallace, N.C., U.S.	142	34.44 N	77.59 W
Wallaceburg	130	42.36 N	82.23 W
Wallachia □⁹	48	44.00 N	25.00 E
Walla Walla	150	46.03 N	118.20 W
Wallingford, Ct., U.S.	136	41.27 N	72.49 W
Wallingford, Vt., U.S.	136	43.28 N	72.58 W
Wallis and Futuna □²	8	14.00 S	177.00 W
Wallula, Lake ⊜¹	150	46.00 N	118.55 W
Walnut, Ms., U.S.	144	34.56 N	88.53 W
Walnut, N.C., U.S.	142	35.50 N	82.44 W
Walnut Cove	142	36.17 N	80.08 W
Walnut Ridge	144	36.04 N	90.57 W
Walpole	136	43.04 N	72.25 W
Walsall	26	52.35 N	1.58 W
Walsenburg	148	37.37 N	104.46 W
Walsrode	30	52.52 N	9.35 E
Walterboro	142	32.54 N	80.40 W
Walter F. George Lake ⊜¹	142	31.49 N	85.08 W
Waltershausen	30	50.53 N	10.33 E
Waltham	136	42.22 N	71.14 W
Walton, Ky., U.S.	136	38.52 N	84.36 W
Walton, N.Y., U.S.	136	42.10 N	75.07 W
Walvisbaai (Walvis Bay)	86	22.59 S	14.31 E
Walvis Bay → Walvisbaai	86	22.59 S	14.31 E
Walworth	138	42.31 N	88.35 W
Wamba ≃	86	3.56 S	17.12 E
Wami ≃	86	6.08 S	38.49 E
Wampum	136	40.53 N	80.20 W
Wamsutter	150	41.40 N	107.58 W
Wanaka, Lake ⊜	98	44.30 S	169.08 E
Wanamingo	138	44.18 N	92.47 W
Wanchese	142	35.50 N	75.38 W
Wanganui	98	39.56 S	175.03 E
Wangen [im Allgäu]	30	47.41 N	9.50 E
Wangerooge I	30	53.46 N	7.55 E
Wanne-Eickel	30	51.32 N	7.09 E
Wanneroo	96	31.45 S	115.48 E
Wanxian	66	30.52 N	108.22 E
Wapakoneta	136	40.34 N	84.11 W
Wapato	150	46.26 N	120.25 W
Wapello	138	41.10 N	91.11 W
Wappapello, Lake ⊜¹	144	36.58 N	90.20 W
Wappingers Falls	136	41.35 N	73.54 W
Wapsipinicon ≃	138	41.44 N	90.20 W
Warangal	70	18.00 N	79.35 E
Warburg	30	51.29 N	9.08 E
Warburton Creek ≃	96	27.55 S	137.28 E
Ward, Mount ▲	98	43.52 S	169.50 E
Warden	150	46.58 N	119.02 W
Wardha	70	20.45 N	78.37 E
Ward Hill ▲²	26	58.54 N	3.20 W
Ware	136	42.15 N	72.14 W
Ware ≃	136	42.11 N	72.22 W
Wareham, Eng., U.K.	26	50.41 N	2.07 W
Wareham, Ma., U.S.	136	41.45 N	70.43 W
Waremme	30	50.41 N	5.15 E
Waren	30	53.31 N	12.40 E
Warendorf	30	51.57 N	7.59 E
Ware Shoals	142	34.23 N	82.14 W
Wargla	82	31.59 N	5.25 E
Warka	30	51.47 N	21.10 E
Warmbad	86	24.55 S	28.15 E
Warminster, Eng., U.K.	26	51.13 N	2.12 W
Warminster, Pa., U.S.	136	40.12 N	75.06 W
Warm Springs, Ga., U.S.	142	32.53 N	84.40 W
Warm Springs, Or., U.S.	150	44.45 N	121.15 W
Warm Springs Reservoir ⊜¹	150	43.37 N	118.14 W
Warner	136	43.16 N	71.49 W
Warner Mountains ⋩	154	41.40 N	120.20 W
Warner Peak ▲	150	42.27 N	119.44 W
Warner Robins	142	32.37 N	83.36 W
Warnow ≃	30	54.06 N	12.09 E
Warrego ≃	96	30.24 S	145.21 E
Warren, Ar., U.S.	144	33.36 N	92.03 W
Warren, Mi., U.S.	138	42.28 N	83.01 W
Warren, Oh., U.S.	136	41.14 N	80.49 W
Warren, Pa., U.S.	136	41.50 N	79.08 W
Warrenpoint	26	54.06 N	6.15 W
Warrensburg, Mo., U.S.	144	38.45 N	93.44 W
Warrensburg, N.Y., U.S.	136	43.29 N	73.46 W
Warrenton, S. Afr.	86	28.09 S	24.47 E
Warrenton, Ga., U.S.	142	33.24 N	82.39 W
Warrenton, Mo., U.S.	144	38.48 N	91.08 W
Warrenton, Va., U.S.	136	38.42 N	77.47 W
Warri	82	5.31 N	5.45 E
Warrington, Eng., U.K.	26	53.24 N	2.37 W
Warrington, Fl., U.S.	144	30.23 N	87.16 W
Warrior	144	33.48 N	86.48 W
Warrnambool	96	38.23 S	142.29 E
Warsaw → Warszawa, Pol.	30	52.15 N	21.00 E
Warsaw, Il., U.S.	144	40.21 N	91.26 W
Warsaw, In., U.S.	144	41.14 N	85.51 W
Warsaw, Ky., U.S.	144	38.47 N	84.54 W
Warsaw, Mo., U.S.	144	38.14 N	93.22 W
Warsaw, N.Y., U.S.	136	42.44 N	78.07 W
Warsaw, N.C., U.S.	142	34.59 N	78.05 W
Warsaw, Oh., U.S.	136	40.20 N	82.00 W
Warszawa (Warsaw)	30	52.15 N	21.00 E
Warta	30	51.42 N	18.38 E
Warta ≃	30	52.35 N	14.39 E
Wartburg	142	36.06 N	84.35 W
Wartburg ⊥	30	50.58 N	10.18 E
Warthe → Warta ≃	30	52.35 N	14.39 E
Warwick, Austl.	96	28.13 S	152.02 E
Warwick, Eng., U.K.	26	52.17 N	1.34 W
Warwick, R.I., U.S.	136	41.41 N	71.22 W
Warwick Channel ⊔	96	13.51 S	136.16 E
Warwickshire □⁶	26	52.13 N	1.37 W
Wasatch Range ⋩	148	40.40 N	111.35 W
Wasco	154	35.35 N	119.20 W
Waseca	138	44.04 N	93.30 W
Washburn	138	46.40 N	90.53 W
Washington, D.C., U.S.	136	38.53 N	77.02 W
Washington, Ga., U.S.	142	33.44 N	82.44 W
Washington, Il., U.S.	138	40.42 N	89.24 W
Washington, In., U.S.	144	38.39 N	87.10 W
Washington, Ia., U.S.	138	41.17 N	91.41 W
Washington, Ky., U.S.	136	38.36 N	83.48 W
Washington, La., U.S.	144	30.36 N	92.03 W
Washington, Mo., U.S.	144	38.33 N	91.01 W
Washington, N.C., U.S.	142	35.31 N	77.01 W
Washington, Pa., U.S.	136	40.10 N	80.14 W
Washington, Va., U.S.	136	38.42 N	78.09 W
Washington □³	132	47.30 N	120.30 W
Washington, Mount ▲	136	44.15 N	71.15 W
Washington Court House	136	39.32 N	83.26 W
Washington Island	138	45.23 N	86.55 W
Washington Island I	138	45.23 N	86.55 W
Washington Terrace	148	41.10 N	111.58 W
Washoe Lake ⊜	154	39.16 N	119.48 W
Wasilków	30	53.12 N	23.12 E
Waskaganish	130	51.30 N	78.45 W
Wasserkuppe ▲	30	50.30 N	9.56 E
Watampone	68	4.32 S	120.20 E
Watatic, Mount ▲	136	42.42 N	71.53 W
Waterbury, Ct., U.S.	136	41.33 N	73.02 W
Waterbury, Vt., U.S.	136	44.20 N	72.45 W

Symbols in the index entries are identified on page 162.

Symbols in the index entries are identified on page 162.

Name	Page	Lat.	Long.
Yanbu'	70	24.05N	38.03 E
Yangjiang	66	21.51N	111.56 E
Yangquan	66	37.52N	113.36 E
Yangtze → Chang ≊	66	31.48N	121.10 E
Yangzhou	66	32.24N	119.26 E
Yanji	66	42.57N	129.32 E
Yankeetown	142	29.01N	82.42W
Yankton	132	42.52N	97.23W
Yanqi	66	42.00N	86.15 E
Yantai (Chefoo)	66	37.33N	121.20 E
Yaoundé	82	3.52N	11.31 E
Yap I	68	9.31N	138.06 E
Yapacaní	118	16.45S	64.18W
Yapen, Pulau I	68	1.45S	136.15 E
Yaqui ≊	108	27.37N	110.39W
Yaraka	96	24.53S	144.04 E
Yare ≊	26	52.35N	1.44 E
Yarí ≊	118	0.23S	72.16W
Yarim	70	14.29N	44.21 E
Yarkand → Shache	66	38.25N	77.16 E
Yarkant (Yarkand) ≊	66	40.28N	80.52 E
Yarmouth, N.S., Can.	130	43.50N	66.07W
Yarmouth → Great Yarmouth, Eng., U.K.	26	52.37N	1.44 E
Yarmouth, Me., U.S.	136	43.48N	70.11W
Yasawa Group II	91	17.00S	177.23 E
Yata ≊	118	10.29S	65.26W
Yass	96	34.50S	148.55 E
Yatagan	48	37.20N	28.09 E
Yatesboro	136	40.48N	79.20W
Yates City	144	40.46N	90.00W
Yatsushiro	66	32.30N	130.36 E
Yatta Plateau ⚹[1]	86	2.00S	38.00 E
Yavari (Javari) ≊	118	4.21S	70.02W
Yavi, Cerro ᴧ	118	5.32N	65.59W
Yazd	70	31.53N	54.25 E
Yazoo ≊	144	32.22N	91.00W
Yazoo City	144	32.51N	90.24W
Ybbs ≊	30	48.10N	15.06 E
Yding Skovhøj ᴧ[2]	22	56.00N	9.48 E
Ye	68	15.15N	97.51 E
Yecla	44	38.37N	1.07W
Yei ≊	84	6.15N	30.13 E
Yell I	26	60.36N	1.06W
Yellow ≊, U.S.	144	30.33N	87.00W
Yellow ≊, In., U.S.	144	41.16N	86.50W
Yellow → Huang ≊	66	37.32N	118.19 E
Yellowhead Pass ⋊	130	52.53N	118.28W
Yellowknife	130	62.27N	114.21W
Yellowknife ≊	130	62.31N	114.19W
Yellow Sea ᵀ[2]	66	36.00N	123.00 E
Yellowstone ≊	132	47.58N	103.59W
Yellowstone Falls ᴸ	150	44.43N	110.30W
Yellowstone Lake ⊜	150	44.25N	110.22W
Yellowstone National Park ♦	150	44.30N	110.35W
Yellville	144	36.13N	92.41W
Yemen (Al-Yaman) ◻[1]	70	15.00N	44.00 E
Yemen, People's Democratic Republic of ◻[1]	70	15.00N	48.00 E
Yenangyaung	68	20.28N	94.52 E
Yen-bai	68	21.42N	104.52 E
Yendi	82	9.26N	0.01W
Yenisey → Jenisej ≊	54	71.50N	82.40 E
Yeovil	26	50.57N	2.39W
Yerevan → Jerevan	54	40.11N	44.30 E
Yerington	154	38.59N	119.09W
Yerupaja, Nevado ᴧ	118	10.16S	76.54W
Yerushalayim (Jerusalem)	70	31.46N	35.14 E
Yesa, Embalse de ⊜[1]	44	42.36N	1.09W
Yeu, Île d' I	36	46.42N	2.20W
Yibin	66	28.47N	104.38 E
Yichang	66	30.42N	111.17 E
Yichun, Zhg.	66	27.50N	114.23 E
Yichun, Zhg.	66	47.42N	128.55 E
Yilan	66	46.19N	129.34 E
Yinchuan	66	38.30N	106.18 E
Yingkou	66	40.40N	122.14 E
Yining	66	43.54N	81.21 E
Yirga Alem	84	6.52N	38.22 E
Yiyang	66	28.36N	112.20 E
Yli-Kitka ⊜	20	66.08N	28.30 E
Yngaren ⊜	22	58.52N	16.35 E
Yogyakarta	68	7.48S	110.22 E
Yokohama	66	35.27N	139.39 E
Yokosuka	66	35.18N	139.40 E
Yola	82	9.12N	12.29 E
Yom ≊	68	15.52N	100.16 E
Yonago	66	35.26N	133.20 E
Yonezawa	66	37.55N	140.07 E
Yonkers	136	40.55N	73.53W
Yonne ≊	36	48.23N	2.58 E
York, Eng., U.K.	26	53.58N	1.05W
York, Al., U.S.	144	32.29N	88.17W
York, Pa., U.S.	136	39.57N	76.43W
York, S.C., U.S.	144	34.59N	81.14W
York ≊	142	37.15N	76.23W
York, Cape ⊁	96	10.42S	142.31 E
Yorke Peninsula ⊁[1]	96	35.00S	137.30 E
Yorkton	130	51.13N	102.28W
Yorktown	142	37.14N	76.30W
Yorkville, Il., U.S.	138	41.38N	88.26W
Yorkville, N.Y., U.S.	136	43.06N	75.16W
Yoro	108	15.09N	87.07W
Yosemite National Park ♦	154	37.51N	119.33W
Yos Sudarsa, Pulau I	68	7.50S	138.30 E
Yōsu	66	34.46N	127.44 E
Young	148	34.06N	110.57W
Youngstown, Fl., U.S.	142	30.21N	85.26W
Youngstown, N.Y., U.S.	136	43.14N	79.03W
Youngstown, Oh., U.S.	136	41.05N	80.38W
Youngsville, La., U.S.	144	30.05N	91.59W
Youngsville, Pa., U.S.	136	41.51N	79.19W
Youssoufia	82	32.16N	8.33W
Ypres → Ieper	30	50.51N	2.53 E
Ypsilanti	138	42.14N	83.36W
Yreka	154	41.44N	122.38W
Ystad	22	55.25N	13.49 E
Ystwyth ≊	26	52.24N	4.05W
Yuan ≊	66	28.58N	111.49 E
Yuanling	66	28.20N	110.16 E
Yuba ≊	154	39.07N	121.36W
Yuba City	154	39.08N	121.36W
Yūbari	66	43.04N	141.59 E
Yucaipa	154	34.02N	117.02W
Yucatan Channel ⋃	108	21.45N	85.45W
Yucatan Peninsula ⊁[1]	108	19.30N	89.00W
Yucca	148	34.52N	114.08W
Yucca Valley	154	34.07N	116.35W
Yuci	66	37.45N	112.41 E
Yueyang	66	29.23N	113.06 E
Yugoslavia (Jugoslavija) ◻[1]	16	44.00N	19.00 E
Yukon ◻[4]	130	64.00N	135.00W
Yukon ≊	132a	62.33N	163.59W
Yulin	66	38.20N	109.29 E
Yuma	148	32.43N	114.37W
Yumen	66	39.56N	97.51 E
Yuncheng	66	35.00N	110.59 E
Yurimaguas	118	5.54S	76.05W
Yü Shan ᴧ	66	23.28N	120.57 E
Yushu	66	33.01N	97.00 E
Yutian	66	36.51N	81.40 E
Yverdon	36	46.47N	6.39 E

Z

Name	Page	Lat.	Long.
Zaanstad	30	52.26N	4.49 E
Zábala ≊	48	45.51N	26.46 E
Zabarjad, Jazīrat I	84	23.37N	36.12 E
Zabid	70	14.10N	43.17 E
Ząbkowice Śląskie	30	50.36N	16.53 E
Žabno	30	50.09N	20.53 E
Zabrze (Hindenburg)	30	50.18N	18.46 E
Zacapa	108	14.58N	89.32W
Zacatecas	108	22.47N	102.35W
Zachary	144	30.38N	91.09W
Zadar	40	44.07N	15.14 E
Zadetkyi Kyun I	68	9.58N	98.13 E
Zadorra ≊	44	42.40N	2.54W
Zafirovo	48	44.00N	26.52 E
Zafra	44	38.25N	6.25W
Żagań	30	51.37N	15.19 E
Zaghouan, Jebel ᴧ	40	36.21N	10.08 E
Zagora ⋊	40	43.40N	16.15 E
Zagorsk	20	56.18N	38.08 E
Zagórz	30	49.31N	22.17 E
Zagreb	40	45.48N	15.58 E
Zagros, Kūhhā-ye ⋊	70	33.40N	47.00 E
Zagros Mountains → Zāgros, Kūhhā-ye ⋊	70	33.40N	47.00 E
Žagubica	48	44.13N	21.48 E
Zagyva ⊜	30	47.10N	20.13 E
Zāhedān	70	29.30N	60.52 E
Zahlah	70	33.51N	35.53 E
Záhony	30	48.25N	22.11 E
Zaire (Zaïre) ◻[1]	86	4.00S	25.00 E
Zaječar	48	43.54N	22.17 E
Zajsan, ozero ⊜	54	48.00N	84.00 E
Zakinthos	48	37.47N	20.53 E
Zákinthos I	48	37.52N	20.44 E
Zákinthou, Porthmós ⋃	48	37.50N	21.00 E
Zakopane	30	49.19N	19.57 E
Zala ≊	30	46.43N	17.16 E
Zalaegerszeg	30	46.51N	16.51 E
Zalău	48	47.11N	23.03 E
Zama	144	32.58N	89.22W
Zambezi (Zambeze) ≊	86	18.55S	36.04 E
Zambia ◻[1]	86	14.30S	27.30 E
Zamboanga	68	6.54N	122.04 E
Zambrów	30	53.00N	22.15 E
Zamfara ≊	82	12.05N	4.02 E
Zamora	44	41.30N	5.45W
Zamora de Hidalgo	108	19.59N	102.16W
Zamość	30	50.44N	23.15 E
Zandvoort	30	52.22N	4.32 E
Zanesville	136	39.56N	82.00W
Zanjān	70	36.40N	48.29 E
Žannetty, ostrov I	56	76.43N	158.00 E
Zante → Zákinthos I	48	37.52N	20.44 E
Zanzibar	86	6.10S	39.11 E
Zanzibar I	86	6.10S	39.20 E
Zapadnaja Dvina (Daugava) ≊	54	57.04N	24.03 E
Zapadna Morava ≊	48	43.42N	21.23 E
Zapadno-Sibirskaja ravnina ≊	54	60.00N	75.00 E
Zapadnyj Sajan ⋊	54	53.00N	94.00 E
Zaporožje	54	47.50N	35.10 E
Zaragoza	44	41.38N	0.53W
Zaranj	70	31.06N	61.53 E
Zárate	120	34.06S	59.02W
Zarautz	44	43.17N	2.10W
Zard Kūh ᴧ	70	32.22N	50.04 E
Zaria	82	11.07N	7.44 E
Zărnești	48	45.34N	25.19 E
Žary (Sorau)	30	51.38N	15.09 E
Záskār Mountains ⋊	70	33.00N	78.00 E
Žatec	30	50.19N	13.32 E
Zavidovići	48	44.27N	18.09 E
Zawiercie	30	50.30N	19.25 E
Zbąszyń	30	52.16N	15.55 E
Zbraslav	30	49.59N	14.24 E
Ždanov	54	47.06N	37.33 E
Zduńska Wola	30	51.36N	18.57 E
Zduny	30	51.39N	17.24 E
Zebulon, Ga., U.S.	142	33.06N	84.20W
Zebulon, N.C., U.S.	142	35.49N	78.18W
Zeebrugge	30	51.20N	3.12 E
Zeehan	96	41.53S	145.20 E
Zeeland	138	42.48N	86.01W
Zeist	30	52.05N	5.15 E
Zeitz	30	51.03N	12.08 E
Zeja ≊	56	50.13N	127.35 E
Zejskoje vodochranilišče ⊜[1]	56	54.28N	127.45 E
Zele	30	51.04N	4.02 E
Zelee, Cape ⊁	94	9.45S	161.34 E
Zelengora ⋊	48	43.15N	18.45 E
Zeletin ≊	48	46.03N	27.23 E
Zelienople	136	40.47N	80.08W
Zell	30	50.01N	7.10 E
Zella-Mehlis	30	50.39N	10.39 E
Zel'onodol'sk	20	55.51N	48.33 E
Zembra, Île I	40	37.08N	10.48 E
Zeml'a Franca-Iosifa II	8	81.00N	55.00 E
Zemun	48	44.50N	20.24 E
Zenica	48	44.12N	17.55 E
Zephyrhills	142	28.14N	82.10W
Zerbst	30	51.58N	12.04 E
Zereh, Gowd-e ⊜[7]	70	29.45N	61.50 E
Zerga, Merja C	44	34.51N	6.17W
Zermatt	36	46.02N	7.45 E
Zeroud, Oued V	40	35.50N	10.13 E
Zeulenroda	30	50.39N	11.58 E
Zevenaar	30	51.56N	6.05 E
Zêzere ≊	44	39.28N	8.20W
Zgierz	30	51.52N	19.25 E
Zgorzelec	30	51.12N	15.01 E
Zhangjiakou (Kalgan)	66	40.50N	114.53 E
Zhangzhou	66	24.33N	117.39 E
Zhanjiang	66	21.16N	110.28 E
Zhao'an	66	23.47N	117.12 E
Zhaotong	66	27.19N	103.48 E
Zhdanov → Ždanov	54	47.06N	37.33 E
Zhengzhou	66	34.48N	113.39 E
Zhenjiang	66	32.13N	119.26 E
Zhitomir → Žitomir	54	50.16N	28.40 E
Zhob ≊	70	32.04N	69.50 E
Zhongshan	66	22.31N	113.22 E
Zhoucun	66	36.47N	117.48 E
Zhujiang Kou C[1]	66	23.36N	113.44 E
Zhuoxian	66	39.30N	115.58 E
Zhuzhou	66	27.50N	113.09 E
Žiar nad Hronom	30	48.36N	18.52 E
Zibo	66	36.47N	118.01 E
Zielona Góra (Grünberg)	30	51.56N	15.31 E
Zigana Dagları ⋊	70	40.37N	39.30 E
Zigong	66	29.24N	104.47 E
Ziguinchor	82	12.35N	16.16W
Žigulevsk	20	53.25N	49.27 E
Žilina	30	49.14N	18.46 E
Zillah	150	46.24N	120.15W
Zillertaler Alpen ⋊	30	47.00N	11.55 E
Zimbabwe ◻[1]	86	20.00S	30.00 E
Zimbor	48	47.00N	23.16 E
Zimnicea	48	43.39N	25.21 E
Zinder	82	13.48N	8.59 E
Zion	138	42.26N	87.49W
Zion National Park ♦	148	37.10N	113.00W
Zionsville	144	39.57N	86.15W
Zipaquirá	118	5.02N	74.00W
Żitomir	30	50.16N	28.40 E
Ziway, Lake ⊜	84	8.00N	38.50 E
Zizhong	66	29.48N	104.50 E
Zlarin	40	43.42N	15.50 E
Zlatoust	54	55.10N	59.40 E
Złocieniec	30	53.33N	16.01 E
Złotoryja	30	51.08N	15.55 E
Złotów	30	53.22N	17.02 E
Znojmo	30	48.52N	16.02 E
Zogno	40	45.48N	9.40 E
Zolfo Springs	142	27.29N	81.47W
Zomba	86	15.23S	35.18 E
Zonguldak	16	41.27N	31.49 E
Zornica	48	42.23N	26.56 E
Zrenjanin	48	45.23N	20.24 E
Zrmanja ≊	40	44.15N	15.32 E
Zuckerhütl ᴧ	30	46.58N	11.09 E
Zug	30	47.10N	8.31 E
Zugspitze ᴧ	30	47.25N	10.59 E
Zuiderzee → IJsselmeer ᵀ[2]	30	52.45N	5.25 E
Zújar ≊	44	39.01N	5.47W
Zújar, Embalse del ⊜[1]	44	38.50N	5.20W
Żukowo	30	54.21N	18.22 E
Zululand ⊙[9]	86	28.10S	32.00 E
Zumbrota	138	44.17N	92.40W
Zuni	148	35.04N	108.51W
Zunyi	66	27.39N	106.57 E
Zürich	36	47.23N	8.32 E
Zürichsee ⊜	36	47.13N	8.45 E
Zutphen	30	52.08N	6.12 E
Zvezdec	48	42.07N	27.25 E
Zvishavane	86	20.20S	30.02 E
Zvolen	30	48.35N	19.08 E
Zweibrücken	30	49.15N	7.21 E
Zweisimmen	36	46.33N	7.22 E
Zwickau	30	50.44N	12.29 E
Zwolle, Ned.	30	52.30N	6.05 E
Zwolle, La., U.S.	144	31.37N	93.38W
Żyrardów	30	52.04N	20.25 E
Żywiec	30	49.41N	19.12 E

Symbols in the index entries are identified on page 162.